WHAT IS CRIMINOLOGY?

WHAT IS CRIMINOLOGY?

Edited by

MARY BOSWORTH AND
CAROLYN HOYLE

University of Oxford

Great Clarendon Street, Oxford OX2 6DP
United Kingdom

Oxford University Press is a department of the University of Oxford. It furthers the University's objective of excellence in research, scholarship, and education by publishing worldwide. Oxford is a registered trade mark of Oxford University Press in the UK and in certain other countries

First Edition published 2011
First published in paperback 2012

Impression: 1

British Library Cataloguing in Publication Data
Data available

Library of Congress Cataloging in Publication Data
Data available

ISBN 978-0-19-957182-6
978-0-19-965992-0 (pbk.)

Printed in Great Britain
on acid-free paper by
Ashford Colour Press, Gosport, Hampshire

Dedication

To my parents, Richard and Michal Bosworth—MB

To my sister and children, Suzanne Vandervell, Jacob Rose and Daniel Rose—CH

Foreword

Criminology tends to be viewed as a lowbrow discipline by folk from other social sciences. Perhaps that is because intellectual standards were once lower in criminology than those of the best criminology today. Perhaps it is also because other social scientists see criminology as a populist field. Naturally, they notice those criminologists who appear on television to speculate on what might be motivating a serial murderer who has not been apprehended, whom the commentator has never met!

Perhaps the negativity is because so many of the social sciences are in decline in the west while criminology flourishes. Some of the most powerful disciplines that dominate prestigious learned academies have seen a drop in their share of student enrolments and therefore in their faculty. My more controversial view is that most social sciences are neither as interesting nor as vibrant as they were in the middle decades of the twentieth century. In contrast, fields such as biology and information technology experienced remarkable intellectual growth in this period by reorganizing their intellectual communities around newer ideas like networked cyberspace, the new molecular biology and by revisiting older notions of evolutionary biology and ecology.

We also see a certain disdain from the continuing, if waning, domination of continental criminology by the discipline of law. Some continental lawyers imagine they study solid, complex stuff with a technically demanding logical core; to these lawyers, their criminologist colleagues seem barely playing at being scholars. They would prefer the intellectual company of a philosopher or even an economist to a criminologist.

I have always been a doubter and dissenter from the disciplinary organization of the social sciences, never a hardcore member of any discipline, including criminology. This commitment to interdisciplinarity means I spend more of my time attending conferences organized by non-criminologists than by criminologists. From this comparative vantage point, and from the perspective of being decidedly not a 'true believer' in criminology as a project to discipline young minds, I am nevertheless inclined to conjecture that criminology deserves its success. And the plural debate in this volume confirms that inclination.

First, consider the populist tag. While some students enrol in criminology because they would like to learn to be a 'profiler' of a kind they have seen in Hollywood crime dramas, they actually learn more important things about crime when they arrive in the class. One might predict our disappointed profilers would drop out after the first year. But the meat of the subject seems to sustain them more than the ephemera that attracted them to enrol.

That meat is still a seductively social kind of scholarship. Despite being drawn to other subjects I enjoy the company of criminologists more than colleagues from those other intellectual communities. Police officers are also wonderful company, interesting people, as are the occupants of prisons, on both sides of the bars. Corporate criminals are gripping conversationalists! A strength of the criminological ethos is that it is engaged with narratives of such lives that cross boundaries. As Alison Liebling puts it, good criminology tends to engage with such people 'appreciatively', taking all accounts seriously, and striving to comprehend their passions, insights and disappointments with life. So, while our aspiring young profiler might arrive thinking what will motivate her is the forensic search for clues from a cadaver, what actually does engage her is a more basic appeal that criminology shares with fiction—narratives of lives that transgress.

Undergraduates also find that criminology is a more human subject than psychology. Rats drove much of the narrative from psychology classes that many of us experienced. Criminology had serious psychology in it, substantively and methodologically, yet it also had the ethnography that so appealed in anthropology classes. And it engendered C Wright Mills's sociological imagination. Ironically, at least for me, it accomplished this better than my sociology classes. A few years later, I came to relish reading the sociological classics. But as an undergraduate, I could cotton onto the idea of a sociological imagination, of seeing institutional and macro-historical explanations for social change, seeing the personal as political, via the more concrete engagement with the crime problem, especially the study of corporate crime and gendered crime. This raises one of the interesting debates in this book: whether in the teaching of criminology what we do is engage students with the contested politics and methods of crime policy more than induct them into a discipline. I think we do, and this is the better part of what we do.

The contributions to this collection illustrate why so many undergraduates find criminology engaging in the development of their personal intellectual biographies. The chapters discuss the narrative, the social structural and the quantitatively rigorous faces of criminology. They also consider the interface between explanatory theory and normative theory that is a strength of much criminology. How could one study something like deterrence only technocratically? If it turned out empirically that boiling criminals in oil in the town square deters crime, we would still feel compelled to ask if this would be right. Integrating explanatory and normative theory tends to improve both (Pettit and Braithwaite 2000).

This book suggests that criminology take debates about social justice seriously. This message resonates elsewhere too; law schools might better engage and serve their students were normative debates, that contest what justice should mean, placed at the centre of learning—procedural justice, formal justice, punitive justice, restorative justice, social justice.

Criminology has its share of intellectual factionalism and epistemological dogmatism, though less than it used to. Yet, overall, a key strength of criminology, compared with most of the social sciences, is that epistemological pluralism is the dominant ethos. If you share my belief that the social sciences have dug themselves into a terrible set of holes, pluralistic openness to diverse tools, and new tools, will be needed to dig toward the light.

A final reason criminology has deserved its comparative success is that it offers material that policy-makers can use. 'Nothing works' nihilism used to be common. Recent decades have seen not only quality research on why institutions like imprisonment can be so counterproductive, but has also identified better investments that can reduce crime, and sometimes increase social justice and victim justice at the same time. These fruits have made criminology more successful than many other social sciences in attracting funding from foundations and the public purse.

Even so, more work needs to be done as politicians and the public do not always wish to believe criminological evidence. My own suspicion is that the social movement for restorative justice, conceived as a long-run agenda of social justice transformation starting with conflict resolution in schools, could educate future generations to be more thoughtful and less automatically punitive in their thinking about how to respond to violence and theft. We are not born democratic and decent; civility is something we must learn in a structured way.

In the early and mid-1990s some of us spent more than a few years avoiding criminology conferences; it seemed more strategic to build evidence-based restorative justice in hybrid researcher-practitioner communities outside the walls of the academy. By the late 1990s, however, criminology had become extremely welcoming to those restorative justice debates that it had previously viewed as marginal. These debates were productively incorporated within criminology's broad church. Again, we might see that kind of history as evidence of a field that is now mature in its openness.

For all those virtues, criminology remains far too Anglophone an intellectual tradition. It also has too weak a comparative imagination, though the rise of higher quality crime research in Asia and at Europe's margins feeds hope, as does work in the south with a postcolonial and a transnational sensibility that has been ably embraced into this volume. Marcus Felson is surely right in his chapter when he says criminology 'does best when considering crime as a very local matter'; yet it is impoverished by the limited set of localities it learns from. An American mentor once described the pages of *Criminology* as applying progressively greater rigour to ever more trivial questions. Little wonder Jeff Ferrell in his chapter 'drifts' away from such journals—akin to the way a delinquent drifts from the discipline of dominant normative orders. Our undergraduate classes are more intellectually engaging than most of the work published in our journals. Still we all learn how to find those pieces of wheat among criminology's piles of chaff. And the contributions to this volume will help us think critically about how to sift.

As I write, I am preparing papers for the 2010 International Peace Research Association conference, and feel glad to be a peace researcher rather than a Peaceologist. I would prefer students to study research methods of general use in the social sciences that can also be applied to crime and theory about particular kinds of crime and particular kinds of institutions. So it surprises me how very useful criminological theory so often proves in the study of peacebuilding.

The editors have done a splendid job of setting up the conversation in this volume, both at the conference in Oxford and in their introductory chapter, and have brought together a stellar collection of contributors. I understand those who the editors say declined the invitation to contribute. There is some virtue in getting on with the job of doing whatever one is best at without devoting large swathes of professional time to navel gazing. Then again, a certain amount of this can be healthy if your navel is worth a look, and I can promise readers some high quality, insightful, gazing here. More than that, we can learn quite a bit from this book about how to retool criminology worksites to be more productive, sharper in their insights, more fun and more just.

John Braithwaite

Reference

P. Pettit and J. Braithwaite (2000), 'Republicanism and Restorative Justice: An Explanatory and Normative Connection', in H. Strang and J. Braithwaite (eds), Restorative Justice: From Philosophy to Practice, Aldershot: Dartmouth.

Acknowledgements

We would like to thank all of our contributors, who bore our frequent 'gentle reminders' with good humour and who have produced such engaging accounts of the field. We would also like to recognize those who participated in the October 2009 conference, including those who did not prepare chapters for the book: Adam Crawford, Liora Lazarus, Benjamin Goold, Julian Roberts, Hans-Jörg Albrecht, and Timothy Endicott. We are fortunate at Oxford to host a thriving post-graduate community, many of whom are grappling with the kinds of issues covered in this book for the first time in their own research. A number of our students helped out with this project at various moments, for which we are grateful: Harry Annison, Emma Kaufman, James Ogg, Sophie Palmer, Hannah Maslen. Finally, as ever, neither the book not the conference could have happened without funding. Thanks to the Centre for Criminology, the Law Faculty Research Support Fund, the Hulme Fund and Oxford University Press for making this possible. In a recent job search in the department, members of staff were asked by a candidate about how colleagues get along at the Centre for Criminology. When the Director, Ian Loader, pointed to the amount of collaborative projects among staff as an indicator of the atmosphere at the Centre, the candidate asked a follow-up: 'but do people do it more than once?' This project, which has involved almost all of the members of the Centre in some capacity, and, in particular, has seen the two of us working together very closely over the past eighteen months, has been both fun and interesting. We certainly would do it again!

Mary Bosworth and Carolyn Hoyle
Oxford, July 2010.

Contents

2. METHODOLOGICAL ALLEGIANCES: HOW SHOULD CRIMINOLOGY BE DONE?

PART II CRIMINOLOGY AND ITS BORDERS

1. THE LIMITS OF THE DISCIPLINE: WHERE DO WE DRAW THE LINE?

2. THE LIMITS OF GEOGRAPHY: DOES CRIMINOLOGY TRAVEL?

List of Contributors

Editors

Mary Bosworth is Reader in Criminology at the University of Oxford and Fellow of St Cross College. She is also concurrently Professor of Criminology at Monash University, Australia. She works on issues to do with race, gender and citizenship with a particular focus on prisons and immigration detention. Her books include: *Engendering Resistance* (Ashgate, 1999), *The US Federal Prison System* (Sage, 2002); *Race, Gender and Punishment* (co-edited with Jeanne Flavin, Rutgers, 2007); and *Explaining US Imprisonment* (Sage, 2010). She is co-Editor of *Theoretical Criminology* with Simon Cole and is currently conducting an ethnography of immigration detention centres in the United Kingdom.

Carolyn Hoyle is Professor of Criminology at the University of Oxford and Fellow of Green Templeton College. She has published empirical and theoretical research on a number of criminological topics including policing, domestic violence, restorative justice and the death penalty. Her publications include: *Debating Restorative Justice* (with Chris Cunneen, Hart Publishing, 2010); *Restorative Justice: Critical Concepts in Criminology* (Routledge, 2009); *The Death Penalty: A Worldwide Perspective* (with Roger Hood, Oxford University Press, 2008); *New Visions of Crime Victims* (co-edited with Richard Young, Hart Publishing, 2002); *Negotiating Domestic Violence: Police, Criminal Justice and Victims* (Oxford University Press, 2000).

Contributors

Katja Franko Aas is Professor of Criminology at the Institute of Criminology and Sociology of Law, University of Oslo, Norway. She has written extensively on issues of globalization, security, border controls, surveillance and uses of information and communication technologies in contemporary penal systems. Her recent publications include: *Technologies of Insecurity* (co-edited with H.M. Lomell and H. O. Gundhus, Routledge-Cavendish, 2009); *Globalization and Crime* (Sage, 2007); *Sentencing in the Age of Information: from Faust to Macintosh* (Routledge-Cavendish, 2005); and *Cosmopolitan Justice and its Discontents* (co-edited with

C. Baillet, Routledge, forthcoming). *Sentencing in the Age of Information* was joint winner of the 2006 Socio-Legal Studies Association Hart Book Prize.

Andrew Ashworth has been at the University of Oxford since 1997, as Vinerian Professor of English Law, Fellow of All Souls College, and a member of the Centre for Criminology. His principal fields of research are criminal law, criminal process, sentencing and related parts of European human rights law. He teaches courses for the undergraduate law degree, for the BCL, and for the MSc in Criminology and Criminal Justice. He was a member (1999–2010) and chairman (2007–10) of the Sentencing Advisory Panel.

Charles Barber is a Lecturer in Psychiatry at the Yale University School of Medicine and Director of The Connection Institute, an advocacy, research and training initiative on mental health and criminal justice issues at The Connection, Inc., a human services and community development agency in Connecticut. He created for the Connecticut Department of Correction a 'best practice' model for community-release programmes. He is the author of *Songs from the Black Chair: A Memoir of Mental Interiors* and *Comfortably Numb: How Psychiatry is Medicating a Nation* (University of Nebraska Press, 2005).

Alfred Blumstein is a University Professor and the J. Erik Jonsson Professor of Urban Systems and Operations Research and former Dean (from 1986 to 1993) at the H. John Heinz III College of Public Policy and Management of Carnegie Mellon University. He has had extensive experience in both research and policy with the criminal justice system since serving on the President's Commission on Law Enforcement and Administration of Justice in 1966–7 as Director of its Task Force on Science and Technology. Dr Blumstein has served on numerous national committees and commissions and his efforts in the academy and public life have been recognized by various awards, including: the 1985 Kimball Medal 'for service to the [operations research] profession and the society'; the 2007 Stockholm Prize in Criminology; the 1987 ASC Sutherland Award; the 1998 Wolfgang Award for Distinguished Achievement in Criminology; and was awarded an honorary degree of Doctor of Laws from the John Jay College of Criminal Justice CUNY. He is a member of the US National Academy of Engineering, a Fellow of the American Association for the Advancement of Science (AAAS) and the American Society of Criminology. His research over the past twenty years has covered many aspects of criminal justice phenomena and policy, including crime measurement, criminal careers, sentencing, deterrence and incapacitation, prison population, demographic trends, juvenile violence, and drug policy.

Ben Bowling is Professor of Criminology and Criminal Justice in the School of Law, King's College London. He was previously Senior Research Officer in the Home Office, Visiting Assistant Professor at John Jay College of Criminal Justice

(City University of New York), lecturer at the University of Cambridge Institute of Criminology and Visiting Professor at the University of the West Indies. He has published widely in the fields of crime and policing and speaks regularly about his work on courses, conferences, television and radio. He has been an adviser to the United Nations, Interpol, the UK Parliament, Home Office and the Foreign & Commonwealth Office. His books include: *Violent Racism* (Oxford University Press, 1998); *Racism, Crime and Justice* (with Coretta Phillips, Longman, 2002); *Policing the Caribbean: Transnational Security Cooperation in Practice* (Oxford University Press, 2010) and *Global Policing* (with James Sheptycki, Sage, 2012).

John Braithwaite is an Australian Research Council Federation Fellow at the Australian National University. His current research returns with Graham Dukes to work on corporate crime in the pharmaceutical industry. Mainly he will spend the rest of his days working on a project called Peacebuilding Compared. Volumes on Bougainville, Solomon Islands and Timor-Leste are on the way to join the first ANU E Press volume called *Anomie and Violence: Non-truth and Reconciliation in Indonesian Peacebuilding.*

David Brown is Emeritus Professor at the University of New South Wales, Sydney, Australia, where he taught criminal law, criminal justice, criminology and penology from 1974 to 2008. He has been active in criminal justice movements, issues and debates for over three decades and is a regular media commentator. He has published widely in the field including thirty chapters in books. He has co-authored or co-edited: *The Prison Struggle* (1982); *The Judgments of Lionel Murphy* (1986); *Death in the Hands of the State* (1988); *Criminal Laws* in four editions (1990); (1996); (2001); (2006); *Rethinking Law and Order* (1998); *Prisoners as Citizens* (2002); and *The New Punitiveness* (2005).

Amanda Burgess-Proctor is an Assistant Professor in the Department of Sociology and Anthropology at Oakland University, US. She received her PhD in Criminal Justice from Michigan State University. Her primary research interests include feminist criminology, criminological theory, intimate partner violence, and intersections of race, class, and gender. She has published articles in *Feminist Criminology, Violence Against Women, Violence and Victims,* and *Women and Criminal Justice.*

Shawn D. Bushway is an Associate Professor of Criminal Justice on the faculty of the School of Criminal Justice at the University at Albany. He received his PhD in Public Policy Analysis and Political Economy in 1996 from the Heinz School of Public Policy and Management at Carnegie Mellon University. His current research focuses on the process of desistance, the impact of a criminal history on subsequent outcomes, and the distribution of discretion in the criminal justice sentencing process.

Pat Carlen, Visiting Professor at Kent University and Editor-in-Chief of the *British Journal of Criminology*, has published eighteen books and many articles on crime and justice. She has given invited lectures in Australia, United States, Netherlands, Denmark, Portugal, Spain, Canada, Austria, Sweden, New Zealand, Hungary, South Africa and Peru, and has conducted research in several of those countries. Selected works have been translated into Japanese, Norwegian, Dutch, Portuguese and Spanish. In 1997 she was awarded the American Society of Criminology Sellin-Glueck Prize for outstanding international contributions to Criminology and in 2010 the British Society of Criminology Award for Outstanding Achievement.

Janet Chan is Professor and Associate Dean (Research) at the University of New South Wales (UNSW) Law School and a Fellow of the Academy of Social Sciences in Australia. Janet's research interests include: reform and innovation in criminal justice, organizational culture, and the sociology of creativity. She has published numerous books and articles on criminal justice and policing issues, including: *Changing Police Culture* (1997); *Fair Cop: Learning the Art of Policing* (with Chris Devery and Sally Doran, 2003); and *Reshaping Juvenile Justice* (2005). In recent years Janet has developed a research interest in the creative practice of artists, scientists and art-science collaborations. She is co-editor (with Leon Mann) of a 2011 volume *Creativity and Innovation in Business and Beyond*. In 2010 she started a collaborative project with Jane Bolitho, Jenny Bargen and Jasmine Bruce on restorative justice for serious offenders. Since 2011 she has led a new research project on understanding legal culture and work stress among Australian lawyers.

Chris Cunneen is Professor of Criminology at Cairns Institute, James Cook University and has a conjoint appointment with the University of New South Wales, Sydney, Australia. He has published widely in the area of juvenile justice, policing, criminal justice policy, restorative justice and indigenous legal issues. His books include: *Indigenous Legal Relations in Australia* (Oxford University Press, 2009); *The Critical Criminology Companion* (Federation Press, 2008); *Juvenile Justice, Youth and Crime in Australia* (Oxford University Press, 2007); *Conflict, Politics and Crime* (Allen and Unwin, 2001); *Faces of Hate* (Federation Press, 1997); and *Indigenous People and the Law in Australia* (Butterworths, 1995). He is the co-author with Carolyn Hoyle of *Debating Restorative Justice* (Hart Publishing, 2010).

Kathleen Daly is Professor of Criminology and Criminal Justice, Griffith University (Brisbane, Australia). She writes on gender, race, crime, and justice; and on restorative, Indigenous, and international criminal justice. First based in the United States 1983–95 (Yale University and the University of Michigan), she travelled to Australia in 1995 as a Senior Fulbright Scholar to study restorative justice. From 1998 to 2006, she received three Australian Research Council (ARC) grants to research restorative justice and the race and gender politics of alternative justice practices. In 2008, she launched an international project on innovative responses to sexual violence, also funded by the ARC; and in 2009, as co-CI, she is participating in a fifth ARC-funded project on legal responses to Indigenous partner violence. In addition to books and edited collections, she has published over seventy articles in journals, edited volumes, and law reviews. She is a Fellow of the Academy of the Social Sciences in Australia, and immediate past President of the Australian and New Zealand Society of Criminology (2005–9).

Aaron Doyle is Associate Professor of Sociology at Carleton University in Ottawa, Canada. His research interests include risk, insurance, and security; experiences of risk in everyday life; criminological theory; crime and media; and visual surveillance. He has published numerous articles in these areas and authored, co-authored or co-edited the books: *Arresting Images: Crime and Policing in Front of the Television Camera; Risk and Mortality; Insurance as Governance;* and *Uncertain Business: Risk, Insurance and the Limits of Knowledge* (all University of Toronto Press); and *Critical Criminology in Canada: New Voices, New Directions* (University of British Columbia Press).

Marcus Felson is Professor at Texas State University, San Marcos, Texas. He is author of *Crime and Nature* (Sage, 2006) and *Crime and Everyday Life* (Sage, 2002) now going into its fourth edition. He originated the routine activity approach to crime rate analysis, and is currently studying the co-offending process. A graduate of the University of Chicago, he received his PhD from the University of Michigan. Professor Felson works on down-to-earth theories with tangible applications. He has been a guest lecturer in many nations, including Argentina, Australia, Belgium, Brazil, Canada, Chile, the Czech Republic, Denmark, England, Estonia, Finland, France, Germany, Hong Kong, Hungary, Italy, Japan, Mexico, Netherlands, New Zealand, Norway, Poland, Scotland, Spain, Sweden, Taiwan, and Turkey. He has given talks on crime to applied mathematicians at several universities, including UCLA, Rutgers, the *Centro de Análisis y Modelamiento de la Seguridad* at the University of Chile, and the *Centro di Ricerca Matematica Ennio De Giorgi* at the *Scuola Normale Superiore* University in Pisa, Italy. He is the author of 'What Every Mathematician should Know about Modeling Crime'.

Jeff Ferrell earned his PhD in sociology from The University of Texas at Austin, and is currently Professor of Sociology at Texas Christian University, United States, and Visiting Professor of Criminology at the University of Kent, United Kingdom. He is the author of the books: *Crimes of Style* (Garland, 1993; Northeastern University Press, 1996); *Tearing Down the Streets* (Palgrave/Macmillan/St. Martin's, 2001/2002); *Empire of Scrounge* (New York University Press, 2006); and, with Keith Hayward and Jock Young, *Cultural Criminology: An Invitation* (SAGE, London, 2008), winner of the 2009 Distinguished Book Award from the American Society of Criminology's Division of International Criminology. He is also the co-editor of the books: *Cultural Criminology* (Northeastern University Press, 1995); *Ethnography at the Edge* (Northeastern University Press, 1998); *Making Trouble* (Aldine de Gruyter,

1999); *Cultural Criminology Unleashed* (Routledge/ Cavendish/Glasshouse, 2004); and *Cultural Criminology: Theories of Crime* (Ashgate, 2010, forthcoming). Jeff Ferrell is the founding and current editor of the New York University Press book series *Alternative Criminology*, and one of the founding editors of the journal *Crime, Media, Culture: An International Journal* (SAGE, London), winner of the Association of Learned and Professional Society Publishers' 2006 Charlesworth Award for Best New Journal. In 1998 he received the Critical Criminologist of the Year Award from the Division of Critical Criminology of the American Society of Criminology.

David Garland is Arthur T. Vanderbilt Professor of Law and Professor of Sociology at New York University. He has taught at the University of Edinburgh and held visiting positions at Leuven University, UC Berkeley, and Princeton University. He is the editor (with Richard Sparks) of *Criminology and Social Theory* (2000) and of *Mass Imprisonment: Social Causes and Consequences* (2001); the founding editor of the journal *Punishment & Society*; and the author of *Punishment and Welfare* (1985), *Punishment and Modern Society* (1990), *The Culture of Control* (2001), and, most recently, of *Peculiar Institution: America's Death Penalty in an Age of Abolition* (2010).

Michael R. Gottfredson is a Professor of Criminology, Law, and Society and of Sociology at the University of California, Irvine, where he also serves as the Executive Vice Chancellor and Provost. He received his AB in 1973 from the University of California, Davis and PhD in 1976 from SUNY at Albany. He is the author or editor (with others) of several books, including: *Control Theories of Crime and Delinquency* (2003); *Personal Liberty and Community Safety* (1995); *The Generality of Deviance* (1994); *A General Theory of Crime* (1990); *Decision-making in Criminal Justice* (1988); *Positive Criminology* (1987); *Policy Guidelines for Bail: An Experiment in Court Reform* (1985); *Understanding Crime* (1980); and *Victims of Personal Crime* (1978). He has published numerous articles in journals, including *Criminology*, *American Journal of Sociology*, *American Sociological Review*, *Advances in Criminological Theory*, and various law reviews. He is a Fellow of the American Society of Criminology, the recipient of the Paul Tappan Award by the Western Society of Criminology for outstanding contributions to the field of criminology, the Distinguished Graduate Award from the Nelson Rockefeller College of Public Affairs and Policy, and the Richard McGee Award for 'Outstanding Contributions to Crime Theory' from the American Justice Institute.

Kevin D. Haggerty is editor of the *Canadian Journal of Sociology* and book review editor of the international journal *Surveillance and Society*. He is professor of sociology and criminology at the University of Alberta and a member of the executive team for the *New Transparency* Major Collaborative Research Initiative. He has authored, co-authored or co-edited: *Policing the Risk Society* (Oxford University Press); *Making Crime Count* (University of Toronto Press); *The New Politics of*

Surveillance and Visibility (University of Toronto Press); and *Surveillance & Democracy* (Routledge).

Kelly Hannah-Moffat is Professor and Vice Dean Undergraduate of the Department of Sociology at University of Toronto Mississauga, where she has been since 1999. She is cross-appointed to the Centre of Criminology and is a Massey College Senior Fellow. She has published numerous articles and books on risk, punishment, parole decision making, gender and diversity. She recently published *Gendered Risks* (with Pat O'Malley, Routledge Cavendish, 2007); 'Restructuring Pre-sentence Reports Race, Risk, and the PSR' *Punishment and Society*, (2010), 12(3) with Paula Maurutto; and 'Under These Conditions: Gender, Parole, and the Governance of Reintegration' *British Journal of Criminology*, (2009), 49:1–20 (with Sarah Turnbull).

Ole Kristian Hjemdal became a sociologist in 1975. From 1981 to 1988 he worked together with Thomas Mathiesen at the Institute of Sociology of Law at the University of Oslo, as a researcher and assistant professor. From 1988 until 1995 he was an associate professor at Oslo University College and then headed the Norwegian Centre for Information and Studies of Violence from 1996 until 2003. In 2004 the Centre became a part of The Norwegian Centre for Violence and Traumatic Stress Studies, where he now heads the section for studies on violence and trauma–adults. His research is on ethnic discrimination and integration of immigrants and ethnic minorities; social work; self-help organization and on interpersonal violence. His latest work has been on violence against pregnant women and on men as victims of family violence.

Tim Hope, Chair in Criminology, University of Salford, Manchester. Between 1974 and 1991 he worked at the Home Office Research and Planning Unit, where he earned a PhD in Sociology from the University of London. He has also held positions with CACI Ltd. and the Universities of Keele, Missouri-St. Louis and Manchester. He has been a visiting research fellow of the Scottish Centre for Crime and Justice Research (University of Edinburgh), the Quantitative Criminology Group of the Cathie Marsh Centre for Census and Survey Research (University of Manchester), and the Vauxhall Centre for Criminology (University of Luton). He was Director of the Economic and Social Research Council Crime and Social Order Research Programme and the Keele Community Safety Group. He is, or has been, an adviser or consultant to the International Centre for the Prevention of Crime, the European Forum for Urban Safety, the Audit Commission for England and Wales, the UK Statistics Commission (on crime statistics), the National Reassurance Policing Programme, the City of St Louis, MO. Police Department, and the Safer Bury Partnership. He is a member of GERN, jointly coordinated (with Dario Melossi) the work-package 'local public policies of crime prevention' of the CRIMPREV Co-ordination Action of the European Union Sixth Framework Programme, and was an expert consultant to the European Commission evaluation of the European

Crime Prevention Network. On the politics of crime control evaluation, he has given oral and written evidence to the House of Commons Science and Technology Committee, contributed to the CRIMPREV Methodology and Good Practice work-package, and published *Critical Thinking about the Uses of Research* (with Reece Walters). He has presented and published papers (some in translation) in the United States, Canada, France, Germany, Italy, Netherlands, Czech Republic, Poland, and Portugal.

Mike Hough is Professor of Criminal Policy at Birkbeck, University of London, and Co-director of the Institute for Criminal Policy Research. Mike has published extensively on a range of criminological topics including policing, crime prevention and community safety, anti-social behaviour, probation and drugs. Current work includes research on sentencing, on drugs, on youth justice and on public trust in justice. He is the President of the British Society of Criminology. His recent publications include: 'Crime and Criminal Justice: Exploring the Policy Options' (with Julian Roberts in *Option for a New Britain*, edited by Varun Uberoi, Adam Coutts, Iain McClean and David Halpern, Palgrave MacMillan, 2009); *Tackling Prison Overcrowding* (edited with Rob Allen and Enver Solomon, Policy Press, 2008); and *Surveying Crime in the 21st Century* (edited with Mike Maxfield, Willan, 2007).

Alison Liebling is Professor of Criminology and Criminal Justice and Director of the Prisons Research Centre at the University of Cambridge Institute of Criminology. She has carried out research on suicides in prison, staff-prisoner relationships, the work of prison officers, small units for difficult prisoners, incentives and earned privileges, prison privatization, values and practices in prison life, and measuring the quality of prison life. She has published several books, including *Suicides in Prison* (1992), *Prisons and their Moral Performance* (2004) and (with Shadd Maurna) (2005) *The Effects of Imprisonment.*

Ian Loader is Professor of Criminology and Director of the Centre for Criminology at the University of Oxford, United Kingdom. He is author of *Civilizing Security* (with Neil Walker, 2007, Cambridge University Press) and *Public Criminology?* (with Richard Sparks, 2010, Routledge) and is currently engaged in research and writing on markets for security.

Monique Marks is based in the Community Development Programme at the University of KwaZulu-Natal. She is also a Research Associate of the Centre of Criminology at the University of Cape Town. She has published widely in the areas of youth social movements, ethnographic research methods, police labour relations, police organizational change and security governance. She has published three books: *Young Warriors: Youth Identity, Politics and Violence in South Africa*; *Transforming the Robocops: Changing Police in South Africa;* and *Police Occupational Culture: New Debates and Directions* (edited with Anne-Marie Singh and Megan O'Neill).

Shadd Maruna is Director of the Institute of Criminology and Criminal Justice at the School of Law Queen's University Belfast where he is also Professor of Justice Studies and Human Development. He received his PhD from Northwestern University. Previously, he has been a lecturer at the University of Cambridge and the University at Albany, SUNY. His book *Making Good: How Ex-Convicts Reform and Rebuild Their Lives* (American Psychological Association, 2001) was named the 'Outstanding Contribution to Criminology' by the American Society of Criminology in 2001. His other books include: *Rehabilitation: Beyond the Risk Paradigm* (Routledge, 2007); *The Effects of Imprisonment* (Cambridge University Press, 2005); *After Crime and Punishment: Pathways to Ex-Offender Reintegration* (Willan, 2004); and *Fifty Key Thinkers in Criminology* (2010, Routledge).

Thomas Mathiesen completed his PhD at the University of Oslo on a prison study in 1965 *(The Defences of the Weak,* Tavistock Publications). He became Professor of Sociology of Law in 1971 and, after retirement in 2003, Professor Emeritus. He is still active at the Department of Criminology and Sociology of Law at Oslo and is author of a number of books on sociology of law, criminology, media power and the silencing power of public administration. A number of his books and articles are published in a wide range of languages. Six of his books are published in English, including: *The Politics of Abolition* (1974) and *Prison on trial* (3rd edn. 2006). He is co-founder, and active member of KROM—The Norwegian Association of Penal Reform, which commenced its activities in 1968. KROM is a pressure group in the field of penal policy, and has inmates, ex-inmates and non-inmates on the board and among its members. Many of Mathiesen's publications are based on his wide experience as a member of this group.

Eugene McLaughlin is Professor of Criminology and Sociology in the Department of Sociology, City University London. He is currently co-director of the *Law, Justice and Journalism Research Centre.* He has written extensively on police governance and reform, police–community relations, the managerialization of criminal justice and contemporary criminological theory. His current research concentrates on the theory and practice of policing in multi-pluralist societies, the news media and crime, and the contemporary knowledge practices of critical criminology. His most recent books are *The Sage Handbook of Criminological Theory* (co-edited with Tim Newburn, Sage, 2010) and *The New Policing* (Sage, 2007). He is also the co-editor of *Public Criminologies* (Special Issue of *Theoretical Criminology,* edited with Lynn Chancer, 2007); *The Sage Dictionary of Criminology* (edited with John Muncie, Sage, 2005) and *Criminological Perspectives: Essential Readings* (edited with Gordon Hughes and John Muncie, Sage, 2002). He is a member of the editorial boards of the *British Journal of Criminology, Crime, Media* and *Culture* and *Theoretical Criminology.*

Linda G. Mills is Professor of Social Work, Public Policy, and Law at New York University. She is also Executive Director of NYU's Center on Violence and Recovery,

NYU's Senior Vice Provost for Undergraduates in the Global Network University, and Associate Vice Chancellor for Admissions and Financial Aid for NYU Abu Dhabi. In her books, *Violent Partners: A Breakthrough Plan for Ending the Cycle of Abuse* (Basic Books, 2008) and *Insult to Injury: Rethinking Our Response to Intimate Abuse* (Princeton University, 2003), Mills challenges current paradigms of domestic abuse and develops a new theory and practice based on empirical research, for rethinking how we respond to violence in intimate relationships. Mills' publications include: 'Circulos de Paz and the Promise of Peace: Restorative Justice Meets Intimate Violence' (with Mary Helen Maley and Yael Shy), *NYU Review of Law and Social Change*, 2009; 'Shame and intimate abuse: The critical missing link between cause and cure', *Children and Youth Services Review*, 2008; 'The justice of recovery: How the state can heal the violence of crime', *Hastings Law Journal* in 2006; 'Fighting for child custody when domestic violence is at issue: A survey of state laws and a call for more research' (with Amy Levin), *Social Work*, 2003; 'The law of white spaces: Race, culture, and legal education' (with Peter Goodrich), *Journal of Legal Education*, 2001; and 'Killing Her Softly: Intimate Abuse and the Violence of State Intervention', *Harvard Law Review*, 1999. Mills is currently directing and producing a documentary called 'Auf Wiedersehen: 'Til We Meet Again', a film that explores the intergenerational transmission of trauma from the Holocaust to 9/11. The film has been invited to several film festivals and recently won an Audience Award, Runner Up for Best Documentary, at the Los Angeles Jewish Film Festival.

David Nelken taught criminology at Cambridge University, Edinburgh University and University College, London before moving to Italy. He is currently Distinguished Professor of Sociology at the University of Macerata, Italy, as well as Distinguished Research Professor of Law at Cardiff University, and Visiting Professor of Law at the London School of Economics. He has been appointed visiting professor of Criminology at the Oxford Centre of Criminology from 2010–13. He is an Academician of the UK Academy of Social Sciences and received a Distinguished Scholar Award from the American Sociological Association in 1985 and the Sellin-Glueck Award from the American Society of Criminology in 2009. His research focuses on white-collar crime, corruption, and comparative criminology. His most recent book is *Comparative Criminal Justice: Making Sense of Difference* (Sage, 2010).

Tim Newburn is Professor of Criminology and Social Policy at the London School of Economics. He is a past President of the British Society of Criminology and author/editor of over thirty books including: *Sage Handbook of Criminological Theory* (ed with McLaughlin, Sage, 2010); *Key Readings in Criminology* (Cullompton: Willan, 2009); *Policing Developing Democracies* (edited with Hinton, London/New York: Routledge: 2008); *Policy Transfer and Criminal Justice* (with Jones, Open University Press, 2007); *Criminology* (Cullompton: Willan, 2007); and *The Politics of Crime Control* (ed with Rock, Clarendon Press, 2006).

Ian O'Donnell is Professor of Criminology at University College Dublin and an Adjunct Fellow of Linacre College, Oxford. Previously he was director of the Irish Penal Reform Trust. His most recent book is *Child Pornography: Crime Computers and Society* (with Claire Milner, Willan, 2007).

Stephan Parmentier studied law, political sciences and sociology at the KU Leuven (Belgium) and the University of Minnesota-Twin Cities (United States). He currently teaches sociology of crime, law, and human rights at the Faculty of Law of the KU Leuven, where he has served as the Director of the Law and Society Institute and the Head of the Department of Criminal Law and Criminology. He has been a visiting professor at the International Institute for Sociology of Law in Oñati (Spain), the University for Peace (San José, Costa Rica) and the University of New South Wales (Sydney, Australia), and a visiting scholar at the universities of Stellenbosch (South Africa), Oxford (United Kingdom) and New South Wales (Sydney, Australia). He was the editor-in-chief of the *Flemish Yearbook on Human Rights* and is the founding general co-editor of the new book *Series on Transitional Justice* (Intersentia Publishers, Antwerp). Parmentier has also has served as an advisor to the European Committee for the Prevention of Torture, the Belgian minister of the Interior, the King Baudouin Foundation, and Amnesty International. His research interests include political crimes, transitional justice and human rights, and the administration of criminal justice. He was the vice-president of the Flemish section of Amnesty International between 1999 and 2002.

Ray Paternoster is Professor in the Department of Criminology and Criminal Justice at the University of Maryland, United States. His research interests include the analysis of offender decision-making, behavioural economics and crime, issues pertaining to capital punishment, criminological theory, desistance from crime, and the transition from adolescence to adulthood. He received his PhD degree from Florida State University in 1978 and has been at the University of Maryland since 1982.

Nicole Rafter teaches in the College of Criminal Justice, Northeastern University, United States. Her research interests include criminological theory, crime films, the history of criminology, and the work of Cesare Lombroso. Her most recent books include: *Origins of Criminology: A Reader* (Routledge, 2009); *The Criminal Brain: Understanding Biological Theories of Crime* (New York University Press, 2008); *Shots in the Mirror: Crime Films and Society* (Oxford University Press, 2006); and a new translation of Lombroso's *Criminal Man* (with Mary Gibson, Duke University Press, 2006). With Michelle Brown, she is currently working on *Criminology Goes to the Movies*, a book examining intersections among films and criminological theories (forthcoming, 2011). She is a Fellow of the American Society of Criminology and winner of its 2009 Sutherland Award.

Beth E. Richie is The Director of the Institute for Research on Race and Public Policy and Professor of African American Studies and Criminology, Law and Justice at The

University of Illinois at Chicago. The emphasis of her scholarly and activist work has been on the ways that race/ethnicity and social position affect women's experience of violence and incarceration, focusing on the experiences of African American battered women and sexual assault survivors. Dr Richie is the author of numerous articles concerning Black Feminism and Gender Violence, Race and Criminal Justice Policy, and The Social Dynamics around issues of sexuality, families and grassroots organizations in African American Communities. Her book *Compelled to Crime: the Gender Entrapment of Black Battered Women* is cited in the popular press for its original arguments concerning race, gender and crime. Her upcoming book, *Black Women, Male Violence and the Build-up of a Prison Nation* chronicles the evolution of the contemporary anti-violence movement during the time of mass incarceration in the United States. Her work has been supported by grants from The Robert Wood Johnson Foundation, The Ford Foundation, and The National Institute for Justice and The National Institute of Corrections. She has been awarded the Audre Lorde Legacy Award from the Union Institute, The Advocacy Award from the US Department of Health and Human Services, and The Visionary Award from the Violence Intervention Project. Dr Richie is a board member of The Woods Fund of Chicago, The Institute on Domestic Violence in the African Community, The Center for Fathers' Families and Public Policy and a founding member of INCITE!: Women of Color Against Violence.

William A. Schabas is Professor of International law, Middlesex University, London; Emeritus Professor of Human Rights Law and Chairman, Irish Centre for Human Rights, National University of Ireland Galway. He is also an Honorary Professor at the Chinese Academy of Social Sciences, in Beijing, and *Professeur Associé* at the Université du Québec à Montréal. He is the author of more than twenty books and 275 journal articles, on such subjects as the abolition of capital punishment, genocide and the international criminal tribunals. His most recent book, *The International Criminal Court: A Commentary on the Rome Statute*, was published by Oxford University Press in 2010. He is editor-in-chief of *Criminal Law Forum*. Professor Schabas was a member of the Sierra Leone Truth and Reconciliation Commission. He is the chairman of the Board of Trustees of the United Nations Voluntary Fund for Technical Cooperation in Human Rights. He is an Officer of the Order of Canada, a member of the Royal Irish Academy, and the current laureate of the Vespasian V. Pella Medal for International Criminal Justice of the Association internationale de droit penal.

Clifford Shearing is the Chair of Criminology and holds the South African Research Chair of Security and Justice in the Faculty of Law at the University of Cape Town where is his also the Director of the Centre of Criminology. His research focuses on the governance of security. His most recent books are *Imagining Security* with Jennifer Wood (Willan, 2007) and *Lengthening the Arm of the Law* with Julie Ayling and Peter Grabosky (Cambridge, 2009).

Lawrence W. Sherman is the Wolfson Professor of Criminology at the University of Cambridge, where he directs the Jerry Lee Centre of Experimental Criminology and the Police Executive Programme. He is also a Distinguished University Professor at the University of Maryland in the Department of Criminology and Criminal Justice. He has designed or directed over thirty randomized field experiments in crime prevention and justice, including twelve restorative justice experiments in Australia and the United Kingdom, as well as evaluations of policies for policing domestic violence, hot spots of crime, and gun crime. He has been elected President of the American Academy of Political and Social Science, the American and International Societies of Criminology, and the Academy of Experimental Criminology.

Natalie J. Sokoloff is Professor Emerita of Sociology, and has been a member of the faculty of John Jay College of Criminal Justice for forty years. She is also a member of the doctoral faculties in Sociology, Criminology, and Women's Studies at the Graduate School, City University of New York. She teaches courses on women, crime, and justice; imprisonment and empowerment; and domestic violence. In 2005 she was doubly honoured with the Outstanding Teaching Award at John Jay College and the Distinguished Scholar Award from the American Society of Criminology's Division on Women and Crime. Some of her recent publications include 'The Intersectional Paradigm and Alternative Visions to Stopping Domestic Violence: What Poor Women, Women of Color, and Immigrant Women Are Teaching Us about Violence in the Family', *International Journal of Sociology of the Family* (American Sociological Association, 2008); 'Expanding the Intersectional Paradigm to Better Understand Domestic Violence in Immigrant Communities', *Critical Criminology* (2008); 'Locking up Hope: Immigration, Gender, and the Prison System', *Scholar and Feminist Online*, 6(3) (2008); 'Impact of the Prison Industrial Complex on African American Women', *Souls: A Critical Journal of Black Politics, Culture, and Society*, 5(4): 31–46; and two critically acclaimed books: *Domestic Violence at the Margins: Readings on Race, Class, Gender and Culture* (Rutgers University, 2005); and *The Criminal Justice System and Women: Offenders, Prisoners, Victims & Workers*, 3rd edn (McGraw-Hill, 2004). Her expansive *Multicultural Perspectives on Domestic Violence: A Bibliography* is available at <www.lib.jjay.cuny.edu/research/DomesticViolence/>).

Richard Sparks is Professor of Criminology at the University of Edinburgh and Co-Director of the Scottish Centre for Crime and Justice Research (<http://www.sccjr.ac.uk/>). Richard's main research interests are in prisons; penal politics; public responses to crime and punishment, and criminological theory. His publications include: *Criminal Justice and Political Cultures* (with Tim Newburn (eds), Willan, 2004); *Criminology and Social Theory* (with David Garland (eds), Oxford University Press, 2000); *Crime and Social Change in Middle England* (with Evi Girling and Ian Loader, Routledge, 2000); and *Prisons and the Problem of Order* (with Tony Bottoms and Will Hay, Oxford University Press, 1996). Richard's current work, in collaboration with Ian Loader, concerns competing accounts of relevance and influence in crime and justice research, and the place of criminology in debates on the public roles of the social sciences. See further I. Loader and R. Sparks, *Public Criminology?* (Routledge, 2010).

Lucia Zedner is Professor of Criminal Justice, Law Faculty and Corpus Christi College, University of Oxford. She first became a Member of the Centre for Criminology at Oxford in 1988 when she was a Prize Research Fellow at Nuffield College. After teaching for five years at the London School of Economics she returned to Oxford in 1994. Since 2007 she has also held the post of Conjoint Professor at the Faculty of Law, University of New South Wales, Australia where she is a regular visitor. She has also held visiting fellowships at universities in Germany, Israel, America, and Australia. Her publications include *Women, Crime and Custody in Victorian England* (Oxford University Press, 1991); *Child Victims* (with Jane Morgan, Oxford University Press, 1992); *The Criminological Foundations of Penal Policy* (co-edited with Andrew Ashworth, Oxford University Press, 2003); *Criminal Justice* (Oxford University Press, 2004), *Crime and Security* (co-edited with Benjamin Goold, Ashgate, 2006), *Security* (Routledge, 2009) and many articles and chapters in the field of criminal justice and security.

WHAT IS CRIMINOLOGY? AN INTRODUCTION

MARY BOSWORTH AND CAROLYN HOYLE

CRIMINOLOGY is booming. Numerous departments, research centres, post-graduate and undergraduate programmes open each year, while new books and journals also proliferate. Such growth is particularly noticeable in the English-speaking world, where Australasia, North America, and Britain are peculiarly enthusiastic consumers and producers of criminological knowledge. Yet, the field is not limited to such places, as witnessed by publications like the *Asian Journal of Criminology* (est. 2006), the *Journal of Scandinavian Studies in Criminology and Crime Prevention* (est. 2000), *Champ Pénal* (est. 2004), the *Pakistan Journal of Criminology* (est. 2009) and in the form of professional groups such as the Sociedad Mexicana de Criminología Capítulo Nuevo León (est. 2008), the South Asian Society of Criminology and Victimology (est. 2010), and the European Society of Criminology (est. 2000). Even San Marino, one of the smallest countries in Europe, has its own society of criminology, the Società Sammarinese di Criminologia (est. 2006).

There are some places where the discipline is weak; whereas criminology was once influential on policy-makers in parts of Latin America, for example, its role there sharply declined during the last decades of the twentieth century (Del Olmo 1999; Elbert 2004). So, too, and notwithstanding attempts to generate an 'Africana criminology' in the *African Journal of Criminology and Justice Studies* and elsewhere (Agozino 2005; 2003), much African criminological scholarship other than that produced in South Africa remains somewhat outside the mainstream of the discipline. Instead, in both these continents, the impact of criminology appears to be most evident in international policy transfer of crime control measures, projects themselves that have origins in criminological research conducted elsewhere (Cohen 1988; Karstadt 2002; Lippens 2004).

In addition to variations in the strength and influence of the discipline, there is little agreement within the field over the contours of the discipline itself. Most obviously, as in other social sciences, there is considerable disagreement among scholars over methodological issues—ie how best to conduct research. More than that, however, the subject-matter and the aims of the discipline are also contested.

Such disagreement has many effects, all of which feed back to the discipline in various ways, though these are rarely considered in any detail within the scholarly literature. We have witnessed, for example, a growing divergence between the two main national producers of criminological knowledge: the United States and the United Kingdom. Whereas once, criminologists opined that 'It is difficult to understand British criminology without writing about the United States. American criminology is a powerhouse of ideas, research techniques and interventions which understandably dominate Western thinking about crime' (Young, 1988: 163), it seems these days that the 'special relationship' between these two nations may, in criminology, as elsewhere, be shifting. Primarily driven apart by methodological concerns, scholars in Britain and America inhabit quite different disciplinary cultures; while in the latter, the discipline is predominantly housed in departments of 'criminal justice' with a target audience of state agents, in the former, 'criminology' remains a point of intersection between a number of academic fields and approaches.

The research culture and position of criminologists in Scandinavian countries like Norway and Sweden differs in subtle but important ways from both Britain and America. Not only is there less social distance and a more parsimonious approach to punishment, but in these countries the relationships between the state agents of control and punishment and the academy is much closer. Criminology in such places continues to be viewed by the state as something useful and important with which to engage.

In comparison, while the Home Office of England and Wales once had close links with the academy, today there seems to be considerable mutual distrust, at least amongst more critical criminologists. Tim Hope and Reece Walters recently called on criminologists to boycott government research, arguing that the government skews, manipulates and distorts criminological research 'for political gain' (Hope and Walters 2008: 9). In a publication that received a good deal of media coverage they argued that: 'Critical scholarship is viewed as unwelcome, unhelpful and is actively discouraged. Any credible independent research that is likely to shed a negative or critical light on the policies and practices of government will not be procured, funded, published or even debated by the Home Office' (ibid.: 12). 'We live in a society where government manipulates or cherry-picks criminological knowledge and produces distorted pictures of the "crime problem".... Academic criminologists must not grant legitimacy to such a corrupt process' (ibid.: 23).

Alongside, and perhaps in response to, the lack of clarity over the impact and purpose of the discipline in the policy arena, in the English-speaking academy there has been a narrowing of the terms of debate as numerous new journals have sprung up for the various constituent subfields of the broader discipline. In the United States, for instance, many of the sub-groups within the American Society of Criminology publish their own journals. Thus, the Division of Women and Crime sponsors *Feminist Criminology* (est. 2006) and the Division of Critical Criminology has long produced its own journal *Critical Criminology* (est. 1989). More broadly speaking, scholars interested in media and crime are likely to publish in *Crime, Media and Culture* (est. 2005) while, since 1997, those who self-identify as 'theoretical criminologists' are drawn to publish in *Theoretical Criminology*. While some general criminology journals remain, typically those produced by (national) professional associations, such as the American Society of Criminology's journal, *Criminology*, the *British Journal of Criminology*, and the *Australian and New Zealand Journal of Criminology*, these traditional bastions of criminological scholarship are facing stiff competition.

All in all, then, it appears that criminology may be fragmenting at the precise moment that, as a discipline, it is so vibrant and successful. In the worst case scenario, the field of inquiry seems at some risk of sinking into a set of cliques where criminologists read the work of others who think like them, write for those very same people and publish only in the journals that they and their colleagues are already reading. All too often, this approach leaves unasked and, therefore, unanswered broader questions about crime, punishment, victimization and justice while also obfuscating disagreements over method, aim, and impact of criminological research.

In this edited collection we have raised these concerns with a group of leading international scholars in order to generate a critical discussion of the state of the discipline. We did not invite contributors to give biographical accounts of how they came to the field but rather, drawing on their own research, to present their view of criminology today and their sense of, and ambitions for, how the discipline might develop in the future. In so doing, this collection seeks to contribute to the rather sparse literature on the intellectual history of criminology.

More established disciplines like history and literature routinely and for some time have devoted considerable energy to mapping their field of inquiry in publications from their subfields of historiography and literary theory. Classic texts of this kind include E.H. Carr's *What is History?* (Macmillan, 1961) and F.R. Leavis's *English Literature in our Time and in our Universities* (Chatto & Windus, 1969). More recently, in the 1990s, Seyla Benhabib, Drucilla Cornell, Judith Butler, and others produced *Feminist Contentions* (Routledge, 1996), in which they engaged in heated debates over the form, future and utility of feminist theory and of gender studies. Such reflexive literature not only maps out the contours of particular arenas of scholarship, it also reinvigorates them by provoking others to engage with the aims and nature of the discipline. We should not shy away from disagreement within our field. Rather, we suggest in this collection, robustly debating such matters is a worthy task for criminologists in its own right, as well as an indicator of a commitment to the criminological endeavour, whatever form that may take.

We do not believe that criminology is actually at risk of dying out; the volume of teaching, research and publication, along with the high public and political interest in crime and punishment preclude this. However, we believe there is good chance of it stultifying somewhat, and of becoming, in some places, little more than an instrumental mechanism of the state for evaluating criminal justice programmes.

By asking the leading international scholars to consider the state and future of criminology we want to acknowledge the debate and fissures within the field, and to challenge the discipline to be more reflexive. In so doing, we do not intend to map out the range of topics and issues that constitute the discipline; there are a number of handbooks that adequately serve this purpose (see, for instance, Maguire *et al.* 2007; Tonry 2001, 2009). Instead, these chapters address the nature of criminology, the challenges facing it today, and where it might be heading.

This collection of specially commissioned chapters charts the intellectual shape of the discipline as it is currently configured. Contributors have taken a normative position, writing from their different perspectives about the way they view the current criminological landscape, about the subjects they choose to research, the approaches they take and the audiences they write for. Using a series of prompts, we asked them to consider the historical and intellectual background to their work and their ambitions for the discipline. As such, the book offers a comprehensive account of the major movements and scholarship in contemporary criminology.

Prompting Debate, Bringing Scholars Together

Contributors were given six prompts to choose from to direct their thoughts to key critical issues in the discipline. They were also all invited to attend a two-day conference in October 2009 at the Centre for Criminology at the University of Oxford to share their papers and ideas. More than half attended.

The prompts we devised were:

1. *What is Criminology For?*

To some extent this first question underpins the entire collection. As a discipline concerned with issues of crime, justice and punishment, criminology by nature would seem to be related to criminal justice policies and state institutions. However, criminologists are by no means agreed on the appropriate form that any engagement with such issues should take. While some conduct research primarily designed to improve, evaluate or implement policy, others consider such matters as entirely outside their sphere of influence or interest.

Recently, discussions have occurred in the journal *Theoretical Criminology* over the responsibilities of criminologists to engage in policy (see, for example, Chancer and McLoughlin 2007; Haggerty 2004). Elsewhere, in the United Kingdom, there is a related discussion emerging over 'public criminology' (Loader and Sparks 2010). In many countries, academics use their scholarship to pursue a human rights agenda and persuade those in power in various jurisdictions to make fundamental changes to their criminal justice systems (McEvoy 2003). Those contributors who opted for this prompt structure their responses around such issues.

2. *What is the Impact of Criminology?*

Building on the first question about the aims of the discipline, this prompt sought to draw out discussions of 'evidence-based' research and the relationship between the academy and policy. Most who responded to this prompt were interested in the efficacy of applied research, yet this question was also answered by those who view the discipline primarily as an intellectual pursuit disconnected from the criminal justice system. Whatever their perspective, we encouraged authors to reflect on the unintended consequences of research and the limited control most of us hold over the use to which our findings are put.

3. *How should Criminology be Done?*

We asked this question in the hope of generating some discussion of research methods. Usually, other than those few scholars who contribute to research methods textbooks, criminologists rarely explicitly address the assumptions underpinning their favoured research techniques. Such reluctance to engage with the research process not only enables a 'methodological lie' to continue, in which results emerge effortlessly from 'hypotheses', but also contributes to internal, unarticulated divisions within the discipline. In particular, in the US context it divides almost absolutely those who conduct qualitative research from those who favour quantitative methods.

Those motivated by a desire to understand what works in reducing crime are likely to believe that criminologists should conduct empirical research as well as theorize about causes of offending. Generally, however, they fall into different camps; with those of a more ethnomethodological bent distinguishing themselves from others who believe that social scientists must adhere to the deductive method in order to produce reliable, falsifiable theories. Criminology for some is very messy; involving time hanging around in the field making sense of a chaotic world. Others trust data generated by methods developed from the natural sciences. For some criminologists raw data are not wanted or needed, indeed may be entirely irrelevant to their academic enterprise. Those essays responding to this prompt address the influence of other disciplines on criminology such as psychology, economics, political science, even the medical sciences, and, for some, the influence of indigenous justice.

4. *What are the Key Issues and Debates in Criminology Today?*

This prompt has generated discussion about where we draw the boundaries in defining 'criminology' as a discipline or a sub-discipline. It has also enabled contributors to address specific issues that have recently become particularly popular within criminology such as security, immigration, and transitional justice. Others focus on older, but still unresolved problems like race and gender, paying particular attention to how such factors intersect.

Basic questions over whether a discipline of 'criminology' actually exists might seem strange in this context yet, as universities increasingly offer criminology as an undergraduate degree, thus defining it as an academic discipline in its own right, some scholars would prefer to view it as no more than a subject of interest to sociologists, lawyers, historians, psychologists etc. For such people, criminology is no more than a 'rendezvous subject' (Downes, as cited in Rock 1997) that pilfers knowledge and methodologies from the key disciplines that traditionally produced criminologists; namely sociology, psychology, and law.

This prompt lead some authors to consider how topics once firmly outside of criminology have recently been drawn in. One obvious example is that of crimes against humanity, the study of which was previously the terrain of political scientists, historians, and international lawyers. It is now becoming an increasingly popular subject of concern for a small group of criminologists and has resulted in some cross-fertilization between political scientists working on transitional justice and criminologists with theoretical and empirical knowledge of restorative justice.

5. *What Challenges does the Discipline of Criminology Currently Face?*

As more and more degree and other academic courses in criminology are developed and as increasingly specialized academic journals and handbooks proliferate, we may be in danger of becoming so parochial that we are incapable of learning from the academic and social world around our discipline, and unable to contribute anything meaningful to that world. Some contributors have reflected on the increasing power of ethics committees and funding bodies in directing and restricting our research, particularly empirical research. While funding crises in some universities may push those who are naturally disinclined to pursue policy-directed empirical research, without adequately drawing on or contributing towards theory-building, the increasingly risk-averse ethics bodies (in the United States in particular) may prevent others from carrying out crucial, if difficult, research with offenders or victims who are deemed to be vulnerable.

6. *How has Criminology as a Discipline Changed over the Last Few Decades?*

This final prompt sought to encourage contributors to reflect on changes in the field. Whilst one or two contributors focus only on the historical journey of criminology in any or all jurisdictions, others reflect on how the challenges and the motivations may be different today than they were when Sir Leon Radzinowicz—widely considered to be the founding father of British criminology—was a young man. Still others discuss the impact of globalization and immigration on a field that has previously been tied to the nation state. Under circumstances of increasing mobility how must criminology respond?

Who is Criminology?

While the explicit question underpinning this collection is '*what* is criminology?' an equally important one to ask of it is '*who* is criminology'? Who, in other words, have we included in this collection and, perhaps more importantly, who is not here? Put in more empiricist terms, what are some of the limitations of the sample of scholars whose views we have canvassed?

On the one hand, our detractors might suggest that this is (another) collection of the 'usual' suspects; primarily qualitative, predominantly Anglo-American and overwhelmingly male and white. Where are the newer voices? And the more marginalized? Where are our non-English speaking colleagues?

On the other hand, however, and perhaps somewhat defensively, we selected contributors as broadly as we could manage given our own spheres of influence and interest. Thus, though we have included some European colleagues, we acknowledge that contributors are primarily drawn from the English-speaking world. Indeed, we would be the first to agree that the contributor list reflects our own perceptions of the field, rather than an objective reality about it. We invited those academics with whose work we were familiar, whose articles and books we had studied as students and chosen for our reading lists once teaching our own students. Some we had worked with, some we counted as friends, but most were chosen because *we* thought they were influential.

There are—according to some—more rigorous ways of determining who the 'leading criminologists' are. Most famously, Ellen Cohn and David Farrington have published a number of articles in different criminology and criminal justice journals over the past twenty years claiming to be able to identify the 'most influential' criminologist in the English-speaking world. While cautioning the reader that citations and influence are not perfectly correlated, Cohn and Farrington claimed, in 1994, that the most-cited criminologists in what they saw as the four major criminology journals[1] during the period 1986–90 were Marvin E. Wolfgang, Alfred Blumstein, James Q. Wilson, and Michael Hindelang (Cohn and Farrington 1994). Two of these men died in the 1980s; we invited James Q. Wilson and Alfred Blumstein to contribute to this publication. Alfred accepted.

A later publication by Cohn and Farrington (2007) showed that between this period and a later one of 1996–2000, the number of cited authors increased by nearly 40 per cent. The most cited authors in this later time period were John Braithwaite, Ken Pease, Julian V. Roberts, and Robert J. Sampson, with John Braithwaite being the most cited across all four journals. We had invited all but one of these men to contribute to the book. While two attended and spoke at our conference and all initially hoped to produce chapters, only John Braithwaite produced a chapter in time for the collection. Cohn and Farrington's (2008) study of the most-cited criminologists in twenty criminology and criminal justice journals (ten US journals and ten international) from 1990–2000 showed that broadening the scope brought Francis T. Cullen and Robert D. Hare into the elite group with Sampson and Braithwaite. We invited neither of these two! Furthermore, Robert Sampson emerged as the most-cited scholar across the journals in 2000, compared with Lawrence W. Sherman in 1995 (who has contributed) and Marvin E. Wolfgang in 1990.

Clearly, even if we can agree on who the leading scholars are, we might not be successful in efforts to include them. In total some thirteen academics turned down our invitation to contribute. In addition, a handful of others who initially agreed, subsequently failed to produce a chapter in time, despite repeated and increasingly cantankerous reminders. While most were positive in their praise for the project, they were either overcommitted with other publications or simply never responded to our emails.

Though perhaps our 'n' is too small from which to draw any conclusions, it was striking that the vast majority of those who turned our invitation down, or did not produce their promised chapter, favoured empiricist, quantitative methods. They also were overwhelmingly based in the United States. Perhaps their reticence reflects our weaker interpersonal ties to them, their busy schedules or other, unknown, factors. Nonetheless, it seemed that the questions we were asking were simply not considered interesting or relevant to some of our quantitative colleagues. In the words of one particularly well-known English criminologist 'Thanks for the invitation but I am afraid that I am overwhelmed by other *more important* commitments and so can't take this one on.' (Our emphasis). He went on to describe in some detail his methodological approach (strongly quantitative), attaching two recently published articles as evidence, and concluded somewhat defensively: 'However, I don't expect that many of your contributors will agree with any of this!'

[1] The *British Journal of Criminology*, *Criminology*, the *Canadian Journal of Criminology*, and the *Australian and New Zealand Journal of Criminology*.

For another US scholar, the project was far too 'British'.[2] This leading criminologist, also with a strong quantitative bent, replied to our invitation to contribute: 'I've not much interest in the questions you want explored. I've never understood why British academics including very capable ones like... and... find the discipline/profession/trade interesting in itself. I think the things I work on are interesting and important (though I've few illusions that what I do affects the real world) but I don't find myself as a person or a type especially interesting or important.... Probably I just lack the necessary imagination to be stimulated by criminology as an end rather than as a means.' Of course some of those who favour the more quantitative approach to gathering data do reflect on the role and influence of criminology, as chapters by both Lawrence Sherman and Alfred Blumstein show, so we can reject the idea that a reflexive criminology must be qualitative. Yet, it seems clear that some of our more numerically-minded colleagues do not see the point of critically assessing the state, nature and impact of our field.

What other problems arose as we put this collection together? In particular, what was the result of placing a premium on seniority? Would recent graduates not have something to say about the field and its divisions? What might justify the slice of professors whose thoughts make up this collection?

Again, this selection was made deliberately, not out of some obsequious view that only senior academics are worth attending to—or because we wanted to record their thoughts before they leave the world of criminology, or even the world[3]—but out of a recognition that most of the contributors are the 'second generation' of modern criminologists; men and women whose writing has and is continuing to contribute to the very shifts in the field that we are interested in. Though criminology emerged in the nineteenth century, it is, for the most part, at least in terms of the academy, a twentieth century discipline, with the first university departments in the United Kingdom established only in the 1950s and 1960s and in the United States somewhat earlier, during the considerable expansion in higher education. Many of the authors in this collection were taught by some of the founding fathers (who were almost exclusively men), in the 1970s and 1980s, and now, having reached the top of their profession, are driving the field.

Making such a selection does, however, come at a cost. Not only does it stifle the voices of those who are less senior, but it both contributes to the Anglo-American bias (since the United States and the United Kingdom were for many years the primary sites of criminological analysis, though perhaps no longer), and, most of all, it skews the number of women and minority contributors. Though female students often dominate our intake, at least in Oxford, and though there are many young women

[2] Despite of course the fact that one of us (Mary Bosworth) is Australian and, as stated below, we sought out contributors from all over the world.

[3] On at least one occasion we found ourselves 'googling' a contributor to ensure that a failure to reply to repeated emails did not reflect their demise; we would not want to hassle a dead person! As far as we could tell, however, they remained hale and hearty, just resistant or uninterested.

teaching in universities around the world, this collection of essays has few papers dealing with matters such as gender, race and class inequalities. Most contributors are white men. Such an effect, given our own personal research interests and theoretical and ideological approach, is rather ironic, and has been both revealing about the state of the discipline and somewhat disheartening. A number of key essays do cover these topics, but this was an area that we had some difficulty in attracting contributors to discuss. Altogether then, our experience in putting together this collection suggests that, notwithstanding the considerable contributions made to our discipline by feminist and minority scholars, race, gender and class, remain still somewhat on the margins.

Structure

The structure of the book reflects the wide range of responses scholars made to our six prompts. It is not, however, organized according to the prompts. Instead, once all the papers were in, we realized that a new structure had emerged, one that we had not envisaged beforehand and one that was based on relations and arguments within criminology and beyond.

Time and again, in their papers, authors reflected on the borders and boundaries, the divisions and challenges within and outside the field. Issues that we had not previously considered, like nationality and transnationalism, seemed to be more important than matters we had thought significant like race and gender. Curiously, too, there is far less commitment to particular approaches, particularly in terms of methodology, than our experience of signing up contributors would suggest. The image of the field that emerges then is a multi-layered one of inward debates, with external commitments, a growing frustration with the state, yet a commitment to working for social justice.

The chapters are arranged so that the book can be read from front to back, in order. Or else, as is more likely, individual pieces can be plucked out and read in isolation. The first half contains seventeen essays that have been organized into three sections, each of which grapples with internal discussions about the state, nature and purpose of the field. The second half of the book follows the same format, with a further seventeen papers grouped into three sections, addressing the relationship between criminology and other disciplines, the state and beyond.

Some papers refer to one another, others do not. Certain themes reappear, while other issues are mentioned only once. While papers from the United Kingdom and the United States predominate, accounts from and of other countries appear as well. In our conclusion to this collection we provide a thematic discussion of the volume and a short description of how each chapter fits into the structure of the book and speaks to the theme of borders.

Conclusion

In their variety, the essays give a clear sense of a field in motion. Criminology is indeed booming, and we hope we have captured some of its dynamism as well as some of its failings in the pages ahead. This is not an exhaustive account of the field, but it is a good beginning.

Mary Bosworth and Carolyn Hoyle
Oxford, July 2010

References

Agozino, B. (2005), Editorial, *African Journal of Criminology and Justice Studies*, 1(1).

_____ (2003), *Counter-Criminology: A Critique of Imperialist Reason*, London: Pluto.

Benhabib, S. *et al.* (1996), *Feminist Contentions*, London: Routledge.

Carr, E.H. (1961), *What is History?*, London: Macmillan.

Chancer, L. and McLaughlin, E. (2007), 'Public criminologies: Diverse perspectives on academia and policy', *Theoretical Criminology*. 11(2): 155–73.

Cohen, S. (1988), *Against Criminology*, New Brunswick: Transaction Books.

Cohn, E. G. and Farrington, D. P. (2008), 'Scholarly influence in criminology and criminal justice journals in 1990–2000'. *Journal of Criminal Justice*, 36: 11–21.

_____ (2007), 'Changes in scholarly influence in major international criminology journals', *Australia and New Zealand Journal of Criminology*, 40: 335–59.

_____ (1994), 'Who are the Most Influential Criminologists in the English-Speaking World?', *British Journal of Criminology*, 34, 2: 204–25.

Del Olmo, R. (1999), 'The Development of Criminology in Latin America', *Social Justice*, 26.

Elbert, C. A. (2004), 'Rebuilding Utopia? Critical criminology and the difficult road of reconstruction in Latin America', *Crime, Law and Social Change*, 41: 385–95.

Haggerty, K. (2007), 'Displaced Expertise: Three Constraints on the Policyrelevance of Criminological Thought', *Theoretical Criminology*, 8(2): 211–31.

Hope, T. and Walters, R. (2008), *Critical Thinking about the Uses of Research*, Centre for Crime and Justice Studies King's College London.

Karstedt, S. (2002), 'Durkheim, Tarde and Beyond: The Global Travel of Crime Policies', *Criminal Justice* (2), 111–23.

Leavis, F. R. (1969), *English Literature in our Time and in our Universities*, London: Chatto & Windus.

Lippens, R. (2004), 'Centre-periphery dynamics, global transition and criminological transfers: Introductory notes inspired by V.S. Naipaul', *Crime, Law & Social Change*, 41: 301–17.

Loader, I. and Sparks, R. (2010), *Public Criminology*, London: Routledge.

Maguire, R. *et al.* (2007), *The Oxford Handbook of Criminology*. 4th edn, Oxford: Oxford University Press.

McEvoy, K. (2003), 'Beyond the Metaphor: Political Violence, Human Rights and "New" Peacemaking Criminology', *Theoretical Criminology*, 7(3): 319–46.

Tonry, M. (2001), *The Handbook of Crime and Punishment*, New York: Oxford University Press.

_____ (2009), *The Oxford Handbook of Crime and Public Policy*, New York: Oxford University Press.

Young, J. (1988), 'Radical Criminology in Britain: The Emergence of a Competing Paradigm', *British Journal of Criminology*, 28(2): 159–83.

PART I

CRIMINOLOGY AND ITS CONSTITUENCIES

1

CONCEPTUAL ALLEGIANCES: WHOSE SIDE ARE YOU ON?

1

CRIMINOLOGY'S PUBLIC ROLES: A DRAMA IN SIX ACTS

IAN LOADER AND RICHARD SPARKS

Programme Notes: Criminology in a Hot Climate

It has become commonplace in recent years to describe the context of crime and penal policy-making as having been politicized. This term signifies that crime in many, but by no means all, contemporary democracies has become a prominent token of electoral competition and that governmental reactions to it are heavily swayed by political calculation and expediency. In this climate, the argument runs, crime policy comes increasingly under the influence of mass media and 'public opinion' and at the mercy of ill-informed and sometimes actively whipped-up popular emotion. The result is a policy environment that is volatile and unstable, one in which it becomes difficult to make reason and evidence the drivers of what is said and done. Such ambitions become at best contested, at worst impossible, in a world where crime and social responses to it have 'heated up' (Loader and Sparks 2010: chapter 3).

This altered context of public debate and policy formation raises anew some old questions about the place and purpose of criminology—indeed, the social sciences generally—in politics and public life. That these questions are 'old' is hard to dispute: they troubled each of sociology's founders in turn and have continued to vex its practitioners ever since (eg, Mills 1959; Gans 1989). They also have a long provenance and special purchase in criminology, a field constituted around a social problem and whose subject-matter is of acute interest to rulers and citizens alike. That these antique questions are generating renewed interest today is evidenced by the lively debate that has followed Michael Burawoy's attempt to outline and defend a 'public sociology' (Burawoy 2005; Clawson *et al.* 2006) and by the fact that this debate has quickly prompted cognate claims and dispute about the public roles of criminology (eg, Chancer and McLaughlin 2007; Sherman 2009). A nerve appears to have been touched: criminologists fret that the flourishing of their field when measured using the standard yardsticks of jobs, degree programmes, conferences, journals, publications, prizes etc. has coincided with a waning of influence on public debate and social action beyond the academy. Criminology has, the worry goes, become a 'successful failure' (Loader and Sparks 2010: chapter 1).

One way of reappraising the issues at stake here is to think afresh about criminology's relation to the present pathologies and unrealized promise of modern politics. In the former case, this means trying to make good on the rather remote and thin understanding that criminology too often has of the world of practical affairs by fostering a better appreciation of the forces that shape the treatment of crime in the contemporary public sphere and the reasons why (social) scientific knowledge about crime does or does not get taken up and used in political debate and governmental action. This, in turn, means acquiring the will, and the necessary tools, to develop understanding of the 'circumstances of politics' (Waldron 1999: 106) and cultivating a 'qualified tolerance' towards those who practise politics as a vocation (Swift and White 2008: 64). This does not, however, mean reconciling oneself to the status quo. In the latter case, reappraisal means reconnecting with and developing those strands of criminological thought which have insisted that crime is 'political' (Taylor, Walton and Young 1973; Cohen 1996) and making explicit the connections that exist—that cannot but exist—between crime and its control and the repertoire of ideas (order, justice, authority, legitimacy, freedom, rights etc.) and traditions (liberalism, but also conservatism, socialism, social democracy, feminism, republicanism, environmentalism etc.) that comprise modern political thought. It involves folding into our understanding of criminological research and public engagement the fact that any discussion of the criminal question encodes in miniature a set of claims about the nature of the good society, and any attempt to answer it—however apparently 'dry', technical, or limited in scope—carries and projects a possible world, a desirable state of affairs that a political or criminological actor wishes to usher into existence.

To think again and in these ways about the intersections between criminology and politics does not dispose of, or render secondary, the question of criminological knowledge and its uses. Having indicated why criminologists might better understand the pathologies of modern politics and be clearer about the relationship of their work to its ideals and possibilities, another set of questions shuffles into view. One presumes that most individuals who spend their time, or in many instances the greater part of their working lives, practising criminology or an allied craft do so because they believe that acquiring knowledge about crime, or justice, or punishment has some value. It also seems safe to suppose that they think the knowledge they produce and disseminate has a quality—a methodological rigour, respect for evidence, or theoretical acuity which enables it to unearth things about the world or see that world in a revised light—that sets it apart from other claims about crime and its control, such as those circulated by politicians, journalists, bloggers, victims groups, offenders, police officers, campaigners, or simply citizens engaged in daily conversation. But what exactly is this 'expertise' and what value and place does it have? Here the following questions begin to emerge: what contribution can criminological knowledge make to shaping responses to crime in a polity which acknowledges crime and punishment to be properly political issues? What in a democracy is the public value of criminology? What is the collective good that criminological enquiry seeks to promote? What modes of intervention—and what institutional arrangements—can best realize that good?

To answer these questions we introduce a new figure, or perhaps more accurately, revive and update an old one. We call this character, following and extending John Locke (1690/1975), the *democratic under-labourer.*[1] We use that figure to elaborate and defend the idea that we can best give coherence to criminology's public purpose by understanding its role as one of seeking to foster and sustain a better politics of crime and its regulation. This figure—the hero or heroine of the drama that follows—emerges from an effort to revisit and revise an earlier treatment of these issues by Garland and Sparks. Garland and Sparks (2000) argued that criminology at the beginning of the twenty-first century faced some strategic choices. It can, they suggested, see itself as a 'kind of specialist under-labourer, a technical specialist... providing data and information for more lofty and wide-ranging debates', or it can take account of the 'social and cultural centrality of crime' and 'embrace a more critical, more public, more wide-ranging role' (ibid.: 18). Some readers of that essay took exception to the starkness of the choice being presented and to what they saw as a devaluing of the role of 'under-labourer' (Hood 2002: 159). We think, on eflection, that they had a point. Perhaps it is better to avoid the language of choices (with the attendant danger that individuals will divide into different camps) and, instead, recover and deploy in the service of a better democratic politics of crime Locke's antique figure of the 'under-labourer'. This, at any rate, is the idea that animates the drama that now ensues.

[1] The term is borrowed, more immediately, from Swift and White (2008) who use it to describe the relation of political theory to real politics.

The Drama of Criminological Engagement

Act 1: Enter the Democratic Under-Labourer

I fear that the Directors' programme notes may have begged too many questions. So let me be clear from the outset. I am not only or mainly focused on matters of public engagement. Nor is my position that criminologists have to be so engaged. To be a democratic under-labourer is to be committed, first and foremost, to the generation of knowledge. For me criminology comprises three distinct but necessary 'moments' or dimensions. We might call these the moment of discovery (primary criminology—finding-out, if you will), the institutional-critical moment, and the normative moment. Let me briefly explain what I mean by each of these and why they are important, indeed indispensable.

I think criminology is properly in the business of producing reliable knowledge about such matters as crime causes, patterns and trends, offender motivations and behaviour, and what measures do or do not prevent crime. I also think it can use this knowledge in a bid to increase the use of and regard for evidence in media and public discourse about crime; to make political game-playing and irresponsibility more difficult than it might otherwise be; and to build a knowledge base for good professional practice. We can, in other words, deploy what we have learned about the causes and distribution of crime, and what does or does not work to control it, as the basis for public education. At the very least criminology can seek—as Stan Cohen once put it—to forbid facile gestures.

But I also think that criminology needs to strive to understand and explain why criminal justice so stubbornly refuses to make room for the knowledge that our field produces and why the criminal question has heated up in recent years and with what effects. The tasks here properly include those that have been the staple of sociological criminology since the 1960s: to examine how 'crime' problems are selected and the meanings of crime and socially and politically constituted; to make sense of media representations of crime, order and justice and their reception; to understand the history, cultures and organizational practices of government bureaucracies and criminal justice institutions; and to situate trends in crime and penality in the wider settings of economic, social and cultural change. There are, in my view, no good reasons to set up these forms of criminological knowledge production in opposition or to prioritize one over the other. To me such polarization makes little sense.

Both of these—the 'primary' and the 'institutional-critical'—are properly thought of as explanatory programmes of research. They have different objects of inquiry—and the practitioners of each sometimes have trouble in recognizing what the others do as serious research—but they are both part and parcel of the contribution that the field, broadly considered, has made to knowledge and understanding of crime, punishment and social control. These explanatory goals do not however exhaust what it means to do criminology. I also think that the field has quite properly a normative dimension. I know not all who call themselves criminologists share this view and would happily leave the normative theorizing to jurisprudence or political philosophy. But I cannot find compelling grounds to accept this. Surely, it is a legitimate part of our job to draw out and articulate what is at stake in criminological and public debate about crime; to clarify the value conflicts and trade-offs that lie therein, and to unearth the claims and aspirations that lie buried in political rhetoric, policy pronouncements and everyday talk about crime. Disciplined theorizing on the ideals that should inform the governance of crime and principled proposals for addressing crime problems differently are central to what it means to do criminology as a democratic under-labourer. In either case, our normative task is to supply a constant reminder that there is always more at stake in crime reduction than reducing crime and hence more to evaluation than finding out 'what works'.

This is not a sermon. So I had better make it clear that I am not instructing criminologists that they each have to 'tool up' in all these areas of enquiry. That is perhaps too much to ask, though I can think of a few admirable examples of people who have achieved this (John Braithwaite, say, or Anthony Bottoms) and areas of enquiry that have clearly benefited from this breadth of approach (such as recent work on legitimacy and criminal justice). My argument is much less about the research strategies of individual criminologists than about the collective organization of the field. It offers a coherent rationale for theoretical and methodological pluralism and exchange. It also gives us reason to be wary of attempts to place theories, topics and methodologies in some kind of hierarchy, or champion any one of them as the only true path.

What, though, of the question of public intervention in disputes about crime? Three things need to be said here. The first is that engaging in public life—being 'political' in some broad sense—does not mean reducing the question of crime to one of political preference, nor positing criminologists as quasi-politicians, nor celebrating folk-wisdom over professional judgement and hard-won knowledge. Our task is to be bearers and interpreters of that knowledge and to bring it to bear on matters of public concern and dispute. It is not, in my view, legitimate to expect politicians to behave like applied scientists (though one from time to time gets the impression that some criminologists think that they should). Similarly, whilst criminological engagement may well benefit from a degree of political nous and requires some political skills, addressing public issues *as a criminologist* does not mean that we simply become politicians, or law enforcers, or victim advocates, or lobbyists. This is not what democratic under-labouring calls for at all.

When they enter public controversies, criminologists need to retain an academic 'formative intention' (if I may borrow a phrase from science studies[2])—an overriding commitment to producing valid knowledge and having that knowledge limit what can legitimately be said and done. Now I, as a democratic under-labourer, have

[2] Collins and Evans (2007).

a generous and capacious account of what counts as knowledge and where it comes from, but my primary attachment remains to that academic formative intention. If criminologists get severed from these intentions and all that flows from them, they lose what is legitimate and valuable about their contribution to a better politics. They also risk the sorry fate of many a self-styled 'public intellectual' these days—too much public, not enough intellectual.

This formative intention need not only constrain however. Nor does it reduce what criminologists can bring to public debate to matters of evidence narrowly construed. It seems obvious to me that criminology enjoys a degree of freedom that many participants in political and professional struggles over crime and justice lack. In particular, criminology can bring to bear a disposition one might hope to find in politics but which often in fact breaks the rules of the political game and exists only at its margins. It is a disposition that refuses to take the social world for granted or accept received political 'imperatives', aims to provoke and unsettle, and poses questions about our responses to crime that insecurity-fuelled and ideology-lite political cultures have forgotten how to ask. Criminology is well-placed to do this because being critical in *this* sense properly forms part of the social scientist's DNA. In other words, criminology can and should bring to public discussion of its subject matter a scepticism that refuses to treat at face value the categories, assumptions and self-understandings that make up 'common sense' about crime and its control. This I think is of great democratic value—arguably of more democratic value than the corrosive cynicism that today passes for 'social criticism' among journalists and the commentariat. But the inclination not to treat present social arrangements as fixed need not confine itself to exposing falsehood and tearing things down. For me, as a democratic under-labourer, it also translates into a willingness to innovate and experiment, to create and to build. Democratic under-labouring has, in other words, an important public role in theorizing and setting forth alternative ways of thinking about and responding to crime—the single most significant recent instance of which one finds in the restorative justice movement. Its task is to sketch and present what political theorist John Rawls calls 'realistic utopias'—proposals for remaking and reimagining the institutional arrangements for fostering security and delivering justice that connect with, and seek to creatively reconstruct, the meanings of current social practices and beliefs in ways that take us beyond the mental and institutional structures of the present.[3] If this is too fancy for some tastes, the Chicago sociologist Andrew Abbott puts it rather better when he says: 'We do not advance into the future by merely getting rid of this of that social problem, important as that may be. We advance by imagining what the future can be.'[4] I wholeheartedly agree.

[3] Rawls (2001). We borrow the notion of remaking and reimagining from R. M. Unger (1987).

[4] Abbott (2006: 208).

We need, finally, to give up on a certain kind of modernist 'hope'—the hope that criminological knowledge can engineer outcomes, end political discussion, trump the ill-informed concerns and perspectives of others. For democrats this hope was always something of a nightmare, one that threatens to drain public life of significance, erase value conflict and moral argument, and replace politics with engineering. This will no longer do. Science these days *is* controversy, not an end to it—something that is even true of natural science (you doubt this?—what about recent disputes over climate change, genetically-modified food or reproductive medicine?). As a democratic under-labourer, I embrace these aspects of the social uses of knowledge. I think the public role of criminology involves generating controversy, opening up and extending debate, challenging and provoking received public 'opinion' and political postures. In these respects, I am happy to line up behind one of Michael Burawoy's central claims about public social science—namely, that it seeks to engage in a dialogue with publics who are already themselves in dialogue. This also means that criminology has an internal relationship with a more deliberative politics of the criminal question, and to what has been called 'argumentative' or 'intelligent' rather than simply 'evidence-based' public policy-making.[5] From this perspective criminological engagement means participating within, and working to facilitate and extend, institutional spaces that supplement representative politics with inclusive public deliberation about crime and justice matters, whether locally, nationally, or in emergent transnational spaces.

You want me to encapsulate all this in a phrase, even a slogan? How about this: intellectual ambition, political humility. For me democratic under-labouring brings coherence to criminology's public role by combining intellectual curiosity and generosity on the one hand, with political modesty, the knowing of one's limits and one's place, on the other. It values the diversity of theories, topics and methodologies that constitute contemporary criminology rather than seeking to establish a new school or brand of criminology: 'under-labouring criminology'—no thanks. While recognizing the importance of embedding criminological intervention in a knowledge base, it does not require this knowledge base to be universally agreed upon or undisputed. Instead, it seeks to accommodate reasonable differences of (expert) criminological focus and view and proposes a civic role that those working from within different perspectives in the field may be able, at least minimally, to put and pursue in common: raising the quality of political argument about crime and thereby contributing 'to the health and robustness of our shared public realm'.[6]

[5] These coinages are taken, respectively, from Hoppe (1999) and Sanderson (2009).

[6] In coming to this conclusion the democratic under-labourer has found especially useful the work of Wilsdon *et al.* (2005), from whom the quote is taken, and that of Swift and White (2008). Those unaccustomed to, or simply annoyed by, this dramatic mode of address can find an extended and more 'academic' account of the democratic under-labouring conception of criminology in Loader and Sparks (2010: chapter 5).

Act II: The Scientific Expert

Scientific expert: The criminologist's role, as I see it, is to produce valid and reliable evidence about what causes crime and what preventative, police and penal programmes work to reduce it. We now have the methodologies and techniques—notably, but by no means only, randomized control trials and systematic reviews—necessary to generate this knowledge and our public task is to brigade and disseminate what we know as freely as possible—to policy-makers, practitioners and to the general public. We also need to create an infrastructure that can extend this knowledge base and put it to practical use—as they have done in medicine. If we can do this, we can base professional practice in policing and criminal justice on what works, we can stop politicians wasting taxpayers' money on vote-winning programmes that are useless at reducing crime, and we can make evidence-based policing a reality, not a piece of rhetoric. I have several worries about what you call 'democratic under-labouring'. I am inclined to think that you are too loose and, frankly, woolly in what you are willing to count as valid and useful knowledge. What you think of as generosity will, I fear, dilute attention and resources from what scientific criminology—and crime science—really can do to make people's lives better (rather than make politics better!). It will also open the door—your protestations to the contrary—to all kinds of things that are really political advocacy dressed up as research. On the other hand you seem unhelpfully focused on criminology when what matters is the application of relevant scientific knowledge, from wherever it comes—medicine, public health, genetics, demography, and so on. But let me be as generous as I can be and accept for the moment the basic contours of what you propose. Does it still not make sense, even then, to operate a division of labour and for me to continue to focus on the research I can do well? You do the political theorizing, and think a lot about the politics of crime if you want to. I will get on with what I have been trained, as a scientist, to do and take forward the kind of criminology that can best serve the public interest.

Democratic under-labourer: I am not asking you to become a political theorist. But I do think we could usefully know more about politics, and the institutional contexts that your work meets. Even in your own terms, this must surely make sense. If you want evidence to matter more in government (a goal I share, by the way) then you need to have some understanding of how politics and government works. But there is more at stake than just this. I know there are some subtle accounts of how scientific evidence might interact with other considerations in shaping public policy—interestingly enough, some of the best of these are to be found in policy fields involving natural science. But in criminology I too often come away with the impression that people are striving to replace politics with calculation. If one aspires to live in an 'evidence-based society'[7], as some of your colleagues advocate, then you need to tell us why this would be so desirable or indeed feasible—and that takes us into the terrain of social and political theory. But there are other political questions

[7] Welsh and Farrington (2001: 166–9).

that cannot so easily be dispensed with here. Your condescension towards what you call 'advocacy research' forgets I think that, in practice, scientific criminologists routinely breach their own firewalls and can be found lobbying politicians in pursuit of their own preferred vision for reducing crime or doing justice. I also think your implicit conception of science's role in policy-making comes too close to a 'public understanding of science' model that is being increasingly discredited, and superseded, in natural science. Is there a place for democratic dialogue in your conception of how crime policy is to be made? If so, what is it?

This brings me, finally, to your insistence on a hierarchy of methods (the famous 'gold standard') and what looks to me to be a related attempt to reduce criminology to programme evaluation. Why do you insist upon this? Can you not see that it is a red rag to a bull among many of those who do not share your chosen conception of what criminology (or programme evaluation) should be? I myself am inclined to be more generous and affirmative than many critics have been. I accept that our field—thanks to your efforts—does know things about what works, what does not work and what is promising in crime reduction—and think there is public value in having that knowledge reckoned with and discussed in debates about policy and practice. I am happy to include this when I advocate a criminology that challenges conventional wisdom and provokes debate. There is a real contribution to be made here—one that others are more likely to recognize when it is not presented as the only contribution criminology can make. It is also more likely to be reconciled with my focal concerns if experimental criminology is recast—drawing, if you like, on the legacy of American pragmatism[8]—as a project that seeks to imbue in both criminology and government a spirit a democratic innovation and collective lesson-learning—in short, a better politics.

Act III: The Policy Advisor

Policy advisor: I think we can best maintain our professional integrity as criminologists if we retain a firm distinction between our research and giving advice or counsel to policy-makers or practitioners based on that research. I want to be able to pursue my own research agenda around the problems and topics that grab my interest—though I work in a department that depends on external research funds, have staff who need jobs, and want to do work that is of relevance to policy debates. This is the core of what I take criminology to be about and it is why I got into it—a core that is not best protected by doing too much of one's research for government.

But I am also happy—in fact, I think it is a professional responsibility—to try to use that research to inform debate and improve policy and practice. So when I am asked to give evidence to a parliamentary committee, or become a member of an

[8] Dewey (1954).

advisory body—and feel I am equipped to contribute something—then I will show up and give my best. I have also made efforts to cultivate working relationships with practitioners in the criminal justice system, especially at senior levels. I find them for the most part a receptive audience, willing to talk (and listen!), open to ideas, and insulated a bit from the pressures that make it so difficult for politicians to 'do the right thing' in our field. By the way, this is not just a one-way street—I have learned a terrific amount from the people I engage with. You may not want to hear this, but I think this is where researchers can really make an impact, partly off-stage, in conversations with and among criminal justice elites. Yet I do not see much room for this in what you call 'democratic-under-labouring'. In fact, I worry that you are a bit sniffy about it.

Democratic under-labourer: I am in no position to be 'sniffy' for I have tried to engage in just the kinds of activity that you describe and, like you, think it is important. There clearly are opportunities here for criminology to make an impact, not only or even mainly at national level, but by getting involved with agencies at sub-national or local level. Think for a moment about the way criminology's relations with the police, or prison service, in Britain, has been transformed in recent decades (generally for the better I should add) and you have some measure and what has been and can be done.

We do however have to reckon with the drawbacks of this form of intervention. There attends the process of advising or counselling criminal justice professionals a certain amount of secrecy—you even indicated that this was a condition of success. But this raises, justifiably, concerns about accountability, and the absence of checks on what advice is being given, which in extremis lead to charges that what is going on here is not public but private criminology. The conditions for the success of this engagement are also, we need to remember, the conditions for it to become too cosy—as relationships and dependencies build, it becomes all too easy to trim what one says (or remain silent in the face of scandal or crisis) in order to avoid jeopardizing the contact. After all, those who run criminal justice agencies often appear to be (and are) good people trying their best to do a difficult job, and one does not want to appear disrespectful.

But I also worry that prioritizing this form of engagement can be a sign of having given up on wider political and public involvement in settings that are more uncomfortable, where there are fewer shared assumptions, and where one is likely to get a rougher ride. Yet arguably today—in a mass-mediated age, where crime and punishment saturate our culture—this is where the action is. If so, our prime task now lies in trying to impact upon public debate and the political process, rather than aligning with professionals against it. My worry, in this context, is that such professional engagement is too defensive, a kind of rearguard action against an emotive, irrational, heated-up public culture. As such, it can begin to look like an attempt to recover the lost world of elite policy-making where decent, like-minded people gather to do what they are convinced is the right thing, and the supposedly 'ill-informed' public are nowhere to be seen. This hardly amounts to a better politics—in fact it is running away from politics.

My reaction would strike the wrong note if it ended at this point. There is much of value in the approach you recommend—and, as I say, I follow it myself. Intervening quietly behind the scenes is often the most effective way to 'speak truth to power', as the old saying goes. It is also, as you say, a way of intervening in public life whilst maintaining the integrity of one's research.

Act IV: The Observer-Turned-Player

Observer-turned-player: I don't want to appear rude but I think you are suffering a high level of delusion, or are at least possessed of the wishful thinking that tends to strike academic criminologists when they contemplate how they might change the world. I used to work in a university and I used to hold to many of the things that you have felt it necessary to call (in that way academics have) 'democratic under-labouring'—do you mind if I don't run that one past the minister! I also continue to share many of the fine sentiments that this idea conveys. But I decided some time back that I was fed up helping to produce lots of valuable knowledge that had little or no effect on policy, so I went to work in government. From that perspective much of what you say strikes me as, if I may borrow a phrase beloved of British civil servants, 'unhelpful'. You are right about one thing though. Most criminologists do not have the foggiest idea how policy-making or politics works, or how to produce research that stands the slightest chance of influencing its outcomes. Too often they write reports (that are too long, badly written, or never nail the point), or give seminars on their research, and then expect policy in that field to implement what they recommend. Dear, oh dear.

It thus seemed to me more useful to try to influence policy and secure greater influence for criminology from the inside, since this, to be blunt, is where the real action is. This is never easy, it involves daily compromises, you lose many more battles than you win, you are enrolled into policies that you think—as a criminologist—are wrong-headed. You also rarely get rewarded for your efforts to tell criminologists how to gain more respect and influence in government. But if you want criminology to influence things—and stand any chance of producing a better politics—this is the place to be, 'inside the machine'. Only from here do you discover how politics really works, know who to talk to to get things done, and be able to exert what little influence criminology can ever have. 'Democratic under-labouring', by contrast, seems to have little interest in—or hope of—making criminology relevant to government. All that stuff about challenging public opinion, proposing alternative ideas, informing debate: the chattering classes will no doubt lap it up as usual. But it will not change a thing.

Democratic under-labourer: Okay, I get the point! I accept that the path you have taken is a difficult and under-appreciated one and that there is value in locating criminology—in physical form—at the heart of government. But you will have heard what I said to the policy advisor about capture, accountability, and the dangers of private criminology: surely these dangers loom even larger along the path that you commend. I also think it is a mistake—as you must surely acknowledge—to think that criminology can only create value, or hope to have effects on the wider world, by turning its face toward government and dancing to the tune played by our current rulers. Didn't C. P. Snow have something to say about all that as long ago as the beginning of the 1960s?[9] Space needs also to be retained for a criminology that raises questions about and challenges the assumptions made by governments (that, as you know, have lately devoted much frenzied and ill-considered attention to fighting crime). Besides, who says that government is the main or only audience? We also need a criminology that engages with other constituencies in the wider civil society—practitioners, campaigners, voters, media, industry. What you, from your standpoint, have become weary or intolerant of, democratic under-labouring strives to revalue and insist upon—not as the only criminological tasks, but as an important part of what criminology has to offer the project of a better, or even alternative, politics of crime and its regulation. What space remains in your vision for styles of work which pose fundamental questions about how our society responds to crime? Criminology must not become simply a Royal Science.

Having said that, I can still respect, as a democratic under-labourer, the mode of engagement you have pursued and now seek to defend. If one believes that criminology matters—and that politics would be better as a result of absorbing the lessons it has to teach—then there are good reasons to have it represented inside the criminal justice system and the institutions of democratic government. It is one route—but only one among many routes—by which one may strive after a more thinking politics.

Act V: The Social Movement Theorist/Activist

Social movement theorist/activist: For me, criminology best serves the causes of a better politics when it aligns itself with those social groupings whose interests are not served by politics as it is currently constituted. My role is to analyse the conditions that give rise to that exclusion and to put my knowledge and skills at the service of those who are excluded—and victimized—by reason of their class, ethnicity, gender, sexuality or age. It is to campaign for human rights and social justice and for a justice system that protects the former and attends to the latter. For over four decades, these causes have been fought for, and in part advanced, by those working from within criminology's critical tradition. Questions of domestic and sexual violence have been placed on the criminological and policy agenda by feminism and women have won new forms of recognition and protection. The racism of the

[9] C. P. Snow (1961).

criminal justice state has been exposed and struggled against; questions of state and corporate crime have been brought to the fore, and new forms of accountability imagined and campaigned for.

As I learned about 'democratic under-labouring' I was uncertain as to whether you shared these commitments. I appreciated what you said about crime being political, and your remarks about the importance of critique, having a normative agenda, and the role of utopian thinking. You rightly point out that engaged activism can be combined with good quality theory and research. Yet you are also far too generous about mainstream scientific criminology, and make assumptions about politics and politicians which seem altogether too conservative (to put it mildly!). So I cannot decide where your allegiances lie. Is democratic under-labouring a form of critical criminology? If so, why not say it?

Democratic under-labourer: I thought I had said it. I tried to make it clear at the outset that for me the institutional-critical and normative dimensions of the subject are integral parts of its task. This involves refusing to take the social arrangements, that we happen to have at present, for granted, and retaining a space for utopian thinking about possible futures. Like many others (including some of the people I have just been talking to, funnily enough) I was drawn into the field and greatly excited by the new criminologies of the 1960s and 1970s. I would never disavow that inheritance and have tried to show that its effects on the field of criminology have been far-reaching and overwhelmingly positive. I confess that I have never been greatly attached to the term 'critical criminology' itself—primarily for the reason Bourdieu never described his project as critical sociology.[10] The reason is that a critical sensibility—the inclination to question the terms in which the social world is conventionally apprehended—ought to be part of what it means to be a criminologist—or any kind of social scientist. Why should those who don't self-identify with critical criminology so easily be exempted from this basic professional obligation? I also view criminology's tendency to divide into camps (which students and colleagues are enticed to join) as a damaging one, not least when it is coupled with a desire to denigrate or expel (rather than wonder what one may learn from) those in other 'factions'. What you said about 'mainstream scientific criminology' rather confirmed these fears—the feeling is, I understand, mutual.

I worry also that what you advocate risks running into a radical version of the dangers I identified in the role of policy advisor—that of suppressing what one knows, or what one says, for the sake of the cause, of making criminological knowledge subservient to—rather than critical servants of—those struggling for a better or alternative politics. There is nothing in the position I outlined that prevents criminologists becoming involved with human rights campaigns, or penal reform groups, or any other social movement. I have taken on such involvements myself. But assuming such commitments *as a criminologist* means being prepared to bring

[10] Bourdieu and Wacquant (1992).

what one knows, and thinks on the basis of that knowledge, to bear on the cause, and not losing the ability to exercise the basic critical sensibility I just alluded to.

There are many excellent reasons why a democratic under-labourer would get so involved in ways that keep alive the spirit and ambition of criminology's critical tradition—there are so many forms of harm and so many injustices that command our attention. What social movement theorists and activists in the field have taught us is that searching for a better or alternative politics of crime means reflexively questioning the claims of contemporary politics to be acting in the public good and finding ways of accommodating the claims for recognition and resources of those constituencies who are excluded by, and from, it. Criminology loses touch with this part of its recent history only at great cost.

Act VI: The Lonely Prophet

Lonely prophet: For me, criminology's main analytical (and political) task is to develop understanding of what you might call 'the big picture'. Our job, which is still relatively neglected in a field seduced by the policy audience and dominated by a small-scale empirical focus and general lack of theoretical ambition, is to develop macro explanations of patterns of crime and social control that set these issues in the context of the global economic, social, cultural, and technological change that whirls around our heads. We must learn from, and continue to build upon, the recent efforts of Garland, Ericson, Pratt, Simon, Jock Young in his later writings, and others. We must couple the staple concerns of criminology to those of social theory and political economy, as Zygmunt Bauman or Loïc Wacquant have shown us, in order to better understand the place that crime and control have come to assume, and play, in our world. Our public task is to learn about these worrisome trends and the—not so good—politics that drive them, and to issue warnings about the dark, illiberal directions that contemporary democracies are heading in under the guise of controlling crime, disorder, and terrorism. The more we can illuminate these dangers for our students, practitioners, and co-citizens, the more they may be mobilized to act against them.

I am pleased to see that what you call democratic under-labouring appears to make ample room for my concerns, though it appears equally (and oddly) generous to those utilitarian forms of criminology that Michel Foucault once famously and rightly ridiculed.[11] So I worry that your misguided consensualism may detract from the important and relatively neglected tasks that lie before us today. I worry too that your sense of politics (better or otherwise) remains too local, or even anachronistically national, and that it will not be up to the challenges of doing justice in a globalizing world. Where, on your list of what it means for criminology to serve a better politics, is the advent of the penal state, the ascendency (and today crisis) of

[11] The reference is to Foucault (1980: 47).

neo-liberalism, the rise of a surveillance society, the flows of crime and crime control across borders, the blurring of internal and external security and so on. Have these escaped your attention?

Democratic under-labourer: Not at all—they are central to the kind of criminology and criminological politics I have proposed, as they must be to any serious attempt to fashion a better or alternative politics of crime. But the 'big', global risks you cite always manifest themselves somewhere, are experienced unevenly in different places; are accorded meaning and responded to within particular mundane and political cultures, and thus always have a 'local' political dimension. All this needs our attention and engagement too. My worry here is that the turn in criminology to making sense of global penal trends (and there is a lot of this kind of work around just now—some very good, some less so) risks losing sight of this unevenness and the lessons we can learn from it. It also floats above the world in a manner that can seem detached from any particular place and its matters of concern. So do not get me wrong. Your issues are important ones and they are also my issues, subject to the qualifications and extensions I have just introduced. There is thus an important and vital role for the lonely prophet, whose company criminologists must value and seek to keep (so maybe you need not be quite so lonely after all). For you vitally bring to our understanding of, and capacity to intervene into, the politics of crime, both an ambitious sociological imagination, and the kind of professional critical sensibility that close policy engagements and situated political commitments sometimes place in jeopardy.

Epilogue: The Value of Criminological Pluralism

This series of imaginary—but not we think unserious or unhelpful—dialogues between the democratic under-labourer and proponents of five established styles of criminological engagement has been intended to clarify what we mean by democratic under-labouring and to draw out certain limitations and strengths of existing positions when measured against the approach we have staked out and defended here. The exchanges have hopefully made clearer what it means to practice the craft of criminology, and to engage in public life, as a democratic under-labourer. They have also hopefully shown that there is much of value in the stances assumed by each of the democratic under-labourer's interlocutors not only taken one by one, but rather more in what they can contribute collectively when assembled together.

These positions are not in our view fixed identities to which people must cleave. Nor should we treat these styles of criminological engagement as exhausting the field of possibilities. Even if they have historically been constituted in opposition to one another there is no compelling reason why their 'advocates' should choose only to stand on their differences or to pass like ships in the night. We are well aware that there are genuine points of epistemological and political disagreement between these positions—we are not in search of 'integration' or woolly-minded consensualism. But there is also much scope for, and value in, encouraging serious debate and exchange. It further seems to us that individuals may take up more than one of these stances at different times depending on the issue that they are addressing, which audiences they are seeking to reach and the aspirations they are pursuing.

The democratic under-labourer, mindful of this, does not seek to stake out a sixth position. Rather we see under-labouring as a sensibility which seeks to emphasize that criminology's public value lies not only in the plurality of theoretical perspectives, focal concerns and methodologies that comprise contemporary criminology, but also in the range of ways it can be put to work in the service of a better politics of crime and its regulation. The default position of many criminologists who justifiably believe that an emotive penal politics threatens the Enlightenment values they hold dear has been to respond by seeking to reinstate a cooler mode of criminological intervention—to bring about, or in some versions return to, a world in which expertise, a calm bureaucratic ethos, and the best evidence prevail. They have also, similarly understandably, sought to insulate the institutions in which policy is decided from the heat of the surrounding political environment. For us there are limits as well as strengths to this kind of strategy. It sometimes appear to represent a retreat from politics, and this raises questions about whether this is either a feasible or desirable posture. The public value of democratic under-labouring, by contrast, lies not so much in 'cooling down' controversies about crime and social responses to it as in working out why they are so hot, helping to build what Loïc Wacquant (2009: 167) calls 'civic firebreakers' against the upsurge of unregulated punitive passions, and in finding ways of addressing the heated passions that crime and punishment prompt as matters of concern and disagreement within practices of deliberative governance (Latour 2004). In these senses the democratic under-labourer is emphatically not a new-fangled invention of ours (still less a new brand of criminology). Rather it is an attempt to recover and put to use today an interpretation of the original civic purposes of the social sciences.

It is with this overarching set of purposes in mind that the democratic under-labourer strives to foster exchange, debate and accommodation between different criminological approaches, and to highlight the costs of criminology's recurring tendencies to exist under conditions of passive toleration and indifference, to engage in hostile bids to colonize the whole field, or to file for divorce and set up in some other, more comfortable home (Loader and Sparks 2010: chapter 1). The democratic under-labourer works, in other words, to mediate criminological difference. He acts, in Latour's terms, as a 'diplomat'—a figure who shuttles between camps in the service of productive co-existence, while always bearing 'the stigmata of the camp he represents' (Latour 2004: 221).

References

Abbott, A. (2006), 'For Humanistic Sociology' in D. Clawson, R. Zussman, J. Misra, N. Gerstel, R. Stokes, D. Anderton, and M. Burawoy (eds), *Public Sociology*, Berkeley: University of California Press.

Burawoy, M. (2005), 'For Public Sociology', *American Sociological Review*, 70: 4–28.

Bourdieu, P. and Wacquant, L. (1992), *An Invitation to Reflexive Sociology*, Cambridge: Polity.

Chancer, L. and McLaughlin, E. (2007), 'Public Criminologies: Diverse Perspectives on Academia and Policy', *Theoretical Criminology*, 11, 2: 155–73.

Clawson, D., Zussman, R., Misra, J., Gerstel, N., Stokes, R., Anderton, D., and Burawoy, M. (eds) (2006), *Public Sociology*, Berkeley: University of California Press.

Cohen, S. (1996), 'Crime and Politics: Spot the Difference', *British Journal of Sociology*. 47, 1: 1–21.

Collins, H. and Evans, R. (2007), *Rethinking Expertise*, Chicago: University of Chicago Press.

Dewey, J. (1927/1954), *The Public and its Problems*, Athens: Shallow Press.

Foucault, M. (1980), 'Prison Talk', in C. Gordon (ed.), *Power/Knowledge: Selected Interviews and Other Writings 1971–1977*, New York: Pantheon.

Gans, H. (1989), 'Sociology in America: The Discipline and the Public', *American Sociological Review*, 54: 1–16.

Garland, D. and Sparks, R. (2000), 'Criminology, Social Theory and the Challenge of Our Times', in D. Garland and R. Sparks (eds), *Criminology and Social Theory*, London: Oxford University Press.

Hood, R. (2002), 'Criminology and Penal Policy: The Vital Role of Empirical Research', in A. E. Bottoms and M. Tonry (eds), *Ideology, Crime and Criminal Justice*, Cullompton: Willan.

Hoppe, R. (1999), 'Policy Analysis, Science and Politics: From 'Speaking Truth to Power' to 'Making Sense Together'', *Science and Public Policy*, 26, 3: 201–10.

Latour, B. (2004), *Politics of Nature: How to Bring the Sciences into Democracy*, Cambridge: Cambridge University Press.

Loader, I. and Sparks, R. (2010), *Public Criminology?*, London: Routledge.

Locke, J. (1690/1975), *An Essay Concerning Human Understanding*, Oxford: Oxford University Press.

Mills, C. W. (1959), *The Sociological Imagination*, Harmondsworth: Penguin.

Rawls, J. (2001), *The Law of Peoples*, Cambridge, MA: Harvard University Press.

Sanderson, I. (2009), 'Intelligent Policy Making for a Complex World: Pragmatism, Evidence and Learning', *Political Studies*, 57: 699–719.

Sherman, L. (2009), 'Evidence and Liberty: The Promise of Experimental Criminology', *Criminology & Criminal Justice*, 9, 1: 5–28.

Snow, C. P. (1961), *Science and Government* (The Godkin Lectures 1960), Cambridge, MA: Harvard University Press.

Swift, A. and White, S. (2008), 'Political Theory, Social Science, and Real Politics', in D. Leopold and M. Stears (eds), *Political Theory: Methods and Approaches*, Oxford: Oxford University Press.

Taylor, I., Walton, P., and Young, J. (1973), *The New Criminology*, London: RKP.

Unger, R. M. (1987), *Social Theory: Its Situation and Its Task*, Cambridge: Cambridge University Press.

Wacquant, L. (2009), *Prisons of Poverty*, Minneapolis: University of Minnesota Press.

Waldron, J. (1999), *Law and Disagreement*, Oxford: Oxford University Press.

Welsh, B. and Farrington, D. (2001), 'Toward an Evidence-Based Approach to Preventing Crime', *The ANNALS of the American Academy of Political and Social Science*, 578: 158–73.

Wilsdon, J., Wynne, B., and Stilgoe, J. (2005), *The Public Value of Science*. London: Demos.

2

SOME ADVANTAGES OF A CRIME-FREE CRIMINOLOGY

MICHAEL R. GOTTFREDSON

In order to answer the question 'what is criminology?', it is necessary to first answer the question 'what is crime?'. If criminology is the scientific study of the causes and consequences of crime, then the first order problem for criminology is to define the proper scope for the field—what might be termed the 'problem of the dependent variable'. It may strike many as odd that this should be so or that there should be any problem answering the question 'what is crime', but a definition of crime for criminology has long been a matter of considerable debate. Undoubtedly the most common answer is provided by reference to the law; that is, by the behaviour classified as a crime in statute. In this standard textbook view, a crime is a behaviour proscribed by the criminal law and the task for criminology is to describe and then explain patterns of criminal law violations and the efforts created to limit them. Others, however, find the appropriate focus of study for criminology not in law but by reference to a discipline or a perspective about individual and collective human behaviour. For these criminologists, crime is defined as an expression of the casual principles of their discipline. For example, for the economist, crime is simply a form of (illegal) work, subject to the same general economic forces as all other work; for the sociologist, crime is the expression of a social norm of one group that violates the social norm of another group, subject to the same general sociological forces governing collective conduct; for the psychologist, crime is an expression of a personality trait (eg, aggression), caused by the same psycho-biological forces determining other traits. This last approach to criminology, which, elsewhere, we have labeled 'substantive positivism' (Hirschi and Gottfredson 1990, 1994), blends a preference for the methodological positivism of science with the dictates of a discipline.

A third way to define the dependent variable for criminology, which may be called the behavioural view, situates illegal acts among the large scope of acts people engage in as they individually and then collectively seek to maximize gain and minimize loss. In this general perspective, crime is part of a much larger set of behaviours that provide (or appear to provide) momentary benefit for the actor but which are costly in a longer term. Many of these behaviours are almost always classified as crimes by societies and thus punished by the sanctions available to the criminal law, but others fall outside the boundaries of criminal law, under the rubric of accidents, substance abuse, or inappropriate conduct for school, work or interpersonal relations. Criminology is, in this view, the study of this set of behaviours, whether or not violations of the criminal law, subject to causal explanations at many levels of analysis and cutting across nearly every discipline (Gottfredson and Hirschi 1990, 1994).

How criminology solves the dependent variable problem will affect the kinds of explanations that are sought, the range of disciplines that are included in the answer and even the public policies that might be expected to change the level and distribution of crimes in a society. So, the answer to the question 'what is criminology?' depends, utterly, on the answer to the question 'what is crime?'.

The Definition of Crime

Restricting criminology to behaviours that violate the criminal law is surely the most common and most commonsensical approach to criminology. This is the view favoured by Paul Tappan (1947) in his famous arguments with the sociologists Thorsten Sellin and Edwin Sutherland as criminology became established as an academic discipline (sociology) in the middle of the twentieth century in the United States (cf, Sellin 1937; Sutherland 1939). The most important modern expression of this approach is provided by Wikström in his presentation of situational action theory: '*Crime* may be defined as *an act of breaking a moral rule defined in criminal law*' (2006: 63, italics in original). Scholars from Tappan to Wikström favour a criminal law solution to the dependent variable problem, in part, because of its precision and objectivity. The feature of criminal law that blends a mental state (intention) with an act violating a shared, important rule, defines an important focus of behaviours with critical commonalities. It is also the definition favoured by the deterrence school in criminology in both its classical form (Beccaria 1764; Bentham 1789) and in modern versions (Becker 1974; Packer 1968).

There are both conceptual and empirical problems with defining the dependent variable for criminology by reference exclusively to the criminal law. A legal definition of crime includes too much and too little. The now substantial body of empirical literature on behavioural patterns related to offending shows a considerable range of problem behaviours that seem to 'go together' with ordinary delinquency and crime. Many types of accidents, much substance abuse, and many other interpersonal problems correlate very highly with delinquency across subjects (for reviews, see Gottfredson 2004; Farrington 2003). In addition, some violations of the criminal law are not easily characterized as harming others in pursuit of short-term personal gain at the risk of longer-term personal cost (eg, some forms of terrorism and civil disobedience (Gottfredson 2005)). Whereas most offenders may be characterized as 'versatile' with respect to ordinary crime, delinquency, and problem behaviours, some offences do not behave in this way. And, as Sellin and others have pointed out, temporal and geographic variability in behaviours that violate the criminal law are problematic for a science of criminology that defines its dependent variable in this way. After all, the forces involved in defining conduct as criminal by political authorities do not in each instance involve behavioural explanations for the conduct. As political science or sociology of law, this is important and extremely interesting. As criminology, it likely heads down the wrong path.

The second common solution to the dependent variable problem, substantive positivism, has been the method most favoured by academic criminology for the last fifty years or so. As the empirical social and behavioural sciences became prominent in universities, scholars from one and then an other discipline applied the constructs of their disciplines in an effort to explain the patterns of crime shown by empirical research consistent with the discipline (Hirschi and Gottfredson 1990). Thus, for some sociologists crime must be a social construct and, it may be argued, can only be explained by other social constructs. Perhaps the best known representation of this view was made by Sutherland and Cressey, who admonished: 'Although crime and criminality are by definition social phenomena, people have for centuries entertained the notion that they are products of nonsocial causes' (1978: 118; see also Hirschi and Gottfredson 1980). Economists argued that crime should be explained by the constellation of pecuniary costs and benefits associated with it, just as other forms of work may be explained (and, at least for crime, the non-pecuniary costs and benefits could safely be ignored (see, especially, Becker 1974)).

Unfortunately for the disciplinary approach to crime-definition, scores of competent researchers throughout the social and behavioural sciences had not learned that their work was impossible. Consequently, criminology today has a significant and rapidly growing body of replicated facts; facts that span the disciplines from individual level interpretation (see, eg, Gottfredson 2007) to the aggregate or social level (eg, Sampson, Raudenbush, and Earls 1997). Indeed, the explosion of high quality research at a variety of levels of measurement requires a theoretical criminology capable of consistent explanations at different levels of measurement and analysis.

There is a better way to define crime and thus address the question 'what is criminology?'. This view, which may be referred to as a 'behavioural' approach, draws on the now substantial body of research about the actual nature of criminal events (see, eg, Gottfredson and Hirschi 1990; Felson 2004) with the objective of seeking to discover whether and to what extent they have common elements. From these elements, the essence of criminal acts for the actor is inferred, allowing for the possibility that they will help to uncover a view of human nature consistent with them. If so, a logical correspondence may be created between acts and actors, permitting the possibility of an internally consistent theory for criminology. In other words, it is possible to create a definition of crime explicitly for the purpose of creating a causal theory, beginning with the nature of crime itself, rather than with socio-political acts that define it for law or with theories that begin with a conception of offenders and suggest what crime must be like. A science of criminology begins by assuming that theories are free (or obligated) to define their own dependent variable and to seek explanations derived from and hence consistent with the phenomena they wish to explain. This is the path followed by control theories of crime (Gottfredson and Hirschi 1990, 1994; Britt and Gottfredson 2003) and by routine activity, lifestyle and situational crime perspectives.

Whether a definition of crime works for science or not is a matter of consistency with fact, of clarity, parsimony, internal consistency and acceptable scope. The behavioural method implies that some acts that the criminal law classifies as crime may not be included in the definition of crime for a theory of criminology; just as some 'non-crime' acts may well be included.[1] For present purposes (seeking an answer to the question 'what is criminology?') it may be illuminating to examine some consequences that a crime-free (in the legal sense) criminology has for some important contemporary issues and to contrast these to expectations drawn from a criminal law-constrained criminology. It will be argued that a behavioural definition of crime has great enabling properties for criminology—just as it has some limitations. One illustration will be offered to suggest how a criminology with its own definition of crime may help interpret research results about crime policy—the rather perplexing empirical findings about general deterrence. First, a brief description of the rationale behind the behavioural concept for crime is necessary.

A Few Key Facts about Crime and Offending

A good deal has been learned recently, from victim surveys, from self-reports of delinquency and from studies of official reports about the nature of most ordinary

[1] Such a possibility presents a difficult semantic problem, of course, for it requires reference to a purpose when we use the word 'crime'—alas, there does not seem to be a good alternative to this problem.

crime (Gottfredson and Hirschi 1990; Felson 1994; Hirschi and Gottfredson 1994). Much, if not most, criminal behaviour is rather mundane, shortsighted, and seemingly adventitious. It produces little gain and engenders considerable long-term negative consequences for the actor. It tends not to be planned long in advance, but rather often seems nearly spontaneous (and, in hindsight, even to the offender to be unaccountable). In result, it can hardly be said to be utilitarian. There are, of course, exceptions, but studies of homicide, family violence, gang assault behaviour, robbery, burglary, and general delinquency depict the nature of the acts as frequently unplanned, rather adventitious, often alcohol involved, and resulting in limited and momentary apparent gain to the offender (Gottfredson and Hirschi 1990).

Thus, for criminology, it is necessary to overcome the stereotype about crime that sociologist Marcus Felson calls the 'ingenuity fallacy'. This is the false image derived from the media (and some theories) that depicts crime as planned, as crafty, as requiring 'tough' offenders. Felson notes (2002: 10) '... most crime as we know it today needs no advanced skills' and 'most crimes involve little planning, plotting, or creativity'. Rather, most common crimes of assault and theft are rather mundane affairs, in which an ordinary temptation causes a young man with little self-control to ignore the long-term consequences of his actions. Most common forms of crime and delinquency are themselves highly opportunistic (ie dependent on the easy availability of a victim or a target or a substance to abuse). Notwithstanding some intricate frauds and the relatively rare well-planned organizational crime and the histrionics of the media, most ordinary crimes and delinquencies provide rather momentary pleasures or gains to the offender (some quick cash, an easy high, or the resolution of an annoyance).

Considerable research also depicts a robust and substantial correlation between misconduct early in life (truancy, incorrigibility, bullying, and theft) and delinquency and crime during adolescence and adulthood. The link between early childhood problem behaviours and crime (including violent behaviour) later in life is reported regularly in a variety of disciplines (for summaries, see Gottfredson and Hirschi 1990; Loeber and Stouthamer-Loeber 1986; Loeber and Dishion 1983; Mischel *et al.* 1988; Sampson and Laub 1995). Research regularly shows that the best predictor of crime is prior criminal behaviour. In other words, research shows that differences between people in the likelihood that they will commit criminal acts persist to a remarkable degree over time. As recently summarized by Farrington, (2003: 223) '... there is marked continuity in offending and antisocial behaviour from childhood to teenage years and to adulthood [citations omitted]. This means there is relative stability of the ordering of people on some measure of antisocial behaviour over time, and that people who commit relatively many offences during one age range have a high probability of also committing relatively many offences during another age range' (see also, Baumeister and Heatherton 1996; Hardwick 2002; Zhang *et al.* 2002).

There is a substantial correlation between the amount of problem behaviours of parents and the level of delinquency of their children. Furthermore, there are strong links between the strength of attachment between children and their parents and level of crime and violence. The effect of family on crime and violence has been a staple of empirical criminology for decades (Gottfredson and Hirschi 1990; Loeber and Dishion 1983; Loeber and Stouthamer-Loeber 1986; Hirschi 1969; McCord and McCord 1959; Glueck and Glueck 1950; Brannigan *et al.* 2002). Indeed, '...the fact that delinquents are less likely than nondelinquents to be closely tied to their parents is one of the best documented findings of delinquency research' (Hirschi 1969: 85).

There is also a close relationship for individuals between their level of violent behaviour and their level of other forms of delinquency and criminal behaviour; a similar correspondence can be found between violent behaviour and other problem behaviours, such as drug use, accidents, illnesses, poor school performance, and employment instability. Offenders by and large do not specialize in one or another form of criminal behaviour, a fact validated in both self-report and in official statistics (Hindelang *et al.* 1981; Osgood *et al.* 1988; Britt 1994; Sampson and Laub 1993; Wolfgang *et al.* 1972). Consider Farrington's summary of the evidence (2003: 224):

> ...offending is versatile rather than specialized....the types of acts defined as offenses are elements of a larger syndrome of antisocial behaviour, including heavy drinking, reckless driving, sexual promiscuity, bullying, and truancy. Offenders tend to be versatile not only in committing several types of crimes but also in committing several types of antisocial behaviour.

Research has extended the versatility finding well beyond the traditional definitions of crime and delinquency, to other problem and health behaviours. As just one example, Junger *et al.* (2001) produced relationships between criminal offending and personal victimization, property victimization, pedestrian and car accidents, falls and tripping in a large nationwide survey of the Dutch population. They conclude, '[a]ll in all, [the data] provide strong evidence for an interpretation that a constellation of problem behaviour is experienced by certain individuals' (2001: 19; see also, Donovan *et al.* 1991; Junger and Tremblay 1999).

A Crime-Based Theory of Crime

These general characteristics of offending and the nature of crime that they presume helped shape the theory of self-control (Gottfredson and Hirschi 1990). Control theorists assume that all people pursue self-interest and that individual behaviour is motivated by the pursuit of pleasure and the avoidance of pain. There are, to be sure, countless constellations of pleasures and pains, from the physical to the emotional, from near term to long term, resulting in a wide variety of control theories. Each assumes, however, that the unrestrained pursuit of these wants in everyday life will inevitably lead to conflict with the wants and rights of others. Consequently, controls are established by social groups (including parents, communities, and states) to channel the pursuit of these wants in ways that minimize harm to others. Aggressive, bullying, and assaultive acts can lead to the immediate satisfaction of wants, only if the longer-term costs are disregarded.

Self-control theory is influenced by the observation that there are considerable differences among people in the tendency to ignore the long-term costs of their actions and that these appear to be established before adolescence. Self-control appears to be established by the actions of parents and other care-givers who teach children to pay attention to the consequences of their behaviour. When a caring adult is present in the developing child's environment and takes an active role in socialization, high levels of self-control are readily produced and appear to become a stable characteristic of the individual (Gottfredson and Hirschi 1990). But sometimes such early care-giving is not present in the child's environment and one result is a greater focus on satisfaction of immediate pleasures at the expense of longer-term goals. When self-control becomes established, the fear of parental disappointment, shame from family and friends, and the loss of affection and respect, and disapproval of those the person cares about are the sanctions of most moment and such concerns become a consistent and forceful part of the self and carried throughout life. Crime and delinquency, force and fraud, tarnish interpersonal relations and they thus deter crime and delinquency to the extent that they exist and are considered. Self-control governs action implicitly and explicitly as variation among people in considering these costs. A very substantial body of research from psychology, sociology and child development is consistent with this model (Gottfredson 2005; Baumeister and Heatherton 1996).

Put another way, self-control is the tendency to delay short-term personal gain for long-term personal and collective interests. Crime and delinquency can provide satisfaction of universal human wants and desires, but only by risking longer-term goals (the avoidance of punishment; the ability to achieve conventional accomplishments like education and employment; interpersonal relationships) and whatever short-tem pain may attend the act. Thus, those with lower levels of self-control are, all things being equal, more likely than those with higher levels of self-control, to behave violently, to commit crime or to engage in delinquent acts. The same characteristics lead to greater involvement with accidents and excessive use of drugs and alcohol.

The nature of self-control thus helps to account for the fact that many delinquencies, crimes and other problem behaviours seem to 'go together', that interpersonal violence, stealing, drug use, accidents and school misbehaviour are commonly found in association. The acts associated with these problems all provide some immediate benefit for the actor (money, pleasure, the end of a troubling dispute), as do many other behaviours. But each also carries with it the possibility of harmful consequences to the actor or to others. What differentiates people is not that such acts may provide benefits, but that some routinely ignore the potential costs and do them anyway. Thus, self-control theory is sometimes called a 'restraint' theory, a theory that focuses on why people do not engage in crime and delinquency rather than why they do (Hirschi, 1969).

Crimes, in this theory, are acts undertaken for short-term or immediate gain without regard to the long-term negative costs to the actor. As events, most ordinary crimes fit this definition, as do many acts which are not necessarily violations of the criminal law—acts that result in accidents (eg, reckless driving) or other problem behaviours (school truancy, interpersonal difficulties, and employment problems). At the same time, some crimes as defined by law do not fit—as for example when the actor has a long-term orientation (such as some forms of terrorism or civil disobedience).

Behavioural-Based versus Legal-Based (Deterrence) Theories in Criminology

We are now in position to contrast a theory-based definition of crime with a legal-based definition. Many such contrasts could be created, but for present purposes it is instructive to focus on the now substantial body of research on the effectiveness of criminal sanctions and the persistent inability to document very significant effects for the certainty and severity of criminal sanctions on the occurrence of ordinary crime and delinquency.

Both the classic school in criminology (eg, Beccaria 1764; Bentham 1798) and the deterrence perspective more recently (Packer 1968; Nagin 1998; Pratt *et al.* 2006) adopt the assumptions of the rational, calculating, actor, weighing costs and benefits of contemplated acts. In the deterrence model, violations of the criminal law are an option for action, constrained by the potential consequences. The important features of these consequences are properties of the criminal sanction—especially the likelihood and the severity of the penalties imposed. In the most influential modern theoretical exposition of this view, the economist Becker (1974) argues that people should be influenced by these in deciding whether or not to commit a crime, just as they are influenced in all other courses of action by consideration of costs and benefits. Variability in sanctions matters, not variations among people in their attention to long-run costs and benefits. The criminal law defines crime for this view by definition, because once behaviour is a violation of the criminal law it is subject to penalties and it is characteristics in these penalties that cause crime. Such a perspective has a good deal of commonsensical appeal and is the view dominant in the criminal justice process (Packer 1974).

For control theories, on the other hand, individual differences in the tendency to weigh the long-term consequences of acts, whether violation of the criminal law or not, are profound. Penalties provided by the criminal justice system, such as arrest, fines, and incarceration, are typically considerably removed in time from the temptations of the acts themselves. Persons with high self-control might well be influenced by such remote consequences, but individuals relatively low in self-control are not. If crimes provide quick, easy and immediate benefits, and little immediate cost, then, like other such acts, those low on self-control will likely undertake them, regardless of the severity of the ultimate punishment. At the same time, individuals with high self-control attend to the non-criminal justice costs of crimes and delinquencies—shame, embarrassment, and loss of affection and regard by family, friends, and community. Since crimes and delinquencies bear such costs, they are likely to be more consequential to those high on self-control, then are criminal penalties, whatever their characteristics. Those with high self-control are easily deterred and thus the severity of sanctions would not be expected to matter much for them either.

This all means of course that the two perspectives make altogether different predictions about the effectiveness of (long-term) criminal justice sanctions or crime prevention efforts. For control theory, far removed criminal sanctions, such as provided by criminal justice processing and punishment, whether certain or not, should have very little consequence for offending. Variations in policing should be understood, in control theory terms, as efforts to effect short-term costs. Their effects should be limited to highly visible, intensive and intrusive 'at the elbow' methods and they should produce no lasting deterrence effects. In other words, deterrence by the criminal sanctions might work best where they are needed the least and work least well where offending is most likely. These predictions seem consistent with the evidence.

Some Evidence about Deterrence and Policing on Crime

The research literature on the effectiveness of the criminal sanction is large and involves many methods and measures, but most recent systematic reviews of the literature find very little evidence of marginal deterrence effects for criminal justice sanctions and practices for most crimes. Pratt (2009: 71) provides a comprehensive and recent summary of the general deterrence literature: '... meta-analysis of forty studies on perceptual deterrence—those that assessed individuals' perceptions of the certainty and severity of punishment—found that these deterrence-based predictors were, at best, only weakly associated with criminal behaviour (see also Paternoster 1987)'. What positive findings there are seem limited to studies that draw on college students' self-reported intentions to offend in scenario-based studies or on 'perceptual' deterrence studies.[2]

[2] It may well be the case that these 'perceptual' deterrence studies actually provide strong support for the role of self-control and help explain why deterrence seems to matter so little: 'Differences across individuals in their perceptions of the certainty and severity of legal sanctions are related to

There are numerous studies of the consequences of variability in the severity of sentencing for crimes and they rather routinely come to the conclusion that harsher sentences do not provide a significant marginal deterrent effect for most crimes. For example, von Hirsch *et al.* (1999) review British sentencing schemes and find that they do not provide a basis for inferring that increasing severity of sentences generally is effective in enhancing deterrent effects (although they conclude that certainty may matter to some degree). Similar results are reported by Nagin (1998) and by Pratt (2006) for US research. The literature also seems to support the notion that those least in need of deterrence by the justice system are the most likely to report they are influenced by it: 'The recent perceptual studies, and a few available studies of actual offending behaviour, provide additional confirmation for the hypothesis that social ties, or the lack of them, affect the deterrent effects of the criminal-justice policies—with persons having strong social ties (ie strong links to families, local communities, etc.) being the more readily deterred by prospects of being apprehended' (von Hirsch *et al.* 1999: 3).

The studies of natural variations in crime rates and incarceration levels across time and space come to much the same conclusion. Blumstein's recent review of the empirical data about the deterrent and incapacitative effects of imprisonment is worthy of citation: 'There has been a massive growth in prison populations since the early 1970's with no comparable effect on crime rates' (general reviews may be found in Blumstein and Wallman (2000: 480)).

Studies of the effects of variation in policing strategies seem also to support the notion that the criminal justice sanctions have little effect of the probability of crime, at least within the bounds of policing generally regarded as acceptable in a liberal democracy (Reiner 2000: 1037; Bayley 1994; Eck and Maguire 2000: 249). On the other hand, highly intrusive 'at the elbow' methods of policing, in which areas are saturated with police to provide an image of constant presence, may have modest crime reduction effects. Relatively immediate sanctions, such as those offered when police are literally present at the scene, can affect the probability of crime for nearly everyone: '. . . the limited evidence available suggests that it is possible that focused attention on small areas with very high numbers of crimes contributed to the overall reduction in violent crime' (Eck and Maguire 2000: 248).

Consistent with control theories, a policeman at the elbow can increase the immediacy of the sanction sufficiently that it will curtail crime in specific places at particular times, but it will evaporate when the surveillance is gone. The 'situational crime prevention' research of Clarke and his colleagues has shown this effect

the likelihood that they will engage in criminal acts because these estimates are a function of (are evidence of) differences in their levels of self-control. These differences and their effects are not altered by changes in the actual certainty and severity of punishment. It is therefore a mistake to treat their perceptions as evidence in favour of 'deterrence theory' as it is ordinarily understood' (Hirschi 2008: 69).

of self-control also—the presence of witnesses or the police, a lock, or the obvious absence of potential gain (no change available) lowers the amount of crime—that is, short-term barriers may work, but not long-term sanction threat (see the excellent review by Bennett 1998; see also, Felson 1994).

The Future of Crime in Criminology

Criminology, as a behavioural science, will be advanced by a more general focus on problem behaviours, by a discipline-free theoretical approach and by lifting the political/legal restrictions to the dependent variable problem. A behavioural science of crime is possible when criminologists break with the tradition of restricting their attention to violations of the criminal law, free themselves from requirements of disciplinary explanations, and focus instead on the empirically observed properties of the events themselves and the tendencies they satisfy. To be sure, some conduct in violation of the criminal law will not then be incorporated into the explanation for crime and some decidedly non-crime will be. But there is little reason to believe *a priori* that a consistent and accurate theory of conduct could be constructed on the basis of the socio-political decisions that result in the criminal law. And, as we have seen, it may well be the case that a crime-free criminology will offer greater insights into the consequences of the criminal law itself.

For theory and research, a crime-free criminology means reducing the focus on delinquency and crime as special or especially motivated behaviour. Situating crime within the bounds of other conduct, subject to the same general principles as all other behaviour, makes criminal behaviour much less problematic or difficult to comprehend. Criminology far too often generates theories with more motivation than the acts entail, more special force that ordinary crime involves. Both public policy and academic theory benefit when the histrionics of the criminal justice system and the media depictions of crime are not allowed to be the basis of our thinking about crime.

When criminology focuses on the true nature of most crime, and its correspondence with other problem behaviours, research will incorporate the methods and findings of a broad range of disciplines and it is likely that effective public policies to confront crime will not focus exclusively or even largely on the criminal justice system. Ensuring success in school and employment, preventing substance abuse and violence, and a focus on the quality of early childhood experiences are likely to replace changes in policing, incarceration, and monitoring as techniques to lower the rate of crime. Limits on the penalties provided by the criminal law will need to be justified on grounds other than deterrent efficacy and crime control will become less important as a justification for investments in the criminal justice system.

REFERENCES

Baley, D. (1994), *The Police for the Future*, New York: Oxford University Press.

Baumeister, R. and Heatherton, T. (1996), 'Self-Regulation Failure: An Overview', *Psychological Inquiry*, 7: 1–15.

Beccaria, C. (1995 [1764]), *On Crimes and Punishments*, Cambridge: Cambridge University Press.

Becker, G. (1974), 'Crime and Punishment: An economic approach', in G. Becker and W. Landes (eds), *Essays on the Economics of Crimes and Punishments*, New York: Columbia.

Bentham, J. (1798), *An Introduction to Principles of Morals and Legislation*, London: Athlone Press.

Bennett, T. (1998), 'Crime Prevention', in M. Tonry (ed.), *The Handbook of Crime and Punishment*, New York: Oxford University Press.

Blumstein, A. and Wallman, J. (eds) (2000), *The Crime Drop in America*, New York: Cambridge University Press.

Britt, C. (1994), 'Versatility', in T. Hirschi and M. Gottfredson (eds), *The Generality of Deviance*, New Brunswick: Transaction.

_____ and Gottfredson M. (2003), 'Control Theories of Crime and Delinquency', *Advances in Criminological Theory, vol. 12*, New Brunswick: Transaction.

Cohen, L. and Felson, M. (1978), 'Social Change and Crime Rate Trends: A Routine Activities Approach', *American Sociological Review*, 44: 588–608.

Donovan, J., Jessor, R., and Costa. F. (1991), 'Adolescent Health Behaviour and Conventionality-Unconventionality: An Extension of Problem-Behaviour Theory', *Health Psychology*, 10, 1: 52–61.

Eck, J. and Maguire, E. (2000), 'Have Changes in Policing Reduced Violent Crime?', in A. Blumstein and J. Wallman (eds), *The Crime Drop in America*, New York: Cambridge University Press.

Farrington, D. (2003), 'Developmental and Life-Course Criminology: Key Theoretical and Empirical Issues—The 2002 Sutherland Award Address', *Criminology*, 41, 2: 221–55.

Felson, M. (1994), *Crime in Everyday Life*, Thousand Oaks: Pine Forge Press.

Glueck, S. and Glueck, E. (1950), *Unraveling Juvenile Delinquency*, Cambridge: Harvard University Press.

Gottfredson, M. (2004), 'The Empirical Status of Control Theories in Criminology' in F. Cullen (ed.), *Taking Stock: The Empirical Status of Theories in Criminology*, New Brunswick: Transaction.

_____ (2005), 'Offender Classifications and Treatment Effects in Developmental Criminology', *Annals of the American Academy of Political and Social Sciences*, 602: 46–56.

_____ (2007), 'Self-Control Theory and Criminal Violence', in D. Flannery, *et al.* (eds), *Cambridge Handbook on Criminal Violence*, Cambridge: Cambridge University Press.

_____ and Hirschi, T. (1990), *A General Theory of Crime*, Stanford: Stanford University Press.

Hardwick, K. (2002), *Unraveling 'Crime in the Making': Re-examining the role of informal social control in the genesis and stability of delinquency and crime*, PhD thesis, Department of Sociology, University of Calgary, Alberta.

Hindelang, M., Hirschi, T., and Weis, J. (1981), *Measuring Delinquency*, Beverley Hills: Sage.

Hirschi, T. (2004), 'Self-Control and Crime', in R. Baumeister and K. Vohs (eds), *Handbook of Self-regulation: Research, Theory and Applications*, New York: Guilford.
_____ (1969), *Causes of Delinquency*, Berkeley: University of California Press.
_____ and Gottfredson, M. (1990), 'Substantive Positivism and the Idea of Crime', *Rationality and Society*, 2: 412–28.
_____ and _____. (eds) (1994), *The Generality of Deviance*, New Brunswick: Transaction.
_____ and _____. (2000), 'In Defense of Self-Control', *Theoretical Criminology*, 4, 1: 55–69.
Junger, M. and Tremblay, R. E. (1999), 'Self-control, Accidents and Crime', *Criminal Justice and Behaviour*, 26: 485–501.
_____, van der Heijden, P., and Keane, C. (2001), 'Interrelated Harms: Examining the Associations between Victimization, Accidents, and Criminal Behaviour', *Injury Control and Safety Promotion*, 8, 1: 13–28.
_____, Stroebe, W., and van der Laan, A. (2001), 'Delinquency, Health Behaviour and Health', *British Journal of Health Psychology*, 6: 103–20.
_____, West, R., and Timman, R. (2001), 'Crime and Risky Behaviour in Traffic: An Example of Cross-Situational Consistency', *Journal of Research in Crime and Delinquency*, 38, 4: 439–59.
Loeber, R. and Dishion, T. (1983), 'Early Predictors of Male Delinquency: A Review', *Psychological Bulletin*, 94: 68–99.
_____ and Stouthamer-Loeber, M. (1986), 'Family Factors as Correlates and Predictors of Juvenile Conduct Problems and Delinquency' in M. Tonry and N. Morris (eds), *Crime and Justice: An Annual Review of Research*, vol. 7, Chicago: University of Chicago Press.
Marcus, B. (2004), 'Self-Control in the General Theory of Crime: Theoretical Implications of a Measurement Problem', *Theoretical Criminology*, 8, 1: 33–55.
_____. (2003), 'An Empirical Assessment of the Construct Validity of Two Alternative Self-Control Measures', *Educational and Psychological Measurement*, 63, 4: 674–706.
Matza, D. (1964), *Delinquency and Drift*, New York: Wiley.
Mischel, W., Shoda, Y., and Peake, P. (1988), 'The Nature of Adolescent Competencies Predicted by Preschool Delay of Gratification', *Journal of Personality and Social Psychology*, 54, 4: 687–96.
Nagin, D. (1998), 'Criminal Deterrence Research at the Outset of the Twenty-First Century', *Crime and Justice: A Review of Research*, 23: 1–43.
Packer, H. (1968), *The Limits of the Criminal Sanction*, Stanford: Stanford University Press.
Pratt, T. (2009), *Addicted to Incarceration*, Thousand Oaks: Sage.
_____, Cullen, F. T., Blevins, K. R., Daikgle, L. E., and Madensen, T. D. (2006), 'The Empirical Status of Deterrence Theory: A Meta-Analyses' in F. Cullen (ed.), *Taking Stock: The Empirical Status of Theories in Criminology*, New Brunswick: Transaction.
_____, Turner, M., and Piquero, A. (2004), 'Parental Socialization and Community Context: A Longitudinal Analysis of the Structural Sources of Low Self-Control', *Journal of research in crime and delinquency*, 41, 3: 219–43.
Reiner, R. (2000), 'Policing and the Police', in M. Maguire, *et al.* (eds), *The Oxford Handbook of Criminology*, Oxford: Oxford University Press.
Sellin, T. (1938), *Culture, Conflict and Crime*, New York: Social Science Research Council.
Sutherland, E. (1939), *Criminology*, Philadelphia: Lippincott.
_____ and Cressey, D. (1978), *Principles of Criminology*, Philadelphia: Lippencott.
Tappan, P. (1947), 'Who is the Criminal?', *American Sociological Review*, 12: 96–102.

Von Hirsch, A., Bottoms, A., Burney, E., and Wikstrom, P-O. (1999), *Criminal Deterrence and Sentence Severity: An Analysis of Recent Research,* Oxford: Hart Publishing.
West, D. and D. Farrington. (1973), *Who Becomes Delinquent?*, London: Heinemann.
Wickstrom, P-O. (2006), 'Individuals, Settings, and Acts of Crime. Situational Mechanisms and the Explanation of Crime', in P-O. Wickstrom and R. Sampson (eds), *The Explanation of Crime: Context, Mechanism, and Development,* Cambridge: Cambridge University Press.
_____ (forthcoming) 'Situational Action Theory', in F. Cullen and P. Wilcox (eds), *Encyclopedia of Criminological Theory.* Thousand Oaks: Sage.
_____ and Treiber, K. (2007), 'The Role of Self-Control in Crime Causation: Beyond Gottfredson and Hirschi's *General Theory of Crime*', *European Journal of Criminology,* 4: 237–64.

3

CRITICAL CRIMINOLOGY: THE RENEWAL OF THEORY, POLITICS, AND PRACTICE

EUGENE MCLAUGHLIN

I have always been just a little bit wary about writing about Critical Criminology and have tended to say 'no thanks' when asked. I was never sure what I could write that would not be either a predictable regurgitation of previous contributions or open to accusations of misrepresentation or both. And of course there is Stan Cohen's (1988: 11) caution that it requires both familiarity and distance; the need to be self-reflective and the avoidance of 'a narcissistic exaggeration of its importance'. Not the easiest of requirements. Nevertheless, probably for generational reasons, I have become much more interested in the intellectual development and diffusion of Critical Criminology as well as the prospects for its renewal. This chapter does not have the space to retrace the complicated pre-historical twists and turns of various Marxist-inspired critical criminologies. Instead, I begin by detailing the theoretical, political and research coordinates of a Critical Criminology that coalesced into an orthodox Marxist position in the course of the 1980s and 1990s. I want then to go on to discuss the challenges now facing Critical Criminology. I do of course need to acknowledge from the outset that, globally, there are several critical criminological communities of identification and articulation and divergent thematic paths. To varying degrees they are antagonistic towards the conventional criminological complex. My primary geographical reference point is the UK as it is the geo-political context that has generated what I view to be the most forceful orthodox position.

Where Were We? The Formation of Critical Criminology

It is impossible to overstate how central the social conflicts of the late 1970s and 1980s are to understanding the consolidation of an orthodox Critical Criminological paradigm in the UK. This strategic 'moment of truth' for Marxist criminology is something that is forgotten in increasingly sanitized conventional histories. Addressing Becker's classic 'whose side are we on?' question at this conjunctural crisis sharpened the analytical differences between Left Realists and Critical Criminologists on the thorny issue of the Marxist conceptualization of the state. Left Realism's development of a working class victimology foregrounded the role of defending a strong social democratic welfare state capable of regulating capitalism and protecting the vulnerable from the predatory criminality associated with competitive individualism. For Critical Criminologists, the social democratic state was in the process being transformed into an authoritarian anti-welfare state determined to police the social crisis and defeat various real or imagined internal and external threats. The 'heightened indignation, zeal and emotional commitment' surrounding a 'politics of injustice', identified by Cohen (1988: 261), is reflected in publications emanating from that period. This chapter does not have the space to include the story of Left Realism. Like Cohen (1988: 17), I believe that the emergence of a Left Realism's revisionist position 'demands our most serious attention in telling the story of anti-criminology' as it represents 'an almost complete reversal of the original enterprise'. It needs also be recognized that the Left Realist 'turn' received a considerable boost from feminist criminologists who wanted to use the 'criminalising power of the state for instrumental and symbolic ends' (Cohen 1988: 245). For a reminder of the details of the Left Realist agenda I would recommend that readers consult Lea and Young (1984); Jones *et al.* (1986); Kinsey *et al.* (1986); Matthews and Young (1986) and Matthews and Young (1992a, 1992b).

Hall *et al.*'s conceptualization of the rationales and workings of the rapidly evolving 'authoritarian state', as articulated in *Policing the Crisis,* was embedded in the neural wiring of Critical Criminology. This explanatory framework was also hard-edged via Poulantzas' (1978: 79) insistence on the routine rather than exceptional role played by the monopoly of violence in the exercise of state power. The brutalizing realities associated with the 'iron fist' in 'the velvet glove' became an article of faith with particular reference to Northern Ireland. Critical Criminology's engagement with broader theoretical developments would also be configured through this Poulantzasian theoretical filter. A portfolio of five theoretical coordinates nest under the 'authoritarian state' thesis that defined Critical Criminology's agenda in the 1980s and 1990s: criminalization; racialization; ideological mystification; penal abolitionism; and praxis. The primary task was identifying the criminalization practices that emanated from and assisted the 'authoritarian state' in its management of structural contradictions (Scraton and Chadwick 1991: 181; see also Scraton 1987). The 'authoritarian state' is grounded in the interests of, not just of, a particular class or of capital, but also in those of 'race' and gender. Classism, sexism, heterosexism, and racism, it was argued, are not isolated phenomena, but become institutionalized as taken-for-granted relations of power, which constitute and determine the punitive policies and practices of the criminal justice agencies. The overriding concern was to demonstrate how the application of the criminal label was not simply a matter of controlling 'criminality' but of constructing and containing political opposition and resistance. Criminalization is one of the most powerful disciplinary strategies available to the 'authoritarian state' because it mobilizes public consent for state action against particular groups if they can be linked to criminal threats.

'Racialization' was the second key allied coordinate. Sim and Gilroy (1983) reiterated Hall *et al.*'s thesis that a carefully cultivated racialized fear of crime, especially when connected to the ideological construction of the 'young, black male criminal', justified both tough police and judicial actions and fuelled 'tough on crime' legislation. As a consequence, not only were certain forms of crime racialized but whole communities were criminalized. An important point here is the insistence that racism is institutionalized in state practices. Although it was more likely to be take-for-granted rather than actually researched, the third coordinate was 'ideological mystification'. Following Hall *et al.* (1978), Critical Criminology recognizes that hegemony-building and the articulation of state power implies an intimate interrelation between coercion and consent. Critical analysis needs to be conscious of the role played by the ideological state apparatuses, particularly the mass media. Hall *et al.'s* reworked 'moral panic' thesis, combined with Herman and Chomsky's (1988: 298) position on the mass media's role in 'manufacturing consent', and a residual attachment to the concept of 'false consciousness' became the default position for explaining rising crime rates, public fear of crime and electoral support for authoritarian populism on law and order issues. For Critical Criminology, 'common-sense' understandings of the crime problem and crime control ideologies are embedded in and reproduced and amplified through media processes and practices (see, for example, Box 1983: 3). In so doing, the media also discharges another crucial ideological role—deflecting public attention from consideration of a much more serious range of social harms, dangers and forms of injustice.

The fourth coordinate was penal abolitionism, which allowed for a trenchant critique of the prison and criminal justice. Developed from Mathiesen (1974), the starting point is the insistence that conventional thinking about crime, criminality and punishment is fundamentally flawed because the 'harms' associated with social life cannot, and should not be, regulated by the criminal justice system. Abolitionism insists that events and behaviours that are criminalized have nothing in common other than the fact that they have been usurped by the criminal justice system. Hence, 'crime' has no ontological reality independent of the definitional processes and enforcement practices of the criminal law and criminal justice system. Social problems, conflicts, harms and antagonisms are an inevitable part of everyday life and therefore cannot be delegated to professionals and experts 'promising' to provide 'solutions'. When professionals intervene, the essence of social problems and conflicts are effectively 'stolen' and re-presented in forms that only perpetuate the problems/conflicts (see Christie 1984). This explains why the criminal justice system is overwhelmingly counterproductive in relation to its objectives. It does not function according to the rationales and legitimations claimed by it, whether they be rehabilitation, deterrence or prevention. Nor does it attend to the needs of victims or offenders because it causes unnecessary suffering and offers little influence to those directly involved. Finally, it cannot protect people from being victimized and is incapable of controlling criminality.

For Critical Criminology, the major risk associated with crime in modern societies is not necessarily criminal victimization, but punitive crime control strategies that facilitate repressive developments. The prison plays the crucial function in the 'authoritarian state' of warehousing 'surplus populations' and the 'dangerous classes'. However, this classic carceral function has taken a novel turn because of the return of the private prison. The private sector is capable of building, equipping and running prisons for whatever purpose is deemed appropriate by the state. The commercial prisons have a built-in 'growth dynamic' because they have a vested interest in seeing an increase both in crime and the public's fear of crime (see Christie, 2004).

The final vital coordinate of Critical Criminology is 'praxis'—the unity of theory, research and political practice intended to transform personal troubles into public issues (cf Mills 1959). To avoid falling into the trap of having its capacities compromised by and incorporated into the repressive apparatus of the state, the preferred mode of intervention would be: working with pressure groups campaigning for reform of the criminal law and/or criminal justice system or miscarriages of justice produced by institutionalized discrimination; participating in community inquiries into contentious criminal justice practices; interrogating official reports into state controversies (rioting, industrial disputes, prison protests, incidents of institutional violence etc.) in order to expose discrepancies in official accounts of 'what really happened'; and publicizing the crimes of the economically powerful, state crimes and human rights violations (for fuller details see Scraton 2004). Counter-hegemonic working practices are extremely important to: concretizing the 'authoritarian state' thesis; clarifying inter-personal ethics; identifying progressive social change; and enabling methodological innovation.

Where Are We Now? A Critical Criminology Orthodoxy

The previous discussion sought to establish how the theoretical and political parameters of Critical Criminology hardened into an orthodoxy. So what of the twenty-first century? A significant number of Critical Criminologists remain confident that the theoretical coordinates of the orthodox paradigm are more relevant than ever to explaining 'new times', particularly in the context of the post 9/11 Global War on Terror (GWOT). Carrington and Hogg (2002), Hillyard *et al.* (2004), Barton *et al.* (2007), and Coleman *et al.* (2009) provide us with an insight as to where Critical Criminology currently stands. Given their genealogy, it is not surprising that the texts are remarkably similar in their endorsement of the parameters of Critical Criminology.

Most notably, there remains an insistence on the 'unity' of critical theory, political practice and research. For Scraton (2002: 35) Critical Criminology is obligated to 'speak truth to power', challenging 'the political and ideological imperatives of official discourse, state sponsored evaluations of official policy initiatives and the correspondence of vocational training to the requirements of the crime control industry'.

'Crime' must continue to be problematized because it has no ontological reality and dominant constructions misrepresent and distort the real problem of crime. Criminalization processes are deemed to be as essential as ever to the functioning of the increasingly authoritarian state. The priority research areas for Critical Criminology remain highlighting: the injustices associated with the relentless expansion of the crisis-prone criminal justice system; state violence; and the crimes committed by the powerful elites. This means that it must also be politically allied to those struggling for social equality and justice and 'those who endure institutionalized harm' at the hands of the states as a result of structural inequalities derived from and sustained by the 'determining contexts' of class, patriarchy, race and age (see also Scraton and McCulloch 2009).

Critical Criminology is scathing in its assessment of the role played by conventional criminologists in the intensification of authoritarian crime-control practices. This is most obvious in the case of state-sponsored managerialist/technicalist criminology and entrepreneurial crime scientists whose stated aim is to devise and sell more effective forms of crime control. However, liberal criminologists are also criticized for continuing to work within the welfarist parts of an ever-expanding crime control complex that legitimize criminalization and management practices.

Consequently, conventional criminology, in its various guises, is viewed as compromised by its institutionalization as a policy relevant rather than an academically autonomous discipline and its willingness to work on the 'inside track' of the state's criminological agenda and preferred methodologies in return for funding, patronage and recognition. For Hillyard and Tombs (2004: 28) 'all too often, the products of criminological reasoning have been used to bolster states, providing rationales for the extension of state activities in the name of more effective criminal justice' (ibid.: 25). In addition, the blind spot of conventional criminology remains its inability to research victimization by the powerful, not least because the state does not recognize nor fund such research. It is imperative for Critical Criminologists to distance themselves from the authoritarian state's ever-expanding criminological agenda rather than pandering to it (Walters 2007). This would also create the opportunity to 'name and shame' those criminologists who are willing to conduct 'tick box' state-sponsored research on a tightly regulated contractual basis with no political consideration of the implications of their work (see also Sim *et al.* 2004).

Equally significantly, Critical Criminology no longer has to expend energy pointscoring with Left Realism as its primary oppositional perspective. Instead, its antipathy is directed towards the latest manifestation of the 'enemy within'—governmentality criminologists who have developed a revisionist post-state position. Inspired by Foucault's (1977, 1978, 1980) analysis of the shift from 'sovereign' to 'disciplinary' power, this perspective prefers to examine the plural, evolving nature of social control, penality, surveillance and governance, foregrounding private and civil spheres of action. Hence, the chain of Critical Criminological references premised as they were on the monopoly of violence of the 'sovereign state', were viewed as too unsophisticated a base from which to explain emergent forms of advanced liberal networks of governance (Shearing and Stenning 1985; see also Rose and Miller 1992; Lianos 2003). However, for Critical Criminology, these criminologists have accepted, in an uncritical manner, superficial anti-statist policy makeovers (such as 'partnerships', 'networks' and 'nodes') rather than researching the changing configuration of state sovereignty and the intensification and extension of the state's disciplinary capacities. For Coleman *et al.* (2009: 7) the defining characteristics of the state have been conveniently airbrushed out of governmentality analysis. The core problem of state violence cannot be resolved theoretically by pretending it does not exist:

> always at the centre of state interventions in violence—or, at a minimum, the threat of violence. Therefore, state violence is always implied or connected to the so-called 'soft' forms of power... Not only are the boundaries of the legitimacy of violence established by law but the power and authority of the state—indeed law itself—is necessarily an intimately bound to violence [Coleman *et al.* 2009: 14].

The 'anti-statist' project work of governmentalists makes them active participants in the state's ideological mystification processes.

Not surprisingly, an age-old question continues to unsettle twenty-first century Critical Criminology - should it abandon what it deems to be the compromised discipline of criminology to the managerial criminologists and crime scientists? Hillyard and Tombs (2004) have advocated a 'social harm' or 'zemiological' perspective, which would take in physical, financial/economic and emotional/psychological harms. They recognize that 'harm is no more definable than crime, and that it too lacks any ontological reality' (Hillyard and Tombs 2004: 20). It is also difficult to identify the range of issues to be encompassed by 'social harm'. However, their arguments in support of moving from a criminological to a production of 'social harms' approach are as follows: it acknowledges the multitude of harms that can affect people in the 'cradle to the grave' life cycle; it recognizes not just individual but also corporate and collective responsibility for actions and non-actions; it prioritizes a social policy rather than criminal justice policy response; it facilitates consideration of 'mass harms' that cannot be handled satisfactorily by the criminal justice process; and it confronts powerful interests and power structures.

Done and to be Done: Renewal in Bewildering Times

As we have seen, orthodox Critical Criminology has entered the new century with its tenets intact. Jock Young (2002: 271) argues that the need for an agenda-setting critical criminological perspective has never been greater. It does, however, have to radicalize itself intellectually so that it can work on the 'fundamental dislocations of justice that occur throughout our social order'. And for Currie (2002: v) the dislocations of justice are global in nature. However, there are serious question marks as to whether orthodox Critical Criminology's portfolio of core theoretical coordinates are all that is required to 'work' on these globalized dislocations of justice.

At this point of the discussion, it is necessary to go back to Stuart Hall's (1988) analysis of the challenges facing the left in radically 'New Times'. He identified a debilitating tendency on the left to construct and inhabit intellectual straitjackets, insisting, first and foremost, on doctrinal adherence to a particular form of understanding. This is the result not only of a defensiveness in the face of dominant neo-liberal agendas but is 'also due to a certain notion of politics, inhabited not so much as a theory, more as *a habit of mind*. We go on thinking a unilinear and irreversible political logic, driven by some abstract entity we call 'the economic' or 'capital,' etc' which can provide a total explanation' (Hall 1988: 275–6). The result is a propositional knowledge base about the state, economy, and the social, and corresponding truth games, that are stifling, operating without either an incisive critique of the status quo or the prospect of progressive alternatives. Hall argued that the failure of the left to renew its analysis in the face of the New Right's multifaceted assault on the post-war settlement rendered it politically paralysed and foregrounded the risk of intellectual irrelevance (ibid.; see also Hall 1996; Hall and Jacques 1989). For Hall, ideological conviction is politically self-defeating—the reality is that politics comes without historical guarantees.

Critical Criminology is once more at a crossroads in terms of the strategic choices available to it. As Bauman (2001a: 28) has argued:

> Crossroads call for decisions about which way to go but the first call, and not at all obvious decision to be taken is to recognize the crossroad as a crossroad—to accept that more than one way leads from here to the future and that sometimes pursuing the future—any future—may require sharp turns.

Critical Criminology can continue to employ the road map that has guided it for over two decades. However, I believe that it should consider a variety of strategic issues that may or may not lead in a different direction. What Hall (1996) requires of Cultural Studies to remain critical and deconstructive can also be applied to Critical Criminology. First, theoretical clarity requires that Critical Criminology must avoid analytical closure. It must make use of its unique (Marxist) intellectual resources but also engage with and when necessary drawn upon a range of viewpoints in order to generate a rigorous critique of its core assumptions and positions. Second, it must be politically engaged in the Gramscian sense. For Hall, the left cannot cut itself off in a near cynical manner from understanding and engaging with the realms of tactical politics and popular cultural transformations.

At a theoretical level it ought to be willing to work through the limitations of its authoritarian state-centred analysis. As was demonstrated in the previous section, Critical Criminology seeks to unmask the 'authoritarian state' in all its guises—'the carceral state'; the 'punitive state'; the 'coercive state'; the 'garrison state'; the 'surveillance state', the 'national security state'; 'the exceptional state' —etc. There are of course restrictions as to how far Critical Criminology can shift conceptually—and politically—in its search for the 'authoritarianism implicit in the liberal state' (Rolston and Scraton 2005: 549). It must be distinct and continue to define its own agenda in opposition to the constitution of conventional criminology at any given moment. However, as Schwendinger and Schwendinger (1970: 57) noted, concepts 'are brought to light and operationalized by the political struggles of our time'. Essentialization and eternalization of the concept of the 'authoritarian state'—as an intellectual 'brake-point' rather than as a cutting edge concept, narrows the possibilities for rigorous examination of the contradictory evidence that is so vital to renewal. By definition Critical Criminology is required to critique, interrogate and unsettle 'the self-evident' and it should do so in a ruthless intellectual manner. However, there is evidence that it has theoretical difficulty in making sociological sense of the complex of risks and uncertainties that define a rapidly changing governmental landscape. Its authoritarian state-centred analysis leaves little space for identification and consideration of contradictions, dilemmas and tensions associated with the due processes of liberal democratic governance. In addition, perhaps it might be more theoretically worthwhile to deconstruct rather than seeking to prove the existence of the authoritarian state. Here we should remember Poulantzas always cautioned against theorizing in a way that exaggerated the coherence, role and capacities of the state. Graham (1990: 56) has noted that theorists can 'pick one or several processes as "entry points" into the infinitely complex and ceaselessly changing social totality'. For her

> an entry point is a starting place in social analysis rather than an essence of social life. Starting with a particular entry point cannot give us a 'better' understanding of the social totality than we would have if we started somewhere else. But it will give us a different understanding, which produces different effects.

Critical Criminology needs to address empirical deficiencies to do with the lack of primary research on the institutional sites of criminal justice and security. Because it is failing to do so, it has, with notable exceptions, increasing difficulty in generating its own 'raw material' and methodological innovation. Its self-proclaimed 'dangerous scholarship' into the practices of the 'authoritarian state' remains heavily dependent on investigative news reporting and official documents for its data. Expanding the Critical Criminological agenda to highlight new forms of discrimination, exploitation, oppression and injustice, cannot overcome the absence of an empirical research programme on the changing nature of criminal justice processes, practices and agencies. This means it is unable to theorize in a rigorous way the politics of criminal justice institutions. To take but one example, I find it remarkable and alarming that despite Critical Criminology's appreciation of Hall *et al.*'s *Policing the Crisis*, the programme of critical research on the police has all but dried up.

With regard to the 'problem of crime', it is almost inevitable that the preferred interventionist stance requires rebalancing. First, in policy terms Critical Criminology continues to have difficulty in identifying or committing itself to progressive policies and practices. The preferred focus is on highlighting repressive practices and reformist policy failures. This version of impossibilism tends to push aside contradictions and tensions and dismisses or downplays progressive developments that, in turn, cut Critical Criminology off from communicating with a far wider audience, and creating strategic alliances with criminal justice professions. The fear of co-option and the quest for a 'replacement discourse' that will move beyond and/or dissolve 'crime' and 'criminal justice' runs the risk of generating political inaction. Second, Critical Criminology remains, again for understandable reasons—normative and practical—remarkably selective in the social harms and injustices it chooses to research and highlight. As was noted above, Critical Criminology has a public responsibility to provoke, irritate and exasperate as the bearer of 'unwelcome news' (Cohen 2002: xiii). It remains quite rightly evangelical in its determination to unearth the crimes of the economically, politically, socially, and militarily powerful (see for example, Green and Ward, 2005; Scraton,2007; Coleman, *et al.* 2009; Hudson and Walters 2009). However, it remains silent, theoretically and politically, on the crime problems that define public debate by utilization of a variety of 'techniques of neutralization', namely historical relativization, ideological mystification, media misrepresentation and moral enterprise and moral panic. The demise of Left Realism's working class victimology as a sharp-elbowed counterbalance has created a fundamental difficulty because Critical Criminology works best with a 'double consciousness' in relation to 'whose side it is on'. Some of the core arguments of Left Realism should be revisited because, as Hall (1980) noted, 'the politically potent themes of crime and delinquency, articulated through the discourses of popular morality, touch the direct experience, the anxieties and uncertainties of ordinary people'. Active engagement with the hotly contested politics associated with disturbing and intractable crime problems that capture the headlines is necessary if we are to think about the pre-conditions for the production of safe societies. This of course requires difficult deliberation on the relationship between individual rights and responsibilities; the possible and preferred role and scope of the state; the politics of law and order; and the purpose of the criminal justice system.

With notable exceptions, there has been a lack of interest in a political economy of conventional criminality in a moment of global shifts in political and economic relations, social insecurity and the erosion and systematic weakening of the state's social authority. Taylor (1999) insists that the political, as well as theoretical, imperative for Critical Criminology should be researching and explaining 'the ever intrusive fear and reality of crime' (Taylor 1999: 4) that are characteristic of neo-liberal 'market societies' defined by a fracturing of the social by competitive individualism. What is significant is his proposition that 'the analysis of crime, in all its different local and transnational forms, must proceed in recognition of the social fact of our times—the rise of the post-Fordist market society' (Taylor 1999: 64). Drawing upon a variety of social theorists, he argues that we are living in the midst of a post-industrial 'social crisis' defined by: under and unemployment; material poverty and social inequality; a fear of falling and fear of 'the other'; a weakening of the nation state; inclusionary and exclusionary practices; consumer culture; changing gender relations; and changing patterns of family and parenting. The disabling and disorganizing features of the global 'market society' in which everything is 'for sale' and social inequalities are normalized, are responsible for generating or intensifying these problems. For Taylor, the priority has to be researching the criminogenic, decivilizing characteristics of neo-liberal market societies, including changing crime patterns particularly related to 'local economies of crime'; the nature of criminal victimization; and the concurrent restructuring of crime control practices (see also Reiner (2007)). This connects across to Young's (2002) championing of a 'cultural turn' in Critical Criminology, suitable to understanding the 'vertigo' associated with the cultural logics of Bauman's 'liquid modernity', defined by: the inability of state institutions to bring or even promise to bring social order and individual security; economic deregulation; the changing nature of interpersonal relations; excessive consumerism; hyper-diversity; flexible moralities; and a fragmented 'public' sphere.

In conclusion, Critical Criminology must of course be understood as a work in progress—it is a demanding, unsettling and oppositional form of scholarship without any guarantees. Stan Cohen (1989: 100) reminds us of the tensions between the requirements of intellectual and political life. Honest intellectual life thrives and depends upon 'a spirit of scepticism, doubt and uncertainty. The answers are provisional; thought is ambiguous; irony is deliberate'. However, political life 'calls for immediate commitments' to social justice and responding to pressing demands for humanitarian help that are 'binding and encourage neither scepticism nor irony'. Managing this tension is not an easy task:

> All we can do, is find the best guide to each one—then confront the tension that results. This is hard going. In the end the only guides are, first, our sense of social justice, and second whatever time we have in the 24 hour day... our task is seemingly impossible: to combine detachment with commitment. There is only one universal guide for this: not to use intellectual skepticism as an alibi for political inaction [Cohen 1989: 123, 127].

References

Barton, A., Corteen, K., Scott, D., and Whyte, D. (eds) (2006), *Expanding the Criminological Imagination*, Cullompton: Willan.

Bauman, Z. (1999), *In Search of Politics*, Stanford: Stanford University Press.

_____ (2001a), *Community: Seeking Safety in an Insecure World*, Cambridge: Polity Press.

_____ (2001b), *Liquid Modernity*, Cambridge: Polity Press.

Bianchi, H. and van Swaaningen, R. (eds) (1986), *Abolitionism: Towards a Non-Repressive Approach to Crime*, Amsterdam: Free University Press.

Box, S. (1983), *Power, Crime and Mystification*, London: Tavistock.

Carrington, K. and Hogg, R. (eds), *Critical Criminology: Issues, Debates, Challenges*, Cullompton: Willan.

Christie, N. (1977), 'Conflicts as property', *British Journal of Criminology*, 17, 1: 1–15.

_____ (1986), 'Suitable enemies', in H. Bianchi and R. van Swaaningen (eds), *Abolitionism: Towards a Non-Repressive Approach to Crime*, Amsterdam: Free University Press.

_____ (1993), *Crime Control as Industry: Towards Gulags Western Style*, London: Routledge.

_____ (2004), *A Suitable Amount of Pain*, London: Routledge.

Cohen, S. (1988), *Against Criminology*, London: Transaction Books.

_____ (1989), 'Intellectual Scepticism and Political Commitment: The Case of Radical Criminology', in P. Walton and J. Young (eds), *New Criminology Revisited*, London: Routledge.

Coleman, R., Sim, J., Tombs, S., and Whyte, D. (eds) (2009), *State, Power, Crime*, London: Sage.

Currie, E. (2002), 'Preface', in K. Carrington and R. Hogg (eds), *Critical Criminology: Issues, Debates, Challenges*, Cullompton: Willan.

Foucault, M. (1977), *Discipline and Punish*, Harmondsworth: Penguin.

_____ (1978), 'Prison talk' in C. Gordon (ed.), *M. Foucault Power/Knowledge: Selected Interviews and Other Writings 1972–77*, Bristol: Harvester Wheatsheaf.

_____ (1991), 'Governmentality', in G. Burchell, C. Gordon, and P. Miller, *The Foucault Effect: Studies in Governmentality*, Chicago: University of Chicago Press.

Gilroy, P., Grossberg, L., and McRobbie, A. (eds) (2000), *Without Guarantees: In Honour of Stuart Hall*, London: Verso Books.

Graham, J. (1990), 'Theory and Essentialism in Marxist Geography', *Antipode*, 22, 1: 53–66.

Green, P. and Ward, T. (eds) (2005), 'State Crime: Special Issue', *British Journal of Criminology*, 45, 4.

Hall, S. (1988), *The Hard Road to Renewal*, London: Verso.

_____ (1996), 'On Postmodernism and Articulation: An Interview with Stuart Hall (edited by L. Grossberg)', in D. Morley and K. Hsing-Chen (eds), *Stuart Hall: Critical Dialogues in Critical Studies*, London: Routledge.

_____, Critcher, C., Jefferson, T., Clarke, J., and Roberts, B. (1978), *Policing the Crisis*, London: Hutchinson.

_____ and Jacques, M. (eds), *New Times: the Changing Face of Politics in the 1990s*, London: Lawrence and Wishart.

Herman, E.S. and Chomsky, H. (1988), *Manufacturing Consent: the Political Economy of Mass Media*, New York: Pantheon Books.

Hillyard, P., Pantazis, C., Tombs, S., and Gordon, D. (2004), *Beyond Criminology: Taking Harm Seriously*, London: Pluto.

_____, Sim, J., Tombs, S., and Whyte, D. (2004), 'Leaving a 'Stain on the Silence': Contemporary Criminology and the Politics of Dissent', *British Journal of Criminology*, 44: 369–90.

Hogg, R. and Carrington, K. (eds) (2005), *Critical Criminology: Issues, Debates and Challenges*, Cullompton: Willan.

Hudson, B. and Walters, R. (eds) (2009), 'Criminology and the war on Terror: Special Issue', *British Journal of Criminology*, 49, 5.

Jones, T., MacLean, B., and Young, J. (1986), *The Islington Crime Survey*, Aldershot: Gower.

Kinsey, R., Lea, J., and Young, J. (1986), *Losing the Fight Against Crime*, Oxford: Blackwell.

Lea, J. and Young, J. (1984), *What is to be Done about Law and Order?*, Harmondsworth: Penguin.

Lianos, M. (2003), 'Social Control after Foucault', *Surveillance and Society*, 1, 3:.412–30.

Matthews, R. and Young, J. (eds) (1986), *Confronting Crime*, London: Sage.

_____, and _____. (eds) (1992a), *Rethinking Criminology: The Realist Debate*, London: Sage.

_____, and _____. (eds) (1992b), *Issues in Realist Criminology*, London: Sage.

Mills, C. W. (1959), *The Sociological Imagination*, New York: Oxford University Press.

Poulantzas, N. (1978), *State, Power and Socialism*, London: Verso.

Reiner, R. (2007), *Law and Order: An Honest Citizen's Guide to Crime and Control*, Cambridge: Polity.

Rolston, B. and Scraton, P. (2005), 'In the Full Glare of English Politics', *British Journal of Criminology*, 45, 4: 547–64.

Rose, N. and Miller P. (1992), 'Political power beyond the state: problematic of government', *British Journal of Sociology*, 43, 2: 173–205.

Schwendinger, H. and Schwendinger, J. (1970), 'Defenders of Order or Guardians of Human Rights', *Issues in Criminology*, 5: 123–57

Scraton, P. (ed.) (1987), *Law, Order and the Authoritarian State: Readings in Critical Criminology*, Milton Keynes: Open University Press.

_____. (2004), 'Defining "Power" and Challenging "Knowledge": Critical Analysis and Resistance in the UK', in R. Hogg and K. Carrington (eds), *Critical Criminology: Issues, Debates and Challenges*, Cullompton: Willan.

_____. (2005), *The Authoritarian Within: Reflections on Power, Knowledge and Resistance*, Inaugural Professorial Lecture Queen's University, Belfast, 9 June 2005 (<http://www.statewatch.org/news/2005/nov/phil-scraton-inaugural-lecture.pdf>).

_____ (2007), *Power, Conflict, Criminalisation*, London: Routledge.

Scraton, P. and McCulloch, J. (eds) (2009), *The Violence of Incarceration*, New York: Routledge.

Shearing, C., and Stenning, P. (1985), 'From the Panopticon to the Disneyworld: The Development of Discipline', in A. N. Doob and E. L. Greenspan (eds), *Perspectives in Criminal Law*, Aurora: Canadian Law Book Co.

Taylor, I. (1982), *Law and Order: Arguments for Socialism*, Basingstoke: Macmillan.

_____. (1999), *Crime in Context: A Critical Criminology of Market Societies*, Cambridge: Polity.

Walters, R. (2007), 'Critical Criminology and the Intensification of the Authoritarian State' in A. Barton, K. Corteen, D. Scott, and D. Whyte (eds), *Expanding the Criminological Imagination*, Cullompton: Willan.

Walton, P. and Young, J. (eds) (1998), *The New Criminology Revisited*, Basingstoke: Macmillan.

Young, J. (1992), 'Ten Points of Realism', in R. Matthews and J. Young (eds), *Rethinking Criminology: The Realist Debate*, London: Sage.

_____ (2002), 'Critical Criminology in the Twenty-First Century: Critique, Irony and the Always Unfinished', in K. Carrington and R. Hogg (eds), *Critical Criminology: Issues, Debates, Challenges*, Cullompton: Willan.

_____ (2007), *The Vertigo of late Modernity*, London: Sage.

4

DISCIPLINARITY AND DRIFT

JEFF FERRELL

A half century or so after its publication, Gresham Sykes and David Matza's (2003 [1957]) article, 'Techniques of Neutralization: A Theory of Delinquency', has settled in as an accepted component of the criminological canon. This canonization is certainly merited; the article offered an important complement and corrective to criminological thinking at the time of its publication, and the innovative 'theory of delinquency' that it presented has been usefully employed by criminologists since. Yet canonization is not without its dangers. Divorced from the broader analysis that Sykes and Matza developed, the model of 'techniques of neutralization' has at times become caricature, its themes recast as a simple checklist of deviant techniques. Likewise, the post hoc contextualization of Sykes and Matza's work within that of 'similar' criminological theories has served in some ways to erase what was distinctive, and distinctively complex, about their analysis. Most broadly, disciplinary comfort with 'techniques of neutralization' as a component of criminological knowledge has masked a subversive possibility: that this model could not only be productively applied *by* criminologists, but *to* criminologists and criminology.

Here I attempt to reclaim 'techniques of neutralization' from the criminological canon and, in so doing, to suggest something of its unrealized potential for analysis and critique. This reclamation project proceeds on three fronts. First, I explore a delicate dialectic essential to Sykes and Matza's (2003: 233) analysis: that between the 'dominant social order' and those who would free themselves, if episodically, from it. Second, I turn the model of 'techniques of neutralization' back on the discipline that has embraced it, utilizing Sykes and Matza's insights as a lens through which to view criminological norms and criminological deviance. Finally, I explore the potential of drift as a form of knowledge, in the hope that some of criminology's participants—perhaps even the discipline itself—might be made to drift.

The Moral Validity of the Dominant Normative System

A shallow reading of 'Techniques of Neutralization'—and one that casts it all too comfortably among conventional 'control' theories of crime—would posit a solid social order from which would-be delinquents episodically free themselves through cheap rationalizations and morally suspect neutralizations. Their bond to the shared moral order temporarily neutralized, they are then vulnerable to drifting into bad behaviour—not as negativistic delinquents fired by oppositional subcultural values (Cohen 1955), but as individuals momentarily lacking the appropriate normative rudder.

In reality, though, Sykes and Matza are making a far different set of claims about society, culture, and crime. For them, the social order is not all that orderly; it is shot through with moral ambiguity and ethical contradiction. 'The normative system of a society', they argue, 'is marked by…*flexibility*; it does not consist of a set of rules held to be binding under all conditions' (Sykes and Matza 2003: 233–4, emphasis in original). Significantly, then, potential delinquents do not neutralize their bonds to a solid social order by utilizing morally ambiguous techniques; they neutralize their bonds to a contradictory social order by employing the same moral ambiguities already extant in social life. Moreover, as Sykes and Matza (2003: 234) take care to point out, these ambiguities constitute 'cultural constructions', social scripts closer to Mills' (1940) vocabularies of motive than to 'idiosyncratic' individual beliefs. As they explicate more fully in a subsequent article (Matza and Sykes 1961), and as Matza (1964: 60–61) reiterates in *Delinquency and Drift*, the social order carries the cultural seeds of its own negation; its loose moral threads remain always ready to be pulled.

At a minimum, then, Sykes and Matza describe a social order in which the boundaries between good and bad, normal and abnormal, law and crime are at best porous and shifting. Referring to the technique of neutralization that denies individual responsibility, they argue that 'it is not the validity of this orientation that concerns us here, but its function of deflecting blame…'; referring to the technique that critiques those who would critique the delinquent, they likewise note that 'the validity of this jaundiced viewpoint is not so important as its function in deflecting condemnation…' (Sykes and Matza 2003: 235, 236). Yet on another level this is precisely what *does* concern Sykes and Matza: the normative validity of a social order that leaves itself open to exemption and critique—that in fact embodies its own exemptions and critique—and so as well the normative validity of those who engage this critique.

Subtitled 'a theory of delinquency', their essay is as much a theory of society—and writing in the mid-1950s, amidst the presumed normative consensus of post-war America, they posit a social order that instead slips between one moral contradiction and another. The episodic delinquent may still in general terms 'recognize the moral validity of the dominant normative system', as Sykes and Matza (2003: 232) argue. It's less clear that Sykes and Matza do.

Or to put it another way: by Sykes and Matza's model, it seems that drift is inherent in an already compromised moral order, with or without the neutralizing techniques of potential deviants. The prerequisites for drifting away from illusions of moral certainty are in place: the ambiguity of dominant moral claims, the situational flexibility of the codes that lawmakers and religious leaders present as inflexible moral absolutes. The potential delinquent notices these contradictions, and invokes them—but the delinquent does not invent them. Sensing the cracks and contradictions in the dominant moral order, the potential delinquent only wedges them open a bit wider so as to set a course of autonomous social action, making manifest existing moral contradictions in an attempt to exit, momentarily, existing social constraints. The moral compromises and subterranean values (Matza and Sykes 1961) that circulate through daily life, complementing and contradicting alleged moral absolutes, constitute the cultural milieu out of which crime and delinquency emerge. In terms of crime and delinquency, Sykes and Matza are suggesting the social order is no more wholly innocent than the youthful drifter is wholly guilty.

In this sense a compromised moral order can be seen to spawn drift as surely as a constipated social order produces strain. In fact, we might say that the moral order of contemporary society is itself *anomic*—anomic not only at the level of the structural contradictions that Merton (1938) mined, but at the level of everyday experience, of everyday moral ambiguity and uncertainty. Echoing (though not citing) Merton's analysis, Sykes and Matza (2003: 237) speculate that, 'on *a priori* grounds it might be assumed that these justifications for deviance [techniques of neutralization] will be more readily seized by segments of society for whom a discrepancy between common social ideals and social practice is most apparent'. On the other hand, they write, it may be that 'this habit of 'bending' the dominant normative system—if not 'breaking' it—cuts across our cruder social categories ...' In either case the gap between 'social ideals and social practice'—we might even say the *strain* of pronounced moral absolutes pulling against the reality of everyday moral contradictions—sets the stage for delinquency and drift. Thou shalt not kill, undermined at every turn, exemptions endlessly taken, by patriotic war reports and the state's own death penalty, not to mention the 'fantasies of violence in books, magazines, movies, and television [that] are everywhere at hand' (Matza and Sykes,1961: 717). Thou shalt not steal, except that every commercial encounter constitutes a swindle and a con, and with this the growing realization that what the large print giveth the small print taketh away (Waits, 1976). Oh, and by the way, young people, know your rights:

> You have the right not to be killed—murder is a crime—unless it was done by a policeman or an aristocrat.... Young offenders, know your rights. You have the right to free speech, as long as you're not dumb enough to actually try it [Strummer and Jones 1982].

Of course, the same social order that harbours these moral contradictions also embodies a host of mechanisms operating to mask them. For some young people, the accumulated entreaties of the priest, the parent, and the teacher—and in the United States, the school police liaison—may suffice in sustaining the moral straight and narrow. For others, the pre-scripted morality of the televised police procedural or the moral drama of the athletic spectacle may, for a time, paper over emerging doubts; for still others, the busy hum of a youthful life may itself be sufficient to keep contradictions at bay. Even when moral contradictions do begin to bubble up through these layers of cultural containment, delinquency still may not occur; certainly not every young person who senses the social order's moral inadequacy turns this sensation into neutralization, drift, and delinquency. Just as for Merton the structural contradictions that spawn strain may or may not be addressed through theft or drugs or conformity, so the moral contradictions that underlie drift may or may not result in delinquency. For both Merton, and Sykes and Matza, sociological criminology preserves human agency while critically situating it at the intersection of social structure, culture, and crime.

For Sykes and Matza, then, the delinquent is the sort of young person who sees past mechanisms of cultural containment—past the moral proclamations of various authorities and the simplistic scripts proffered by popular morality tales—so as to perceive the inherent contradictions and inconsistencies underlying the moral order. Moreover, the successful delinquent acts on these insights, invoking them as techniques of neutralization so as to engineer a temporary exit. In this sense the young delinquent is a *natural social critic and activist*, perhaps because not yet fully socialized into the shared illusions of moral certainty, but in any case standing sufficiently outside the taken-for-granted dualities of good and bad, law and crime, to see them as forms of cultural artifice. That is, the delinquent operates *as a critical sociologist*.

Regarding 'denial of responsibility' as a technique of neutralization—the claim that 'delinquent acts are due to forces outside of the individual and beyond his control'—Sykes and Matza (2003: 234, 238) note that 'the similarity between this mode of justifying illegal behaviour assumed by the delinquent and the implications of a 'sociological' frame of reference or a 'humane' jurisprudence is readily apparent'. They then add in a footnote: 'A number of observers have wryly noted that many delinquents seem to show a surprising awareness of sociological and psychological explanations for their behaviour and are quick to point out the causal role of their poor environment'. Perhaps Sykes and Matza are here being 'wry' themselves—but even if so, they are also confirming the trajectory of their own analysis: towards a 'surprising' affinity between the delinquent's world view and the sociologist's. The technique of neutralization that involves 'denial of injury'—that is, the delinquent's sense that 'his behaviour does not really cause any great harm despite the fact that it runs counter to the law' (Sykes and Matza 2003: 235)—likewise sounds suspiciously similar to the critical criminologist's critique of low-order criminalization, punitive drug laws, and victimless crime. As for the 'condemnation of the condemners'—the delinquent's claim that those in power are often 'hypocrites, deviants in disguise', police often 'corrupt, stupid, and brutal', teachers and parents 'always' inclined toward favoritism and abuse—well, not always, but as any good sociologist would tell you, certainly more often than those police and teachers and parents would have us believe. And as regards the delinquent's 'appeal to higher loyalties'? 'The conflict between the claims of friendship and the claims of the law, or a similar dilemma', Sykes and Matza (2003: 236) remind us, 'has of course long been recognized by the social scientist (and the novelist) as a common human problem'.

Sykes and Matza, it turns out, have undertaken far more than a simplistic 'control theory' of moral order and deviance from it—have accomplished more even than a sophisticated and nuanced 'theory of delinquency'. In suggesting that the delinquent mindset time and again mirrors that of the sociologist or criminologist—embodies, even, something of the sociological imagination—they have also suggested that the sociological/criminological mindset embodies something of the delinquent's. Wryly or otherwise, Sykes and Matza have aligned sociological criminology not with agents of social control, *but with the drifters and the delinquents.* What are we to make of this?

Disciplinarity and Drift

As a starting point, we might remember that a 'dominant normative system' can operate not only at the broad societal level posited by Sykes and Matza, but within smaller social groups, subcultures, and professional associations. These smaller associations may well embody something of the broad normative order, of course, while also developing their own internally dominant norms. Following Sykes and Matza's analysis, we would also expect that their dominant normative systems would embody a host of inconsistencies and contradictions, and so remain ripe for neutralization and drift—if only a delinquent or a sociologist will take notice and take action.

The discipline of criminology offers one such normative system. As a discipline, criminology provides both formal and informal normative guidelines for professional conduct generally, and for the appropriate undertaking of criminological research and analysis specifically. Moreover, as a 'social science', the discipline of criminology promotes a set of normative standards regarding objectivity, replicability, and the accumulative advancement of knowledge. Criminology's professional associations provide one important repository of these normative standards. The

American Society of Criminology (ASC), for example, straightforwardly states that its members include 'students, practitioners, and academicians from the many fields of criminal justice and criminology', and that these members 'pursue scholarly, scientific, and professional knowledge concerning the measurement, etiology, consequences, prevention, control, and treatment of crime and delinquency'[1]. While the ASC does not elaborate on the moral and ethical frameworks for this scholarly work, the British Society of Criminology (BSC) does, by way of its *Code of Ethics for Researchers in the Field of Criminology*. Among its many moral injunctions, the BSC code advises criminologists to:

- refrain from laying claim, directly or indirectly, to expertise in areas of criminology which they do not have;
- correct any misrepresentations and adopt the highest standards in all their professional relationships with institutions and colleagues whatever their status....;
- promote equal opportunity in all aspects of their professional work and actively seek to avoid discriminatory behaviour. This...includes an obligation to avoid over-generalizing on the basis of limited data....;
- base research on the freely given informed consent of those studied in all but exceptional circumstances. (Exceptional in this context relates to exceptional importance of the topic rather than difficulty of gaining access)...;
- seek to maintain good relationships with all funding and professional agencies in order to achieve the aim of advancing knowledge about criminological issues and to avoid bringing the wider criminological community into disrepute with these agencies....;
- recognize their obligations to funders whether contractually defined or only the subject of informal or unwritten agreements....;
- seek to avoid contractual/financial arrangements which emphasize speed and economy at the expense of good quality research and....[2]

All of this might seem a morally valid and internally consistent system by which a discipline defines itself and sets the terms of scholarly and professional conduct for its members. But of course, as Sykes and Matza would remind us, it is nothing of the sort. It is instead a disciplinary moral order beset by contradiction and inconsistency, both in conceptualization and in practice, and all of this only half-hidden behind professional protestations otherwise. To begin with, the various injunctions that make up this moral order 'seldom if ever take the form of categorical imperatives', operating instead 'as qualified guides for action, limited in their applicability in terms of time, place, persons, and social circumstances' (Sykes and Matza, 2003: 233). The ASC provides its members no formal code of ethics; the BSC's guidelines overtly acknowledge 'exceptional circumstances', and in any case 'do not provide

[1] <www.asc41.com>, accessed 5 March 2010.

[2] <http://www.britsoccrim.org>, accessed 5 March 2010.

a prescription for the resolution of choices or dilemmas surrounding professional conduct in specific circumstances. They provide a framework of principles to assist the choices and decisions that have to be made also with regard to the principles, values and interests of all those involved in a particular situation'. Equally important, 'subterranean values' circulate throughout the discipline, around and below these provisional injunctions—that is, values 'which are in conflict or competition' with formal disciplinary morality 'but which are still recognized and accepted by many' (Matza and Sykes 1961: 716) within criminology.

The potential disciplinary deviant, then, understands criminology's moral order to be a provisional accomplishment rather than a collective categorical imperative. The potential deviant likewise watches and listens with care, measuring the distance between disciplinary self-definition and disciplinary practice, and hearing amidst injunctions to 'correct any misrepresentations' and 'promote equal opportunity' other sorts of values being promoted. As with the potential social delinquent described by Sykes and Matza, the potential disciplinary deviant in this way engages a partial *sociology of criminology* and, if successful, utilizes this sociological perspective to neutralize disciplinary bonds so as to drift outside their orbit.

Denial of responsibility: The discipline is larger than I am. I don't decide which theories or methods are accepted—but I do have to survive—so if that means misrepresenting my areas of expertise a bit, so be it; I'll learn as I go. Plus, my teaching and administrative work leave me little time for my own research and writing—I don't have time to look up every citation and cross-check every quote. Worse, the senior people in my department set unreasonable standards for advancement, so why shouldn't I have my graduate students mark my students' papers, or do a little uncredited research for me? You know, I used to think I was some sort of Mannheimian (1936) free-floating intellectual, but increasingly I realize that I'm 'more acted upon than acting' (Sykes and Matza 2003: 235).

Denial of injury: If I order some textbook examination copies and then sell them to a used book buyer, the big book publishers 'can well afford it' (Sykes and Matza 2003: 235)—and besides, just look at the paltry royalties they're paying me on my own book. That marking and research I'm having my graduate students do will serve them well in the long run; it's part of the professional socialization process. And that research grant I just received? That big granting agency can afford for me to take a little extra money off the top. And if they want me to churn out a quick survey, to 'emphasize speed and economy at the expense of good quality research', well, they're the ones paying for it—and, really, who's going to read the report anyway?

Denial of victim: I support the rule of submitting a manuscript to only one journal at a time, but the last time I sent a manuscript to this journal it took them six months to get back to me, so I'm simultaneously submitting my latest manuscript to them and to another journal. And speaking of journal articles: did you see the critique of my work that ------ inserted into that theory article she just published? I try to be fair, 'to avoid over-generalizing on the basis of limited data', but I'm using this last little study I did to mount a critique of her whole theoretical framework.

Condemnation of the condemners: The reviewers that rejected my latest journal submission obviously weren't sharp enough to understand my ideas—and who are they to tell me what makes for good criminology anyway? That Institutional Review Board that rejected my research proposal because I didn't adequately explain my informed consent procedures? Not one member knows what it is to do real field research, and certainly not on an issue as important as mine. And that negative review I got last year from the department chair? Please—it's been so long since he did any good scholarship he wouldn't know it if it bit him.

Appeal to higher loyalties: I promised my publisher the manuscript by the first of the year, but my father's been ill and needing my care—so, yeah, I value my career, but first things first. Meanwhile, here in the department, we're long overdue for curriculum revision—but if we get rid of those outdated courses on 'race and crime', what's old Dr. ---------- going to teach? He's only two years from retirement; we can wait. And that student in my theory class, the bright one with two kids, just now coming back to school, who needs a 'B' to keep her scholarship? Maybe it's better to make sure she gets that 'B' this one time than to grade her work as critically as I know I should.

Now I leave it to you, dear reader: Are these idiosyncratic accounts of individual moral failing, or evidence of shared 'cultural constructions', perhaps even subterranean values, circulating widely within the discipline of criminology? As C. Wright Mills might put it, are these not the sorts of ideas and emotions that we have all experienced on occasion, discussed with close colleagues, joked about at criminological conferences—that is, the very sorts of shared vocabularies of motive that link personal experience to social context? If so, then two conclusions follow. First, these shared moral constructions emerge in part from criminologists' own analysis of their discipline, from a kind of informal sociology of knowledge and sociology of organization that criminologists apply to the discipline of criminology as they make their way through it. Like Sykes and Matza's drifting delinquents, criminologists throughout their careers often see past their discipline's own self-proclaimed moral standards, its formal moral order, so as to catch sight of its structural contradictions. That is, they develop an experiential *sociology of criminology*. And yet, secondly, even as these sociological insights serve at times to neutralize one's bond to the discipline's 'dominant moral system', they do not necessarily spawn systematic disciplinary deviance. Instead, as with Sykes and Matza, they allow for episodes of drift, for the sorts of fleeting moral uncertainty that may or may not lead to double submissions or fudged citations or questionable student evaluations.

Just as criminologists develop in the course of their careers an informal sociology of criminology, then, Sykes and Matza's techniques of neutralization suggest a *criminology of criminology*—a model by which we can account for ongoing, episodic disjunctions between formal disciplinary self-definition and deviant disciplinary practice. And it seems they suggest something else as well: a different sort of sociology of knowledge, a deeper sort of disciplinary analysis, and a distinct sort of epistemic drift.

Cultural Criminology as Drift

A discipline's 'dominant normative system' of self-definition and self-policing operates not only in the realms of research ethics and funding guidelines. It operates also in the realms of intellectual tradition and paradigmatic preference. As encoded in theory and methodology handbooks and introductory textbooks, and as much so in submission categories for professional meetings and submission standards of professional journals, a discipline defines itself through its own self-proclaimed intellectual heritage, and enforces this definition through mechanisms of intellectual inclusion and exclusion. In the case of criminology, this sort of intellectual boundary maintenance generally invokes the discipline's tradition of scientific and social scientific inquiry into crime and its prevention, with the discipline's contemporary configurations of theory and method understood as advancing this science of crime and crime control. The American Society of Criminology, it will be recalled, unambiguously asserts that criminologists 'pursue scholarly, scientific, and professional knowledge concerning the measurement, etiology, consequences, prevention, control, and treatment of crime and delinquency'. Criminological textbooks generally reproduce this disciplinary self-image, and with equal assurance. Criminology, they say, 'uses scientific methods to study the nature, extent, cause, and control of criminal behaviour' (Seigel 2008: 2); criminology is 'built around the scientific study of crime and criminal behaviour...' (Schmalleger 2004: 14); criminologists 'scientifically study the nature and extent of crime...' (Glick 2005: 5).

As before, though, Sykes and Matza's analysis would suggest that this normative system, like others, embodies its own contradictions and exceptions—and that some criminologists may well notice these contradictions and mine them for their neutralizing effects. Further, it would suggest that criminologists most keenly and critically aware of criminology's disciplinary contradictions—that is, criminologists most oriented to a sociology of criminology—would be those most inclined to drift outside the discipline's intellectual boundaries. A brief revisiting of Sykes and Matza's techniques of neutralization—this time in the realms of criminology's intellectual traditions and preferred paradigms—reveals something of this dynamic.

Denial of responsibility: I'd like to be at peace with my discipline, but there's just too much pulling me away from it, too much of interest outside the bounds of criminology as a 'social science'. It's not my fault—I'll be trying to read the latest issue of *Criminology* or the *British Journal of Criminology*, but I'll get seduced by a documentary film on domestic violence or an old blues song about a murder, and I swear,

I'll realize that I've learned more about crime from them than from my own professional journals.

Denial of injury: Violating criminology's social scientific self-image and its standards of 'scientific' inquiry can only benefit criminology in the long run. Just look at Marx and Kropotkin, Park and Polsky, Becker and Matza—they were more activists and essayists and freelance investigators than 'social scientists', and yet their work was essential to criminology's development. And notice how often and how thoroughly past orthodoxies of 'scientific' criminological theory and method have been discredited; as Feyerabend (1975) would point out, this tells me that my job as a progressive criminologist is to undermine the current orthodoxy, not endorse it.

Denial of victim: I didn't start this fight; orthodox criminology did. I'd like to believe in the discipline and its potential, but the exclusionary absurdity of claiming a 'science' of something as culturally complex as 'crime' forces me to critique my own discipline. Likewise, the self-congratulatory 'scientific' claims of convenience-sample survey researchers and governmental statisticians beg for a response—and beg to be confronted, lest they devolve criminology into some sort of narrow academic actuarialism.

Condemnation of the condemners: Those who claim criminology's positivist heritage as a science of crime are either historically ignorant or 'hypocrites' (Sykes and Matza 2003: 236). Criminology's positivism was founded in fraud, performance, and cultural imperialism (Morrison 2004); today that fraudulent tradition sustains itself with samples, surveys, and statistics that by design ignore the very meaning and experience of crime in the interest of 'speed and economy', career advancement, and governmental funding. Those who today enforce contemporary criminology's intellectual standards sometimes seem like 'latter-day cabalists', their claims '... astonishingly close to the mystical beliefs of Pythagoras and his followers who attempted to submit all of life to the sovereignty of numbers' (Postman 1985: 23).

Appeal to higher loyalties: Times are too desperate to plod along with the normal science of contemporary criminology; we must have a criminology that can engage effectively with the crises of late modernity. To the extent that the discipline increasingly confounds 'the many fields of criminal justice and criminology' (ASC), it is also increasingly likely to side with state funding, state power, and state definitions of crime, and so to avoid this very sort of critical engagement. Criminology is an intellectual perspective, not a religion—and if that perspective today needs radical reinvention, so be it. I'm a citizen and an intellectual first, a criminologist second.

A criminologist who notices these disciplinary deficiencies may nonetheless retain a certain loyalty to the discipline's subject-matter and analytic potential—may, that is, continue to self-identify as a criminologist—while nonetheless drifting time and again outside the discipline's normative bounds. For such a criminologist, the sense that criminology's claims of 'science' are largely delusional may serve to neutralize bonds not to criminology as such, but to criminology *as a science*, and so to promote criminological exploration beyond social scientific bounds. Abandoning journal articles and governmental tables, this criminologist may drift in any number of directions: toward art or literature, folk culture or journalism, or some other alternative form of criminological inquiry.

In fact, this model seems to apply quite clearly to one of contemporary criminology's more prominent alternative approaches: cultural criminology. Certainly cultural criminologists have worked to widen criminology's subject-matter to include media representations, subcultural styles, and other 'cultural' phenomena that interconnect with crime and crime control. More significantly, though, they have sought alternative modes of criminological analysis and communication—cultural modes, broadly speaking—and have grounded this quest in a neutralizing critique of orthodox criminology and its claims to social scientific status. While cultural criminology has remained conversant with certain criminological theories oriented toward social interaction and cultural meaning, then, it has drifted away from more positivistic forms of criminological analysis and toward the analytic sensibilities of cultural studies, cultural geography, art, music, literature, and political theory. Likewise, cultural criminologists have overtly critiqued what they see as the shallow pseudo-science of conventional criminological methodologies, embracing instead an ethnographic sensibility that emphasizes shared meaning, experience, and emotion (Ferrell, Hayward and Young 2008). In addition, cultural criminologists have critiqued the (pseudo)scientific culture of criminological communication—the culture of passive third person writing and distended statistical tables—and have attempted to develop an alternative criminological culture that incorporates performance, narrative, 'true fiction', photography, and documentary filmmaking. Just as Sykes and Matza's drifting delinquents remain engaged with the larger moral order while episodically drifting from it, many cultural criminologists maintain their master status as criminologists while at the same time drifting from criminology's current intellectual and disciplinary configurations.

And yet, in the case of cultural criminology and otherwise, there seems to exist a dynamic that Sykes and Matza's model does not quite capture. Addressing the specific nature of delinquency and drift, Matza (1964: 28, emphasis in original) argues that

> drift stands midway between freedom and control. Its basis is an area of the social structure in which control has been loosened, coupled with the abortiveness of adolescent endeavor to organize an autonomous subculture, and thus an independent source of control, around illegal action. The delinquent *transiently* exists in limbo between convention and crime ... he drifts between criminal and conventional action.

Here drift is defined primarily in the negative, as a sort of social and cultural vacuum characterized by the absence of both conventional control and autonomous (subcultural) action. Relatedly, drift is conceptualized as a transient state of cultural 'limbo' in which the delinquent remains suspended, temporarily, between the more clearly defined poles of 'freedom and control', or 'criminal and conventional action'. Yet drift can mean more than traversing a temporary absence of meaning, more than haphazard movement between two fixed points. Drift itself can *produce* meaning, and can constitute a particular form of deviant knowledge. Drift can even be addictive, particularly as a way of knowing—and so those who are continually caught up in it, those who grow accustomed to it, can come to constitute, if not an 'autonomous subculture', then certainly something more than isolated, episodic deviants. Put simply, juvenile delinquents or cultural criminologists may not abandon the 'dominant normative system' so as to commit fully to a 'competing or countervailing' (Sykes and Matza 2003: 231–2) subculture. But they may commit to drift itself, and so embrace certain nomadic tendencies.

A closer look at cultural criminology's development reveals just these sorts of tendencies, and with them alternative forms of knowledge. For many cultural criminologists, the unorthodox forms of method, theory, and communication just mentioned are meant to promote not a fully-formed criminological counterculture, but rather an open-ended process of wandering intellectual exploration. Moreover, many of cultural criminology's unorthodox perspectives *themselves* embody this drifting, nomadic sensibility. By way of reflexive explication, the remainder of this chapter will drift among some of these perspectives. In the spirit of this sort of drifting knowledge, the discussion will not stay long in any one place, seeking as it does the comparative insights of the nomad over the solid understandings of the intellectual settler.

...the literary and political figure of the *flaneur*—the urban drifter, the aimless wanderer of the city's streets and alleys—has long referenced not only a quintessential form of urban experience, but a particular sort of urban knowledge. The flaneur's endless wanderings produce a holistic, emergent sense of the city, less attuned to any one location than to the webwork of cultural spaces and social interactions that animate city life. In this sense the flaneur knows the city, maps and remaps the dynamics of the city, in ways unavailable even to...

...architects and cartographers and city planners, who know the city more as a form of static, abstract, and rational organization. As de Certeau (2008: 158, 160, 162) argues, those who walk and wander the city write a different sort of 'story' about it, a story 'shaped out of fragments of trajectories and alterations of spaces'. This story in turn produces a 'proliferating illegitimacy', a 'rich indetermination', that reclaims knowledge of the city for its inhabitants, and so humanizes the urban experience. Or, if the goal is not only to humanize everyday experience but to revolutionize it, then there is...

...the *derive*, a particularly potent form of drift. As conceptualized and practised by radical Situationists of the mid-twentieth century, the derive is a form of ongoing spatial drifting designed to induce disorientation, and with this disorientation new possibilities of knowledge and perception. To wander a street rather than to hurry down it, to lose oneself in an otherwise familiar city, the Situationists argued, is to inaugurate a 'revolution of everyday life' (Vaneigem, 2001), to begin a 'discarding of the maps made by work and consumption and habit' (Ferrell, 2006: 197), and so to know one's life and one's environment on new terms. All of which I suppose I knew on some level, but never really understood, until I...

...began a life of digging through other people's trash (Ferrell 2006). Wandering from trash pile to trash pile, traversing the city's back alleys, I soon realized that I had remapped a city that I thought I knew well, reinvented it as a place of possibility and surprise. Moreover, the stumbling discovery of discarded items and their accidental juxtapositions invested them with new meanings, suggested insights and ideas that I couldn't have imagined otherwise. And overriding all this was another scrounger's insight: just because something is discarded doesn't mean it's drained of worth. Could all this be true of criminology as well? Perhaps we should wander among criminology's discards, rediscover lost texts, seat Cohen's *Delinquent Boys* next to Erikson's *Wayward Puritans* just to see what they'll say to each other, cut and paste new bricolages from criminology's forgotten canon. In doing so we might also create...

...*temporary autonomous zones* (Bey, 1985), fleeting intellectual spaces in which we would be free to wander away from accepted definitions, to imagine new perceptual possibilities. After all, precise definition and delimitation often serve to retard the process of inquiry, to mask the useful uncertainty of the subject at hand. Just ask Richard Grant (2003: 270–1)...

...who, in commenting on the difficulty in defining various nomadic groups, and in particular a loose group of train hobos known as the FTRA, notes that the initials 'FTRA' apparently referenced at first 'Fuck the Reagan Administration', later something like 'Free to Tramp and Ride Alone', and now mostly 'Freight Train Riders of America'. Grant comments also on the FTRA's (appropriately) uncertain origins. 'It was founded by Daniel Boone under a bridge in Libby, Montana, or maybe Whitefish, Montana, in 1981, or 1983, or 1985', Grant writes. 'Daniel Boone can't remember because he was drunk and high at the time, and has done his best to stay drunk and high every since.' And of course any or all of that could be a mistake as well, but then again...

...maybe mistakes can usefully neutralize normative assumptions and promote a sort of wandering creativity. Robert K. Merton (in Cullen and Messner 2007: 6) has noted the difference

> between the finished versions of scientific works...and the actual course of inquiry.... Typically, the scientific paper or monograph presents an immaculate appearance which reproduces little or nothing of the intuitive leaps, false starts, mistakes, loose ends, and happy accidents that actually cluttered up the inquiry.

Art historians now recognize that much of the art of Man Ray, Kandinsky, de Kooning, Duchamp, Rauschenberg, and Pollock emerged out of mistakes and misperceptions, out of misfired clay and cracked printing presses (Lovelace1996). Anarchists and punks celebrate their own sort of drifting knowledge; as the anonymous author of the wandering travelogue *Evasion* (2003:12) says, 'I always secretly looked forward to nothing going as planned. That way, I wasn't limited by my imagination. That way anything can, and always did, happen.' Writers like David Shields even propose that a new sort of intellectual and artistic movement is underway, one based in 'randomness, openness to accident and serendipity' (David Shields in Sante 2010: 17). So maybe...

...in the spirit of Sykes and Matza, drift can offer criminologists new ways of knowing, can teach us something about drifters and about the social order from which they wander. And maybe, in the balance between disciplinarity and drift, criminologists would sometimes do well to embrace their nomadic tendencies.

References

Anonymous (2003), *Evasion*, Atlanta: CrimthInc.

Bey, H. (1985), *T.A.Z.*, New York: Autonomedia.

de Certeau, M. (2008), 'Walking in the City', in S. During (ed.), *The Cultural Studies Reader*, Abingdon: Routledge.

Cohen, A. (1955), *Delinquent Boys*, New York: Free Press.

Cullen, F. and Messner, S. (2007), 'The Making of Criminology Revisited', *Theoretical Criminology*, 11, 1: 5–37.

Ferrell, J. (2006), *Empire of Scrounge*, New York: New York University Press.

_____, Hayward, K. and Young, J. (2008), *Cultural Criminology: An Invitation*, London: Sage.

Feyerabend, P. (1975), *Against Method*, London: Verso.

Glick, L. (2005), *Criminology*, Boston: Pearson.

Grant, R. (2003), *American Nomads*, New York: Grove.

Lovelace, C. (1996), 'Oh No! Mistakes into Masterpieces', *ARTnews*, 95, 1: 118–21.

Mannheim, K. (1936), *Ideology and Utopia*, London: Routledge.

Matza, D. (1964), *Delinquency and Drift*, New York: John Wiley and Sons.

_____, and G. Sykes, (1961), 'Juvenile Delinquency and Subterranean Values', *American Sociological Review*, 26: 712–19.

Merton, R. K. (1938), 'Social Structure and Anomie', *American Sociological Review*, 3: 672–82.

Mills, C. W. (1940), 'Situated Actions and Vocabularies of Motive', *American Sociological Review*, 5, 6: 904–13.

Morrison, W. (2004), 'Lombroso and the Birth of Criminological Positivism', in J. Ferrell *et al.* (eds), *Cultural Criminology Unleashed*, London: Routledge.

Postman, N. (1985), *Amusing Ourselves to Death*, New York: Penguin.

Sante, L. (2010), 'The Fiction of Memory', *The New York Times Book Review*, 14 March, 17.

Schmalleger, F. (2004), *Criminology Today*, 3rd edn, Upper Saddle River: Pearson.

Seigel, L. (2008), *Criminology: The Core*, 3rd edn, Belmont: Thompson.

Strummer, J. and Jones, M. (1982), 'Know Your Rights', *Combat Rock*, CBS.

Sykes, G. and Matza, D. (2003 [1957]), 'Techniques of Neutralization: A Theory of Delinquency', reprinted in E. McLaughlin *et al.* (eds), *Criminological Perspectives*, London: Sage.

Vaneigem, R. (2001 [1967]), *The Revolution of Everyday Life*, London: Rebel Press.

Waits, T. (1976), 'Step Right Up', *Small Change*, Asylum.

5

THE GLOBAL FINANCIAL CRISIS: NEO-LIBERALISM, SOCIAL DEMOCRACY, AND CRIMINOLOGY

DAVID BROWN

Introduction

In a festschrift to David Downes published in 2006 Robert Reiner noted the 'mysterious disappearance of social democratic criminology', going on to ask if it was dead—'or is it still alive and capable of returning?' (2006: 7). Reiner's conclusion was that 'there is ... some potential for a more overt espousal of social democratic criminology', a task he pressed the following year in *Law and Order: An Honest Citizen's Guide to Crime and Control* (2007). The 'mysterious disappearance' of social democratic criminology echoes the 'unravelling' of 'penal welfare', the 'eclipse of the solidarity project' (Garland 1996: 447, 463) and the postulated 'death of the social' or the advent of the 'post-social age' (Rose 1996: 328, 353). Social democracy, the solidarity project, penal welfarism and 'the social' are all it seems, like John Cleese's parrot, somewhat comatose, victims of the onslaught of neo-liberalism, the 'market society; 'the risk society', the 'crime control complex', 'governmentality', 'turbo-capitalism' and various other more metaphorical characterizations of life in 'late modernity'.

Global Financial Crisis

In 2008 a financial crisis swept the globe, as the deregulated US mortgage home loan market collapsed under the weight of unpaid loans resulting from risky lending practices and unlimited credit, much of it outside the traditional bank sector in hedge funds and investment banks. The crisis spread to the banking and financial markets worldwide, wiping trillions off international markets; a Bank of England Report estimated 'total losses in financial wealth towards the end of 2009 Q1 were equivalent to around 50% of world GDP' (Bank of England 2009: 13). In an attempt to stem rapidly rising unemployment rates the leaders of the neo-liberal 'Washington consensus', the United States and United Kingdom, embarked on a Keynesian rearguard pump priming operation injecting billions of taxpayer funds into propping up selected industries such as car manufacturers GM and Chrysler and financial organizations like AIG, and bailing out or nationalizing key large banks such as Lloyds, the Royal Bank of Scotland and HBOS in the United Kingdom and Citigroup and Bank of America in the United States. 'Almost half of the world's largest banks received direct government support' (ibid.: 17) and the scale of support to UK, US and euro area banking systems 'would exceed US$14 trillion' 'equivalent to around 50% of these countries annual GDP' (ibid.: 20). 'Turbo-charged' (Young 2007: 14, quoting Luttwak 1995) or 'casino' capitalism had come a cropper, bringing on the worst recession since the 1930s, plunging many into unemployment, undermining the credibility of the market fundamentalism of neo-liberal ideologues and prompting a mass public backlash against the culture of consumption, greed and excess symbolized by bankers awarding themselves annual bonuses of many times the average wage, attempting to continue their gladhanding after the crash but now with public rather than account holder funds.

The radical left, which for decades had addressed many a meeting, rally and publication with a tirade about the impending crisis of capitalism, constantly about to implode under the weight of its internal contradictions, was largely silent in the face of this actual crisis of capitalism, seemingly better equipped to battle the rhetorical 'immanent' version. It was left to governments across the political spectrum to grapple with the financial crisis, their major weapons being classic Keynesian and social democratic intervention in the market, socializing losses, engaging in public spending programmes to limit rises in unemployment and attempting to achieve increased regulation of the finance and banking sectors. The extent to which these interventions will be successful and the widespread public dissatisfaction with capitalism can be turned into a programme of increased regulation and wealth redistribution along social democratic and environmentally responsible lines, as against simply jump starting demand, remains to be seen. In one poll only 11 per cent of people surveyed across twenty-seven countries thought free market capitalism was working well while a majority in fifteen out of twenty-seven countries polled wanted their governments to be more active in owning or directing control of their nations' industries and a majority in twenty-two out of twenty-seven countries supported governments distributing wealth more evenly (BBC poll 9 November 2009).

Crisis, Criminology, and Contestation

This then is the political conjuncture in which the authors of this volume ponder the question: 'What is Criminology?' My intention in this contribution is not to argue 'for' a social democratic criminology (on which see Reiner 2006, 2007) so much as to suggest that this broader economic, political and social context of a 'global financial crisis' provides a backdrop, casting into relief current boundaries of criminology, permeated and made fluid in criminology's recent cultural turn. This cultural turn has reinvigorated criminology, providing new objects of analysis and rich and thick descriptions of the relationship between criminal justice and the conditions of life in 'late modernity' (and no shortage of inventive metaphors). Yet in comparison with certain older traditions that sought to articulate criminal justice issues with a wider politics of contestation around political economies and social welfare policies of different polities, many of the current leading culturalist accounts tend in their globalized convergences to produce a strangely decontextualized picture in which we are all subject to the zeitgeist of a unitary 'late modernity' which does not differ between, for example, social democratic and neo-liberal polities, let alone allow for the widespread persistence of the pre-modern. One effect of these globalized 'fluid modernity' accounts (however unintended) is to depoliticize, diminishing and devaluing the agents, spaces, practices, and discourses of contestation (Brown 2005).

My argument will be that contrary to this globalizing trend there are signs within criminology that life is being breathed back into social democratic and penal welfare concerns, habitus, and practices. I will discuss only three of these signs: the emergence of neo-liberalism as a subject of criminology; a developing comparative penology which recognizes differences in the political economies of capitalist states and evinces a renewed interest in inequality; and what I would like to think of as a nascent revolt against the 'generative grammar' (Garland, 2001: 18), 'pathological disciplinarities' (Carlen 2005: 430) and 'imaginary penalities' (Carlen 2008) of neo-liberal managerialism.

The focus will be mainly on penology and will be conducted at a level of generality, drawing chiefly on Australian and UK experience and examples. A few stirrings and signs do not a resurrection make and, as *The Life of Brian* suggested, signs are open to very different interpretations and can lead in very different directions. Financial crises and ensuing recession can lead to an extension of neo-liberalism and policies such as cuts to public services, but they can also 'create tipping points away from neo-liberalism. There may be an alternative form of global modernity that is either social democratic or one that is nationalist, protectionist, authoritarian or xenophobic' (Walby 2009: 425). A recognition that the future is not inevitably neo-liberal is in sharp contrast to a battery of defeatist pronouncements from leading left wing thinkers, perhaps best encapsulated in Perry Anderson's oft-quoted statement that:

> For the first time since the Reformation there are no longer any significant oppositions –that is systematic rival out-looks—within the thought world of the West; and on a world scale either ...Whatever limitations persist to its practice, neo-liberalism as a set of principles rules undivided across the globe; the most successful ideology in world history. (Anderson 2000: 17; quoted in England and Ward 2007:1])

If contestation is to be recuperated in the face of this sort of fatalistic hyperbole, both more generally and in criminology, it might be helpful to relinquish the rigid periodization that produces a history of epochs, one superseding the other, rolling all before it burying the past, a valourization of rupture over continuity, the new over the old. The proclamations of the death of the social, the demise of the solidarity project and penal welfarism, and speculation on the death, suicide or murder (Reiner 2006: 7) of social democratic criminology are, as Garland notes, 'a kind of counter-rhetoric' not an 'empirical description. The infrastructures of the welfare state have not been abolished or utterly transformed. They have been overlaid by a different political culture, and directed by a new style of public management.' The destiny of penal welfarism is 'not to be dismantled, but to become the problematic institutional terrain upon which new strategies and objectives are continually built' (Garland 2001: 174). Rather than being flattened, blown or washed away, social democracy and penal welfarism are partly submerged, reshaped, blended, reconfigured, hybridised, 'recalibrated'. Political, economic and social policies promoting social solidarity are still part of political struggle and in many countries and regions (especially in Latin America) attract increased popular support, often overt, sometimes displaced.

The Emergence of Neo-Liberalism as a Subject of Criminology

The origins of neo-liberalism are widely seen to lie in the theories promoted by the University of Chicago economist Milton Friedman and his associates in the 1950s.

Key policies—which were first championed by General Pinochet in Chile, after he overthrew the democratically elected Socialist Allende Government—included free trade, privatization, deregulation, and welfare state retrenchment (Harvey 2005; Klein 2007). England and Ward (2007: 11–2) provide four different understandings of neo-liberalism: as an ideological hegemonic project; as policy and programme; as state form; and as governmentality. In as much as criminologists engage with neo-liberalism it is predominantly in the fourth sense, as governmentality. Assisted perhaps by the standing of its Foucauldian heritage, governmentality has been assimilated into criminological debate, especially in the areas of crime prevention, underpinning established concepts such as 'responsibilization', 'criminologies of the self', 'governance at a distance', the 'government of populations', and the rise and rise of risk technologies (Garland 1997).

Few criminologists have explicitly tackled neo-liberalism as policy and programme although, as I shall argue later, Pat Carlen's work provides a devastating critique of its effects in the penal realm. Other researchers have traversed neo-liberal policy effects in discussions of issues such as the politics of crime control (Newburn and Rock 2006), police reorganization (McLaughlin and Murji 2000), and New Labour criminal justice policies (McLaughlin, Muncie and Hughes 2001), to mention but a few. Still other criminological work either discusses some inflection or other of neo-liberalism and its effects without calling it such, or focuses on an allied (and different, although sometimes conflated) concept such as globalization (eg Aas 2005, 2008). Jock Young's *Vertigo* (2003) although hardly mentioning neo-liberalism by name, provides a Mertonian (Young 2003) cultural critique of the processes of transgression, insecurity, resentment, and vindictiveness heightened by neo-liberal restructuring. In David Garland's *The Culture of Control* (2001) overt reference to neo-liberalism plays a minor role compared to the processes of social and cultural change described as 'the coming of late modernity' (ibid: viii). Late modernity is linked to a second force, the 'free market, socially conservative politics' (ibid: x). It is the articulation of free market ideology (neo-liberalism) with neo-conservativism that is vital: the 'volatility' of law and order is a consequence of the instability of this articulation. This approach is directly challenged by Loic Wacquant in his recent book *Punishing the Poor* (2009) where Wacquant puts neo-liberalism in the driving seat and sees Garland's 'hysterical denial' and 'acting out' punitive 'criminologies of the other' (Garland 1996) as an essential function of neo-liberalism itself. 'The root cause of the punitive turn is not late modernity', Wacquant asserts, 'but neo-liberalism, a project that can be indifferently embraced by politicians of the Right or Left' (Wacquant 2009: 305).

Neo-liberalism for Wacquant is a 'transnational political project' consisting of four 'institutional logics': 'economic deregulation'; 'welfare state devolution, retraction, and recomposition' to support the 'intensification of commodification' and discipline labour; 'the cultural trope of individual responsibility which invades all spheres of life'; and 'an expansive, intrusive, and proactive penal apparatus' 'to contain the disorders generated by diffusing insecurity and deepening inequality' (ibid.: 306–7). While trumpeting the small state mantra neo-liberalism turns out to 'beget 'big government' on the twofold frontage of workfare and criminal justice'. In short, '... *the invasive, expansive, and expensive penal state is not a deviation from neo-liberalism but one of its constituent ingredients*' (2009: 308, emphasis in original). In Wacquant's account then, 'it is not just the policies of the state ["mating restrictive workfare with expansive prisonfare"] that are illiberal but *its very architecture*', constructing a 'Janus-faced Leviathan' and demonstrating that 'neo-liberalism is constitutively corrosive of democracy' (2009: 312, 313, emphases in the original)

If this sounds somewhat functionalist, Wacquant in both a prologue and a 'theoretical coda' invokes Bourdieu against 'the functionalism of the worst' ... 'which transmutes the historically conditioned outcome of struggles, waged over and inside the bureaucratic field to shape its perimeter, capacities, and missions, into a necessary and ineluctable fact'. (ibid: 313, xx) The difficulty is that these admirable sentiments tend to bookend such a passionate treatment of the 'Poverty of the Social State' and the 'Grandeur of the Penal State', including a brave chapter on sex offenders as the new pariahs to be 'hunted down' as 'privileged targets', that the cumulative effect (on this reader at least) was a sense of overwhelming inevitability, in the face of which, contestation does not seem to have much place, appearing briefly in 'How to Escape the Law and Order Snare' (ibid: 281–6). But this more programmatic section towards the end of the book which includes exhortations to 'defend the autonomy and dignity of the occupations making up the Left arm of the state, social worker and psychologist, teacher and specialized educator, housing coordinator and child-care worker, nurse and doctor' (ibid.: 285) comes as somewhat of a surprise after nearly 300 pages in which these occupations appear to have been swept aside in the 'surge of the penal state' (ibid.: xix) or caught up in the 'assistantial–correctional mesh' (ibid.: 98). Similarly, exhortations to halt the 'seemingly harmless semantic drifts' (ibid.: 284) might be applied to the drift from 'castaway categories' (ibid.: 4), 'subproletariat' (ibid.: 12), 'marginalized fractions of the working class' (ibid.: 69) to 'the dross of the market society', 'social' and 'human detritus' (ibid.: 273). While such formulations may be metaphorical, they illustrate the more general danger of positing such a sweeping 'planetary dissemination' (ibid.: 20) of the neo-liberal political project as to run the danger of reinscribing and reinforcing that which is being decried.

What this very perfunctory survey suggests is that neo-liberalism has not figured directly as a central subject in criminological work but that this may be changing. Such developments are promising. For in as much as it is named and seen as a legitimate criminological object, neo-liberalism, (or more usefully neo-liberalization—see later), particularly in its guise of 'policies and programme', is a better focus for discussion than the vague concept of 'late modernity', which can only be described, celebrated or deplored, but not contested, for it is not an identifiable subject possessing agency but an epochal description or characterization, a condition, stage or state, to which it is impossible to attribute causality (cf the processes or programmes of modernization). At the same time, and to put it over-crudely, in as much as criminologists have grappled with neo-liberalism, the results have tended to engender either a resigned sense of inevitability (some might call it a 'quietism') at the march of 'governmentality', risk, 'responsibilization' and 'government at a distance' or alternatively and infrequently, militant denunciations of the ravages of neo-liberalism which tend to see it as hegemonic ideology or state form and overplay its unitary character, effects, and reach. Both these tendencies foreclose or attenuate the forms of actually existing and potential contestation and resistance, in a subtle and unintended way extending the power of neo-liberalism.

Comparative Penological Analysis: Political Economy and Inequality

Eugene McLaughlin argues in his chapter that 'with a couple of notable exceptions there has been an abandonment of interest in political economy/materialist analysis of crime and social transformation' (this volume). Ian Taylor's last book *Crime in Context* (1999) is indeed a major exception. But in the emerging field of comparative penology the work of Cavadino and Dignan (2006), Lacey, (2008) and Pratt (2008) constitutes a serious attempt to engage in a comparative analysis of political and cultural economies and their penal tendencies, to explain the significant national differences in imprisonment rates and the measures of penal tolerance and severity which underlie them.

The new comparative criminology builds on earlier comparative work (Downes 1988) in particular that of Esping Anderson who makes a threefold distinction between liberal market economies, conservative corporatist, and social democratic forms of 'welfare regimes' (1990, 1999), what Walby describes as a 'varieties of capitalism' approach (Walby 2009: 29) further developed by Hall and Soskice (2001). Applying this basic classification to the 'penal tendencies' (Cavadino and Dignan 2006: 15, Table 1.1), imprisonment rates, and 'attitudes to punishment' of the political economies of selected advanced western style democracies, those countries with the highest imprisonment rates are 'neo-liberal' countries with liberal market economies, followed in turn by 'conservative corporatist', 'social democracies', and 'Oriental corporatist', all with 'coordinated market economies' (ibid.: 22, table 1.2). Similarly, attitudes to punishment are broadly, but not so neatly, in line with the different types of political economy (ibid.: 30, table 1.3). This type of comparative analysis highlighting difference rather than similarity can be applied to the considerable regional variation in imprisonment rates, the use of the death penalty, private prisons, three strikes legislation and mandatory minimums in the United States between states (Zimring and Hawkins 1991; Barker 2006; Newburn 2006) and in

Australia between the Northern Territory and other Australian states and between Victoria and New South Wales (Australian Prison Project 2009).

The argument is that the socio-cultural, political and economic variables affecting the capacity to deliver inclusionary and reintegrative criminal justice policies (which should be the aim of liberal democracies) vary in different forms of democracy around the 'liberal/coordinated market economy' distinction. As Lacey argues, 'liberal market systems oriented to flexibility and mobility have turned inexorably to punishment as a means of managing an excluded population consistently excluded from the post-Fordist economy' while 'coordinated systems which favour long term relationships—through investment in education and training, generous welfare benefits, long term employment relationships—have been able to resist the powerfully excluding and stigmatizing aspects of punishment' (Lacey 2008: 109; see also Pratt 2008; Beckett and Western 2001; Downes and Hansen 2006).

Cavadino and Dignan caution: 'penality remains irreducibly relatively autonomous from any particular factor or combination of factors, however powerful' (ibid.: 36). In much comparative work, the crucial significance of race and colonialism/post colonialism in the production of imprisonment rates is underplayed. By and large the neo-liberal political economies are also former colonial or post-colonial countries with very high indigenous and racial minority imprisonment rates (cf the social democracies). But partly cutting across this, immigrants or foreign nationals are massively over-incarcerated across the European Union (Wacquant 2006). The link between inequality and levels of punishment (Cavadino and Dignan 2006: 29) is extended by Wilkinson and Pickett who mount a broader argument outside criminology, summarized in the title of their book: *The Spirit Level: Why More Equal Societies Almost Always Do Better* (2009), an excellent example of a highly successful public intervention outside but of relevance to criminology which can be articulated to a broader politics of defending and recuperating social democracy.

Whatever the limitations of this type of work so far, it has several benefits. First, it returns political economy and a concern about inequality to criminology centre stage. Second, in its interest in different 'varieties of capitalism' and links between these differences and levels and forms of punitiveness, penal regimes and strategies, it serves to undermine the dominant tendency common in 'late modernity' type analyses to see homogenizing globalized convergence everywhere. Third, it restores social democracy to consideration as an established variety of welfare regime and polity, in a way that opens up debate around its capacity to resist or 'adjust' to 'neo-liberal drift' (Ellison 2006). Fourth, it invites criminologists to think about how their research might be articulated with political policies and programmes that combat exclusion, inequality, loss of trust, resentment, and other criminogenic forces.

Challenging the 'Pathological Disciplinarities' and 'Imaginary Penalities' of Neo-Liberal Managerialism

The new neo-liberal discourses and practices of managerialism are indicative of a more general struggle over the 'habitus' of the public service, welfare and criminal justice fields, crudely posed as an opposition between the older penal welfare traditions and the new neo-liberal managerialism that centres on risk. Garland describes habitus as a 'kind of generative grammar that structured the standard language, the standard thinking, and the standard practices of the actors and agencies who operated within the field' (Garland 2001: 18). Working life in bureaucratic and public service institutions, is increasingly characterized by manic micro-management, over-regulation, mission statements, obsessive auditing and monitoring, measurement by performance indicators or 'KPIs', targets, quality assurance reviews and benchmarking, all of which require the adoption of a form of management speak in which verbs are turned into nouns and opacity is preferred over clarity, or seen as an indication of theoretical sophistication. It is a world ever 'progressing forward', largely without agents, where the passive voice reigns supreme, intellectual workers are 'content providers' and in the university sector vice-chancellors rejoice when they see the 'balance of trade' running in favour of 'their' particular university, one measure of which is 'grants walking in the door exceeding grants walking out'. Risk is the touchstone of much of this frenzied activity, with new formulations of risk emerging almost daily, requiring new strategies, policies, task forces, and units to formulate protective response measures. Measures which have a tendency to both devolve responsibility downwards, protecting management, and to require the particular sector's front line workers, be they police, prison or probation officers, or academics, to depart from their primary professional service and performance tasks and construct 'virtual' accounts of their activities that signify compliance with the new risk averse strictures.

Measurement, Audit, KPIs, and Risk

Measurement is the touchstone of all things; if it cannot be counted, reduced to a 'metric' or graph, it is of little value. The annual reports of courts are full of tables about delay; the speed of processing cases quantified into weeks and months is now the key performance measure; notions like the quality of justice (or education, or health and welfare) being far too nebulous to be measured. The various agencies of government: prisons, courts, hospitals, schools, universities, have become more and more performance driven, self-referential systems evaluated by quantitative criteria, primarily how many inmates/cases/patients/students/complaints have been processed, in what time and at what cost. The audit measures of 'efficiency' and 'effectiveness' have less and less connection to social effects and more and more to 'outputs' and management of the 'enterprise', particularly the management of risk, central to which is the *political* risk of 'scandals' (eg, prison escapes; parolees reoffending). The clearest and most unremarked upon example of risk as a driver in the criminal justice system is rapidly rising rates of remand imprisonment, now running at 25 per cent of all prisoners in Australia, constituting an unacknowledged process of preventive pre-trial detention.

Risk management also permeates academia. Research is subject to lengthy and complicated 'ethics' clearance applications so that remaining in the library involves less risk than interviewing real people and theoretical speculation is the safest of all. Academic promotion is increasingly dependent on gaining external research grants and increased rates of publication, judged on elaborate ranking exercises that produce a new round of 'metrics'. There has been a massive expansion of part-time staff on short-term contracts and in many places an increase in class sizes; a deterioration in staff–student ratios; a reduction in face-to-face teaching hours; the abolition of lunch hours and an expansion of teaching time slots to include weekends and additional 'summer and winter' semesters and 'intensive courses' so that university 'plant' can be utilized '24/7' and '24/12'; the compression and trimming of degree content, the proliferation of newly 'badged' degrees offering 'compact' versions of existing degrees and greater possibilities for 'double dipping' in the chase for fees; and bonuses for senior management who oversee the intensification of teaching, research and grant production.

Welcome to the world of the new neo-liberal managerialism in the university sector. The idea of the university as an 'ivory tower' immune from the 'real world' is risible; current levels and forms of managerialism are toxic, counterproductive and unsustainable. Academic researchers, criminological or otherwise, need to confront the ways in which the neo-liberal restructuring of the university sector is a 'variable' in their own research, affecting in myriad ways the available funding, methodology, conduct, content, and publication of research, in what it is possible or 'wise' to say.

'Imaginary Penalities' and 'Pathological Disciplinarities'

In the prison sphere Pat Carlen has perhaps done the most to examine the effects of neo-liberal managerialism. As she puts it:

> ...the old modernist construct of the class bound, gendered and/or discriminated-against prisoner seems to have been somewhat lost. ...Yet as every prison officer and probation officer knows, and notwithstanding the rhetoric's and prejudices of programming and audit, prisoners today have the same social characteristics as of yesteryear and many prison staff are puzzled as to the relevance of the proliferation of rules, regulations and audit to making prisoners' in-prison experiences less damaging and their post-prison careers more law abiding [Carlen 2005: 429].

In a later study based on an unnamed Australian women's prison Carlen coined the term 'imaginary penalities' (Carlen 2008) to describe the way in which prison staff spent much time constructing paper trails of compliance, supporting and justifying reintegrative prison programmes which were not actually being offered as they were designed for sentenced prisoners and the prison held mainly remanded prisoners. Officers responded creatively to audits 'as if' they were actually running programmes 'posited upon imaginary prisoners (they were short-term remand rather than sentenced), imaginary programmes (they were not running) and imaginary 'back up' in the community (neither 'back up' nor 'community' existed)' (ibid.: 5). Carlen's work struck an immediate chord with many academics who recognized in requirements to navigate the templates, questionnaires, KPI's and audits of academe, a parallel imaginary or virtual world to that of the real classroom. Indeed once alerted to this concept it seems to pop up everywhere (ibid.: xv), as the following two recent Sydney examples show. In the first, hospitals were creating 'virtual beds' that did not actually exist, enabling patients who were physically still in the emergency section to be taken off the waiting lists, lowering the head count and meeting KPI's. In the second, corrective services were keeping as many as 1,700 people per month in police cells in Central Station, three times higher than the numbers recorded in statistics, holding them in a 'pseudo gaol' to keep prison numbers down. All creative ways of meeting KPI's that are unrealistic, beyond control and unfunded; what we used to call fraud or dishonesty is now creative accounting to meet performance indicators.

Carlen argues that 'too often, rules are eventually cherished and embellished as being ends in themselves—at which point they become 'disciplinarities' (2005: 430). Moreover, where these disciplinarities become 'untrammelled' and 'unquestioned' they lead to atrophy and become 'pathological', constraining innovation. Carlen's suggestion for 'stopping the disciplinary rot presently atrophying rehabilitation attempts both within and outside the prison walls might be by having a clear agenda for the supersession of disciplinary governance by democratic rule usage' (ibid.: 431). Contesting disciplinary governance involves developing an agenda composed of several elements: a reassertion of leadership largely abdicated to KPIs; a coherent overarching strategy; the remoralization of prison personnel cowed by the blame shifting onto middle management and prison officers for failing to meet KPIs; penal probity involving conversations about what prisons can and cannot do—eg 'limit the damage done to prisoners and the harm done to society'; recognition of cultural diversity to combat the damage and pains engendered by monocultural prison organization and programmes; a principle of minimal carceralism to develop a 'conversation questioning the security value-added of every prison practice that is justified in the name of prison order and security'; and social realism which would lead to the recognition of the limits to the gains to be made from in prison programmes and the need to expand programmes of prisoner resettlement, accommodation, access to medical, welfare, educational and employment programmes after release (Carlen 2005: 432–436).

Carlen is careful to point out that many previous official reports have produced similar recommendations but they remain largely unimplemented, because, she argues, 'the disciplinary cancer' of KPIs, psychological programming and auditing has got 'such a stranglehold on the penal body politic that only a determination to cut it out root and branch' will allow the emergence of creative and democratic rule-making 'in the interests of prisoner resettlement' (ibid.: 436). Her argument can be extended to all manner of institutional settings beyond the criminal justice system, including education, health, welfare, indeed the political institutions themselves, in a revolt against the sclerosis induced by neo-liberal management practices and their desiccated grammar of KPIs, audits, and measures that have become ends in themselves.

Conclusion

Struggles over neo-liberal reconfiguration and the grammar, mentalities and practices through which it is achieved have been multiple, both within criminology and outside; the examples chosen are but three manifestations among many, standing alone but also interlinked. It is not suggested that neo-liberalism is the 'author' or sole 'cause' of 'pathological disciplinarities' or risk-based audit managerialism and 'imaginary penalities'. Clearly disciplinarities and managerialism have a much older provenance than neo-liberalism. What is suggested is that neo-liberalism has inflected disciplinarities in the direction of the 'pathological' and away from 'democratic rule usage' (Carlen 2008: 431). Similarly, in relation to managerialism, the suggestion is that neo-liberal formulations of risk, KPIs and audit criteria with their emphasis on narrowly defined notions of 'efficiency' and 'cost', increase the tendency for audit measures to become inward looking ends in themselves, eschewing more broadly defined social aims and outcomes that were and are aspirations under social welfarist and social democratic regimes, however much they might be difficult to measure, flawed or unmet in practice. In as much as neo-liberal ideologists and sections of the left see neo-liberalism as having 'vanquished' or 'superseded' social democracy and 'the social' my argument is, first, that any neo-liberal ascendancy is, in criminological terms, significantly criminogenic, and second, that however battered and bruised, a reconfigured 'penal welfarism' and the 'solidarity project' have shown a resilience, both in criminology and more generally, a resilience which might be strengthened in the context of the global financial crisis. More specifically, a political project of reconnecting penal policy with social and economic policy, which might be articulated to a broader political narrative of recuperating aspects of social democratic heritage from the excesses of neo-liberalism, has been suggested as a counter to the criminogenic and anti-social consequences of neo-liberal restructuring.

Two key aspects of such an articulation would be, more narrowly, to redirect resources from the burgeoning prison sector into practical assistance with ex-prisoner resettlement, and more generally to connect penal policy explicitly to social and economic policy by rerouting it from the exclusive terrain of individual culpability, so familiar in tabloid, talk-back, and political discourse. To point to socio-economic determinants in explaining crime, is not, as Nicola Lacey notes, 'inconsistent with judging it adversely or with holding offenders accountable' (2008: 200). Those social determinants, the culturalist turn in criminology and the excitement of 'edgework' notwithstanding, are depressingly familiar and repetitive, delivering up expanding prison populations of racial and ethnic minorities, the unemployed, the mentally ill, the sexually and physically abused, the state wards, the homeless, the poor, the marginal, the previously incarcerated, and the inhabitants of particular housing estates, and particular geographical regions.

One of my reasons for emphasizing the resilience of penal welfarism is that, at least in the Australian context, and I suspect elsewhere, conversations with front-line criminal justice workers—be they police, defence lawyers or prosecutors, judicial officers, probation, parole and prison officers, youth and social workers—often quickly turn to the material force of the social and economic determinants of crime, albeit not in these exact terms. Few of these criminal justice workers have been seduced by the popular punitive siren call of the shock jocks, tabloids and politicians: that crime is simply a manifestation of evil or fecklessness, a matter of individual responsibility best met by severe punishment. Invariably the talk turns to drug and alcohol use and abuse, mental illness, poor education and job prospects, dysfunctional families, family violence, rehabilitation, resettlement difficulties, the inadequacy of post-release services, the quandaries involved in recognizing all these precipitating factors and at the same time dealing ethically and responsibly with the individuals before them within the limits of their powers, responsibilities and resources, and so on. Contrary to populist portrayals of this sort of talk as the province of 'do-gooding elites' who 'don't live in the real world' and have never been victims of crime, these workers/professionals have a much more 'realistic' and practical picture of crime issues stemming from their daily work than those media commentators who use crime stories to accentuate division and controversy, run racial 'anti-elites' and other agendas, or the politicians who offer a quick 'tough on crime' thirty-second media grab in response.

The symbolic politics of law and order feeds on the abstract, the emotive and the discursive but falters at the specific and the practical, a domain in which it takes only a little digging to discover a considerable commitment among those actually working in the field to due process and penal welfare values and practices, along with a recognition that these values and practices are under increasing attack and sometimes require clothing or disguising in the new forms of managerial discourse. One of the limitations of a predominantly discourse analysis of the 'new punitiveness' is that it tends to conflate discourse with non-discursive practice, in the process missing much of the cynicism, irony and contempt often underlying the lip service being paid to the new neo-liberal management speak, the desiccated and forked tongues of KPIs, 'imaginary penalities' and 'virtual' audits.

In case my argument for reconnecting penal and social and economic policy, and articulating it to a broader social democratic narrative is read as simply a call for an unproblematic 'public criminology', then it bears remarking that such calls underestimate the complexity of the relationships between theory, government, and politics, all of which are semi-autonomous domains having their own conditions of existence, rationalities, institutional means, technologies, languages, modes of deportment, practices, and limits which are not reducible to a particular criminological or political theory or practice or given historical agents (Hogg 1996: 46). Processes of articulation are dependent on constantly shifting alliances and discursive constitutions of the subjects, agents, strategies, terms, and outcomes under discussion, for there are no '*a priori* agents of change', 'privileged points and moments of rupture' (Laclau and Mouffe 1985: 178–79) or underlying relations of unity merely waiting to be realized. Subject positions can no longer be constituted *a priori* according to particular privileged locations or essential subjectivities; social movements derive their progressive character through their discursive constitution (Brown 2008: 232–4). Prisoners for example, are plural, not unified, subjects—unities being a matter of construction, not attribution based on location. A politics of articulating penal, economic and social policy with social democracy must encompass tensions and struggles within dominant forces, contrary to the romantic notion of resistance as 'property of the left' (O'Malley 2000: 162). A penal reorientation such as shifting resources from prison to prisoner resettlement requires specific operational programmes fashioned within the prevailing public, political, media, bureaucratic, fiscal, cultural and governmental means and limits—means and limits themselves subject to calculation and change.

As far as criminology's institutional means, technologies, modes of deportment and practices are concerned, a notable feature of the papers presented at the conference leading to this volume was the relative lack of attention devoted to the teaching of criminology, as against the conduct and nature of criminological research. This is despite the fact that the majority of 'criminologists', loosely defined, hold teaching positions and are required to move between teaching, research and administration, roles that involve differential limits, requirements and ethical challenges. One strategy among many in the teaching role is to conceive of teaching as a transmission process, a nodal or network point through which questions, challenges, knowledge, research, policy, legal and political strategies, the voices and aspirations of excluded groups, can all be relayed between students, social movements, politicians, criminological colleagues, criminal justice agencies, the media, and the general public. This is not a prescription but a personal preference or aim. It is an approach fairly common among the ranks of 'critical criminologists' in the Australian context where, as I have argued elsewhere, criminology's historical institutional location largely within law schools, while perhaps limiting theoretical sophistication, has produced an engaged, committed, reformist stance that has often been campaign oriented and social movement driven, and has involved both shifts in and out of government-commissioned research and a disposition to be involved in media, political, and popular forums and debates (Brown 2002: 96–101). Among the consequences of this history are that the often unhelpful dichotomy between 'administrative' and 'critical' criminologists is less marked than in the United Kingdom or United States and that the recent call for a 'public criminology' has been met with a little bemusement as a call for more of the same.

The reference to 'reformist' in positive terms in the previous paragraph highlights another quieter argument that has underpinned this chapter, given that throughout much of the 60s, 70s and 80s radical politics and critical criminology, 'reformist' was a term of abuse. The argument has been that a small contribution to resuscitating the solidarity project might be made by abandoning the Marxist heritage of hostility to social democracy of the 'renegade Kautsky' type. If opportunities presented in the current crisis of neo-liberalism as a political programme are to be seized, it is vital to argue strongly against market intervention solely to restore demand and 'business as usual', backed by cuts to public services, and in favour of forms of market intervention that restructure and regulate the market in social directions, requiring greater environmental sustainability, reducing income differentials, curbing cultures of greed and gambling in the financial sector, reconfiguring the tax system in a progressive direction and investing in public transport and other infrastructure promoting community based sharing networks that are not based on a constant increase in consumerism, consumption, and narcissism.

If neo-liberalism is seen not as an ideology, but as a *process* involving, to use the title of England and Ward's book, a 'reconfiguration of states, networks and peoples', a process of '*neo-liberalization*' that is partial, uneven and contested, then it is arguably open to subversion in more democratic and equalizing directions. To draw out these possibilities it would be helpful to argue the benefits and continued relevance of social democracy and penal welfarism in a context of an actual crisis of capitalism. Reiner, paraphrasing Rosa Luxemburg, argues that 'on present trends the choice is social democracy or barbarism' (Reiner 2006: 39). Certainly socialism or barbarism are not the only choices, there are degrees of difference in capitalist polities and in the life chances of their citizens which are the subject of political and policy choices, choices which although sometimes fine have real effects; in these sometimes narrow spaces and small graduations, many people live.

The Boundaries of Criminology and Evangelism

To return to the title of this collection and the issue of the boundaries of criminology, the argument above in favour of situating criminology in the broader conjuncture of the global financial crisis and a critical interrogation of neo-liberalism, reconnecting penal policy with economic, social and public policy, along with the utilization of interdisciplinary sources such as some from social geography and political sociology, illustrates an approach to the status of criminology of the 'rendezvous discipline' sort (Downes, cited in Rock, 1997: 20). As David Garland put it in his plenary address at the World Criminology Congress in Barcelona in 2008:

> Instead of aspiring to an autonomous discipline, we should work for an expansive criminology that operates as a bridging subject—a subject that poses specifically policy-oriented, social-problem questions using general theoretically oriented, social scientific concepts in a way that enriches and empowers both [Garland 2008: 4].

I share Garland's fears that an autonomous criminology might be narrowing rather than 'bridging', confined to secure boundaries, such as state defined crime, readier to burn bridges not only to foundational disciplines such as sociology, politics and law, but also to new disciplines and fields that might open up in the course of pursuing 'policy-oriented, social problem questions'. In relation to teaching criminology there are also benefits in posing 'policy-oriented, social-problem questions' rather than pitching a tent in an already mapped, neatly surveyed and bounded disciplinary field. Theory is not its own justification and requires testing against an empirical or non-discursive dimension particular to time and place, or face rejection or modification. In my view, approaches to teaching criminology as an unfolding tour through the major theories/theorists can often produce a deadening effect on student interest and enthusiasm. Whereas starting with a social problem, a controversy, a case, specific to time and place, before moving out in spirals, painting in context and making connections across disciplinary boundaries, raising questions, theories, and histories for consideration as they seem to assist in developing understanding, rather than as templates or teleologies to be asserted, more readily arouses student interest and engagement and highlights the promise and excitement of criminology.

Finally, on the question of evangelism, raised in Pat Carlen's chapter (and see Carlen 2009), her criticisms are similar to ones I have previously raised under a complementary title, 'Losing my Religion' (Brown 2002); namely a reflection on no longer being enamoured of the self-evident, taken for granted virtues of an implausibly underdog status claiming critical criminology and its sometimes denunciatory, exclusionary and totalizing claims and practices. The problem is not, as Carlen points out, the championing of 'critical, cultural and public criminologies', the more of which generally the better, as exemplified in the work of Jock Young, Elliot Currie (indeed Pat Carlen herself), but the prescription of 'what types of intellectual work may contribute (or not) to this latest rebranding of academic criminology' (Carlen, this volume). As this chapter has illustrated, I for one still warm to the proselytisers siren call, indeed echo it, but hopefully as aspiration rather than prescription. Wandering the highways and byways of our 'engaged rather than detached, and eccentric rather than self enclosed' field (Garland ibid: 20), inspiration and refreshment is often found in seemingly unlikely places, including some previously visited in different circumstances, not so very long ago. Those places look, and are, different now, 'reconfigured' to use the lingo; green fields have sprouted golden arches and parking lots, but under bridges and alongside railway tracks, rather than (or as well as?) 'hundreds of tiny theatres of punishment' (Foucault 1978: 113)—allotment gardens are returning to life. This chapter has suggested that criminologists would do well to join the diggers there for a chat.

References

Anderson, P. (2000), 'Renewals', *New Left Review*, 1: 5–24.

Aas, K. F. (2005), 'The Ad and the Form: Punitiveness and Technological Culture', in J. Pratt *et al.* (eds), *The New Punitiveness*, Cullompton: Willan.

_____ (2008), *Globalisation and Crime*, London: Sage.

Australian Prison Project (2009) (<www.app.unsw.edu.au>).

Barker, E. (2006), 'The Politics of Punishing: Building a State Governance Theory of American Imprisonment Variation', *Punishment and Society*, 8: 5–32.

Bank of England (2009), *Financial Instability Report*, Issue 25, 26 June.

BBC (2009), *Press Release*, 'Global poll: Wide dissatisfaction with capitalism 20 years after fall of Berlin Wall', 9 November 2009, <www.bbc.co.uk>, accessed 30 November 2009.

Beckett, K., and Western, B. (2001), 'Governing Social Marginality: Welfare, Incarceration and the Transformation of State Policy', *Punishment and Society*, 3: 43–59.

Brown, D. (2002), 'Losing my Religion: reflections on Critical Criminology in Australia' in K. Carrington and R. Hogg (eds), *Critical Criminology*, Cullompton: Willan Devon.

_____ (2005), 'Continuity, Rupture or just more of the 'Volatile and Contradictory'? : Glimpses of New South Wales' Penal Practice behind and through the Discursive' in J. Pratt *et al.* (eds), *The New Punitiveness*, Cullompton: Willan Devon.

_____ (2008), 'Giving Voice: The Prisoner and Discursive Citizenship' in C. Cunneen and T. Anthony (eds), *The Critical Criminology Companion*, Sydney: The Federation Press.

Carlen, P. (2005), 'Imprisonment and the Penal Body Politic: The Cancer of Disciplinary Governance' in A. Leibling and S. Maruna (eds), *The effects of Imprisonment*, Cullompton: Willan.

_____ (2008), 'Imaginary Penalities and Risk-Crazed Governance' in P. Carlen (ed.), *Imaginary Penalities*, Cullompton: Willan.

_____ (2009), 'Review of "The Critical Criminology Companion"', *British Journal of Criminology*, 49: 276–9.

Carrington, K., and Hogg, R. (2002), *Critical Criminology: Issues, Debates, Challenges*, Cullompton: Willan Devon.

Cavadino, M., and Dignan, J. (2006), *Penal Systems: A Comparative Approach*, London: Sage.

Downes D. M. (1988), *Contrasts in Tolerance: Post War Penal Policy in the Netherlands and England and Wales*, Oxford: Clarendon.

_____ and Hansen, K. (2006), 'Welfare and Punishment in Comparative Perspective', in S. Armstrong and I. McAra (eds), *Perspectives on Punishment*, Oxford: Oxford University Press.
Ellison, N. (2006), *The Transformation of Welfare States*, London: Routledge.
England, K and Ward, K. (eds) (2007), *Neo-liberalization: States, Networks, Peoples* Mass.: Blackwell.
Esping-Anderson, G. (1990), *The Three Worlds of Welfare Capitalism*, Cambridge: Polity.
Foucault, M. (1978), *Discipline and Punish*, New York: Pantheon Books.
Garland, D. (1996), 'The Limits of the Sovereign State: Strategies of Crime Control in Contemporary Society', *British Journal of Criminology*, 36,4: 445–71.
_____ (1997), '"Governmentality" and the Problem of Crime', *Theoretical Criminology*, 1, 2: 173–214.
_____ (2001), *The Culture of Control*, Oxford: Oxford University Press.
_____ (2008), 'Criminology and the Academic Field' Plenary Address, World Congress of Criminology, Barcelona, July.
Harvey, D. (2005), *A Brief History of Neo-liberalism*, Oxford: Oxford University Press.
Hall, P. A., and Soskice, D. (eds) (2001), *Varieties of Capitalism: The Institutional Foundations of Comparative Advantage*, Oxford: Oxford University Press.
Hogg, R. (1996), 'Criminological Failure and Governmental Effect', *Current Issues in Criminal Justice*, 8, 1: 43–59.
Klein, N. (2007), *The Shock Doctrine*, London: Penguin.
Laclau, E., and Mouffe, C. (1985), *Hegemony and Socialist Strategy*, London: Verso.
Lacey, N. (2008), *The Prisoners' Dilemma*, Cambridge: Cambridge University Press.
Luttwak, E. (1995), 'Turbo-Charged Capitalism and its Consequences', *London Review of Books*, 17, 21: 6–7.
McLaughlin, E., and Murji, K. (2000), 'Lost Connections and New Directions: Neo-Liberalism, New Managerialism and the Modernisation of the British Police', in K. Stenson and R. Sullivan (eds), *Crime, Risk and Justice*, Cullompton: Willan.
_____ Muncie, J. and Hughes, G. (2001), 'The Permanent Revolution: New Labour, New Public Management and the Modernization of Criminal Justice', *Criminal Justice*, 1: 301–18.
Newburn, T. (2006), 'Contrasts in Tolerance', in T. Newburn and P. Rock (eds), *The Politics of Crime Control*, Oxford: Oxford University Press.
_____ and Rock, P. (2006), *The Politics of Crime Control*, Oxford: Oxford University Press.
O'Malley, P. (2000), 'Criminologies of Catastrophe? Understanding Criminal Justice on the Edge of the New Millennium', *Australian and New Zealand Journal of Criminology*, 33, 2: 153–67.
Pratt, J. (2008), 'Scandinavian Exceptionalism in an Era of Penal Excess', *British Journal of Criminology*, 48: 119–37; 275–92.
_____, Brown, D., Brown, M., Hallsworth, S., and Morrison, W. (eds) (2005), *The New Punitiveness*, Willan Devon: Cullompton.
Reiner, R. (2006), 'Beyond Risk: A Lament for Social Democratic Criminology' in T. Newburn and P. Rock (eds), *The Politics of Crime Control*, Oxford: Oxford University Press.
_____ (2007), *Law and Order: An Honest Citizen's Guide to Crime and Control*, Cambridge: Polity Press.
Rock, P. (1997), 'Sociological Theories of Crime', in M. Maguire, R. Morgan, and R. Reiner (eds), *The Oxford Handbook of Criminology*, 2nd edn, Oxford: Oxford University Press.

Rose, N. (1996), 'The Death of the Social? Re-Configuring the Territory of Government', *Economy and Society*, 25, 3: 327–56.

Taylor, I. (1999), *Crime in Context*, Cambridge: Polity Press.

Wacquant, L. (2006), 'Penalization, Depoliticization, Racialization: On the Over-Incarceration of Immigrants in the European Union', in S. Armstrong and I. McAra (eds), *Perspectives on Punishment*, Oxford: Oxford University Press.

Wacquant, L. (2009), *Punishing the Poor: The Neo-liberal Government of Social Insecurity*, Durham and London: Duke University Press.

Young, J. (1999), *The Exclusive Society*, London: Sage.

_____ (2003), 'Merton with Energy, Katz with Structure: The Sociology of Vindictiveness and the Criminology of Transgression', *Theoretical Criminology*, 7, 3: 389–414.

_____ (2007), *The Vertigo of Late Modernity*, London: Sage.

Walby, S. (2009), *Globalization and Inequalities*, London: Sage.

Wilkinson, R., and Pickett, K. (2009), *The Spirit Level: Why More Equal Societies Almost Always Do Better*, London: Allen Lane.

Zimring, F., and Hawkins, G. (1991), *The Scale of Imprisonment*, Chicago: University of Chicago Press.

6

AGAINST EVANGELISM IN ACADEMIC CRIMINOLOGY: FOR CRIMINOLOGY AS A SCIENTIFIC ART

PAT CARLEN*

THE main argument of this essay is that because academic criminology is a scientific art, it is unfortunate that three of the most exciting perspectives in criminology today—those academy-based criminologies which have variously self-branded as

* I thank: Mike Maguire, Jacqueline Tombs, and Anne Worrall for their encouraging comments on the first draft of this chapter; Ian Loader for stimulating and imaginative comments, queries, and strictures on subsequent drafts; David Brown for being an encouraging and stimulating discussant of the paper given at the conference *What is Criminology* (Centre for Criminology, Oxford University, 30 September – 2 October 2009); and Mary Bosworth and Carolyn Hoyle for being most kindly and forbearing editors.

'critical', 'cultural' or 'public'—at times reveal evangelistic tendencies that pose a threat to their capacity for the open debate that each of them espouses. Other brand-name academic criminologies have, over the years, been frequently endangered by the same tendencies (see Carlen 1998) but, because of the promise and dangers inherent in their twin allegiances to both academic criminology and criminology politics, and also because of the desirability of such socio-political commitments, if criminology as a scientific art is to have any social significance, I think it is important that the evangelistic strains in critical, cultural and public criminologies should be confronted. In my view, they are the least desirable, and potentially most self-damaging, aspects of the best of contemporary academic criminology.[1]

The Terrain

By 'criminologies' I am referring to any discourses that make knowledge claims about the making, breaking, or enforcement (or not) of the criminal laws of any jurisdiction—whether these claims are rooted in common sense, politics, ethics, or whatever. The list is never-ending, can be variously parcelled-up and named and, even then and thereafter, can redivide and coalesce anew to accommodate as many new, individual, popular, political, and policy discourses as may ever attempt to explain 'crime'. From such a perspective, academic criminology is just one among a range of views on the causes of crime and the nature of justice, though in this article I focus solely on academic criminology. Specifically, I am concerned that critical, cultural and public criminologies in particular have evangelistic tendencies which are inappropriate to the scientific principle of open and ongoing enquiry.[2]

The focus of the essay is narrow. I do not analyse academic criminology as an ascribed profession (that is, as a profession that has its status nowadays primarily ascribed to it by an institution rather than by a discipline), though it is that too. And although I concede that the institutionalized professionalization and disciplining of scientific inquiry has had, and continues to have, effects on both the fashioning of academic ethics and the shaping of knowledges, questions about the effects of institutional governance on the shaping of academic criminology are bracketed-off from the inquiry here.[3] Rather, this essay broadly defines academic criminology as being a set of multi-faceted and often opposed scientific practices aiming either to explain or

[1] I do not discuss here the many institutionalized threats to academic criminology itself, eg the refusal of some senior academics to recognize any perspectives other than their own as having any scientific merit whatsoever; and the managerialism in universities which has been so corrosive of academic production in the United Kingdom.

[2] Similar concerns were expressed by Brown (2002) in relation to critical criminology and Pratt (2006) in relation to restorative justice.

[3] For good discussions of the impact that institutionalization has had on sociology see Clawson *et al.* (2007). For criminology, see Loader (1998) and Hope (2008).

analytically deconstruct crime phenomena. The arguments of this first part, therefore, are based on the following foundational assumptions about academic criminology as a scientific practice and a scientific art. Specifically, it is assumed that:

1. because criminology is a science, it should be: open; constantly recognizing, questioning, and, if necessary, destroying the conditions of its own existence; and neither 'trimming' its questions to make them politically correct or expedient, nor 'clubbing'—that is, pulling its punches—either to conform to contemporary academic fashions or political prejudices, or in response to disciplinary bullying by either political or academic powers-that-be;
2. only academic and extra-academic acceptance of the potential of communicable scientific practices to create new knowledge of crime phenomena endow academic criminology with its claims to be heard as one distinct criminological voice among the many others that may, variously, stake their claims to be heard on entirely different criteria: for instance, on the grounds that they represent 'the people' or various ethical, political or religious stances, or . . . just plain old common sense;
3. academic and scientific criminology should try not only to think the unthinkable about crime, but also to speak the unspeakable about the conditions in which and by which it is known. (The latter is an essential prerequisite for both critical and cultural criminology.);
4. scientific criminology may employ technical knowledge (eg, statistics, modelling) in furtherance of the scientific project of new knowledge production;
5. the pursuit of science is also forever in opposition to the discipline within which it is necessarily institutionalized. In short, academic criminology must constantly be on guard against any evangelistic tendencies which obfuscate the New either by overwrapping it in reductionist and oppositional critiques of the Old, or by bending it to assuage a variety of differently located and variously manifested institutional and public appetites (see, for instance, Cain (1989) on 'transgressing criminology' and Loader (2009) on the usefulness of the concept of appetite for criminological analyses of security and crime phenomena);
6. scientific criminology has to work on a contradiction: it has to recognize and cherish its constitutive ideologies (those both within and without academia) if it is to create the New out of the archival affects and effects of the already known. This latter balancing act is especially important for critical and public criminologies. It is in the discovery and creation of the New out of the *bricolage* of the Old that criminology becomes a scientific art form.

The rest of the essay is divided into three parts: the first will outline the main tenets of critical, public and cultural criminologies and locate their importance to contemporary criminological thought; the second will argue against the evangelistic strains in these three criminologies; and the last will argue for criminology as a scientific art-form.

For Critical, Cultural, and Public Criminologies

Although critique is a necessary component of all scientific endeavour, the term *critical criminology* was coined to distinguish it from types of empirical work typically conducted or commissioned by government agencies concerned with addressing crime as a social problem. In much (though not all) official research and discourse on crime, the nature of criminal law, criminal justice, and lawbreaking remain uncontested and the focus is primarily on the crimes of working class males. By contrast, critical criminology draws on writings by historians, Marxists, feminists, psychoanalysts, anthropologists, and other modern and postmodern theoretical perspectives to call into question and repose the questions to be asked about crime and criminal justice. Indeed, I would suggest that, ironically, it was only as a result of the advent of critical criminology that, in the United Kingdom at any rate, the discipline of criminology was reinvigorated sufficiently to put up a successful fight to become recognized and institutionalized as a university discipline independent of its parent disciplines of law and/or sociology. Nowadays, moreover, critical criminologies can also lay claim to some leading international criminologists. It could even be argued that critical criminology *is* the mainstream in UK academic criminology now. With such success behind them, therefore, the continued need of critical criminologists to engage in oppositional evangelism is puzzling. Yet, in one of the latest and certainly one of the most stimulating edited books of critical criminology to come out of Australia (Anthony and Cunneen 2008), many of the authors, though denying that there is a dominant mainstream criminology in Australia, still suggest that the strategic rationale for critical criminology is that it is required to oppose the mainstream. And that claim can also still be heard in the United Kingdom. Moreover, opposition to the 'mainstream' is frequently the main justification for the proselytizing strains in cultural and public criminologies, too. But although all three evangelistic strains against the 'mainstream' are to a certain extent correct in their critiques, they are not *entirely* correct, though for slightly different reasons in each case. While the root cause of critical criminologies' misplaced evangelism is a failure to recognize their own success in already colonizing the 'mainstream', the proselytizing claims of cultural and public criminologies additionally suggest a refusal to acknowledge that, though rebranding old theories (in the case of cultural criminology) and old practices (in the case of public criminology) under a new label may well satisfy institutional demands for non-stop innovative publishing and, in the case of public criminology, social relevance, such nominalist rebrandings, if made independently of any additional creativity, do much more for the disciplinary management of knowledge than they do for knowledge production.

Cultural criminologies, like critical criminologies, are concerned with being critical, their main emphasis being on 'the centrality of meaning, representation and power in the contested construction of crime' (Ferrell, Hayward, and Young 2008: 2). I happen to agree with this emphasis and with every other objective of their collective endeavour. However, given that the centrality of meaning, representation and power has been a taken-for-granted assumption in academic criminology since at least the 1960s, I find it difficult to understand why a new and distinct label was required at the beginning of the twenty-first century. But the salient point to be noted in support of my argument that cultural criminology is high in evangelistic rhetoric is that its most well-known proponents refer to it as 'a collective project', call others to join them in various types of 'activism' (as do critical and public criminologists, incidentally) and make claims to espouse a very broad range of perspectives which, together, they claim, have resulted in cultural criminology emerging as 'a distinct criminology in the cultural tradition', and one, moreover, which might be best described as a 'loose federation of outlaw intellectual critiques' (Ferrell (2007: 99), quoted in Ferrell, Hayward, and Young (2008: 210). In that case, one might ask, why risk diminishing the various 'outlaw' intellectual critiques by drawing them all altogether under one label?

Public Criminology focuses on the possible and/or desirable relationships between the academic criminology profession and politics. Like public sociology (see Burowoy 2005), public criminology is directed at making its academic project relevant to the lives and concerns of people beyond the university (see Uggen and Inderbitzen 2006) and its proponents include many who are even better known as critical or cultural criminologists (eg Currie 2007; Young 2007). It is, of course, not surprising that critical criminologists, committed to calling into question the taken-for-granted meanings of law, crime and criminal justice, should want both to engage with public concern about crime and to disseminate perspectives and arguments that run counter to the criminologically illiterate and toxic representations of criminal justice issues as peddled by the mass media and politicians. Academic criminologists who have the requisite skills and make the time to become public intellectuals, campaigners or journalists have existed as long as the discipline itself, and their influence has often (though not always) been profound and progressive. Amongst living criminologists, Jock Young and Elliot Currie stand out as two amongst many critical, cultural and public criminologists who have tirelessly practised what they preach. Sociologist Loic Wacquant, moreover, has achieved international public intellectual status with his writings on crime and the penal state without ever engaging in any self-branding of himself or his work (Wacquant 2004, 2009). What I object to about the recently attempted institutionalization of public criminology, however, is that its proponents, instead of merely canvassing for others to join them in an avowedly political endeavour (about the desirability of their work having an effect beyond the academy) conflate their personal morality/politics with a scientific art form (academic criminology) and then by labelling the whole bundle as public criminology are overly prescriptive about what types of intellectual work may contribute (or not) to this latest rebranding of academic criminology. OK, other schools of criminology are playing the same political game of legitimating only one type of academic criminology, but the critical criminologies (and cultural and public criminology can here be subsumed under the critical label without violence being done to them) with their essential commitment to openness and critique, cannot risk fighting essentialist positions even by merely nominally essentialist means. For at the moment when a critical, cultural, or public criminology is recognized, or recognizes itself as such, its institutional, political, or policy influence may well be strengthened but its freedom to imagine the new is compromised: certain questions can no longer be asked and all those refusing the label are 'othered'. Blessed are the others, say I.

Against Evangelism in Critical, Cultural, and Public Criminologies

I turn now to some of the claims evangelistic writings make about 'the good news' they bring under the 'critical', 'cultural' and 'public' labels and argue that:

1. the evangelistic turn in criminology is to be regretted because, in evangelistic criminology there is a greater emphasis on what criminologists should *be* as moral people, rather than what they should *do* as practising academic criminologists;
2. the evangelistic turn not only involves a call to arms against the conventional criminology pre-conditional to the existence of more radical criminologies but, too frequently, does not go beyond an oppositional to a creative stance;
3. the evangelistic turn, instead of focusing on the new, is usually characterized by much maligning of quantitative criminology and a reinventing of the wheels of all other criminologies;
4. evangelistic criminology too frequently involves a proselytizing tendency towards silencing and closing-off alternative ways of knowing (though I should acknowledge here that all three gospels under consideration insist that that they welcome all kinds of work—so long as it is critical);
5. as both critical and cultural criminologies refuse to define themselves, except in terms of difference from 'mainstream' or conventional criminologies, it has to be assumed that the surest way of being critical or cultural is to self-define as being opposed to the 'mainstream', and then summon others to collaborate in reinventing a new mainstream in place of that which has purportedly just been demolished.

Evangelism in science or social science in general is not new and what I am going to write in the rest of this ironically anti-sermonizing sermon could be said of a whole number of other niche criminologies (eg 'Marxist' or 'feminist') whose practitioners also apparently have a need to attach a promotional tin can to their tails. John Pratt, for instance, in 2006 criticized the evangelism of proponents of restorative justice (RJ), commenting that 'in much of the RJ literature, and in many of the conventions and conferences held to discuss it, there is something of a crusading, evangelical fervour. It has taken on the identity of some inherent, self-evident, taken-for-granted 'good''... and he continues:

We should note, though, that this is not the first time such a thing has happened in the development of modern penality. Earlier criminal justice reform movements have assumed similar 'divine' qualities, with their advocates taking on evangelical roles. That is to say, their reform initiatives have been projected as beyond reproach, shining out against the darkness of the unreformed areas of criminal justice they challenge; indeed, criticism is seen almost as sacrilege, put about by those on whom its light has yet to shine [Pratt 2006: 47].

And I am glad that Pratt emphasizes that he is talking about evangelical 'movements'. For, in talking of evangelism in criminology, I am *not* referring to people, and certainly not to those who have been exercised by methodological questions and the associated epistemological or moral dilemmas; or to those who have focused on the relationships between academic research, politics and policy; and nor to those who make policy recommendations directly related to their own, or other people's academic arguments or research findings. Moreover, I accept that rhetoric is part of argument and I am not referring to writers who employ rhetoric in making their arguments. In fact, I am not referring to people at all. I am referring solely to writings which, under newly-named brands of criminology, make apostolic and imperialistic pronouncements about what are the fit and proper questions, sources of funding, methods, and epistemological and ontological assumptions not just for their own new knowledge project, but for any other which hopes to make a contribution to knowledge about crime or the criminal justice system. Such writings do not seek to convince by argument but instead seek followers to join them—not as workers on specific projects, but as *believers* in a particular brand of criminology. And it could very well be argued that criminological evangelism is practised because it is the most effective strategy for protecting and nurturing the New in the face of old establishment and 'disciplinary' opposition. To some extent, I agree. It is the old paradox of creativity versus discipline (or knowledge versus ideology, non-stop revolution versus routinization—however one prefers to parcel up the existential conundrum). Even so, I would like to use the rest of this space to argue first that, in so far as evangelism seeks for adherents to a perspective on the basis of oppositional rhetoric rather than creative analysis, it is antagonistic to scientific endeavour; and, second, that maybe the way out of the creative versus disciplinary paradox is to concentrate on doing criminology as a job rather than on being some kind of partisan criminologist. Of course, critical and cultural criminologies *are* creative, and public criminology certainly advocates doing criminology as a job of political intervention. It is their evangelizing tendencies on which this piece focuses; and the evangelizing features shared by all three evangelistic movements and which, I also think, are detrimental to academic criminology are:

- a tendency only to define themselves in opposition to mainline or conventional criminology;
- an ahistorical tendency to reinvent the wheel;
- reiteration of conversion calls to those practising non-brand-name 'other criminologies' to join the new orthodoxies;

- an emphasis on criminological subjectivity (*being* critical, *being* reflexive, *being* public) rather than on the more achievable objects of *doing criminology.*

On Being Critical (and Reinventing the Wheel)

The first rhetorical device of the evangelistic turn in criminology is to lump together all criminology that does not call itself critical or cultural into something called 'conventional criminology' and then write most of it off as having nothing whatever to contribute to the critical or cultural endeavour. Yet when these critical and cultural criminologies turn to specifying the distinctiveness of their own perspectives they spend a considerable time reinventing the very same wheel that they have already written off in their spin against conventional criminology.

For what can it mean to 'be a critical or cultural criminologist'? I had always assumed that a stance of constant critique is the distinguishing feature of academic work. Yet critical criminologists are engaged in a more specific, and, incidentally, quite limiting, critique. The self-consciously critical/cultural stances in criminology are most frequently rooted in a creed that, after making the rather self-evident observation that criminology takes an ideologically-tainted concept, ie crime, as its subject-matter, teaches that it is therefore the prime duty of critical and cultural criminologists to expose either the injustices which stem from, or the cultural understandings inherent in, conventional criminology's foundational lie, ie that it is concerned equally with all forms of lawbreaking. Yet where does that get one in terms of conducting a piece of research? It might of course determine the *choice* of research, but why should it dictate the method? And *is* there a critical or cultural method? There is nothing inherently critical in ethnography for instance, just as there is nothing inherently non-critical in quantitative methods.

More importantly, if one is employed as an academic, is 'critical intent' enough? Conversely, is it impossible for a 'non-critical' criminologist (an administrative criminologist', say) to contribute to the critical endeavour? I would answer 'No' to both these questions. Yet, within the evangelistic strains in criminology there seems to be an assumption that as criminologists sow, so shall they reap; in other words, that so long as they go into a project intending to be critical or on the side of the (critical, cultural, or publicly-spirited) angels, the ensuing theory will have the hoped-for critical power or benign effect. Unfortunately, it is not as easy as that. Theories and their effects have conditions of existence that mean they constantly oscillate between the new and the ideological, and any individual social theorist is not only but one amongst many of those conditions, but is also a product of those conditions. Social scientists' knowledge of their own conditions of existence too, is at any one time, forever partial and forever changing, so that even if critical criminology aspirants can make the correctly critical choices in theoretical *and* political terms, they still may fail in their criminological projects because of conditions beyond their control... or simply because they are not very good at what they do.

Moreover, even if, on their own criteria, critical criminologists succeed, they will not be able to control either the way their critical theory is used—any more than any other scientist can—or its discursive effects. For example, parts of the theory may either be incorporated into conservative or repressive discourses, or used to justify practices far removed from those hoped for by the theorist. Conversely, an administrative criminologist working on a small canvas according to conventional technical protocols (eg, statistical analysis) may well contribute as much (or more) to new knowledge about the working of contemporary criminal justice as the self-consciously critical theorist. Yet in the writings of critical criminologists there seems to be a rather positivistic 'othering' of those criminologists whose methods and ideological assumptions do not quite mesh with those of the evangelistic discourses of critical, cultural and public criminologies, and this, ironically, in its tendency towards discursive closure, is, I would have thought, antagonistic to the critical project to which all three evangelistic streams lay claim.

On Being a Cultural Criminologist (and Reinventing the Wheel)

As for 'cultural criminology': for sociological criminologists (and many other criminologists) culture has always been central to their study of crime, as in the theories of Durkheim, Merton, symbolic interactionists and subcultural theorists, to name but a few. This being so, it is difficult to see what is distinctly new about cultural criminology. As far as I can see, it is a lot of new wine in an old bottle. Moreover, when cultural criminologists are faced with going beyond saying that every social phenomenon has multiple meanings to explaining why some meanings win out over others, they appear to lose their bottle altogether. For, apart from lauding ethnographic methods, they give few clues as to how multiple meanings are to be 'unravelled', and by whom; and that conundrum is but one of the many old and extraordinarily difficult problems likely to confront any social theorist who privileges 'multiple meanings' as both objects and methodological tools of research. Other questions arise too. Where do cultural criminologists place themselves and their writings in relation to 'the collective experience of everyday life'? Can they do more than record and reflect? If meanings are to be contested, which meanings are to be contested, by whom and why? Moreover, in answering these questions, where are the boundaries to be drawn (if at all?) between ontology, epistemology, method, and politics; between art and argument? How are we to make communicable sense of what each of us can experience via our senses, and intuit via empathy? Are Shakespeare's *Hamlet* and *Macbeth* examples of critical, cultural, or public criminology? After all, each is a play about the life and times of a royal and serial murderer. Scepticism aside, it could well be contended that it is the very uncertainty of the cultural dynamic which makes it difficult for cultural criminologists to go beyond description and prescription to actually jumping off the cultural fence and attempting to *explain* why crimes and criminal justice take the forms they do at any one time. But, if that is the case, why call their project cultural *criminology*? For although I can see what is *cultural* about cultural criminology, I cannot see what is *criminological* about it.

To date, cultural criminology has provided incisive insights into the cultural mix of subjective meanings of much behaviour seen as either deviant or inexplicable by critical observers marching to a different tune, but it does not and cannot address the question as to why certain people routinely fall foul of the law in very mundane ways (ways certainly not involving the excitement of 'edgework') and are then routinely rounded up and officially clobbered for it.[4]

On Being a Public Criminologist (and Reinventing the Wheel)

And finally, maybe the presently fashionable call for criminologists to make their research findings more accessible to the general public, and engage more with public debates about crime, is the most anachronistic war cry of all. For, British criminology, at least, has always been public in terms of some criminologists variously being involved in campaigning, addressing professionals working in the criminal justice system, being involved with lawbreakers, government ministers and civil servants, and engaging in public debate via the media and various local government forums. Sure, all this activity has not achieved much, but it is wishful thinking (or arrogance) to assume that if criminologists wrote in more easily understandable prose, or talked in the media more frequently, or all took jobs as government advisors, that either the public at large or politicians would interpret their research findings in the way the critical or cultural or public criminologists might hope or expect. And which publics are being referred to? It is not much use convincing the powers-that-be that some research indicates that imprisoning lawbreakers seems to make them more likely to commit crime in the future if the public hearing this is hearing it with different priorities in mind. I think of two adjacent American states: in one, criminologists convinced the public, judges and an economizing executive that imprisonment and its associated recidivism are so expensive that it would cost the state less to put money into non-custodial projects. This advice was followed and there was an almost immediate reduction in the numbers being imprisoned; in the neighbouring state, by contrast, the same message was given to politicians whose main concern was to keep employment rates up. They too embraced the criminologists' message; more prisons were built.

I understand the reasons why some criminologists are frustrated by their inability to affect crime policy, and I appreciate that in making the plea for a public criminology they are acting from moral or political motives to improve the quality of criminal justice. But except in cases where academic criminologists are already bound by a funding contract or an access agreement as to where, when and how they disseminate their findings, where they choose to publicize and promulgate a

[4] A part of this section was previously published in Carlen (2009).

particular interpretation of them should be seen as a matter of theoretical, personal, moral and political choice, not stemming from any institutionalized academic or professional imperatives. And I do not believe that reflexivity is a panacea for all these critical ills.

Because I have always found the usage of the term 'reflexivity' so vacuous when applied to scientific methodology, I had at this point to look up how criminology methods textbooks define it; and they usually exhort criminologists, especially qualitative researchers, to reflect on their methods—on possible sources of bias, possible suppressions of certain meanings etc. And in one sense that is fairly simple. We know if we have suppressed some data in order to protect someone, we know whose side we are on in an industrial dispute, we know our political, religious and ethical beliefs. What we do not know, and what our publics cannot know, is how these domain assumptions have affected our knowledge product and whether it has made it less or more valuable for the purpose for which it was crafted. Of course, there are all kind of analyses publics can apply—logical, discursive, statistical—but the objectivity of the knowledge will depend upon the desire for a certain object that publics hold. I do not mean by this that publics only believe what they want to believe. I mean that theoretical products become objects of knowledge if they are recognizable as such according to criteria shared by both author and audience—though their precise status (value) as knowledge objects may be continuously contested, eg some will claim that they are ideological products, some that they are new knowledge products. And their status will change according to the uses to which they are put and the balance of powers contesting them.

So, it seems to me that instead of wasting gallons of ink on deciding whether or not criminologists are partisan, critical, or reflexive, it might be more productive of new criminological knowledge if academic criminology were to concentrate on doing a good job in terms of fulfilling a desired object of research—which might well be pure, applied, political, or campaigning research and conducted according to any one of an unlimited range of transparent research methods. And if you have the talent, time and opportunity, by all means be critical, cultural and go public, just as the inclination takes you. But don't evangelize. Just do it.

Criminology as a Scientific Art

Kristeva (1975: 73) explicitly warns 'those committed to the practice of challenge' *against* the frequent temptation to 'abandon their discourse as a way of communicating the logic of that practice'. Foucault is less patient with theorists who, now under the signs of 'democratic communication' and 'progressive politics' once more attempt to claim authorial control over the effects of a discourse: 'they do not want to lose *what they say*, this little fragment of discourse' (Foucault 1978:26). But they *will* lose what they say and neither the intelligibility (or not) of the discourse, or its legitimacy (or not) nor its accessibility (or not) remain in authorial control (Burton and Carlen 1979: 136).

By this stage, it might well seem that in talking against evangelism in criminology I have myself been evangelizing against the evangelizers. Not so. Like Groucho Marx, I do not want to join anyone else's club, and I wouldn't want them to join mine—even if I had one. I have chosen to argue against the evangelistic tendency in critical, cultural and public criminologies, only because I think these perspectives are very important dimensions of the criminological endeavour and because I myself have been pleased to practise all three. I also know enough about the contradictions in these perspectives to admit that although the evangelistic tendencies are there, much more is there too, and to that extent, it could be claimed that I have been very unfair in elevating the evangelistic dimensions above all others. None the less, and although some critical, some cultural and some public criminologists will think I should know better, I am unrepentant. Academic and political activities are *not* reducible one to the other and, accordingly, and despite my commitment to the aspirations of the critical, cultural and public projects in criminology, their evangelism is, as I have already said, to be regretted. However, I think and hope that the critical, cultural and public gospels are falling on stony ground. For, when I look at what academic criminologists actually do (as opposed to reading about what they are being exhorted to do by the evangelizers) it does seem to me that *when they are actually doing academic work*, instead of *being* partisan by trying to meet evangelizing demands for critical, cultural or public relevance, a majority still *do* criminology as artisans rather than as partisans.[5] (For debate on partisanship, see Becker (1967) and Gouldner (1973).)

By 'artisan' I am referring to a state of working consciousness that is ready to give, sell or lend its professional expertise to many different types of enterprise, different because each of them requires a different type of practice and expertise. For there are all kinds of jobs to be done by criminologists and there are many different ways of doing them. Thus criminologists practising criminology as a scientific art may well prefer to practise pure research but feel they can usefully lend their expertise to a government agency to do applied research in order to produce desired knowledge, eg the numbers of people who go out of prison homeless—and why. Or they may choose a research project in pursuit of a political aim—to gather information in the hope that it will be useful to support a political argument. Or they may suspend their own research priorities in order to address a question posed

[5] I base this statement on my observation of the many criminologists whose work I have read and observed over the years, many of whom will also have called themselves critical criminologists, many of whom will have assumed, as I always have, that crime is, amongst other things, a cultural phenomenon and many of whom, too, will have also thought they were engaging in public criminology via teaching, campaigning, and contributing to government commissions and research.

by a campaigning group. In each of the last three cases—the applied, the political and the campaigning—they may well not like the uses to which the results are put (and will be even more disappointed when they are ignored!), but they will know that when they take on the job. All they can do is make a judgement before they accept an assignment, thereafter do it to the best of their ability and professional ethics and then fight over the uses to which it is put. But why, you might well ask, take on these types of applied, politically-motivated and campaigning jobs in the first place?

The primary motivation is usually an intellectual curiosity—and that curiosity will often be compounded of a good dose of sociological imagination on the one hand and scientific curiosity and expertise on the other. And the interest will be in the artful production of new knowledge—on puzzling over something—maybe data but maybe just a hunch or observation of a social phenomenon—and then getting something produced. And sometimes that curiosity will be critical in terms of producing some previously unthought of knowledge, but sometimes it will be only investigative, producing descriptions that the researchers themselves can make nothing of, but which may well become critical in someone else's work. Of course, being curious is not enough. Criminologists as artisans are, in my opinion, professionally bound to do the job according to their craft criteria, ethical and methodological, and to make those craft criteria explicit—though as I have already said, I do not think that it is possible for anyone to know or make known whether all the criteria have been met.

In *all* research, there is the possibility of critique. In pure research there is from the beginning the self-conscious desire to think the unthinkable, to make explicit the previously hidden and to imagine the new. But critique can be a state of mind in all research—and the new is just as likely to be crafted when doing applied research, so long as curiosity and imagination go hand in hand with the routine application of tried and tested research methods.

Lastly, and what undermines all the craft and the critique, is the necessary commerce and politics; and I am not talking about the institutional pressures to bring in money, to publish in one type of publication rather than another, or the selling of the product to the audience. I refer to the discursive abyss into which many writers fall in the act of writing; the difficulties of distinguishing between the representational and the analytic; the sense of loss as the product is shrunk into authorial discourse; and the puny creative reward as authorial discourse is absorbed into, or destroyed by, other discourses. Thereafter, of course, it may play a bit part in some other writer's (or even a policy-maker's) grand product; but it will be lost forever to the would-be originating authors. Which is the ultimate reason why (and despite the fact that I have spent this entire chapter arguing otherwise!) it does not really matter whether criminologists style themselves critical, cultural, public, Marxist, feminist and/or . . . whatever.

References

Anthony, T. and Cunneen, C. (2008), *The Critical Criminology Companion*, Sydney: Hawkins Press.

Becker, H. (1967), 'Whose Side are we on?', *Social Problems*, 14: 239–47.

Brown, D. (2002), '"Losing my Religion: Reflections" on Critical Criminology in Australia' in K. Carrington and R. Hogg (eds), *Critical Criminology*, Cullompton: Willan.

Burrawoy, M. (2005), 'For Public Sociology' 2004 American Sociological Presidential Address', *American Sociological Review*, 70: 4–28.

Burton, F. and Carlen, P. (1979), *Official Discourse*, London: Routledge and Kegan Paul.

Cain. M. (ed.) (1989), 'Introduction', in *Growing Up Good*, London: Sage.

Carlen, P. (1998), 'Criminology Ltd: The Search for a Paradigm', in P. Walton and J. Young (eds), *The New Criminology Revisited*, Basingstoke: Macmillan.

_____ (2009), 'Review of Thalia Anthony and Chris Cunneen (eds), "The Critical Criminology Companion"', *British Journal of Criminology*, 49, 2: 276–9.

Clawson, D., Zussman, R., Misra, J., Gerstel, N., Stokes, R., Anderton, D.L., and Buroway, M. (eds) (2007), *Public Sociology*, Berkeley: University of California Press.

Currie, E. (2007), 'Against Marginality: Arguments for a Public Criminology', *Theoretical Criminology*, 11, 2: 175–90.

Ferrell, J. (2007), 'For a Ruthless Cultural Criticism of Everything Existing', *Crime, Media Culture*, 3, 1: 91–100.

_____, Hayward, K., and Young, J. (2008), *Cultural Criminology*, London: Sage.

Foucault, M. (1978), 'Politics and the Study of Discourse', *Ideology and Consciousness*, 3: 7–26.

Gouldner, A., 'The Sociologist as Partisan', in A. Gouldner (ed.), *For Sociology: Renewal and Critique in Sociology Today*, New York: Basic Books.

Hope, T. (2008), 'The First Casualty: Evidence and Governance in a War Against Crime', in P. Carlen (ed.), *Imaginary Penalities*, Cullompton: Willan.

Kristeva, J. (1975), 'The System and the Speaking Subject', in T. A. Sebeock (ed.), *The System and the Speaking Sign*, Lisse: Peter de Ridder Press.

Loader, I. (1998), 'Criminology and the Public Sphere: Arguments for Utopian Realism', in P. Walton and J. Young (eds), *The New Criminology Revisited*, Basingstoke: Macmillan.

_____ (2009), 'Ice Cream and Incarceration: On Appetites for Security and Punishment', *Punishment and Society*, 11, 2: 241–58.

Pratt, J. (2006), 'Beyond Evangelical Criminology: The Role and Significance of Restorative Justice', in I. Aertson, T. Daems, and L. Robert (eds), *Institutionalizing Restorative Justice*, Cullompton: Willan Publishing.

Uggen, C., and Inderbitzen, M. (2006), 'Public Criminologies'. Paper presented at the 2006 Annual meetings of the American Sociological Association, Montreal <www.soc.umn.edu/~uggen/uggen_inderbitzin_TC2006.pdf>.

Wacquant, L. (2004; Eng. Edn., 2009), *Punishing the Poor: The Neoliberal Government of Social Insecurity*, Durham and London: Duke University Press.

Young, J. (2007), *The Vertigo of Late Modernity*, London: Sage.

2

METHODOLOGICAL ALLEGIANCES: HOW SHOULD CRIMINOLOGY BE DONE?

7

SHAKE IT UP, BABY: PRACTISING ROCK 'N' ROLL CRIMINOLOGY

KATHLEEN DALY

AT many criminology conferences, there is the conference dinner and, with luck, a dance band. At these events, criminologists of all theories, methodologies, and ideological persuasions gather to shake it up. We twist, jump, hop, twirl, gyrate, and move, some more wild, sweaty, sexy, and expressive than others. But the general mood is abandonment, leaving the academic role behind, getting out of our skins, and being on the floor as a group. If conference life is a 'ritual occasion ... [that can] bring out the worst in people, [where] you have to work hard to remain a decent human being' (Cohen 1995: 33, 45), the dance band floor is a singularly unifying occasion. It helps me to identify what is needed to bring out the best in people doing criminology.

A key text that inspires my essay is Nils Christie's lament about the boring qualities of criminology. 'How can it be like this?' he asks. 'How come that so much criminology is dull, tedious and intensely empty as to new insights?' This is especially perplexing when, as he observes, criminology is 'based on material from the core areas of drama... conflict..., danger..., catastrophe, abuses and sacrifice'; and yet it is 'still so trivial' (Christie 1997: 13). His answer is that criminology is 'over-socialized' by schooling, conventional thinking, state-generated data and state-determined questions, and overly short time frames that leave 'too little time for dreaming' (ibid.: 19). I build on Christie's ideas by outlining some practices of rock 'n' roll criminology, by which I mean ways of shaking up how we do our work.

Like any type of music, rock 'n' roll has a complex history, and I selectively highlight elements that resonate for me and with my use of the term as a metaphor. I cannot conduct a scholarly review of the music literature on rock 'n' roll, but will take my chances with the Wikipedia entry for 'Rock and Roll'. A blend of blues, country, and gospel, the genre became immensely popular in the 1950s and early 60s with significant cultural impact (p. 1). Rock 'n' roll music was associated with 'breaking boundaries and expressing the real emotions that people were feeling, but didn't talk about'. It combined white and black forms of musical expression, breaking down racial segregation, and 'encouraging racial cooperation and shared experience' (p. 8). The 'songs described events and conflicts that most [adolescent] listeners could relate to', encouraging a youth culture (p. 8). Described by one writer as creating a 'global psychic jailbreak' (p. 1), rock 'n' roll evolved into new musical forms in the mid 1960s and beyond. In imagining a rock 'n' roll criminology, I would like to encourage forms of criminological research and writing that press the boundaries of convention and conformity.

Styles of Criminology

As is the case in other fields, we think of criminology as having different schools of thought, methodological approaches,[1] and political-ideological positions. As a student in sociology, this is how I learned the field; and like so many others, I began to understand variation and differences across the field and to see students and colleagues using this mental map. I want to argue against viewing criminology and ourselves in this manner. We need a new aesthetic, which does not deny differences of theory, methodology, or politics and ideology, but which views the enterprise and our judgements of the value of the work we do in a different way.

We need to shift our mental maps of the field from 'schools' to 'styles' of doing criminology. By styles, I mean the differing ways of conducting and communicating research. A major impediment in the field is that many think that there are just one or two styles. When reading what are regarded as top-rated journals in

[1] Drawing from Creswell and Piano Clark (2007: 4), *methodology* refers to the broader, philosophical framework or set of assumptions used; *design*, to 'the plan of action' that links methodological assumptions to specific methods; and *methods*, to specific techniques of gathering and analysing research materials.

criminology, this is often (although not always) the message communicated. These journals, eg *Criminology* or *British Journal of Criminology*, contain articles that typically use one style—what I term Standard Scientific—of conducting and communicating research. We see a familiar template with the headings of introduction, theory, methods, findings, and discussion. This template is not confined to journals that typically publish statistically-based research; it is also seen in those publishing interview or ethnographic material. It is the discursive frame and orientation of the author using Standard Scientific that makes it distinctive, not the methodologies, research designs, or methods used.

There is a place for Standard Scientific, of course, but it is one of many styles that we should be practising and appreciating in the field. There are many others, too many to review here, but I name and describe several to encourage their use. They include the Contemplative Review, the Synthesis, the Non-Standard Scientific, and the Send Up. These styles are practised by a variety of analysts, that is, across all types of theoretical, methodological, and ideological positions. Variation is evident, however, in the degree to which an author is successful; and this is distinguished by dynamic, clear, and compelling communication. I shall give a few examples of essays or writers that demonstrate the style, but there are many more who come to mind.

The Contemplative Review takes a broad problem (or set of problems) in an area, and asks questions about or examines the problem from several positions. Some questions may be answered, but others may not be. The aim is to address the complex qualities of a problem, at times drawing from extant theories or empirical material, and to make sense of it. Examples of this form are Tony Bottoms' (1998) consideration of trends in sentencing and his (2003) sociological analysis of claims and facets of restorative justice, and Barbara Hudson's (1998) reflection on the problems raised for informal and restorative justice by sexual and racial violence. The Contemplative Review may require the writer to step back and 'suspend belief' on commonly accepted ways of thinking; and, in so doing, the field may be advanced by looking at a problem in a fresh light.

The Synthesis takes stock of a large body of theory or research (or both) with the aim of making sense of it: empirical patterns or conceptual themes are identified and assessed, varied approaches or debates are canvassed and compared, and disparate bodies of work are brought together. The Synthesis may sum up an older, well-known field of knowledge; or it may introduce and elucidate a new field, eg 'feminist criminology' or 'cultural criminology'. The aim is to assemble and depict a wide view of what is known or occurring, and to do so compactly, accessibly, and with an analytical focus or a framework of analysis. Without the latter, it is not a synthesis, but a review of the literature. The Synthesis can be carried out with different goals in mind: to establish evidence-based policy, to set a more general policy direction, or to develop new theoretical understandings. Among the examples are David Garland's (1990) theoretical synthesis of punishment and Doris McKenzie's (2006) review of correctional strategies. Such work would be more prevalent in policy-related areas if Elliott Currie's (2007) argument for a 'public criminology' were to be taken up.

The Non-Standard Scientific aims to be scientific, that is to produce authoritative knowledge, but to do so in ways different from the Standard Scientific. This style can take many forms, but what I have in mind are discursive frames and author orientations in conducting and communicating well-theorized empirical work, which break with the tenets of positivism.[2] One tenet is separation of the author from the subject(s) of research; a second is separation of the author from the written text; and a third is separation of the author from the reader. I recognize my limits: I am not a rhetorician, discourse analyst, or specialist in interpretive social science. However, stated briefly, Standard Scientific presumes that authority and objectivity are best achieved through a *separation* of author from the research subject(s), the written (or spoken) text, and the reader. Non-Standard Scientific challenges this understanding of authority and objectivity. Its practitioners may choose research topics to research that flow from their biographies or, in other ways, relate to their lives. In conducting research, they may become close to those they study, forming relations over several years. In writing and communicating, they may bring themselves into the research as an actor and participant, and they may relate to readers directly.[3]

This style is most likely seen in field studies or ethnographic research, where the author is part of a group and participates with group members, albeit in varied ways. In keeping with my theme of rock 'n' roll criminology, I would like to imagine that Non-Standard Scientific could also be practised by those who are more comfortable and familiar with a positivist methodology, but who want to shake it up and try another style. This is a significant methodological shift, but it may bring personal and professional rewards, and moments of intellectual breakthrough. For example, Karen McElrath (2001) describes her shift in identity as confirmed quantitative analyst to a believer in qualitative approaches. This came about when she moved to Queen's University, Belfast, and became 're-socialized' into new academic values, including a greater appreciation of qualitative methods (p. 3). This change occurred with the encouragement of colleagues to work on qualitative projects, coupled with McElrath's commitment to learn new ways of thinking, 'to play the role of student once again' (p. 3). Non-Standard Scientific invites reflection on how we relate to the people and phenomena we study, and how we communicate what we learn to others.

Of all the styles considered here, the Send Up is the least practised and rarely seen. This is a pity for the growth and dynamism of the field, and we should be encouraging more of this style. The Send Up reflects on the foibles, insecurities, egotisms,

[2] The term post-positivism is often used today and is more accurate, but for simplicity, I use positivism.

[3] Some authors may have little discernible presence in a text, others present their views and emotions in footnotes, and still others write themselves into the text as research participants.

self-interests, and existential qualities of 'being' a criminologist. It may also consider the nervous ticks, turgid speaking and writing styles, and repetitive and boring features of criminology. Criminology needs comedy and satire, whether in written or spoken form, and anyone who has the gift for it should be encouraged to practise and perform. The contributions to the field would be great: it would help to lift the spirits of practitioners and to break loose from tired and conventional ways of thinking, and perhaps in the process, to become more creative. A sense of 'breaking loose' comes when we can laugh at ourselves, and it may help to alter or refocus settled ways of thinking and knowing. It may also help to create a sense of existential 'we-ness'. I look forward to the day when the American Society of Criminology's Sutherland Award recipient does not deliver the standard 'serious' address, but rather gives us profound insights in the form of jokes, sketches, stories, and impersonations. It takes a special talent to carry this off, and it is not encouraged in graduate school or professional life. Little wonder, then, that we see so little of it. It could be a nice income earner for those considering retirement. Stan Cohen's (1995) Send Up of 'conference life' is exemplary.

Clarity

The end product of doing criminology is written and spoken texts.[4] These may or may not be read or listened to, and they may have significant or minimal impact. It is surprising how little is said in theory or method textbooks, or in introductions to the field, about the importance of writing, and its corollary, speaking, for effective communication. Thousands of articles in criminology journals alone are published each year, with countless others in social science, humanities, and law journals. Drawing from *Journal Citation Report* for 2008, produced by Thomson Reuters (formerly by The Institute for Science Information or ISI), the journal having the highest impact factor (IF) in 'criminology and penology' is *Criminology*, at 2.34 (*Science Watch*, 7 June 2009). Translated, this means that, on average, each article published in *Criminology* during 2006 and 2007 was cited an average of 2.34 times in the journals indexed by the Web of Science in 2008. For comparison, the impact factors for other journals in the top ten are 1.80 (*Crime & Delinquency*), 1.30 (*British Journal of Criminology*), 1.23 (*Journal of Quantitative Criminology*), and 1.19 (*Punishment & Society*). Despite the well-recognized problems with impact factors, particularly in the social sciences, they are a chastening reminder for anyone who takes pride in publishing articles in highly ranked journals. Few people seem to be citing the articles, at least soon after they are published, although a higher number may be reading them. Why are some texts more likely to be read and grasped? What is it that we, as readers, are looking for?

[4] I do not consider mixes of speech and visual forms, which are likely to increase in our work.

We desire clear, lucid, and lively ways of understanding complex problems about human existence and accounts of that existence. The two—human existence and accounts of it—cannot be separated in the work we do, which poses significant challenges for any depiction of our social and physical worlds. We inevitably work with approximations of human experience and behaviour, understood through several layers of social construction. The form of writing, especially its clarity, is one dimension, but there are others. Do the ideas engage us? Do they inspire or help us to see problems in new ways?

Quality and Originality

An elusive feature of our work is quality and originality. In a project directed by Michèle Lamont, she and her colleagues conducted interviews with fellowship proposal reviewers in the humanities and social sciences in the United States to determine how the reviewers arrived at judgements of quality and originality, and how they decided which proposals merited funding (Guetzkow *et al.* 2004). The reviewers were guided by stipulated criteria, including 'clarity, significance, feasibility, and, in some broad sense, quality' (pp. 194–5), but how were these qualities translated into practice?

Two criteria were most often mentioned: originality, followed closely by clarity. These were then followed by 'social relevance, interdisciplinarity, feasibility, importance, breadth, carefulness, usefulness, and 'exciting'' (Guetzkow *et al.* 2004: 196, fn. 6). Focusing on the dimensions of originality, the authors learned that the most frequently mentioned element was 'original approach', followed by original theory, topic, method, or data. These findings for the humanities and social sciences differ from those in studies of science, where the production of an 'original theory' and 'original results', normally in the form of 'making a new discovery', are what is most valued (ibid.: 197). Further, the *meanings* of original theory or results differ from those in the sciences. Original theory was in the form of 'connecting or mapping ideas' or producing a 'synthesis of the literature'; and original results, in the form of 'new interpretations' (ibid.: 197). The broader term, 'original approach', refers to the general direction of a project, including its 'perspective, angle, framing, points of emphasis, questions, unique take, or view' (ibid.: 199). The more specific elements of theory, method, or data that are embedded in a 'new approach' are the 'juxtaposition of ideas' that are not normally put together, 'creative combinations of ideas, sources, or methods,' and 'new ways of combining' (ibid.: 199). These elements are ideally what we would want to see and encourage as part of rock 'n' roll criminology: juxtaposition and creative combinations of concepts and methods.

Also of relevance to rock 'n' roll criminology, the elements associated with originality were related in reviewers' minds to the *moral qualities* of researchers. The applicants judged to have original proposals were described as 'adventurous, ambitious, bold, courageous, curious, independent, intellectually honest, risk-taking... and challenging the status quo' (ibid.: 203). By contrast, those whose proposals were judged not to be original were depicted as 'conformist, complacent, derivative,... hackneyed, lazy, parochial, pedestrian, tired' *and* as 'fashionable, trendy,... slavish, "riding on the band wagon" or "throwing around buzz words"' (ibid.: 203). Guetzkow *et al.* say that these descriptors condensed judgements of a researcher's 'intellectual authenticity': 'independent and dynamic scholars are authentic, whereas phoney scholars are lazy or worse, trendy' (ibid.: 203). To be an authentic scholar, then, means not reproducing the status quo *nor* following the latest trends (ibid.: 204), both of which are types of conformity. Instead, the message from Guetzkow *et al.* is to follow one's interests and passions, take chances, and think for oneself.

In reflecting on this last point, I was reminded of Christie's (1997) first 'block against insight': a lack of 'access to self'. In the process of learning authoritative understandings of crime and justice, students downplay their life experiences and insights. This is reinforced in schools, and then in universities, where learning continues to be based on a 'schooling' model of socialization and of filling empty vessels with authorized knowledge. Christie recognizes that 'there is a tension, some would say outright conflict, between socialization and innovation' (p. 17). However, he worries that universities, which should be sites of both 'transmitting cultural heritage' and challenging that heritage (ibid.: 16), are increasingly focused on the former, to the neglect of the latter. Access to self and 'trusting [one's] own experiences' (ibid.: 17) are increasingly stymied in university learning. It is little wonder, then, that conformity to the status quo or to trendy ideas is a safe path, one that many graduate students and academics elect. For Christie, as for proposal reviewers in Guetzkow *et al.*, this produces trivial insights. Taking risks, being true to one's self, having a passion for pursuing ideas—all are constitutive of an 'intellectual authenticity' that is highly regarded in the field, but paradoxically not encouraged. I would want to reinforce the point, however, that no matter how original or passionate the ideas, they must also be communicated clearly. Without clarity, originality cannot be readily discerned.

Near Data Research

Christie (1997) draws a useful distinction between distant and near data research, and he suggests that the former is more likely to produce 'findings of triviality' than the latter. Distant data are 'already processed data', such as official counts of crime, which 'have been given their officially designated meaning' (p. 21). Typically, they are called 'hard data,' the reference being to numerical representations of categories and action, which, if gathered in sufficient quantities, can be subject to statistical analyses. By contrast, near data, also termed 'soft data', are interpretations that social science researchers themselves make while observing acts and actors. They usually require many observations of a smaller number of people and acts because the researcher has 'to be there'. To Christie, this raises a 'mystery' (ibid.: 21). To paraphrase, why are many observations of a smaller number of acts or actors believed to be less 'honourable ... in certain scientific circles' than a few observations on a larger number of acts or actors? Christie's principle concern is that too much criminology is based on state-processed files, where the notion of 'crime' is not sufficiently problematized, when it should be.

There is another element of distant data research that troubles me even more. There is too much distance between the researcher and the actors and the action, that is from 'being there'. My point is not that quantitative studies have no value, because of course they do, depending on their data quality. Rather, I am concerned with how researchers may orient themselves to the material, including the terms and language used to describe patterns and relationships. The tools of quantitative research are just that: *tools* for understanding, interpreting, and explaining complex patterns. They do not substitute for understanding and explanation. This point is lost on some analysts, who may be caught up in statistical precision and statistical interpretation more than in the complexities of the social phenomena under examination. Such tunnel vision arises, I believe, because analysts lack a sense of 'being there', of being on the inside of complex social phenomena and the worldviews of participants, as much as this is possible or practicable.

One way to address this problem is that distant data research should be linked to the relevant near data research, or researchers should approximate 'being there', whether by observation or experience, or more vicariously, by reading of others' observations or experiences. Of course, some areas of criminological investigation are not readily observable nor directly experienced. For these, we may need to rely on texts and traces of conversations and actions, which may include distant data or approximations of near data. My point is that those relying upon distant data should aim to bring themselves as near as they can to the phenomena they are describing or attempting to understand.

Compared to sample surveys or other methods of assembling large quantitative datasets, near data research is less often practised. In general, and here I have in mind field research, researchers' activities are physically and psychologically more taxing. It requires time to enter the field, establish a field presence, and negotiate one's identity and relationships with others. Field work needs desk work: time spent on reflecting and writing on the day's activities, typically with field notes going to the hundreds of pages, with interview transcripts also going to the hundreds of pages. Writing about what one has observed and learned takes a special skill in weaving 'action' with 'analysis', identifying themes, and moving between observed activity and accounts of it by participants. If carried off successfully, the author can take us into worlds of action and meaning that many of us would not otherwise have known.

The work gives us a sense of proximity to action and behaviour; we learn how people negotiate self, identities, and relationships to others and to social and legal authorities; and we hear the argot in use that crystallizes meanings, world views, experiences. This sense of proximity may also be glimpsed by in-depth interviews and re-interviews with people.

Selected examples of near data research are Lisa Maher (1997) on sex work and the street-level drug economy in Brooklyn, Jeff Ferrell (1997) on graffiti groups in Denver, and Robert MacDonald and colleagues (2006) on marginal youth in Teesside. In the spirit of rock 'n' roll criminology, I would like to imagine that Terri Moffit or David Farrington would want to talk with several Teesside youth 'at the sharp end' about how they 'live through conditions of social exclusion' (MacDonald 2006: 373). If they did, I wonder, would these scholars' categories of analysis change? Would they think differently about pathways into and out of crime?

I wish to press this point further. All of us are caught up in favoured and familiar ways of 'doing criminology'. Some say that they have an aversion to numbers and could never participate in a statistical study; others say that unless they have a large number of cases, they cannot produce useful knowledge. Some believe that field experimental designs produce the most authoritative knowledge. They forget that this design can be applied to a selected set of problems, and they overlook the ways in which the knowledge produced is restricted to a particular range of cases, often for good ethical reasons. No one method, design, or methodology can have a claim to superior knowledge. All have a role and may produce a 'truth' of some type, and all are partial and limited.

Those who engage in distant data research need to suspend belief on their favoured concepts and understandings by reducing the distance between them and the phenomena they are studying. They can achieve this goal by confronting, appreciating, or utilizing near data research, or approximations to it. Likewise, those who engage in near data research could create more distance between themselves and the phenomena they are studying. The value to distance is the ability to learn more, albeit perhaps superficially, about a larger number of cases or people. From this, we may be better able to discern patterns and variability. By shaking up our individual ways of 'doing criminology', we move from our comfort zones, become unsettled, and in the process, orient ourselves to problems in more imaginative and creative ways. There is an unfortunate skew in the field today: an over-reliance on distant data research, when all of us would benefit by near data research, or approximations to it. We also require more pluralistic and juxtaposed approaches to theory and methodology.

Pluralism and Juxtaposition

I am mindful of the theoretical and methodological cautions by Garland (1990) and Creswell and Piano Clark (2007) when contemplating the mixing or combining of theories and methodologies. Garland's (1990) analysis of the theories of Durkheim, selected Marxists, Foucault, and Elias to inform a sociology of punishment could, he said, 'all too easily collapse into an arbitrary eclecticism ... an intellectual tangle of incompatible premises, ambiguous concepts, and shifting objects of study' (p. 279). Rather than trying to 'add together' these theories, he had a *pluralistic* objective in 'the construction of a rounded sociological account of penality'. Likewise, in putting forward the case for mixed research designs, Creswell and Piano Clark (2007) identify the different stances taken by practitioners on whether different 'worldviews' (eg, positivist, constructionist, advocacy and participatory) can be combined. Some believe it is possible to combine them, whereas others do not.

In earlier work on gender, race, and sentencing (Daly 1994), I took the latter position. I was persuaded by Richardson (1990: 118) that logico-scientific and narrative modes of reasoning were 'irreducible to each other and complementary', each providing 'a distinctive way of ordering experience and constructing reality'. I said that knowledge producers needed to become more bilingual in seeing the strengths of statistics and storytelling in creating truth claims about 'justice' in sentencing, and that research practices should *oscillate* between their familiar methodological home pole and another pole. I still believe that this is the case, although I remain open to new ways of representing social realities as these are inevitability constrained by language and discursive fields.

Pluralism and juxtaposition are particularly evident feminist perspectives in criminology (see Daly 2010), although they are not limited to this domain of inquiry. As a practitioner in the area for over three decades, I am struck by an increasing appreciation of the diverse ways of constructing knowledge (often condensed to broad categories of empiricism, standpointism, and deconstruction), and a desire for more inclusive and imaginative understandings of inequalities and 'difference'. Several examples will suffice.

In the 1980s, two distinctive trajectories emerged within feminist research in criminology: 'real women' and 'woman of discourse' (Daly and Maher 1998). Both were prompted by major challenges to 1980s feminist theorizing: one, by black and racialized women's critiques of dominant white analyses; and the other, by post-structuralistic critiques of positivism and dualisms in western thought. Although each has different emphases and theoretical orientations, it became evident to many of us that one cannot fully depict 'real women' without reference to the discursive fields by which girls or women are constructed or construct themselves. Likewise, one cannot assume that analyses of 'women of discourse' necessarily reflect girls' and women's identities and lives they lead. Ideally, then, the aim is to interpolate 'the discursive' and 'the real', not an easy task because each comes with its own set of theoretical referents and specialized vocabularies. Successful examples include Bosworth (1999), Maher (1997), Mason (2002), and Miller (2001).

Understanding difference, inequalities, social standpoints, and social relationships, which include multiple and contingent relations of sex/gender, race or ethnicity, class, age, sexuality, nationality, religion, and the like, is a significant task. Standard criminological approaches typically assume categorical and static approaches, for example by statistical comparisons of black and white men and women's rates of arrest for violent crime. These may provide some insight into aggregate group-based differences, using distant data, but they do not give us a sense of action, dynamics, process, and the fluidity of identities and subjectivities, nor of how the world appears from different perspectives or social locations. There are many ways to explore these complex realities (see Daly 1998*a*, 2010 for approaches and examples). I give two examples from my research. The first is 'breaking boundaries' by shifting a research angle of vision; the second is finding political common ground across 'difference', conflict, and inequalities.

Using materials from the New Haven felony court study (Daly 1994),[5] I decided to take a different angle of vision: rather than analyse racial-ethnic differences in the court's treatment of female defendants, I wondered how black women, as a group, related to the court (Daly 1998*b*). In particular, I was interested in the multiple positions of black women to 'white justice': as mothers, wives, girlfriends, and others who supported lawbreaking sons and daughters; and as crime victims and defendants. How did they challenge, negotiate, or agree with 'white justice'? An important finding was that black women were most often present in the court and its records as mothers, girlfriends, or spouses of defendants. Crime victims or defendants, who are typically at the centre of most criminological research, were in the minority. I came away from the research with the realization that if we wished to gain a deeper appreciation of how gender and race prejudice work in the court through the eyes and experiences of black women, we would learn as much from family members connected to cases, as from lawbreakers and victims.

I use the term 'race and gender politics of justice' to refer to the differing emphases that racialized minority and feminist groups take in seeking justice. In general,[6] racialized groups give greater emphasis to offenders' interests; feminist groups, to victims' interests. Is it possible to address these conflicting interests, or are they forever in tension? I have proposed an 'intersectional politics of justice', which could assist in changing antagonistic relations toward more constructive and progressive ones (Daly 2008). My application is to debates concerning alternative justice practices, including restorative justice and contemporary indigenous justice practices, where there are conflicting interests between offenders and victims, race and gender groups, and the rights of individuals and collectivities. To address these, I propose that justice should not be viewed as a zero sum game, that we must engage in intersectional thinking by taking the positions of other group members, and that victims and offenders have rights that cannot be compromised by collectivities.

[5] These were pre-sentence reports and transcripts of judicial sentencing remarks.

[6] Of course, there are exceptions to this dualism.

Pluralism and juxtaposition, and associated ways to combine, interpolate, intersect, or shift one's angle of vision, offer fresh ways to address problems. They force one to look again, in a different way, on what the problem is. They can provide new metaphors and concepts, and they push us out of our comfort zones into new areas of inquiry, new ways of learning and seeing. They may provide openings for us to glimpse and appreciate theories or methodologies that are not our favoured ones, but are worth trying, if only once. This may create a wider vision and understanding of the criminological field, which is renewed not by repetition in well-grooved places, but by breaking out of the tracks.

Last Dance

Some are critical of criminology for not addressing this or that problem or for dealing with it in too limited a way. 'Criminology' is not an actor. It is a discipline or specialism, which depends for its knowledge production, problem focus, and critical posture upon its individual practitioners. Yes, there is a socializing and 'schooling' environment that we are brought into and that moulds and pushes us in certain directions. However, we are not helpless, unthinking pawns in a field of knowledge. If, as Christie thinks, a good deal of criminological knowledge is trivial, we cannot blame the field for this. Rather, we must take responsibility for changing and reinvigorating it, for shaking it up.

Enter rock 'n' roll criminology. I have suggested an alternative mapping of the field, with a greater emphasis on styles of criminology, proposing that we need to experiment with and be appreciative of a range of styles. Originality and quality are elusive terms, but they collect around the notion of a researcher's 'intellectual authenticity', which is associated with taking chances, challenging the status quo, but not conforming to fashionable trends. Elements of originality and quality include juxtaposition and combination, whether of theories, concepts, ideas, methodologies, methods, and the like, although novelty for its own sake is not recommended. Clarity and liveliness in writing and speaking is essential. I suspect that much of what Christie finds 'dull, tedious and intensely empty' about criminology stems from lifeless and dull texts and styles of communicating.

I have called attention to an over-reliance on distant data research, with its most troubling feature being too much distance of a researcher from 'being there'. To compensate, I suggest that distant data researchers attempt to bring themselves closer to the phenomena they are studying by relying on near data research or approximations to it. The more general message of rock 'n' roll criminology is that everyone can benefit from shaking up their favoured ways of 'doing criminology', by stepping out of their well-grooved tracks, and by listening and engaging with those whose work is different or unfamiliar. All of this requires some degree of release from our respective 'psychic jails', our conventional ways of working, doing what is comfortable, familiar, and known. We may take some comfort in recognizing that others on the rock 'n' roll dance floor are ready to break out of jail too.

References

Bosworth, M. (1999), *Engendering Resistance: Agency and Power in Women's Prisons*, Aldershot: Ashgate/Dartmouth.

Bottoms, A. (1998), 'The Philosophy and Politics of Punishment and Sentencing', in C. Clarkson and R. Morgan (eds), *The Politics of Sentencing Reform*, Oxford: Clarendon Press.

_____ (2003), 'Some Sociological Reflections on Restorative Justice', in A. von Hirsch, J. Roberts, A. Bottoms, K. Roach, and M. Schiff (eds), *Restorative Justice & Criminal Justice: Competing or Reconcilable Paradigms?*, Oxford: Hart Publishing.

Christie, N. (1997), 'Four Blocks against Insight: Notes on the Oversocialization of Criminologists', *Theoretical Criminology*, 1, 1: 13–23.

Cohen, S. (1995), 'Conference Life: The Rough Guide', *Scottish Journal of Criminal Justice Studies*, 1: 33–50.

Cresswell, J. and Piano Clark, V. (2007), *Designing and Conducting Mixed Methods Research*, London: Sage.

Currie, E. (2007), 'Against Marginality: Arguments for a Public Criminology', *Theoretical Criminology*, 11, 2: 175–90.

Daly, K. (1994), *Gender, Crime, and Punishment*, New Haven: Yale University Press.

_____ (1998a), 'Gender, Crime, and Criminology', in M. Tonry (ed.), *The Handbook of Crime & Punishment*, New York: Oxford University Press.

_____ (1998b), 'Black Women, White Justice', in A. Sarat and M. Constable (eds), *Crossing Boundaries: Traditions and Transformations in Law and Society Research*, Evanston: Northwestern University Press and American Bar Foundation.

_____ (2008), 'Seeking Justice in the 21st Century: Towards an Intersectional Politics of Justice', in H. V. Miller (ed.), *Restorative Justice: From Theory to Practice, Vol. 11, Sociology of Crime, Law and Deviance*, Bingley: JAI Press.

_____ (2010), 'Feminist Perspectives in Criminology: A Review with Gen Y in Mind', in E. McLaughlin and T. Newburn (eds), *The Handbook of Criminological Theory*, London: Sage.

_____ and Maher, L. (1998), 'Crossroads and Intersections: Building from Feminist Critique', in K. Daly and L. Maher (eds), *Criminology at the Crossroads: Feminist Readings in Crime and Justice*, New York: Oxford University Press.

Ferrell, J. (1997), 'Criminological Verstehen: Inside the Immediacy of Crime', *Justice Quarterly*, 14, 1: 3–23.

Garland, D. (1990), *Punishment and Modern Society: A Study in Social Theory*, Chicago: The University of Chicago Press.

Guetzkow, J., Lamont, M., and Mallard, G. (2004), 'What is Originality in the Humanities and Social Sciences?', *American Sociological Review*, 69, 2: 190–212.

Hudson, B. (1998), 'Restorative Justice: The Challenge of Sexual and Racial Violence', *Journal of Law and Society*, 25, 2: 137–56.

MacDonald, R. (2006), 'Social Exclusion, Youth Transitions and Criminal Careers: Five Critical Reflections on "Risk"', *The Australian and New Zealand Journal of Criminology*, 39, 2: 371–83.

MacKenzie, D. (2006), *What Works in Corrections*, Cambridge: Cambridge University Press.

Maher, L. (1997), *Sexed Work: Gender, Race and Resistance in a Brooklyn Drug Market*, Oxford: Clarendon Studies in Criminology.

Mason, G. (2002), *The Spectacle of Violence: Homophobia, Gender, and Knowledge*, New York: Routledge.

McElrath, K. (2001), 'Confessions of a Quantitative Criminologist', *ACJS Today*, 24, 4: 1, 3–7.

Miller, J. (2001), *One of the Guys: Girls, Gangs and Gender*, New York: Oxford University Press.

Richardson, L. (1990), 'Narrative and Sociology', *Journal of Contemporary Ethnography*, 19, 1: 116–35.

Science Watch (2009), 'Journals Ranked by Impact: Criminology & Penology', Sci-Bytes—What's New in Research, Week of 7 June 2009, accessed 9 March 2010.

Wikipedia, The Free Encyclopedia (2010), 'Rock and Roll', accessed 8 March 2010.

8

CRIMINOLOGY'S DISNEY WORLD: THE ETHNOGRAPHER'S RIDE OF SOUTH AFRICAN CRIMINAL JUSTICE

CLIFFORD SHEARING AND MONIQUE MARKS

Introduction

In many ways South Africa can be described as a Disney World. It is stunningly beautiful and is a land filled with an array of places of adventure and fun. It also has a diversity of peoples (characters) leading to its depiction as the 'rainbow nation'. Yet beyond this happy surface is a more hidden reality, often not seen by those that visit this country for its fun and fantasy. Fifteen years after its transition to democratic governance, South Africa remains an extremely divided and unequal society plagued by high crime rates, memories of colonial oppression, and varied lived realities. For the wealthy citizens (still predominantly white but increasingly more diverse) it is a playground, for the poor (predominantly black) citizens it is a very different terrain of struggle and hardship (see, for example, Mbembe 2004). And while the state has a developmental project, many non-state governance arrangements exist to make up for government service delivery deficits and to provide alternative governance arrangements where government agencies (like the police) are still viewed with distrust or as simply inadequate (Kotzé 2000).

The stark inequalities and unevenness of daily life in South Africa are the result of a long history of (double) colonization. While South Africa gained independence from Britain in 1910, it only gained formal recognition from the Commonwealth of Nations in 1931. But the end of British colonialism did not represent the end of colonialism in South Africa. Indeed, key South African intellectuals such as Harold Wolpe described the reality of South African politics and economics as 'colonialism of a special type'. What this meant was that South Africa was, until 1994, a territory occupied by the colonized and the colonizer. In this system, the black majority were colonially oppressed by the white minority, many of whom had viewed themselves as previously colonized. The liberation struggle in South Africa therefore centred on the abolition of the colonial white state and the creation of a democratic state based on the principles of majority rule (Wolpe 1990). 'Liberation' was formally achieved in 1994 when South Africa held its first democratic elections.

However, the legacy of the two forms of colonialism have left deep scars and South Africa today can best be described as a struggling post-colony that mirrors, and indeed is an emblem of, a global reality that many view as 'global apartheid' (Titus 1996; Castells 1998). South Africans continue to live markedly unequal lives where class and race continue to intersect. The rural/urban divide epitomizes this dual existence, but even in the cities, wealth and poverty, formal economy and informal economy, rest side by side. Mbembe's description of Johannesburg is a very vivid reminder of this:

> Contemporary downtown Johannesburg visually resembles other African cities in the aftermath of decolonization: a matrix of plural styles, a striated, striped city that concatenates the most formal and modern with the most informal... Behind its disorderly convulsions and apparent formlessness, there is a recognition that the metropolis is fundamentally fragmented and kaleidoscopic—not as an art form but as a compositional process that is theatrical and marked by polyphonic dissonances [Mbembe 2004: 400].

The colonial, and an even wider eurocentric/western, legacy has to be accounted for in 'doing' criminology in South Africa since it impacts on forms of crime and deviance, meanings attributed to crime and social control, and the variety of governance arrangements that existed in a fractured society. Doing criminology in places like South Africa requires research methods that allow for an understanding of variant meanings and lived experiences as well as a wide array of coping strategies within a complex social reality.

Chris Cunneen (in this volume) has argued for a criminology that takes account of postcolonial realities. Such a criminology, he suggests, would compel us to think more seriously about 'the relationship between race and criminalization, the development of identities of resistance, and various processes of transformative justice'. It would also 'draw our attention to broader questions of social and political power, matters of legitimacy, political authority and consent—all of which presuppose how we understand and define crime and crime control'. A postcolonial perspective does not assume universal laws and legitimacy, but instead looks for alternate forms of agency and meaning in regard to crime, punishment, and social ordering. This perspective, he argues, has the potential to fundamentally break with dominant eurocentric/western narratives that are generally state-centric.

If we are to take this perspective seriously in doing criminology, we would need to think more creatively about the questions that we are trying to answer. These may differ somewhat from the questions that are asked in western democracies. The questions that need to be answered, we believe, include the following: Why are criminal acts so violent in nature? To what extent are state criminal justice bodies viewed as legitimate? What alternative, non-state criminal justice arrangements exist and how do they intersect with state nodes of criminal justice? What meanings do South Africans attribute to the transformation (postcolonial) project? What imaginings should guide policies and practices aimed at democratic, equitable and fair governance of security? How do we map out and explain the complex and pluralized criminal justice arrangements? What is the role of the state in creating safer and more just realities where hybrid political arrangements are most evident?

There are many ways in which these questions can be answered. Criminologists could, for example, conduct quantitative studies that focus on levels of crime and violence. They could do surveys, which seek out (very broad) opinions and attitudes about crime, justice and institutional change (such as of the police and the court system). This kind of research is important and without doubt it provides us with sets of statistics to inform theorizing as well as crime-prevention and combating strategies. Criminologists could also examine, and analyse, the myriad polices meant to shape institutional change, such as the reform of the state criminal justice system. This research is vital as it allows us to frame the structural changes that have taken place, particularly since the transition to democracy. These forms of research provide us with vital framing information. However, such research falls short of fulfilling the requirements of the agenda we have outlined.

What is required in addition is research that is more qualitative in nature—research able to provide insights into the divergent meanings that the range of actors (both those with power and those more marginalized) give to crime, violence and transitional justice. If we rely exclusively on positivist approaches to doing criminology in places like South Africa, we lose sight of the fragmented, fragile and fluid nature of criminal justice arrangements and the meanings that individuals and groups ascribe to them.

We require ethnographic research that allows us to get a nuanced grip on the divergent complex arrangements that exist to govern crime and to restore justice. Beyond this, we believe that those who do criminology should adopt a critical stance that will enable them to imagine new realities, which take account of historical and present injustices that will enable them to envisage new and safer futures.

This chapter is divided into three parts. In the first part we explain what we mean by ethnography and provide examples from our own ethnographic research endeavours. Second, we explore ways of transforming knowledge and imaginings into action or practice. Here we explore the notion of praxis as discussed by Marx and Engels in the *German Ideology* (1947). We maintain that the point of doing social research is not merely to contemplate the world, but to change it—a position that is, despite conventional understandings, not in conflict with Weber who saw the choice of research topics as value driven. In the final section we argue that southern places should be viewed as sites of knowledge creation.

The Case for Ethnography and Case Studies

Within the field of criminology there is a rich history of ethnographic studies. These date back to Frederic Thrasher's book, *The Gang* (1927), Klockars work on deviant subcultures (1979), Howard Becker's work on *Outsiders* (1963), Polsky's (1967) work on hustlers, Jock Young's composition on *The Drugtakers* (1971) and Stanley Cohen's study of *Folk Devils and Moral Panics* (1972). Indeed, much of criminology's most fundamental work has emerged out of ethnographic research that some have dismissed as idiosyncratic and impressionistic (Adler and Adler 1998). More recent ethnographies include Joan Moore's (1991) work on homeboys and homegirls in the Barrio, Felix Padilla's (1992) work on gangs as an American enterprise, and the work ('Reading Difference Differently?') of Coretta Phillips and Rod Earle (2010) on identity and race in prisons. However, ethnography has been, and continues to be, a 'minority tradition' within criminology (Maguire 2000). As Adler and Adler (1998) put it, ethnography is often viewed as an 'academic vice', and is not taken seriously by 'mainstream' criminologists. This is unfortunate as ethnographic studies have generated appreciative understandings that would be 'difficult if not impossible to obtain through any other method' (Yates 2004).

There are many reasons for the marginalization of ethnographic approaches to doing criminology. Ethnographies are viewed as 'messy' (Maguire 2000), risky to both researchers and research subjects (Inciardi 1993), and as failing to meet the requirements of scientific research that include validity, reliability and generalizability (Brewer 2004). Traditionally, ethnographies are time-consuming and as a result are not viewed as a way of finding immediate solutions for 'pressing' problems. As a result of these perceived weaknesses of the ethnographic approach, criminology has edged toward a discipline obsessed with surveys, statistics and other 'objective' methodologies (Ferrell 2009). There are very serious consequences to this positivistic creep. As Ferrell (2009) puts it, criminological research has become impenetrable to every day citizens and to those wanting to effect change in times of national and global crisis. The mystics of objective (state-serving) criminology—obsessed with scientific inquiry, mathematical inquiry and dispassionate analysis—has encouraged a mainstream criminology that is devoid of human emotion and human action (Ferrell 2009).

Given this state of affairs within criminology, it is not surprising that there have been calls for criminologists to return to the messy, unpredictable work of ethnography:

> We invite residents of Hotel Criminology to leave the hotel room for a while. Go into the streets, into living rooms and corporate bedrooms, into juvenile lockups. Situate yourself as close as you can to the perpetrators of crime and deviance, to the victims, to the agents of legal control; put yourself as best you can and for as long as you can, inside their lives, inside the lived moments of deviance and crime. You won't experience it nicely, and if the danger and hurt become too much, be glad of it. Because, as near as you will ever get, you have found your way inside the humanity of crime and deviance [Hamm and Ferrell 1998, cited in Goldsmith 2003: 124].

European-based policing scholar, Maurice Punch, also reminds us of the rich history of policing ethnography and calls for a revival of ethnographic studies in the contemporary (and transitory) policing world:

> The field of policing was built on a set of ethnographies from the sixties and seventies which are not only dated but which focused predominantly on patrol work in the rough areas of large cities. There is a need for a new generation of ethnographers scrutinising detective work and specialised units, rural policing, small town policing and policing in transient societies such as South Africa, the former Soviet republics, Northern Ireland and so on. There may be elements in the current academic life that are inimical to field studies but we need some new faces... but with new conceptual lenses... the new crop of ethnographers would inform us of what is happening at the 'sharp end' in diverse settings [Punch 2003: 4].

These are important reminders of the need for a place for ethnography within criminology. In the South African context, these reminders are very welcome as we struggle to understand the meanings and effects of transition and difficult lived-realities in a place where people struggle daily with violence, high levels of crime and inept state agencies. If we are to answer the questions we outlined in our introductory comments we need to step out of our distant and distinct comfort zones, as Hamm and Ferrell (1998) suggest. We need to situate ourselves as actors with our own agency and (acknowledged) subjectivities in the uncomfortable spaces of shambolic state criminal justice institutions and within communities most affected by crime, violence and disorder.

South African criminology is plagued by the same blindness as criminology in the rest of the world. Most researchers who focus on issues related to criminology are most comfortable with the kind of research that is quantifiable, policy directed (and therefore quick to do), and desktop based. Yet there are researchers/academics who have broken free from these shackles and have produced wonderfully detailed accounts of institutional and community life. The authors have both in different ways played a small part in this and will discuss our own contributions to this 'alternative' criminology later.

Amongst the ethnographers who have situated themselves at the sharp end of criminological studies are Jonny Steinberg and Antony Altbeker. Both Altbeker and Steinberg have explored 'the social meanings of people in the setting by close involvement in the field' (Brewer 2004: 313). They have taken the time to 'understand people's actions and their experiences of the world, and the ways in which their actions arise from and reflect back on those experiences. Altbeker, in his book *The Dirty Work of Democracy: A Year on the Streets with the South African Police Service* (2005) shadowed police units who respond to cases of murder, armed robbery, gangsterism and domestic violence. His book provides a fascinating, fly-on-the-wall account of how street-level policing works and why it so often does not. It offers unique insight into the men and women behind the badge and into the world they confront. What he demonstrates through his rich descriptions is that cops are loved and hated, praised and blamed. Altbeker takes us inside this unique and strange profession, and provides us with an account that is both nuanced and reflective.

In his second book, *South Africa: A Country at War With Itself* (2007) Altbeker provides us with a close-up account of both what is unusual about police work and what is mundane (Dixon 2008). He provides a first-hand account of what it means to live in the uglier (less Disney-like), parts of South Africa. He is able to provide a clear picture of the hardness of life in the disadvantaged black townships and the horrible reality of domestic violence that takes place in the private spaces of people's homes. He pierces beneath the language of 'police transformation' and takes us behind the horrifying statistics that have numbed most South Africans. His observations enable Altbeker to fundamentally question explanations of South Africa's crime rate that are premised on poverty and inequality. While his theoretical contribution and his resultant recommendations have been questioned (see Dixon 2008), there can be no doubt that this book provides us with a far finer-grained account of what is really happening in the South African crime and policing scene than any statistical report or policy analysis ever could.

Jonny Steinberg is an ethnographer of international acclaim. In his fourth ethnographic book, *Thin Blue: The Unwritten Rules of Policing South Africa* (2008) Steinberg argues that policing in crowded urban space is like theatre. Only here the audience writes the script, and if the police do not perform the right lines, the spectators throw them off the stage. In vivid and eloquent prose, Steinberg takes us into the heart of this drama, and picks apart the rules South Africans have established for the policing of their communities. What emerges is a lucid and original account of a much larger matter: the relationship between ordinary South Africans and the government they have elected to rule them. He provides us with evidence of the very fragile, untrusting and fluid relationship between the police and local communities.

Steinberg uncovers the unwritten rules of policing and the hidden engagements between South Africa's citizens and its police force. Beyond this, Steinberg reveals the intricate ways in which communities (both rich and poor) police themselves, sometimes in collaboration with the police and private security actors, sometimes not. Implicit throughout his book is an acknowledgement that the policing field is plural or nodal in character. Steinberg brings complex theories to light in his very accessible writing. In so doing he simultaneously provides us with a contemporary 'sharp end' description, and theoretically informed explanations, of South Africa's policing landscape. He demonstrates how ethnography is not mere storytelling, but rather an approach that allows us to test existing theories, build new explanations and be able to do this in ways that make sense to a readership beyond academia. Steinberg shifts our understandings and our imaginings in fundamental ways, while entertaining us with his vivid descriptions and brilliantly crafted interpretations.

We have fronted Steinberg and Altbeker's work because they are exemplars of a new face of South African ethnography. Like any good ethnographer, both believe that doing good and meaningful social science involves entering people's lived realities and developing a 'close association and familiarity with the social setting' (Brewer 2004: 312). They are prepared to do the 'dirty work' (Hughes 1958) of social research by leaving 'Hotel Criminology' and getting into grimy police vehicles and stepping onto the dusty and dangerous streets of South Africa's shambolic townships. In doing this, they knowingly placed themselves in risky situations.

The authors of this chapter have engaged in ethnographic work and have never bought into preoccupations with 'objectivity' and neutral representations of the social world that do not recognize the place of values in selecting subject-matters. We enter the research field knowing that we do so with our own personal identity, personalities and histories—again something that Weber recognized. Our research is impacted and determined by our multiple 'positionalities'—as researchers, social advocates, teachers, and citizens. And through our engagement in the field, our imaginations are fired, our understandings of real-lived social realities are refined, and our capacity to impact on change processes is enhanced as a result of building trust and familiarity. Our ethnographic endeavours are based both within communities (mostly marginalized) and organizations (of the police in particular).

In our view, organizational ethnographies are as important as ethnographies of those who are marginalized in one way or another. Organizational ethnographies, such as ethnographies of the police, allow us to investigate how organizational actors, like the police, cope within their bureaucratic environment. They allow us to explore, from the inside, the practical reasoning of those at the top and the bottom of the organization. Ethnographies also provide us with the techniques to explore what shapes discretion and how decisions are made in everyday encounters. Knowing what makes police tick and how they understand their own working reality is particularly crucial in periods of transition when police are expected to act differently in response to legal and policy changes that they (generally) had no place in creating.

Marks immersed herself in a South African police unit over a period of three years (see Marks 2004). The aim of this ethnographic endeavour was to explore what the change process meant to the police and whether or not they were able to enact new policies and the 'skill' taught in training courses. This ethnographic journey allowed for a first-hand understanding of the difficulties and dilemmas of change for police officers in a period of transition. What became apparent was the incongruity between everyday behavioural responses and formal statements of change as captured in policy statements. Through listening to stories and reminiscences it was possible to gain an empathetic (albeit not sympathetic) understanding of police officers' attachments to the past and their resultant resistance to some of the new organizational demands.

An ethnographic approach provides researchers with a way to examine cultural knowledge that police officers share and use to interpret their experiences. It allows researchers to comprehend complex value systems that are fashioned or transmitted by organizational folklore, stories, and memories, that can only be grasped through ongoing engagement with police members in their own 'natural' environment (Schwartzman 1993).

Such understandings would never have been possible without forging trust. This required taking the time to be there, to listen, and to participate in the daily working lives of the police. Ethnographies of the police in places like South Africa test the researcher—her staying power and her willingness to be in the crime and grime. It means subjecting oneself, as researcher, to dangerous situations. While most researchers, including ourselves, would choose to avoid engaging in dangerous fields (Lee 1995) this is not always possible. Ethnographers cannot always dissociate from acts of violence, even when such acts are considered unjustifiable and even iniquitous. The very people who engaged in acts of violence (not an unusual occurrence in a police organization) are usually the same people who are struggling with processes of personal and organizational transformation. They are also the same people who allow researchers like ourselves to participate in their daily (sometimes exceptional) activities. Being in the field observing (and indirectly participating in) acts of violence presented a unique opportunity to understand an important facet of the organizational culture of police, which would not be captured or easily interpreted if more indirect research tools were used.

A similar conclusion was arrived at by Winlow *et al.* (2001), in their ethnographic study of bouncers in pubs, clubs, and bars. The chief researcher observed, and even participated in, acts of violence, which, he claims, was necessary for him to be able to conduct the research as a covert ethnographer. Winlow *et al.* acknowledge that such involvement did, of course, raise ethical questions. They argue that these were not ignored, but 'were placed secondary to the pragmatics of getting a job as a bouncer and keeping it' (2001: 543). Researching 'violent groups', they posit, is often unpredictable and ethnographers are forced to change roles and renegotiate interactions, often on the terms of the researched group. Certainly not all ethnographers (and certainly not many, if any, ethics committees), however, would agree with their decision to place research pragmatics above ethical and moral considerations.

Ethnographic research, even in exciting contexts like paramilitary police units, is not always exhilarating or glamorous. To maintain existing relationships and develop new ones, it is important to spend time just 'hanging around'. In the case of the study of the Public Order Police unit in South Africa, this meant endless hours in the offices of police officers talking about anything from how the unit was functioning, to family crises, to politics, to new personal business ventures. These informal interactions were crucial not only to building trust and familiarity, but to coming to grips with the everyday and more mundane thought processes of the police, as well as their everyday interactions with one another. It can also involve attending, and even actively participating in, formal meetings and workshops—it is here that I became a participant-as-observer. Such participation not only indicates a real willingness to understand the police organization in all its varying facets, it also provides a mechanism for keeping abreast of the formal processes taking place such as policy initiatives as well as planning and evaluation processes.

The ethnography of the police briefly described above allowed us to answer some questions about institutional change and the meanings that individual actors attribute to transitional moments. Questions about localized arrangements for governing security required different types of ethnographies. Shearing spent a number of years observing and participating in peace processes in the disadvantaged townships in and around Cape Town. The Zwelethemba Peace Committees were actively engaged in projects that combined peacemaking with 'doing justice' in a restorative manner (Shearing and Johnston 2005). Shearing wanted to discover how these peace committees do (and should) engage with state actors such as the police. He wanted to find out how safety networks operate at the most local level and he was actively involved in processes aimed at making the peace committees sustainable and accountable. He was also concerned with how more indigenous forms of justice articulate with state justice and with what structures and processes need to be set in place for communities to feel that justice is done when crimes were committed or when community conflicts needed to be resolved. Shearing's ongoing involvement with the Zwelethemba project was not simply a storytelling exercise. It was a project that has uncovered the complex nexus of security governance in South Africa and has been the ground upon which theories of nodal governance and restorative justice have been built (see Froestad and Shearing 2007). The questions Shearing asked coincide directly with the agenda of a postcolonial criminology—he sought to explore and develop processes within the boundaries of the constitution, but which left aside the criminal law's concern with the past, with establishing guilt and accordingly meting out punishment.

In doing this research Shearing left the comfort of the suburbs to spend significant periods of time in the dusty and often dangerous spaces that are generally hidden from view to those who prefer to see the Disney World aspects of Cape Town. Indeed, Cape Town is internationally known as one of the most beautiful cities in the world with its stunning oceans and magnificent beaches. Cape Town is the playground of the rich and famous. But Cape Town, like the rest of South Africa, has multiple realities, both dark and light. It is precisely this dual character that establishes it not only as a desirable tourist destination but also as an emblematic city in today's world of the very rich and very poor.

Similarly in Durban, Marks and her co-authors (including Shearing and Jennifer Wood) have tried to map out the complex reality of the policing landscape. This has meant using a range of ethnographic techniques (participant observation, in-depth interviews and documentary analysis) to make sense of the variety of policing arrangements that exist in Durban. This includes simply being around, what Christine Hentschel (2010) has recently termed being a 'flaneur'—an apt term to describe Shearing's observations in Disney World (Shearing and Stenning 1985) or Goffman's (1961), in his observations of children on a carousel. This has involved exploring a range of cases where policing is carried out by multiple actors. From the middle class suburbs of the Berea, to the informal trading hubs of Warwick Triangle, to the crime-ridden townships of Newlands East and Wentworth, Marks and her co-authors have explored, first hand, how local communities have come together to create safer neighbourhoods (see Marks, Shearing and Wood 2009; Marks and Wood 2010; and Marks and Bonnin 2010).

Away from the relative comfort of the university offices and the official statements of the police about decreasing crime rates, what is clear is that most policing in Durban is not done by the police. Community safety groupings/associations have emerged to identify and resolve threats to security. Sometimes their solutions include the police; often they do not. And even when the police are called upon they very often fail to respond in ways that are deemed legitimate or effective by local communities. Euro-American, state-centred understandings of criminal justice do not apply easily in the postcolony, not even in suburbs that are relatively advantaged. As Steinberg has so eloquently shown, community groupings determine how policing should be done and communities carefully select whom to form alliances with in creating safer spaces (for wider African perspective see Baker 2010; see also Hills 2000).

Making sense of this reality is not always an easy task. In places like Warwick Triangle and Newlands East, members of community safety groupings arm themselves with weapons (often live ammunition) and they acknowledge (once trust has been established) that they use deadly force when the public police fail to respond to calls for their intervention in the fight against violent crime. The use of force (often outside of the law) may be unsettling to those who do not understand the hard livings of people confronted on a daily basis by real threats to their safety and an unresponsive/inept public police agency. The challenge to ethnographers (including ethical ones) in these circumstances is not to automatically apply commonly assumed universalistic norms in interpreting localized lived realities and coping strategies.

It is interesting to note that some of the key discoveries made by Shearing, Marks, Steinberg, and Altbeker coincide. This is an important point to make in the face of the questioning of the generalizability of ethnographic studies. While each of us focused on different parts of the country, patterns emerge not only within our own individual research but between our research projects. What these ethnographies have provided is a relatively comprehensive, though diverse and nuanced, picture of South Africa's policing landscape. For us, this in itself validates the use of ethnography. But this is not what gives ethnography its special leverage. What is perhaps most significant about ethnography is its richness as a source of challenge to existing theory and its ability to generate new and innovative hypotheses.

There are other important gains to be made from doing ethnography within criminology. First, ethnographies provide a wide audience with scholarly evidence and interpretations that are interesting and understandable (Young 2011 forthcoming). Second, they allow for less fixed questions, which in turn create the space for researchers to understand the reality of societies which are fluid and contradictory. This is particularly important to take into account in countries in transition. Third, good ethnographies are built, we believe, on spending time in particular environments thus allowing for building trusting relationships between researchers, practitioners and those affected by crime, disorder, and social ordering. Such trust is not easily achieved in societies where state agencies are fearful of scrutiny and where ordinary people mistrust those who claim to have intellectual capital. Fourth, those who do ethnography demonstrate that researchers too are political and social agents with multiple positionalities that they are prepared to 'expose'. They are engaged and not distant. They have a direct and often personal stake in the peoples and institutions they are trying to understand, and even assist.

But perhaps most significantly, as the above suggests, the value of ethnography lies in its ability to pierce the 'reality' membrane through learning first hand about complexity and the changes that are taking place and need to take place in the future. In short, ethnography takes us a step away from what Jock Young calls 'cosmetic criminology', a criminology that 'would have us believe that crime and many other social problems are mere blemishes on the body politic which can be dealt with by superficial administrative measures' (Young 2011 forthcoming, no pages). A critical ethnographic mindset often prompts us to try to find ways of changing unjust realities in ways that make sense to those whose meanings and experiences are (or should be) the focus of social research. It allows us to imagine possibilities beyond abstracted and administrative solutions.

Praxis Criminology—Engaging in Change Processes

We argued in our introduction that criminology focused researchers in places like South Africa need to take seriously Karl Marx's notion of praxis. Criminology needs to move beyond understanding the world to changing it. Research, especially in countries like South Africa, should be actionable, both for those who are powerful and those who are marginalized. Research needs to inform change agendas in ways that are practically feasible. To be practicably feasible in our recommendations and imaginings, we need to understand the lived realities of social actors and contradictions of the social realities in which they live and work.

Shearing's ethnographic journey with the Zwelethemba project did not end at the point at which he had uncovered the particular and intricate ways in which justice is restored and safety problems are resolved in the townships around Cape Town. Shearing worked together with a group of active community members to create a model that both reflected and added structure to existing practices and structures. The Zwelethemba model was jointly created providing a set of formalized structures and processes for dealing with localized disputes and community defined deviances (see for example Froestad and Shearing 2007; Roche 2002).

The time spent by Marks and her co-researchers exploring the workings of community safety groupings in Durban has also had practical outcomes. Once the research process was complete, a workshop (hosted jointly with the Municipality) was held that brought together a range of actors interested in community-generated safety initiatives. Participants included members of the community safety groupings, police and private security organizations who form part of localized safety networks. At this workshop the researchers provided an overview and an interpretation of their research findings. In light of the researchers findings participants were asked to devise principles that would underpin a manual to be used to create and sustain community safety groupings. Workshop participants also deliberated on the various challenges to the effective working and recognition (by government bodies) of community safety groupings.

Following the workshop a 'How to' manual for forming sustainable community safety groupings' was produced (Marks, Dobson, and Bonnin 2009). The manual was formally launched by the Ethekwini Municipality (Durban) in October 2009. Over a thousand people attended, mostly community members active in local safety initiatives. Initially launched in English, it has now been translated into isiZulu, as a result of requests by local community activists for whom English is a second language. The manual is currently being used by the municipality to establish new community safety groups that mobilize local community capacity to create safer neighbourhoods. In August 2010 a workshop will be held with community members and fieldworkers from the Safer Cities Department to review and revise the manual having reflected on localized experiences of using the manual.

There are many examples that could be given of how the research that we have conducted has been utilized to effect change and bolster community-directed safety initiatives. However, we will use the above examples to reflect upon what makes research 'actionable' and practically relevant. We have three main reflections.

First, we did not enter into the research field as emotionally detached. We selected our research projects because we feel passionately about community justice and were sceptical (politically and theoretically) about state-directed and dominated initiatives. We were, and are, also committed to contributing to the deepening of democracy and justice in South Africa. These passions and commitments motivated us to leave our comfort zones (albeit on temporary bases) to enter into the more difficult worlds of those who are confronted daily by crime, insecurity and government agencies that are unable to deliver on the developmental promises. We believe that some of the best (action-oriented) criminology is done when there are 'strong emotions at work' (Young 2011, forthcoming). Research participants are most likely to respond positively to the findings of researchers who are personally invested in their wellbeing and their future.

Second, research is most likely to be put to practical use if the subjects of the research have been actively involved in the research process. For this to occur, research participants need to know that their knowledge, experiences and meanings are taken seriously and that they are able to contribute directly to the interpreting of research findings. In this respect we are advocates of a participatory action research approach. The PAR approach uses collaboration to overcome the traditional gap between research and practice (Whyte 1991; Geva and Shem-Tov 2002). Ideally, research subjects are directly involved in the research process from problem identification, to research design, to data collection and analysis, and, thereafter, to dissemination and uptake of research findings. The action research encounter is one where 'equal partners meet, enter into dialogue and share different kinds of knowledge and expertise...' (Jordan 2003: 190). Rather than the traditional research model where there is a rigid distinction between researcher and subjects and a quest for objectivity, PAR focuses on a 'dialogical relationship between theory and practice' (Jordan 2003: 188) where knowledge is generated within the everyday world of participants. PAR contrasts sharply with the conventional model of 'pure' research in which members of organizations and communities are treated as passive subjects (Whyte 1991: 20). PAR approaches are most likely to render sustainable change if research subjects (whether state actors or community activists) are seen as change agents capable of being reflective about their beliefs and their practices.

Third, in devising and evaluating change processes we need to take account of the social, political and historical realities in which change agents are embedded. We need, as Jock Young (2011 forthcoming) puts it, to apply the sociological imagination in doing criminology. How change processes emerge, the form that they take and their sustainability, are in large part shaped by where the actors come from, how much power and leverage they have, the extent to which the state supports change efforts, and the ways in which change agents engage with other actors and institutions. For example, community safety networks are most likely to succeed if there is some degree of social cohesion in the local area, if government bodies like the police are prepared to recognize and support these groupings, and if there are tangible benefits derived from participating in such groupings. Having access to material resources might also enhance the sustainability of community safety groupings. In addition, as the field in which change projects are embedded transform, so too will the form that projects such as the Zwelethemba model transform. Doing action research can be compared to a roller coaster ride. As we buy our tickets for the ride we might have some idea of what to expect, but the ride will always be bumpy, surprising, and sometimes disappointing. Yet those who are passionate about adventure parks will continue to hop on the rides knowing that they will always exhilarate.

South–North Learnings

When Shearing was growing up in Durban, a coastal city on the South Africa's east coast within a politically dominant white English-speaking constituency the words 'made in England' signified quality as did the words 'by appointment to her Majesty the Queen'. 'Made in England' signified a product made to the highest standards of excellence. 'Made in England' acquired its meanings from a wider understanding that to be European was to be better and to be English was to be better still. White South Africans not surprisingly sought to take advantage of this cache by referring to themselves as Europeans. The flipside of this was, of course, that to be non-European, whether one was referring to person or a jar of jam, was to be not as good.

This hegemonic mentality pervaded everything, and it certainly pervaded his education as a white South African. Everything about it was European in orientation and focus. As an apprentice sociologist he was taught many of the classic European—though not Marx and Engels—as well as more recent text of American-based scholars—authors like Parsons, Homans, Berger, and many others. As he began to think about where to continue his studies his thoughts inevitably moved to North America and eventually he studied at University of Toronto and at the New School for Social Research in New York, where he had truly wonderful experiences learning from the likes of Carl Mayer, Peter Berger, Stanley Diamond, Hannah Arendt, and Aron Gurwitsch.

Shearing had from the very moment of his birth been immersed within a colonial mentality. He had been raised within an African context, but he had been raised as a westerner. He was raised as a thoroughly colonized South African—proud to be a 'South African' but barely aware of the African continent of which he was a part, despite its very evident presence. As Braithwaite and Drahos (2006) have argued, within such a worldview it is the symbolic centre that defines the aspirations, the hopes and the standards of excellence of the periphery.

When Shearing returned to South Africa in the early 1990s as apartheid was drawing to a close, in the hope that he might be of service to a promised 'new' South Africa, he found himself within a very similar context to the one he had left. South Africa was, and still remains, pervaded by a sensibility that makes clear in a myriad ways that 'the West knows best' (Brogden and Shearing 1991).

This Euro-American mentality remains widely shared within South Africa, and much of Africa, and it is most certainly the dominant mentality of the many donor agencies that have offered to assist in building a new South Africa (van der Spuy 2000) and a new Africa (Baker 2010). This has been particularly true with respect to the governance of security and justice. Good governance here is governance that takes place through western institutions and is pervaded by the sensibilities that are embedded within them. No matter how much has worked, and is working, within other institutional arrangements, it is exceedingly difficult to get these ideas and practices recognized as worthy of attention unless they can be fitted into a wider context of western institutions (Ellis 2009).

In recent years, however, there have been significant conscious attempts on the part of those doing criminology in the 'south' to 'decolonize their minds' (Ellis 2009). African realities are now interpreted through a lens that accounts for the specificities of context, while not abandoning global theories that make sense of these realities. The fact that most governance (of security and other public functions) takes place outside of the state is now seen as having deep historical roots and cultural significance in Africa. In this regard, Africanist scholar, Stephen Ellis makes the very important point that 'most African societies have been governed throughout their existence without reference to political entities that we would today recognise as states... In fact, according to the historian John Lonsdale, 'the most distinctively African contribution to human history could be said to have been precisely the civilized art of living fairly peaceably together *not* in states' (Ellis 2009: 11).

It is not surprising then, as the ethnographic studies by Steinberg, Shearing and Marks *et al.* demonstrate, that most criminal justice activity takes place outside of the state. The notion of nodal security governance, while first formulated by Shearing on his visit to Disney World, was refined and exemplified in his fieldwork in Zwelethemba. Indeed, the theorization of nodal security governance is now viewed as deeply embedded in the South African and even African reality (See Baker 2010)—indeed the very term 'security governance' that is now widely used presumes a polycentric governance reality. But equally important, this theorization has been transported to the North. Nodal security governance understandings have now become a part of the discourse of many who do criminology throughout the world. These understandings have even been introduced into the language and policies of police organizations in the United Kingdom, Canada, and Australia (see Wood and

Dupont 2006). Southern learnings are impacting directly on criminological theorizations in, and of, the North.

None of this is to imply that a decolonization of the academic mind has taken place in places like South Africa. Far from it. However, increasingly, African criminologists are discovering the importance of the identity and history of the African postcolony. An intellectual renaissance is occurring that accounts for the complexity, failings and wisdoms that Africa has to offer global criminology. Places like South Africa are emblematic of complex realities with complex solutions. But the fact that they are transitionary spaces means that they are often more open to new sets of questions and innovative solutions. And while the specificities of these spaces cannot be denied, the questions asked here resonate with questions that are asked in the 'developed' North. For across the world those who do criminology are grappling with questions such as, who the police should be in a world of pluralized governance; and how marginalized communities can act upon the criminal justice landscape in ways that enhance feelings of safety and justice. Those who do criminology, whether based in the South or the North, are compelled more than ever to situate themselves in local and global realities and to jointly imagine ways of achieving a safe, peaceful and equitable world. The nexus lies not just in our social realities but in our intellectual learnings and sharings. The postcolony provides us with a much needed space for critical reflection on lived realities and on how to do criminology.

References

Adler, P. and Adler, P. A. (1998), 'Forward: Moving Backward', in J. Ferrell and M. Hamm (eds), *Ethnography at the Edge: Crime, Deviance and Field Research*, Boston: Northeastern University Press.

Altbeker, A. (2005), *The Dirty Work of Democracy: A Year on the Streets with the SAPS*, Johannesburg and Cape Town: Jonathan Ball.

_____ (2007), *A Country at War with Itself: South Africa's Crisis of Crime*, Johannesburg and Cape Town: Jonathan Ball.

Baker, B. (2010), *Security in Post-Conflict Africa: The Role of Nonstate Policing*, Boca Raton: CRC Press.

Becker, H. (1963), *Outsiders: Studies in the Sociology of Deviance*, London: Free Press.

Braithwaite, J. and Drahos, P. (2000), *Global Business Regulation*, Cambridge: Cambridge University Press.

Brewer, J. (1990), *Ethnography*, Buckingham: Open University Press.

_____ (2004), 'Ethnography', in C. Cassel and G. Syman (eds), *Essential Guide to Qualitative Methods in Organisational Research*, London: Sage.

Brogden, M. and Shearing, C. (1991), *Policing for a New South Africa*, New York: Routledge.

Castells, M. (1998), *End of Millennium, The Information Age: Economy, Society and Culture*, Vol. III, Cambridge, MA; Oxford, UK: Blackwell.

Dixon, B. (2008), 'South Africa: A Country at War with Itself', *Transformation*, 68: 136–40.

Cohen, S. (1972), *Folk Devils and Moral Panics,* London: MacGibbon and Kee.

Ellis, S. (2009), *South Africa and the Decolonization of the Mind,* Inaugural lecture delivered upon accepting the position of VU University Amsterdam Desmond Tutu Chair holder in the areas of Youth, Sports and Reconciliation, at the Faculty of Social Sciences of VU University Amsterdam on 23 September.

Ferrell, J. (2009), 'Kill Method: A Provocation', *Journal of Theoretical and Philosophical Criminology,* 1, 1: 1–22.

Froestad, J. and Shearing, C. (2007), 'Beyond Restorative Justice: Zwelethemba, a Future-focused Model using Local Capacity Conflict Resolution', in R. Mackay, M. Bosnjak, J. Deklerck, C. Pelikan, B. van Stokkom, and M. Write (eds), *Images of Restorative Justice Theory,* Frankfurt: Verlag fur Polizeiwissenschaft: 16–34.

Geva, R. and Shem-Tov, O. (2002), 'Setting Up Community Policing Centres: Participatory Action Research in Decentralised Policing Services', *Police Practice and Research: An International Journal,* 3, 3: 189–200.

Goffman, E. (1961), *Encounters: Two Studies in the Sociology of Interaction—Fun in Games and Role Distance,* Indianapolis: Bobbs-Merrill.

Goldsmith, A. (2003), 'Fear, Fumbling and Frustration: Reflections on doing Criminological Fieldwork in Colombia', *Criminology and Criminal Justice,* 3: 103–25.

Hamm, M. and Ferrell, J. (1998), 'Confessions of Danger and Humanity', in J. Ferrell and M. Hamm (eds), *Ethnography at the Edge: Crime, Deviance and Field Research,* Boston Northeastern University Press.

Hills, A. (2000), *Policing in Africa: Internal Security and the Limits of Liberalization,* Boulder: Lynne Rienner.

Hentschel, C. (2010), *The Spatial Life of Security,* PhD thesis, University of Leipzig.

Hughes, E. (1958), *Men and Their Work,* Glencoe: The Free Press.

Inciardi, J. A. (1993), 'Some Considerations on the Methods, Dangers and Ethics of Crack House Research', in J. A. Inciardi, D. Lockwood, and A. E. Pottieger (eds), *Women and Crack Cocaine,* New York: Macmillan.

Jordan, S. (2003), 'Who Stole my Methodology? Co-opting PAR', *Globalisation, Socieities and Education,* 1, 2: 185–200.

Klockars, C. (1979), 'Dirty Hands and Deviant Subcultures', in C. Klockars and F. O'Connor (eds), *Deviance and Decency: The Ethics of Research with Human Subjects,* Beverly Hills: Sage.

Kotzé, D. (2000), 'The Political Economy of Development in South Africa', *African Security Review* 9, 3: online.

Lee, R. (1995), *Dangerous Fieldwork,* Qualitative Research Methods Series No. 34, Thousand Oaks: Sage.

Maguire, M. (2000), 'Researching Street Criminals in the field: A Neglected Art?' in R. King and E. Wincup (eds), *Doing Research on Crime and Justice,* Oxford: Oxford University Press.

Marks, M. and Bonnin, D. (2010), 'Generating Safety from Below: Community Safety Groups and the Policing Nexus in Durban', *South African Review of Criminology,* 41, 1: 56–77.

_____, Dobson, R., and Bonnin, D. (2009), *Community Action for Safer Neighbourhoods. Safer Cities Project,* Durban: Durban Municipality.

_____, Shearing, C., and Wood, J. (2009), 'Who Should the Police Be? Finding a New Narrative for Community Policing in South Africa', *Police Practice and Research: An International Journal,* 10, 2: 145–55.

_____ and Wood, J. (2010, forthcoming), 'South African Policing at a Crossroads: The Case for a "Minimal" and "Minimalist" Public Police', *Theoretical Criminology.*

Marx, K. and Engels, F. (1947), *The German Ideology*, New York: International Publishers.

Mbembe, A. (2004), 'Aesthetics of Superfluity', *Public Culture*, 16, 3: 373–405.

Moore, J. (1991), *Going Down To The Barrio: Homeboys and Homegirls in Chicago*, Philadelphia: Temple University Press.

Padilla, F. (1992), *The Gang as an American Enterprise*, Piscataway: Rutgers University Press.

Perez, D. and Shtull, P. (2002), 'Police Research and Practice: An American Perspective', *Police Practice and Research: An International Journal*, 3, 3: 169–87.

Philips, C. and Earle, R. (2010), 'Reading Difference Differently?: Identity, Epistemology and Prison Ethnography', *The British Journal of Criminology*, 50, 2: 360–78.

Polsky, N. (1967), *Hustlers, Beats and Others*, Harmondsworth: Pelican.

Punch, M. (2003), *Summary Remarks of the International Police Conference at Kentucky University*, 12–14 June, unpublished. Permission received from the author to use these notes.

Roche, D. (2002), 'Restorative Justice and the Regulatory State in South African Townships', *British Journal of Criminology*, 42, 3: 514–33.

Schwartzman, H. (1993), *Ethnography in Organisations*, Newbury Park: Sage Publications.

Shearing, C., and Johnston, L. (2005), 'Justice in the Risk Society', *The Australian and New Zealand Journal of Criminology*, 38, 1: 25–38.

_____ and Stenning, P. (1985), 'From the Panopticon to Disney World: The Development of Discipline', in A. N. Doob and E. L. Greenspan (eds), *Perspectives in Criminal Law: Essays in Honour of John Ll. J. Edwards*, Toronto: Canada Law Book.

Spradley, J. P. (1979), *The Ethnographic Interview*, New York: Holt, Rinehart, and Winston.

Steinberg, J. (2008), *Thin Blue: The Unwritten Rules of Policing South Africa*, Johannesburg and Cape Town: Jonathan Ball.

Thrasher, F. (1927), *The Gang: A Study of 1,313 Gangs in Chicago*, Chicago: University of Chicago Press.

Titus, A. (1996), *Unravelling Global Apartheid: An Overview of World Politics*, London: Polity.

Van der Spuy, E. (2000), 'Foreign Donor Assistance and Police Reform in South Africa' *Policing and Society*, 10: 343–66.

Whyte, W. F. (ed.) (1991), *Participatory Action Research*, Newbury Park: Sage.

Winlow, S., Hobbes, D., Lister, S., and Hadfield, P. (2001), 'Get Ready to Duck: Bouncers and the Realities of Ethnographic Research on Violent Crime Groups', *British Journal of Criminology*, 41: 536–48.

Wolpe, H. (1990), *Race, Class and the Apartheid State*, Trenton: Africa World Press.

Wood, J. and Dupont, B. (2006), *Democracy, Society and the Governance of Security*, Cambridge: Cambridge University Press.

Yates, J. (2004), 'Criminological Ethnography: Risks, Dilemmas and their Negotiation', in G. Mesko, M. Pagon, and B. Dobovsek (eds), *Policing in Central and Eastern Europe: Dilemmas of Contemporary Criminal Justice*, Faculty of Criminal Justice, University of Maribor, Slovenia.

Young, J. (1971), *The Drugtakers*, London: McGibbon and Kee.

_____ (2011, forthcoming), *Criminological Imagination*, Cambridge: Polity Press.

9

ORIGINS OF CRIMINOLOGY*

NICOLE RAFTER

LIBRARIES have shelves full of histories of criminal justice—accounts of the development of policing, courts, prisons, the insanity defence, and so on—but relatively little on the history of criminology. Related fields such as anthropology, psychology, and sociology have broad historical overviews of their sciences; why not ours? One answer to that question surely lies in a problematic understanding of 'science.' Over time criminologists have tended to adopt what one might call the gold-digging model of doing science, interpreting their work as a search for truth—for a definitive cause of crime, or at least an unshakable scientific step in that direction. If we dig deeply enough, according to this model, and work with sufficiently powerful tools, we will eventually hit pay dirt—at which point we can toss the debris of earlier efforts in the trash heap.

To think in historical terms undermines the gold-digging model, for it negates the promise of scientific certainty and raises uncomfortable questions about the nature of science as a truth-seeking enterprise. It implies that we have to develop another model, not the gold-digging model that leaves us without a past but a processual model that conceives of criminology more like a river, an ongoing effort flowing through time, hitting rocks, absorbing currents from other fields, picking up new methods or concepts as it travels, eddying back to reconsider earlier findings, sometimes allowing work—even good work (Bursik, 2009)—to wash up on the river's

* This essay is in part an adaptation of the introduction to Nicole Rafter (ed.), *Origins of Criminology: Readings from the Nineteenth-Century* (Abingdon: Routledge/ Cavendish, 2009).

banks. To create a history of a science requires conceiving science as an enterprise in time.

This essay focuses on early attempts to explain crime scientifically, efforts that began in the late eighteenth century and continued very nearly till the end of the nineteenth century, when the term 'criminology' finally came into use and the field became a discipline—meaning a relatively distinct area of study. This chapter has two parts. In the first, I offer a synthetic overview of criminology's European and American origins. I do not try to answer the question, '*What is criminology?*', but I do try to suggest how some of the field's originators would have answered that question. In the next part I identify three key themes in ninetheenth century criminology: the nature of moral insanity (which today would be called psychopathy); evolution and its implications for understanding lawbreaking; and crime as a social phenomenon. In conclusion, looking to the future, I argue that a key challenge for criminology in the decade ahead is to develop a history—not a fixed account that will never be rewritten, because each generation has to reinterpret its past, but an in-depth account of its origins and of its work as an ongoing endeavour.

European and American Origins

Introductory textbooks, in their obligatory two-and-a-half-page genuflection to the past, often identify Cesare Beccaria as the first criminologist. This is nonsense if we define 'criminology' as scientific efforts to understand crime. Beccaria's small volume *On Crimes and Punishments* (1764/1986) is not a criminological text, nor does it attempt to be scientific; rather it is a treatise on the nature of law—on the legal changes that autocratic governments should make to reduce crimes. True, implicit in Beccaria's philosophy of punishment is a theory about the causes of crime. In Beccaria's view, man is a rational being, capable of making self-interested choices. If the laws are clear, administered fairly, and punitive in proportion to crimes, no sensible person will break the law. 'Tangible motives,' he writes (1964/1986: 7), are 'required sufficient to dissuade the despotic spirit of each man from plunging the laws of society back into the original chaos'. These tangible motives are the punishments established for lawbreakers. Beccaria took the causes of crime—human greed and self-centeredness—for granted.

Criminology in fact began as a series of cottage industries—small, minimally-specialized workshops in which researchers worked to explain crime as an aside to their central occupations, such as running a lunatic asylum or collecting national statistics on courts and prisons. In the nineteenth century these makeshift centres of production—which often consisted of little more than a desk and a sheaf of notes on criminal cases—were scattered thinly around western Europe and the eastern United States—one in Philadelphia, another in northern Italy, and still others in Perth

(Scotland), London, Lyon, New York, Paris, and Vienna. It took about 100 years for the work of the early scholars—Benjamin Rush in Philadelphia, Cesare Lombroso in Turin, J. Bruce Thomson in Perth, Henry Maudsley in London, Alexandre Lacassagne in Lyon, Richard Dugdale in New York, André-Michel Guerry in Paris, Richard von Krafft-Ebing in Vienna—to gel into 'criminology'.

Until late in the nineteenth century, researchers involved in the production of what we now call criminology may have been in contact with only two or three other specialists conducting similar work. (For ease of reference, I will call these researchers 'criminologists', even though few would have understood or accepted the label). They might have established such contacts through personal correspondence and journal subscriptions (for example, some psychiatric journals had a 'developments abroad' section to keep members up to date). Some maintained a standing order with foreign booksellers for works on a particular subject such as criminal insanity. Later in the century criminologists built networks by attending conferences such as the international congresses of criminal anthropology convened between 1886 and 1914 (Kaluszynski 2006). They also started contributing articles on their research to specialized journals such as the *Archivio di psichiatria, antropologia criminale e scienze penali* founded by Lombroso in 1880 and the *Archives de l'Anthropologie Criminelle* founded by Alexandre Lacassagne in 1886. Slowly, the production of criminological knowledge lost its cottage-industry character and started to resemble the factory-like process with which we are familiar today.

Barriers to Criminology's Development

Over and above geographical distance, two other obstacles to communication separated those who studied crime and criminals: language barriers and the fact that criminology had not yet been conceptualized as an independent field of study. Both obstacles slowed the field's development.

That some criminologists could not read publications in more than one language or converse with foreign colleagues impeded coalescence of the field. French tended to be the *lingua franca* for nineteenth century investigators. The French—Guerry and his fellow statistician Adolphe Quetelet, the alienist Philippe Pinel, the degeneration theorist Bénédict August Morel, the anthropologist Léonce Manouvrier, and the forensic physician Lacassagne—produced much of the period's criminological theory, and French translations of texts written in other languages gave well-educated Italians, Germans, and Britons access to work generated elsewhere. (For example, Lombroso's *L'uomo delinquente* or *Criminal Man*, arguably the most significant single text in nineteenth century criminology, was translated into French about a decade after its first, 1876, Italian publication, but not even partially into English until 1911, and not completely into English until 2006). However, many Americans knew no language other than English, a disadvantage that not only kept them from communicating with Europeans in the developing field but also doomed them to lack of sophistication.

A prime example can be found in the work of Richard Dugdale, the New York City businessman who pioneered in the study of heredity and crime. While absence of biographical information makes it difficult to tell whether Dugdale was monoglot or simply undereducated (or both),[1] he evidently knew nothing of contemporary French degeneration theory, which in the mid- and late-nineteenth century constituted the most important criminological concept in Europe. Remarkably, he all but reinvented degeneration theory in his classic study *The 'Jukes': A Study in Crime, Pauperism, Disease, and Heredity* (1877); but with a stronger background Dugdale could have related his findings to the theory of degeneration that Morel (1857) and other French writers had been elaborating for years. His charts might have been less confusing, his observations more coherent, and his conclusions less subject to misinterpretation.

At the opposite end of the spectrum from Dugdale were criminologists who could read several languages. These included Krafft-Ebing, the German psychiatrist, and Lombroso, the Italian criminal anthropologist. For his pioneering study *Psychopathia Sexualis* (1886/1892), Krafft-Ebing gathered examples from both his own patients and works by others; he could hardly have produced so comprehensive a survey of sexual deviations without access to literatures produced in several languages. Lombroso could read English, French, and German and had correspondents in countries from Argentina through Russia; these contacts enabled him to learn (for instance) of the latest developments in American theory and practise in a matter of months. Because his method, like Krafft-Ebing's, was one of amassing examples, he too benefited immeasurably from being multilingual. But few contemporaries had his linguistic skills or were such omnivorous consumers of research produced elsewhere.

An even greater obstacle lay with the fact that criminology had not yet been conceptualized as a field of study. If the first researchers tended to resemble workers in cottage industries, labouring in separate specialities to produce, piecework, their own theories of offending, that was partly because criminology's territory had not yet been named. Most of it belonged to other intellectual territory—anthropology, evolutionary science, jurisprudence, phrenology, physiology, statistics, and (especially) psychiatry. Nor is there evidence that any of the early researchers other than Lombroso, the self-styled 'criminal anthropologist,' were anxious to adopt new professional identities. But then, there was as yet no such thing as a criminologist and

[1] Dugdale was born in Paris, where his father was engaged in business, but both parents were English and he moved to London when he was seven (slightly later to the United States). Due to ill health, his education was spotty. The only biography seems to be Shepard (1884). For more on Dugdale's unfamiliarity with sources which might have boosted his sophistication, see Rafter (2008).

no such thing as 'criminology', a marketplace where they might display their wares, trade ideas, and make a pitch for their own theory.

Stages in Criminology's Early Development

The field formed in two phases. The first, the cottage-industry phase, began in the late eighteenth century, when the Philadelphian physician Benjamin Rush (1786/1815) began to study moral insanity, and lasted till Lombroso published *Criminal Man* until 1876. During this period of inchoate but rich theorizing, the French laid the basis for criminal statistics; phrenologists such as Franz Joseph Gall (1835) and Johann Gaspar Spurzheim (1834) formulated the first general theory of crime; lawyers and physicians debated the nature of criminal insanity; journalists such as Henry Mayhew (1862) in England and Edward Crapsey (1872) in New York investigated the urban underworld, sometimes speculating on the causes of criminal behaviour; and Friedrich Engels (1845/1993) developed an economic explanation for crime. In an intriguing interpretation of this early period, the historian Karen Halttunen (1998) argues that during it American culture changed its basic explanation for murder from that of the common sinner found in late eighteenth century execution sermons to that of the moral monster found in nineteenth century Gothic narratives. It would be useful to look for parallel processes in Europe, for Halttunen maintains (1998: 6) that the Gothic imagination profoundly shaped 'the modern liberal concept of criminal and mental "deviance" and what should be done about it' (also see Ystehede 2008).

Moral-monster explanations fed directly into the second phase of criminology's early development, starting with Lombroso's *L'uomo delinquente* (1876), which argued that the worst criminals are born criminals and demonstrated that criminology could become a science in its own right. The new field was born, and if at first its relations to anthropology, psychology, psychiatry, and statistics remained unclear, those who were studying crime and criminals at least could now think of themselves as labouring on roughly the same scientific project. A core of knowledge began to form, although much of it was hotly contested. This second phase ended in the early 1890s, when the term 'criminology' became the name for the new field. Britons became familiar with the term when Havelock Ellis published *The Criminal* (1890), his compendium of criminal anthropology (also see Garland, 1985). Americans learned of it when Arthur MacDonald published *Criminology* (1893), another compendium of criminal anthropology, this one an intellectual hash but nonetheless the first book to bear that title. While there had been criminology (scientific research on crime and criminals) in earlier decades, now there was 'criminology', a way of thinking about that research as a single, if amoeba-like, field.

However, this development should not be viewed as a teleological enterprise carrying us to the promised land of present-day criminology. As historian David Garland explains (1994: 17), we should not regard eighteenth- and nineteenth-century writings 'as proto-criminologies struggling to achieve a form which we have since perfected'; rather, 'it seems more appropriate to accept that there are a variety of ways in which crime can be problematized and put into discourse, and that "criminology" is only one version among others'.

Histories of criminology's early development have been slow to materialize and, again, the reasons lie with language barriers and nomenclature. Once more, the fact that early researchers wrote in a variety of languages has been a major obstacle. To produce a synthetic history of nineteenth century criminology, with its rich multiplicity of theories and empirical studies, one would need to read English, French, German, and Italian, for starters[2] (Spanish would probably be a good idea, too, to take Spain and South America into account). This difficulty is slowly being overcome as the key documents are translated into English, which has replaced French as the *lingua franca* of scholarly research in criminology, and as Google's book programme speeds up access to key documents. In addition, an international conference on the history of criminology held in Florence, Italy, in the 1990s, encouraged cross-fertilization among scholars working in English, French, German, and Italian (Becker and Wetzell 2006) and helped overcome the field's 'collective amnesia' (Laub 2004: 2) about its roots.

Still, it is still not easy to write a history of something that lacks a name. Historians (in so far as they have examined criminology at all) have tended to focus on the period *since* the 1890s, when *criminology* was so christened (for example, Beirne 1988; Laub 1983). And even then, their studies have often concentrated on a particular country or figure—a perfectly valid and useful procedure, but one that needs supplementation. We also need to know the nineteenth century history of the field, when it was in the process of formation, and we need cross-national comparisons.[3]

Key Themes in Nineteenth Century Criminology

Among the major interests or preoccupations of nineteenth century criminologists, three were overriding and very nearly ubiquitous: those of moral insanity; evolution and its implications for understanding the causes of crime; and crime as a social phenomenon. While these concerns did not surface in every criminological tract of the period, they constituted major themes or undercurrents that coursed through wide range of theoretical writings.

[2] Some of the groundwork has already been laid; see, for example, Davie (2005); Frigessi (2003); Garland (1985); Gibson (1998, 2002, 2006); Mucchielli (2006); Rafter (1997, 2008); Wetzell (2000). This list is not a full bibliography but merely an indication of the sorts of sources available.

[3] For cross-national work see, in addition to sources already cited, d'Agostino (2002); Becker (2006); Beirne (1993), (1994); Bondio (2006); Wetzell (2000); Foucault (1977); Gould (1981); Leps (1992); Mannheim (1972); Nye (1976); Pick (1989); Regener (2003); Rock (1994). Again, this list is not intended as a full and definitive bibliography but merely as an indication of available sources.

Moral Insanity

Throughout the century, psychiatrists with an interest in crime tried to explain why some offenders seemed undeterrable and particularly vicious. Time and again, these psychiatrists returned to the puzzle of people who committed crimes repeatedly, sometimes obsessively, no matter how much punishment or treatment they received. Such people, they found, tend to commit crimes that are gruesome and pitiless, thus demonstrating an inability to identify with their victims. Criminology began with efforts to scientifically understand this sort of offender.

Theorists used different terms to identify the condition that caused repeat, apparently uncontrollable, offending: moral derangement, moral insanity (the most popular label), mania without delirium, degeneration, moral imbecility, incorrigibility, inborn criminality, hereditary unfitness. But although the labels differed, the goal was the same: to explain the actions of morally insane offenders. Theorists concluded that moral insanity was a state or condition, not a set of behaviours. This was a significant innovation for, previously, crime had been understood as behaviour and punished as such. Cesare Beccaria and other members of the eighteenth century classical school of criminology had been concerned only with criminal acts, not with criminality. But nineteenth century theorists who grappled with repeat, remorseless behaviour conceived its cause as an innate condition, that of being morally insane (or degenerate, or incorrigible, and so on). Those in this state (they reasoned) must lack the moral sense, a faculty or ability present in law-abiding people; or at least their moral sense must be in a state of decay, causing them to devolve or go backward down the evolutionary ladder. It seemed clear that the problem lay in offenders' brains; moral insanity was a biological condition, not a social problem (Rafter 2008).

The theme of moral insanity shaped another preoccupation of nineteenth century criminology: the habitual offender. Repeat offenders had been recognized in earlier periods, but they had been regarded more as annoyances than as a special type of offender, and certainly not as a special breed with suspect biology, as habitual offenders became in the work of mid- and late-nineteenth century commentators such as Lombroso (2006) and Thomson (1870). Ideas about moral insanity flowed into explanations of habitual offenders as incorrigibles, even born criminals. Criminal justice officials, frustrated by their inability to detect habitual offenders who changed names or residences, were keenly interested in better methods of identification. These they found, first in Alphonse Bertillon's method of measuring and photographing offenders (1896) and later in fingerprinting (Galton, 1892).

Suspicion that some of the worst offenders might actually be morally insane, and thus not criminally responsible, ignited an acrimonious debate over the nature of insanity and proper use of the insanity defence. On one side were the psychiatrists who argued that moral insanity, even though it did not involve hallucinations and complete loss of contact with reality, was really a mental illness whose victims should be spared from the most severe punishments. Opposing them were other psychiatrists and legal theorists who argued that men and women who were putatively morally insane were actually normal in all respects but one—their criminal tendencies—and thus not insane at all. Those on the first side tended to accept scientific determinism, their foes to endorse free will. And proponents of moral insanity endorsed the idea, increasingly important as the century wore on, of crime as an illness. In their view, the criminal is not corrupt but sick. 'Deprived of the sense of duty and of free will,' wrote the French psychologist Prosper Despine (1868: 541), 'the criminal... decides his course of action only in accordance to his strongest desires, desires that are involuntary manifestations of the depraved instincts with which he was born'. Despine's view was almost universally shared by proponents of the moral insanity explanation of serious, repeat offending.

Evolution

Criminology was inevitably shaped by the most disturbing idea of the nineteenth century, the theory that organisms change biologically through the generations. Evolution was not a concept that Darwin pulled out of a hat in 1859, when he published *The Origin of Species*. Decades earlier, educated people had become aware that dinosaur bones and rock strata contradicted the Biblical story of God creating everything, unchangeably, in a single moment, and they had started to come to terms with evolution's implications. The criminological result was the theory of degeneration, according to which some people evolve while others devolve or go backward toward a condition of lesser complexity and savagery (Pick 1989; also see Hodgen 1964: chapter 7). Darwin's work reinforced (or seemed to reinforce, for it was often misunderstood) such speculation.

Degeneration theory, built on the assumption that acquired characteristics such as a tendency toward alcoholism or thievishness could become ingrained and inherited, grouped criminals with paupers, the insane, idiots, and other degenerates. At first, proponents such as Dugdale (1877) believed degeneration to be a reversible and perhaps even curable condition: by avoiding alcohol, working assiduously, and generally living upright lives, criminals could acquire new and better characteristics and eradicate the old; and although the process of acquiring new traits might take several generations, at least their descendants would not grow up to face the gallows. But as the century wore on and crime and pauperism proved to be intractable problems, theorists became more pessimistic; they replaced their original 'soft' determinism with a 'harder' hereditarianism, according to which criminality and other social problems were fixed in degenerates' germ plasm. 'Of the true thief,' explained the English psychiatrist Henry Maudsley (1874: 31), 'as of the true poet it may truly be said that he is born, not made.'

Pivotal was Richard Dugdale's *'Jukes'* study (1877). Himself a 'soft' hereditarian (at least most of the time), Dugdale proposed environmental changes such as better education to improve the family lines of criminals and paupers. However, his readers took '*The Jukes*,' with its foldout genealogical charts showing the flow of degeneration through the generations, as proof positive of the 'hard' hereditarian position. Obviously, they concluded, it is foolish to attempt to rescue an unfit family such as the Jukes, and much better to stop its members from reproducing. Dugdale's study inspired the first American eugenics programme (Rafter 1992).

Like other members of the educated classes, most nineteenth century criminologists accepted the tenets of so-called scientific racism, according to which whites are the best evolved of all the races. Scientific racism often became part of evolutionary explanations of criminal behaviour: the worst offenders are like savages, closer to Hottentots and other black-skinned primitives than to normal white people, with their well-evolved moral sense (eg, Lombroso 2006). In this case as in that of degeneration theory, explanations based on ideas about evolution pointed to a biological problem: criminals' brains must be more primitive than those of well-evolved whites. Far from being common sinners, as riddled with original sin as anyone else, criminals were now Gothic monsters, strangers among the civilized (Hurley 1996; Rafter and Ystehede 2010). This change was one result of criminologists' efforts to come to terms with evolutionary theory.

Crime as a Social Phenomenon

While some criminologists endorsed a racist eugenics, vilifying the criminal's body, others concentrated on studying crime as a social phenomenon. A central task was identifying key variables. Among the first variables to be examined were age and sex (for examples, see Carpenter (1857) and Lieber (1833)). Another, perhaps oddly, was weather—a variable whose relationship to crime fascinated nineteenth century criminologists. Yet another was social class—the theme of the great nineteenth century investigations of the underworld. Rapid population growth and industrialization had distended cities with vast numbers of the poor, living in conditions of appalling squalor. The journalist Henry Mayhew was one of the first to investigate the dimensions of the social class variable. 'In the first portion of *London Labour and the London Poor*', read an advertisement for Mayhew's monumental mid-century investigation,

> the respectable portion of the world were for the first time made acquainted with the habits and pursuits of many thousands of their fellow-creatures, who daily earn an honest livelihood in the midst of destitution, and exhibit a firmness and heroism in pursuing 'their daily round and common task' worthy of the highest commendation. Yet these had long been regarded as the dangerous classes, as men and women who were little higher than Hottentots in the scale of civilization! The publication of Mr. Mayhew's investigations, illustrated by the recitals of the people themselves, for the first time led to a knowledge of the poorer world of London, of which the upper classes knew comparatively nothing [in Mayhew and Binny 1862: iii].

In his follow-up volume, *The Prisons of London,* Mayhew turned his attention to those who 'are in reality the dangerous classes, the idle, the profligate, and the criminal', exposing their social relationships with the great city that bred them (Mayhew and Binny 1862). Urbanization now joined other factors as an important social variable. Some investigators visited the city, as Edward Crapsey (1872) did the 'nether side' of New York; others lived in it, as Friedrich Engels (1845) did in Manchester, but they were all interested in understanding the interrelated effects of social class and urbanization.

The century ended with a burst of sociological theorizing. Gabriel Tarde (1912/1968), the distinguished French jurist and sociologist, was unpersuaded by criminal anthropology and instead sought to discover the 'laws of crime...in a special application of the general laws which appear to us to govern social science' (p. 321). The general law from which he derived his criminology was that of imitation, the human tendency to copy the behaviour of others. (To identify which others were most imitated and to explain why were among the tasks Tarde assigned himself.) Although Tarde's specific theory has not stood up, his more general repudiation of biological explanations was influential, as was his insistence that crime is part of social life. Émile Durkheim, another French sociologist, took this reasoning a step further, boldly concluding that crime is not something we should hope to eradicate but rather 'normal because a society lacking it would be completely impossible'. Indeed, crime 'is a factor in public health, an integral part of all healthy societies' (Durkheim, 1895/1960: 66). In the 1890s Edward Alsworth Ross, the well-regarded American sociologist, introduced the concept of social control (Ross 1901); his analysis of the containment of deviance, while not particularly successful in its own right, provided a conceptual tool useful to later sociologists—who conceived of deviance and control as two sides of one coin—and to historians of social control systems. Also at the century's end, the American sociologist W. E. B. DuBois (1899) showed the world how to analyse race sociologically.

As criminologists worked to understand the social nature of crime, they developed statistical tools, the first of which were ongoing, national censuses of criminals. They had to decide what to count, how to count it, and how often to count it. They also had to decide what to do with census information. France was the first nation to organize such a census and address these issues, as it did under the direction of Andre-Michel Guerry, a lawyer turned statistician. Guerry's work (1833) was almost immediately seconded by that of Adolphe Quetelet (1835), who argued that since crime statistics fluctuate only slightly from year to year, crime must exist apart from the individual offender and be in some sense embodied in society itself. The implications of the series of crime statistics were profound and complex, affecting not only criminological theory but also politics and jurisprudence, as Tarde observed in his book *La Criminalité comparée* (1890: v-vi):

Everywhere, in France and abroad, notably in Italy, matters of crime and punishment are all the rage. An unarguable need for reforms is felt here, provoked not only by the outburst of crime but by increasingly clear awareness of the nature and causes of this evil thanks to progress in statistics. This entirely new source of information, which habituates the contemporary public to seeing social facts in huge bulk, no longer confused and dubious like earlier generalizations about crime but precise and exact in every detail, leads to the view that all social questions are matters of governance.... The criminologist [*criminaliste*] can no longer be simply a jurist, exclusively concerned with the sacred rights of the individual...; it is necessary to be a statistical philosopher, concerned above all with the general interest.

With the advent of crime statistics, neither the individual judge nor the statesman nor the general public could avoid viewing crime as a social matter.

What was Criminology, and What will it Be?

If criminology's originators had been asked '*What is criminology*?' they would not have understood the question, for they worked as anthropologists, or prison reformers, or psychiatrists, or statisticians, and they had never heard of 'criminology'. Many of them were freelancers, and even those who worked for the state—British prison physicians, French statisticians, Italian professors, US census-takers—had not been directed by their governments to discover the causes of crime. They simply thought they could do it. They were curious.

Over the nineteenth century, their projects broadened—from understanding the morally insane, for example, to explaining all offending; and as fears of the so-called dangerous classes grew, their work attracted more attention and funding. In retrospect, it seems clear that nineteenth century criminologists developed national identities—the British, medical and penological; the French, sociological and liberal; the Italians, anthropological and control-oriented; the Americans, perhaps eugenical—but much more research is needed to give a clear picture of national differences. Specialized journals such as those founded by Lombroso and Lacassagne intensified those national differences but, paradoxically, they also helped unify the fledgling field by bringing its subject-matter in being. If today the specialization of journals fragments criminology, dividing it into ever narrow sub-specialities, the opposite was true in the nineteenth century, when the few specialized journals produced the first literature for a field that as yet had little substance and few reference points.

What challenges does criminology face in the years ahead? One, certainly, is the challenge of writing its own history. We already have bits and pieces of that history—excellent work on the development of criminology in specific countries, on the work of specific criminologists, and on specific phenomena such as the congresses on criminal anthropology; but much more research is needed to fill the gaps on criminology's origins. We need more translations—for example, English translations of the work of Bénédict Auguste Morel (1857), the great degenerationist. We need histories of criminological statistics and biographies of key figures in the discipline's past such as Pauline Tarnowsky, the first female criminologist (see, for example, Tarnowsky 1899). We need studies of national variations in the reactions to criminal anthropology and research on the development of ideas about habitual offenders. Most of all, we need synthetic international overviews that can help us overcome our forgetfulness about criminology's past, especially about the pre-1900 period of which we are particularly ignorant.

References

Beccaria, C. (1764/1986), *On Crimes and Punishments*, with Notes and Introduction by David Young, Indianapolis: Hackett Publishing Company.

Bertillon, A. (1896), *Signaletic Instruction*, Chicago: The Werner Company.

Bursik, R. J. Jr. (2009), 'The Dead Sea Scrolls and Criminological Knowledge: 2008 Presidential Address to the American Society of Criminology', *Criminology*, 47, 1: 1–16.

Carpenter, M. (1857), 'On the Importance of Statistics to the Reformatory Movement, with returns from Female Reformatories, and Remarks on them', *Journal of the Statistical Society of London*, 20, 1: 33–40

Crapsey, E. (1872), *The Nether Side of New York; or, the Vice, Crime and Poverty of the Great Metropolis*, New York: Sheldon and Company,

Darwin, C. (1859), *The Origin of Species*, repr., London: Penguin, 1968.

Davie, N. (2005), *Tracing the Criminal: The Rise of Scientific Criminology in Britain, 1860–1918*, Oxford: Bardwell Press.

Despine, P. (1868), *Psychologie Naturelle: Étude sur les Facultés Intellectuelles et Morales*, Paris: F. Savy.

DuBois, W. E. B. (1899), *The Philadelphia Negro*, Philadelphia: University of Pennsylvania Press.

Dugdale, R. L. (1877), *'The Jukes': A Study in Crime, Pauperism, Disease, and Heredity; also Further Studies of Criminals*, New York: G. P. Putnam's Sons.

Durkheim, É. (1895/1960), *Les Règles de la Méthode Sociologique*, repr. Paris: Presses Universitaires de France.

Ellis, H. (1890), *The Criminal*, London: Walter Scott.

Engels, F. (1845/1993), *The Condition of the Working Class in England*, D. McLellan (ed.), Oxford: Oxford University Press.

Ferri, E. (1898), *Criminal Sociology*, New York: D. Appleton and Company.

Fletcher, J. (1849), 'Moral and Educational Statistics of England and Wales', *Journal of the Statistical Society of London*, 12, 2: 151–76.

Gall, F. J. (1835), *On the Functions of the Brain and of Each of Its Parts*, 6 vols, W. Lewis, Jr. (trans.), Boston: Marsh, Capen, and Lynn.

Galton, F. (1892), *Finger Prints*, London: MacMillan.

Garland, D. (1985), 'British Criminology before 1935', *The British Journal of Criminology*, 28, 2: 1–17.

_____. (1994), 'Of Crimes and Criminals: The Development of Criminology in Britain', in M. Maguire, R. Morgan, and R. Reiner (eds), *The Oxford Handbook of Criminology*, Oxford: Clarendon Press.

Guerry, A-M. (1833), *Essai sur la Statistique Morale de la France*, Paris: Chez Crochard.

Hurley, K. (1996), *The Gothic Body: Sexuality, Materialism, and Degeneration at the fin de siècle*, Cambridge: Cambridge University Press.

Kaluszynski, M. (2006), 'The International Congresses of Criminal Anthropology: Shaping the French and International Criminological Movement, 1886–1914', in P. Becker and R. Wetzell (eds), *Criminals and their Scientists: The History of Criminology in International Perspective*, Cambridge: Cambridge University Press.

Lieber, F. (1833/1970), 'Preface and Introduction of the Translator', in G. de Beaumont and A. de Tocqueville (eds), *On the Penitentiary System in the United States and its Application in* France, repr., New York: Augustus M. Kelley.

Lombroso, C. (1876), *L'uomo delinquente studiato in rapporto alla antropologia, alla medicina legale ed alle discipline carcerarie*, Milan: Hoepli.

_____ (2004), *Criminal Woman, the Prostitute, and the Normal Woman*, Durham, NC: Duke University Press.

_____ (2006), *Criminal Man*, Durham: Duke University Press.

MacDonald, A. (1893), *Criminology*, New York: Funk & Wagnalls.

Maudsley, H. (1874), *Responsibility in Mental* Disease, London: Henry S. King and Co.

Mayhew, H., and Binny, J. (1862), *The Criminal Prisons of London and Scenes of Prison Life*, London: Griffin, Bohn, and Company.

Morel, B-A. (1857), *Traité des Dégénérescences Physiques, Intellectuelles et Morales de l'Espèce Humaine*, Paris: J. B. Baillière.

Pick, D. (1989), *Faces of Degeneration: A European Disorder, c. 1848– c. 1919*, Cambridge: Cambridge University Press.

Quetelet, A. (1835), *Sur L'Homme et le Développement de ses Facultés*, vol. 2, Paris: Bachlier.

Rafter, N. H. (1992), 'Claims-Making and Socio-Cultural Context in the first U. S. Eugenics Campaign', *Social Problems*, 39: 17–34.

_____ (1997), *Creating Born Criminals*, Urbana: University of Illinois Press.

_____ (2007), 'Crime, Film and Criminology: Recent Sex-Crime Movies', *Theoretical Criminology*, 11, 3: 403–20.

_____ (2008), *The Criminal Brain: Understanding Biological Theories of Crime*, New York: New York University Press.

_____ (ed.) (2009), *Origins of Criminology: Readings from the Nineteenth-Century*, Abingdon: Routledge/Cavendish.

_____ and Ystehede, P. (2010), 'Here be Dragons: Lombroso, the Gothic, and Social Control', in M. Deflem (ed.), *Popular Culture, Crime, and Social Control*, Emerald/JAI Press.

Ricoeur, P. (2004), *Memory, History, Forgetting*, Chicago: University of Chicago Press.

Rosenau, P. M. (1992), *Post-Modernism and the Social Sciences*, Princeton: Princeton University Press.

Ross, E. A. (1901), *Social Control: A Survey of the Foundations of Order*, New York: Macmillan.

Rush, B. (1786/1815), 'An Inquiry into the Influence of Physical Causes upon the Moral Faculty, Oration before the American Philosophical Society in Philadelphia, February 27, 1786', in B. Rush (ed.), *Medical Inquiries and Observations*, 4th edn., Vol. 1. Philadelphia: M. Corey.

Savelsberg, J. J., and Sampson, R. J. (2002), 'Introduction: Mutual Engagement: Criminology and Sociology?', *Crime, Law and Social Change*, 37: 99–105.

Shepard, E. M. (1884), The Work of a Social Teacher. Being a Memorial of Richard L. Dugdale', *Economic Tracts* XII: 1–14, New York: Society for Political Education.

Spurzheim, J. G. (1834), *Phrenology, in Connexion with the Study of Physiognomy*, Boston: Marsh, Capen and Lyon.

Tarde, G. (1890), *La Criminalité* Comparée, Paris: Ballière et Félix Alcan.

_____. (1912/1968), *Penal Philosophy*, repr. Montclair: Patterson Smith.

Thomson, J. B. (1870), 'Psychology of Criminals', *Journal of Mental Science*, 16: 321–50.

von Krafft-Ebing, R. (1886/ 1892), *Psychopathia Sexualis*, Philadelphia and London: The F. A. David Co.

Wines, F. H. (1888/2009), 'Introductory remarks, Report on the Defective, Dependent, and Delinquent Classes of the Population of the United States, as returned at the Tenth Census (June 1, 1880)' in N. Rafter (ed.), *The Origins of Criminology: A Reader*, Abington: Routledge.

Zerubavel, E. (2003), *Time Maps: Collective Memory and the Social Shape of the Past*, Chicago: University of Chicago Press.

10

HAVE I GOT NEWS FOR YOU? MEDIA, RESEARCH, & POPULAR AUDIENCES

LINDA G. MILLS

In this era of pundits and specialists, presidents on talk shows and prime ministers on television, comedians reporting the news, and newscasters using valuable air-time to feud with their rivals—all for the purpose of influencing popular opinion or the course of a policy debate—even the study of criminal behaviour benefits from the publicity generated by a newsworthy story. The interface of scholarship and the web, and the breakdown of traditional news hierarchies both multiplies the sites of possible publicity for criminology, and provides new opportunities and media for dissemination and for the potential impact on the course of policy-making in relation to the study of crime. In speaking on behalf of those criminologists whose work influences politics or politicians, we should all recognize that this is a new era for engaging the media. To answer the question: what is criminology and criminological research, we must include some notion of the relevance of our work to a broader audience and how that work can be disseminated in this new technological age.[1]

The first impact of the multiplicity of media and the proliferation of zones of influence is the scope of the pundit's visibility.[2] Experts multiply, academic celebrity becomes currency, and at the same time, the skills necessary for the transmission of expertise—qualification—become a matter of acclamation, audience approval, and ratings, which are not necessarily equivalent.[3] Think of the role of US Secretary of State, Colin Powell, in presenting the case for the Iraq invasion to the United Nations (King and Ensor 2003). His legitimacy was in the form of satellite photos of indistinct purported mobile chemical weapons sites, and his rhetorical trump card was a tiny vial of what might have been anthrax (CNN.com 2003). His position and notoriety were his qualification. Consider the impact of former President Bill Clinton on the release of a journalist in Korea (Kessler 2009), former Vice-President Al Gore on climate change (Msnbc.com 2007), or Brad Pitt, Angelina Jolie, Madonna, Sir Bob Geldof and George Clooney (to name a few) wielding the might of stardom to 'change the world'.

Similarly, the news media, twenty-four hours, seven days a week, both feed off celebrity and become celebrated themselves. President Obama brought his health care message to the people by appearing on five talk shows in one day (Stanley 2009). On the flipside, Jon Stewart, host of a late night satirical news half hour in the United States, interviews politicians for a young electorate who would otherwise get no news at all (Associated Press 2004). Political careers are made and broken on the comedy shows these days and numerous leaders around the world monitor such programmes as the Daily Show, the Colbert Report, the Tonight Show and David Letterman, for their own ratings and for the latest cultural trends (Kurtz 2004). Certainly in the United States, but also in the United Kingdom, we have come to depend on experts who tell us 'what's really going on'; but the experts transpire, all too often, to be entertainers.[4]

[1] The National Science Foundation in the United States is but one example of a research funding agency that now requires grant applicants to describe the 'broader impact' of their research, which is becoming increasingly more important. See, for example, 'NSF Strategic Plan for FY 2006–2011: Investing in America's Future' (NSF 06-48). For a UK example, see 'The Research Excellence Framework: Second Consultation on the Assessment and Funding of Research, Higher Education Funding Council for England' which provides that research will be judged according to its 'impact'. 'Significant additional recognition will be given where researchers build on excellent research to deliver demonstrable benefits to the economy, society, public policy, culture and quality of life'. Available at: <www.hefce.ac.uk/Pubs/HEFCE/2009/09_38/> (accessed 27 February 2010).

[2] This was first studied in relation to television, most famously by Bourdieu (1988) and by Régis Debray (1981, 2000) in a series of books on mediology and academia. On the conflict between 'charismatic authority' and academic judgment, see Post (2009); and for a position that deplores academic forays into public sphere *tout court*, see Fish (2008).

[3] For a recent empirical study of academic judgment and the (failing) attempt to separate evaluation from impact and visibility, see Lamont (2009).

[4] For a UK example, consider the long-running *Have I Got News for You?*, described as a 'comedy quiz show that grills celebrity contestants on the week's top stories and news'.

All this suggests, as scholars of popular culture have long asserted, that things have also changed for researchers and academics, especially for those whose work is designed to influence important policy issues or debates. For example, my own work in domestic violence, which focuses, at least in part, on the overall effectiveness of treatment options for abusive partners, is, frankly, *only* relevant *if* my findings have such an impact. I will argue that it is not only a matter of how intelligent someone is or whether they have studied an issue, but now it is increasingly a question of whether researchers have the ingenuity necessary to proselytize and place their work on the relevant shows. The importance of a scholar's findings or messages is as likely to turn on an ability to court publicity and embrace the culture of the news cycle as it is to rely on the legitimacy of the academic work.[5] We are likely to feel persuaded by the media-based specialists employing these principal techniques if they are skilled in presenting plausible narratives in accessible forms and if their sound bite-friendly stories appear to be authentic and compelling.[6]

The popularization of research findings in the form of newsworthy narratives, in contrast, say, to presenting a scientific theory or finding at a conference or poster session, is perhaps most pronounced when it comes to the issue of crime. This may be in part due to the fact that of the top ten most popular television shows in the United States, four of them involve the investigation of crimes, the workings of the criminal justice system, or are otherwise related to understanding the criminal mind (*NCIS, The Mentalist, CSI, NCIS: Los Angeles*) (USA Today 2009). The third and fourth most downloaded television shows around the world are *24* and *Prison Break* (Guardian. co.uk 2009). These realities do not even begin to capture the popularity of the genre of crime to a populace: think of the centrality of *Law and Order* or its spin-offs, including *CSI*, in how we have come to think of victims and perpetrators of crime. This is not just an American phenomenon. *Law and Order* has been syndicated around the world, is revered by audiences far and wide, and has largely been viewed by the public as a vehicle for the popularization of victims' rights (Podlas 2008).

My personal experience with the popular media suggests that they seek not only an articulate and witty presenter, but someone who has a newsworthy and marketable storyline.[7] These stories need to be told in terms familiar to the programme's viewers and by someone cognizant of the celebrity status of the host. What, for

[5] See Bourdieu (1998) for the argument that this reduces the academic to the laws of market and commodity; and Lecourt (2001) for an acute account of the retraction of scholars from the public sphere. On the other side, Wark (2004) suggests the possibilities and potentials of web based knowledge and dissemination.

[6] New media offer new forms of rhetoric and law, with visual advocacy becoming increasingly important both theoretically and practically. For an overview, see Feigenson and Speisel (2009). For a discussion of the intersection of law and film, see Sherwin (2009). On the shifting boundaries between text, film and law, see also Goodrich (2009).

[7] I have prepared for and appeared on shows such as *Good Morning America*, *Oprah* and *The O'Reilly Factor*, to name a few; I have been featured in such popular publications as the *New York Times Magazine*, and quoted in *People, Glamour, Harpers and Queen* and *Cosmopolitan*. I have blogged for

example, does Oprah Winfrey want her audience to hear? When Bill O'Reilly seeks a five-minute interview, what is his angle? Invariably, it is a dramatic story, a surprising fact, a compelling theory. The question this essay addresses is: how do scholars generate these stories and what possibilities and pitfalls are presented to researchers who choose to develop such narratives?

In my own research, I often find myself moving between the social scientific data and the biographical, moral and institutional stories that lie behind them; I am both the popular commentator and a traditional researcher. As I have come to learn, for research to be directly relevant to lay audiences, it must be accessible, topically relayed and entertaining. Newsworthy narratives make the research visible, media currency and potentially a part of public and policy discourse.

Given my research interests, it was never a question of *whether* I would tell stories, but rather which stories I would tell. Trained as a lawyer and a critic, my viewpoint often ran contrary to myths that were promoted by advocates telling 'stories'. I often feel a moral and scientific responsibility to tell a counter-story. So too, all the popular shows on which I have appeared have wanted a 'good story'.

Not everyone thinks that the propensity of popular culture to rely on sound bites and stories in this new media age is a good thing. The prolific and prolix judge, Richard Posner, scion of conservative legal scholarship and populist public intellectual, has argued that the quest for publicity has turned respectable contemporary intellectuals such as Elaine Scarry, Ronald Dworkin and even Akhil Amar into errant pundits.[8] The search for the newsworthy narrative, the shocking fact, or the effective soundbite has placed the desiderata of extended airtime in advance of scholarly protocols and disciplinary boundaries. There is, Posner suggests, a law of diminishing returns: the likely veracity of the scholar expert's public statements are in inverse ratio to their degree of publicity.[9]

On this score, I challenge Posner's monolithic and somewhat disingenuous antagonism to the new media and its role in the transmission of intellectual opinions and

Psychology Today. Each of my interactions with producers or reporters reinforces my sense of their desire for research defined by its audience impact.

[8] Elaine Scarry wrote several articles on her theory of the electro-magnetic causes of celebrated airplane crashes and is duly noted (Posner 2001: 92) as an instance of punditry unsupported by disciplinary competence—she is a Professor of English. Ronald Dworkin is pilloried for being a signatory to an advertisement published in the *New York Times* on 10 November 2000 asserting that 'there is good reason to believe that Vice-President Gore has been elected President by a clear constitutional majority of the popular vote and the Electoral College'. The advertisement was also signed by Robert DeNiro, Bianca Jagger, Paul Newman and Joanne Woodward and so, for Posner, epitomized the conflation of the academic and the entertainment worlds (ibid.: 113–6). According to Posner, Akhil Amar was simply wrong on the role of the Supreme Court in *Bush v Gore* (ibid.: 39).

[9] Posner (2001: 77) writes, 'In the public-intellectual market there are no enforceable warranties or other legal sanctions for failing to deliver promised quality, no effective consumer intermediaries, few reputational sanctions, and, for academics at any rate, no sunk costs—they can abandon the public-intellectual market and have a safe landing as full-time academics.' He notes earlier: 'academics are not apolitical; would that they were. Rather, they are political naïfs, prigs about power' (ibid.: 75).

research outcomes by suggesting that we can have the best of both worlds.[10] I explore these popular opportunities through a particular aspect of the rhetoric of storytelling and its growing significance in criminology and in public and progressive advocacy work. I argue that, for good or ill, persuasion is frequently more important than argument or fact—topicality and an accurate sense of the audience will as likely persuade as strict adherence to the work of interviewing or theory development. We have to acknowledge that, whether we like it or not, facility with the media and skill in telling stories now have a significant place in the realm of science. Acknowledging this fact, however, comes with significant responsibilities, which I will try to illuminate in the realm of qualitative research and its impact.

Through three very different stories drawn from distinct intellectual projects, in what follows I will explore the reliability and ethics of storytelling as a means of popular dissemination of research, and then analyse the pitfalls and possibilities associated with the efforts taken by scholars to gather those stories. Here, I focus on both how qualitative research is gathered and the responsibilities that are involved in presenting it.

For one of the stories, I talk openly about the person I am describing; for the other two, I neither reveal their identities nor many of the specifics of the stories, given concerns for the confidentiality of the subjects. Still, I hope to convey the insights I learned from getting to know the subjects of these narratives in order to provoke debate on the methodologies of collecting such stories and their appeal to popular audiences.

Secrets

A few years ago, I was collecting stories for a piece I was writing on domestic violence when I was introduced to a subject I very much wanted to interview—I will call him Sean. I have deliberately concealed his name and the details of his life and work in order to protect his identity.

Sean was a fascinating man who had done remarkable work in the field of violence prevention. He had a stunning history of victimization in an intimate relationship, which he relayed to me in great detail. I was so taken by his story that I spent many hours on the phone with him learning about what he did, how he did his work, and how he had come to be so passionate about his commitment to others who were in violent situations. We would often be interrupted in our phone sessions when he would be called away to a crisis. We would arrange to talk a few hours later in order

[10] See also Goodrich (2003), arguing that the relation between scholarship and the media has to be understood in less immediate and more diffuse terms. Duxbury (2001) offers an intriguing dissection of the (not inconsiderable) influence of legal academics upon judges and judgment writing in three jurisdictions.

to finish our discussion, at which point I would hear afresh what the latest cases were that he was handling.

I was especially interested in the stories he would listen to—in this case, stories about violence, and how he handled the stress of the job. I was clearly compelled by his own story, what had motivated him to enter the field, and how his own life experiences had influenced him to do his work. He described in vivid detail how he had been deeply affected by violence and how that experience had motivated him to advocate on behalf of others. I had positioned him prominently in the piece I was writing and believed that his story was crucial to my argument.

As the piece was close to being published, I would talk to him regularly to check a fact or confirm a date. I would push him to recall with precision, both his own story and the stories of his clients, so that I could portray his character accurately, as well as the contours of his interactions. As I encouraged this truthfulness, I was reminded of the numerous headline-grabbing authors who had exaggerated their stories for a good read—the humiliation Oprah Winfrey felt when James Frey, author of *A Million Little Pieces,* was found to have lied about certain facts that he presented in his memoir of addiction and alcoholism. I was clearly doing something different. After all, I was a scholar and a social scientist and my stories could be relied upon.

When the piece went to the publisher, I was satisfied. I had done what all good qualitative researchers are trained and expected to do—I had verified my facts over and over again, and when I was unsure, or my subject equivocated, I had qualified them. I was enjoying the best of both worlds—storytelling and science—and the impact of combining these effects would be visible to fellow scholars and the public alike.

Imagine my surprise when I received an urgent email from Sean, just as the piece had been returned to me in 'proof'. He must talk to me, he said, 'it was important'. The only problem was that he had to travel for a week and could not talk to me until he returned. What did that mean, I wondered? 'Should I stop the presses?' I asked him via email. 'Maybe', he suggested. I did what any good researcher would do—I held the piece back.

When we finally connected a week later, he explained that although everything he had told me was true, he had omitted one important detail: he was a woman at the time that he had personally experienced violence. He had transitioned to being a man over the last several years, and because he had always thought of himself as a man (even when he was a woman) he had simply omitted this fact when he told me his story. The discovery that Sean was a transsexual changed everything. This was no longer a story about a man who had been abused by a woman. Rather, assuming that I was going to be factually accurate, this was a story of two women—one abusive toward the other. While a story of a lesbian couple's violence was obviously an important one, I was presented with two issues that needed to be addressed.

First, I was not telling a story about an abusive lesbian relationship. Rather, I was describing the phenomenon and dynamic of a woman who was abusing a man. More importantly, Sean did not want me to tell a story of lesbian violence. He insisted that because he had always felt like a man—even though he was biologically a woman at the time he had experienced the violence—it was not accurate to tell the story as one of violence between two women.

Perhaps it goes without saying, but I did not publish the story of Sean's relationship in any detail. No matter how much time I had invested in this story (in the end, it was over 40 hours of research and writing), I could not publish it in the way Sean hoped I would.

What lesson did I learn? I learned that there are limits to story-telling. Just as Oprah had to come to terms with the fact that James Frey had not quite told his readers the whole truth, I had to come to terms with the fact that despite my investment in Sean, he still had secrets to hide. Understanding what makes people exaggerate their stories for a good read, or in Sean's case to hide his identity as a transexual, is an important beginning point. Sean clearly had good reasons not to reveal his gender history. He feared repercussions if it was known that he was a transexual—his fears were certainly not unfounded. His anti-violence work was important to him and his community; taking the risk of exposure of his gender identity could forego everything he had worked so hard to achieve.

But what did that mean for either qualitative research in criminology or public storytelling or both? The reason we do quantitative research is because the law of numbers cancels out the risk of one person's lies. We rely on rigorous experimental designs with large populations to tell us what's really happening if and when we make our discoveries. Does this mean that we should not gather or tell stories? Yes, at one level. But, at the level of policy change or influence over public opinion, we *have* to tell stories, make the scientific human, engage the audience, and document the real as it is encountered by its subjects. The lesson learned from Sean is that researchers should not become overly invested in their subjects. Doing so can blind one to simple and important aspects of the story and its context. But even so, our subjects can be charming—and it is difficult to maintain a distance as we come to know their stories in an intimate way. Although Sean decided ultimately to disclose (to me) his true gender identity, other subjects may not feel that same level of trust. The lure of Sean's story and the power of his experience engaged me as a researcher in precisely the manner and with all the excitement that I wanted for my audience as well.

Guilty on the Inside

Over many years of research in the field of domestic violence, I have come to know very well a woman named Brenda Aris. Brenda was convicted of second degree murder in Riverside, California after she shot her sleeping husband, Rick Aris, following a decade of unrelenting abuse. Brenda served nearly ten years in prison for this crime after having been given a sentence by a local judge of fifteen years to life. Governor Pete Wilson took pity on Brenda's story and commuted her sentence in 1993 (Mydans 1993). She was released from prison in 1997 (DeSantis 1997).

Brenda is famous not only because she received a commutation in her sentence from a Republican governor, but also because she was the subject of an important Court of Appeals case in California that overturned the law regarding the admissibility of battered woman's syndrome evidence.[11]

When I first met Brenda, my research on her case was wide-ranging and involved talking to everyone who had been touched by it. I wanted to understand exactly what had happened at her trial and why this abused woman had been given a life sentence. I was completely sympathetic to a story that seemed nothing short of outrageous—a woman was convicted of second degree murder by a judge who refused to consider certain facts or allow the jury to understand them. After I interviewed Brenda's defence attorney, I was more convinced than ever of Brenda's story, and especially outraged by the role the jury (and particularly the forewoman) had played in manipulating the outcome. I decided to interview Louise Biddle, the juror forewoman who was, in large part, responsible for Brenda's conviction.

Ms Biddle agreed to discuss the case with me and welcomed me into her home. She described her own experience of coming to know Brenda at trial, including the fact that she believed Brenda deserved a murder conviction, a long prison sentence, and more. Indeed, Louise would have convicted Brenda of first degree murder if she could have convinced the other jurors of such an outcome. What surprised me most was not that Louise told me that she herself had witnessed abuse as a child, that her fiancée had been murdered and the culprit never found, incidents that had obviously influenced her prejudicial view of Brenda. Rather, what was most surprising was that meeting Louise had the unexpected effect of influencing my assessment of Brenda's story and what she had done.[12]

As sympathetic as I was to Brenda, I began to view her relationship with her battering husband as more complicated than she had initially described it to me. It was not a simple abuse story: a horrible man abusing a weak woman, as Brenda had often come to tell it herself. It was a love story gone terribly wrong with Brenda returning time and time again to a man who was abusive towards her. And while Brenda was clearly not responsible for any of Rick's violence, there was still a dynamic in this relationship that needed to be acknowledged and in which Brenda had played a role.

[11] *The People of the State of California v Brenda Denise Aris*. 215 Cal. App 3d 1178; 1989. Brenda's case made legal history when the judge refused to allow an expert to testify at her trial regarding Brenda's actions on the night she killed Rick and the fact that they stemmed from years of abuse. Her appeal was particularly devastating because although the court ruled that in future cases, battered woman's syndrome evidence should be admitted in cases like Brenda's, in her own case, the appellate court did not believe it would have made a difference in the jury's verdict. See p. 1199. Brenda served eight more years in prison after the Court of Appeal's decision.

[12] This story is told in some detail in Mills (2003: 81–2; 2008: chapter 3).

My evolving view of Brenda and her relationship with Rick did not mean that I thought she deserved to spend her life in jail. She and I both agreed that a five-year sentence would have been fair given that she had shot and killed a sleeping man, a man she loved, the father of her children, and someone who had beaten her for many years. But we did disagree, at least to some extent, about how we viewed the events that led up to Rick's death.

While this became apparent a few years after I first met Brenda, it was most pronounced as I started to tell her story in ways that diverged from her view of what happened. This tension was particularly acute when I chose to publish my assessment that Rick may have had homosexual propensities (see Mills 2008: 54). After reviewing several police reports, I came to believe that Rick's behaviour toward women, including Brenda, may have been motivated by his own self-hatred and the difficulty he had coping with his conflicted sexual identity. Although I believe that Brenda could have ultimately lived with my assessment of her husband's sexual preference, it was especially difficult for one of her daughters, who did not believe my judgment to be true. Even if it was true, she did not want to see such an allegation (and the accompanying evidence) in print.

As scholars, we need to come to terms with the fact that when we insert ourselves into people's lives in these intimate ways and start to tell their stories, we can actually end up tearing their well-established narratives apart. It is important that we understand that before we start asking a lot of questions about someone's life story, that doing so can wreak havoc in unexpected ways. We need to prepare our subjects for these possibilities while still encouraging them to share their stories. While we need to describe the facts and analysis as we see them, we also have to be accountable to the people whose stories we seek and then tell. This is especially true in this era of media proliferation—through YouTube, the Internet, and email—stories are spread in myriad and unexpected ways. Since none of us can predict where our stories will end up, it is important that we be thoughtful about what we choose to release and how our interpretations can affect the lives of our subjects.

Thin Ice

Recently, my work has turned towards the Holocaust. Trauma and its effects has always been at the heart of my research, and so it is no surprise, given my mother's experience of flight from Nazi Austria when she was thirteen, that I would focus my research efforts in that direction. About three years ago, Peter Goodrich (my husband) and I began preparing for a film we were proposing to make about my mother's journey to the United States. The project started off quite innocently—the next generation's journey back to understand what happened when a family escaped the Nazis. We were especially interested in teaching our ten-year-old son about this history and what better way to do it than by gathering these accounts on film.

The project quickly became far-reaching when we came upon an archive in Vienna that had been discovered in 2000, in an abandoned building owned by the Jewish community (Backman 2007). Stashed away in that building were over a million records, documenting the complicated relationship that existed between the Jewish Community in Vienna during Nazi occupation and Adolf Eichmann, otherwise known as the 'Architect of the Holocaust'. What we learned from the historians who were reconstructing the history was that the leaders of the Jewish Community in Vienna during the Nazi era, had to strike a bargain with Eichmann, both for their own survival and the survival of the Austrian Jewish Community (Rabinovici 2011, forthcoming). From their vantage point, the Jewish Community in Vienna had no choice (Arendt 1963).[13]

I was immediately struck by the complexity of what we had discovered. Had the Jewish leaders collaborated with Adolf Eichmann to save Jews or only to save themselves? On balance, was their relationship a necessarily evil? Had their organizational efforts actually facilitated the deaths of Austrian Jews? We were faced with Hannah Arendt's controversial argument in her reports of the Eichmann trial that the Jewish Community leaders were collaborators (Arendt 1963). At the same time, it was hard not to concur with Doron Rabinovici's (2011, forthcoming) account of the history who had concluded that Vienna's Jewish Community leaders were 'powerless' to act in any other way. We also discovered the startling fact that of the 185,000 Jews who were living in Austria in 1938, 135,000 of them survived the war (Gilbert 1988: 2). These were good outcomes, comparatively speaking: it is estimated that 90 per cent of Polish Jews, for example, were killed between 1938 and 1945 (PolishJews.org 2000).

As we started to interview our star witnesses for the film—young historians and archivists who were reconstructing these records and the history of the Jews during the Holocaust—we discovered that they had their own family histories. With only 5,000 or so Jews in Vienna these days, it was not surprising that at least some of those who are responsible for preserving these wartime records and for administering the payment of reparations, have their own family relationships to Nazism. And while some of those we interviewed were quite insightful and even ashamed of their family connections to Nazis, others were very much uninterested in unearthing the role their ancestors may have played in the extermination of the Jews.

As a therapist, I felt that some of these Viennese and non-Jewish historians had not recognized—to the extent *I felt* was appropriate—their own familial links to a Nazi past. For me, it was important that they explore and understand their histories and how those histories brought them to this Jewish reconstruction work. I believed it was significant that we 'reconcile' as people with divergent and painful histories, for them as descendants of perpetrators, for me as victim, and that we seek answers

[13] This point lies at the heart of Arendt's controversial analysis. See also, *The Specialist: Portrait of a Modern Criminal*, 1999. [Film] Directed by Eyal Sivan. France: Amythos Productions.

to questions together: what does it mean to live with this family legacy? How does it differ when the legacy is of perpetrator as opposed to victim? Yet my new Austrian friends were not always attuned to what some may call a New York Jewish propensity for analysing their family histories. I was the Woody Allen in this story and they were perfectly happy noting their past and not examining it.

The dilemma became particularly acute when we were making directorial decisions about how to depict our Viennese colleagues. Would we emphasize their limited insight in order to highlight the fact that they seemed to be denying their histories? Doing so could have the effect of portraying them as latent Nazis, something I both did not want to do, but also knew was not true. These historians were (surprisingly) sympathetic to Jews (and Israel) today. If we did not depict the denial, however, were we being honest about what we thought was a crucial discovery? Plus, we had come to rely on these experts and to respect their scholarly work. We certainly did not want to undermine their credibility.

These questions plagued our work as we made our way through the editing process. In the end, it became important to present both sides—my Woody Allen-esque perspective, fascinated by family backgrounds—as well as their side, that their Nazi relatives were not them *per se*, and they were not responsible for the violence their relatives had inflicted on the generations that came before them. I took away from this experience the importance of telling many sides of a story. Whereas staying true to my perspective was important, (as in the Brenda Aris case example), it was also important to represent the subject's perspectives which is both of scientific value and a more complete story.

Research and Relationships, Accuracy, and Audiences

In summary I derive three important lessons from the stories I have shared. First, as in Sean's story, partial truths or incomplete facts are always going to be a necessary evil when gathering stories—social scientists who utilize stories must always keep this reality in mind and should never hesitate to remind audiences of the pitfalls of storytelling. Second, the story gatherer's projection and perspective cannot be untangled from how the story is ultimately presented. Scholars should be challenged to self-reflect candidly upon their own investments and their countertransferences as a first step towards doing good scholarship, but they should also never fail to diverge from a subject's version of events.[14] As in Brenda's story, having the capacity to discuss with the people we interview all the possible effects of storytelling, is crucial from an ethical point of view. Conversing in this way must be done before dissonances are discovered—a skill even the most experienced researchers must continue

[14] For an elaboration on the usefulness of self-examination, see Mills (1999: 576–586).

to develop. Third, and correlatively, one's desire to present an issue in sharp focus can sometimes become more important than the pursuit of context, history, and the needs of the subjects and relationships being analysed. Beware: sharp distinctions can manipulate the presentation of a topic that calls for greater (not lesser) nuance. As was evident when we made our film, entertainment involves conflict—it is compelling to pit expert against expert, one viewpoint against another. But such stark positions may not convey the subtleties and complexities of the story you should tell. Qualifiers and clarifiers should be readily employed to avoid Judge Posner's strictures while still allowing for the stories the new media seek.

For those scholars and researchers in criminology who want to have a greater influence over their audiences and the behaviour and policies that intersect with their work, I suggest that the burden on us as qualitative investigators is more significant than the meticulous quantitative researcher who counts each subject and categorizes every behaviour. While the lines on the ledger sheet are less clear, and the draw of the media far stronger, the benefits of such work are vitally important. We should tell the stories on news programs and talk shows, but never forget to qualify them. We should take it upon ourselves to educate audiences about the reliability of the findings of qualitative research while still remembering the power of storytelling. **Law and Order** makes a difference to people because they see themselves in those stories. As scholars with the stories of our subjects in hand, we too can make a difference. The possibilities, I would suggest, should be embraced, but not without recognizing the pitfalls.

References

Arendt, H. (1963), *Eichmann in Jerusalem*, New York: Penguin.

Associated Press (2004), 'And Now the News: For many Young Viewers, it's Jon Stewart', *Msnbc.com*, 4 March 2004 (<www.msnbc.msn.com/id/4400644>/, accessed 16 November 2009).

Backman, M. (2007), 'Vienna Cache is One of Largest Holocaust Archives', *New York Times* 4 June 2007 (<www.nytimes.com/2007/06/04/arts/04iht-archive.1.5987074.html>, accessed 16 November 2009).

Bourdieu, P. (1988), *Homo Academicus*, Cambridge: Polity.

_____ (1998), *Television*, New York: Free Press.

CNN.com (2003), 'Transcript of Powell's U.N. Presentation', *CNN.com*, 5 February 2003. (<www.cnn.com/2003/US/02/05/sprj.irq.powell.transcript.05/index.html>, accessed 16 November 2009).

Debray, R. (1981), *Teachers, Writers, Celebrities*, London: Verso.

_____ (2000), *Transmitting Culture*, New York: Columbia University Press.

DeSantis, J. (1997), 'Battered Wife Set Free: Woman Who Killed Abusive Husband Released From Prison', *Daily News*, 14 February 1997: 2.

Duxbury, N. (2001), *Jurists and Judges: A Study of Influence*, Oxford: Hart Publications.

Feigenson, N. and Speisel, C. (2009), *Law on Display: The Digital Transformation of Legal Persuasion and Judgment*, New York: New York University Press.

Fish, S. (2008), *Save the World on Your Own Time*, New York: Oxford University Press.

Gilbert, M. (1988), *Atlas of the Holocaust*, Oxford: Pergamon Press.

Goodrich, P. (2003), 'The Perspective Law of the Ego: Public Intellectuals and the Economy of Diffuse Returns', *Modern Law Review*, 66, 2: 294–307.

_____ (2009), 'Screening Law', *Law and Literature*, 21, 1: 1–23.

Guardian.co.uk. (2009), 'The Guidelines: A Torrent Indeed, *Guardian.co.uk*, 5 September 2009 (<www.guardian.co.uk/culture/2009/sep/05/downloaded-us-tv-shows-2009>, accessed 19 November 2009).

Kessler, G. (2009), 'N. Korea Releases U.S. Journalists: Pardon Issued After Bill Clinton Meets with Kim Jong Il', *The Washington Post*, 5 August 2009. (<www.washingtonpost.com/wp-dyn/content/article/2009/08/04/AR2009080400684.html>, accessed 16 November 2009).

King, J. and Ensor, D. (2003), 'Powell: Iraq Hiding Weapons, Aiding Terrorists', *CNN.com*, 6 February 2003. (<www.cnn.com/2003/US/02/05/sprj.irq.powell.un/index.html>, accessed 16 November 2009).

Kurtz, H. (2004), 'The Campaign of a Comedian: Jon Stewart's Fake Journalism Enjoys Real Political Impact', *Washington Post*, 23 October 2004, <www.washingtonpost.com/wp-dyn/articles/A55440-2004Oct22.html>, accessed 16 November 2009).

Lamont, M. (2009), *How Professors Think: Inside the Curious World of Academic Judgment*, New York: Oxford University Press.

Lecourt, D. (2001), *The Mediocracy: French Philosophy Since the Mid-1970's*, London: Verso.

Mills, L. G. (1999), 'Killing Her Softly: Intimate Abuse and the Violence of State Intervention', *Harvard Law Review*, 113, 2: 551–613.

_____ (2003), *Insult to Injury: Rethinking Our Response to Intimate Abuse*, Princeton: Princeton University Press.

_____ (2008), *Violent Partners: A Breakthrough Plan for Ending the Cycle of Abuse*, New York: Basic Books.

Msnbc.com (2007), 'Gore, U.N. Climate Panel win Nobel Peace Prize', *Msnbc.com*, 12 October 2007. (<www.msnbc.msn.com/id/21262661/>, accessed 16 November 2009).

Mydans, S. (1993), 'Clemency Plans Denied in 14 Abuse-Defense Cases', *The New York Times*, 30 May 1993: 121.

Podlas, K. (2008), 'Guilty on All Accounts: Law & Order's Impact on Public Perception of Law and Order', *Seton Hall Journal of Sports and Entertainment Law*, 18, 1: 1–40.

PolishJews.org. (2000), *Holocaust* (<www.polishjews.org/shoah/shoah4.htm>, accessed 16 November 2009).

Posner, R. (2001), *Public Intellectuals: A Study of Decline*, Cambridge, MA.: Harvard University Press.

Post, R. (2009), 'Debating Disciplines', *Critical Inquiry*, 35, 4: 749–72.

Rabinovici, D. (2011, forthcoming), *Eichmann's Jews: The Jewish Administration of Holocaust Vienna 1938–1945*, Polity Press, translating D. Rabinovici (2000), *Instanzen der Ohnmacht. Wien 1938–1945. Der Weg zum Judenrat*, Vienna: Jüdischer verlag.

Sherwin, R. (2009), 'Imagining Law as Film (Representation without Reference?)', in A. Sarat, M. Anderson, and C. O. Frank (eds), *Law and the Humanities. An Introduction*, New York: Cambridge University Press.

Stanley, A. (2009), 'For President, Five Programs, One Message', *New York Times Online*, 20 September 2009 (<www.nytimes.com/2009/09/21/us/politics/21watch.html>, accessed 16 November 2009).
USA Today (2009), 'Nielsen Ratings for week of Nov. 2', *USA Today*, November 2009 (<www.usatoday.com/life/television/news/nielsens-charts.htm>, accessed 16 November 2009).
Wark, M. (2004), *Hacker's Manifesto*, Cambridge, MA: Harvard University Press.

11

SORT CRIMES, NOT CRIMINALS

MARCUS FELSON

You never get clarity… as long as a word is used by twenty-five people in twenty-five different ways [Ezra Pound 1963].

Words are the daughters of earth; things are the sons of heaven [Samuel Johnson 1755].

Introduction

CRIMINOLOGY is the study of crime, including: its regularities and variations; how it is carried out and how it is avoided or thwarted; when it occurs and where; its precursors and consequences; its targets and modus operandi; how it is intertwined with other activities; and its diverse participants, including offenders, victims, police, bystanders, witnesses, and anybody else whose presence or absence affects crime occurrences or who are impacted by those occurrences. Criminology as a field succeeds best when it focuses on crime, not criminals. It does best building on tangible features of crime and worst when it seeks to predict and explain the criminal and non-criminal tendencies of individuals. It works best when modeling itself on the natural sciences and worst when modelling itself on the physical sciences. It does best when considering crime as a very local matter, and worst when exaggerating globalism at the expense of local events. It does best when studying symbioses among criminal and non-criminal activities, and worst when treating crime as an isolated set of behaviours. It does best studying crime within a larger set of human needs and tendencies, and worst when it views criminal needs and tendencies as unique or special. It does best with highly focused research and worst with research articles making massive claims. These problems can be remedied by refocusing on crime rather than criminals. In addition, using the life sciences rather than the physical sciences better enables us to think about and study crime. To do this, we need a clear mind about how to define crime.

It is easy to make a mess of crime definitions by mixing up two distinct questions: First, what crimes do people commit—before anything is done about it? Second, how does the justice system *act* after it decides a crime has occurred? The second question brings with it many more complexities: Whether a crime happened *this time;* whether *this person* did it; whether the accused are *treated* equally by the justice system; and how people in different places and times act or do nothing. This chapter seeks to answer *only* the first question—what crime is *before* something is done about it.

Each person who survives to age 30 spends 148,920 hours in the prime crime-prone ages, 13–29. Those hours are highly uneven in how they expose that person to challenge and risk, cooperation and conflict, temptation and repulsion, indifference and control. Those hours include moments in solitude, in small groups, and in crowds; with family, with close friends, with casual acquaintances, with total strangers, and with various mixes of acquaintanceship. It brings together people and things, or pushes them apart. For a million people there are almost 150 billion hours in young ages during which life ebbs and flows, sometimes producing crime opportunities.

On a subset of occasions, a person takes advantage of those crime opportunities. In a subset of those occasions, something or someone counteracts the offender's actions. In still fewer cases, official agencies respond to those offenders, defining and classifying them in the process. Classification serves an administrative purpose. It is also a central feature of science. Born in 1707, Linnaeus synthesized our knowledge of flora and fauna with a classification scheme alive and well today.[1] The Linnean system is very elaborate, but it also offers synthesis and simplicity, so one can learn about plants and animals in stages. Even though no one person knows all of it, naturalists all over the world can converse in the same scientific language using the same categories of life (see Slaughter 1982).

Classification and Science

The life sciences depend upon that classification, and an entire field of biology is devoted to its growth. That is not to say that naturalists agree on everything about

[1] For an account of the life and work of Linnaeus, the University of Uppsala maintains a website titled LinnéOnline, at <www.linnaeus.uu.se/online/index-en.html>.

classification, but they have a working consensus on enough of it to allow joint progress. That progress depends on a distinction between observation and classification. Observation is a first step upon which classification depends. But there are so many observations that keeping them in order becomes a problem. To assist their own minds, naturalists work very hard to sort information. That makes it easier for them to teach and to discuss.[2]

Classifications in biology have a *basis* in reality, but they are still *human conventions* to help people talk to one another about nature. Note well that *many important features of life are not part of the classification scheme, but are still part of science.* In other words, life scientists use only a part of their knowledge for sorting, while the rest of it they bring in later. They do this, not because the rest of knowledge is less important, but because not all knowledge is amenable to drawing lines and sorting distinct entities within a hierarchical scheme. Thus many variations in life transcend the categories of Linnaeus and his forbears, but those categories are still needed to keep botany and other fields from losing their way.

The substantive nature of a scientific topic has a great impact on how scholars sort things. The physical sciences often deal with building blocks that are exactly the same; electrons do not have personalities and do not seem to make their own decisions. Any variations in what they do follow laws of a deterministic sort. The life sciences differ fundamentally from the physical sciences because living things have individuality, at least to some extent, and because they tend to be more surprising than dead things. Such a claim does not deny that surprises occur in the physical world, or that rocks vary in size, and that they seem alive as they roll down the hill. (For a sample of discussions about free will, determinism, and science, see Machamer and Wolters (2007).) But in the end the life sciences deal with life, so we cannot study trees and orangutans in quite the same way we study pebbles.

Life scientists sometimes use mechanical laws, but in the end they must allow for variations among organisms within a single species, as well as inconsistent movements and actions by a single organism as it goes through life. No two amoebas are alike, and one amoeba does not move in exactly the same manner every moment of the day. This is not an argument for phenomenology, but rather for recognizing that scientific strategy will differ for the life sciences. Those strategies include devising a wider conceptual repertoire than the physical sciences use. Those strategies also include normative agreements among naturalists to help organize information.

Such strategies explain why naturalists form committees. They meet every year or so to decide how newly discovered species should be classified, and perhaps to reclassify some species based on new information. The classification process is partly science and partly human convention for human purposes. After the meeting, somebody probably leaves unhappy about something, and botanists will tell

[2] Alfred North Whitehead (1941) emphasized the marriage of factual information and general principle to produce modern science.

their graduate students why they do not agree with a given decision. But practical decisions enable the life sciences to make progress. The life sciences define millions of species and use them to organize information. They smooth out some of the individual variations within species for conceptual simplicity. They then sort species into kingdoms, phylums, families, etc. At the same time, of course, the concepts and categories of a vast number of life sciences look beyond these categories, considering how diverse species breathe and live. (For example, see work on plant taxonomy in Stuessy (2009).) This brings us to the definition of life.

Life has seven special attributes: organization, adaptation, metabolism, movement, growth, reproduction, and irritability. A pebble is not highly organized, does not adapt to its environment, has no short-term metabolism, cannot move about, does not grow in its life cycle, and cannot reproduce. If you poke a pebble, you cannot irritate it; it will not bite you. Even low level animals have these seven attributes. That is what makes them alive.

Humans, as the most advanced form of life, are especially likely to vary both between and within a single life. So it is bizarre to study people with simpler models and classifications than life science uses. Although humans are more complex than any other single species, humans are far less complex than the million other species together. By learning how to study and organize information about so many species, the life science offers important tools for studying people, including their criminal behaviour, and doing so without getting too lost.

Classification and Criminology

Criminologists do best to follow the life scientists, not the physical scientists, because crime has all the attributes of life. It involves organization, usually at a rudimentary level, but sometimes beyond that. It adapts to new opportunities and is affected by outside pressures. It has a daily metabolism, varying greatly by hour of day. (See Felson 2006.) It moves over space. It grows and recedes. It responds to reproduction and demographic processes, as youths reach crime-prone ages and age out. Specific provocations affect its occurrences. Crime is alive, and criminology must be too.

The role of genetics in the life sciences deserves some attention. On the one hand, genes are more important for classifying diverse species. The genetic differences between a paramecium and an elephant are dramatic, and the elephant did not learn to be so in school. On the other hand, many social sciences mistakenly believe that biology is a purely genetic field of inquiry. Genetics is only one of the topics in the life sciences. In particular, ecologists and naturalists spend a lot of time studying *non-genetic* interdependencies in the environment, and do so with greater sophistication than most social sciences. We can best learn how to conduct and organize non-genetic inquiry by watching life scientists do just that.

More than a century of criminological research and thinking has produced two general approaches to classification. The first approach is to classify persons by their relationship to crime. The second approach is to classify fairly large chunks of urban space by crime levels and by social variables thought to generate crime motivation. Both of these efforts have failed. The failures have been evident for at least sixty years, during which further progress has been nil. Yet we see little willingness to admit these failures and move on to a better approach. The ability to predict who will become an offender has made virtually no progress since Glueck and Glueck (1950). Offenders are too uneven. Those offending early usually stop. Those offending late usually offended early, but that is calculating backwards. Some predictive success is claimed when predicting crime from crime, but such forecast is not based on independent information. Failing to explain offender v non-offender, many criminologists sought to predict very serious offenders—a task less prone to failure, but still not successful. Others have shown that advanced drug abusers were once incipient drug abusers, hardly insightful. It may make sense for correctional departments to classify individuals under their supervision, but we cannot build a science on such classifications. It makes sense to classify someone as a violent offender if you have to pick what part of the prison to put them in. But most violent offenders commit mostly non-violent offences. And some classified as non-violent later engage in violence. You cannot build physics on electrons that change their mind about who they are.

At one point, the only real source of independent variables was census data for units of 50,000 persons. Discovery of the delinquency area was worthwhile and a part of the story. But subsequent work shows repeatedly that a high crime area includes very low crime blocks and corners, and that relatively few addresses or micro areas within these areas drive their crime rates up (see Eck and Weisburd 1995). Thus, crime location is much more precise. It makes no sense anymore to say that Brixton's general culture is criminal when Brixton's crime varies every 35 metres.

The attribution of crime to particular racial, ethnic, or economic groups should have died in 1943 when Austin Porterfield showed that his students at Southern Methodist University had committed roughly the same crimes as the local designated juvenile delinquents. This is not to deny local or human variations, but they appear to be a matter of degree. The difference between the tough and the genteel is that the tough start their misbehaviour younger and stay longer, and are better able to take over turf than the genteel. But middle class youths commit too many violations to justify a class- or race-based criminology.

Indeed, criminology must divorce itself from rigid classifications of people and city sections. To make progress, it is necessary to begin classifying crimes, not criminals; and studying crime in terms of very local areas, not entire 'social areas'. However, to get there one must first abandon the notion that crime-motivation is a special thing.

The first concept to abandon is 'expressive violence'. This confusing and vague idea allows us to link any frustration indirectly to crime. Indirectness is the bane of science because it gives us no specific mechanism and therefore is subject to intellectual and empirical legerdemain. To say that my having a bad life experience makes me violent in other settings really says almost nothing without offering specific mechanisms. To be sure, such mechanisms are sometimes offered (Berkowitz 1993), but these mechanisms are often confusing (see evaluation by Tedeschi and Felson 1994).

All violence is instrumental, even if it is not always wise or sensible in the long run. Offenders make decisions in the short run, often in a split second. As explained by Tedeschi and Felson (1994), those decisions have one of three purposes. First, an offender might seek to get somebody else to do what he wants, or to take something he wants. These offences are often easy to understand. Second, an offender might act to restore his self-image. Thus if you made me look bad, I might commit violence against you or slash your tyres, even if I get no money back. My crime made some sense at the time, even if I regret it after going to jail. Third, an offender sometimes wants to punish someone else for wrongdoing as he sees it, even if he is not personally the direct victim of the person he punishes. You weren't nice to that pretty lady, so I will punish you for what you did, because I think you deserve it. Offender instrumentalism goes beyond immediate gain in tangible goods, beyond tangible goals. The offender's thinking is always central to understanding crime.

Because individuals vary in how they think, variations and surprises are possible in the world of crime. Yet variations in self-control or other individual traits cannot be the fundamental source of a classification scheme. Those variations are a matter of degree, making any boundaries difficult to draw. Even though human classification schemes are always artificial to some extent, those schemes should have some basis for drawing clear lines most of the time. Moreover, each individual varies from hour to hour, day to day, month to month, and year to year. Thus we cannot divide the population the way we divide species in terms of criminal action.

Ultimately we must make criminal acts themselves the classifying basis. The most important classification is a dichotomy: is it a crime or is it not? We must define crime in order to define criminology, and in order to proceed with further classification.

Defining Crime

We are aware that every local jurisdiction defines crime by its local law and enforcement. Although Canada has one criminal code for the whole nation, the United States has fifty-two, one for each state, plus the District of Columbia, plus the federal system. In addition, each locality has certain criminal ordinances. It is easy to say therefore that crime is not definable. But naturalists have dealt with and solved

problems like this. We have no kangaroos roaming the United States, but American and Australian naturalists agree that kangaroos are mammals and have common species names. They can converse. Americans and Germans have different laws about prostitution, and jurisdictions vary internally in their enforcement, but this does not prevent us from finding common ground.

To study crime properly, we need to know its universal features. We need to find a general definition that applies in all countries and all places, and that takes natural history into account. If you give me a list of all human behaviours, I should be able to tell you which ones are crimes and which ones are not. I should do this in very few words, being very practical. Such a definition should not try to serve all purposes. It should not try to specify who is really guilty. Nor should it promise to count up every crime that real people do in real life.

I am looking beyond a *local* definition of crime, or one period of history. I am searching for a *natural history definition* of crime. Like the life sciences, extinct forms are still classified. A classification is cumulative over time—categories are added but usually not removed. Forms that appear on one continent but not another are still included. A definition of crime must consider both the behaviour of people and the behaviour of the justice system. Justice is a living process. Laws grow, meander, respond to stimuli, and stray from what is written. Not only do laws change names and coverage, but they vary from place to place. How, then, can we use earthly laws to define crime in a consistent fashion? Naturalists can help us think in terms of overall natural history, going beyond any one patch of land or moment in time. They have experience with definitions as devices assisting human comprehension. The challenge is to *use* information from diverse justice systems over history and over nations without allowing that information to produce disorder.

How can we make sense of crime when the criminal law has thousands of oddities and when laws on the books might never be enforced? To do so requires distinguishing *rare* crime from *odd* crime. Rare crime is criminalized in various societies, but seldom happens or is discovered. Odd crimes are not taken seriously by officials and might have to be excluded from the crime category. Naturalists handle these issues fairly well. A sheep born with three legs is not declared to be a new species. On the other hand, a rare species of bird can be defined if its members have some normalcy and generality, despite paucity.

A good naturalist has a local eye, but a comprehensive mind. A naturalist studies specifics without giving up generalities. Confronted with variation, a naturalist simply defines a larger category and then subdivides it. Thus 'mammal' is a universal category, but specific mammal species are not universal. Similarly, we have universal categories of crime, even though specifics differ among jurisdictions. A comprehensive definition of crime can take natural variations into account, too. It allows us to expand, divide, and link categories, as necessary.

Just as naturalists can code extinct dinosaurs, we can code extinct crimes, such as witchcraft. If naturalists can handle plant colourings that vary within a category, we can handle crime variants, too. If naturalists can code ugly species, we can include crimes defined by tyrants to reduce individual liberty, even if we disapprove of such laws. Thus *crime* can include behaviours that I personally think *should not* be banned, and *non-crime* can include behaviours I think *should* be banned. A scientist avoids mixing up what *is* and what *ought to be*. If you forget that, you will confuse yourself and everybody else. A comprehensive crime definition transcends natural variations, finds a common denominator among them, and allows observers to classify variants later—while excluding odd laws.

A natural history definition of crime takes into account formal law, citizen violations, and official responses to such violations. A crime is:

- any *identifiable behaviour* that
- an *appreciable number* of governments
- has *specifically prohibited* and
- formally punished.

This fifteen-word comprehensive definition of crime requires that a law must be stated and enforced some time in human history. Some part of a law must be written for it to help define crime. Thus prehistoric people had no crime in the formal sense. Yet a crime can exist if the law is *not entirely* written down, so long as the banned behaviour is specific and official.

I used the phrase 'appreciable number' for a reason. This threshold removes illegal acts that are quirks of a particular place, but have no general significance as crime. Thus if a single tribe in Borneo considers something illegal within its realm, that would not automatically be defined as crime in natural history terms. We can say for practical reasons that, to be a crime, a behaviour must have been banned by at least ten societies in history, and its violation must have been punished on at least fifty occasions in each of these societies. That eliminates the oddities. It also reminds us that human definition is a human process, helping scientists around the world and even in different ages to organize and share information in consistent fashion. The definition process must come to terms with *both* regularity and variation. To do so, oddities must be cut off and set aside, while variants are worshipped and organized. Doing so requires a practical rule distinguishing oddities from variants, and such a rule was just provided.

I have learned to appreciate the *Webster's Dictionary* definition of crime: 'an act or the commission of an act that is forbidden or the omission of a duty that is commanded by a public law and that makes the offender liable to punishment by that law'. The most important difference between the dictionary definition and the one offered here is my emphasis on accumulating historical experience. Moreover, I have excluded crimes of omission, which often are difficult to pinpoint in time and space, so they are antithetical to my tangible thinking. However, I do not ban taking these into account at a later date, so long as the definer can specify a specific time and place when an offender failed to perform required duties.

As stated at the outset, this chapter excludes from the definition process how the justice system *acts* after it decides a crime has occurred. This chapter seeks to define crime *before* something is done about it, disregarding whether and how society responds in any specific instance. So long as *some* offenders have been sanctioned some time in history for something they really did, we can define that action as crime. Crime considers behaviours prohibited by *formal governments.* It excludes most bad behaviours of everyday life—which are handled outside government and have little to do with criminal law. Of course, governments can prohibit a behaviour, yet act against it only occasionally. A crime by definition does not require the justice system to act every time. It requires that a specific behaviour, with an identifiable target of action, be formally prohibited (by an appreciable number of governments), that this prohibition be subsequently violated, then that the violator be formally sanctioned (in an appreciable number of cases).

Thus, crime's comprehensive definition includes past and present crimes, and leaves room for future crimes. At least for now, the list includes crimes that occur rarely (yet are not oddities), are found here but not there, then but not now, or now but not then. Like species, the list of crime types never shrinks, even with extinctions. The list grows longer as new criminal laws are enacted and acted upon; old legal codes are discovered along with evidence they were used; vague prohibitions are made specific, and enforced; or existing prohibitions are violated and sanctioned for the first time under criminal law. You now have a rule for deciding what is a crime.

You can usually designate a crime by asking a few questions. Did at least a few societies designate a specific behaviour to be criminal? Did somebody engage in that behaviour after it was banned? Did that society punish some offenders formally for their violations? If all three responses are positive, the behaviour is a crime by the natural history definition. If one of the answers is negative, the behaviour is excluded. This definition of a crime can incorporate the many variants of prostitution law or drug violations, even if not all variants are in force at all times and places. One then can study the many natural variations in crime just as naturalists study the distributions of rabbits, amphibians, or orchids.

Vague and ill-defined offences, such as unspecified 'disorderly conduct' or nonspecific 'loitering', cannot fit the comprehensive definition, even if they are listed as illegal in a particular jurisdiction. Only if police procedures, custom, or case law make such a prohibition reasonably clear and specific could it be added to the comprehensive list. So, too, a definition of crime must *never* include all or most human behaviour. The definition committee might need a new rule in the future about what strange laws to omit. But violations should not be removed simply because they are strange. If a silly law is widely used, it remains a part of natural history.

Our assignment is now simpler. We might not agree on what *should* be criminalized. But we can probably agree that a behaviour has often been *treated* criminally. Those from different nations can discuss prostitution as a crime—in terms of the natural history definition—then consider how their local variations in law affect the behaviour and its consequences. If an Australian and a British police officer read this chapter, each will have a different view of prostitution as a crime, in terms of their own laws. But *despite their national differences, they can agree totally that prostitution is a crime in terms of the inclusive historical definition.* This practical distinction allows us to find commonality in the face of variation.

We now have a comprehensive crime definition based on crime's natural history, taking into account governments as part of human behaviour. This definition also helps us to classify our general list of crimes further. A taxonomy is a living system, growing new limbs, expanding and adapting over decades and centuries. Since Linnaeus, naturalists have named, coded, and classified some 1.5 million types of living things. If Linnaeus returned to life today, he would recognize his taxonomy in broad terms; but naturalists could still give him a good briefing.

Classifying requires cooperating. It is not handed down from heaven, but rather represents a human effort to work together. A classification scheme does not use all of nature's details. Instead, it uses a *subset* of those details to help systematize the rest. To organize what we know and want to know about crime, we must decide what unit to classify. We cannot get very far classifying people. As several chapters have shown, offenders are highly inconsistent. For more than 100 years, offenders have defied the classifiers. To confuse the classifiers: 'violent offenders' commit mostly property offences. As I have shown elsewhere (Felson 2006), most offenders are generalists. 'Property offenders' suddenly do something violent. Non-offenders become offenders, and offenders become non-offenders. Thus a burglar today might be a shoplifter tomorrow or stay on the right side of the law for months at a time. Differentiating offenders *as people* is not a dependable enterprise. That is why a crime taxonomy needs to classify types of criminal *acts*, not criminals.

A Natural Taxonomy of Crime

The current definition of crime in tangible terms leads towards a taxonomy of crime types, independent of any single legal system. I have presented this taxonomy at great length elsewhere (Felson 2006), but its main organizing principle is that every criminal act has a physical story. An offender works his way towards a target, then acts upon it. That physical story provides an excellent tool for organizing a taxonomy of crime types that transcends the diverse legal systems among nations and eras. Wherever and whenever, an offender moves along a path toward that target—encountering barriers, sometimes overcoming them, often with the use of tools; at last converging with the crime target.

This very general physical story applies to a vast variety of specific crime types and makes possible a single taxonomy of crime. The paths that can be followed might be physical, organizational, or electronic, but they are paths nonetheless. We can use that information to classify crime. This general and natural taxonomy of crime can be used in many places and across multiple eras. It is based on tangible behaviour in the real world. The proposed taxonomy of crime builds on *crime's universal features*—as defined by the offender's motion towards the target (or object) of the crime.

Conclusion

Whether we are defining crime or classifying it, we do best to work with the physical world. Science at large long ago discovered that it must interpret phenomena in terms of and relationship to the physical world, and that it must use that world to help scientists themselves organize information so they can understand it and communicate. That world transcends legal systems and ages. Even though technology may change the transport, weapons, and crime targets over time, the physical world and physical problems remain. Even the electronic system of communication has paths, barriers, tools, and convergences. Even organizations have within them a variety of linkages and blockages.

By proceeding in this manner, we can make a list of all crimes in the natural history of humans during eras of formal government, allowing for variations among jurisdictions as part of natural history. Then we can classify those crimes by their socio-physical characteristics as offenders proceed towards their targets, without being burdened by jurisdictional differences in how crimes are classified. Perhaps our greatest challenge in definition and organization is to find a way to use our intellects, without letting our minds get lost in the woods. Crime's own physical requirements provide tangible landmarks so scholars keep in touch with crime itself and avoid losing sight of one another.

As Samuel Johnson noted, 'A blade of grass is always a blade of grass, whether in one country or another' (cited in Piozzi 2007). Our broad crime definition is not limited by local variations in law, by oddities of local law, or by who is the culprit, what the justice system does afterwards, or whether somebody was unjustly treated. Those are important issues, but should not confuse the task at hand—finding a comprehensive definition for crime that helps sort out which behaviours fit and which do not. This chapter offers a crime definition that can be put to work, and a tangible set of categories defined to be useful in many times and places. After all, definitions are human devices to help us make sense of nature, else why do we have them?

References

Berkowitz, L. (1993), *Aggression: Its Causes, Consequences, and Control*, Philadelphia: Temple University Press.

Eck, J. and Weisburd, D. (1995), 'Crime Places in Crime Theory', *Crime Prevention Studies*, 4: 1–33.

Felson, M. (2006), *Crime and Nature*, Thousand Oaks: Sage Publications.

Glueck, S. and Glueck E. (1950), *Unraveling Juvenile Delinquency*, New York: The Commonwealth Fund.

Johnson, S. (1755), 'Preface', *A Dictionary of the English Language*, online at Vassar College Library Special Collections, accessed 19 October 2005.

Kelloway, E. K., Barling, J., and Hurrell, J. J. (eds) (2006), *Handbook of Workplace Violence*, Thousand Oaks: Sage Publications.

Machamer, P. and Gereon W. (eds) (2007), *Thinking about Causes: From Greek Philosophy to Modern Physics*, Pittsburgh: University of Pittsburgh Press.

Piozzi, H. L. (2007), *Anecdotes of Samuel Johnson, 1741–1821*, Project Gutenberg (<http://infomotions.com/etexts/gutenberg/dirs/etext00/andsj10.htm>, accessed 9 May 2010).

Pound, E. (1963), 'Interview' in G. Plimpton (ed.), *Writers at Work*, New York: Viking Press (*The Paris Review Interviews*, 2nd edn).

Slaughter, M. M. (1983), *Universal Languages and Scientific Taxonomy in the Seventeenth Century*, Cambridge: Cambridge University Press.

Stuessy, T. F. (2009), *Plant taxonomy: The Systematic Evaluation of Comparative Data*, New York: Columbia University Press.

Tedeschi, J. T., Felson, M., and Richard, B. (1994), *Violence, Aggression, and Coercive Actions*, Washington: APA Books.

Whitehead, A. N. (1941), *Science and the Modern World*, New York: Macmillan.

12

STUDYING DESISTANCE FROM CRIME: WHERE QUANTITATIVE MEETS QUALITATIVE METHODS

RAYMOND PATERNOSTER AND SHAWN BUSHWAY

KARL Marx (Marx 1969: 387–8) once argued, sardonically, that one function of the criminal in society is that he helps keep criminology professors employed:

> A criminal produces crimes. If we take a closer look at the connection between this latter branch of production and society as a whole, we shall rid ourselves of many prejudices. The criminal produces not only crimes but also criminal law, and with this also the professor who gives lectures on criminal law and in addition to this the inevitable compendium in which this same professor throws his lectures onto the general market as 'commodities'.

We are not going to be nearly as sarcastic (nor, unfortunately, as insightful) as Marx was, but in our essay we would like to discuss what we think criminology is for, and how it might fruitfully be done. We will discuss these two issues within the substantive context of what we think is one of the most exciting areas of theorizing and research in the field today—the study of how once active criminals stop participating in crime. To us, the question, 'what is criminology for', is a relatively simple one to answer, and a very good place to start this essay.

The main thing (but not the only thing) that criminology does is to study the causes of crime and therefore *make causal inferences about crime*. Now, we are going to interpret this question so broadly that it would cover the study of conformity as well (the just-mentioned quitting of crime), as well as the study of reactions to crime (since police, court, or prison officials may cause crime to diminish or worsen). Few would dispute that many academic criminologists are interested in understanding the causes of crime. This study has become more conceptually complex in recent years as criminologists have carved out many different dimensions of crime. These dimensions include the initiation into or what is frequently called the 'onset' of crime, continuation or persistence in crime, criminal escalation (committing crimes that are more serious than before), criminal de-escalation (committing crimes that are less serious than before), criminal specialization or the lack of specialization (the 'generality' of crime), and even the study of not committing crime or the desistance from crime. In spite of these conceptual complexities, it remains true that the kind of academic criminologists alluded to by Marx are interested in understanding the causes of crime. We would also argue, perhaps more controversially that even policy-makers, criminal justice officials at every level, and academic criminologists who study criminal justice practices do nevertheless have to be interested in understanding the causes of crime. We say this because most criminal justice policies have as their base goal crime reduction. Even policies that seem to be about fairness and equity have at least a partial goal of crime reduction, because civilians who believe that the process is not fair might actually commit more crime. If we were to ask, 'well why do you think crime will be reduced if we do this?', the answer is likely to take some form of a causal explanation. For example, if we were to ask those in the criminal justice system why they advocate enhanced penalties for offenders who carry a gun during a crime, they would say that enhancing the penalty for carrying a gun makes the crime more potentially costly and would-be criminal offenders would refrain from carrying a gun because if caught they would want to avoid the extra penalty. The expectation that enhanced penalties would reduce gun-carrying crimes is predicated upon deterrence theory. If the theory is misguided, that is if it is not an accurate depiction of the world, then the policy is likely to fail.

If both academic and practitioner criminologists are interested in understanding the causes of crime, then they are interested in theories of crime and more specifically the *evaluation of theories of crime*. Theories of crime are essentially explanations as to what the causes of crime (or the reaction to crime) are. Academic criminologists are interested in evaluating theory from the perspective of pure science—they want to know if their theoretical description of the world has what the sociologist Alvin Gouldner (1970) once called 'cognitive validity'—the extent to which the theory fits the facts. Practitioner criminologists are as interested as academic criminologists in evaluating theory because a theory that has cognitive validity will provide more successful policy programmes. In a nutshell, then, criminology is essentially about evaluating theory. Stated differently, the common ground that unites different specific topical areas of criminology as well as academic v 'real world' criminologists is the concern with making and evaluating *causal inferences* or *causal statements* about crime that are derived from theories.

We have stated above that the implications generated from theory must be *observable implications*. How criminologists evaluate theories, therefore, is by collecting empirical observations—data—and subjecting these observations to analysis, which, if properly done, will lead to accurate causal inferences about the cognitive validity of the theory. This means that criminologists use theory to generate observable implications about the world and apply analytical procedures to see if the implications of theory correspond to the data. The partner of good theory in criminology (and good practice we would hasten to add), therefore, is good empirical research methods and sound analytical tools that can investigate the observable implications of the theory. It would logically follow from this, then, that a theorist should clearly spell out all of the observable implications of her theory (King *et al.* 1994). It would also seem reasonable that the more observable implications that a theory can generate, the more tests of the theory that can be conducted, and the greater our confidence in the theory. This kind of hypothesis testing is what makes criminology a social science.

Now, it is often thought, even amongst criminologists themselves, that there are two distinct and separate classes of methodological or analytical tools available in criminology to study crime—quantitative tools and qualitative tools. Quantitative tools use measures that are easily quantifiable to study processes and the relationships between variables, often with large numbers of cases. Qualitative data uses measures or observations that are not easily quantifiable to study processes and the relationships between variables, often with small numbers of cases. Most of us trained to be criminologists are trained to think *either* in quantitative or qualitative terms and we do one type of research or the other and are derisive, or dismissive, of those that use the other method. We think that there is only one 'true' way to obtain causal understanding. This type of one-sided thinking is dunderheaded and, frankly, a waste of time. There are not two but one logic of causal inference in criminology—that based on the counterfactual—and both qualitative and quantitative methods can and should follow the same logic and procedures of causal inference (King *et al.* 1994, 1995).

Quantitative tools are tools that frequently involve the estimation of some mathematical model that is believed to be an accurate depiction of the verbal theory (Blalock

1969). In other words, the statistical model is merely a mathematical representation of the observable implications of the theory. One of the advantages of the mathematical model is that the implications are clearly and lucidly depicted in the model. An example of a frequently used mathematical tool in criminology is the ordinary least squares (OLS) regression model. In this quantitative tool, the researcher believes that some continuous dependent variable (eg the number of crimes a person has committed over some time period) is equal to the additive linear influence of some collection of independent or explanatory variables. The purpose of the regression model is to provide greater precision and clarity than that provided by a verbal description of the theory. The more precise mathematical model of the theory can then be put to empirical test with collected observables or data. As an example, in 1969 the American criminologist Travis Hirschi (1969) articulated a theory of delinquency which he called social control theory. The essence of Hirschi's social control theory is that delinquency is more likely to occur when a youth has weak emotional attachments to conventional others like parents and teachers, when they are committed to few conventional goals like getting good school grades, when they are not involved in conventional activities like after-school clubs, and when they have weak moral beliefs in the validity of rules. A quantitative criminologist would test Hirschi's theory by collecting data on these four elements of the social bond and delinquency and estimating an OLS regression equation that might look something like this:

$$y_i = \alpha + \beta_1 \text{ Attachments} + \beta_2 \text{ Commitments} + \beta_3 \text{ Involvements} + \beta_4 \text{ Moral Beliefs} + \varepsilon_i \qquad (1.0)$$

where y_i is the value of delinquent acts committed by person i

One of the attractive features of social control theory is that it makes some clear predictions about the observable implications of the theory that are captured by equation 1.0: (1) each of the four elements of the social bond should be related to delinquency independent of the others, and (2) the sign of each of the regression coefficients should be negative. Additional implications could also be generated from a careful reading of Hirschi (1969) such that conventional attachments have positive effects on commitments, involvements and beliefs. Other implications could be generated that if found to be true would provide support for social control theory and cast doubt on the cognitive validity of competing theories. For example, since social control theory asserts that high conventional aspirations inhibit delinquent conduct while strain theory asserts that it generates offending, a negative regression coefficient for aspirations would support the former and be 'bad news' for the latter. The more of these observable implications that could be generated the more confidence we would have in the theory.

Qualitative tools have a very old pedigree in criminology, at least in American criminology. In their series of delinquent life histories, Clifford Shaw and Henry

McKay produced some of the first and still some of the best qualitative accounts of the causes of delinquent behaviour (Shaw 1930, 1931). Ironically, they also produced some of the first detailed quantitative studies of the causes of delinquency (Shaw and McKay 1942), but these two components were never fully integrated into a unified causal inference system for the theory of social disorganization. The qualitative accounts of Shaw and McKay stand apart from and are frequently seen to be directed at a different aspect of delinquency than their quantitative account. Finestone (1976), for example, has argued that the life histories narratives are *illustrative* at the individual social psychological level of the process of social disorganization that goes on at the structural or sociological level. Finestone (1976: 25) argued that 'the life history data [was used] to communicate the more intangible nuances of the social life of the local community'. From a very early point in the history of the discipline then, the work of the Chicago theorists set up a bifurcation between quantitative and qualitative methods. While quantitative (statistical) methods do the 'heavy lifting' of formally testing the causal implications of theory, qualitative methods are used for 'illustrative purposes' or are used 'to communicate the more intangible nuances' of crime, but not for testing causal inferences. One prominent contemporary qualitative criminologist, Jody Miller (2009: 2) recently wrote that qualitative data are virtually never used to test the causal inferences of theory but 'appear as supplemental, descriptive data that provides 'colour' and 'flash' to liven up quantitative analyses'. Qualitative data analysis, in other words, are not used to evaluate theory or test the observable implications of theory but are relegated to the role of making such quantitative analyses more interesting.

A good example of this is a well-known book on desistance by Laub and Sampson (2003). This work contains detailed and very sophisticated quantitative analyses about the process by which the Glueck boys desisted from crime as men, but also includes excerpts from interviews with the subjects involved in the study where the narratives provided simply illustrate conceptual points reported in the quantitative tables. For example, the quantitative analyses revealed the importance for desistance for some of these men having an emotionally satisfying relationship with their spouse. Provided narratives include excerpts from the interviews where some men are quoted as saying that having a 'good woman' was instrumental in their quitting crime. However, in no case, did the researchers show us that those who desisted appear to value their partner differently than those who did not. This illustrates Miller's point quoted above that qualitative analyses simply provides 'colour' and 'flash' but are never put to work at the crucial task of evaluating the observable implications of the theory.

The reason that qualitative analyses have not been equal partners with quantitative analysis in evaluating theory is that these techniques are frequently thought, even by those who use them, to be best used for purposes other than testing the observable implications of theory. In one of the frequently cited handbooks of qualitative research by one of the most renowned qualitative researchers, Norman

Denzin (Denzin and Lincoln 1998) is most emphatic about the different purposes of quantitative and qualitative analysis. He argues (1998: 9) that the qualitative researcher is one who is interested in the *interpretative understanding* of social events and that this:

> implies an emphasis on processes and meanings that are not rigorously examined, or measured (if measured at all), in terms of quantity, amount, intensity, or frequency. They seek answers to questions that stress how social experience is created and given meaning. In contrast, quantitative studies emphasize the measurement and analysis of causal relationships between variables, not processes.

Denzin is not alone in his position that qualitative analysis is historical, interpretative, and subjective in getting at the hidden meaning of social experiences for those who have them, and not at all concerned with being a part of positivistic science's interest in evaluating the causal implications of theory. In large measure, qualitative methods are seen by most criminologists as a 'soft' set of methods, best used for describing and revealing and not for testing hypotheses or evaluating theory.

In this essay, we argue that there should not be this bifurcation between the two sets of methods. Following a lead set more than a decade ago by the political scientists Gary King and his colleagues Robert O. Keohane and Sidney Verba (1994: 4, 1995), we believe that both types of methodological approaches should be used in the evaluation of criminological theory and that 'all good research can be understood—indeed, is best understood—to derive from the same underlying logic of inference'. What unifies both quantitative and qualitative analyses, what makes them equal partners in doing good science, is the adherence to a common set of rules of causal inference. As a platform for making causal inference, we suggest that both quantitative and qualitative researchers should be concerned with evaluating counterfactual conditions.

As an example, if we wish to know the causal effect of some event on crime, say the effect of a stable job on desistance from crime, then the causal effect of a stable job can be assessed by taking the difference between two outcomes:

Outcome 1: Y is the number of crimes committed by person X in the year during which he had stable employment.

Outcome 2: Y' is the number of crimes committed by person X in the same year under the same conditions had he not had stable employment.

The inferential problem, of course, is that we do not and indeed cannot observe both outcomes; we have either outcome 1 *or* outcome 2, so we never are able to observe for certain the causal effect. Paul Holland (1986) has termed this problem *the fundamental problem of causal inference*, and it is a fundamental problem because it simply cannot be solved—not by better data nor by more sophisticated statistical techniques. We simply cannot observe both outcome 1 and outcome 2. But what we wish to do either by creating appropriate research designs or collecting sufficient data is approximate the comparison of counterfactual conditions to get at the causal effect. In other words, try to get around the fundamental problem of causal inference. For example, the purpose of randomization in experimental design is to create a control group that is the counterfactual condition to the treatment group. The purpose of careful and comprehensive collection of data in observational studies is to enable researchers to mimic through quantitative statistical control what they cannot control via research design. Regression-based models such as that shown in equation 1.0 are somewhat clumsy attempts to create the counterfactual condition by 'controlling for' other variables. Propensity score-matching methods are more transparent attempts to create counterfactual conditions. Each of these strategies tries to get around the fundamental problem of causal inference not by observing the same observation under two conditions but by creating two *comparable* observations, one of which experiences the explanatory variable in question (the 'treatment'), one of which does not. The causal effect estimated is the difference in the dependent variable between these two observations that are assumed to be comparable in all important ways except for the explanatory variable. King *et al.* (1994) refer to this as the assumption of unit homogeneity.

Although an analysis of counterfactual conditions is a staple of recent quantitative analysis, it has not often been used in qualitative analyses. Our point is that it can, and should, be. Shadd Maruna (2000) in his book, *Making Good*, moves in the direction of using qualitative tools to evaluate the causal implications of theory (see also Hagan and McCarthy 1998). After outlining a theory of desistance wherein offenders who quit crime are argued to reconstruct their criminal past so it is consistent with their current views of themselves as good people, Maruna explicitly tries to test some implications of the theory with personal interviews wherein he attempts to create counterfactual conditions by matching desisting offenders with those who continued in their life of crime. Though an important step in the direction we advocate, his research does not fully integrate quantitative analyses with his interview narratives, and even seems to acquiesce in the traditional view that qualitative methods are poorly suited to lift the weight of causal analysis. For example, he states (Maruna 2000: 38) that 'although phenomenological research can supplement our understanding of how changes in the environment affect individual cognition, these findings can do little to prove or disprove the overall importance of jobs, marriage, or rehabilitative treatments for the wider population. More traditional methodologies, using correlations and large-scale random samples, are far better suited than narratology for this purpose'. We are in complete agreement with Maruna's analytical approach in *Making Good*, but our more general epistemological view is more assertive than Maruna's in that we think that both qualitative and quantitative data can evaluate counterfactual conditions.

We would like briefly to illustrate what we mean by equalization and integration of quantitative and qualitative methods in the analysis of counterfactual conditions with the same substantive example as Maruna's—the study of desistance from crime. We have elsewhere articulated a theory of criminal desistance that argues that the process of quitting crime involves a gradual sequence that involves a growing dissatisfaction with a life of crime, and a change in one's personal identity (Paternoster and Bushway 2009). We argue that criminal offenders have working identities as someone who among other things has and can commit criminal acts. This working identity remains operational as long as it is thought to be successful—that on average it nets more benefits than costs. Gradually, however, the working identity of 'offender' becomes less and less satisfying. The process is a measured one and only occurs when perceived failures in and dissatisfactions with different areas of life become linked—being an offender is not financially useful, it becomes seen as physically too dangerous, the perceived costs of imprisonment loom more likely and greater, and the cost to one's social relationships seem too high to pay (Baumeister 1994). When these life dissatisfactions around a criminal identity become linked, they are more likely to be projected into the future, and the person slowly discovers that he would like to change—to be something and someone else. This perceived sense of a future or possible self as a non-offender and the fear that without change one faces a bleak and highly undesirable future, is what provides the initial motivation to break from crime. Movement toward the institutions that support and maintain desistance (legitimate employment, association with conventional others) is unlikely to take place until the possible self as non-offender is contemplated and at least initially acted on. The growing discontent they feel begins to lead offenders to weaken their commitment to a current working identity as offender because they begin to entertain an identity in the future that does not include crime and that they wish to work toward—what we term the positive possible self. In addition to the pull provided by the possible self of a non-offender, they have in their self schema the push of a feared self. The feared self is the negative dimension of their possible self and includes an image of themselves in the future that they fear they may become—a destitute, criminal offender, isolated from family, who may easily die in prison or die from drugs. The change in identity and movement from offender to desisting ex-offender involves among other things a change in preferences or tastes and a change in social networks such that the desisting offender no longer desires many of the things they once did, they avoid the 'life as party' (Shover 1996), and former criminal associates. What this means is that desisting offenders break from their past in terms of their identities, their social networks, and their preferences (among other things) so that a break from crime is both metaphorical and as we will argue below, analytical.

We have earlier in this essay argued that the evaluation of theory is best undertaken by generating as many of the observable implications of the theory as possible and subjecting them to empirical analysis. Here we would add quantitative and qualitative analysis. We can, therefore, generate observable implications that we can assess with quantitative data and with qualitative data. More directly, we are applying our qualitative tools to evaluate the casual implications of our theory that we have laid out in the same manner and with the same evidential credibility as our quantitative analysis. For the quantitative component of the evaluation of our theory, we have argued that one observable implication of our identity theory of desistance is that it should be manifested as a structural break in an individual level time series of offending. That is, explanatory factors should have different effects on offending before and after the identified break in offending: things that mattered before (drug use, wild friends) will matter less or not at all while things that did not matter before (holding a steady job, being a good parent and spouse) matter or matter more.

For decades now quantitative criminologists have been analysing time series of offending data, but at the aggregate level and not at the individual level. For example, Pridemore *et al.* (2008) recently published a paper where they examined the relationship between the Oklahoma City bombing and the events of 11 September and monthly homicide counts at the local, state and national level. In one analysis they had a count of the number of homicides in Oklahoma County for 120 months, sixty-three months before the Oklahoma City bombing and fifty-seven months after. These are the kinds of aggregate-level, time-series data most criminologists are used to seeing, data on some criminal event from some aggregate level over some long period of time. We suggest that time-series data can be used at the *individual level* as well. For example, the Cambridge Study in Delinquency Development (CSDD) has collected conviction data on a sample of approximately 400 South London boys from age 12 to age 50. These thirty-eight years of offending data for each youth are time-series conviction data at the individual level and we can profitably use these thirty-eight years of conviction data to estimate an individual level times series of offending probability. We have suggested that our identity theory of desistance is essentially a story of structural breaks. Support for our theory can therefore be developed with quantitative methods by examining the time series for structural breaks.

Although there are multiple forms of structural breaks, one version implies that that there are two sets of parameters across time periods.

$$Y_t = \begin{cases} \alpha_a + \rho_a Y_{t-1} + e_{at} \text{ if t} < \text{T} \\ \alpha_b + \rho_b Y_{t-1} + e_{bt} \text{ if t} \geq \text{T} \end{cases} \quad (1.1)$$

Criminological theorists have not formally discussed structural breaks in the context of individual time series, but we see elements of structural breaks in some desistance theories including our identity theory. For example, the notion of age-graded causal factors is consistent with the idea that the value of coefficients on some time-varying variables vary over time. For example, if employment is inversely related to offending during adulthood but not during adolescence (Uggen 2000), we have structural coefficients that vary with time, which could generate time-varying α or ρ in equation 1.1. Uggen's work, much like our identity theory of desistance, describes a structural break in an individual time series. Our identity theory is only plausible if there is empirical evidence in favour of structural breaks. And, assuming that there are structural breaks, the distribution of age at which the breaks occur would be an important fact that desistance theories would need to explain. For our identity theory, we would need to predict the timing of the structural break across individuals using our focus on the possible self. We would predict the arrival of the structural break to occur around times when an accumulation of negative life events leads to a realization on the part of the individual and a structured attempt to create a change in the way that individual interacts with her world. It is unclear whether the data would support a detailed analysis of the nature of the structural break, but it is at least possible that this type of analysis could distinguish between different versions of desistance theory.

We briefly illustrate our point with some preliminary time-series analysis of the youth in the CSDD data (Farrington *et al.* 2006). Recall that the CSDD is a prospective longitudinal survey of 411 South London males. Data collection began when the boys were eight years old and conviction data were obtained for these boys from age 10 to age 50. We create an estimate of the probability of conviction for each year of age. Although we estimated continuous trajectories of latent probability of conviction over the thirty-eight years for all 411 subjects, we will focus only on three individuals, displayed in Figure 1, who follow what we believe most people would agree are desistance trajectories. The *individual time series* for these three subjects from age 12 to 50 follow the classic age-crime curve with an increasing probability of conviction up through adolescence followed by a declining probability with desistance from crime beginning in the mid-twenties until the time series ends at age 50. Some of the observable implications of our identity of desistance would be whether these particular time series could indeed be described as a structural break, and whether we could find theoretical covariates like social networks and preferences whose sign and/or magnitude would change before and after the identified break. A person before the structural break is presumed to be comparable to the same person after the break except with respect to explanatory variables that we are interested in. In terms of unit homogeneity, the person is acting as his/her own control group.

We move now to briefly discuss the qualitative strategy that is complementary to this statistical analysis of individual time series. The critical point to keep in mind is our argument that there is a common logic of causal inference that unifies quantitative and qualitative analyses. In other words, qualitative researchers are not exempt from the fundamental problem of causal inference. No less than in statistical analysis, in order to make valid causal inferences the qualitative analyst must get around this fundamental problem by making a reasonable assumption of unit homogeneity, or the comparability of compared observations. One way to do this would be to intensively interview and study a subject before and after they have had a structural break that was identified in a quantitative analysis of their individual time series. For example, qualitative information could conceivably have been obtained from person # 35 in Figure 1 in his early years before he became involved in crime, during his peak

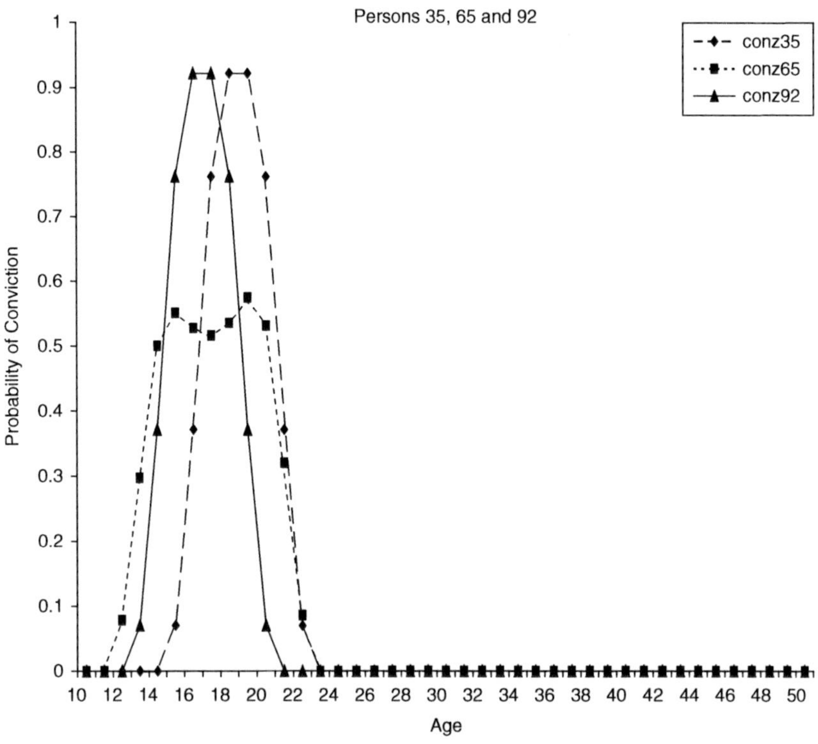

Figure 1 Desistance Patterns for Three Subjects from South London Data

criminal period, and in the early years of desistance. Richly detailed narrative information could be collected with respect to such factors as what his working identity was, what conception he had of himself in the future (his possible and feared selves), his social network, and involvement in activities that either supported or resisted his current identities (see Baskin and Sommers 1998 for an example of this type of work). In the complete absence of narrative data, a narrative story about person # 35's life could still be reconstructed from the available data in the CSDD dataset. If the identity theory of desistance we outlined is true, we would expect to see changes in expressed preferences, social relationships, and working and possible identities. Because the person differs in ways other than identified explanatory variables (such as age alone), before and after the structural break, the assumption of unit homogeneity would still be problematic. However, keep in mind that this information would still contribute information about the theory and that one of our goals is to generate as many observable implications of the theory as possible. This approach could complement other quantitative and qualitative efforts to evaluate the theory.

One such complementary qualitative approach would be to find a person in the CSDD data set who was comparable in as many ways as possible to person #35 up to the age offending was initiated but did not experience a structural break in their individual time series. Recall that since we are unable to return person #35 in time and have him mature to age 50, we can, however, observe what happens to a comparable person (the assumption of unit homogeneity) who did not experience a structural break in the time series. As with quantitative analyses, however, we have no guarantee that the units are homogeneous and cannot directly test the unit homogeneity assumption. However, we have generated yet another observable implication of our theory which we examine with qualitative data which speaks directly to the issue of making a causal inference and is not used simply to provide narrative flourish.

Another complementary strategy might be to select cases for qualitative analysis that are different with respect to the extent to which subjects did or did not desist from crime. Here we argue for selecting cases for intensive analysis that differ *across a range of the dependent variable*—offenders who persist in crime at a high level, those who flirt with desistance or who exhibit intermittency in offending, and those who like those in Figure 1 desist. A retrospective examination of the events in the past lives of these different subjects would speak to the plausibility of both a structural break with crime, identity change, and the cluster of factors we hypothesize are related to an identity change. This strategy is similar to the case-control method frequently used in epidemiological research. We must be clear that we are not suggesting that we select cases with *particular values* of the explanatory variables in mind. That is, we do not want to select desistance cases that we knew involved identity change and persistence cases that did not. This is precisely the practice of using qualitative data to provide descriptive and narrative support for quantitative analysis that we argue against in this essay. Rather, selecting cases across a range of the dependent variable and then engaging in detailed qualitative retrospective analysis provides some information with respect to the plausibility of a causal connection between the explanatory variables we are interested in and our dependent variable.

Conclusion

Criminology is the social science that evaluates theoretical explanations of the causes of crime. The goal is to use both deductive and inductive approaches to generate theories that reflect some part of the reality of the process that generates crime at both the individual and group level. These theories do not need to be complete. Their value derives from their ability to create generalizable insights about what caused crime in a particular situation such that a practitioner could take steps to prevent such crime in the future. An approach that essentially argues for a separate theory for each and every situation disregards the value of theory. Theory is valuable precisely because it can help the criminologist predict and anticipate the crime-generation process across cases. Such broadly applicable insight should then, in theory at least, help practitioners construct effective crime-prevention techniques.

Hot-spot policing is a good example of this type of theory building which then generates a productive crime fighting strategy. Situational crime theorists argued that criminal activity tends to be concentrated in environments that have a number of favourable characteristics. As a result, the theory predicts that crime will not be randomly distributed across space, but will rather be concentrated in certain very identifiable places. Social science observational research has shown that this is in fact the case. Hot-spot policing takes the next logical step and argues that policing should be focused on these 'hot spots' rather than on all space equally. The central argument here is that other spaces will not be as conducive to crime, (if they were, crime would have concentrated there instead of the places in which crime did occur), and therefore, crime will not be simply displaced to a new space.

Our discussion of desistance theory has a similar value. If desistance is a process that is instigated by a change in identity which is then slowly reconstructed over time, then policies should be constructed that support and reward this change in identity. Policies and practices that act as if such change is neither possible nor plausible undercut the desistance process and should be changed. If, on the other hand, desistance is nothing more or less than the aging of the organism, then policies and practices in the criminal justice system can be focused on other concerns, such as population management, without concern that the policies and practices will have a criminogenic affect.

In this essay, we have gone to great lengths to argue that qualitative and quantitative data are equally useful in the scientific enterprise that is criminology. Both types of data can, and should be, used to test theoretical claims deductively. Both types of data can and should be used to generate insight inductively into the types of theories that might be useful in the first place. Neither type of data is inherently better than the other, and analysts that specialize in one type of research should not act as if they are engaged in a separate and distinct exercise from those who specialize in the other. Ideally, both types of data can be used to test the theoretical implications generated by theory in the same analytical work. But, it is a mistake if qualitative data are used to simply highlight insights generated by the quantitative data. It would be equally problematic if quantitative data were used to simply support, rather than test, the findings from qualitative data.

The irony that this essay is written by two criminologists known for quantitative analysis is not lost on us. But our point is not to simply assert that we value qualitative data, and qualitative data analysts. Rather, we want to invite all criminologists to recognize that, regardless of method, we are all engaged in the same scientific enterprise, and can and should therefore hold ourselves to the same basic standards of the scientific enterprise, whether we are using qualitative or quantitative data. The fundamental core of this enterprise is the creation of a useful counterfactual. In social science, unlike lab science, we cannot create 'true' counterfactuals where identical specimens are exposed to different treatments. However, we can work hard to create plausible comparison groups who are similar to each other on as many characteristics as possible. We would like to see all criminologists engage in more discussion of their counterfactuals, which after all, identifies their causal test. The more we explicitly recognize our roles as scientists, the better our tests will be. Better tests should create better theory—and by inference, better policy.

References

Baskin, D. R. and Sommers, I. B. (1998), *Casualities of Community Disorder: Women's Careers in Violent Crimes*, New York: Westview Press.

Baumeister, R. F. (1994), 'The Crystallization of Discontent', in T. F. Heatherton and J. L. Weinberger (eds), *Can Personality Change?*, Washington: American Psychological Association.

Blalock, H. M. (1969), *Theory Construction—From Verbal to Mathematical Formulations*, Englewood Cliffs: Prentice-Hall.

Farrington, D. P., Coid, J. W., Harnett, L., Jolliffe, D., Soteriou, N., Turner, R., and West, D. J. (2006), *Criminal Careers Up to Age 50 and Life Success Up to Age 48: New Findings from the Cambridge Study in Delinquency Development*, London: Home Office.

Finestone, H. (1976), 'The Delinquent and Society: The Shaw and McKay Tradition', in J. F. Short, Jr. (ed.), *Delinquency, Crime and Society*, Chicago: University of Chicago Press.

Gouldner, A. W. (1970), *The Coming Crisis of Western Sociology*, New York: Basic Books.

Hagan, J. and McCarthy, B. (1998), *Mean Streets: Youth Crime and Homelessness*, New York: Cambridge University Press.

Hirschi, T. (1969), *Causes of Delinquency*, Berkeley: University of California Press.

Holland, P. (1986), 'Statistics and Causal Inference', *Journal of the American Statistical Association*, 81: 945–60.

King, G., Keohane, R. O., and Verba, S. (1994), *Designing Social Inquiry*, Princeton: Princeton University Press.

_____, _____, and _____. (1995), 'The Importance of Research Design in Political Science, *American Political Science Review*, 89: 475–81.

Laub, J. H. and Sampson, R. J. (2003), *Shared Beginnings, Divergent Lives: Delinquent Boys to Age 70*, Cambridge, MA: Harvard University Press.

Maruna, S. (2000), *Making Good: How Ex-Convicts Reform and Rebuild Their Lives*, Washington: American Psychological Association.

Miller, J. (2005), 'The Status of Qualitative Research in Criminology', Proceedings from the National Science Foundation's Workshop on Interdisciplinary Standards for Systematic Qualitative Research. (<http://www.wjh.harvard.edu/nsfqual/>).

Marx, K. (1969), *Theories of Surplus Value*, Vol. I, Moscow: Foreign Languages Publishing House.

Paternoster, R. and Bushway, S. (2009), 'Desistance and the 'Feared Self': Toward an Identity Theory of Criminal Desistance', *Journal of Criminal Law and Criminology* 99, 4: 1103–56.

Pridemore, W. A., Chamlin, M. B., and Trahan, A. (2008), 'A Test of Competing Hypotheses about Homicide Following Terrorist Attacks: An Interrupted Time Series Analysis of September 11 and Oklahoma City', *Journal of Quantitative Criminology*, 24: 381–96.

Shaw, C. R. (1930), *The Jack Roller*, Chicago: University of Chicago Press.
_____ (1931), *The Natural History of a Delinquent*, Chicago: University of Chicago Press.
_____ and McKay, H.D. (1942), *Juvenile Delinquency and Urban Areas*, Chicago: University of Chicago Press.
Shover, N. (1996), *Great Pretenders: Pursuits and Careers of Persistent Thieves*, Boulder: Westview Press.
Uggen, C. (2000), 'Work as a Turning Point in the Life Course of Criminals: A Duration Model of Age, Employment, and Recidivism', *American Sociological Review*, 65: 529–46.

13

CRIMINOLOGY AND THE ROLE OF EXPERIMENTAL RESEARCH

MIKE HOUGH

THIS chapter discusses the role of experimental research in policy-focused criminology. It makes some fairly simple points, that nevertheless need making, in response to a current tendency to overstate the contribution that particular research methods can make to the discipline. The context on which the chapter draws is British, but I hope that the conclusions drawn have wider applicability and relevance. My argument is this: the questions with which policy-focused criminology grapples range from the simple to the very complex; experimental research methods have a value in answering questions of middling complexity; but they are useful in answering neither very simple questions nor very complex ones; criminologists should not artificially restrict themselves to examining issues of middling complexity, by insisting that experimental research methods should lie at the heart of the discipline.

The Context[1]

For as long as I have being doing criminology, there have been tensions within UK criminology between researchers at the 'applied' end of the spectrum and their more traditionally academic colleagues. Government research, and government-sponsored research, tends to be largely atheoretical, or rather, it implicitly accepts the conceptual frameworks within which political and governmental debate about crime and its control are conducted. This body of work tends to be narrowly focused, and addresses specific policy questions. In general it is empirical, quantitative and increasingly incorporates a cost-benefit assessment. It is overwhelmingly short-termist—designed to answer the question whether whatever is being evaluated is having an immediate impact; and it tends to be uncritical, in the sense that it does not (or cannot) question general government policy. Rather, it assesses whether the evidence favours investment in one policy tactic as opposed to another. Traditionally in the United Kingdom this sort of research has either been carried out by government departments (primarily the Home Office and, since 2007, the Ministry of Justice) researchers, by governmental bodies with auditing functions (such as the National Audit Office and the Audit Commission), or by academics on contract to government departments. Increasingly, though, 'niche consultancies' are also carrying out this sort of work.

In contrast, there is a growing body of academic research which is much more theoretically orientated, and substantially detached from policy dilemmas—even when crime policy is the focus of its attention, as indeed is often the case. Typically this work is concerned with conceptual rather than empirical analysis, and in so far as it engages with empirical work is as likely to draw on qualitative as quantitative work. Probably the best known and the most cited British criminologist at the moment is David Garland (eg, Garland 2001, 2002)[2]. His work is an extended commentary on government crime-control policy that is nevertheless largely detached from the day-to-day questions with which politicians and their advisors have to grapple.

There is no necessary reason why this divergence should have occurred. Research can be both theoretically engaged and empirically grounded. Indeed it should be a source of concern if there were not a vigorous interplay between theoretical and empirical work. In practice, however, criminology feels as uncomfortably polarized as it has been at any time since the 1970s.

Over the last decade this polarization has become more obvious, because the atheoretical empiricism of government criminology has become more obvious. 'Evidence-led policy' became a watchword throughout the New Labour administration (1997–2010), even if in reality politicians and their officials were sometimes quite cavalier in their approach to evidence. The metaphor that informed governmental approaches to policy research in this (and other) fields was that of the toolbox. The job of policy researchers

[1] The themes in this section are discussed more fully in Hough (2010), and in Morgan and Hough (2007).

[2] Despite being based in the United States for many years.

was to evaluate which tools worked and which did not, thus filling the policy toolbox with a set of tools from which practitioners could make an appropriate selection.

Unsurprisingly given this perspective on policy research, the early and mid 2000s saw an increasing attachment to systematic reviews of the evaluative literature reviews amongst some grouping of academics and amongst government research managers. Several have nailed their colours to the mast of the Campbell Collaboration[3]. The basic idea behind this initiative, itself modelled on the Cochrane Collaboration in the healthcare field, is that one should be systematic in assembling and reviewing research evidence, admitting only those studies that achieve acceptable methodological standards.[4] The threshold for inclusion of studies should be set individually for each review, in the light of available evidence. For example, the Maryland Scale of Scientific Methods is often used as a filtering device.[5] In this, randomized controlled trials are rated as the gold-standard—the highest quality research. The ambition is that with sufficient investment in high quality research, a body of knowledge will be built up over time that would tell criminal justice managers what works in crime control in much the way that the National Institute for Health and Clinical Excellence (NICE) offers guidance to health managers about what treatments represent a good investment for the National Health Service.

Perhaps the clearest statement of the ambitions of the 'experimentalist' criminologists is to be found in Sherman (2009: 16). He sketches out the evidential utopia that the Campbell Collaboration hopes to create as follows:

> Whether you are a crime victim, a police superintendent, a Magistrate, or a probation officer, you will be able to go to www.campbellcollaboration.org to find out exactly the same kind of information [as is provided by the Cochrane Collaboration in relation to health treatments]. What is the most effective strategy to prevent auto theft? Do burglar alarms work? What can I do to protect my daughter from chronic domestic violence by her partner? What sentence is optimal for a chronic burglar? All these questions deserve to have answers from the Campbell Crime and Justice Group. [Sherman, 2009:16].

By implication, evaluative research evidence not meeting the methodological standards specified in the protocols for Campbell systematic reviews—which constitutes the vast majority of criminological evaluation—will presumably be consigned to the dustbin of research incompetence.

[3] See Hollin (2008) for a discussion. I and colleagues have argued elsewhere that this is best understood as an understandable response to the disappointing results of a very large-scale research programme established in the first years of the current administration for evaluating the Crime Reduction Programme. See Hough (2003), Maguire (2003).

[4] See <www.cochrane.org> for details of the Cochrane Collaboration, and <www.campbell collaboration.org/> for details of the Campbell Collaboration.

[5] The Maryland Scale assigns evaluative studies into 1 of 5 categories, according to the form of experimental control that is used to help to attribute causality. The highest score is reserved for studies that use randomized controlled trial methods. Systematic reviews usually exclude all studies that fall into the lowest two categories, and some include only the top, or the top two, categories. The scale provides a measure of internal validity, but does not take account of external validity.

Some Concerns

My concern with the Campbell approach is that it risks being very wasteful of the criminological evidence that has been accumulated over the years. By placing experimental research at the centre of policy-focused criminology it devalues a great deal of valuable evidence that has been accumulated at great effort and cost.

I have no ideological opposition to randomized controlled trials and their less methodologically muscular cousins that use quasi-experimental designs. Nor do I have any opposition to the idea of *system* in reviewing policy evidence. It is important for reviewers to be clear and explicit about their rules for searching for evidence, and about their rules for admitting or rejecting evidence. It is systematic reviews that follow rules *inappropriate to the object of study* that are objectionable.[6] An important question to ask is whether the rules for sifting evidence that have gained currency in the Campbell Collaboration and in governmental criminology are the right ones. The answer that I shall offer in this chapter is that these rules are too narrow, and that in effect they rule out consideration of the more complex—and interesting—questions that criminological research can address.

I want to suggest that evaluative research questions fall at varying points on a continuum of complexity. Some are so simple that they do not require any experiments to answer them. Some are so complex that no formal experiment will be of any use. Some fall in the middle ground where an experimental trial is precisely what is needed. Policy-relevant criminologists need to be clear about where their research questions fall on this continuum. It strikes me as doctrinaire to argue that criminologists interested in policy questions must *necessarily* address only those questions of middling complexity that are suitable for experimental research. To illustrate my argument, I shall offer examples of policy questions that fall at either end of the spectrum, as well as ones that occupy the middle ground. Readers must forgive me for a tendency towards *reductio ad absurdum,* but overstating the argument gives it clarity.

Questions that are Too Simple for Experiment

Not every research question that involves attribution of causality needs an experiment to establish the causal relationship. A crude example is that of the preventative impact of capital punishment on offenders. The *general deterrent* effects of capital

[6] The most common form of mismatch is to specify inappropriately restrictive rules. Our Home Office-funded evaluation of Drug Treatment and Testing Orders (Turnbull *et al.* 2000; Hough *et al.* 2003) is typically excluded from systematic reviews using the Maryland Scale, as lacking adequate comparison groups. So too is the Scottish equivalent (McIvor 2004). In combination the two studies say a great deal about the order's effectiveness, however. But reviews which wastefully throw away such evidence necessarily exclude such comparative insights.

punishment are notoriously hard to establish, but the impact on the offenders themselves is unequivocal. Once killed, people do not reoffend, and it is execution that achieves this outcome. We take for granted that death robs people of agency, and the evidence for this is direct observation.[7]

This may seem a specious example, but it is worth noting that medical researchers have also voiced frustration with the idea that all knowledge has to be underpinned by experimental evidence. The point has been amusingly made in a well-known article published in the *British Medical Journal* that offers a parody of a systematic review examining the life-saving efficacy of parachutes (Smith and Pell 2003). The nicely-turned joke in this paper is that the effectiveness of parachute use in preventing 'death and major trauma' cannot be assumed, because there is only 'anecdotal evidence' about its impact, with no reliable body of RCT evidence about the effectiveness of this particular usage. The 'conclusions' offered by the authors are as follows:

> Only two options exist. The first is that we accept that, under exceptional circumstances, common sense might be applied when considering the potential risks and benefits of interventions. The second is that we continue our quest for the holy grail of exclusively evidence based interventions and preclude parachute use outside the context of a properly conducted trial. The dependency we have created in our population may make recruitment of the unenlightened masses to such a trial difficult. If so, we feel assured that those who advocate evidence based medicine and criticise use of interventions that lack an evidence base will not hesitate to demonstrate their commitment by volunteering for a double blind, randomised, placebo controlled, crossover trial [Smith and Pell, 2003:1460].

The article's serious point, of course, is that observational data can be crucial—and overwhelmingly sufficient—in answering some forms of evaluative question. To take a criminological example, the effectiveness of DNA analysis in linking biological samples to suspects is no longer in doubt; it 'works' as surely as parachutes save pilots' lives. And the evidence that established the low probability of 'false positive' matches was observational, rather than experimental. The policy questions that remain relate to the cost-effectiveness of different levels of investment in DNA analysis. The evidence helps answer these questions tends again to be observational rather than experimental.

Questions that Demand Experiment

There are, of course, many questions about cause and effect which demand and require experimental research. The clearest example is that of pharmaceutical drug trials where impressions about effectiveness derived from simple observational data

[7] Excepting the possibility of paranormal intervention.

can mislead. Where people are given a therapeutic drug, there are likely to be placebo effects, on the one hand, and selection effects, on the other.[8]

Pharmaceutical treatments are especially suitable for randomized control trials because the number of confounding factors tend to be reasonably limited and the circumstances under which the experimental treatment is taken are similar to the everyday settings in which people take their medicines. Drug trials thus tend to have both internal and external validity. That is, they can establish cause and effect in the experimental setting; and the results can be generalized to real-world settings.

Are there criminological questions of equivalent complexity? Certainly there have been a few RCT experiments in the field and many more quasi-experimental studies. The simplest way to get a feel for this work is to visit the Campbell Collaboration website and examine the systematic reviews that relate to offending and policing. The best of these, such as Lipsey and colleagues' (2007) review of cognitive behavioural treatment (CBT) programmes, are very useful and informative. This reviews fifty-nine studies, of which nineteen were RCTs. It shows that in aggregate, CBT programmes outperformed controls in terms of recidivism by 25 per cent. This review demonstrates that experimental evaluation is possible of programmes in which a clearly defined intervention is delivered to populations of offenders. It greatly adds to our knowledge by drawing together the studies in a single meta-analysis. The review very clearly summarizes the results of a large number of studies, in a way that allows one to get a reasonable sense of their internal validity. The extent to which they achieve external validity is an important question to which I shall return.

The least exciting of the systematic reviews on the Campbell Collaboration website have more of the qualities of the fanciful review of parachute effectiveness described above. They tend to conclude that very few methodologically adequate studies have been conducted to date, and one must be cautious about drawing any firm conclusions whatsoever. There is no great harm in a Rumsfeldian process of conversion of 'unknown unknowns' into 'known unknowns'—but the question presents itself whether the researchers might not have made a greater contribution to knowledge using a different reviewing approach.

Questions that are Too Complex for Experiment

Many criminological questions have a strong normative dimension to them, even if we prefer to ignore this. Whatever else it may be, the criminal justice system is at least in part an enterprise intended to make people behave well towards each other, and to be respectful of each other's rights. In other words criminal justice institutions are engaged in one of the most complex social functions. To make the case

[8] Selection effects occur in this context when sub-groups who are more (or less) likely than others to show spontaneous recovery are more (or less) likely to complete a course of drugs.

that complex social functions lie beyond evaluation, I propose to take as an example policy questions about the value of cultural education which are in important ways cognate with questions about how best to make people respect others' rights.

The idea is fundamentally embedded in our educational and social systems that the acquisition of culture is in some way inextricably linked to people's 'moral performance'.[9] At the heart of the liberal tradition is the idea that one becomes a better person for exposure to the best traditions of the visual, musical and literary arts. Defining precisely what is meant by 'better' in this context is complex, but it usually refers to achieving a rounded appreciation of the human condition—a tragic perspective—that predisposes people to treat others with tolerance and sympathy. Large investment decisions are premised on this belief. Why else would ministries of culture support their national art collections and subsidize their national opera companies? Why else would universities invest so heavily in the humanities?[10] Our attachment to this belief can be demonstrated by those (usually fictional) characters who are the exception that proves the rule. Blofeld, the villain in several Bond films, draws his dramatic power from the paradoxical combination of cultural sensitivity and amorality.

One might expect that a government committed to evidence-led policy would have submitted these beliefs about the linkage between exposure to culture and moral performance to the rigorous scrutiny of evaluative research. Why has no equivalent to the Campbell and Cochrane Collaborations been established for accumulating evidence about 'what works' in the cultural field in improving moral performance? Many questions spring to mind:

- is the romantic tradition in music more morally improving than the classical?
- Is contemporary fiction inferior to the great nineteenth century novels in engendering a tragic vision?
- Are the works of Young British Artists as morally uplifting as Goya and Picasso's Guernica?

I invite readers to construct their own experimental research design to evaluate questions of this sort that will help guide the investment decisions of the UK Treasury and the Department of Culture, Media and Sport. My own current favourite is to mount a randomized controlled trial in which young adult subjects are randomly allocated into three groups, and then exposed for a prolonged period exclusively to one of three categories of music:[11] late-modern ironic pop (eg, Lily Allen, Lady Gaga); representatives of 'high culture' (perhaps Mahler, Bruckner and Richard

[9] I borrow the term from Liebling (2004).

[10] A glib answer to this question is that universities are consumer-led bodies that respond to demand—but this simply relocates the value placed on cultural activities to society as a whole.

[11] Sub-samples of around 100 per condition should have sufficient statistical power to identify gross differences between genres.

Strauss' late works); and a selection of recent winners of the Eurovision song context.[12] The experiment would involve pre-test and post-test self-report measures of sensitivity to the human condition, measures of well-being and self-report measures of preparedness to engage in altruistic behaviour.

Assuming that experiments of this sort will exist only as thought-experiments, I enjoy them partly because of their inherent absurdity, and partly because they illustrate the reasons why the impact of complex social behaviour lies beyond the reach of quantitative experimental research. The idea is that progressive *immersion* in a cultural tradition over a lifetime can have a value, rather than *forced consumption* of discrete elements of it. The artificiality of the experiment would totally fail to capture the complex processes that the 'moral value of culture' hypothesis implies. In the argot of research methodologists, the experimental exposure to the different conditions would bear so little relationship to the real-life contexts in which people listened to different sorts of music that the experiment would have no external validity—or generalizability—whatsoever. The internal validity of an experiment of this sort might nevertheless be high, if the problems of maintaining 'programme integrity'—and the ethical issues raised by over-exposing subjects to Eurovision champions—could be overcome.

Where Should the Centre of Gravity of Policy-Focused Criminology Fall?

It is a question of choice—made collectively by funders and policy researchers—where the 'centre of gravity' of policy research should fall. Proponents of the Campbell approach, in arguing for a focus upon knowledge supported by experimental evidence, clearly believe that the key questions for policy research are those of middling complexity. Others, including myself, think that many of the most important questions to which criminal policy needs answers are more akin to those about culture and moral performance. That is, they have a subtlety and complexity that places them beyond the reach of experimental research.

This is not to deny *any* role for experimental criminological research. Well-conducted experiments can establish the presence or absence of cause and effect in an intervention. This can sometimes come in the shape of 'debunking' research, such as the work on the ineffectiveness of boot camps (see the Campbell Collaboration review by Wilson *et al.*, 2005) and the classic evaluation of the DARE drug education programme by Rosenbaum and Hanson (1998). Sometimes it comes in the shape of confirmatory research, demonstrating that a particular approach has value—as in the evaluations of CBT discussed above (Lipsey, 2007).

[12] For the benefit of readers beyond Europe, this annual television contest has become notorious for the insipid quality of songs put forward by the contestant countries.

Advocates of the Campbell approach such as Sherman (2009: 16) argue that in terms of building a robust evidence base, it is still early days, and that if we take the right decisions now about research strategy—and invest in methodologically solid research programmes—in time the evidence base will develop: each piece of experimental research will add cumulatively to our knowledge. I am more sceptical. I have suggested that processes designed to make people behave well are highly complex. A particular feature of this complexity is the reflexivity of these processes.

Making people behave well is a highly reflexive process in the sense that the meanings attributed to the process by those involved in it will affect the outcomes.[13] This means that the effectiveness of interventions will be highly context-specific. What works in one culture at one time may well be ineffective in other settings and at other times.

If I am right to stress the reflexivity of processes of social control, the implication is that demonstrably successful programmes such as CBT may work only in those settings that are culturally appropriate for them. It seems improbable that they would have had any purchase in Victorian England; one can only speculate whether they will be as effective as they are at present in twenty-five years' time.

There is some evidence that speaks to this issue. An important series of studies carried out by the Home Office in the mid-1990s graphically demonstrated the limits in generalizability from evaluative research in this field. The first study (Friendship *et al.* 2002), examining the first four years' experience of a cognitive skills programme working with offenders in prisons, showed considerable impact. However in a later replication of the evaluation (Falshaw *et al* 2003; Cann *et al.* 2003) when the programme was rolled out to prisons on a larger scale, the effectiveness of the programme appeared to evaporate. The authors suggest, amongst other things, that changing levels of motivation amongst prisoners or staff could explain the difference.[14]

These studies graphically illustrate a potential problem for evaluative research: evaluations with robust methods of causal attribution, such as RCTs and quasi-experimental designs with properly matched control groups, tend to have high internal validity, but often have limited external validity. Let us accept, in this case, that the initial study had established incontrovertibly a link between the cause and the effect for the particular groups of offenders and workers under evaluation. However strong this internal validity, the study's external validity—the ability to generalize to other circumstances—may be quite limited. Even if the initial study reached the right conclusion, there are plenty of reasons for doubting whether the programme will work the same magic with other offenders and workers in other settings. In this respect, experimental research into criminal justice differs fundamentally from

[13] There is a discussion to be had about the extent to which the prescription of pharmaceutical drugs is a similarly reflexive process, but *on the whole* it is safe to assume that statins—or paracetamol, or aspirin—will achieve their intended effect regardless of the meanings that participants construct of the process.

[14] There are other possible explanations. There might have been problems of matching in the—quasi-experimental—design that biased the first study towards success, for example.

pharmaceutical trials, where generalizability, at least within broadly similar settings, is usually high.[15]

What research strategies should be pursued in fields characterized by their extreme complexity? It is *not* to invest in a huge programme of randomized controlled trials—though, as I have argued, there is a place for experimentation. Policy-focused criminology would do better to construe its task as the construction and testing of middle-level theories about how to change people's behaviour.[16] Choices about strategies and tactics needs to be made on the basis of middle level theories about what is likely to work best.

What counts as a middle-level theory? Well, the ones to which I subscribe about changing people's behaviour for the better include the following: that effective social control pays proper attention to normative issues; that achieving change is a human process, in that the quality of relationship will be a key determinant of outcome; that the personal qualities of agents of social control are important; that effective social control turns on the legitimacy conferred on the agent of change and on the process for achieving change; that legitimacy flows from fair and respectful treatment.

The research strategy for testing such middle-level theories needs to be as multifaceted as the subject is complex. Evidence in support of them may *sometimes* be found in experimental research, sometimes in quantitative surveys, sometimes in qualitative work. If policy focused criminology is to remain healthy, it needs to do what it does best—which is to construct and test middle-level theories about the maintenance of social order. These middle-level theories can bring insight and perspective to policy. In my view this is the real contribution that criminology—whether theoretical or empirical—has actually made to policy.

Why this Methodological Debate is Important

Someone coming to the questions afresh might conclude that criminologists are over-preoccupied about methodological minutiae. However, the debate about what counts as evidence for policy decisions is of great importance. If only that evidence which has been accumulated through experimental research is treated as reliable, then criminal policy will only make choices from a sub-set of relatively crude and simple policy options. Questions about the need for justice and humanity in social control are at the same level of complexity as those about the relationships between culture and moral performance. If we adopt research methods that are insensitive to these issues, we shall do a serious disservice to criminal policy.

[15] Eg UK doctors would probably accept the clear US evidence about the effectiveness of statins in lowering cholesterol as a good guide to outcomes in this country.

[16] Ironically, Sherman's own work is full of very creative examples of such middle-level theories, as Tilley (2009) argues.

References

Cann, J., Falshaw, L., Nugent, F., and Friendship, C. (2003), *Understanding What Works: accredited cognitive skills programmes for adult men and young offenders*, Home Office Findings No. 226. London: Home Office <www.homeoffice.gov.uk/rds/pdfs2/r226.pdf>.

Falshaw, L., Friendship, C., Travers, R., and Nugent, F. (2003), *Searching for 'What Works': an evaluation of cognitive skills programmes*. Home Office Findings No. 206. London: Home Office.

Friendship, C., Blud, L, Erikson, M., and Travers, R. (2002), *An evaluation of cognitive behavioural treatment for prisoners*, Home Office Research Findings 161. London: Home Office.

Garland, D. (2002), 'Of Crimes and Criminals: The Development of Criminology in Britain' in M. Maguire, R. Morgan, and R. Reiner (eds), *The Oxford Handbook of Criminology*, 3rd edn, Oxford: Oxford University Press.

_____ (2001), *The Culture of Control: Crime and Social Order in Contemporary Society*, Oxford: Oxford University Press.

Hollin, C. (2008), 'Evaluating offending behaviour programmes: does only randomisation glisten?' *Criminology and Criminal Justice*, 8, (1): 89–106.

Hough, M., Clancy, A., Turnbull, P. J., and McSweeney, T. (2003), *The Impact of Drug Treatment and Testing Orders on Offending: two-year reconviction results*, Findings 184. London: Home Office.

_____ (2010), 'Gold standard or fool's gold: the pursuit of certainty in experimental criminology', *Criminology and Criminal Justice*. 10, 1: 11–22.

Liebling, A. (2004), *Prisons and their Moral Performance*, Oxford: Oxford University Press.

Lipsey, M., Landenberger, N. A., and Wilson, S. J. *Effects of Cognitive-Behavioral Programs for Criminal Offenders*, Campbell Collaboration <www.campbellcollaboration.org>.

McIvor, G. (2004), *Reconviction following Drug Treatment and Testing Orders*, Edinburgh: Scottish Executive Social Research.

Morgan, R. and Hough, M. (2007), 'The Politics of Criminological Research', in R. King and E. Wincup (eds), *Doing Research on Crime and Justice*, Oxford: Oxford University Press.

Rosenbaum, D. P. and Hanson, G. S. (1998), 'Assessing the effects of school-based drug education: A six-year multilevel analysis of project D.A.R.E', *Journal of Research in Crime and Delinquency*, 35, (4): 381–412.

Sherman, L. W. (2009), 'Evidence and liberty: the promise of experimental criminology', *Criminology and Criminal Justice*, 9, (1): 5–28.

Smith, C. S. and Pell, J. P. (2003), 'Parachute use to prevent death and major trauma related to gravitational challenge: systematic review of randomized controlled trials', *British Medical Journal*, 327: 1459–61.

Tilley, N. (2009), 'Sherman v Sherman: realism v rhetoric', *Criminology and Criminal Justice*, 9, (2): 135–44.

Turnbull, P. J., McSweeney, T., Webster, R., Edmunds, M., and Hough, M. (2000), *Drug Treatment and Testing Orders: Evaluation Report*. Home Office Research Study No. 212. London: HMSO.

Wilson, D. B. MacKenzie, D. L., and Ngo Mitchell, F. (2005), *Effects of Correctional Boot Camps on Offending* The Campbell Collaboration 2005, Campbell Collaboration <www.campbellcollaboration.org>.

3

POLITICAL ALLEGIANCES: WHAT IS CRIMINOLOGY FOR?

14

CRIMINOLOGY AND SOCIAL JUSTICE: EXPANDING THE INTELLECTUAL COMMITMENT

BETH E. RICHIE

Introduction

In an attempt to broaden the discussion about the intellectual goals and methodological approaches that define the field of criminology, this chapter will present the case for including the notion of social justice—both theoretically and as a matter of praxis—for consideration in the future directions that the discipline of criminology might take. I do so as a way to challenge the epistemological tendency to bifurcate the understanding of what criminology is where, on the one hand, a community of scholars advocate that criminology should be understood principally as a theoretical discipline concerned primarily with generating ideas about the social context of the law and the philosophical meanings associated with social contracts, norm violations and other matters related to rights, privileges and obligations; while on the other hand, an esteemed cohort of criminologists focus on producing applied or policy-oriented research that explores solutions to the problems of crime (see, *inter alia*, Barry 2005; Ellis, DeKeseredy, and Alvi 2005; Miller 1999; Petersillia 1991; Quinney 2003; Young 2002). The goal of this essay is neither to engage in this debate nor to expose the problems associated with the existence of fractions in the field; rather, I argue that scholars, policy-makers, interventionists and activists, regardless of their orientation to the primary function of criminology, should prioritize the intellectual work in the discipline that contributes to the creation of a more just society.

This essay begins by offering reflections on what I mean by 'advancing social justice' in the context of criminology. First, I offer a conceptual definition drawing on the work of political philosophers, social scientists and other scholars whose work has focused on how ideas about law, rights, and crime are linked to social institutions and their influence on the problem of social inequality. Next, I present a set of normative assumptions that provide a rationale for my argument followed by a discussion of why criminology, as a discipline, has a unique obligation to engage in work that is directed towards contributions to a more just society because of the very position that it assumes in the intellectual and professional landscape. I will use the case of women and substance abuse as an illustration of my point and conclude this essay with a brief discussion of some of the challenges that such an approach might create for scholars interested in advancing the field of criminology.

The Conceptualization of Social Justice within the Context of Criminology

The concept of social justice is studied by political philosophers, social scientists, legal theorists and critical scholars who are trained in interdisciplinary fields, like Black Feminist Theory and Critical Race Theory (Collins 2000; Delgado and Stefancic 2001). Outside the academy, religious leaders have used the concept to claim a kind of ethical imperative to motivate certain behaviour, while public policy-makers apply the language of social justice to promote initiatives that are designed to reallocate resources, and community activists invoke the term to signal a commitment to working for economic and political equality and advancing human rights (Capeheart and Milovanovic 2007). Indeed, there is evidence of both a common, everyday consensus about the meaning assigned to 'social justice' as well as a contested sense of 'who owns it' and what people mean symbolically and practically when referring to it. This sense of rhetorical ambiguity creates an interesting conceptual situation, on the one hand, wherein the term social justice is deployed to establish a kind of moral superiority about assumed shared social commitments to core social values (like freedom or opportunity) without empirical measures to justify a set of concrete outcomes that would determine if those values were actualized.

The general consensus about a commitment to social justice with only a vague agreement about what the concept means and how to achieve it can create practical and intellectual opportunities for criminologists in so far as there is an audience that—despite definitional imprecision—has accepted some notion of justice as a common social goal (Capeheart and Milovanovic 2007). This situation gives theorists a space and empiricists an opportunity to do the work with important public support. It means that some scholars can concern themselves with theories of social justice—as political philosophers might—while at the same time, as social researchers, we can design empirical tests of what social justice looks like and what difference it makes. Finally, the broad understanding of the role that criminology plays in creating a more just society establishes a legitimate space for criminologists to explore how organizations, policies, and programme initiatives work to increase or decrease social inequality on key measures and then to partner with community activists in collaborative efforts to change them. For the purposes of my discussion, I will argue that it is important that criminologists resist the instinct to define social justice narrowly and instead take advantage of the common consensus; immersing ourselves in the various streams of the discipline to craft a social justice agenda for the divergent intellectual positions in the field.

The broad conceptualization that I am using in this essay posits social justice as a signifier of a range of conditions that would expand opportunity for those who have been constrained by their social position or lack of access to institutional privileges. This includes creating a set of circumstances where disadvantaged groups or individuals who experience injustice are compensated for their plight. It means using a methodological approach that takes our understanding of social problems into account and links individual pathology and social deviance to the role of institutions and the state in creating disadvantage. Social justice, in this sense, incorporates a range of macro variables (such as race, class and gender) and takes on a corrective role in responding to the social inequality that results from institutionalized forms of domination by restoring rights, creating opportunity, and strengthening the social position of those who suffer the most in contemporary society because of structural racism, persistent sexism and exploitation of poor people.

More concretely, criminologists might consider the following theoretical questions regarding social justice. Is social justice accomplished through the meeting of needs of groups who are structurally and systematically disadvantaged by reallocating resources or by expanding opportunity in some way that equalizes contributions to society and subsequent access to social benefits (Frazer 2003)? Is it most helpful to those in precarious positions within the criminal legal system (as people who break the law or victims whose rights are denied) to establish what is 'deserved' by individuals within the system or what the system should accomplish for the larger social good? (Miller 1999) Other theoretical inquiries into questions of social justice have looked at issues of power, democracy, and the centrality of relationships between citizens, social movements and the state (Young 2002). Related research would explore how notions of citizenship vary by legal status and how that status changes based on adherence to hegemonic gender norms, ethnic group identities and dominant cultural expectations (Yuval-Davis 1997). And finally, what role does the broader social condition play in crime and victimization rates where the practice of withholding benefits both causes and results from social inequality? These are the kinds of theoretical questions that criminologists might ask in the pursuit of understanding what social justice is and how it works as a criminological variable.

A second area of inquiry is introduced when social justice is considered from the standpoint of measuring social inequality, its impact on opportunity, and how these are linked to public safety and responses to lawbreaking. Criminologists have amassed an important body of literature that attempts to put the theory of social justice to empirical test, developing measures of how social justice (or the corollary injustice) affects crime rates and how, in turn, lawbreaking and victimization influences social status and other problems. These analyses are focused on concerns like the experiences of groups with fewer resources when they or their neighbours break the law, on the consequences of unequal access to legal benefits of those who are charged with crime, and how to assess the impact of unequal opportunity on recidivism rates (Clear 2009; Jenness 2004; Kelley 2000; Western 2007).

Lastly, a cluster of criminological researchers have dedicated their scholarly work to advancing social justice by looking at the processes of the criminal legal system and how they could be improved (Hawkins 2003; Western 2007). In this area of research, scholars design studies that evaluate the role that institutions play in increasing or decreasing the negative consequences of crime. This literature asks questions like: what motivates the criminal legal system to act in certain ways? What 'types' of justice is deployed by which institutions? What are the social and political priorities that guide an organization's process? What is a 'fair' institutional response both for people who break the law and for people who are victimized? And, perhaps most essentially, at the level of organizations, how do we ensure that the system does not unfairly disadvantage the social actors who, because of injustice, find themselves in it?

In each of these domains, the question of understanding social justice as a factor in the creation of crime is not to be misunderstood as an issue that cannot accommodate discussions of personal responsibility, free will, or agency on behalf of social actors. Rather, the point is that whether evaluating the role of criminal legal institutions, measuring and testing inequality, or advancing new theoretical frameworks, the field of criminology is enhanced by considering social justice as part of both the overall research agenda and criminological praxis.

Theories that Influence Normative Assumptions Regarding Criminology and Social Justice

There are a set of normative assumptions that frame the conceptualization of social justice in the field of criminology and the arguments that I am making in this chapter. These assumptions are drawn from various critical theoretical paradigms that have influenced social sciences, the humanities, and contemporary legal scholarship. They are offered here to suggest that criminologists, who are interested in intellectual work that results in social justice, need to become conversant in epistemological and methodological approaches that are organized around a set of explicit assumptions.

A key starting place is the orientation that Black Feminist Theory brings to thinking about social justice as an intellectual goal (Collins 2000; Potter 2006; Young 1980). Advanced by sociologist Patricia Hill Collins, this paradigm argues that research reflects values, despite claims that some scholars make that their work is pure and objective. Our work is not based on a neutral set of theoretical or paradigmatic positions, but rather it has biases that need to be made explicit in order for consumers of research to understand the perspectives and interests that frame the research in the first place. In the case of criminology, there is a tendency for scholarship to reflect the interest of those in powerful academic institutions who study crime in rigidly controlled disciplinary boundaries and in political institutions that understand lawbreaking as principally a problem of deviance and social control (Garland 2001; Lattuca 2001). Criminology needs to be intentional in its work that challenges these taken-for-granted biases and assumptions in order for it to be useful in the pursuit of social justice (as opposed to furthering the injustices experiences by marginalized groups).

Critical Race Theory is a second theoretical paradigm that has influenced the normative assumptions that are influential in advocating that social justice work be carried out by criminologists (Delgado and Stefancic 2001). In particular, this theoretical paradigm promotes the use of alternative methodological approaches and argues that those most impacted by problems of crime and justice should be included in prioritizing the research questions. Equally important, results should include a reflexive orientation to intervention strategies (Hesse-Biber and Piatelli 2007; McIntyre 2008). That is, Critical Race Theory argues that some aspects of criminology, like other intellectual traditions, should be explicitly dedicated to understanding how social changes could be operationalized as a way to decrease inequality and equalize power and resources.

Finally, theories of intersectionality help criminologists understand how—as a discipline constituted of interdisciplinary scholars—we are particularly well prepared to raise questions about how multiple identities and systems of inequality converge at the point of connection to the criminal legal system to further disadvantage stigmatized groups (Burgess-Proctor 2006; Crenshaw 1991). These paradigms provide important intellectual and methodological tools to criminologists interested in social justice such that we are better prepared to respond to broad questions about, for example, human rights within the context of international detention or more specific questions about how restorative justice and community accountability factor into responses to violent victimization. They serve to substantiate the claim that because the very substance of our work centres on understanding justice, we are obligated to do something about it as part of our intellectual mission. The normative assumption that I am making here is that as the discipline organized to study protection, desistance from crime, and freedom from threats and suffering, we are fundamentally obligated to engage in broader discussions about how to create a society where everyone has access to these benefits.[1]

An Illustration of Social Justice Criminological Work

The discussion of the conceptual definition and the normative assumptions, which assert that criminology should play a key role in the creation of social justice, becomes more salient when applied to a specific example. I have chosen to focus on women and illegal substance abuse for a number of reasons. First, there are extensive data that link women's use of drugs and their subsequent involvement in illegal activity (Bush-Baskette 2004; Richie 1996). This activity, in turn, leaves women vulnerable to the long arm of the criminal legal system, which results in their growing presence in the population who are incarcerated in the United States (Daly and Tonry 1997). This over-representation is mirrored by other groups who are similarly situated and under the surveillance and control of the criminal legal system in this country (Mauer 1999; Spohn and Spears 2003). This leaves them vulnerable to long-term social, economic, and political disenfranchisement.

It is also the case that there is growing consensus among theoretical as well as primarily policy-oriented criminologists that substance abuse has been misclassified as a crime problem when it might be better understood as a problem of social injustice—of economic and other disadvantages (Baum 1996; Drug Policy Alliance Network; Logan 2004). Indeed, substance abuse among women is a problem that links several spheres of social injustice, including health and mental health disparities that lead to lawbreaking, insufficient or inadequate rehabilitation and treatment options that lead to staggering recidivism rates, and the perilous impact of

[1] To be clear, it is *not* my assumption that all social scientists, legal scholars, or philosophers should be engaged in reconfiguring social institutions, but rather that a body of critical studies should be included in the disciplinary framework somewhere. I make these strong assertions because criminologists study the very social institution that is primarily involved with dispensing justice, namely the criminal legal system.

felony disenfranchisement on individual and community stabilization (Drug Policy Alliance Network, 2001; <www.drugwarfacts.org/cms/node/64>). Finally, the problem of substance abuse, while not concentrated in disadvantaged communities, has had a much more serious impact on low-income neighbourhoods where there are high rates of victimization and a lack of community services. This aggregate picture is one that should compel criminologists to look at the role of social justice in the problem of women's substance abuse given the extent of the problem and its reflection of social inequalities.

A review of the literature reveals several epistemological trends in the data that describe the problem. One body of research looks at individual-level psychological analyses of causation. Other studies attempt to recognize the link between substance abuse and other social problems such as poverty and violence. There are important accounts of the ways that certain groups of women are disproportionately affected by the problem and significant evaluation research of programme effectiveness and model intervention strategies. Much of this is very good research that stands up to the most ambitious standards of scientific rigour; the research questions are good ones, the methodological approaches are sound, the samples are appropriate, and the analytic strategies are well thought out. In the aggregate, while the conclusions from this body of work illuminate many of the factors that are important to the understanding about women and their drug abuse in contemporary society, they do not, in general, focus on questions that are key to formulating a social justice analysis of the problem.

The approach that is most prevalent in the literature looks at individual pathology, disorganized families, strained neighbourhoods, rates of prior victimization and other crime, weak social networks, and other factors as if they are natural conditions in our social order (Richie 2007). These 'risk factors' are described and quantified, but not analysed as part of a larger macro category of social injustice. For example, it is noted that women who use illegal substances have a higher rate of victimization, but gender violence is seldom linked to its root causes—male domination—or theorized as a problem of power relationships between both individuals and within relationships of the state. An alternative to this essentialized narrative would look at the link between public policy decisions about matters of inadequate housing, lack of work, poor educational opportunities, or subordinate gender roles as topics to be measured and included in the analysis of the factors that lead to the increase in women's substance abuse. It would include other issues as well, like degrading interactions with social institutions, social stigma, and punitive criminal justice policy that affect women's sense of self-worth and might predispose them to substance abuse. Matters of institutional neglect of low-income communities, the role of certain policing on certain types of substances (but not others), the racial and class hierarchies in political processes that allocate resources and benefits, and historical patterns of harsh treatment by the criminal legal system would also be included.

Theoretical Questions Related to Social Justice and Women's Substance Abuse

A new set of theoretical questions regarding women's substance abuse emerge as significant if criminologists look at social justice as a macro level variable. In addition to the very important work of exploring the link between women's substance abuse and conditions in their family of origin, the role of their peers in risk-taking behaviour, women's individual reactions to stress or other individual factors that predispose them to the risk of substance abuse, asking questions about the role of injustice opens a broader area for researchers to explore. Such questions might include an exploration of the movement of substance abuse from the domain of health research into the criminal justice sphere and the ways that the social construction of crimes reflects broader social interests. In addition, it might be important to incorporate neo-liberal theories of the welfare state in order to conduct an analysis of the role that economic marginalization played in women's involvement in the illegal drug trade, or feminist theories of power and domination to understand the role that gender oppression played in women's use of drugs with their partners. Multi-cultural theory or intersectional analyses would help explain how institutional policy influences women's inability to comply with treatment protocols or conditions of treatment. Exploring these and related areas would allow researchers to expose the role that macro level forces play in women's substance abuse—not as a way to diminish or compete with the importance of individual characteristics—but as a way to look for additional causal factors and other solutions.

Measuring Social Justice as a Factor in Women's Substance Abuse

When social justice is included as a variable to be measured as part of the research design then it can be treated as an analytic category. Here, I am not only suggesting that an operationalized notion of social justice be included on data collection instruments (survey instruments, questionnaires or interview schedules), but that researchers define and quantify the concept in such a way that participants' responses and/or field observations can be interpreted as issues of social justice *even if* they are not defined in precisely those terms by the women substance abusers who make up the sample being studied. This approach is consistent with the normative assumptions extracted from Black Feminist Theory, Critical Race Theory, and Intersectionality. For example, in the same way that depression is measured, injustice could be operationalized in concrete terms that were defined by those women who experience it and generalized to others and tested for validity. It must be recognized that there is an important literature that attempts to quantify related terms, such as 'empowerment' or 'self efficacy', however in the research on substance abuse, an analytic category that includes elements of social justice is underdeveloped. To remedy this would be an ambitious and important scientific project, one that would serve not only to possibly decrease substance abuse among women but also help the discipline of criminology to move towards including more social justice work.

Social Justice Agenda as an Intervention Programme

In addition to expanding the theoretical understandings about social inequality, drugs and crime and attempting to measure the role that lack of social justice plays in the rates of women who use illegal substances, introducing social justice as a research question allows for a new set of possibilities around intervention research and scholars' engagement in social change work. What would an intervention programme that included social justice in its goals look like? Who or what would be the 'target' of the intervention? What activities would be included in the therapeutic menus offered to those who are suffering? What would the role of punishment or other state sanctions be in responding to the problem? How would programme success be measured? What policy changes would be required?

These types of questions are being asked by a growing cohort of scholar/practioners who are interested in advancing a different kind of social justice intervention on problems that marginalize groups in our society. These include programmes that build community-organizing skills that engage so-called 'clients' in action research that is aimed towards social transformation as opposed to only providing social services. The field of women's substance abuse treatment research could benefit from and build on this work were it to embrace the notion of social justice research. This would include multi-method criminological studies and analytical strategies that privilege those who are most affected as the people who validate knowledge about the problem. In addition, studies that look at resistance as well as protective factors would also serve the goal of advancing understanding of the relationship between women, drug abuse and social justice.

I have used the example of women and substance abuse to illustrate the possibilities for a richer, more nuanced, and expanded understanding of the problem if criminologists would assume that creating social justice is part of our work. Such an approach would reposition the notion of social justice as a key area of criminological inquiry at the theoretical, empirical, public policy, and applied level.

Conclusion

In this essay, I have argued that regardless of whether scholars understand themselves to be primarily concerned with theory, policy-making, intervention, or social activism, criminologists have the responsibility to include attention to social justice as one of the outcomes of our intellectual work. The particularities of this imperative are embedded in the topics that we study (issues of rights, safety, and the law) as well as our interdisciplinary tradition that connects us with critical theories that constitute other disciplines (Black Feminist Theory, Critical Race Theory, and Intersectionality). Indeed, we might have a particular role to play because of our role as researchers, policy-makers, advocates and activists who study the very social institution that is primarily involved with dispensing justice—namely the criminal legal system. In addition, the common consensus that supports social justice as a value and the various claim-makers that use the term as a marker of their moral, political, and ethical positioning leave the field in a critical position to take up the issue with intellectual rigor and active engagement. These features create a solid argument and a strong theoretical and empirical platform for developing new theoretical paradigms, asking new conceptual questions, designing new measurement tools, analysing public policies, and engaging activities designed to create social change.

Accepting this opportunity means addressing the challenges that accompany it. First, it is not clear that the field has evolved in such a way that scholars are prepared or willing to take up the rigorous demands of becoming conversant in critical methodologies and paradigms that support the study of social justice. Criminology, like other disciplines, comprises various intellectual stakeholders who may not be willing to relinquish hold on their epistemological positions. Academic departments, scholarly journals, funding agencies, and professional organizations constitute a kind of power elite who have an interest in advancing work that reflects dominant traditions and paradigms. Taking up new questions related to social justice will require shifts in both paradigms and power.

A second challenge is that the work towards social justice will remain at the level of rhetoric unless efforts are made to broadly operationalize it. It bears repeating that my assertion is that the conceptual imprecision is an advantage in so far as it offers a wide range of intellectual projects to take shape. However, it could also feed intellectual ambivalence if there are not some concrete outcome measures that will be used to evaluate the impact of our work.

The example of women and substance abuse provides some insights into what this work might look like. It allows for the creation of a set of recommendations about how research on women and drugs could serve a goal of a broad social justice agenda as well as advancing a paradigm shift for the discipline as a whole. Is including social justice as a goal of criminology a viable intellectual and/or political idea? That is yet to be seen. Surely, it is worthy of discussion among criminologists as we contemplate the future direction of the discipline and as long as there is such clear social injustice to be conquered.

References

Barry, B. (2005), *Why Social Justice Matters*, Malden: Polity Press.

Baum, D. (1996), *Smoke and Mirrors: The War on Drugs and the Politics of Failure*, Boston: Little, Brown and Company.

Burgess-Proctor, A. (2006), 'Intersections of Race, Class, Gender, and Crime: Future Directions for Feminist Criminology', *Feminist Criminology*, 1: 27–47.

Bush-Baskette, S. (2004), 'The War on Drugs and the Incarceration of Mothers', in P. J. Schram and B. Koons-Witt (eds), *Gendered (In)Justice: Theory and Practice in Feminist Criminology*, Long Grove: Waveland Press, Inc.

Capeheart, L. and Milovanovic, D. (2007), *Social Justice: Theories, Issues, and Movements*, New Jersey: Rutgers University Press.

Clear, T. (2007), *Imprisoning Communities: How Mass Incarceration Makes Disadvantaged Neighborhoods Worse*, New York: Oxford University Press.

Collins, P. H. (2000), *Black Feminist Thought: Knowledge, Consciousness, and the Politics of Empowerment*, 2nd edn, New York: Routledge.

Crenshaw, K. (1991), 'Mapping the Margins: Intersectionality, Identity Politics, and Violence against Women of Color', *Stanford Law Review*, 43, 6: 1241–99.

Daly, K. and Tonry, M. (1997), 'Gender, Race, and Sentencing', *Crime and Justice*, 22: 201–52.

Delgado, R. and Stefancic, J. (2001), *Critical Race Theory: An Introduction*, New York: New York University Press.

Drug Policy Alliance Network, 'What's Wrong with the War on Drugs?', *Drugpolicy.org*. (<www.drugpolicy.org/drugwar/>, accessed 5 March 2010).

_____ (2001), 'The War on Drugs is a War on Women of Color', *Drugpolicy.org*, August 2001. (<www.drugpolicy.org/about/position/race_paper_women.cfm>, accessed 5 March 2010).

Ellis, D., DeKeseredy, W. S., and Alvi, S. (2005), *Deviance and Crime: Theory, Research, and Policy*, 3rd edn, New York: LexisNexis/Anderson.

Fraser, N. (2008), *Scales of Justice: Reimagining Political Space in a Globalized World*, New York: Columbia University Press.

Garland, D. (2001), *The Culture of Control: Crime and Social Order in Contemporary Society*, Chicago: University of Chicago Press.

Hawkins, D. F. (2003), 'On the Horns of a Dilemma: Criminal Wrongs, Civil Rights, and the Administration of Justice in African American Communities', in D. F. Hawkins, S. Myers, and R. N. Stone (eds), *Crime Control and Social Justice*, Santa Barbara: Greenwood Publishing Group.

Hesse-Biber, S. N. and Piatelli, D. (2007), 'Holistic Reflexivity: The Feminist Practice of Reflexivity', in S. N. Hess-Biber (ed.), *Handbook of Feminist Research: Theory and Practice*, Thousand Oaks: Sage Publications.

Jenness, V. (2004), 'Explaining Criminalization: From Demography and Status Politics to Globalization and Modernization', *Annual Review of Sociology*, 30: 147–71.

Kelly, M. (2000), 'Inequality and Crime', *The Review of Econonmics and Statistics*, 82, 4: 530–9.

Lattuca, L. R. (2001), *Creating Interdisciplinarity: Interdisciplinary Research and Teaching among College and University Faculty*, Nashville: Vanderbilt University Press.

Logan, E. (2004), 'The Wrong Race, Committing Crime, Doing Drugs, and Maladjusted for Motherhood: The Nation's Fury over 'Crack Babies'', in P. J. Schram and B. Koons-Witt (eds), *Gendered (In)Justice: Theory and Practice in Feminist Criminology*, Long Grove: Waveland Press, Inc.

Mauer, M. (1999), *Race to Incarcerate*, New York: New Press.

McIntyre, A. (ed.) (2008), *Participatory Action Research*, Thousand Oaks: Sage Publications.

Miller, D. (1999), *Principles of Social Justice*, Cambridge, MA: Harvard University Press.

Petersillia, J. (1991), 'Policy Relevance and the Future of Criminology', *Criminology*, 29, 1: 1–15.

Potter, H. (2006), 'An Argument for Black Feminist Criminology: Understanding African American Women's Experiences With Intimate Partner Abuse Using an Integrated Approach', *Feminist Criminology*, 1: 106–24.

Quinney, R. (2003), 'Criminology as Moral Philosophy', in D. F. Hawkins, S. Myers, and R. N. Stone (eds), *Crime Control and Social Justice*, Santa Barbara: Greenwood Publishing Group.

Richie, B. E. (2007), 'Women and Drug Use: The Case for a Justice Analysis', *Women and Criminal Justice*, 17, 2: 137–43.

_____ (1996), Compelled to Crime: The Gender Entrapment of Battered Black Women, New York: Routledge.

Rose, D. and Clear, T. (1998), 'Incarceration, Social Capital, and Crime: Implications for Social Disorganization Theory', *Criminology*, 36, 3: 441–80.

Spohn, C. C. and Spears, J. W. (2003), 'Sentencing Drug Offenders in Three Cities: Does Race/Ethnicity Make a Difference', in D. F. Hawkins, S. Myers, and R. N. Stone (eds), *Crime Control and Social Justice*, Santa Barbara: Greenwood Publishing Group.

Western, B. (2007), *Punishment and Inequality in America*, New York: Russell Sage.

Young, I. M. (2002), *Inclusion and Democracy*, New York: Oxford University Press.

Young, V. D. (1980), 'Women, Race, and Crime', *Criminology*, 18, 1: 26–34.

Yuval-Davis, N. (1997), 'Women, Citizenship and Difference', *Feminist Review*, 75: 4–27.

15

A NEW LOOK AT VICTIM AND OFFENDER—AN ABOLITIONIST APPROACH

THOMAS MATHIESEN AND
OLE KRISTIAN HJEMDAL*

Old News

It is old news in criminology that prison figures are soaring in a majority of western countries. In the forty-three European countries with populations of at least 250,000, prison populations rose in twenty-six between 1998 and 2001. In western Europe there were increases in eleven out of eighteen countries, and in central

* The basic idea on the relationship between victim and offender, in the latter part of this paper, was first presented by sociologist Ole Kristian Hjemdal. The idea was further developed in the Norwegian edition of Thomas Mathiesen's book *Prison on Trial*. The idea is not presented in the English edition, and is developed for the first time in English in this publication. The remainder of the chapter contains joint perspectives.

and eastern Europe there were increases in fifteen out of twenty-five countries (Walmsley 2001). The United States provides the most serious western example. As of 30 June 2008, state and federal correctional authorities had jurisdiction or legal authority over 1,610,584 prisoners, with an additional 785,556 inmates confined in local jails. The overall population, of 2,396,240 inmates, had increased by 19 per cent (373,502 inmates) since the end of 2000 alone. As of 30 June 2008, one in every 131 US residents was held in custody in state or federal prisons or in local jails. It amounted to 789 prisoners per 100,000 inhabitants. Some states, such as California, had a still higher number of prisoners per 100,000. During the six months ending 30 June 2007, the prison population in the United States increased by 1.6 per cent; 0.8 per cent during the same period in 2008. Sixteen states reported small decreases in their prison populations, while the prison populations in the remaining thirty-four states increased. The growth had slowed down in eighteen of the thirty-four states. We can infer that in close to half of the thirty-four states, prison populations kept increasing at least as fast as before.[1]

Despite nuances, the total increases since 2000 are horrendous. And the trends go further back, at least until the 1980s. What should we do about it?

Various Approaches

Criminology provides various approaches. One of them may be called *boundary acceptance*. The boundaries of the prison are kept intact. The conditions that are part and parcel of the penal and prison system are accepted as boundaries to be taken for granted. Attempts are made to find and underscore the kinds of criminology that governments are listening to and responding to in penal policy, without the boundaries being crossed or violated. Criticism may occur, but only within these boundaries—literally these walls.

One variety of boundary acceptance is based on *individual explanations* of deviance and crime. The hope is that genetics, biology, psychology, various pedagogical approaches like cognitive skills programmes, anger management programmes, cognitive behavioural therapies and the like are called in, which may improve things on the individual level. Strategies of individual incapacitation, in which risk

[1] The number of prisoners in the United States per 100,000 in 2008 is kindly supplied by Professor Borge Bakken of Hong Kong. Otherwise the source is the Office of Justice Programs, US Department of Justice, press release 31 March 2009. Due to the combination of various sources of data, the figures given are (close) approximations.
Note that among inmates held in custody in prisons or jails, black males were incarcerated at 6.6 times the rate of white males. One in 21 black males was incarcerated at midyear 2008, compared to one in 138 white males. As of mid 2008, black males (846,000) outnumbered white males (712,500) and Hispanic males (427,000) among inmates in prisons and jails. About 37 per cent of all male inmates at mid 2008 were black (down from 41 per cent for mid 2000).

assessments based on a variety of techniques have a prominent place, have likewise gained prominence. A wide range of studies in the 'What Works' tradition, a treatment orientation that has supplanted the 'Nothing Works' thinking from the 1960s and 1970s, have rekindled hope (Lipsey 1995). Alternatives such as community sentences, conflict resolution boards and electronic surveillance in the home are being tried in some countries.

The trouble with the various trends and studies based on an individual understanding of crime is that their effectiveness in terms of recidivism is to a very considerable extent scant (Mathiesen 2007). Under rigorous controls various carefully designed measures based for example on psychological and pedagogical preconditions may work to some extent, but such rigorous controls and carefully designed measures are rarely present in our prisons. Our closed prisons are to a large extent boisterous places where drugs are taken in large quantities, and where prisonization—to use Donald Clemmer's (1940) classical term—is an inherent ingredient.

Furthermore, alternatives such as community sentences and conflict resolution boards tend to become add-ons to the prison system rather than true alternatives to it. At the eleventh hour parliaments will vote in such a manner that the measures will be opened not primarily as alternatives to unconditional sentences, but rather as alternatives to conditional sentences or even more lenient control efforts. This is a story that goes far back into the history of 'alternatives'. As Stanley Cohen (1985) has pointed out so eloquently, the total control system seems to swell rather than shrink, at least in many places. To be sure, important exceptions exist (McMahon 1992), but this is a general tendency. It might be added that reliance on the fiscal crisis, arguing that it is too expensive to build or maintain prisons (which has recently become a line of thinking in the US state of California), appears likely to be only a short-term method that will melt away when the economy changes. It is not based on an intrinsic wish to decrease prison figures.

A second variety of boundary acceptance is based on *social or societal explanations* of crime and delinquency. Reference is made to collective morality, which presumably is waning, class conflict and status discords, demography, ethnicity (often combined with class), geography and culture and so on—as well as their practical applications in terms of strategies of collective incapacitation—where whole groups or categories are targeted As in the case of boundary acceptance of the individual variety, the intentions may partly be humanistic and critical of important societal dimensions (class and ethnicity are cases in point), but it is difficult to see the practical results, and measures are often strongly repressive and quite ineffective. In Norway two related examples come to mind: A so-called 'VIC project', in which VIC stands for 'very important criminals' who are closely monitored and taken off the streets when apprehended, and a 'broken windows project' imported from New York, which is another variety of the same. In New York as well as in Norway the 'broken windows' approach is one of many examples of repressive measures that do not yield desired results. Demographic factors and other factors are at work.

The crime rate has gone down in cities and towns also where a 'broken windows' approach is not applied.

A third and final variety of boundary acceptance, where the prison as such is not attacked, but rather accepted, should also be mentioned. We are thinking here of various *critical approaches* to the existing prison system, which keep the boundaries up and the prison as a solution intact. Arguments like: the prison does not work as a preventive measure; the costs of control are greater than the gains; crime is a cultural construction that remains uninfluenced by prison; proposals to reduce the number of prisons; to have more open prisons and fewer closed ones; decriminalization of certain behaviour patterns that currently are criminalized (the use of softer drugs), and the like, are fair enough as criticisms, but do not tear down the walls. Generally speaking, criticisms and proposals like these are well meaning and are mustered by enthusiasts with good intentions. We cannot shrug them off like many of us did in the 1970s. Reforms may be important to prisoners, and they may also have some positive long-term functions. But, by keeping boundaries up, the authorities may easily ward them off as methods to reduce significantly prison populations.

Abolitionism

If the goal is to reduce the number of prisoners and prisons effectively, a much bolder attack on the prison which can transcend system boundaries is in order as a line of thinking. The line of thinking must be broad, essentially demanding a fundamental change in western criminal policy. This is the crux of an *abolitionist* approach to criminal and penal policy.

An abolitionist, whether a scientist, a teacher, or a person practising their trades, is not a person who is preoccupied with what we would call system justification. He/she is not a person who is preoccupied with refining the existing. Their wish is to get rid of the existing, like some people close to 2,000 years ago got rid of (the remnants of) the Roman Empire, or like others more recently, in many countries, got rid of slavery and the death penalty. To be sure, many forces operated in the direction of these major historical examples of abolitions. Yet, in quite a few places slavery and the death penalty are not abolished. In addition, one can find examples of their return under new names. Nevertheless, in many places they may be seen as major, more or less full-scale abolitions.

More concretely, and having worked with the issues involved in abolitionism in the realm of penal and prison policy for roughly forty years, we have, over time, delineated several different *lines* of abolitionist thinking. Here we will briefly mention three of them.

First, *abolitionism may be seen as a stance.* It is the attitude of saying 'no'. This does not mean that the 'no' will be answered affirmatively in practice. A 'no' to prisons will not occur in our time. But as a *stance* it is viable and important. This does not mean that we have not been preoccupied with concrete abolitions. In the Norwegian context, we have been strongly engaged in getting forced labour for alcoholic vagrants abolished (it was in fact abolished in 1970). We were also engaged with getting the borstal, or youth prisons, abolished (they were in fact abolished in 1975). We have done this through our work in the Norwegian prison movement (KROM—the Norwegian Association for Penal Reform, established in 1968 and still going strong). But we have (also in the context of KROM) been preoccupied with fostering and developing an abolitionist stance (in Norwegian *holdning*, and in German the much better word *Stellung*); a constant and deeply critical attitude to prisons and penal systems as human (and inhumane) solutions. Many forces, at the workplace as well as in the private sphere, operate in the direction of softening the abolitionist stance, and one therefore has to be on constant alert to maintain and develop it.[2]

Second, *abolitionism may be seen as an important academic exercise*. While maintaining and advocating an abolitionist stance to penal and prison matters in the external world, the abolitionists who are engaged academically have the academic site as a concrete workplace. In the academic world, in contrast to life outside that is full of compromises, pressures, pitfalls and loud noise, it is possible to think in a clear and principled way. The main point with abolitionism as an academic exercise is that the context provides an opportunity to think and loudly express new ideas; think and loudly express what may be imagined although it is not yet anywhere near practical policy. It was possible, for example, for Louk Hulsman (1997) to ponder deep questions such as: what will it take to have not only prisons, but also penal policy as a whole, abolished? Is it possible to develop a new language supplanting the criminal justice language, and to have criminal law supplanted by civil law? Is it possible to create a civil rather then penal frame of reference in society?

The pressures within the academy to follow the mainstream and remain within a criminal law and penal frame of reference are very strong indeed. Producing research grants, getting tenure as well as a whole range of other social pressures are at work in favour of the mainstream. But in the western world the academy is one of the few places where basic views outside the mainstream may be upheld and loudly voiced.[3]

Abolition as a stance and academic abolitionism are two forms of theoretical abolitionism present in a time where the actual abolition of prisons lies in the future, out of our reach. Both are viable and important. But there is also another possibility, a third form of abolitionism, which is as viable and important as the others. It brings in a third dimension, where a retreat to the safe haven of the academy or a mere

[2] For a further understanding of this line of abolitionism, see Mathiesen (2008).

[3] The present brief statement about abolitionism as an academic exercise is inspired by, but partly different from, Louk Hulsman's conception of 'academic abolition'. Hulsman takes academic abolition to mean, *inter alia*, the development or reconstruction of a different language with which to talk about 'problematic situations' (see Hulsman 1997).

dimension of a staunch *no* is combined with 'expeditions' and actions favouring basic change in the outside world, *notably at key points in our prison and penal policies and culture*. This third form of abolitionism crosses boundaries with stamina and resolve, brings in deep and prolonged interaction with those who are subject to the so-called criminal justice system—the prisoners—and is, up to a point, practical. But it consciously leaves aside many of the practical technicalities and compromises that all too quickly make system boundaries arise once again.[4] It is an art (see, for example, Christie 2004).

This is the line we advocate for *a new criminology*, to counterbalance the very strong tendency in the discipline towards boundary acceptance of one or more of the kinds indicated earlier in this chapter.

An example is in order.

Victim and Offender

The relationship between *victim and offender* strikes at the core of criminal policy. Though victimless crimes certainly abound, the relationship is nonetheless key. Turn the key, and another criminal policy may emerge.

The victim has received increasing attention during the past couple of decades. The plight of the victim, or of his or her relatives, is often compared with the situation of the offender. In public debate it is frequently said that while the offender receives large doses of help and support, the victim receives next to nothing. This, it is maintained, is out of balance and an unjust arrangement. Presumably, the tables should be turned: The victim should receive much more support of various kinds and the offender, less, so that the relationship between victim and offender is brought into balance.

We propose a different way of looking at the relationship between victim and offender. We have in mind victims of offenders who today serve time in prison, or of offenders who would have served time in prison if they had been caught. Our analysis is meant as a sketch, an idea that needs further development, and is in line with an abolitionist way of thinking.

Our point of departure is that it serves the victim little to have the offender reported to the police and possibly imprisoned. First, the victim largely receives little or nothing from it. An exception would be the minimum pleasure of naked revenge on the part of the victim. Though such a sentiment is understandable, we do not accept it as a legitimate function of imprisonment. Second, revenge is an 'open' feeling: as a sentiment it is never fully satisfied and legal punishment of the perpetrators does

[4] New debates and conflicts over abolition may occur when academics and prisoners become engaged in a common social movement. However, it is our experience, after 40 years of work in KROM (see above), that many such conflicts may be solved in a long-term perspective.

not reduce the victims' feelings of revenge (Orth 2004); stiffer sentences usually lead to further demands for revenge, and so on in an unending circle. Third, our present system is of rather marginal importance to most victims. Few victims (in Norway 15–20 per cent) report cases of violence to the police, and when property crimes are reported the main reason is to release the insurance rather than having the offender sentenced. The main reason for not reporting violence is that victims do not think it will be of any help (which, by the way, is quite correct as the chances of being exposed to further violent episodes is not influenced by reporting to the police). Also, in cases where crimes against the person are in fact reported, sentencing does not usually follow. For example, in over 80 per cent of all reported rapes, charges are for various reasons dropped. To use the victim as an argument for a more repressive policy misses the target completely, not only because it does not help the victim to have the offender imprisoned, but also because the large majority of victims are out of reach of present-day criminal policy (Hjemdal 2002).

On the side of the prisoner, and again contrary to popular opinion, it serves the offender little to be imprisoned. The pains of imprisonment are sharp, often as knives, and prisons are not service institutions but disciplinary control systems. Those who are imprisoned systematically constitute one of the most poverty-stricken strata in society, and remain so after serving a prison sentence.

Imprisonment, then, is a solution for neither victim nor offender.

'Victimology' has, through the past couple of decades, become an important research area. Nevertheless, criminal policy does not cease to focus on the offender. The offender is the object of criminal policy. They are to blame, and they are to be punished.

We take the position that a radical change should take place in the very focus of criminal policy. The position may be seen as a concrete implementation of an abolitionist approach. Our proposal is to *move the focus of attention in criminal policy completely away from the offender, and over to the victim.*

Traditionally, the offender and the victim are seen in relation to each other. They are two sides of the same coin. What we propose, is to untie the relationship between the two. We propose to use Occam's razor[5] on the tie, and make the victim *rather than* the offender the object of criminal policy.

This idea is fundamentally different from the more traditional notion of restorative justice. At the core of restorative justice is the understanding of crime as a conflict relationship between a victim and an offender. In restorative justice the role of the criminal justice system is to prepare the parties for solving the conflict between themselves. The main objective of restorative justice is to repair the damage and restore the relationship between the parties. Our notion presupposes a much

[5] Occam's razor can be popularly stated as 'when you have two competing theories that make exactly the same predictions, the simpler one is the better'. The principle is attributed to 14th-century English logician and Franciscan friar, William of Occham.

stronger role on the part of the state, in which—to repeat—the state moves the very focus away from the offender and over to the victim.[6] But conflict resolution may come in as one of the many ways of providing a new social dignity on the part of the victim (and offender). We return to this later.

Our notion means that the efforts of society should not consist of adjusting the right punishment to the crime committed by the offender, but that the efforts of society should rather consist of adjusting the correct help to the victim. The measures taken by society should not be escalated, in the form of pain or punishment, relative to the guilt and damage done by the offender, but the measures taken by society should be escalated, in the form of help, relative to the situation and damage done to the victim. In short: rather than operating with a scale of punishment related to the offence, we should operate with a scale of help related to the harm experienced by the victimized person.

It is a foreign thought, and we should therefore acquaint ourselves with it. Once again, the heart of the matter is to adjust the efforts of society as help to the victim *rather than* punishment of the offender. The crux of the matter is to escalate the measures of society as help relative to the situation and damage on the part of the victim *rather than* escalating them as punishments relative to the offender's guilt and damage done.

The heart of the matter, then, is a brand new criminal policy, a criminal policy that also would decrease anxiety in society, something which traditional criminal policy does not do. As Box and Hale (1982, 1985) have suggested, lawmakers and courts may be seen as 'anxiety barometers', as institutions that, through their decisions, reflect the anxiety of society. But they *do* nothing to the anxiety. The policy that we propose would *do* something with the anxiety by the shifting of attention mentioned above.

Such concentration on help to the victim could conceivably take three general forms:

First, the *symbolic form*. Symbolic rehabilitation is important in a number of cases: institutionalized sympathy, rituals expressing sorrow, stronger forms of rehabilitating honour through personal and public conversations and forms of being together, adequate resources for treatment in a wide sense of the word where *this* is wanted. And peace and quiet, no interference, where *that* is wanted.

Second, the *material form*. Life insurance in the real sense of the word is important. Here this means that all members of society automatically, from birth on, are economically insured against crime, and that the insurance is released in very simple ways, without complicated and degrading efforts on the part of the victim. It is curious, however, that our advanced social democratic state has not already instituted this, but has left it to private initiative. A general life insurance from birth on would among other things have wiped out the class differences that exist today as far as insurance goes. The poverty of imprisoned offenders usually makes it impossible for

[6] In this sense it is different from the model of restitution proposed by Randy Barnett (1977).

offenders to compensate damages, at least when the damages are more than trivial. It would have to be a state insurance. A low insurance tax for all citizens from birth on would make it possible for the state to pay damages, at least in cases where the damages are above a certain level.

Today's state compensation to victims of violent crimes is only a beginning. Over and above economic insurance and standard compensation, concrete support for rehabilitation of material structures that have been damaged, similar support for rehabilitation of the human situations that have been damaged, would be important. You can say that it is not always easy to rehabilitate, even when it is in the material sense. But within today's system *nothing* is rehabilitated or rebuilt, and much can after all be done in this respect.

Third, the *social form*. This is the place where a new contact between victim and offender could be relevant. It presupposes an active interest on the part of both parties.

Today's conflict resolution boards could be one model. Generally crime, at least of the traditional kind, may be viewed as a communicative act, a sidetracked attempt to say something. When we consider it important that what is being said is said in a manner which is acceptable, further communication may be facilitated, and arrangements for that purpose should be established. But at times—indeed, quite often—such communication is not desired by one or both parties, or is impossible to arrange for other reasons. Obviously, communication of this kind cannot be established as long as the offence remains undetected or unresolved. Nevertheless, the social form is far from being exhausted as a way of thinking. For those who have been exposed to street violence, the establishment of networks of a protective and rehabilitative kind, especially in the sense of reducing anxiety, would be important. For those who have been subjected to violence in the private sphere, today's crisis centres for battered women and men could provide a model. As violence in the private sphere is being uncovered, we understand how important the establishment and further development of protective centres would be, and how important it would be to give those who are employed there all the resources they need for running the centres. For battered women and men, and for those who have been exposed to more subtle but threatening victimization, it would be important (as supplements to the protective centres) to develop roles for persons who could be called in and act as go-betweens. Roles of this kind are almost totally lacking in our society today.

These are just suggestions—a whole host of social measures as well as symbolic and material methods may be envisaged. But what about the cost? We have mentioned a life insurance against criminal damages for all citizens from birth, which would imply a small insurance tax on everyone. The insurance would be a non-profit matter, so the tax would be low. But it would require an administrative bureaucracy (a danger would be that this bureaucracy could grow large; this would have to be prevented), and the many other arrangements that would be relevant and necessary would be costly. Who would pay, over and above the insurance tax?

Keep clearly in mind our point of departure: the crux of the matter is to escalate the measures of society as help relative to the situation and damage on the part of the victim, *rather than* escalating them as punishments relative to the offender's guilt and damage done. In other words, the point is an installation of a new kind of justice. This would lead to a drastic reduction of the prison population, which is part and parcel of the abolitionist approach. In turn this would involve a similarly dramatic reduction of costs in the construction and maintenance of prisons. We do not consider it our task here to present a detailed budget, just to present the idea. The money saved would certainly cover the expenses of help to victims. Also of the utmost importance: it would help cover a large part of the expenses that would have to be geared towards *help to the offender.* To repeat, we know the offenders who are imprisoned are regularly extremely poor. They lack education, housing, jobs, in large numbers they are drug addicts, alcoholics, and the like. Saved money would have to be divided between the ranks of victims and the ranks of offender. There would be money enough through saved prison expenses.

We hear the cry: what of protection of society? What of incapacitation of the offender, collective and selective? What of the deterrence of the offender and also of others who are not yet inside the walls? These are large questions. Our answers to them are given in detail in Thomas Mathiesen's (2006) book *Prison on Trial.*[7] A large collection of data—a whole library of empirical studies—suggest that prison is a failure in terms of all the standard justifications of imprisonment.

Perhaps there is a lower threshold or floor in terms of imprisonment under which we cannot go without doing some harm to society. In Britain, the United States, and many other countries we are very far indeed from that floor today. It is time to change our priorities, carving out a basically new criminal policy in our societies.

We have just presented an idea of such a change. It would have to be carved out in practice. In practice it would be a long drawn-out process, with pitfalls and struggles. From the start it would involve a mode of thinking that is critical but also constructive rather than just concentrating on the difficulties. Perhaps, above all, it would involve a basic change in the cultural climate of our society.

Conclusions

Quite a few years ago, the French sociologist Pierre Bourdieu (1977) coined the term *doxa* to stand for that which is taken for granted, that which is not questioned because it is common knowledge to everyone in the tribe. *Doxa* has hegemony. If debates do occur on issues in *doxa* (and they often do in the western world), they are

[7] Also out in Norwegian, Swedish, Danish, German, Italian, Spanish, and Taiwan mandarin, and currently being translated into mainland mandarin.

frequently *orthodox*: while frequently sensational in terms of media coverage, the coverage often takes for granted and therefore neglects the basic issues involved. Ethnomethodologists have touched on such hidden dimensions of societal communication long before Bourdieu, without using his terminology. At times, however, debates become *heterodox*, touching on deep issues. Struggles may then occur, for example, over critical issues in criminal policy. Heterodox opinions are often relegated to marginal journals and newspapers outside the mainstream. But sometimes they become threatening to basic dimensions in *doxa*. They become real battles. Such struggles may make the world better, but also worse—there are historical examples of both. It is our hope that our new look at the victim and offender makes (some) people think outside of standardized patterns, outside of *doxa*, to make the world better. It would also help open up for a new and exciting science of criminology, which thinks outside the box, and which is not restricted by boundaries.

References

Barnett, R. (1977), 'Restitution: A New Paradigm of Criminal Justice', *Ethics*, 87, 4: 279–301.

Bourdieu, P. (1977), *Outline of a Theory of Practice*, Cambridge: Cambridge University Press.

Box, S., and Hale, C. (1982), 'Economic Crisis and the Rising Prisoner Population in England and Wales', *Crime and Social Justice*, 17: 20–35.

_____, and _____ (1985), 'Unemployment, Imprisonment and Prison Overcrowding', *Contemporary Crises*, 9, 3: 209–28.

Christie, N. (2004), *A Suitable amount of Crime*, London: Routledge.

Clemmer, D. (1940), *The Prison Community*, Boston: Christopher Publishing House.

Cohen, S. (1985), *Visions of Social Control*, Cambridge: Polity Press.

Hjemdal, O. K. (2002), 'Holder politiets arbeid mål?' ('Is the Work of the Police up to Standard?'), in A. Skodvin (ed.), *Polititjenestemann og akademiker* (Police Officer and Academic), Oslo: Norwegian Police University College.

Hulsman, L. (1997), 'Themes and Concepts in an Abolitionist Approach to Criminal Justice', *Dordrecht*, 22 September 1997 (<www.loukhulsman.org/Publication/>).

Lie, E. M. (2009), 'Law og orden i New York' ('Law and Order in New York'), *Aftenposten*, 23 September 2009.

Lipsey, M. W. (1995), 'What do we Learn from 400 Research Studies on the Effectiveness of Treatment with Juvenile Delinquents?', in J. McGuire (ed.), *What Works: Reducing Reoffending Guidelines from Research and Practice*, London: Wiley.

Mathiesen, T. (2006), *Prison on Trial*, 3rd edn, Hook: Waterside Press.

_____ (2007), 'Fra 'Nothing Works' til 'What Works'—Hvor store er forskjellen?' ('From 'Nothing Works' to 'What Works'—How Great is the Difference?'), in H. von Hofer and A. Nilsson (eds), *Brott i välfärden. Om brottslighet. Utsatthet og kriminalpolitik* (*Crime in Welfare. About crime, Vulnerability and Penal Policy*), Festskrift till Henrik Tham (Homage volume in honour of Henrik Tham), Stockholm: Kriminologiska Institutionen.

_____ (2008), 'The Abolitionist Stance', paper presented at the International Conference on Penal Abolition (ICOPA XII), 23 July 2008, printed in *Journal of Prisoners on Prisons*, 17, 2: 58–63.

McMahon, M. (1992), *The Persistent Prison? Rethinking Decarceration and Penal Reform*, Toronto: University of Toronto Press.

Orth, U. (2004), 'Does Perpetrator Punishment Satisfy Victims' Feelings of Revenge?', *Aggressive Behavior*, 30: 62–70.

Walmsley, R. (2001), *European Prison Populations: Recent Growth and how to Reduce it*, London: Home Office.

16

REMEMBERING CRIMINOLOGY'S 'FORGOTTEN THEME': SEEKING JUSTICE IN US CRIME POLICY USING AN INTERSECTIONAL APPROACH

NATALIE J. SOKOLOFF AND AMANDA BURGESS-PROCTOR*

* The authors thank Beth Huebner and Fred L. Pincus for their helpful comments on an earlier draft of this manuscript.

Introduction

THE 2008 Annual Meeting of the American Society of Criminology featured four high-profile presidential sessions organized by then-president Bob Bursik. One session focused on issues related to politics and crime, and included a moderated discussion about criminologists using our research to inform crime and justice policy. Among the panelists was Charles Wellford of the University of Maryland and the National Academy of Sciences, who encouraged contemporary criminologists to focus less on identifying the causes and correlates of crime and more on improving justice in the United States. According to Wellford, justice is a 'forgotten theme' in the field of criminology.

In this chapter, we address the concern that justice is criminology's 'forgotten theme'. After briefly outlining the failure of contemporary mainstream criminology to engage with justice, we summarize the intersectional framework, which we believe offers criminology an important tool both for identifying inequalities and for working to improving justice. To illustrate, we use an intersectional approach to examine how problematic crime policy can lead to injustices for marginalized groups: specifically, how the US War on Drugs has contributed to the mass incarceration of poor Black[1] and increasingly Latina women. We employ an intersectional approach to analyse this problem in two ways. First, guided by its attention to a range of inequalities, we use the intersectional framework to uncover the disproportionate incarceration of marginalized women and, then, to illuminate how restrictive public policies for former drug offenders have ravaging consequences for poor Black and Latina women, and for the marginalized communities to which they return from prison. Second, guided by its emphasis on advancing social justice, we use the intersectional framework to offer specific research and policy suggestions that can help ameliorate some of the injustices for marginalized women as they return to their home communities from prison. In this way, we hope to encourage a reorientation of criminology that focuses less on explaining crime and more on advancing justice for our most marginalized populations.

Inequality, Crime, and Justice in Contemporary Criminology

Modern positivist criminology emerged in nineteenth-century France during a time when the 'dangerous classes' threatened public order (Beirne and Messerchmidt 2010; Shelden 2001). Early criminologists struggled to establish theirs as a discipline capable of scientifically analysing and predicting the behaviour of the criminal

[1] In the United States, Black and African Americans are used interchangeably (eg, see Potter 2006), but do not include other ethnic groups like Asians as in England.

class, whom the fledgling prison system had largely failed to contain (eg, see Balbi and Guerrey 1829; Quetelet 1831). Many early scholars applied the scientific method to criminal behaviour in a 'self-conscious' effort to identify causes and correlates of criminal offending, and that intellectual orientation persists in much of the field to this day (Beirne and Messerchmidt 2010: 92).

Notwithstanding the discipline's traditional focus on offending etiology and control, elements of criminology have always been concerned with justice (see, for example, Beccaria [1764] 1819). Starting in the 1960s and 1970s, a whole host of critical criminologists (including Marxist, critical race, and feminist scholars) began to analyse and critique injustices in the criminal legal system.[2] This scholarship highlighted class-, race-, and gender-based disparities in the treatment of offenders and victims, and questioned the relevance of mainstream theories of criminality that had developed almost exclusively using samples of white, working class or impoverished men and boys. We have, in other words, several decades of critical scholarship revealing serious race, class, and gender disparities in the processing of offenders and victims in the criminal legal system. What remains somewhat absent, however, particularly in mainstream criminological literature, is a robust theoretical framework that accommodates the *interplay between* and *simultaneity of* these factors (see Burgess-Proctor 2006 for a review; Price and Sokoloff 2004).

From our perspective, then, criminology requires reorientation along two important dimensions. First, we must move away from single-focus conceptualizations of inequality toward those that recognize the socially structured linkages between race, class, gender, and other systems of power. Second, we must focus less on only scholarly pursuits that seek to explain offending in favour of those that recognize—and, more importantly, work to correct—inequities caused by problematic crime policy. Contemporary criminologists seeking to accomplish these aims are wise to consider a framework that both attends to intersecting sources of inequality *and* emphasizes pursuing justice for groups marginalized by intersecting race, class, and gender systems.

The Intersectional Approach

Intersectionality is a theoretical framework that guides research, activism, and thinking. It concentrates on the lived experiences of different groups of women (and men), giving voice to those who historically have been silenced. Intersectional scholars are primarily concerned with *socially structured systems of inequality* and *relationships between groups in society*; they use this framework both to guide their empirical research and to advance particular policies and social justice goals.

[2] Belknap (2001) uses the term 'crime processing system' instead of 'criminal justice system' in order to reflect the system's emphasis on processing offenders rather than promoting justice. Likewise, in this chapter we use the term 'criminal legal system' out of similar concerns.

The concept of intersectionality was first used by US legal scholar Kimberlé Crenshaw to analyse the interaction of race and gender in work force discrimination (1991) and battering (1994) in the lives of Black women. Indeed, the first intersectional scholars were Black women and other women of colour who, living at the intersection of the feminist and civil rights/Black studies movements, felt marginalized by both white women *and* Black men (Richie 2005; Sudbury 2005).[3] These Black women demanded acknowledgement of their experiences from white feminists and Black critical race activists alike.

Several guiding principles of an intersectional framework are relevant for any attempt to reorientate criminology toward improving justice for marginalized groups. First, the socially structured systems of race, class, and gender are not seen as a series of isolated variables. Instead, intersectionality considers the effects of race, class, gender, and other facets of social location to be *multiplicative rather than additive* (Andersen and Collins 2004). Thus, the overall effect of these intersecting systems in determining one's social location is greater than the sum of their individual influences. Second, intersectionality entails more than a politics of 'inclusion' or 'assimilation', in which the experiences of many different groups of women are incorporated into a white, heterosexual, middle class framework. Rather, intersectionality requires an entirely new approach in which *marginalized groups are the centre of analysis, organizing, and social change* (Sokoloff 2008). Intersectionality also affirms individual agency by acknowledging that women in constrained or oppressed social locations make choices to resist oppression in different ways (Abraham 2000; Lamphere and Zavella 1997). Third, and most important, the intersectional approach is committed to *advancing social justice* to improve the lives of marginalized members of society (Andersen and Collins 2004; Weber and Parra-Medina 2003). The commitment to justice inherent to the intersectional approach is crucial for feminist criminological praxis (Burgess-Proctor 2006), including working for reformation of problematic crime policy.

Intersectionality is particularly useful for studying inequality and injustice in the criminal legal system because it attends to the complex ways race, class, gender, and other systems of power interconnect such that certain groups become more vulnerable to criminal legal system control. A powerful example of this is the US War on Drugs, which has contributed to the mass incarceration of marginalized women who then become subject to restrictive state and federal policies for ex-offenders. Below we demonstrate how an intersectional framework recasts our understanding of the impact the War on Drugs, mass incarceration, and restrictive ex-offender policies have on marginalized women, while offering criminologists a tool for reforming

[3] Heteronormativity or heterosexuality was assumed, and many of the Black and other women of colour challenging white male and female and Black male dominance were lesbians as well (Richie 2005).

these policies so as to improve justice for the people and groups they most severely disadvantage.

The War on Drugs and the Mass Incarceration of Marginalized Women

The experiences of contemporary incarcerated US women are defined by the monumental increases in incarceration that occurred during the last three decades of the twentieth century. Kathleen Daly and Meda Chesney-Lind (1988: 525) memorably described this period as one of 'equality with a vengeance', in which harsh punishments developed in response to crimes committed mostly by poor, violent male offenders were uncritically extended to women. For example, mandatory minimums, three strikes, and truth-in-sentencing laws often were applied to women in the name of equal treatment. These 'get tough' crime control policies lead to the incarceration of more people for longer periods of time, while reducing their opportunities for diversion, parole, or rehabilitation. Women were increasingly swept into this penal dragnet, despite committing a disproportionate number of non-violent drug and lower-level economic crimes (Sabol, West, and Cooper 2009; Steffensmeier and Schwartz 2004). Thus, even as the proportion of women incarcerated in state facilities for violent crimes fell from 48.9 per cent in 1979 to 34.8 per cent in 2003 (Greenfield and Snell 1999; Harrison and Beck 2006), during this period women's overall incarceration rate steadily increased, outpacing men's growth (Huebner, DeJong and Cobbina 2009; The Sentencing Project 2007).

At the start of the 1970s, there were 5,600 women in US prisons (Currie 1998), a figure that had changed only slightly since 1936 (Simon 1993). Beginning in the 1980s, however, women's incarceration rates climbed steadily, so that as of 2008 there were 105,300 women in prison (Sabol, West, and Cooper 2009). Combined with the 99,673 women in jail (Minton and Sabol 2009), there were over 200,000 incarcerated women in the United States in 2008.[4] Further, an additional 836,872 women were on probation and parole in 2008 (Glaze and Bonczar 2009).[5] Summing these figures yields a shocking result: *currently more than one million women are under control of the criminal legal system.*

[4] The *rate* of incarceration for both men and women actually has been *slowing* in the 2000s, as money for prisons has become scarcer and slightly fewer people are being incarcerated for drug crimes. Importantly, the decline in incarceration for drug crimes has led to a decrease in both the number and rate of incarceration for Black men and women (Sabol, West, and Cooper 2009). Nevertheless, Black women and men continue to be overrepresented in prison today.

[5] This figure is important because, according to Glaze and Bonczar (2009), one-third of all women who enter prison do so for a 'technical violation' of probation or parole that leads to revocation, rather than for committing another crime.

The War on Drugs is a major factor behind the massive increase in women's incarceration. The ever-toughening drug laws and correctional policies of the last three decades have resulted in women's incarceration increasing at a faster rate than men's in recent years, largely as a result of women's disproportionate participation in drug-related crimes (Bloom, Owen, and Covington 2003; Deschenes, Owen, and Crow 2007; Huebner, DeJong, and Cobbina 2010).[6] As it has for the general population of women offenders, the War on Drugs has sharply affected poor women of colour (primarily Black and secondarily Latina), as they are disproportionately arrested and incarcerated for drug offences (Diaz-Cotto 2007; Sudbury 2004). For example, in 2008 the federal and state imprisonment rate for Black women (149 per 100,000) was twice as high as for Latinas (75 per 100,000) and three times as high as for white (50 per 100,000) women (Sabol, West, and Cooper 2009: 2, table 2). Similarly, Black women were three times as likely as white women to be incarcerated in prison or jail in 2005, while Latinas were 69 per cent more likely than white women to be so incarcerated (The Sentencing Project 2007). This has led some to suggest that the War on Drugs is really a 'War on Poor Black Women' (Bush-Baskette 1998; Russell-Brown 2004).

Other women disproportionately affected by the War on Drugs include those who are uneducated, unskilled, and/or sporadically employed (Bloom, Owen, and Covington 2003).[7] Many others also are heads of household and/or mothers of young children (Glaze and Maruschak, 2008), further adding to their (economic) marginalization. Additionally, imprisoned women often have serious, long-term substance abuse problems (Belknap 1996; Greenfield and Snell 1999; McClean, Robarge, and Sherman 2005), are in poor health (often with complications of HIV, asthma, diabetes, hypertension, STIs and reproductive health problems (Freudenberg 2005)),[8] and have histories of childhood or adult victimization and abuse (Greenfield and Snell 1999). As the multiplicity of their marginality makes clear, an intersectional framework decentres an essentialist notion of 'women', understands that not all women are alike, and is the most appropriate lens for viewing the complexity of disadvantage in the lives of incarcerated women affected by the US War on Drugs.

[6] The role of intimate partner violence (IPV) is especially important in this context, as research indicates that some battered women self-medicate with illegal drugs as a survival strategy (eg, see Rogers *et al.*, 2003), while others are forced into drug sales by their abusive partners (eg, see Richie 1996). Others are criminalized for using drugs —primarily crack — while pregnant, thereby making reproduction a crime primarily for poor Black women (Roberts 1997; Duley 2006). Still others rely on the state to prosecute and incarcerate abusers, which 'fuel[s] prison expansion... [and] perpetuates a culture of systemic violence against women by not addressing the structural inequalities upon which this type of violence relies' (Duley 2006: 88).

[7] In New York state prisons about two-thirds of men and women have neither a high school diploma nor a GED. In New York City jails this figure jumps to 90 per cent, with 50–70 per cent of adult prisoners reading below the sixth grade level in English (Fine *et al.*. 2003).

[8] See Mallik-Kane and Visher (2008) for a discussion of similar health problems among returning women.

Applying Intersectionality: How Restrictive Ex-Offender Policies Disadvantage Marginalized Women and their Communities

Restrictive crime policies place almost impossible burdens on those marginalized women who are leaving prison, and on the communities to which they return. Financial penalties—including fines, fees, costs, surcharges, forfeitures, assessments, reimbursements, and restitutions—may be imposed on many convicted criminals. Though little recognized, these penalties form serious impediments to ex-offenders' successful reintegration (Rosenthal and Weissman 2007). In addition, of the 13 million former and current prisoners living in the United States today, 792,220 are women (Felony Disenfranchisement Rates for Women 2008); and the vast majority of all ex-offenders cannot vote. Thirty-five states prohibit ex-felons from voting while on parole, thirty have similar prohibitions for felony probationers, and two states deny voting rights to *all* ex-offenders after they complete their sentence (Petersilia 2003; The Sentencing Project 2008). However, marginalized women convicted of felony drug offences are subjected to a host of additional restrictions that exacerbate their already vulnerable social status. An intersectional framework better reveals the nature and extent of these 'post-incarceration sentences' (Allard 2002: 27) on marginalized women, as we describe below.

First, laws at both the state and federal levels require public housing facilities to deny residence to convicted felons, including drug offenders (Petersilia 2003). As a result, women leaving prison with limited financial means may be forced to seek alternative forms of shelter. However, many incarcerated women were either homeless (up to 40 per cent in some studies; see Richie 2001) or inadequately housed before *entering* jail or prison (McClean, Robarge, and Sherman 2006), so subsidized housing may be one of very few options available to these returning women. Moreover, these same women may not reside with parents, grandparents, partners, friends, relatives, or children who live in public housing facilities, as entire families can be evicted for providing housing to ex-offenders (Nieves 2002). Public housing facilities are disproportionately located in poor, urban communities of colour; therefore, women returning to these communities feel the disparate impact of public housing bans. Thus, marginalized women with felony drug convictions are placed at increased risk of homelessness and other substandard housing options, such as returning to an abusive ex-partner or relative (Allard 2002).

Second, the Felony Drug Provision (FDP) of the 1996 Welfare Reform Act permanently bans receipt of cash assistance and food stamps for anyone convicted of a drug felony (sale or possession). Although states were able to opt out of the FDP, only eight[9] have done so; the remaining forty-two states enforce the ban in full (twenty-two states) or in part (twenty states; Allard 2002). Data collected from

[9] States opting out of the ban are: CT, MI, NH, NY, OH, OK, OR, VT, and DC.

twenty-three of those forty-two states reveal that between 1996 and 1999, an estimated 92,000 women were affected by the FDP (Allard 2002). Largely due to race- and gender-based socio-economic inequalities making them highly susceptible to poverty and thus over-represented in the welfare system, Black and Latina mothers are disproportionately disadvantaged by the lifetime welfare ban (Allard 2002).

Third, in many states people with felony convictions are banned from certain employment sectors, including civil service careers. In all states, former offenders are restricted from working as beauticians and nurses; and in most from child care, education, and home health care (Petersilia 2003)—jobs that are heavily Black and female. Thus, the very jobs requiring little formal education or training to which poor women of colour with limited employment options otherwise might gravitate are unavailable to women with felony drug convictions. For Black women, these employment restrictions are particularly harsh given race-based employment segregation that denies them jobs based on their race and criminal history, no matter how minor (Reid 2002).

Fourth, victim service agencies may refuse to offer treatment and resources to women with criminal convictions. In some cases, programmes perform background checks on women who call for assistance because their funding requirements forbid service provision to ex-prisoners (Richie 2001). Denial of victim services is especially problematic for marginalized women—including women of colour (Sokoloff and Pratt 2005), poor women (Purvin 2007; Sokoloff and Pratt 2005), and immigrant women (Bui 2004; Raj and Silverman 2002; Sokoloff 2008)—who are at greater risk of intimate partner abuse than their majority-group counterparts. These policies are particularly harmful to Black women, who have some of the highest victimization rates for rape, intimate partner abuse, and murder in the country (Della Giustina 2006; Hampton *et al.* 2003; Rennison and Planty 2003; Websdale 1997). For Black women, lack of access to victim services exacerbates (and is exacerbated by) the intensity of poverty, segregation, and isolation within poor Black communities to which formerly incarcerated drug offenders typically return (see Hampton *et al.* 2003; Richie 2001; Sokoloff and Dupont 2005).

Finally, the communities to which many marginalized women drug offenders return after prison likewise are in very poor condition (Clear 2006; La Vigne *et al.* 2003). As Richie (2001) notes, most poor women of colour leaving prison return to a small number of communities with the very same conditions they left when they entered prison: disenfranchised communities with limited economic, social, and political resources. Affordable housing, jobs, and health care are limited at best, and seriously limited community resources are further inhibited by the women's inadequate education and their criminal records. These women face multiple, competing demands as they simultaneously try to regain custody of minor children, juggle childcare, search for housing and employment, and try to enroll in a substance abuse treatment programme, which often is a condition of their release (Freudenberg *et al.* 2001; McClean, Robarge, and Sherman 2006; Richie 2001).

In short, in the United States, the experiences of poor Black (and Latina) women returning from prison, their families, and the communities to which they return are simultaneously raced, classed, and gendered in powerful ways.[10] Whereas examining one source of inequality at a time offers a narrow view of the consequences of problematic crime policies for marginalized women ex-offenders, using an intersectional lens helps us see the broad scope of the injustices these policies incur for women and communities marginalized by intersecting systems of race, class, and gender.

Conclusion: How Intersectional Criminology can Improve Justice for Marginalized Women and their Communities

We opened this chapter with remarks from Dr Charles Wellford at the 2008 American Society of Criminology Annual Meeting, during which he called justice a 'forgotten theme' in criminology. Therefore, it seems fitting to conclude with the 2009 presidential address by ASC president Todd Clear, a vocal critic of the mass incarceration movement. In his address, Clear (2010) confronts criminologists' reluctance to engage in policy reform, noting, 'Some of us have tried to use the [disciplinary] knowledge as a tool for improving the justice system; others—perhaps most of us—have not' (p. 19). Clear urged contemporary criminologists to embrace the 'production of justice' in the application of our work to public policy (ibid: 13). Mirroring our arguments here, Clear highlighted the devastating consequences of mass incarceration—especially for poor minority communities—to emphasize the need for criminologists to embrace a focus on justice in public policy.

An intersectional approach offers a useful corrective as it enables—and even *requires*—scholars to apply their knowledge to both inform and reform public policy (Burgess-Proctor 2009; see Hull, Scott, and Smith 1993). One prominent example of this type of community activism occurred with women of colour working in the anti-violence against women movement. They understood that efforts to curb violence against women of colour required the empowerment of marginalized battered women for personal *and* social change that demanded an intersectional framework. Most important, because of this, they have had a measure of success in translating academic knowledge into community action as they work in coalitions with

[10] While our focus in this chapter has been on US drug policy, similar patterns have emerged in other nations. For example, Sudbury (2004) identifies the *prison industrial complex* as a profitable relationship between corporations, politicians, the media, and state correctional institutions that 'generates the racialized use of incarceration as a response to social problems rooted in the globalization of capital' (p. 224). This prison industrial complex, combined with the globalization of the War on Drugs, also has led to the incarceration of poor women of colour in Canada, Britain, and many European countries.

researchers and grass roots activists and organizations (see Incite! Violence Against Women of Color 2006; Smith 2005; Sokoloff 2008).

The efforts of women of colour anti-violence activists serve as a model for contemporary criminologists to extend their scholarship beyond academia by fighting unjust social policies and actively promoting just social policies. Specific suggestions for criminologists to accomplish these aims include:

- send executive summaries of our published journal articles to state or local policy-makers to increase visibility of research that documents when policies are problematic;
- publicize our work to the media so that important research results are shared beyond academia;
- advise state legislators to opt out of restrictive federal policies (like the Felony Drug Provision, public housing bans for ex-offenders, occupational bans, etc.);
- encourage congressional leaders to repeal lifetime bans on any rights and privileges (voting, welfare, etc.) for ex-offenders;
- form coalitions and partnerships with community agencies (for example, groups working on behalf of women serving time in and returning from prison) to work for changes at the local or state level;
- create public forums to discuss the underlying structural inequalities that lead to the over-incarceration of marginalized women. Use creative arts, such as videos, as a means of community education and discussion for both personal *and* social change.

We sincerely hope that contemporary criminologists heed the call to 'remember' justice, and to work not only for policy change, but real social change, using an intersectional framework in this endeavour. In this way, we can begin to uncover and challenge the social processes underlying problematic criminal legal policies and work toward a more socially just criminology and society.

References

Abraham, M. (2000), *Speaking the Unspeakable: Marital Violence among South Asian Immigrants in the United States*, New Brunswick: Rutgers University Press.

Allard, P. (2002), *Life Sentences: Denying Welfare Benefits to Women Convicted of Drug Offenses*, Washington: The Sentencing Project.

Andersen, M. and Hill Collins, P. (eds) (2004), *Race, Class, and Gender*, 5th edn, Belmont: Wadsworth.

Balbi, A. and Guerry, A-M. (1829), *Statistique Comparée de L'état de L'instruction et du Nombre des Crimes dans les Divers Arrondissements des Académies et des Cours Royales de France*, Paris, France.

Becarria, C, (1819), *An Essay on Crimes and Punishment*, Philadelphia: Nicklin.

Belknap, J. (1996), *The Invisible Woman: Gender, Crime, and Justice*, 2nd edn, Belmont: Wadsworth.

Bierne, P. and Messerschmidt, J. W. (2010), *Criminology: A Sociological Approach*, 5th edn, New York: Oxford University Press.

Bloom, B., Owen, B., and Covington, S. (2003), *Gender Responsive Strategies: Research, Practice, and Guiding Principles for Women Offenders*, Washington: National Institute of Corrections.

Bui, H. (2004), *In the Adopted Land: Abused Immigrant Women and the Criminal Justice System*, Greenwich: Greenwood.

Burgess-Proctor, A. (2006), 'Intersections of Race, Class, Gender, and Crime: Future Directions for Feminist Criminology', *Feminist Criminology*, 1, 1: 27–47.

_____ (2009), 'Looking Back, Looking Ahead: Assessing Contemporary Feminist Criminology', in H. Copes and V. Topalli (eds), *Criminological Theory: Readings and Retrospectives*, New York: McGraw-Hill.

Bush-Baskette, S. R. (1998), 'The War on Drugs as a War on Black Women', in S. L. Miller (ed.), *Crime Control and Women: Feminist Implications of Criminal Justice Policy*, Thousand Oaks: Sage.

Clear, T. R. (2007), *Imprisoning Communities: How Mass Incarceration Makes Disadvantaged Neighborhoods Worse*, Oxford: Oxford University.

_____ (2010), 'Policy and Evidence: The Challenge to the American Society of Criminology: 2009 Presidential Address to the American Society of Criminology', *Criminology*, 48, 1: 1–25.

Crenshaw, K. (1991), 'Demarginalizing the Intersection of Race and Sex: A Black Feminist Critique of Antidiscrimination Doctrine, Feminist Theory, and Antiracist Politics', in K. Bartlett and R. Kennedy (eds), *Feminist Legal Theory*, Boulder: Westview.

_____ (1994), 'Mapping the Margins: Intersectionality, Identity Politics, and Violence Against Women of Color', in M. Fineman and R. Mykitiuk (eds), *The Public Nature of Private Violence*, Taylor andFrancis/Routledge, Inc.

Currie, E. (1998), *Crime and Punishment in America*, New York: Henry Holt.

Daly, K. and Chesney-Lind, M. (1988), 'Feminism and Criminology', *Justice Quarterly*, 5: 497–538.

Della Giustina, J-A. (2010), 'The Impact of Gender, Race, and Class Discrimination on Femicide Rates', in V. Garcia and J. Clifford (eds), *Female Victims of Crime: Reality Reconsidered*, Upper Saddle River: Prentice Hall.

Deschenes, E., Owen, B., and Crow, J. (2007), *Recidivism among Female Prisoners: Secondary Analysis of the 1994 BJS Recidivism Data Set*, Long Beach: California State University.

Diaz-Cotto, J. (2007), 'Latina Imprisonment and the War on Drugs', in M. Bosworth and J. Flavin (eds), *Race, Gender and Punishment: From Colonialism to the War on Terror*, New Brunswick: Rutgers University.

Duley, K. (2006), 'Un-Domesticating Violence: Criminalizing Survivors and U.S. Mass Incarceration', *Women and Therapy*, 29, 3/4: 75–96.

Faith, K. (2004), 'Progressive Rhetoric, Regressive Policies: Canadian Prisons for Women' in B. R. Price and N. J. Sokoloff (eds), *The Criminal Justice System and Women: Offenders, Prisoners, Victims and Workers*, 3rd edn, New York: McGraw-Hill.

Felony Disenfranchisement Rates for Women (2008), *The Sentencing Project*. (<www.sentencingproject.org/doc/publications/fd_bs_women.pdf>, accessed 12 March 2010).

Fine, M., *et al.* (2003), 'Changing Minds: Going to College at a Maximum Security Prison', *Women, Girls, and Criminal Justice*, 4, 2:17–18, 25–31.

Freudenberg, N., Daniels, J., Crum, M., Perkins, T., and Richie, B. E. (2005), 'Coming Home from Jail: The Social and Health Consequences of Community Reentry for Women, Male Adolescents, Their Families and Communities', *American Journal of Public Health*, 95: 1725–36.

Glaze, L. and Bonczar, T. (2009), *Probation and Parole in the United States, 2007—Statistical Tables*, Bureau of Justice Statistics, NCJ 224707. (<http://bjs.ojp.usdoj.gov/content/pub/pdf/ppus07st.pdf>, accessed 1 December 2009).

_____ and Maruschak, L. (2008), *Parents in Prison and Their Minor Children*, Bureau of Justice Statistics Special Report, NCJ 222984. (<http://bjs.ojp.usdoj.gov/index.cfm?ty=pbdetail&iid=373>, accessed 10 December 2009).

Greenfield, L. and Snell, T. (1999), *Women Offenders*, BJS Special Report, NCJ 175688.

Hampton, R., Oliver, W., and Magarian, L. (2003), 'Domestic Violence in the African American Community', *Violence against Women*, 9, 5: 533–57.

Harrison, P. and Beck, A. (2006), *Prisoners in 2005*, Washington: Bureau of Justice Statistics.

Huebner, B., DeJong, C., and Cobbina, J. (2010), 'Women Coming Home: Long-term Patterns of Recidivism', *Justice Quarterly*, 27, 2: 225–54.

Hull, G., Bell-Scott, P., and Smith, B. (eds) (1993), *But Some of Us Are Brave: All the Blacks Are Men, All the Women Are White: Black Women's Studies*, New York: The Feminist Press at CUNY.

Incite! Women of Color Against Violence (2006), *Color of Violence: The Incite! Anthology*, Boston: South End.

Lamphere, L. and Zavella, P. (1997), 'Women's Resistance in the Sunbelt: Anglos and Hispanas Respond to Managerial Control', in E. Higginbotham and M. Romero (eds), *Women and Work: Exploring Race, Ethnicity, and Class*, Thousand Oakes: SAGE.

La Vigne, N., Thomson, G. L., *et al.* (2003), *A Portrait of Prisoner Reentry in Ohio*, Washington: Urban Institute.

Mallik-Kane, K. and Visher, C. (2008), *Health and Prisoner Reentry: How Physical, Mental, and Substance Abuse Problems Shape the Process of Reintegration*, Washington: Urban Institute.

Mauer, M. and Chesney-Lind, M. (eds) (2002), *Invisible Punishment: The Collateral Consequences of Mass Imprisonment*, New York: New Press.

McClean, R., Robarge, J., and Sherman, S. (2006), 'Release from Jail: Moment of Crisis or Opportunity for Female Detainees', *Journal of Urban Health*, 83, 3: 382–93.

Minton, T. and Sabol, W. (2009), *Jail Inmates at Midyear 2008—Statistical Tables*, Bureau of Justice Statistics, NCJ 225709. (<http://bjs.ojp.usdoj.gov/content/pub/pdf/jim08st.pdf>, accessed 1 December 2009).

Nieves, E. (2002), 'Drug Ruling Worries Some in Public Housing', *New York Times*, 28 March 2002.

Petersilia, J. (2003), *When Prisoners Come Home: Parole and Prisoner Reentry*, New York: Oxford University Press.

Potter, H. (2006), 'An Argument for Black Feminist Criminology: Understanding African American Women's Experiences with Intimate Partner Abuse Using an Integrated Approach', *Feminist Criminology*, 1, 2: 106–24.

Price, B. R. and Sokoloff, N. J. (eds) (2004), *The Criminal Justice System and Women*, 3rd edn, New York: McGraw-Hill.

Purvin, D. (2007), 'At the Crossroads and in the Crosshairs: Social Welfare Policy and Low-Income Women's Vulnerability to Domestic Violence', *Social Problems*, 54, 2: 188–210.

Quetelet, A. (1831), *Recherches sur le Penchant au Crime aux Différens Age*, Brussels, Belgium.

Raj, A. and Silverman, J. (2002), 'Violence against Immigrant Women: The Roles of Culture, Context, and Legal Immigrant Status on Intimate Partner Violence', *Violence against Women*, 8, 3: 367–98.

Reid, L. (2002), 'Occupational Segregation, Human Capital, and Motherhood: Black Women's Higher Exit Rates from Full-Time Employment', *Gender and Society*, 16, 5: 728–47.

Rennison, C. M. and Planty, M. (2003), 'Nonlethal Intimate Partner Violence: Examining Race, Gender, and Income Patterns', *Violence and Victims*, 18, 4: 433–43.

Richie, B. (1996), *Compelled to Crime: The Gender Entrapment of Battered Black Women*, New York: Routledge.

_____. (2001), Challenges Incarcerated Women Face as They Return to Their Communities: Findings from Life History Interviews', *Crime and Delinquency*, 47, 3: 368–89.

_____. (2005), 'A Black Feminist Reflection on the Antiviolence Movement', in N. J. Sokoloff and C. Pratt (eds), *Domestic Violence at the Margins*, New Brunswick: Rutgers University.

Roberts, D. (1997), *Killing the Black Body: Race, Reproduction, and the Meaning of Liberty*, New York: Vintage/Random House.

Rogers, B., McGee, G., Vann, A., Thompson, N. and Williams O. J. (2003), 'Substance Abuse and Domestic Violence: Stories of Practitioners that Address the Co-Occurrence among Battered Women', *Violence against Women*, 9, 5: 590–8.

Rosenthal, A. and Weissman, M. (2007), *Sentencing for Dollars: The Financial Consequences of a Criminal Conviction*, Center for Community Alternatives. (<www.communityalternatives.org/pdf/financial%20consequences.pdf>, accessed 10 January 2010).

Russell-Brown, K. (2004), *Underground Codes: Race, Crime and Related Fires*, New York: New York University.

Sabol, W. J., West, H. C., and Cooper, M. (2009), *Prisoners in 2008*, Washington: Bureau of Justice Statistics.

Shelden, R. (2001), *Controlling the Dangerous Classes*, Boston: Allyn and Bacon.

Simon, R. (1993), 'Women, Crime, and Justice', in B. Forst (ed.), *The Socio-Economics of Crime and Justice*, New York: M. E. Sharpe.

The Sentencing Project (2007), *Women in the Criminal Justice System: Briefing Sheets*, Washington (<www.sentencingproject.org/doc/File/Women%20in%20CJ/women_cjs_overview(1).pdf>, accessed 8 December 2009).

The Sentencing Project (2008), *Felony Disenfranchisement Laws in the United States*, Washington (<http://sentencingproject.org/doc/publications/fd_bs_fdlawsinus-March2010.pdf>, accessed 12 March 2010).

Sokoloff, N. J. (2008), 'The Intersectional Paradigm and Alternative Visions to Stopping Domestic Violence: What Poor Women, Women of Color, and Immigrant Women Are Teaching Us about Violence in the Family', *International Journal of Sociology of the Family*, 34, 2:153–85.

_____ and Dupont, I. (2005), 'Domestic Violence: Examining the Intersections of Race, Class, and Gender—An Introduction', in N. J. Sokoloff and C. Pratt (eds), *Domestic Violence at the Margins*, New Brunswick: Rutgers University.

_____ and Pratt, C. (eds) (2005), *Domestic Violence at the Margins: Readings in Race, Class, Gender and Culture*, New Brunswick: Rutgers University.

_____, Raffel-Price, B., and Flavin, J. (2004), 'The Criminal Law and Women', in B. Raffel-Price and N. J. Sokoloff (eds), *The Criminal Justice System and Women*, 3rd edn, New York: McGraw-Hill.

Steffensmeier, D. and Schwartz, J. (2004), 'Trends in Female Criminality: Is Crime Still a Man's World?' in B. Raffel-Price and N. J. Sokoloff (eds), *The Criminal Justice System and Women*, 3rd edn, New York: McGraw-Hill.

Sudbury, J. (2004), 'Women of Color, Globalization, and the Politics of Incarceration' in B. Raffel-Price and N. J. Sokoloff (eds), *The Criminal Justice System and Women*, 3rd edn, New York: McGraw-Hill.

_____. (2005), 'Introduction to Incite! – Critical Resistance Statement', in N. J. Sokoloff and C. Pratt (eds), *Domestic Violence at the Margins*, New Brunswick: Rutgers University.

Travis, J. (2005), *But They All Come Back: Facing the Challenges of Prisoner Reentry*, Washington: Urban Institute.

Weber, L. and Parra-Medina, D. (2003), 'Intersectionality and Women's Health: Charting a Path to Eliminating Health Disparities', in M. Texler Segal, V. P. Demos, and J. J. Kronenfeld (eds), *Gender Perspectives on Health and Medicine: Key Themes*, Oxford: Elsevier.

Websdale, N. (1997), *Understanding Domestic Homicide*, Boston: Northeastern University.

West, H. and Sabol, W. (2009), *Prison Inmates at Mid-Year 2008—Statistical Tables*, Bureau of Justice Statistics, NCJ 225619, Washington (<http://bjs.ojp.usdoj.gov/content/pub/pdf/pim08st.pdf>, accessed 2 September 2009).

17

POSTCOLONIAL PERSPECTIVES FOR CRIMINOLOGY

CHRIS CUNNEEN

Introduction

This chapter argues for the importance of a postcolonial perspective in criminology. It is a perspective that has the potential to offer new theoretical insights, and to expand the discipline in an engaged and reflexive endeavour that is cognisant of cultural and historical difference. To date, postcolonial theory has had greater impact in areas such as literature, law, politics, and sociology than it has in criminology. Rather than delve into the intricacies of postcolonial theory, I want to approach it here as a *perspective* that can significantly enhance the vision of criminology. Following writers like Edward Said and Gayatri Spivak, I suggest that postcolonialism is a perspective that demands we recognize the ongoing and enduring effects of colonialism on both the colonized and the colonizers. Colonization and the postcolonial are not historical events but continuing social, political, economic, and cultural processes. The postcolonial exists as an *aftermath* of colonialism and it manifests itself in a range of areas from the cultures of the former imperial powers to the psyches of those that were colonized. In this chapter I explore the potential of a postcolonial perspective: from understanding the relationship between colonization, state crime and the over-representation of marginalized peoples, to an appreciation of indigenous art as a site for criminological investigation.

Legal theorists have used postcolonial approaches to understand the role of law in the colonial process, as well as how the ideological effects of colonial laws continue to have relevance today, and may well continue to have exploitative consequences. They have sought to demonstrate the effects of transplanting western laws onto colonial peoples as part of the process of empire building in a range of areas from intellectual property law and land law to international law and questions of sovereignty. More fundamentally, scholars have questioned the claims to universality of western-based law and jurisprudence. Yet, with few exceptions (eg, Agozino 2003, 2004, 2005; Blagg 2008; Cunneen 2007, 2008; Morrison 2006; Sumner 1982), these ideas have not been taken up to any great extent or as a systematic approach within criminology. Part of the problem is that 'taking the American and European criminological tradition as our point of departure, whether right or left realism, critical theory or administrative criminology—is that they all tend to operate without a theory of colonialism and its effects' (Blagg 2008: 11; see also Cohen 1988). Having said that, it is clear that postcolonial perspectives have informed many writers—particularly those working on issues of race and criminalization and in discussions of crime, development and underdevelopment—from Hall *et al.* (1978) and Sumner (1982) onwards. Sumner, for instance, argued that an historical perspective on criminal law 'must inevitably turn us towards colonialism ... crime is not behaviour universally given in human nature and history, but a moral-political concept with culturally and historically varying form and content' (Sumner 1982: 10). This relativist position on the nature and definitions of crime is distinct from a 'labelling' perspective because a postcolonial perspective sees crime as a category contextualized through the material practices and ideologies of colonial states and by the resistances of colonized peoples.

Postcolonial writers have generally drawn a distinction between two major forms of colonialism: those lands that were colonized for the purposes of settlement (eg, north America, New Zealand, Australia, and South Africa) and those that were colonized for the purposes of economic exploitation (eg, large parts of Africa, the Indian subcontinent, and south-east Asia). It is worth considering in more detail the implications of this conceptual division for criminology, particularly in relation to the long-term outcomes of these differing forms of colonialism. One clear historical effect is that in the former settler countries there are ongoing demands by indigenous minorities for political recognition of self-determination, reparations and compensation for historical injustices and effective responses to contemporary forms of discrimination. Indigeneity is a key concept in our understanding of how criminal justice systems function in former settler societies as well as a site for innovative approaches (eg, circle sentencing, restorative justice, etc.). In addition, to the extent that slavery was a key strategy for economic development in some settler societies (eg, the United States) the long-term impoverishment of formerly enslaved peoples provides a fundamental link to current patterns of over-representation of racial minorities in the criminal justice system.

For large parts of the world, colonialism involved significant economic exploitation of labour and resources, and fundamental changes to social structures and political life. What is the role of criminology in understanding the nature of crime and crime control in the non-western former colonies from the Caribbean to the Pacific, Asia, and Africa? Can criminology have a role unless it develops a theory of colonialism and its effects? The dominant intellectual frameworks of criminology were established in the west with a view of understanding and explaining the phenomena of crime and crime control within specific western contexts. Part of the process of 'decolonizing' criminology is to see that criminology is a product of a particular set of narratives within western social sciences—a set of narratives that were 'fashioned in relation to the experience of the [European] Diaspora and in the construction of complexly stratified societies within and around the urban conurbations of Western cities' (Blagg 2008: 202). The criminological imagination falters when confronted with genocide and dispossession, and with peoples who demand that their radical difference, their laws and customs, their alterity to the west be recognized. We are beginning to see the silences of western criminology being challenged with the specific development of a postcolonial perspective in African criminology, particularly in the writings of Biko Agozino (2003, 2004, 2005).

To the extent that the 'colonial question' has engaged criminology it has been partly through the concept of *diaspora* and the movement of former colonized peoples from the periphery to metropolitan centres. Colonialism and former colonized peoples have had a presence in criminology (and critical legal studies and cultural studies, where they intersect with criminology) where the *diaspora* of former colonized peoples have appeared in western states (usually as a 'crime problem'). The concept of the *diaspora* provided critical writers like Hall (1978; see also Morley and Chen 1996) and Gilroy (1987) with the opportunity to link racialized crime constructs with colonialism. For Hall *et al.* (1998), Black youth and the Black working class in Britain had two intersecting histories: the history of the British working class and the history of Caribbean labour. We also see a similar perspective in the analysis of those working on race and criminalization from Keith (1993) and Solomos (1988, 1993) through to Bowling and Phillips (2002) where the criminal justice system is analysed as one of the key mechanisms through which ideas about race are constructed. More recently, some criminologists exploring globalization (Aas 2007a, 2007b; Findlay 1999, 2008) have noted that criminology is still primarily developed in the former colonial centres, and that the criminological enterprise lacks a coherent theoretical understanding of colonialism and postcolonialism. Despite some exceptions like those noted above, much of the work on globalization and criminology is still distinctly Eurocentric. Human trafficking, the war on terror, illegal immigrants and the transnational flow of peoples are still approached largely as a 'problem' for western states.

What would a postcolonial perspective on criminology look like? At the outset, I would emphasize that a postcolonial perspective for criminology can provide both theoretical insights and grounded policy analysis. A postcolonial perspective in criminology does not need to eschew evaluative approaches or empirical research but it should proceed from a critical and reflexive framework that questions the centrality of a western understanding of crime and control. A postcolonial vision for criminology can engage with public policy formulation and debates, but it does so from a theoretical grounding that recognizes the importance of history, particularly through understanding of the long-term impact of colonization and imperialism, and it does so through an analysis of the structures of sentiment and ideology that determine the intersections of race, crime, and punishment. A postcolonial perspective suggests a number of issues and conceptual standpoints. I do not lay claim in this essay to be any more than suggestive of some possible avenues for exploration.

Human Rights and State Crime

Broadly speaking, a postcolonial perspective opens up criminology to a more intellectually robust understanding of human rights and state crime. It also provides an opportunity to question the historical foundations of criminology as part of the imperialist project (Morrison 2006). I want to explore the potential relationship between state crime and human rights through reference to indigenous peoples in colonial settler societies. As I explore further below, indigenous people have been victims of profound historical injustices and abuses of human rights over the last several centuries that can be at least partially understood in the context of state crime—the modern political state developed through the systematic abuse of peoples who are now minorities within developed states. Furthermore, contemporary criminal justice systems within those states are often seen as disregarding or undermining respect for indigenous people's human rights. A postcolonial perspective also allows us to understand how contemporary indigenous claims to human rights protections can impact on current criminal justice processes, and how those claims might broaden our understanding of reform and change within the criminal justice system.

Historical Injustices and Human Rights Abuses

We know the widespread role of state institutions, often sanctioned by law, as the perpetrators of some of the greatest crimes against humanity. Modern political states have been responsible for the murder of millions of people even when deaths in wars, judicial executions, etc. are excluded (Green and Ward 2004: 1). The modern political state has been integral to the commission of genocide and other human rights abuses. Genocide and modernity have gone hand in hand (Bauman 1989), and the specific modernity of genocide is that the vastness and totality of 'final solutions' could only be pursued by the modern state with access to resources, administrative capacities and lawmaking functions (Gellately and Kiernan 2003: 4). This is at the heart of our contemporary understanding of state crime. That genocide, the 'crime of all crimes', should have been absent from criminology for so long deserves full explanation in itself (Morrison 2004). A part of the problem has been the positivist approaches in law and criminology that define 'crime' as a breach of state criminal law, and count crimes from the data driven by state agencies. Within such state-centric discourses it is difficult to conceptualize the incidence and nature of state crime.

A postcolonial perspective broadens our understanding of state crime because it draws attention to the connections between the colonial development of the modern political state and the globalized nature of gross violations of human rights of indigenous and former colonized peoples. In other words, the modern political state is built on the human rights abuses of colonized and enslaved peoples. Indeed racism, slavery and its consequent effects in Africa and America could be the subject of much criminological research. If we turn our attention specifically to the claims concerning historical injustices and human rights abuses against indigenous peoples we find that there are multiple layers of state crime. At the highest level is the claim that particular colonial practices against indigenous people constituted genocide. Below genocide are claims of mass murder, racism, ethnocide (or cultural genocide), slavery, forced labour, forced removals and relocations, the denial of property rights, and the denial of civil and political rights (Cunneen 2007).

In many cases claims for reparations and remedies for these abuses dominate political relations among indigenous peoples and the state in countries like Canada and Australia. A postcolonial perspective places contemporary demands for reparations and compensation for historical injustices as a legitimate subject area for criminology. If we see these systematic abuses as a form of crime then demands for redress are not simply questions of law and politics, they are also questions with which criminology might fruitfully engage. Such an engagement might involve documenting and understanding the way state agencies were involved in various practices (such as mass murder), or analysing the techniques through which states deny culpability (Cohen 2001), or developing conceptual frameworks and analysis of how processes for reparations might work—particularly given criminology's interests in punishment, offender-victim relations, and restorative justice.

Human Rights Abuses and the Contemporary Relations between Indigenous Peoples and Criminal Justice Systems

Contemporary indigenous peoples are found across many nations and total some 370 million people. As distinct peoples they have retained social, cultural, economic, and political characteristics that distinguish them from the dominant societies in which they live. Indigenous peoples are also among the most disadvantaged and vulnerable groups of people in the world (Permanent Forum on Indigenous Issues 2006).

The experiences of colonization varied depending on when it occurred, where and by whom. However there are commonalities found in indigenous peoples' relations with dominant criminal justice systems in former colonial settler societies both in the English-speaking societies of north America, Australia, and New Zealand, as well as the former settler colonies of central and south America. A common factor relevant to criminology is the massive over-representation of indigenous peoples in state criminal justice systems. Generally the data (where available) shows that indigenous people are more likely to be apprehended by police, more likely to be prosecuted, more likely to be convicted, and more likely to be sentenced to imprisonment (see Cunneen 2007: 247–8 for a summary). There have been major inquiries into the relationship of indigenous people with the criminal justice system, particularly in Australia (the Royal Commission into Aboriginal Deaths in Custody) and Canada (the Manitoba Aboriginal Justice Inquiry, and the Royal Commission into Aboriginal Peoples).

A postcolonial perspective in criminology approaches the question of racial and minority over-representation from a position grounded in the experiences of colonized peoples. Those experiences tend to see over-representation not as a matter of crime and punishment *per se*, but rather as an extension of dispossession and the abuse of human rights. A postcolonial perspective forces criminology to leave the relatively comfortable zone of positivist definitions of crime and to consider how marginalized peoples may view criminal justice intervention as unjust. Western liberal democratic states define their criminal justice systems as neutral, fair and universal in their application, indeed their legitimacy demands that these principles be upheld. Yet it is clear that many indigenous peoples see state criminal justice systems as oppressive. In general positivist approaches in criminology assume the legitimacy of the criminal justice system and seek to answer questions relating to frequency and causes of crime and the efficacy of criminal justice responses. A postcolonial perspective starts by questioning these assumptions and analysing how criminal justice systems can have the effect of entrenching the marginalization of minority peoples.

Collective Rights and Criminal Justice Systems

The process of reasserting indigenous collective rights, such as recognition of indigenous law and governance, self-determination, or self-government, may require significant institutional change on the part of state criminal justice agencies. Given that a central component of the indigenous critique of policing and the criminal justice system has been that indigenous rights have been ignored, it would be naive to think that the political demands of indigenous peoples would not also require substantial institutional reform. Henriksen (1998: 32) has discussed four existing ways of arranging indigenous autonomy and self-government, including:

- indigenous autonomy through contemporary indigenous political institutions (for example, Saami parliaments in the Nordic countries);

- indigenous autonomy based on the concept of an indigenous territorial base (for example, the Comarca arrangement in Panama, the Torres Strait Regional Authority in Australia, or Native American jurisdictions in the United States);
- regional autonomy within the state (for example, the Nunavut territory in Canada or indigenous autonomous regions in the Philippines);
- indigenous overseas autonomy (for example, Greenland home rule).

I simply make the point that political claims to self-determination have significant implications for state-based criminal justice systems. Rather than seeing these claims as a problem—as existing states and their institutions tend to do—a postcolonial perspective for criminology can envision the potential fragmentation of centralized criminal justice systems as an opportunity for responsive change and greater community-driven development.

The right of self-determination is also often linked to indigenous claims of sovereignty. Sovereignty can have multiple meanings in the context of indigenous political claims. It can refer to the historical claim that indigenous people have never relinquished sovereignty—particularly pertinent in Australia where there were no written treaties recognized by the Crown. Or it can be used to refer by indigenous people to the residual and unextinguished rights to self-government and autonomy that were recognized to varying degrees through treaties in New Zealand and north America. More generally, the political claim of a right to self-determination implies the right and ability to exercise some level of sovereign power—even if within the boundaries of existing nation states.

Sovereignty in international law is usually seen as inextricably tied to territory:

> Sovereignty demands a territory over which the governmental authority of the sovereign extends. Control over territory is the most essential element of sovereignty... Territory thus represents both the encompassing limits of a state's jurisdiction over its resident population and the barriers to outside jurisdiction [Royster 1995: 1–2].

However, sovereignty is also a dynamic concept with transformed meanings in different political and historical contexts. It is neither static nor absolute. Despite the apparent claims of the nation state to a concept of sovereignty that privileges a particular political relationship and concept of power, sovereignty is in a state of flux. From an indigenous perspective, it can be conceptualized in terms of jurisdictional multiplicity and divisibility rather than monopoly and unity. A postcolonial perspective sees sovereignty in terms of multiplicity and decentres state power, particularly in relation to defining and controlling crime.

While sovereign power remains central to the nation state, trends towards globalization have also seen the state deal with competing modes of governance. Although 'the liberal-democratic nation-state retains a central role in redistributing elements of sovereign power and national jurisdiction' (Stenson 1999: 67), there has also been a 'redistribution' of sovereign powers. In the criminal justice area, we can see sovereign power moving out of the state to international bodies for courts and policing

(United Nations and regional-based courts, regulatory bodies, investigatory bodies, and so forth). Sovereign power can also be seen as moving downwards to more regional and local spheres of government and governance such as multi-agency crime control partnerships (Stenson 1999: 68).

The redistribution of sovereignty may also provide avenues and gaps for the development of shared jurisdictions or shared sovereignty. The challenge that indigenous claims to sovereignty and self-determination pose for criminology are both theoretical and practical. The theoretical challenge is to understand that basic categories and definitions of crime are fundamentally circumscribed by historical and political contexts. The very legitimacy of the institutions used to control crime is not universally accepted. The praxis issue this raises is: how do we develop legal institutions which are capable of dealing with multiple jurisdictions and differential citizenship claims? In other words, how do criminal justice institutions develop in a manner that can deal fairly with competing citizenship demands and maintain legitimacy for different social groups?

Finally in this discussion on human rights, it is worth making the point that the concept of universal human rights has been much debated within critical and postcolonial theory (see for example Davies 2002: 186–93). In liberal democracies, the rule of law is understood as a universal principle and a fundamental good. Equality before the law and equal protection of the law are seen as the defining features of a legal system built on the rule of law. A postcolonial perspective does not necessarily argue against these principles and the rights they bestow but rather demonstrates the way in which marginalized and colonized peoples are constrained in their capacity to enjoy these protections and rights. Part of the constraint arises from the social and economic position of marginalized groups, as well as racialization and the lack of tolerance of cultural diversity. There is a palpable tension between a universal principle like equality before the law and the recognition of cultural difference, and this tension is constantly played out in law, policy, and practice.

The State, 'Nation' and Crime

A postcolonial approach demands that we consider issues of state power, and one area where state power is often neglected is in its power to define citizenship and belonging. There is an extensive literature on the relationship between nation and the 'imagined community' (Anderson 1996). A postcolonial approach emphasizes the way the state defines itself as synonymous with the nation. Nationalism constructs the 'people', but does so through a process of excluding and forgetting. The limits of belonging to the nation can also become the boundaries of the moral community. To be outside the moral community is to be susceptible to the violence of the state. Discourses on nationalism and the state also bear directly on definitions of crime and criminality. Sumner (1990) has argued that the censure of crime attempts to unify and publicize a vision of the nation and its morality. Crime is seen as a threat to national unity, and criminalization is a key part of the building of the nation through processes of exclusion. Thus, 'notions of crime control, the crime wave, the crime zone, crime as a social problem, and the breakdown in law and order, [are presented] as signs of a moral malaise threatening the constitutional integrity of the state' (Sumner 1990: 49).

Related to this concept of censure is the view that the criminal justice system has a determining role in actually constituting social groups as threats and in reproducing a society built on racialized boundaries. In Keith's (1993: 193) terms, 'the process of criminalization itself now constitutes a significant racializing discourse'. Over the last decade the impact of globalization has lead to discussion of the deep-seated insecurity within liberal democracies and the role of the state in representing itself as the guardian of sovereignty and internal and external security (Bauman 2000; Lianos and Douglas 2000). These three processes are interrelated: punishment is a moral censure reinforcing the boundaries of the nation, crime is fundamentally racializing in drawing its exclusionary boundaries, and the state, at a time of diminishing power in the face of globalization, is eager to exert its power in maintaining internal order. A postcolonial perspective insists in arguing the relevance of these processes to criminology.

Exclusionary practices in the west are about keeping out the human tide of people moving from the third world (Weber 2002; Weber and Bowling 2008), as well as controlling racialized minorities *within* the national boundaries. The racialized minorities within first world nation states may include both ethnic and racial groups who have immigrated or arrived as refugees (the *diaspora* of the formerly colonized and enslaved), as well as indigenous groups. The racialization and criminalization of minority groups excludes and isolates those groups of people from the assumed national consensus. The exclusionary processes of criminalization undermine citizenship rights (where they have been granted). Criminalization legitimates excessive policing, the use of state violence, the loss of liberty and diminished social and economic participation. Criminalization also permits an historical and political amnesia in relation to the effects of colonial processes and role of imperial powers in structuring international economic and political relations. Racialized groups are transformed into a 'law and order' threat to national unity and the longer-term reasons for their economic and social dislocation conveniently forgotten.

A postcolonial perspective enables a much wider focus for criminology: questions of sovereignty and citizenship become core concerns; an analysis of criminal justice as a set of racializing practices become fundamental; and human rights are not seen as a peripheral component of criminology but essential to the task of explaining the position of marginalized peoples.

The Postcolonial Critique of Positivism

The importance, noted above, of seeing formal rights within the context of substantive inequality raises a more general issue of the relationship between western law and marginalized peoples. Postcolonial legal theorists have engaged in a broad-ranging challenge to liberal positivism (see, for example, Fitzpatrick 1992; Darian-Smith and Fitzpatrick 1999; Kapur 2005). Notions of legal neutrality, formal equality, legal objectivity have been met with the objective conditions of substantive inequality, particularly as they are reflected in the conditions of marginalized populations (Roy 2008: 319). Western legal traditions based on liberal positivism have generally excluded the possibility of other law coexisting within its territory (Davies 2002: 277). These claims to absolute sovereignty have undermined the legitimacy of the laws of colonized peoples—which are often characterized as partial, incomplete, and customary (Cunneen and Schwartz 2007). The questions raised by a developing postcolonial jurisprudence have barely impacted on criminology.

The critique of legal neutrality and objectivity and the questioning of the exclusive and universal claims of western law have diverse implications for criminology. Both definitions of crime and the institutional determination of criminality can no longer be seen as separate from, or independent of, the broader claims of western discourses of dominance. Crime and crime control are embedded in the experiences of colonization. This has significant implications for how we might explain the over-representation within criminal justice systems of colonized, formerly colonized, or enslaved peoples. Positivist criminology understands racial or ethnic over-representation as the result of essentially individualized factors that can be determined from aggregate populations (eg, rates of offending and reoffending, living in crime-prone neighbourhoods, single parent families, prior child abuse or neglect, high levels of unemployment, low levels of education, and so forth). These factors can be separated, quantified, measured and put through a regression analysis. 'Race' is reproduced, not as a social relation, but an individualized factor that may or may not shows signs of statistical significance.

By way of contrast, a postcolonialist perspective argues that the individualized factors identified above are embedded in the historical experience of colonization and dispossession. It is the relationship between the processes of colonization and criminalization that need to be excavated and explained. A postcolonial approach refuses to take offending rates at face value, arguing that such rates are not 'knowable' apart from the agencies that identify and process crime. We cannot discount the contribution of institutional practices and legal frameworks within which criminalization and the use of imprisonment are embedded (Cunneen 2006: 340). Further, these institutional practices are caught within broader dominant relationships which reproduce marginalized peoples as criminal subgroups.

A postcolonialist approach emphasizes the perspective of the marginalized in both understanding and in responding to 'over-representation' in the criminal justice system. For example, Blagg (2008), when discussing Australian indigenous peoples and criminal justice, argues that white society's decision to name actions as 'criminal' silences the kind of dissent possible when these actions are named another way. The criminalization of indigenous resistance to colonization silences criticism of the mass dispossession and the theft of land. 'Many Aboriginal people maintain that dispossession, loss of land and culture, the desecration of Aboriginal sites, the breakdown of skin and moyete systems (traditional rules for identifying appropriate marriage partners), the unwillingness of white authorities to acknowledge the jurisdiction of Aboriginal law have *direct and immediate* relevance to both criminal behaviour and to processes of criminalization' (Blagg 2008: 16). He argues that attempts by the state to eliminate, restructure and reconstitute Aboriginal identity in the interests of the colonizer is the core issue rather than criminal offending *per se* (Blagg 2008: 3).

The contrasting approaches between positivist and postcolonial approaches to over-representation have important ramifications for policy, particularly when government-funded institutes are dominated by one paradigm. Blagg's attack on positivism is a reaction to what he perceives as the approach by positivist criminologists to 'tick the Aboriginal box' when researching indigenous justice issues such as over-representation, without ever attempting to understand indigenous perspectives. It is not that indigenous people are ignored—quite the contrary; they are the object of intense scrutiny and intervention. However their understanding and explanations for their own predicament viz-a-viz western law and justice is ignored. For criminological positivists, race and Indigeneity become reduced to potential risk factors for involvement with the criminal justice system, akin to prior offending history or age.

Rethinking Evidence: Non-Literate Societies and the Role of Art and Performance

I noted above that postcolonial approaches seek to instate the voices and perspectives of the colonized within criminological discourse. One example of how this might be achieved is through an understanding of the role of art and performance in indigenous societies. In societies that do not rely on written texts, law is often expressed through various forms of art—such as painting, sculpture, dance and song, which have a special place in reproducing social, moral and religious meanings. In short, if law is not reproduced through the written text it will be reproduced in other forms (Cunneen 2010). A postcolonial perspective, particularly combined with a cultural criminological approach, offers the potential to revalorize alternative conceptions of the expression of law. Understanding how law is constituted through art and performance, rather than law as written text, has implications for how we consider criminological and legal 'evidence'.

As I have argued elsewhere (Cunneen 2010), there is a sense in which indigenous art *unhinges* colonial law as an abstract expression of power and grounds it firmly in the lived experiences of Aboriginal people. Art can become a rich source of ideas, documentation and insight into the inner workings of the state and more specifically criminal justice institutions, and the modes of resistance engendered by oppression. Methodologically, art becomes both a window on the experiences of victimization, and a source of documentation of disturbing criminal events (such as mass murder) where the criminal justice institutions of the colonial state have chosen to ignore or deny the existence of such events. A postcolonial approach to criminology provides the opportunity to shift the epistemological priority given to certain forms of knowledge, and to treat seriously the importance of alternative ways of seeing and knowing.

To take just one example: Aboriginal art has been an important tool for reproducing knowledge about massacres—particularly where the existence of mass murders has been denied by the colonial state. The work of artists contributes to the evidence and continuity in knowledge of local accounts by indigenous people of massacres that are not necessarily recorded or acknowledged in any colonial official documentation. Art becomes a material dimension to the oral history and oral testimony of indigenous people. There is thus a materiality to historical accounts separate from the official written historical documents that tend to privilege (and exculpate) the colonial authorities. For criminologists interested in state crime, the image functions as an evidentiary tool for the existence of officially sanctioned crime. For example, there has been longstanding official denial of the massacres of indigenous people in the Kimberleys of Western Australia during the early twentieth century. Yet the existence of these massacres and the events surrounding them has been reproduced in oral stories, as well as dance and art. Traditional art forms by painters like Rover Thomas, Timmy Timms, and Queenie McKenzie depict a number of massacres in the Kimberleys. Dance ceremonies convey similar knowledge (see Cunneen 2010: 122–7).

A different contemporary set of perspectives on crime and victimization is portrayed through various indigenous interpretations of the meaning of theft. Counting, describing and analysing property crime is the daily domain of criminologists. Yet indigenous depictions and understandings of theft provide an alternative way of seeing. For example, Ian Abdulla paints of the theft of food by indigenous people from 'white people'. There is a naturalness to this 'crime' that is viewed both as survival and depicted without any sense of shame, guilt, or remorse (Arthur and Morphy 2005: 124). Theft also has radically different interpretations than simple definitions of 'property'. Colonial expectations of the disappearance of indigenous people led to large-scale collections of cultural artefacts and human remains of indigenous people in public museums and private collections. Over the last several decades there has been a movement to return human and cultural remains to their communities. indigenous artists have depicted the colonial theft of indigenous body parts and cultural artefacts (see for example Judy Watson's three 1997 paintings titled *Our Bones in Your Collections*, *Our Hair in Your Collections* and *Our Skin in Your Collections*, Art Gallery of New South Wales, nd: 168). Perhaps the most distressing and destructive part of colonial processes in settler societies was the forcible removal of children from their families and communities ('the Stolen Generations'). The policy has been referred to as genocide and has been subject to litigation and demands for reparation (for a summary see Cunneen 2008). Indigenous women artists in particular have dealt with themes arising from the Stolen Generations. Many of these works are incredibly personal and poignant and deal with the trauma and pain caused by these forced removals (for further discussion see Cunneen 2010: 132–3).

A postcolonial perspective rethinks the meaning of evidence and provides an opportunity to break the positivist epistemological frame which tends to dominate both criminological and legal theory and practice. Indigenous cultures utilize rich and complex oral and artistic traditions as an essential part of the communicative process. In contrast to performance and painting, techniques of writing, record-keeping and official documentation have been an essential part of imperial culture. Indeed, record-keeping was integral to the project of colonization: it is the tool for describing, itemizing and controlling the colonized Other. It is also the stuff of mainstream criminology—for example, the crime figures that endlessly repeat the offending rates of minority peoples. To understand the perspective of colonized and marginalized peoples we need to look more broadly at what constitutes evidence—evidence of crime and victimization from the perspective of the marginalized.

Identity and Healing

The notion of the 'Other' is key to postcolonial perspectives. It is a concept that assisted in understanding how categories and images of non-European peoples have been constructed by the west in the social, legal and economic interests of the west. The dichotomy of European and Other have seen non-European peoples relegated to inferior status—their culture and laws subservient to the universal claims of western civilization. Postcolonial perspectives require a particular focus on the construction of race and the way race is constituted and given meaning through various discursive practices. This point has particular resonance for criminology given, as we have already noted, that the institutional practices of the criminal justice system can be seen as a significant constitutive process in the construction of race. Criminology as a discipline, and a discursive practice that produces racialized difference, is also problematized. The racialized construction of offenders not only defines the offender in terms of race, it also constructs the *apparent* non-racialized vision of the normal, respectable and responsible citizen.

When we see criminology as a racialized discourse, as a system of meanings that produce knowledge and practice about crime and race, we can begin to understand how the discipline controls both the mode of representation and their meaning. The discourse controls the process through which we understand crime and deviance (eg, the legitimation of statistical representations of, for example, juvenile crime and its causes) and the symbolic meanings we attach to those representations (for example, black youth as crime-prone). In the case of racialized criminality we see simultaneously the offender as racial and the racialized individual as criminal. As Fanon once remarked, 'not only must the black man be black; he must be black in relation to the white man' (Fanon 1967: 202). The colonized is forced to exist individually and as an embodiment of race: an embodiment that is increasingly overladen with significations of criminality. A postcolonial perspective places the problem of identity as a core category within criminology.

One consequence of the importance of identity for colonized peoples, and the need to reconstruct identity in the face of colonial strategies to circumscribe, define and control the identity of the colonized, is the approach taken towards reforming and rehabilitating offenders. From my experience working with indigenous groups, there is a different understanding about how you change unacceptable criminal behaviour. Generally, there is a greater focus on healing and community-controlled programmes for offenders. One of the consequences of this is the tension that is created between indigenous approaches and state-controlled interventions. In the current period we see an institutional emphasis on criminogenic needs and the various behavioural modification programmes put in place as a result of the identification of these needs. Approaches defined by criminogenic need are clearly in the ascendancy, as opposed to approaches that are more community driven or rely on community involvement and directly target greater social inclusion. This emphasis has important ramifications for marginalized groups because, although they are most likely to be the subjects of these programmes as offenders, they are also less likely as community members to be part of the professionalized interventions.

I am not suggesting that therapeutic approaches should be completely avoided. However, the danger is that government favours those approaches that it can closely administer, control and monitor—and these tend to be programmes reliant on expert interventions that further privilege-dominant definitions of crime and disavow the voices of marginalized peoples. They also tend to be programmes that are 'off-the-shelf' and perhaps only slightly modified for specific experiences of marginalized peoples. They are generally not programmes that are organic to indigenous people and their communities, or their needs and experiences. If we reflect on indigenous developed programmes[1] it is evident they start at a different place to conventional individualized programmes. Indigenous programmes start with the collective indigenous experience. Inevitably, that involves an understanding of the collective harms and outcomes of colonization, the loss of lands, the disruptions of culture, the changing of traditional roles of men and women, the collective loss and sorrow of the removal of children and relocation of communities. Individual harms and wrongs are placed within a collective context. On the one hand, offenders are dealt

[1] In the Australian context these are programmes like Red Dust Healing, Ending Offending, Ending Family Violence, and Journey to Respect.

with as individuals responsible for their own actions; their pain and the forces that propel them to harmful behaviour towards themselves and others are confronted. However, they are *understood* within a collective context of the experience of indigenous peoples in a non-indigenous society. The explanatory context, the explanation for behaviour, is within the collective experiences of the marginalized.

In this sense indigenous programmes are unique because they seek individual change within a collective context. Mainstream programmes (such as cognitive behavioural therapy programmes) cannot achieve that—they do not understand individual change as part of a collective experience. This is why indigenous programmes and indigenous people prioritize the concept of healing: healing is quintessentially and simultaneously an individual and collective experience. It is far more expansive than a notion of rehabilitation: it is concerned with simultaneously healing one's self and community. Individual and collective grief and loss become core issues that programmes need to address rather than only focusing on criminogenic need. Mainstream programmes simply ignore the nexus between oppression and liberation, between collective grief and loss and individual healing. Indigenous healing programmes start from this nexus; they begin with understanding the outcomes and effects of longer-term oppression, and move from there towards the healing of individuals.

Many of the innovative developments in indigenous justice (such as community justice groups or women's community patrols) arise from a *disbelief*: a disbelief in the functionality and the legitimacy of state-centred institutional responses. For the most part, criminalization and incarceration are seen as destructive avenues that cause further family and social disintegration and do not change the behaviour of the perpetrator. The disbelief in the criminal justice system as reformatory or rehabilitative is hardly surprising given that most colonized and formerly colonized peoples have had firsthand experience of police, courts and prisons over many generations.

Conclusion

I have set out to develop an approach to criminology that would enable the discipline to break free from the charge of Agozino (2004) and others that criminology inherently serves the interests of colonialism. A postcolonial perspective can develop and enrich criminology, bringing to light the discipline's silences and absences, foremost among these being questions of genocide, human rights and imperialism. This approach allows us to explore fundamental questions such as the relationship between race and criminalization, the development of identities of resistance, and various processes of transformative justice. It draws our attention to broader questions of social and political power, to matters of legitimacy, political authority and consent—all of which presuppose how we understand and define crime and crime control.

A postcolonial criminology necessarily requires consideration of the long-term outcomes and effects of colonialism, and there are manifold issues for criminology that emerge from this including indigenous political demands for self-determination, the position of formerly colonized and enslaved peoples within the metropolitan centres of former colonial powers, and the role and function of western criminology in developing or third world nations. A postcolonial perspective also focuses our attention on questions of genocide and human rights. An analysis of the systematic abuse of human rights has both an historical and contemporary dimension. A criminology informed by a postcolonial perspective has much to offer discussions and debates around redress, reparations and compensation for historical injustices—in most cases these are after all claims by victims for an effective response to criminal acts. A postcolonial criminology also has much to offer an analysis of contemporary debates around human rights abuses of racialized minorities from deaths in custody to institutional racism.

Finally, I want to suggest that a postcolonial criminology offers insights for policy engagement. Law and criminology tend to situate marginalized groups within a false universalism in terms of their capacity to seek protection of law and their experience as law's subjects (as either victims or offenders). Yet a postcolonial perspective shows that marginalized peoples have less capacity to utilize legal protections, that principles of fairness and equality seem remarkably absent when the marginalized are being criminalized, and that crime and justice are experienced within particular socio-cultural and historical frameworks. Criminology has a suite of standard offerings from sex offender treatment programmes to domestic violence policies. A postcolonial criminology might require us to radically rethink why these policies, programmes or initiatives are not taken up, or are less effective, or simply do not work with particular marginalized and racialized communities. Ultimately we are required to ask broader questions about crime, victimization, punishment and justice, and to provide a more nuanced understanding of social reality.

References

Aas, K. F. (2007a), 'Analysing a World in Motion: Global Flows Meet "Criminology of the Other"', *Theoretical Criminology*, 11, 2: 283–303.

_____ (2007b), *Globalization and Crime*, London: Sage.

Agozino, B. (2003), *Counter-Colonial Criminology: A Critique of Imperialist Reason*, London: Pluto.

_____ (2004), 'Imperialism, Crime and criminology: Towards the Decolonisation of Criminology', *Crime, Law and Social Change*, 41: 343–58.

_____ (2005), 'Crime, Criminology and Post-Colonial Theory: Criminological Reflections on West Africa', in J. Sheptycki (ed.), *Transnatioal and Comparative Criminology*, London: Glasshouse Press.

Anderson, B. (1996), *Imagined Communities*, London: Verso.

Art Gallery of New South Wales (nd), *Tradition Today. Indigenous Art in Australia*, Sydney: Art Gallery of New South Wales.

Arthur B. and Morphy, F. (2005), *Macquarie Atlas of Indigenous Australia*, North Ryde: Macquarie University Press.

Bauman, Z. (1989), *Modernity and the Holocaust*, Cambridge: Polity Press.

_____ (2000), 'Social Issues of Law and Order', *British Journal of Criminology*, 40; 205–21.

Blagg, H. (2008), *Crime, Aboriginality and the Decolonisation of Justice*, Annandale: Hawkins Press.

Bowling, B. and Phillips. C. (2002), *Racism, Crime and Justice*, London: Longman.

Cohen, S. (1988), *Against Criminology*, New Brunswick: Transaction Books.

_____ (2001), *States of Denial. Knowing about Atrocities and Suffering*, Cambridge: Polity Press.

Cunneen, C. (2006), 'Racism, Discrimination and the Over-Representation of Indigenous People in the Criminal Justice System: Some Conceptual and Explanatory Issues', *Current Issues in Criminal Justice*, 17, 3; 329–46.

_____ (2007) 'Criminology, Human Rights and Indigenous Peoples', in S. Parmentier and E. G. M. Weitekamp (eds), *Crime and Human Rights*, Oxford: Elsevier.

_____ (2008), 'State Crime, the Colonial Question and Indigenous Peoples' in A. Smuelers and R. Haveman (eds), *Supranational Criminology: Towards a Criminology of International Crimes*, Antwerp: Intersentia Press.

_____ (2010), 'Framing the Crimes of Colonialism: Critical Images of Aboriginal Art and Law', in K. Hayward and M. Presdee (eds), *Framing Crime: Cultural Criminology and the Image*, London: Routledge.

_____ and Schwartz, M. (2005), *Customary Law, Human Rights and International Law: Some Conceptual Issues*, Background Paper No. 11, Perth: Law Reform Commission of Western Australia.

Darian-Smith, E. and P. Fitzpatrick, P. (eds) (1999), *Laws of the Postcolonial*, Ann Arbor: University of Michigan Press.

Davies, M. (2002), *Asking the Law Question*, 2nd edn, Sydney: Law Book Company.

Fanon, F. (1967), *Black Skins, White Masks*, New York: Grove Press.

Findlay, M. (1999), *The Globalisation of Crime*, Cambridge: Cambridge University Press.

_____. (2008), *Governing Through Globalised Crime*, Uffculme: Willan Publishing.

Fitzpatrick, P. (1992), The Mythology of Modern Law, London: Routledge.

Gellately, R. and Kiernan, B. (eds) (2003), *The Spectre of Genocide: Mass Murder in Historical Perspective*, Cambridge: Cambridge University Press.

Gilroy, P. (1987), *There Ain't No Black in the Union Jack*, London: Hutchinson.

Green, P. and Ward, T. (2004), *State Crime. Governments, Violence and Corruption*. London: Pluto Press.

Hall, S., Critcher, C., Jefferson, T., Clarke, J., and Roberts, B. (1978), *Policing the Crisis: Mugging, the State and Law and Order*, London: Macmillan.

Henriksen J. (1998), 'Implementation of the right of Self-Determination of Indigenous Peoples within the Framework of Human Society', Paper presented to the *UNESCO*

Conference on the Implementation of the Right to Self-Determination as a Contribution to Conflict Prevention, Barcelona, Spain, 21–27 November 1998.

Kapur, R. (2005), *Erotic Justice: Law and the New Politics of Postcolonialism*, London: Glasshouse Press.

Keith, M. (1993), 'From Punishment to Discipline', in M. Cross and M. Keith (eds), *Racism, The City and The State*, London: Routledge.

Lianos, M. and Douglas, M. (2000), 'Dangerization and the End of Deviance', *British Journal of Criminology*, 40: 261–78.

Morley, D. and Chen, K. H. (1996), *Stuart Hall: Critical Dialogues in Cultural Studies*, New York: Routledge.

Morrison, W. (2004), 'Criminology, Genocide and Modernity: Remarks on the Companion that Criminology Ignored', in C. Sumner (ed.), *The Blackwell Companion to Criminology*, Oxford: Blackwell Publishing.

_____ (2006), *Criminology, Civilisation and the New World Order*, Abingdon: Routledge Cavendish.

Permanent Forum on Indigenous Issues (2006). *About UNPFII/ History*. (<www.un.org/esa/socdev/unpfii/en/history.html>).

Roy, A. (2008), 'Postcolonial Theory and Law: A Critical Introduction', *Adelaide Law Review*, 29: 315–57.

Royster, J.V. (1995), 'The Legacy of Allotment', *Arizona State Law Review*, 27, 1: 1–78

Solomos, J. (1988), *Black Youth, Racism and the State*, Cambridge: Cambridge University Press.

_____. (1993), 'Constructions of Black Criminality' in D. Cook and B. Hudson (eds), *Racism and Criminology*, London: Sage Publications.

Stenson, K. (1999), 'Crime Control, Governmentality and Sovereignty' in R. Smandych (ed.), *Governable Places: Readings on Governmentality and Crime Control*, Aldershot: Ashgate.

Sumner, C. (ed.) (1982), *Crime, Justice and Underdevelopment*, London: Heinemann.

_____. (ed.) (1990), *Censure, Politics and Criminal Justice*, Milton Keynes: Open University Press.

Weber, L. (2002), 'The Detention of Asylum Seekers: 20 Reasons Why Criminologists Should Care', *Current Issues in Criminal Justice*, 14, 1: 9–30.

_____ and Bowling, B. (2008), 'Valiant Beggars and Global Vagabonds: Select, Eject, Immobilize', *Theoretical Criminology*, 12, 3: 355–75.

PART II

CRIMINOLOGY AND ITS BORDERS

1

THE LIMITS OF THE DISCIPLINE: WHERE DO WE DRAW THE LINE?

18

PUTTING CRIME BACK ON THE CRIMINOLOGICAL AGENDA

LUCIA ZEDNER*

Introduction

CRIMINOLOGY is flourishing and yet it is striking how little contemporary criminological scholarship really engages with crime. Where once crime was the subject of intense sociological enquiry—witness the outpourings of anomie, control, structural, cultural, and sub-cultural theories—it now risks slipping from criminological view. The waning of the sociology of deviance within the academy has resulted in a corresponding decline in study of the aetiology, social meaning, and construction of crime (Sumner 1994). Criminological library shelves are stacked with books and journals on policing, probation, criminal process, the trial, sentencing, penal theory, and practice, but far fewer about crime itself. In Britain, and elsewhere too, crime has become the elephant in the room, a tacitly acknowledged presence, a 'normal fact of

* My thanks are due to the editors, to participants at the 'What is Criminology?' conference, Oxford 2009, in particular my respondent Adam Crawford, and to Alessandro Spena for their comments and constructive suggestions on an earlier draft.

every day' (Felson 2002), so taken for granted that it is rarely addressed by the very discipline whose founding raison d'être was its study. This is all the more surprising given that criminology lacks a distinguishing theoretical framework, distinctive science, or methodology, and owes what cohesion it possesses to crime as its focus and justifying rationale (Rock 2007).

This is not to say that crime is wholly absent from criminological writings. Crime is commonly invoked as a signifier of institutional failure—implicated in the breakdown of the family, the exclusion of unruly youth from school, and the disorder of the inner city (Ericson 2003: 32). Crime is implicit in the study of penal populism, moral panics, political campaigns, and policy-making, not least in Simon's striking insight that we are now 'governed through crime' (Simon 2007). Crime statistics are habitually cited by politicians, public servants, and journalists as indicators of moral decline or markers of the failure or success of policy initiatives. However, precisely what is being counted is rarely subject to critical scrutiny. True, reducing crime remains a focus of concern. Rational choice theory and its offshoot, routine activity theory, focus on the motivations and circumstances of crime so as to target responses more effectively (Felson and Clarke 1998; Clarke 1995). So-called 'crime science' promotes a new technicist approach to crime reduction that rejects conventional criminology as unworldly and ineffective (Read and Tilley 2000; Laycock 2008). Yet neither is a substitute for a direct engagement *with* crime. What crime is and what it should be appears no longer to be of much interest to criminology.

Policing, criminal justice, and punishment are, of course, worthy objects of criminological attention. For crime is not just a matter of what is legislatively defined as such but what criminal justice officials actually target, investigate, prosecute, and punish. Understanding how crime is constructed by the media, politics, and public opinion, by policing, and the criminal justice process is an important antidote to the 'law in the books' approach whose traditional focus on doctrinal law, to the exclusion of context, has been the subject of such robust criticism (Norrie 2001; Lacey, Wells, and Quick 2003). This said, if criminology is not to morph unreflectively into policing, probation, or criminal justice studies, or become a mere adjunct to policy-making, it needs to revive its core interest in crime and in the whys and wherefores of criminalization.

By strange coincidence, the loss of criminological interest, one might even say faith, in crime has coincided with a revitalization of interest in criminalization by criminal lawyers whose scholarship asks hard questions about what crime is and what it should be. This chapter examines the relative decline of criminological concern with crime and takes issue with claims that criminology should relinquish crime in favour of other organizing concepts such as 'conflict', 'dispute', or 'harm'. It argues that crime needs to be put firmly back on to the criminological agenda by making questions of criminalization as much a focus of criminological as of legal enquiry. It considers what criminology can contribute to criminalization debates and, no less importantly, what criminology has to learn from criminal law. Given concerns about rampant over-criminalization, developing clear limiting principles for criminalization is a potentially powerful means of restraint (Husak 2008). It is also a means of providing a much-needed stimulus to normative theorizing within criminology at a time when the discipline has fallen prey to a brand of professional pessimism that inhibits creative thinking about crime (Braithwaite 2000: 64; Zedner 2002). Last but not least it furnishes a way of refocusing a discipline that risks sprawling beyond any clearly delineated boundary and losing a collective sense of its scope and purpose.

Beyond Crime?

In so far as criminology engages with crime at all it increasingly does so negatively, questioning its very utility as an organizing concept or analytical tool. The recasting of crime as a dispute owned by the parties to it (Christie 1977) is one of the most important and enduring challenges to the concepts of crime and punishment, and spawned the restorative justice movement (Braithwaite 1989; Hoyle and Young 2002; von Hirsch *et al.* 2003). No less striking is an emerging school of thought that crime is simply too restrictive a concept to be useful to criminology. According to this account, crime relies on fictitious claims to ontological reality; criminal liability is attributed by dubious means; and as an inherently individualizing concept it fails to capture serious social harms inflicted by groups, organizations, and states (Friedrichs and Schwartz 2007; Pemberton 2007; Hillyard *et al.* 2005). These arguments lead proponents to conclude that we should abandon crime in favour of a 'social harm perspective' that does not differentiate between those harms labelled criminal and other types of harm (Hillyard *et al.* 2004: 2). They suggest that 'a disciplinary approach organized around a notion of social harm may prove to be more productive than has criminology' (Hillyard and Tombs 2007: 9; Hillyard 2005). Interestingly, this attack is motivated partly by the valid observation that 'criminology has largely failed to be self-reflective regarding the dominant, state defined notion of "crime".... The issue of what crime is, is rarely stated, but rather simply assumed' (Hillyard and Tombs 2007: 11). All true: yet this is hardly a reason for abandoning the category of crime, still less criminology. Rather it should be a spur to concerted engagement with the scope and nature of crime, the principles upon which it is defined and the legal structures in which it is inscribed.

Let us consider briefly the chief arguments and suggest some reasons why they fail to undermine the claims of crime as an organizing concept. A central claim is that it makes no sense to distinguish between criminal and other harms:

> in reality there is nothing intrinsic to any particular event or incident which permits it to be defined as a 'crime'. Crime—and criminals—are fictive events and characters in the sense

that they have to be constructed before they can exist. Crime is thus a 'myth' of everyday life' [Hillyard and Tombs 2007: 10].

This assertion fails to recognize that the construction of crime is necessarily a normative exercise and one in which criminology, alongside criminal law, has an important role to play in determining which principles should underpin its definition, policing and punishment. Even if crime is in some sense a 'myth' it is unclear that harm is any less a myth. Ericson and Doyle's analysis of the contested status of syndromes like post-traumatic stress disorder and whiplash powerfully debunk the idea that harm has any greater claim to ontological reality (Ericson and Doyle 2004: chapter 3).

In a legal system grounded on individual autonomy there are good reasons to identify criminal wrongdoing and to punish those who perpetrate it. Failure to do so constitutes a denial of individual autonomy. As von Hirsch argues, it is tantamount to treating offenders as 'tigers might be treated in a circus, as beings that have to be restrained, intimidated, or conditioned into compliance because they are incapable of understanding why biting people (or other tigers) is wrong' (von Hirsch 1993: 11). He rightly insists that 'treating the actor as someone capable of choice, rather than as a tiger, is a matter of acknowledging his dignity as a human being' (von Hirsch 1993: 11). Punishment differs from other governmental responses to social problems in that its very purpose is to attribute liability and convey blame for wrongdoing and, in so doing, to acknowledge the individual as an autonomous moral agent. By contrast a social harm perspective neither addresses fundamental issues of moral agency, wrongdoing, and blameworthiness that lie at the heart of the criminal law nor delivers censure and sanction of the sort supplied by punishment (von Hirsch 1993: 11; von Hirsch and Ashworth 2005). To claim that punishment is not 'effective' (Hillyard and Tombs 2007: 10) assumes a consequentialist justification for punishment that does not engage with the attribution of moral responsibility for crime integral to a retributive system of justice.

None of this is to propose that criminology adopt an uncritical stance toward the category of crime or state responses to it: far from it. There is much in the foundations, structures, and articulation of crime through the criminal law that invites critical scrutiny and reform. But that need not, and should not, entail abandoning crime as a legal category. Critical engagement with criminal law and penal theory permits difficult questions to be asked about the ways in which offences are arrived at, how they are defined and structured, to whom they are applied, and the consequences that should follow. Criminology makes possible a fully social understanding of crime capable of addressing questions such as whether socio-economic circumstances should count in mitigation; what account should be taken of age, race, or gender; and how equality might be achieved in an unequal society (Hudson 1998).

Second, it is said that criminal law's construction of crime emphasizes individual over collective, corporate, or state responsibility. In so far as this is true it need not imply ditching criminal responsibility but rather redefining liability in ways that better recognize and respond to the criminal liability of companies, groups, and governments. Where the moral bases of the criminal law are wrong, outdated, or out of line with our collective conscience, the case for reform is strong. But this is hardly a ground for dispensing with the legal category of crime altogether. Moreover to the extent that the criminal law fails adequately to penalize crimes of the powerful, the city, or the state it is questionable whether this the fault of law itself or rather the ways in which it is enforced (or not enforced) through the criminal process. To say that fraudulent city bankers or wayward states are not prosecuted vigorously enough for their misdemeanours is not the same as saying that the criminal law is incapable of so doing.

Criminology is further charged with colluding in the failure to address questions of power: 'since its inception, criminology has enjoyed an intimate relationship with the powerful, a relationship determined largely by its failure to subject to critique the category of crime' (Hillyard and Tombs 2007: 16). Yet this is only partially true: the uneasy relationship that criminology has had, and continues to have, with the state defines no more than part of its practice. Those who accept official government commissions or funding do not inevitably or invariably lose their independence and critical edge—far from it. Criminologists have suffered government attempts to compromise their integrity and constrain their intellectual property but, individually and collectively, they have sought to resist this. The discipline's historical roots may lie closely entwined with the interests and projects of the state. But the subsequent formation of an independent, critical corpus of criminological scholars not wholly reliant upon government funding or access, protected by university tenure, and more than willing to criticize the decisions of those in power has substantially moved criminology from being a 'governmental' to 'governance' project (Ericson 2003: 42; Zedner 2003).

To the extent that the problem lies outside the legal category of crime and in the realm of power politics, it is unclear that moving 'beyond criminology' would liberate new conceptions of harm from the hierarchical political relations and interest group politics that have bedevilled it thus far. That crime has been mobilized to serve sectional interests, that it takes particular forms, and targets particular social and ethnic groups does not mean that it is incapable of reform. Nor does it mean that any alternative concept would be free from the effects of these embedded structural inequalities. If powerful constituencies mobilize crime for their own political ends, what reason have we to think that social harm, or indeed any other conceptual category (dispute or conflict, for example), would be immune?

A fourth argument given for abandoning the category of crime is the claim that it gives insufficient weight to harm. Yet harm, quite as much as fault, is central to criminal liability: a fact that those who propose moving beyond criminology scarcely acknowledge. The harm principle, famously articulated by Mill,[1] is central

[1] Namely 'that the only purpose for which power can be rightfully exercised over any member of a civilized community, against his will, is to prevent harm to others' (Mill 1979 edition: 68).

to criminal liability and provides a powerful guide as to what may and what may not legitimately be criminalized. Recall too that it is harm, not fault, which underwrites the strict liability crimes that make up the majority of criminal offences. Prevention of harm is also a powerful mover behind the proliferating array of preventive offences that seek to avert harms before they occur. Inchoate offences, crimes of possession, and of prevention, together with the growing number of hybrid civil-criminal preventive orders (such as anti-social behaviour orders (ASBOs), serious crime prevention orders, and control orders) all find their primary justification in preventing harm.

Finally, it is said that responding to social harm by criminalizing necessarily entails 'ratcheting up and broadening the aims of the criminal justice system' (Hillyard *et al.* 2004: 2). This charge fails to acknowledge that criminalization is a normative exercise that is as much about delimiting the state's power to punish. It also fails to recognize that criminalization endows the defendant with important procedural protections that do not attend other similarly coercive measures such as civil preventive orders or regulatory contracts. Whilst over-criminalization certainly constitutes a 'ratcheting up', permitting coercive measures to be imposed upon individuals without the protections of the criminal process constitutes an instance of under-criminalization equally worthy of criminological concern (Ashworth and Zedner 2010a). Just as restorative justice has attracted criticism for failing to ensure due process for those accused of wrongdoing (von Hirsch *et al.* 2003), so other non-criminal measures that entail compulsion or coercion risk depriving individuals of important procedural and human rights protections. In short, before criminologists capitulate to the call to abandon crime (and with it criminology) they might think more critically about the claims made for alternative approaches and consider the positive restraints and protections entailed in criminal law and procedure.

Criminologists hardly lack awareness of the limits of their endeavour and those of criminal justice as means of controlling crime. Crime surveys expose a dark field of crime unknown to the police; policing studies demonstrate how much policing is carried out by social institutions other than the formal police; and studies of attrition rates reveal how little crime reaches the trial stage. Recognizing the limits of criminal justice institutions and the fact that much deviant behaviour remains unknown, policed in other ways or subject to other regulatory systems, is not tantamount to saying crime and criminalization are unimportant. To the contrary, analysing the bases of criminalization, the procedures and institutions of criminal justice remains a core task not least because they concern some of the most coercive exercises in state power. Only if we have a clear analytical and normative conception of crime, backed by a strong account of what procedural consequences should follow, can criminology maintain its independent existence distinct from other areas of public policy and regulation.

The Criminalization Project

If moving beyond criminology is not the answer, what might it take to reinvigorate criminological interest in crime and to restore criminological confidence in the merits of its own enterprise? One potentially fruitful candidate is the criminalization project, a vibrant intellectual endeavour that invites renewed normative attention to questions such as: What is the basis of 'moral wrong' and how should fault be ascribed? Which categories of wrongs so offend the interests of others as to be rightfully labelled criminal? What are the distinguishing features of 'harm' and 'offence'? What forms does and may crime take? What procedural and institutional structures does its prosecution require? And which principles and values should inform the imposition of criminal liability?

The criminalization project is relatively new and, so far, pursued mainly by criminal lawyers, legal theorists and philosophers (Ashworth 2009; Lamond 2007; Tadros 2007; Duff 2007; Kleinig 2008). Yet it opens up a possible rapprochement between the adjacent disciplines of criminology and criminal law whose relationship, if not actively hostile, has scarcely been warm and friendly. While there are sound reasons for maintaining a distribution of duties consistent with the talents, qualities, and proclivities of different disciplines, respecting disciplinary boundaries need not mean that criminology should simply abandon criminalization to the criminal lawyers. Thinking critically about crime, what justifies criminalization, why, and according to what principles, sits squarely within the remit of criminology and deserves more criminological attention than it has received so far.

One possible explanation is that, despite their evident proximity, criminologists and criminal lawyers appear to be unwilling bedfellows, their backs turned firmly against one another. Lacey observes: 'it is almost as rare to find a criminology text which concerns itself with the scope and nature of criminal law as it is to find a criminal law text which addresses criminological questions about the idea of crime' (Lacey 2007: 179). Since the development of socio-legal studies, critical legal studies, and legal realism, criminal law has begun to show itself more receptive to criminological research. The law-in-context movement has done much to ensure that lawyers cannot and do not confine themselves to the study of law in the books (cf Ashworth this volume). But the traffic has been largely one way. Although lawyers have become more willing to consider criminological insights into the construction of crime, criminology remains loath to acknowledge the relevance or importance of criminal law. In short, the efforts made by social scientifically-minded lawyers to engage with criminological research have not been met by an equal willingness by criminologists to address how law frames their discipline.

The fact that the criminalization project has been colonized by legal theorists is curious because although one motive is to articulate a general theory of criminalization—with attendant principles and values that are clearly the stuff of jurisprudence and philosophy—an underlying driver is a solidly sociological concern about the rapid pace of criminalization (Husak 2008: chapter1). Overcriminalization results from too great a readiness by governments to criminalize as a response to social and political problems. The desire to curb this tendency (quite as much as any analytic or normative interest) is the driving force behind much criminalization scholarship. Given that the criminalization project has such a clear sociological impetus; it is all the more perplexing that it attracts so little criminological interest.

In part this may be the consequence of a fairly settled division of labour between criminal law and criminology, notwithstanding their ostensible common interest in crime. Crudely put, criminal law concerns itself with identifying the forms of behaviour, action or inaction, the structure of offences, the underlying legal principles, and component elements that, in the absence of justification or excuse, give rise to criminal liability. For criminal law theorists and legal philosophers an obvious way of resisting overcriminalization is to develop a stronger account of what should and should not be criminalized. They focus on articulating principles and values to guide and restrain those who formulate and approve new criminal laws, as well as those who administer them. By contrast, criminology has tended to focus its attention on the politics and social construction of crime, on practices of policing, prosecution, and punishment. This division has some merits, not least it acknowledges and plays to the specific methodological training and disciplinary expertise of criminal lawyers and criminologists. But there are costs to too rigid a boundary between the two disciplines (Lacey 2007: 181). Questions like 'what counts as a good reason to criminalize' and 'what values should the criminal law embrace' might seem better left to the lawyers, but they are inseparable from questions of politics, policing, and enforcement that are the very stuff of criminology.

Criminalization might better be conceived as simultaneously an analytic project concerned principally with taxonomy; a normative project concerned with principles and values; and a sociological project concerned with the socio-economic and political motors of criminal justice practice. Its focus could profitably extend to the welter of interpretive and regulatory practices through which the extensive, untidy variety of malign human behaviour is translated into categories of formal criminal liability. Understood this way the potential contribution of criminology becomes clear. Left to the lawyers, theorizing about crime risks remaining fixed on questions about the philosophical foundations of the criminal law and the general principles of criminal liability. Without criminological input normative theorizing about crime is liable to proceed free from the inconvenient truths revealed by a fully grounded, empirically rigorous, and sociologically rich understanding of the ways in which crime is actually policed and prosecuted. Without attention to the political and social processes by and through which crime is constructed and mediated; the administrative, financial, and political drivers of and constraints upon prosecution and punishment; and the social, cultural and professional contexts in which criminal justice agents act there is a danger that a largely artificial account of crime—as consistent with the model principles of the general part[2]—continues to dominate debates about criminalization.

A vital role of criminology is to provide evidence of how criminalization occurs not only on the pages of the criminal law statutes and law reports but in the complex interactions between news media, politicians, and public opinion; in decision-making and exercise of discretion by criminal justice officials; and throughout that tortuous entity the criminal process. Criminology also has much to say about power relations, not least those of class, race, and gender, which lie behind the decision to criminalize and inform the practices of policing and punishment. It reveals the contingent factors, cultural assumptions and prejudices, and political imperatives that underpin the decision to render an act, or omission, criminal. Criminalization might also address larger political questions about the role of the state, its authority over and obligations to citizens; what kind of criminal law serves a liberal democracy, and what responsibilities states have in new areas such as transnational and international crime and terrorism. None of these questions can be addressed without the study of the *Realpolitik* of global, national, and local political and socio-economic structures and relations that criminology is so well placed to undertake.

Why Crime Matters

Clearly, criminology has much to contribute to deliberations about criminalization, but what in turn has criminology to gain from greater engagement with the criminal law? Unless they happen to have a legal background, most criminologists ply their trade without recourse to a criminal law textbook and still less to the statutes or codes, law reports, and other legal instruments that define the very offences about which they write. Seen one way this might seem sensible, leaving criminal lawyers to study the formal rules of conduct and procedure that define criminal liability frees criminologists up to do what criminologists do best. Seen another way this collective turning away from criminal law might be regarded as an extraordinary, wilful blindness by criminologists to the definition, structure, and scope of the very offences that are their raison d'être.

While this tendency is not unique to common law jurisdictions, it derives in part from the contingency of a division that is by no means universal. As Lacey observes, 'to Continental European eyes, the Anglo-American separation of criminal law and criminal procedure, and indeed of criminal law and sentencing, appears extraordinary' (Lacey 2007: 181). In other jurisdictions where the very word for criminal law refers directly to its penal consequence, for example in French *droit pénal*, German *Strafrecht* or Italian *diritto penale*, criminal lawyers are more aware of the sanction-

[2] That is the body of criminal law principles that are said to be common to all criminal offences regardless of their substantive scope or focus. See Shute and Simester (eds) 2002.

conferring function of the criminal law and criminologists more directly appreciate the legal framework in which policing and punishment occurs. In the common law world it is too easy for criminal law and criminal justice to appear to be categorically distinct; the historic irrelation between the two obscures their mutual dependence (Nelken 1987).

Another possible reason for the relative reluctance of criminology to engage with law derives from its suspicion of normative theorizing. Garland claims that criminology's 'claim to be an empirically grounded, scientific undertaking sets it apart from moral and legal discourses' (Garland 2002: 7). Yet this sets up too sharp a distinction (Ericson 2003). It derives partly from the fact that criminology, no less than economics, is a dismal science inclined to negativity and critique, and less positively disposed toward normative theorizing (Zedner 2002: 364–5). Criminologists are apt to think that detached, ironic observation of malfunction, failure, or paradox is a worthy substitute for positive critical endeavour. An important exception is penal theory, a field in which normative theorizing flourishes, where a sophisticated literature engages with jurisprudence, philosophy, and political theory to formulate persuasive accounts of why and how state punishment might be justified (Lacey 1988; Braithwaite and Pettit 1990; von Hirsch 1993; Zimring and Hawkins 1995; von Hirsch and Ashworth 2005). Yet even here much penal theory proceeds without direct engagement with the criminal law. A desert-based theory of punishment, for example, would seem to presume a criminal law grounded in moral wrongdoing. The fact that more than half the statutory offences are crimes of strict liability that require no proof of fault, and many others are little more than regulatory offences, raises questions about how justifiable it is to punish where moral wrongfulness is not at issue. The same criticisms might be made of consequentialist theories of punishment. How defensible is incapacitation as a justification if only a small proportion of crimes pose a serious threat of harm? And what place has restorative justice in respect of regulatory offences and victimless crimes? Closer integration of criminal law and penal theory would address these questions head on and stimulate debate about punishment that engages more directly with the originating grounds for criminalization.

This imperative to address questions about what crime is and what it should be is made more urgent by radical changes in the scope, procedure, and sanctioning of crime that together alter the landscape of crime control (Ashworth and Zedner 2008). To the extent that criminology is constituted as a discipline by its commitment to the study of crime, shifting definitions of crime and changing practices of criminalization have direct ramifications for its scope and limits. Three major areas of change stand out as of particular importance: they can broadly be categorized as substantive, temporal, and procedural.

First, substantive changes in the subject-matter and scope of criminal liability expand the potential remit of criminological endeavour. Areas either newly subject to criminalization, affected by more extensive criminal laws, or intensive policing include (but are not confined to) border control, immigration, human trafficking, crimes of the state, genocide, terrorism, financial and corporate malpractice, environmental harm, and anti-social behaviour. These disparate areas have rapidly become objects of criminological research and writing. The openness and receptivity of criminologists to new objects of enquiry is to be welcomed. But unlimited expansion risks depriving the discipline of its historic boundaries and collective sense of its common object of enquiry. More importantly, the willingness to govern through crime that this expansion of criminal liability connotes has major ramifications not only for the imposition of punishment, which has increased rapidly in many western jurisdictions, but for the very nature of civil society. Critical engagement with the questions like 'Are these appropriate objects of criminalization?', 'Might they better or more appropriately be regulated by other means?', would have a much needed restraining influence upon the propensity to criminalize.

Second, a growing concern with risk and security has created a pressure for earlier intervention, extending inchoate liability for attempts and conspiracy and even pre-inchoate liability to impose fault pre-crime or in respect of risks that may never eventuate. The temporal shift manifests itself not only in greater resort to forms of inchoate liability but also liability for preparatory offences and crimes of possession (Ashworth and Zedner 2010b). Together these threaten to replace post hoc punishment for wrongs done with pre-emptive liability for risk creation or in respect of putative future harms well ahead of wrongdoing. These temporal changes have the power to reconstitute the very parameters of crime and as such pose major intellectual challenges for criminology quite as much as for criminal law (Zedner 2007). To the extent that criminology is defined by crime, the rise of risk threatens radically to reconfigure or even render the discipline redundant. If criminology is not to be passively modified or passed over by these developments a more active discussion about the proper limits of criminal liability is needed.[3]

Third, changing modes of regulation result in more and more deviant behaviour being made the subject of regulatory, administrative, civil and other procedural instruments: witness the rise of civil preventive measures, administrative penalties, and contractual obligations. As a consequence, criminalization comes to be defined as much by what is occurring outside the boundaries of the criminal law as within it (Ashworth and Zedner 2010a; Crawford 2009). Though they may result in quasi-punitive sanctions, coercive measures pursued through civil or administrative channels beyond the criminal process deny their subjects important protections. The expanding use of contractual and other regulatory measures is thus altering the very boundaries of criminal liability, challenging conventional conceptions of crime, and appropriate responses to it. Criminalization is supplemented by alternative, but no less potent, forms of regulation and low level policing is undertaken by housing officers and social services as well as by the police proper. Attention to the ways in

[3] That debate is only now under way; see, for example, Ashworth and Zedner 2010b; Hudson 2009.

which crime control is pursued not only in criminal but also civil, administrative, and regulatory channels raises pressing questions about the limits of crime and the very scope of criminology.

Crime is, by one honourable definition, that which is the subject of the criminal process. In the words of Glanville Williams, 'crime is an act capable of being followed by criminal proceedings' (Williams 1955: 130). The gravity of the charge laid and the consequences of conviction call for the protections of the criminal process. Yet this doctrine is increasingly being eroded by proceedings conducted in civil or administrative channels that target wrongdoing or offensive behaviour and are punitive in their effect. The abuse of alternative channels to pursue punitive ends while evading the human rights protections inherent in the criminal process has been recognized and condemned by the Strasbourg Court. It has ruled that the question of whether or not a person is charged with a criminal offence and thereby entitled to the full protections of Article 6 ECHR is not a matter of nomenclature but for the court to determine by looking at the substance and impact of the measure.[4] This so-called anti-subversion doctrine seeks to prevent governments from pursuing de facto criminal proceedings in civil law channels to evade the protections that would otherwise apply (Ashworth 2004; Zedner 2007). Yet it is only partially successful in resisting the trend toward alternative procedural forms that deny the defendant the protections due. Crawford has observed how:

> new technologies of control introduced under the banner of tackling anti-social behaviour in Britain have appropriated and advanced a logic of regulation in ways that are both highly problematic in themselves, and that collectively foster an assault on many key criminal justice values and principles, notably due process, proportionality and special protections afforded to young people [Crawford 2009: 811].

Procedural side-stepping may be cheaper, quicker, more 'effective', and thus attractive to governments seeking less onerous evidential standards, more relaxed admission of hearsay or secret evidence, and freedom from the requirements set by human rights instruments. Its deliberate erosion of the principled protections that adhere to the criminal process and properly apply to those accused of crime should be as central a topic of criminological concern as it is now for criminal law theory. Decriminalization may be a desirable goal but it can safely be pursued only once we have a clear sense of the grounds upon which we legitimately criminalize in the first place and a fully developed conception of procedural justice beyond the criminal law.

Conclusion

This chapter has suggested just some reasons why criminology should hesitate to abandon the category of crime in favour of other organizing concepts and why it

[4] See *Engel v Netherlands* (1976) 1 EHRR 647.

might engage more enthusiastically with questions about what crime is and what it should be. At a time when criminalization is arguably losing its distinctiveness as a mode of regulation and being eroded and usurped by civil orders and alternative regulatory strategies, it is arguable that criminology risks losing its focus and its very raison d'être (Shearing 2001; Braithwaite 2000). Committing criminology to thinking critically about criminalization would serve the dual function of instituting a much needed revival of normative theorizing and of putting crime squarely back onto the criminological agenda. Determining the boundaries of crime is a proper subject of criminological enquiry: one to which criminology has much to contribute and from which it has much to gain, not least because doing so serves to delineate more clearly the precincts of criminology itself. Criminology presupposes crime but presupposing alone is not enough. Defining crime entails analytical, political, and moral choices, the making of which ought to lie high on the criminological agenda. Anything less would seem to be a failure of professional responsibility.

References

Ashworth, A. (2004), 'Social Control and Anti-Social Behaviour Order: the Subversion of Human Rights?', *Law Quarterly Review*, 120: 263–91.

_____ (2009), *Principles of Criminal Law*, 6th edn, Oxford: Oxford University Press.

_____ and Zedner, L. (2008), 'Defending the Criminal Law: Reflections on the Changing Character of Crime, Procedure, and Sanctions', *Criminal Law and Philosophy*, 2: 21–51.

_____ and _____. (2010a), 'Preventive Orders: A Problem of Under-Criminalization?' in R. A. Duff *et al.* (eds), *The Boundaries of the Criminal Law*, Oxford: Oxford University Press.

_____ and _____. (2010b), 'Preventive Justice and the Limits of the Criminal Law', in R. A. Duff and S. P. Green (eds), *Philosophical Foundations of the Criminal Law*, Oxford: Oxford University Press.

Braithwaite, J. (1989), *Crime, Shame and Reintegration*, Cambridge: Cambridge University Press.

_____ (2000), 'The New Regulatory State and the Transformation of Criminology', in D. Garland and R. Sparks (eds), *Criminology and Social Theory*, Oxford: Oxford University Press.

_____ and Pettit, P. (1990), *Not Just Deserts: A Republican Theory of Justice*, Oxford: Oxford University Press.

Christie, N. (1977), 'Conflicts as Property', *British Journal of Criminology*, 17: 1–15.

Clarke, R. V. (1995), 'Situational Crime Prevention', in M. Tonry and N. Morris (eds), *Crime and Justice: An Annual Review of Research*, Chicago: University of Chicago.

Crawford, A. (2009), 'Governing through Anti-Social Behaviour: Regulatory Challenges to Criminal Justice', *British Journal of Criminology*, 49: 810–31.

Duff, R. A. (2007), *Answering for Crime: Responsibility and Liability in the Criminal Law*, Oxford: Hart Publishing.

Ericson, R. (2003), 'The Culture and Power of Criminological Research', in L. Zedner and A. Ashworth (eds), *The Criminological Foundations of Penal Policy*, Oxford: Oxford University Press.

_____ and Doyle, A. (2004), *Uncertain Busines: Risk, Insurance and the Limits of Knowledge*, Toronto: University of Toronto Press.

Felson, M. and Clarke, R. V. (1998), *Opportunity Makes the Thief: Practical Theory for Crime Prevention. Police Research Series No. 98*, London: Home Office.

_____ (2002), *Crime and Everyday Life*, 3rd edn, London: Sage.

Friedrichs, D. O. and Schwartz, M. D. (2007), 'On Social Harm and a Twenty-First Century Criminology', *Crime Law and Social Change*, 48: 1–7.

Garland, D. (2002), 'Of Crimes and Criminals: the Development Criminology in Britain', in M. Maguire, R. Morgan, and R. Reiner (eds), *The Oxford Handbook of Criminology*, 3rd edn, Oxford: Oxford University Press.

Hillyard, P., Pantazis, C., Tombs, S., and Gordon, D. (2004), *Beyond Criminology: Taking Harm Seriously*, London: Pluto Press.

_____, _____, _____, and _____. (2005), *Criminal Obsessions: Why Harm Matters More than Crime*, London: Crime and Society Foundation.

_____ and Tombs, S. (2007), 'From 'Crime' to Social Harm?', *Crime Law and Social Change*, 48: 9–25.

Hoyle, C. and Young, R. (2002), 'Restorative Justice: Assessing the prospects and pitfalls', in M. McConville and G. Wilson (eds), *The Handbook of Criminal Justice*, Oxford: Oxford University Press.

Hudson, B. (1998), 'Doing Justice to Difference', in A. Ashworth and M. Wasik (eds), *Fundamentals of Sentencing Theory*, Oxford: Clarendon Press.

_____ (2009), 'Justice in a Time of Terror', *British Journal of Criminology*, 49, 5: 702–17.

Husak, D. (2008), *Overcriminalization: The Limits of the Criminal Law*, Oxford: Oxford University Press.

Kleinig, J. (2008), *Ethics and Criminal Justice: An Introduction*, Cambridge: Cambridge University Press.

Lacey, N. (1988), *State Punishment: Political Principles and Community Values*, London: Routledge.

_____ (2007), 'Legal Constructions of Crime', in M. Maguire, R. Morgan, and R. Reiner (eds), *The Oxford Handbook of Criminology*, 3rd edn, Oxford: Oxford University Press.

_____, Wells, C., and Quick, O. (2003), *Reconstructing Criminal Law: Perspectives on Crime and the Criminal Process*, 3rd edn, Cambridge: Cambridge University Press.

Lamond, G. (2007), 'What is a Crime?', *Oxford Journal of Legal Studies*, 27, 4: 609–32.

Laycock, G. (2008), 'Special Edition on Crime Science', *Policing*, 2, 2: 149–53.

Mill, J. S. (1979), *On Liberty*, Harmondsworth: Penguin.

Nelken, D. (1987), 'Criminal Law and Criminal Justice: Some Notes on their Irrelation', in I. Dennis (ed.), *Criminal Law and Criminal Justice*, London: Sweet & Maxwell.

Norrie, A. (2001), *Crime, Reason and History: A Critical Introduction to Criminal Law*, London: Weidenfeld & Nicolson.

Pemberton, S. (2007), 'Social Harm Future(s): Exploring the Potential of the Social Harm Approach', *Crime Law and Social Change*, 48: 27–41.

Read, T. and Tilley, N. (2000), *Not Rocket Science? Problem-solving and crime reduction. Crime Reduction Series Paper 6*, London: Home Office.

Rock, P. (2007), 'Sociological Theories of Crime', in M. Maguire, R. Morgan, and R. Reiner (eds), *The Oxford Handbook of Criminology*, Oxford: Oxford University Press.
Shearing, C. (2001), 'Punishment and the Changing Face of Governance', *Punishment and Society*, 3, 2: 203–20.
Shute, S. and Simester, A. P. (eds) (2002), *Criminal Law Theory: Doctrines of the General Part*, Oxford, Oxford University Press.
Simon, J. (2007), *Governing Through Crime: How the War on Crime Transformed American Democracy and Created a Culture of Fear*, New York, Oxford University Press.
Sumner, C. (1994), *The Sociology of Deviance: An Obituary*, Buckingham: Open University Press.
Tadros, V. (2007), *Criminal Responsibility*, Oxford: Oxford University Press.
von Hirsch, A. (1993), *Censure and Sanctions*, Oxford: Oxford University Press.
_____ and Ashworth, A. (2005), *Proportionate Sentencing: Exploring the Principles*, Oxford: Oxford University Press.
_____, Roberts, J., Bottoms, A., Roach, K., and Schiff, M. (eds) (2003), *Restorative Justice and Criminal Justice*, Oxford: Hart Publishing.
Williams, G. (1955), 'The Definition of a Crime', *Current Legal Problems*, Oxford: Oxford University Press.
Zedner, L. (2002), 'Dangers of Dystopias in Penal Theory', *Oxford Journal of Legal Studies*, 22, 2: 341–66.
_____. (2003), 'Useful Knowledge? Debating the Role of Criminology in Post-war Britain', in L. Zedner and A. Ashworth (eds), *The Criminological Foundations of Penal Policy*, Oxford: Oxford University Press.
_____ (2007), 'Pre-Crime and Post-Criminology?', *Theoretical Criminology*, 11, 2: 261–81.
_____ (2007), 'Seeking Security By Eroding Rights: The Side-Stepping of Due Process ', in B. Goold and L. Lazarus (eds), *Security and Human Rights*, Oxford: Hart Publishing.
Zimring, F. E., and Hawkins, G.(1995), *Incapacitation: Penal Confinement and the Restraint of Crime*, New York: Oxford University Press.

19

TRANSCENDING THE BOUNDARIES OF CRIMINOLOGY: THE EXAMPLE OF RICHARD ERICSON

AARON DOYLE, JANET CHAN, AND KEVIN D. HAGGERTY

Introduction

Criminology lost a world leader with the death of Richard Ericson in 2007. Ericson was one of the pre-eminent criminologists of the last forty years and one of the most cited (see, for example, Cohn and Farrington 2007). This chapter uses Ericson's work as a case study to demonstrate the potential for criminology to reach widely in its contributions to knowledge, transcending conventional boundaries. It responds to the editors' question 'How should criminology be done?' by examining how Ericson's work (especially later in his career) pushed the boundaries of conventional criminology outward into new substantive areas of research, towards interdisciplinarity, and towards making broader theoretical contributions that transcend the particular empirical concern with crime and criminal justice. Zedner (this volume) calls for a renewed focusing of criminology on the core concept of crime. In counterpoint, we use the example of Ericson's research to spotlight how some of the best work in the field can move beyond the conventional foci of criminology and have a wider reach and import. Because of the cultural and institutional centrality of crime and its control, crime can often become the pivot on which broader understandings of social life can turn. The most famous example is of course *Discipline and Punish* by Foucault (1977), which saw the particular case of the prison as paradigmatic for a much wider range of contemporary institutional life. Here we discuss how Ericson's work provides a set of key further illustrations of transcending criminology's conventional boundaries.

Criminology as a Field of Knowledge Production

First, it is useful to consider what we mean in this context by criminology. Rather than thinking of criminology as a discipline or as a substantive area of research, criminology can be conceptualized as a form of practice that produces knowledge and discourse on crime, deviance, control and justice. This knowledge production takes place within a *field* that is a 'space of conflict and competition' over power and resources (Bourdieu and Wacquant 1992: 17). A key is that the field of criminology is not easily defined: modern criminology is said to be 'a composite, eclectic, multidisciplinary enterprise' (Garland 1997: 19), its attachment to disciplines is loose (Pavarini 1994) and its boundaries are unclear (Chan 1996). Moreover, the field is said to be fragmented (Ericson and Carriere 1994), 'messy' (Ericson 2003: 53) and in a 'permanent state of precariousness and crisis' (Pavarini 1994: 51).

Ericson himself argued that criminology is simultaneously a policy field, a legal field, and a system of academic disciplines: 'Criminologists are in perpetual motion among empirical research, policy rhetorics, and policing initiatives' (2003: 31). The production of criminological knowledge has primarily taken place within higher education institutions. Depending on its history as a field in different countries, criminology has lived in a range of academic sites: law, social science, professional schools, or interdisciplinary units. In imitation of Borges' (1964) description of the classification of animals in a Chinese encyclopedia (famously quoted by Foucault (1970) and others), Ericson concluded that:

> A Western encyclopedia might classify criminology as '(a) law, (b) justice, (c) power, (d) order, (e) legitimation, (f) welfare, (g) business, (h) government, (i) a discipline, (j) undisciplined, (k) disciplinary (a form of power/knowledge), (l) *et cetera*, (m) population health, (n) a dog's breakfast [Ericson 1996: 15–16]

John Braithwaite may well add 'regulation, child development, restorative and procedural justice' to the list (2000: 223). Ericson has argued, however, that the diversity of academic criminology does not imply that criminology is 'a pluralistic and level playing field':

> Like all fields, it is subject to perpetual struggles over jurisdiction in terms of a division of expert knowledge and labour (Abbott 1988). Criminological jurisdiction... rises and falls according to how it is located in university organization (powerful and prestigious faculties); paradigms (the success of abstraction about crime and security in taking jurisdiction from others and creating new jurisdiction); research funding (access to and influence over major foundations and other funding agencies); publications (prestigious publishers, and a hierarchy of preferred journals), and professional associations (association with professional power, such as law and medicine) [Ericson 1996:17].

Academic criminology is thus a space of struggle over academic capital, scientific authority, and symbolic and social capital (Chan 2000). What is of interest for our purposes here is the somewhat paradoxical interaction between tendencies to stray from the conventional criminological project and the capital that one may accrue as a result.

One element of the habitus of criminology that appears to be shared by many of its practitioners is a proclivity to reflect on criminology's own (theoretical, policy, or institutional) failures. This focus on failure is part of the reflexive nature of criminology, demonstrated by the compulsion of some strands of criminology to evaluate criminal justice initiatives and the eternal vigilance of critical criminology over undesirable effects of crime control. As Hogg has pointed out, the irony of criminological failures is that they have not inhibited the growth of the discipline (1996). He quotes Stan Cohen's confession to illustrate his point:

> Every attempt I have ever made to distance myself from the subject, to criticize it, even to question its very right to exist, has only got me more involved in its inner life... The more successful our attack on the old regime, the more we received PhDs, tenure, publishers' contracts, and research funds, appeared on booklists and examination questions, and even became directors of institutes of criminology and received awards from professional associations [Cohen 1988: 8].

Sometimes tied to their concerns about the various failures of the criminological project, a number of high profile criminological researchers have tried to distance themselves from criminology or sought to develop their interests in other fields. (In other cases, as with Ericson, the goal in broadening interests may have been more simply to follow interests and avoid intellectual stagnation.) Somewhat ironically, these criminological researchers whose attentions have wandered have continued to be venerated within criminology, in part because the insights they draw from 'outside' have in fact enhanced the richness of criminological practice. At the same time, as we will argue, the best such work in turn may considerably enrich study in fields beyond what is conventionally understood as criminology. The work of Ericson is a case in point. Ericson was a criminologist whose stature in and contributions to the field were tied in part to reaching beyond the conventional boundaries of criminology, as we will now discuss.

Ericson's Contributions

Ericson's research was exclusively conducted within academic institutions. He was initially educated in sociology but completed his PhD at the Institute of Criminology of the University of Cambridge. His institutional appointments—which spanned multiple departments at various stages including sociology and law in addition to criminology—followed a rapid upward trajectory from assistant professor to professor and then director of the Centre of Criminology at the University of Toronto. His research undoubtedly placed him as one of the most prolific and important scholars in the field of criminology. His position in the field was characterized by a trajectory of successes in securing research grants and prestigious fellowships, the supervision of more than 50 postgraduate students, and the publication of numerous books and papers. From 1972 to 2007 he published twelve books, five monographs, eight edited volumes and over 100 journal articles and book chapters. This body of work made valuable contributions, not only on a range of conventional criminological topics such as law, justice, policing and crime control, but also concerning other institutions not normally understood to be the foci of criminology, such as the news media and the insurance industry. Furthermore his work not only drew on and incorporated tendencies in social theory but in turn made important contributions to broader debates, such as those pertaining to risk and security. Ericson's way of doing criminology was thus characterized in part by transcending the substantive boundaries of criminology, by making connections with other disciplines, and by making significant innovative contributions to social theory.

Transcending the Substantive Boundaries of Criminology

One of Richard Ericson's most important innovations was expanding the range of institutions normally studied by criminologists, in order to examine some new institutions that produce crime and justice. Ericson's work crossed many boundaries and covered a diversity of research areas and theoretical avenues (see Haggerty, Doyle, and Chan, forthcoming). Ericson's criminology focused on institutions, on the institutional production of knowledge and on how this is imbued with power relations. It was not focused on etiological questions about why people might or might not commit crime. Throughout his research career, Ericson steered away from such questions as, to him, they missed the point. For him, crime was not a naturally given phenomenon; instead, certain acts *become* crimes through highly variable institutional practices of categorization, monitoring and processing. Consequently, to understand crime, one must understand the various institutions that lay claim to the crime issue, including, as we will discuss, some institutions that are not traditionally considered to be part of the criminal justice system, such as the news media and insurance organizations. An 'institutional' approach to criminology involves studying the institutions that help to establish and process certain phenomena as crimes, and studying some of the distinctive governmental techniques used by these institutions, such as surveillance, risk management and mobilizing accounts in the media.

At one level, Ericson was a social constructionist in that the focus of his work was on the institutional production of knowledge. In all of his studies, Ericson continually returned to questions about the power and paradoxes of official knowledge. This involved scrutiny of the production of official accounts, of shifts in the types of knowledges that institutions use to govern populations, of divergent institutional logics and structures for communicating knowledge, and of institutional decision-making in contexts of imperfect knowledge. Ericson had a particular concern with the interfaces between institutions and how knowledge moved or translated between them.

His first books covered more conventional criminological topics such as the labelling perspective (Ericson 1975a), the identities of young offenders (Ericson 1975b), police patrol work (Ericson 1982), police detectives (Ericson 1981), and the criminal courts (Ericson and Baranek 1982). However, his focus on the institutional production of knowledge, on the interface between institutions, and on how knowledge moved and was translated between them soon led him to consider institutions that are not conventionally considered topics of criminological research. Thus, he shifted his research focus in the 1980s to the news media as another key institution that produces crime and deviance. His trilogy of media books with Patricia Baranek and Janet Chan (Ericson, Baranek, and Chan 1987, 1989, 1991) provide a path-breaking analysis of the mass media as a complex institution made up of a diversity of organizations, technologies and people, interacting and negotiating with other social institutions in the production of crime news that is shaped by organizational, political, and technological constraints. The three books are set against the larger backdrop of a theory of the knowledge society, where power-knowledge represents the key dimension of hierarchy. They were based on ethnographies of six major urban print and broadcast news organizations, as well as qualitative and quantitative analysis of their content. The research included extended direct observation of the news-making process, numerous interviews with news personnel at various organizational levels and with ninety-three key news sources in four institutional arenas: the police, courts, legislature and private sector. It examined the news process from assigning stories and reporting to editing, even devoting a chapter to the process whereby letters to the editors are selected for publication. The third of these books, *Representing Order,* used a thorough content analysis of six television, radio and print news outlets to reveal that crime, law and justice stories make up roughly one-half of all the news (although this varies between outlets). The results of seeing the news media through a criminological lens were innovative theoretically: the authors argued that the news media are a central agency of social control that joins with the legal system to represent order, and that concerns with deviance and control have become the primary defining characteristics of newsworthiness. They highlighted many similarities between media discourse and legal discourse and showed how they are intertextually related in constituting the realities of social order, including what Ericson *et al.* described as the key elements of morality, procedural form and hierarchy.

Although the three books began from a criminological orientation, they also made a series of important contributions to media studies. Indeed they became some of the most important and most cited ethnographies of news production. The authors concluded that journalists have a critical location in the knowledge society, as transformers of specialized bureaucratic knowledge into common sense. Yet their legitimacy often depends on that of the powerful 'authorized knowers' they quote. In contrast to other research, these findings suggest that journalists are often aware that their work is interpretive in nature, 'investing facts with significance'. Another key finding that contrasted with previous research on the news media was that there is pervasive conflict in the newsroom, not only with interpersonal bases and over resources, but also for ideological reasons. Ericson and his co-authors also made a key theoretical turn in audience research, shifting the focus from researching influence on individual audience members to understanding media influence on institutional audiences like the police or government. In short, then, Ericson and co-authors offered a rich and unique approach to the news media by analysing them as a central institution of social control alongside of and enmeshed with the criminal justice system; in doing so they contributed a great deal not only to criminology but, beyond that, to media studies.

Later, Ericson made a bold and challenging move by turning his focus to insurance, an institution of comparable scope and importance to the criminal justice system and the news media, but one much less in the public and academic spotlights and much less 'sexy' in academic terms, and one which had never been the subject of such a research project. His two books *Insurance as Governance* (Ericson, Doyle, and Barry 2003) and *Uncertain Business* (Ericson and Doyle 2004a) provide a painstakingly detailed analysis of insurance as a vital institution of modern governance and examine the array of public and private justice measures that insurers dispense through risk management

In the context of the insurance research, Ericson and Doyle asked what 'crime' means when private institutions like insurance companies are tasked more and more with security provision. For example, the books studied a major crackdown on claimant fraud by insurance companies, and asked what it meant to say such fraud is a 'crime' when it is largely defined and dealt with internally by insurance companies (see especially Ericson and Doyle 2004b). They found that perceived fraud was dealt with outside the criminal justice system in all but a small minority of cases:

> Instead, the crackdown mostly deploys the notion that fraud is a 'crime' as a way to deny claims, particularly from less desirable customers, and to cut costs. The criminal justice system is invoked for symbolic purposes as a deterrent, and police play a supporting role supplying information to insurance investigators on suspected claimants, often for a fee....

> Despite insurers' public rhetoric concerning the immorality of the crime of fraud, and the fact that moral evaluation of particular claimants is often key in the decision to proceed with fraud investigation, in industry practice the dominant morality by far is one of expedience. In an increasingly privatized society, the practical definition of 'what is insurance fraud' becomes whatever is consistent with the smooth flow of business' [Ericson and Doyle 2004b: 122].

The insurance books are set in the context of 'risk society', conceptualizing the criminal justice system as part of a broader set of intersecting public and private institutions that, instead of being focused on deviance, order, and control, organize the production and distribution of knowledge of risk in order to produce security. Ericson and collaborators drew upon 224 interviews with individuals in private and government insurance institutions, and with insurance consumers, to demonstrate that insurance has long been overlooked as a key institution of governance, and that private insurance becomes particularly prominent as the state progressively withdraws from direct service provision. Insurers involve themselves in governance through producing knowledge about risks and making them calculable, using actuarialism to create risk pools, binding populations together legally, protecting against loss of capital, managing risks through surveillance, and serving as a social technology of justice. In expanding the criminological focus to this rarely studied institution, Ericson and co-authors also helped kindle the emergence of the sub-field of insurance studies.

Ericson returned to what might be regarded as more mainstream criminology in his final book *Crime in an Insecure World* (Ericson 2007). Yet this book has a much broader theoretical sweep than most criminology, and shows how criminological issues can be understood as central to social thought more broadly. Ericson traces the history of liberalism and of risk and uncertainty and argues that the 'problem of uncertainty' has now replaced the problem of order and is central to many aspects and agencies of neo-liberal governance. Ericson contrasts Hobbes' Leviathan—the sovereign state as guardian and protector—with a second Leviathan of the 'biblical social imaginary... This Leviathan is uncertainty, a monstrous body that leaves only death and destruction in its wake. Like the smouldering twin towers of the World Trade Centre, this imaginary signals catastrophe and the need for precaution at all costs' (Ericson 2007: 32).

Ericson argues that criminalization has become the leading response to such uncertainty, including a trend towards precautionary logic and 'criminalization of the merely suspicious'. This criminalization becomes mobilized through what Ericson calls counter-law or law against law: 'new laws are enacted and new uses of existing law are reinvented to erode or eliminate traditional principles, standards and procedures of criminal law that get in the way of preempting imagined sources of harm' (Ericson 2007: 24). Empirically the sweep was also very wide, as he examined this process across the realms of national, social, corporate and domestic security, from the US's Patriot Act to anti-social behaviour orders to surveillance of health insurance benefit claimants to the policing of the homeless through the 'Safe Streets Act' in Canada.

In short, then, through this series of path-breaking works, Ericson progressively broadened the scope of criminological research by pushing the criminological study of institutions beyond the traditional triumvirate of policing, courts and corrections.

Making Connections with Other Disciplines

Richard Ericson's criminology was interdisciplinary: while firmly rooted in the intellectual traditions of sociology, Ericson's approach to doing criminology was never confined by disciplinary boundaries. As pointed out earlier, disciplinary diversity is one of the hallmarks of criminology as a field of knowledge production, but while most academic scholars are located in a specific discipline both intellectually and institutionally, Ericson's interdisciplinary scholarship was reflected in his multiple appointments in law, sociology and criminology. The media and crime volumes (Ericson *et al.* 1987, 1989, 1991) drew on and contributed to the sociology of deviance, sociology of knowledge, media and cultural studies, anthropology, political science, and the social psychology of organizations. Similarly, his books on risk society and on insurance (Ericson and Haggerty 1997; Ericson *et al.* 2003; Ericson and Doyle 2004b) engaged with and developed insights not only in criminology and socio-legal studies, but also science and technology studies, organizational and occupational studies, sociology of risk and insurance studies. An important distinction between Ericson's approach and many scholarly attempts at reaching out to other disciplines is that Ericson's connections with scholars from other disciplines were significant rather than perfunctory outside of criminology, as evidenced by the edited volumes involving these scholars (see Ericson and Stehr 2000; Ericson and Doyle 2003; Haggerty and Ericson 2006). Ericson's work was regarded as a key influence in creating the interdisciplinary fields of surveillance studies (Wood 2002) as well as insurance studies.

Contributions to Social Theory

Ericson also frequently moved beyond criminology to look at major social theoretical developments to inform his work. He was neither a strict constructionist nor a structuralist; instead he combined detailed studies of interactions with an analysis of the structural constraints under which people operate. His intellectual trajectory began with labeling theory and symbolic interactionism and expanded to include many influences drawn from, for example, media studies, the sweeping risk society theorizing of Beck, and post-Foucauldian analysis of governmentality. Ericson's books are situated in macro-level analyses, for example, of the knowledge society (Ericson, Baranek, and Chan 1987, 1989, 1991), the risk society (Ericson and Haggerty 1997; Ericson and Doyle 2004a), and neo-liberal governance (see especially Ericson, Doyle, and Barry 2003) but they move skilfully between micro, institutional, and macro levels of analysis. In *Negotiating Control*, for example, Ericson brilliantly made use of Goffman's (1959) and Giddens' (1984) refinement of the notion of 'front' and 'back regions and extended this social-psychological framework for analysing individuals' 'presentation of self' to the 'sociological level of how organizations protect and present their activities by policing spatial regions and knowledge' (Ericson, Baranek and Chan 1989: 9).

A key point is that Ericson's criminology did more than simply draw on broader social theory; in turn it also fed back on and reworked such theory, making wider theoretical contributions. To give another example, *Policing the Risk Society* (Ericson and Haggerty 1997) is not only a book about policing, but, in the broader theoretical literature on risk, is the most noteworthy and sustained effort to synthesize the perspectives of Beckian and Foucaudian scholars. The authors broadened out from what some might see as a relatively narrow empirical concern with police bureaucracy and information processing to show how these mundane developments in policing captured a broader social shift that called for a rethinking of the major social theoretical positions on risk, again showing how crime and control could be a pivot on which much wider understandings of social life can turn. In *Policing the Risk Society*, Ericson returned to the area of policing but employing a substantially different orientation from his earlier celebrated research (Ericson 1981, 1982). In parallel to the insurance research, this book situates the police in the context of the rise of risk-based forms of governance. Here, the emphasis is on how the police, through their increasingly regimented, formatted and controlled information work, serve the risk-management needs of a host of institutions external to the police. Representing the police in this way necessitated that the authors move from the usual focus on police frontline work to study the large volume of mid-level managers in policing, whose role is dominated by structuring, processing, categorizing and conveying risk-relevant information. This empirical example in turn led them to develop a theory of the risk society more generally that synthesized key elements of Beck with work by Foucauldian scholars on risk. Ericson and Haggerty moved outward from a particular focus on crime and policing to argue that all major institutions could now be seen to be organized in forms of bureaucracy and surveillance directed at the production of knowledge of risk for the provision of security. Conceptions of risk are now displacing conceptions of normality and deviance as a dominant mentality about people and populations. Risk society is characterized by a negative logic, focusing on the distribution of 'bads' rather than the distribution of 'goods'. It is increasingly oriented toward the future and its colonization. Risk society is characterized by increasing, continuous, often very rapid reflexivity about risk.

This reflexivity and emphasis on risk calculation only leads to increasing awareness of the partially unknown level of risk and a dark affective colouring of uncertainty and insecurity—leading to the demand for yet more knowledge about risk. There are ongoing battles for hegemony among risk institutions and science is losing ground to other institutions. Professions are reorganized in accordance with risk logic—professionalism is increasingly embedded in systems rather than experts.

The authors thus drew together in an innovative way the theorizing of Giddens and Beck on risk and reflexive modernization with the Foucauldian literature on bio-power and governmentality—the risk profiling and regulation of populations by a fragmented myriad of state and private institutions—plus an eclectic variety of other literature. In doing so, they moved far beyond their initial concern with policing to make a much broader social theoretical contribution beyond the realm of criminology.

Conclusion

Using the example of Richard Ericson's later research, we have argued here that the best work in our field can push conventional criminological boundaries outward, expanding its substantive concerns, connecting with other disciplines and making significant wider social theoretical contributions. In terms of expanding criminology's substantive foci, there remain ample potentially fruitful opportunities to follow Ericson's lead in pushing the boundaries of the institutions we study if we want to fully understand crime, deviance, and their regulation. For example, at the end of his life Ericson was commencing a large project on coroners, who are not only key figures in establishing vital medical facts in some of the most high profile criminal cases, but also may be a prominent institution of reflexive when coroner's inquests help publicize controversial cases and make policy recommendations. Other examples of institutions that deserve greater attention include the International Olympic Committee or FIFA, who at highly celebrated moments coordinate a host of intensive policing/security measures that can produce lasting changes in security (Boyle and Haggerty 2009). Other institutions worthy of similar criminological attention might include, for example, emergency planning departments, various think tanks dealing with different types of risk and security, and financial regulators.

Ericson's successful ventures outwards empirically and theoretically are one positive consequence of the multidisciplinary, loose and eclectic field that criminology has become. He belonged to the category of criminologists we identified earlier, who have both enriched the field of criminology and gained stature within it paradoxically by moving outward from its established boundaries. Ericson's work demonstrated the centrality of crime to a broad range of social institutions. He showed us again the potential of working outward from the example of crime and its control to make wider theoretical contributions to our understanding of social life more generally.

References

Abbott, A. (1988), *The System of Professions. An Essay on the Division of Expert Labour,* Chicago: University of Chicago Press.

Borges, J. L. (1964), 'The Analytical Language of John Wilkins, in R. L. C. Simm (trans.), *Other Inquisitions, 1937–1952*, Austin: University of Texas Press.

Boyle, P. and Haggerty, K. (2009), 'Spectacular Security: Mega-Events and the Security Complex', *International Journal of Political Sociology*, 3, 3: 257–74.

Bourdieu, P. and Wacquant, L. (1992), *An Invitation to Reflexive Sociology*, Chicago: University of Chicago Press.

Braithwaite, J. (2000), 'The New Regulatory State and the Transformation of Criminology', *British Journal of Criminology*, 40: 222–38.

Chan, J. (1996), 'The Future of Criminology: An Introduction', *Current Issues in Criminal Justice*, 8, 1: 7–13.

_____. (2000), 'Globalisation, Reflexivity and the Practice of Criminology', *Australian and New Zealand Journal of Criminology Millennium Issue*, 33, 2:118–35.

Cohen, S. (1988), *Against Criminology*, New Brunswick: Transaction Books.

Cohn, E. G. and Farrington, D. P. (2007), 'Changes in Scholarly Influence in Major International Criminology Journals', *The Australian and New Zealand Journal of Criminology*, 40, 3: 335–59.

Ericson, R. V. (1975a), *Criminal Reactions: The Labelling Perspective,* Farnborough: Saxon House [Heath].

_____ (1975b), *Young Offenders and Their Social Work*, Farnborough: Saxon House [Heath].

_____ (1981), *Making Crime: A Study of Detective Work*, Toronto: Butterworths.

_____ (1982), Reproducing Order: A Study of Police Patrol Work, Toronto: University of Toronto Press.

_____ (1995), 'The News Media and Account Ability in Criminal Justice', in P. Stenning (ed.), *Accountability for Criminal Justice*, Toronto: University of Toronto Press.

_____ (1996) 'Making Criminology' *Current Issues in Criminal Justice*, 8(1): 14–25.

_____ (2003), 'The Culture and Power of Criminological Research', in L. Zedner and A. Ashworth (eds), *The Criminological Foundations of Penal Policy: Essays in Honour of Roger Hood,* London: Oxford University Press.

_____ (2006), 'Publicizing Sociology', *British Journal of Sociology*, 56, 3 :365–72.

_____ (2007), *Crime in an Insecure World*, Cambridge: Polity.

_____ and Baranek, P. (1982), *The Ordering of Justice: A Study of Accused Persons as Dependents in the Criminal Process,* Toronto: University of Toronto Press.

_____, _____, and Chan, J. (1987), *Visualizing Deviance: A Study of News Organization*, Toronto: University of Toronto Press.

_____, _____, _____ (1989), *Negotiating Control: A Study of News Sources*, Toronto: University of Toronto Press.

_____, _____, _____ (1991), *Representing Order: Crime, Law, and Justice in the News Media*, Toronto: University of Toronto Press.

_____ and Carriere, K. (1994), 'The Fragmentation of Criminology', in D. Nelken (ed.), *The Futures of Criminology,* London: Sage.
_____ and Doyle, A. (eds) (2003), *Risk and Morality,* Toronto: University of Toronto Press.
_____ and _____. (2004a), *Uncertain Business: Risk, Insurance, and the Limits of Knowledge,* Toronto: University of Toronto Press.
_____ and _____. (2004b), 'Criminalization in Private: The Case of Insurance Fraud', in Law Commission of Canada (ed.), *What Is A Crime? Defining Criminal Conduct in Contemporary Society,* Vancouver: University of British Columbia Press.
_____, _____, and Barry, D. (2003), *Insurance as Governance,* Toronto: University of Toronto Press.
_____ and Haggerty, K. D. (1997), *Policing the Risk Society,* Toronto: University of Toronto Press, and Oxford: Oxford University Press.
_____ and Stehr, N. (eds) (2000), *Governing Modern Societies,* Toronto: University of Toronto Press.
Foucault, M. (1970), *The Order of Things,* New York: Pantheon.
_____ (1977), *Discipline and Punish,* New York: Vintage.
Garland, D. (1997), 'Of Crimes and Criminals: The Development of Criminology in Britain', in M. Maguire *et al.* (eds), *The Oxford Handbook of Criminology,* Oxford: Oxford University Press.
Giddens, A. (1984), *The Constitution of Society,* Cambridge: Polity Press.
Goffman, E. (1959), *The Presentation of Self in Everyday Life,* New York: Double Day.
Haggerty, K., Doyle, A., and Chan, J. (eds) (forthcoming), *Breaking Criminological Convention: Collected Essays of Richard Ericson. Pioneers of Modern Criminology Series,* Surrey: Ashgate.
_____ and Ericson, R. V. (eds) (2006), *The New Politics of Surveillance and Visibility,* Toronto: University of Toronto Press.
Hogg, R. (1996), 'Criminological Failure and Governmental Effect', *Current Issues in Criminal Justice,* 8, 1: 43–59.
Pavarini, M. (1994), 'Is Criminology Worth Saving?', in D. Nelken (ed.), *The Futures of Criminology,* London: Sage.
Wood, D. (2002), 'Foucault and Panopticism Revisited', *Surveillance and Society,* 1, 3: 234–9.
Zedner, L. (this volume), 'Putting Crime back on the Criminological Agenda'.

20

CRIMINOLOGY'S PLACE IN THE ACADEMIC FIELD*

DAVID GARLAND

I

Contemporary criminology is, in some respects, a remarkable success story. It has certainly come a long way fast. The idea of a distinct science of crime and criminals is a very recent one, having been around for no more than 130 years. The word itself -'criminology'—did not exist prior to 1890 when it was first used (in its French language version) as a non-partisan alternative to some other strange new names that had recently appeared—'criminal anthropology', 'criminal psychology', 'criminal sociology', etc.—each of which claimed its subject-matter for a different discipline. In Britain, when the earliest training courses appeared in the 1930s, many of them were taught by prison medical officers or psychiatrists (Garland 1985; Garland 2002). The subject entered the universities only after the Second World War, when the first institutes and departments began to take shape. When I enrolled in my

* This is a revised version of an address presented to the World Congress of the International Society of Criminology in Barcelona in July 2008 and subsequently published in *International Annals of Criminology*, vol. 46 no. 1, 19–39. The author is grateful to Erin Braatz and Gretchen Feltes for research and bibliographical assistance and also to the Filomen D'Agostino and Max Greenberg Research Fund of the NYU Law School. Joachim Savelsberg and Marie Gottschalk are also to be thanked for some very helpful comments as the speech was being revised for publication.

first criminology class at Edinburgh University in 1974, criminology was still very much a newcomer in the academic world and the recently established criminology department at Edinburgh was one of only a handful in the UK (Radzinowicz 1962, 1999). Today, criminology is a standard part of the undergraduate curriculum in universities all over the world and more and more universities offer postgraduate degrees and doctorates. Particularly in the United States, the United Kingdom, and Australia, the number of college majors, university departments, and even entire colleges dedicated to criminology and criminal justice studies is rapidly increasing (Baars-Schuyt 2001; Bisi 1999; Kerner 1998).

Criminology's professional organizations have also grown. The International Society of Criminology (ISC)'s World Congress attracts 1,000 delegates. The new European Society of Criminology, begun only a few years ago, boasts members from forty-six different countries (Aebi and Kronicz 2008). Dozens of countries have national criminological associations, with membership ranging from thirty-five in the Slovak Criminological Society, to 900 in the British Society of Criminology, to 3,500 in the American Society of Criminology.

Quantitative change produces qualitative change and growth of this scale and rapidity brings institutional and intellectual consequences. As criminology has expanded, attracting more students, more scholars and more research funds, it has gradually changed its character and its position in the academy. Whereas previously criminology existed in universities as a postgraduate specialism or as a strand in a broader undergraduate education, today it increasingly takes the form of a free-standing, autonomous subject, with criminology degrees, criminology departments and criminal justice colleges increasingly operating independently of other academic disciplines.

In an article published in 2006, ISC President Tony Peters noted this tendency and commented as follows: 'An undeniable change in the historical position of... criminology has taken place.... Instead of being a servant or auxiliary discipline in legal, social or even medical sciences, criminology [has become] an autonomous, often independent, entity' (Peters 2006). Professor Peters welcomed these developments for the most part. But he also raised questions, asking 'what is the added value of this autonomous profile?' In this chapter I offer a response to Professor Peters' question by reflecting on the nature of criminology today and on the question of its 'independence'. I will argue that, as criminology becomes more autonomous, with its own 'majors', undergraduate degrees, and criminal justice colleges, the dilemmas and difficulties that affect the subject become more pronounced and more difficult to manage. I will argue that much of criminology's intellectual and institutional strength stems from its integration with, and its rootedness in, a number of other, more fundamental disciplines and that the shifts in criminology's place in the academic field threaten to undermine these sources of strength and status. And I will claim that, paradoxically, criminology's newly-won 'independence' is liable to reduce the extent of its autonomy from government. At a time when developments in the government funding and control of higher education threaten the autonomy of even the most basic, well-established disciplines (Ericson 2003: 59), this is a danger that criminologists ought not to ignore.

As it grows more autonomous, institutionally and intellectually; as it increasingly trains recruits by immersing them primarily in its own literature; as its practitioners focus more and more on criminology's own research agendas; and as they proceed to publish only in its own journals, criminology will tend to become more inward-looking and will lose its vital connection to the more basic disciplines (cf Savelsberg and Sampson 2002). A criminology that reproduces itself internally will tend to narrow itself intellectually. The resulting loss of connection with the basic disciplines, I will argue, is liable to produce negative consequences—not just in intellectual terms (important as these are) but also in respect of the subject's relation to government and its position in the university.

I will suggest therefore that the possibility of an 'independent' criminology ought to be regarded as a temptation to be resisted rather than a goal to be embraced. Instead of aspiring to an autonomous discipline, those of us who do criminological research and scholarship should work for a criminology that is intellectually and institutionally integrated in the wider university. The vision of criminology that I have in mind is one that would operate as a multi-disciplinary, policy-oriented subject, addressing problems of crime, criminal justice, security, and punishment in a variety of ways and drawing upon a range of academic disciplines. It would be a criminology that links the world of policy with the world of scholarship by posing policy-oriented, social-problem questions using theoretically-oriented, social science concepts in a way that enriches both.

II

I began by pointing to some signs of criminology's success—above all, its rapid expansion and increasing capacity to attract students, scholars and research funds. These developments are impressive and significant. But let me also point to some troubling aspects of the present. Instead of focusing on quantitative expansion, let me raise some qualitative questions: about the kinds of knowledge criminologists produce; about criminology's relation to power; and about criminology's position in the academy. In the interests of making a clear and forceful argument, I present these points baldly and with little nuance. It ought to be acknowledged, however, that my information is largely drawn from the United States and the United Kingdom and that criminology's history, character and institutional location vary greatly from place to place (Johnson 1983; Becker and Wetzell 2006).

Let me begin by identifying five issues that seem troubling to me:

1. Criminology may have expanded its place in the university but its position in the academic field is uneven and sometimes weak. In some countries, the subject

is located in elite research universities and graduate programmes but elsewhere it is situated in less highly-ranked institutions where vocational training takes precedence over academic research. As for the research undertaken, in many places it appears increasingly to be responsive to the short-term needs of government departments rather than to basic questions of theoretical inquiry or scientific replication (Ericson 2003; Austin 2003; Chan 2000; Laub 2004). Pressure to deliver rapidly produced, 'useful' knowledge is a problem for all academic disciplines, probably increasingly so, but criminology, because of its problem-focused orientation, is especially vulnerable.

2. Criminology has more students than ever, but the undergraduate students that it now attracts may be relatively less well-qualified than the selected post-graduate students who used to form the subject's recruits and less well-qualified than other undergraduates who enroll in the more basic disciplinary programmes. This appears to be the case, for example, in the United States, where the movement towards independent criminology and criminal justice programmes is already well-advanced (Nieswiadomy 1998).
3. Colleges and universities are currently establishing more and more criminology majors and undergraduate criminology degrees but the proper goals and content of an undergraduate criminological training remain uncertain. In many such programmes in the United States, for example, the orientation is vocational rather than academic. It is worth asking ourselves to what extent training personnel for the criminal justice state ought to be a central characteristic of the criminological enterprise, and what effects a further expansion of 'applied' criminology is likely to have on the subject as a whole.
4. Criminology has become increasingly independent in institutional terms, and as it becomes more autonomous it becomes less deeply rooted in what were once its constitutive disciplines (Savelsberg and Sampson 2002; Savelsberg, Cleveland and King 2004). As criminology develops the institutional characteristics of a free-standing academic discipline—degrees, departments, journals, textbooks, etc.—its relation to other disciplines becomes less organic and less well integrated. And as these theoretical linkages attenuate, the intellectual richness of criminological thought, and the broader interest of criminological findings, will tend to diminish.
5. Criminology has grown in size but it has not grown commensurately in theoretical range or intellectual ambition. As Richard Sparks and I have argued elsewhere, criminologists have been slow to respond to many of the challenges of our times (Garland and Sparks 2000). We were slow to identify America's drift to mass imprisonment as it unfolded from the 1970s onwards: it was not until the late 1990s that studies began to address this development and its social consequences. We have been slow to engage with the emerging world of international criminal law, with crimes of genocide, war crimes and crimes against humanity, all of which entail complex problems of etiology, prevention, punishment and

control (Savelsberg 2010; Hagan and Rymond-Richmond 2009; Hagan, Rymond-Richmond and Parker 2005; Brannigan 1998; Yacoubian 2000; Day and Vandiver 2000; Roberts and McMillan 2003—all draw attention to this neglect). And we have been surprisingly slow to introduce criminological theory and research findings into debates about terrorism and the so-called 'war on terror' with the result that today's most pressing security issues are discussed in the public sphere in ways that are innocent of all criminological theory (for recent antidotes, see Rosenfeld 2002; Savelsberg 2006; Hogg 2007; Hamm 2005; Mythen and Walklate 2006; Clarke and Newman 2006; Zedner 2009). One reason for this pattern is that criminology tends to be topic-focused rather than theory-driven. Where a research agenda is motivated by theoretical questions, new cases of the general phenomenon are attractive subjects for investigation. Where research is focused on a set of already-existing topics, lateral thinking of this kind is less liable to occur.

III

So an expanded criminology is not an unproblematic one. And criminology's position in the academy and its relations with more basic disciplines raise important questions that we ought to consider. In order to clarify the institutional and intellectual issues that these developments entail, I want to draw attention to some of the fundamental characteristics of the criminological enterprise. Drawing on my prior work (Garland 1985; 1988; 1992; 2002) and that of others (Ericson 2003; Savelsberg and Sampson 2002; Savelsberg, Cleveland, and King 2004; Zedner 2003). I will suggest that criminology is eclectic, contested and governmental. I will also argue that although criminology has certain 'disciplinary' attributes, it is not a discipline in the full scientific sense.

Criminology is not a Discipline

Contemporary criminology has all the organizational attributes of a discipline but it lacks the intellectual core around which disciplines usually form. Like any academic subject, criminology has both intellectual and organizational dimensions. Intellectually, it consists of a body of accredited and systematically transmitted knowledge (including exemplary 'paradigmatic' texts, established theoretical frameworks, and data and research findings that are regarded as robust); approved procedures and techniques of investigation; and various clusters of questions that make up the subject's research agendas. These intellectual materials and activities are loosely organized by means of a 'discipline'—the standard organizational form of the modern academy (Garland 2002). The discipline establishes and enforces norms of evidence and argument; evaluates contributions to knowledge; fixes and revises the canon of exemplary theory and research; oversees the training of students; and distributes status and authority among accredited practitioners. These disciplinary functions are carried out by various institutions—peer-reviewed journals, professional associations, conferences, funding agencies, and so on—which make up the material infrastructure of the enterprise (Abbott 2001).

There is nothing especially unusual or interesting about this—in all of these organizational and institutional respects, criminology is no different from any other academic discipline. The interesting question is a prior intellectual one: how and why did this rather inchoate, eclectic, practical subject come to form the basis of an academic discipline in the first place? This is a puzzle because, unlike most other academic disciplines, criminology has no distinct theoretical object and no distinct method of inquiry of its own (Garland 1985; Savelsberg and Sampson 2002).[1] Where other, more fundamental disciplines have formed around a distinctive scientific object, specified and constituted by the science's own theoretical and methodological practices, criminology addresses a pre-given object (crimes and criminals) which it derives from a non-scientific social practice—namely, the criminalization processes of the criminal justice state.[2]

Criminology is Eclectic

Criminologists address themselves to topics that bear upon crime and its control. The list of topics is long and diverse, as a glance at the conference programme of any ASC, BSC or World Congress meeting will show. Criminologists investigate these topics by means of quantitative and qualitative methods, using data sets of every description, drawing upon a whole gamut of theoretical perspectives, and with a variety of ideological and political slants. In their teaching and research, criminologists draw on other disciplines, most notably sociology, psychology, political science and law but also history, anthropology, public health, biology, economics, operations research, and so on.

One of the constitutive dynamics of criminology is the incessant raiding of other disciplines for new ideas with which to pursue, renew and enrich the criminological

[1] Savelsberg and Sampson (2002) use the term 'discipline' to refer to an academic field with a distinctive, self-generated intellectual core of problems and concepts—and they argue, correctly in my view, that criminology is not, in that sense, a discipline. My own usage is rather different, referring to the *organizational* practices that constitute and regulate criminology as a demarcated academic field. Many academic subjects are, of course, disciplines in both senses of the term. Criminology is not. As I argue here, the field of criminology lacks a coherent, self-generated, scientific object because its objects of study (crime, criminals, control) are given to it by extra-scientific processes.

[2] The criminological study of 'crime' differs from the economic study of 'choice' and 'utility', or the political science study of 'power', or the physicist's study of 'atoms' not because the former is a worldly object and the latter are not. It differs because the process of specifying the object of study is, for the other sciences, a theoretical practice internal to the science, whereas in criminology, that process of specification is typically undertaken by criminal justice actors on the basis of legal and political criteria, not scientific ones.

project. As a form of knowledge, criminology is shaped only to a small extent by its own theoretical logic and logic of inquiry. Its epistemological threshold is a low one, by which I mean that the concepts and knowledge-claims of other disciplines easily enter criminological discourse. These relatively low barriers have the effect of making criminology open to radical innovation but also prone to the intellectual disorganization of eclecticism and fragmentation (Ericson and Carriere 1994; Garland 2002).

Criminology is Contested

Given this eclecticism and diversity, there will always be competing visions of what criminology ought to be. Criminology as experimental science; criminology as social science; criminology as policy prescription; criminology as security management; criminology as criminal justice training; criminology as public health; criminology as public discourse—are some of the best known (Sherman 1998, 2005; Petersilia 1991; Balvig, Christie, and Tham 2008; Sarat and Silbey 1988; Uggen and Inderbitzin 2006).

There are also competing conceptions of criminology's proper position in the academic field. Among the most important of these visions are the following: (i) criminology as an independent, stand-alone discipline (Radzinowicz 1962; Wolfgang 1963); (ii) criminology as a sub-field within other more fundamental disciplines (Savelsberg and Sampson 2002); and (iii) criminology as a dissolving pathway into larger studies of regulation, or peacemaking, or human rights violations, and so on (Braithwaite 2000; 2003; Pepinsky and Quinney 1991; McEvoy 2003). To this list of possibilities I would add one more, a conception of criminology that might be described as *dialogic* and *multi-disciplinary*. A dialogic, multi-disciplinary criminology would not be a new project so much as a way of articulating, in a self-conscious manner, what criminology has often been when it has been at its best—namely, an integrative enterprise of translation and exchange; a dialogic enterprise that undertakes the work of criminological inquiry in on-going conversation with the diverse academic disciplines that bear upon its subject-matter; a bridging subject connecting the practical world of crime control with the academic disciplines of social science and law.

Criminology is Governmental

Let me return to a question I raised previously. Criminology's eclecticism and the absence of any object of analysis that it can call its own, make its emergence as a 'discipline' appear puzzling. How did this disparate bundle of policy-related inquiries come to acquire the status of a distinct academic subject? How did criminology achieve its current position in the academic field and in the institutions of higher education?

The solution to this puzzle lies, I believe, in criminology's external clients (which is to say government agencies and criminal justice institutions) and its perceived ability to further governmental interests by bringing its knowledge to bear on crime policy and the practice of criminal justice (Foucault 1977; Garland 1992; Abbott 2001: 69, 134). Criminology's basic organizing principle is the empirical study of crime and its control—which is to say, the study of a legally-defined entity and a state-directed practice. In contrast to the sciences and fully-constituted academic disciplines, criminology's object of study is not a scientifically-specified entity but instead a state-defined social problem and the set of state and non-state practices through which that state-defined problem is managed. As a consequence, criminology is intimately (at the epistemological level) and directly (at the social level) tied into government (Garland 2002).

This governmental dimension was especially obvious in the early years when the subject flourished in the prison, the courtroom, and the juvenile justice hall—a flourishing that was directly encouraged by government support and sponsorship (Garland 1988, 2002). Criminology's subsequent location in the university has obscured this knowledge-power link to some extent and alleviated some of the problems that stem from being too identified with government, but the linkage and the problems remain nonetheless (Garland 1992). Criminology's material support and social status continue to rest in large part upon its perceived utility and value for government. Even within the academy, university authorities and administrators value the subject as much for its ability to attract research funds and student numbers as for its distinguished academic achievements. It is therefore no surprise that criminology—with its ability to attract large numbers of undergraduates and government research grants—has flourished in recent years when universities have suffered budgetary reductions and have been under pressure to be more 'relevant' and 'vocational'.

IV

Criminology's dual commitment to government *and* to the academy, to policy *and* to science, sets up a series of recurring problems and tensions for criminology and its practitioners. My argument is that as criminology becomes institutionally and intellectually more autonomous, these tensions will tend to intensify and become increasingly difficult to manage.

Tension No. 1: Criminology's Relations with Government

The central difficulty that stems from criminology's dual commitment is familiar to researchers in every discipline, namely the struggle to maintain academic integrity while seeking government access and research funding (Mazower 2008). But for criminologists this problem has a more fundamental aspect that is less often noted and less easily dealt with—and it has to do with criminology's epistemological relation to government.

We should remind ourselves of important questions that have emerged at various critical moments in the history of criminology, only to be forgotten again as the subject's normal routines reassert themselves.[3] Is it scientifically legitimate for an academic subject to derive its concepts, its categories, its questions, and its objects of study from state institutions? Should criminology's objects of study be legal categories, governmental problems, and institutional products that are given to it by state practices and political processes? Is criminology obliged to understand the categories of 'crime', 'offender', and 'victim' in accordance with the meanings given to them in the legal process? Must it accept the theories of action and responsibility implicit in legal discourse and court decisions? Or alternatively, ought criminology to reconstitute these categories and theories in its own terms, as is done, for example, in the sociology of deviance? In dealing with these dilemmas, practical considerations (of relevance, of influence, of funding, of communication) may press in a different direction than scientific considerations. How ought criminologists to manage these tensions?

The solution lies, I believe, in the company that criminology keeps. Or to be more precise, in the character of the academic interactional field (Abbott 2001) within which criminology is located and in the intellectual exchanges in which it is routinely involved. It lies in criminology's capacity to establish dialogue with contiguous academic subjects and to bridge the gap between its practical domain and the academic disciplines that can provide resources for conceptualizing it.

Let me offer a concrete illustration. A criminology that investigates state-defined criminal offences and state-identified offenders ought to be in constant dialogue with a sociology of deviance that refuses to take these terms as unproblematic givens. (For example, criminology achieved a major theoretical advance when, in the 1960s, a number of young criminologists who had engaged with symbolic interaction theories then emerging in American sociology used these ideas to challenge criminological positivism and the whole approach to crime and control that it involved.) Such dialogues can take place in many ways—in departmental meetings, at conferences, in undergraduate lectures, in the evaluation of manuscripts submitted to journals, or in the understanding that sociology graduates bring to postgraduate criminology programmes. Where this kind of dialogue routinely takes place, it acts as a healthy reminder that the law's categories are social constructions that can be questioned, and that the state's conceptions of 'normal' and 'deviant' are the outcome of political processes that are historically contingent, subject to change and open to challenge. Such conversations also bring into focus the extent to which criminalizing and penological practices are bound up with wider social processes, not just in the etiology of criminal conduct but in the prior constitution of processes of legislation,

[3] Recall Edwin Sutherland's debate with Paul Tappan about the definition of crime, or the impact of the sociology of deviance in the 1960s, or the Schwendingers' challenge in the 1970s, or the writings of Nils Christie or Louk Hulsman.

criminalization and penalization. They remind criminologists of the links between crime and social issues such as stratification; labour markets; urban ecology; class, race and gender; family relations and the life course; and political economy.[4]

Criminology's institutional location viz-a-viz other disciplines, and viz-a-viz disciplinary journals, conferences, graduate students, and so on is liable to produce intellectual consequences for the subject. Wherever routine, sustained, structural relations are established between criminology and other disciplines—and reproduced through processes of faculty hiring, graduate student recruitment, textbook writing, etc.—criminology can retain its practical focus and yet draw intellectual resources (data, concepts, theories, methods, trained personnel) from contiguous disciplines. These intellectual resources become much less accessible wherever criminology asserts its autonomy and sets itself apart institutionally.

I should note that, in proposing this bridging, dialogic solution, I am refusing a more radical suggestion that criminology ought to entirely reject state definitions, abandon its focus on 'crime', and reconstitute itself on an altogether different basis (cf Schwendinger 1975). I refrain from this more radical choice because it seems to me undeniable that the state's legal categories and institutional definitions—whatever one may think of them politically and epistemologically—are real and powerful. They shape our world, they organize our lives, they determine the fates of millions of people. To reject these categories, to give them no place in our analyses, would be to opt out of an engagement with the real world—an engagement that has always been one of criminology's chief virtues.

Instead of turning away from these real-world facts and institutional categories, criminology ought to engage with them. But such an engagement cannot be unmediated or uncritical. We ought to view these state-defined categories for what they are: a specific regime of truth, made possible by specific institutions, specific social relations and definite balances of power. And before folding these phenomena into our analyses we ought to respecify and reconstitute them in accordance with criminology's theoretical and methodological commitments. This was the elementary lesson taught decades ago by Kitsuse and Cicourel (1963) when they showed that official crime data are data about institutional practices relating to crime, rather than data about crime as such, and by Barry Hindess (1973) who showed that the provenance of such data was no bar to its usefulness, so long as its processes of production were understood and folded into our interpretations of its meaning. Because a policy-oriented governmental criminology is prone to forget these truths, or else to neglect them in the pursuit of funding and relevance, it is important to develop on-going involvements with disciplinary settings in which these fundamental theoretical and methodological issues are debated—and not to confine criminology's

[4] I illustrate my point here by referring to criminology's links with sociology, but one could make the same point by reference to the other disciplines with which criminology carries on conversations—psychology, law, history, political science, and so on.

methodological discussions to the more specialist, technical problems involved in handling and interpreting crime data. Such involvements and interactions provide a crucial counterweight to the pull of the policy audience (Sarat and Silbey 1988) and we ought to seek institutional arrangements that make them a matter of routine.

Tension No. 2: Criminology's Role as Policy Adviser

From its nineteenth century origins to the present day, criminology has provided data, research findings and expertise to governmental (and non-governmental) authorities. The role of policy adviser brings definite benefits: research funding and access; an opportunity to shape policy and serve the public good; training and employment opportunities for students; and an insider knowledge that enhances the criminologist's credibility and public authority (Radzinowicz 1962; Ericson 2003). The danger, however, is that criminology will become a wholly-owned subsidiary of the criminal justice state, with the criminal law dictating its object of study, government agencies dictating its research questions, and politicians and the press dictating its frames of relevance.

This Foucauldian image of criminology as power-knowledge in the service of a disciplinary state is an ever-present danger, given the subject's basic disposition and orientation (Foucault 1980). If criminology has escaped that fate and succeeded in creating a critical distance and a measure of scholarly integrity, it is due to its position in the academic field and its connections with other academic disciplines (Garland 1992). To the extent that it changes that position, to the extent that it loosens these connections, to the extent that it becomes an independent entity that stands on its own, criminology thereby makes itself more vulnerable to being co-opted by government.[5]

Am I suggesting that criminology ought to disengage from all government involvement and that criminologists should cease giving policy advice? Am I adopting the view of Stanley Cohen (1985: 238) who declared: 'It is simply not our professional job to advise, consult, recommend or make decisions'? Or that expressed by John Hagan (1989: 257–8) when he suggested that criminology should be subsumed into an explanatory sociology, completely unconcerned with policy matters?[6] Or of

[5] As Savelsberg and Sampson (2002) argue, 'criminology's isolation from sociology comes at great cost'. They note that 'as criminology closes itself off from other academic disciplines, it opens itself up to extra-scholarly interests, especially those of the state'. They conclude that this process ought to be resisted, and that 'concern with disciplinary credentials [and autonomy] should be replaced by a renewed focus on intellectual ideas'. See also Savelsberg, King and Cleveland (2002) for empirical evidence supporting these claims.

[6] In his more recent work, Hagan appears to have revised his view. His new book about Darfur (Hagan and Ryland-Rowlands 2009) argues that criminology ought to come to terms with genocide and the causal processes underlying it. In the course of his argument, he makes it clear that he envisages a policy role for criminologists, providing international courts and organizations with evidence and expertise that can help justify and direct humanitarian intervention.

Nils Christie, who insists that criminology should be 'problem-raising' rather than a 'problem-solving?'[7]

No, I am not. Nor is there any need to do so, since the issue should be understood as a matter of 'also/and' rather than 'either/or'. Criminology would quickly cease to exist if it gave up its ambition to improve penal policy and offer crime control advice, thereby ignoring the interests of its external clients. But a policy-oriented criminology has its best chance of remaining detached, critical, and intellectually alive if it is taught alongside, and in dialogue with, the kinds of criminology that Cohen and Hagan and Christie have in mind: criminologies that are critical, explanatory, or avowedly trouble-making.

The 'policy-oriented criminologist', the 'academic sociologist of crime', the 'critical criminologist'—these are three different job descriptions (and working personalities) and they each imply a different vision of what criminology should be. But there is no reason why our subject has to commit itself exclusively to one or other of these visions. The field of criminology can fruitfully contain all three kinds of scholarship and facilitate the cross-fertilization of each by the others. Theoretical and critical work stands to gain from an engagement with the details of institutional practice and the messy complexities of policy-making. Policy advice can benefit from an understanding of the theoretical frames and critical perspectives that bear on the subject. A broad field composed of different ways of doing and conceiving criminology, and drawing on a range of different disciplines and perspectives—that is an arrangement that has worked well for criminology in the past and is, I believe, the arrangement we should seek to foster in the future.

Tension No. 3: Criminology's Position in the Academic Field

Criminology's secure location in the academic world and its status as a field of scholarly inquiry respected by its academic peers are, it seems to me, of paramount importance for the intellectual and institutional health of the subject. Criminology's academic integrity and status as a university-based subject are also, as I have suggested, crucial in managing the subject's relations with government. It is therefore worrying that criminology's position in the academic hierarchy has often been an ambiguous one, and that stand-alone criminology (or criminal justice) degrees are—at least in the United States—often associated with colleges where teaching and vocational training take precedence over research and scholarship.

This status problem is linked to some of criminology's essential characteristics. As I have argued, criminology is organized around a policy problem and largely consists of empirical studies that produce local knowledge. In the academic hierarchy, 'problem-oriented fields' of this kind are typically less prestigious than fundamental

[7] Quoted in Zedner and Ashworth (2003: 16)

disciplines (Abbott 2001).[8] This status differential derives from the difference in the kinds of knowledge produced by these different kinds of subject. The basic academic disciplines produce 'portable knowledge' and transferable analytical skills that are more competitive, more enduring, and more valuable over time, compared to the localized 'problem-based knowledge' of subjects like criminology. Why are they more valuable? Because 'portable knowledge' has the power of abstraction, enabling it to address new situations and new problems by means of principles learned in other settings. This contrasts with 'problem-based knowledge' which tends to be more local and more limited in its application. The two forms of knowledge are also intellectually distinct in another prestige-relevant respect: the former aspiring to theoretical depth and analytical understanding, the latter more focused on surface description and practical know-how.

Policy-specific research has important, real-world value, as does vocational training. And criminology would not exist in the university system today were it not for its capacity to provide these practical benefits. But a university-based subject will ultimately be evaluated in terms of the university's intrinsic institutional values, and these are fundamentally to do with the quality and depth of scholarship, research achievement and theoretical understanding. Criminologists ought therefore to take care that the expansion of their subject and its increasing 'independence' do not develop at the cost of its research capacity and academic standing.

Here is another reason why criminology ought to remain close to its constitutive disciplines. Only by drawing on the fundamental disciplines, and contributing to them in turn, can criminologists hope to sustain the scholarly erudition, intellectual depth, and theoretical insight that have always marked the very best criminological writings and that bring prestige and status in the academic world. A criminology that trains its own PhDs, hires its own graduates, and sets its own research agenda may properly regard itself as an independent discipline. But if, in achieving that goal, it confines itself to applied research, problem-focused analyses, and local knowledge, it will have undercut its capacity to attract academic status and prestige and the institutional benefits that flow from these.

Tension No. 4: The Training of Criminologists

Criminologists ought to be trained in one or other of the basic disciplines prior to specializing in crime and punishment. It is not enough to be introduced to these disciplines in passing, as part of a criminology degree: all too often such 'introductions' are a diluted and distorted form of disciplinary training, offering lightweight versions of the real thing, trimmed and tailored to fit into a criminology curriculum. And this problem is likely to grow worse over time. At present, criminology graduate programmes are mostly staffed by faculty trained in one or other of the basic

[8] As Andrew Abbott (2001: 134) points out, 'status differences... keep the disciplines in superior power. Criminology departments hire from sociology departments, but seldom vice versa'.

disciplines—sociology, psychology, law, and so on. But as the subject's institutional independence grows, criminology graduate programmes will increasingly be staffed by faculty with criminology graduate degrees with the result that the institutional relation of these programmes to the basic disciplines will become ever more distant, their intellectual connections ever more attenuated.

To thrive as an academic discipline, criminologists have to compete on equal terms with other social scientists and lawyers. When criminologists write about their research and present their findings in a sociological, psychological, historical or legal mode, they ought not to be amateurs or self-trained outsiders. When criminology programmes recruit students and faculty, they ought to be able to attract the best and the brightest of these other disciplines, and they ought to export criminological ideas and findings back into these other disciplines. It seems to me that the more independence criminology acquires, the more it moves away from the basic disciplines, the more difficult it is to achieve these kinds of exchanges and the academic vitality that comes with them.

There are several sources of status and power in the university system—student numbers, research income, policy impact, media presence—and criminology does relatively well on each of these dimensions. But the primary measure of academic achievement is quality and distinction in scholarship. On this measure, criminology has a more mixed record. If criminology is to thrive in academic settings, criminologists have to aspire to the highest scholarship and reconnect with the fundamental concerns of social science and the humanities.

Creating an independent criminology that disengages institutionally from these larger disciplines is likely to lead to intellectual disengagement as well. Something of the sort has already occurred in the United States. During the first half of the twentieth century, crime and its control were central topics of research in the sociology departments of America's leading research universities: think of the Chicago School, for example, or of Edwin Sutherland's department at Indiana. In the 1960s, the US government attempted to professionalize criminal justice and, to that end, funded a massive expansion of criminological training, much of it based in new criminal justice colleges. The subsequent expansion of this applied, vocational criminology and the rise of these self-standing criminal justice programmes led to a diminution of the subject's status, and prompted the gradual abandonment of the specialism by the sociology departments of all the leading research universities. Until very recently, there was hardly a sociologist of crime and punishment to be found in any of them—with major consequences for the kind and quality of work done on criminological topics.[9] Over the last decade, this process has been partially reversed, and the leading sociology departments are once more hiring and training specialists in crime

[9] See Savelsberg, Cleveland, and Ryan (2004) for empirical evidence about the way that institutional location (criminal justice programme or sociology department) shapes research and theory choices.

and punishment—but only because America's penal system has grown to the point where it has become a major engine of social organization and stratification that can hardly be ignored by mainstream sociology (Western 2007).

Let me be clear. I am not objecting to the existence of criminology institutes or criminology departments. Some of our most important scholarship on crime, control and punishment has come from such places. Nor am I saying that criminology undergraduate degrees cannot be academically first rate. But I am saying that criminology ought not to distance itself from the disciplines that supply its intellectual energy and inspiration—and the move towards institutional autonomy threatens to bring this about.[10]

V

I have described some of the risks entailed in criminology becoming an independent specialism—the risk that it will be cut off from the basic disciplines, the risk that government will extend its influence, and the risk that the subject will lose academic prestige. There is a final risk: namely that an independent criminology will tend to fragment into distinct specialisms unconnected by any overarching theory.

Specialization is a characteristic process in any academic discipline (Dogan and Pahre 1989) but it is an especially powerful dynamic in the field of criminology, given its focus on specific institutions, problems and policies. Prison studies; police studies; probation studies; sentencing studies; treatment studies; victim studies; juvenile studies; violence studies; crime prevention studies; fear of crime studies.....the list goes on, each one a growing subfield poised to spin off from the larger discipline.

There are obvious benefits of specialization, but the most salient drawback of this process is its negative effect on the communication and exchange of ideas. Wherever specialisms proliferate, the tendency is for conversation across the field to decline. Criminologists end up as so many specialists with little to say to each other, with negative consequences for collective learning.

In most academic fields there are two centripetal forces that work to unify research and generate conversation between researchers. One is *topic* and the other is *theory*.[11] Topics bring scholars together but the inherent disposition of *topic* is a drive towards concreteness and specificity. Scholarship that is organized around a topic tends to become ever more specific, ever more specialized. The more scholars there

[10] As the work of Savelsberg *et al.* shows (2002, 2004), the capacity to sustain serious connections between academic subjects is determined by institutional arrangements, organizational routines, and the structurally-conditioned habits and orientations of individual academics. It cannot be left to good intentions.

[11] Methodological discussion can also have this effect, but I am going to ignore that for the moment.

are in the field, the more the field can support numerous specialisms. The more topic specialisms there are, the more fragmented the field becomes. In the end, there is little to talk about outside the rooms where small specialist groups discuss the arcane details of their speciality topic.

The tendency of *theory*, in contrast, is towards abstraction and generalization. Its aim is to include ever more data, ever more processes, ever more situations, and ever more topics in its scope. It strives to link causal arguments and to build unified explanations. Different topics cease to be unconnected specialisms and become, instead, cases, which is to say, multiple opportunities for analysis and inclusion under the aegis of a general explanatory theory. Theory gives rise to conversation and community—or else to focused conflict and disputation. It operates to unify the field in collective projects that transcend particular research and esoteric specialisms.[12]

Theory can, of course, divide an academic field just as it can unify it. But whether it unifies or divides, theory *organizes*, it generates collective conversations, it pulls researchers into a dialogue with one another, moving them beyond their immediate data and specialism to engage with larger questions. Theoretical discussion and debate enhance individual scholarship and serve the collective good of the subject. It is theory that provides the intellectual resources to take on new challenges and new problems, thereby extending our explanatory range and enabling us to engage with new issues as they emerge. Theory is what enlivens and energizes an academic subject. And since theory is generated by processes of abstraction rather than by engagement with specific problems, the vitality of the criminological field largely depends on criminology's continued connection with the disciplinary settings in which abstraction and theorizing are facilitated and rewarded.

VI

My argument has been that although criminology has an institutional base and a problem-oriented core, its most important intellectual sources are eccentric, off-centre, originating from outside the subject itself. If I may personalize the matter for a moment, I would offer my own experience as testament to this. If I were to list the texts that have been most important to me in my work, they would not be the 'classics' of mainstream criminology—though I have engaged with these classics and learned a great deal from them (especially those such as Merton's 'Social Structure

[12] Here we ought to take our lead from the field of anthropology—a discipline in which each individual scholar engages in specialist field research and ethnography, focused on a particular place and particular people. Given this characteristic, anthropology would likely have become utterly fragmented but for the discipline's strong commitment to social theory—a commitment that is institutionalized in textbooks, university curricula, graduate training, journals, and the overall status system of the discipline.

and Anomie', Matza's *Delinquency and Drift* or Cohen's *Delinquent Boys* that were themselves steeped in broader intellectual currents). My most useful exemplars have been works that loomed on the horizon of criminology, on its margins, most of them coming at crime and punishment from well beyond the criminological domain. In addition to the central thinkers of the sociological tradition (Marx, Weber, above all, Durkheim) I think of the work of figures like Paul Hirst, Stuart Hall, Gareth Stedman Jones, Michel Foucault, Jacques Donzelot, Nikolas Rose, Norbert Elias, Clifford Geertz, Pierre Bourdieu, Ian Hacking, and Mary Douglas. These authors were not 'criminologists' in any recognizable sense. And none of their inspirational works was generated out of criminology's core concerns. But every one of them advanced criminological understanding and helped redefine what criminology might be. Every one of them altered the ways in which criminologists could frame their questions, opening up new theoretical understandings in ways that were ultimately productive for the field as a whole.

If criminology is to continue to realize its potential as an academic subject and not just a governmental one, if it is to continue producing scholarship of the highest quality and achieve its rightful place in the academy, it needs to remain dialogic rather than detached, eccentric rather than self-enclosed, grounded in multiple disciplines, not floating independent of them. It is not an autonomous criminology we need, but a dialogic criminology able to embrace and engage an intellectual world that sometimes begins where an independent criminology would likely leave off.

References

Abbott, A. (2001), *Chaos of Disciplines*, Chicago: University of Chicago Press.

Aebi, M. and Kronicz, G. (2008), 'ESC Annual Report 2007' in *Criminology in Europe: Newsletter of the European Society of Criminology*, 7, 2: 3–15.

Austin, J. (2003), 'Why Criminology is Irrelevant', *Criminology and Public Policy*, 2, 3: 557–64.

Baars-Schuyt, A. (2001), 'Overview of Criminology in Europe', *European Journal of Criminal Policy and Research*, 9: 301–13.

Balvig, F., Christie, N., and Tham, H. (2008), 'Whither the Stockholm Prize?', *Criminology in Europe: Newsletter of the European Society of Criminology*, 7, 1: 1–9.

Becker, P. and Weltzell, R. (2006), *Criminals and their Scientists: The History of Criminology in Historical Perspective*, New York: Cambridge University Press.

Bisi, R. (1999), 'Teaching and Professional Training in Criminology', *European Journal of Crime, Criminal Law and Criminal Justice*, 7: 103–29.

Braithwaite, J. (2000), 'The New Regulatory State and the Transformation of Criminology', *British Journal of Criminology*, 40: 222–38.

_____ (2003), 'What's Wrong with the Sociology of Punishment?', *Theoretical Criminology*, 2, 1: 5–28.

Chan, J. (2000), 'Globalization, Reflexivity and the Practice of Criminology', *Australian and New Zealand Journal of Criminology*, 33, 2: 118–35.

Clarke, R. V. and Newman, G. (2006), *Outsmarting the Terrorists*, New York: Praeger.

Cohen, A. (1955), *Delinquent Boys: The Culture of the Gang*, New York: New York Free Press.

Cohen, S. (1985), *Visions of Social Control*, Cambridge: Polity Press.

Day, E. and Vandiver, M. (2000), 'Criminology and Genocide Studies', *Crime, Law and Social Change*, 34; 43–59.

Dogan, M. and Pahre R. (1989), 'Fragmentation and Recombination of the Social Sciences', *Studies in Comparative International Development*, 24, 2; 56–73.

Ericson, R. (2003), 'The Culture and Power of Criminological Research' in L. Zedner and A. Ashworth (eds), *The Criminological Foundations of Penal Policy*, Oxford: Oxford University Press.

_____ and Carriere, K. (1994), 'The Fragmentation of Criminology' in D. Nelkin (ed.), *The Futures of Criminology*, London: Sage.

Foucault, M. (1977), *Discipline and Punish: The Birth of the Prison*, London: Allen Lane.

_____ (1980), 'Prison Talk', in C. Gordon (ed.), *Michel Foucault: Power/Knowledge*, Brighton: Harvester.

Garland, D. (1985), 'The Criminal and his Science', *British Journal of Criminology*, 25, 2: 109–37.

_____ (1988), 'British Criminology Before 1935', in P. Rock (ed.), *A History of British Criminology*, Oxford: Oxford University Press.

_____ (1992), 'Criminological Knowledge and its Relation to Power: Foucault's Genealogy and Criminology Today', *British Journal of Criminology*, 32, 4: 403–22.

_____ (2002), 'Of Crimes and Criminals: The Development of Criminology in Britain', in M. Maguire, R. Morgan, and R. Reiner (eds), *The Oxford Handbook of Criminology* 3rd edn, Oxford: Oxford University Press.

_____ and Sparks, R. (2000), 'Criminology, Social Theory and the Challenge of Our Times, *British Journal of Criminology*, 40; 189–204.

Hagan, J. and Rymond-Richmond, W. (2008), *Darfur and the Crime of Genocide*, New York: University of Cambridge Press.

_____, _____, and Parker, P. (2005), 'The Criminology of Genocide: The Death and Rape of Darfur', *Criminology*, 43, 3: 525–61.

Hamm, M. (2005), 'After September 11: Terrorism Research and the Crisis in Criminology', *Theoretical Criminology*, 9, 2: 237–51.

Hindess, B. (1973), *The Use of Official Statistics in Sociology*, London: Macmillan.

Hogg, R. (2007), 'Criminology, Crime and Politics before and after 9/11', *Australian and New Zealand Journal of Criminology*, 40, 1: 83–105.

Johnson, E. (1983), *International Handbook of Contemporary Developments in Criminology*, 2 vols, Woodport: Greenwood Press.

Kerner, H.-J. (1998), 'The Global Growth of Criminology' *International Annals of Criminology*, 36, 1: 27–42.

Kitsuse, J. and Cicourel, A. (1963), 'A Note on the Uses of Official Statistics', *Social Problems*, 11, 2: 131–9.

Laub, J. (2004), 'The Life Course of Criminology in the United States: The American Society of Criminology 2003 Presidential Address', *Criminology*, 42, 1: 1–26.

Matza, D. (1964), *Delinquency and Drift*, New York: John Wiley.

Mazower, M. (2008), 'Mandarins, Guns and Money', *The Nation*, 6 October: 36–42.

McEvoy, K. (2003), 'Beyond the Metaphor: Political Violence, Human Rights and "New" Peacemaking Criminology', *Theoretical Criminology*, 7: 319–46.

Merton, R. (1938), 'Social Structure and Anomie', *American Sociological Review*, 3: 672–82.

Mythen, G. and Walklate, S. (2006), 'Criminology and Terrorism: Which Thesis? Risk Society or Governmentality?', *British Journal of Criminology*, 46: 379–98.

Nieswiadomy, M. (1998), 'LSAT Scores of Economics Majors', *Journal of Economic Education*, 29, 4: 377–9.

Pepinsky, H. and Quinney, R. (1991), *Criminology as Peacemaking*, Indiana University Press, Bloomington.

Peters, T. (2006), 'The Academic Status of Criminology', *International Annals of Criminology*, 44, 1: 53–63.

Petersilia, J. (1991), 'Policy Relevance and the Future of Criminology', *Criminology*, 29, 1: 1–15.

Radzinowicz, L. (1962), *In Search of Criminology*, Cambridge, MA: Harvard University Press.

_____ (1999), *Adventures in Criminology*, London: Routledge.

Roberts, P. and McMillan, N. (2003), 'For Criminology in International Criminal Justice', *Journal of International Criminal Law*, 1: 315–38.

Rosenfeld, R. (2002), 'Why Criminologists Should Study Terrorism', *The Criminologist*, 27, 6: 1–4.

Sarat, A. and Silbey, S. (1988), 'The Pull of the Policy Audience', *Law and Policy*, 10, 2–3: 97–166.

Savelsberg, J. (2006), 'Underused Potentials for Criminology: Applying the Sociology of Knowledge to Terrorism', *Crime, Law and Social Change*, 46: 35–50.

_____ (ed.) (2007), *Against Narrow, Distorted, and Unconscious Adaptations of Theory*, Special Issue of *Crime, Law and Social Change*, 42 (with contributions by Ross Matsueda, John Hagan & Holly Foster, Mark Cooney, James F. Short, Jr., and Savelsberg).

_____ (2010), *Crime and Human Rights: Criminology of Genocide and Atrocities*, London: Sage.

_____, J. Cleveland, L., and King, R. (2004), 'Institutional Environments and Scholarly Work: American Criminology, 1951–1993', *Social Forces*, 82, 4: 1275–302.

_____ and Flood, S. (2004), 'Period and Cohort Effects in the Production of Scholarly Knowledge: The Case of Criminology, 1951–1993', *Criminology*, 42, 4: 1009–41.

_____, King, R., and Cleveland, L. (2002), 'Politicized Scholarship? Science on Crime and the State', *Social Problems*, 49, 3: 327–48.

_____ and Sampson, R. (2002a), 'Mutual Engagement: Criminology and Sociology', *Crime, Law, and Social Change*, 37, 2: 99–105.

_____ and _____ (eds) (2002b), *Mutual Engagement: Sociology and Criminology?*, Special issue of *Crime, Law and Social Change*, 37, 2, (with contributions by James F. Short, Jr., John Hagan, Diane Vaughan, Susan Silbey, and an introduction by Savelsberg/ Sampson).

Schwendinger, H. and Schwendinger, J. (1975), 'Defenders of Order or Guardians of Human Rights' in I. Taylor, P. Walton, and J. Young (eds), *Critical Criminology*, Routledge, London.

Sherman, L. (1998), 'Criminology and Crime Prevention in the 21st Century', *International Annals of Criminology*, 36, 1: 43–52.

_____ (2005), 'The Use and Usefulness of Criminology, 1751–2005', *Annals of the American Academy of Political and Social Science*, 600: 115–35.

Uggen, C. and Inderbitzin, M. (2006), 'Public Criminologies', paper presented at the 2006 annual meetings of the ASA, Montreal.

Western, B. (2007), *Punishment and Inequality in America*, New York: Russell Sage.
Wolfgang, M. (1963), 'Criminology and the Criminologist', *Journal of Criminal Law and Criminology*, 54: 155–62.
Yacoubian, G. (2000), 'The (In)significance of Genocidal Behavior to the Discipline of Criminology', *Crime, Law and Social Change*, 34; 7–19.
Zedner, L. (2003), 'Useful Knowledge? Debating the Role of Criminology in Post-War Britain', in L. Zedner and A. Ashworth (eds), *The Criminological Foundations of Penal Policy*, Oxford: Oxford University Press.
_____ (2009), *Security*, London: Routledge.
_____ and Ashworth. A. (2003), 'Introduction' in L. Zedner and A. Ashworth (eds), *The Criminological Foundations of Penal Policy*, Oxford: Oxford University Press.

21

WHY CAN'T CRIMINOLOGY BE MORE LIKE MEDICAL RESEARCH?: BE CAREFUL WHAT YOU WISH FOR

SHADD MARUNA AND CHARLES BARBER

THIS chapter is about the intersection between criminology and psychiatry and therefore it is appropriate that our own backgrounds are a mix of those two fields (although neither of us dare speak on behalf of any wider group). We suggest that there is a large movement afoot to make criminological research more akin to a version of the medical model found in psychiatry. After reviewing research and practice in psychiatry, however, we conclude instead that psychiatry might have as much to gain from criminological research traditions as the other way around.

The theme of this chapter emerged, appropriately enough, in a brainstorming session at a probation conference the two of us were attending. The conference facilitated a number of small-group discussions between academics and practitioners, with an agenda to think big about the future of 'corrections'. The discussion at our table was going brilliantly. None of the participants had ever met one another before, but we all were in agreement that the criminal justice system was fundamentally flawed and that a substantial part of the problem involved the disconnection between research and practice in the field. So far, so good.

Then it happened. Someone at the table drew a parallel between corrections and medicine. 'I mean, can you imagine if medicine operated like corrections does? Rolling out treatments that had never been tested. Ignoring evidence that interventions don't work or even that they make patients worse!' Everyone laughed, and then the conversation hit its stride. The group decided that their blue-sky proposal to report back to the wider conference would be to make corrections more like a medical science. Correctional workers should be trained in the same way medical practitioners are, and criminological research should become like medical research, in particular employing random-control trials of the latest interventions in advance of their wider introduction. 'That would be amazing', they all agreed. 'Revolutionizing corrections by making it a real science! How different our prisons and probation offices would look.'

The two authors stayed quiet at this point, despite our excitement at the earlier part of the group's discussion. This medical model fantasy was one both of us have heard countless times before.[1] (When the group reported its conclusions to the rest of the conference, members were surprised that several of the other groups had essentially the same recommendation.) Some of our hesitations, of course, emerged from the well-known problems of trying to marry a medical model to a justice model, that have been rehearsed endlessly in criminological debates, but never better than by writers like Anthony Burgess (1968) in *A Clockwork Orange* or C. S. Lewis (1953) in his remarkable essay 'A Humanitarian Theory of Punishment'. Justice is about desert and requires a notion of human agency that is at complete odds with a medical model of behaviour. However, the conference participants were not recommending a 'strong' version of the medical model. They were not talking about replacing judges with treatment experts or trading retribution for *Clockwork Orange*-like men in white lab coats. They were, instead, pushing for the rather softer version of the medical model—the idea that if crime reduction is a goal of the criminal justice system, then such efforts should be based on sound empirical foundations. This seems fair enough.

[1] Perhaps the only criminological fantasy as oft-repeated as the medical model one is the econometric one of 'Why can't criminology be more like economics?' Of course, no one has been heard to repeat the latter lament since at least the market crash of 2008. Now, few people believe that economists have all the answers for the economy let alone all the other problems of the world.

The problem that the two of us had, in listening to this, however, was the insistence that the guide for such a rational system could be found in the world of medicine. One can understand this impulse, of course. Whereas society's ability to reduce recidivism among prisoners is probably not much better today than it was fifty years ago, the medical world has (with its far greater resources devoted to research) made tremendous progress in combating diseases such as polio, tuberculosis, and rubella. Yet, despite occasional ill-chosen metaphors (eg, 'plagues' of delinquency), crime is not anything like polio. Burglary, rape, homicide, and embezzlement are behaviours—things that people do to others—not inflictions passed through microscopic organisms.

As such, the *only* field of medicine with even the slightest parallels to criminology is psychiatry. After all, psychiatric symptoms, like crimes, also typically involve behaviours (people talk loudly to themselves, act erratically, become withdrawn, etc.) that puzzle and disturb others in society. Indeed, some of the symptoms of psychiatric disorders (eg, physical aggression, drug use) even correspond with those behaviours that societies criminalize. Even this is nothing like a perfect parallel, of course. The behavioural symptoms of mental illnesses such as depression or schizophrenia are thought to be involuntary and unwanted, whereas many criminal behaviors are clearly the result of deliberate, often 'rational', decisions on the parts of actors. Moreover, the best research evidence suggests that the overlap between violence and mental illness is actually rather small (see Monahan *et al.* 2001) and probably simply a result of the high rates of drug use among the mentally ill. Still, it should be clear, if correctional research is to aspire to be more like the medical model, as the conference panelists dreamed, then the *absolute best* that criminology could aspire to would be to one day be more like psychiatric research.

This is why the two of us were unable to share the enthusiasm of our fellow conference attendees. It struck the two of us that if criminologists and correctional practitioners knew more about this history of psychiatric research as detailed in Barber's (2008a) book *Comfortably Numb: How Psychiatry is Medicating a Nation*) (see also Petersen 2008), they too might not be quite so eager to sell out our own practices for these supposedly greener pastures. The attendees at the conference, for instance, might be dismayed to know that the longtime editor of the highly prestigious *New England Journal of Medicine* reluctantly resigned her post after two decades as editor, concluding 'It is simply no longer possible to believe much of the clinical research that is published, or to rely on the judgment of trusted physicians or authoritative medical guidelines'—citing psychiatric research as the worst offender (Angell 2009: 12). That is a fairly huge statement about the state of psychiatric science. Could this really be the great medical model to which we in criminology aspire?

It was out of this realization that the idea for this chapter was hatched, and this chapter is for them—the very well-intentioned and inspirational individuals in criminology and 'offender management' who seek to improve the evidence base for our work. In this chapter we first outline what we see as this medical model dream and how it has played itself out in psychiatry. We then offer some of the known 'side effects' of this medical model fantasy. That is, we talk about some of the problems that psychiatry has faced historically and in contemporary practice that have been exacerbated as much as they have been alleviated by clinging on to a medical model paradigm. Finally, we suggest some alternatives to the medical model, again drawing on research in psychiatry, and conclude by seeking to draw lessons for criminology.

Importantly, our overall argument is not entirely critical of psychiatry. There are, of course, some real scare stories in the history of psychiatric endeavours with which most readers will already be familiar (to some degree the history of the mad house rivals even that of the prison for horrific abuses of power). At the same time, psychiatry has also made some tremendous advances as well that have indeed improved the lives of many. Our argument, however, is that many of these advances have actually emerged from research that is *outside* the mainstream of the traditional medical model. That is, much of what we find exciting about psychiatric research today is emerging out of research that is on the margins of the discipline—not the mainstream medical journals that criminologists sometimes seeks to emulate. Indeed, ironically, much of this research—involving case studies and longitudinal research of lives over time—resembles traditional criminological research far more than the medical model designs favoured in the psychiatric mainstream. We conclude by arguing that psychiatry may have as much to learn from criminology as the other way around.

The Medical Model Dream in Psychiatry

A Very Short History of Psychiatry

As Nikolas Rose points out, most existing histories of psychiatry take on the form of self-serving hagiographies with a familiar structure—in the beginning, there was cruelty and confusion, but as the field became progressively more scientific over time, conditions have continuously improved. Rose (1996) argues that such histories are written 'in the future anterior' (p. 43). That is, the message of this narrative is: Yes, mistakes were made, but stick with us and things will just get better and better as the years go by. In fact, in fifty years we will probably have the whole thing cracked.

The real history of psychiatry is of course not so neatly linear. Psychiatry's history can broadly be divided into three overlapping eras: Asylum Psychiatry, Community Psychiatry, and Corporate/Biological Psychiatry.[2] Asylum Psychiatry began around 1800 with the founding of a series of hospitals for the mentally ill. By 1904, there were 150,000 patients in US psychiatric hospitals. Asylum Psychiatry reached its

[2] The formulation of the distinct entities of Community and Corporate Psychiatry is David Healy's (2002).

peak about 1950, when that census reached well over a half a million (Shorter 1977: 34). Community Psychiatry can (somewhat ironically) be tied to the invention of Thorazine, the first antipsychotic medication, in the early 1950s, which led to the opening of the doors of state psychiatric hospitals. Finally, Corporate/Biological Psychiatry began with the introduction of Prozac. Each of these iterations of psychiatry has featured entirely different treatments, and each has represented a paradigm shift in how psychiatry was conceived and conducted. While the field has in fact progressed demonstrably through each of these eras, each era has been marked by excesses and highly questionable if not unethical practices. In other words, to view the evolution of psychiatry as a steady march towards ever more refined and elegant scientific certainties—the medical model—is not justified by much of the actual history of the field.

The impetus behind Asylum Psychiatry was often well-intentioned and of course justified on the grounds of the medical model version of science of its day. Based on the theory that the natural world was curative, many hospitals were established in sylvan settings. However, the actual treatment that took place in those settings, particularly during the first half of the twentieth century, was often barbaric. In 1916, at a state hospital in New Jersey, Dr Henry Cotton, believing that germs from tooth decay led to insanity, removed patient's teeth and other body parts, such as the bowels. In so doing, he killed almost half of his patients (Whitaker 2003: 80–2). In 1933, Manfred Sakel induced hypoglycemia in patients through the injection of insulin, thereby putting his patients into an insulin coma. The American champion of the lobotomy, Walter Freeman, roamed the United States as a veritable Johnny Appleseed of the technique, which amounted to jamming an ice pick through the patient's eye sockets and destroying the frontal lobes (ibid.: 134). A successful operation, in Freeman's view, was one in which the patient became adjusted at 'the level of a domestic invalid or household pet' (ibid.: 124). Between 1935 and 1950, around 20,000 American psychiatric patients were subjected to such treatments.

There were two prongs of Community Psychiatry—one has proved to be generally a success, and the other a global disgrace. The successful part was the establishment in the 1920s and 1930s of office-based practice for, typically, 'worried well' patients. Psychotherapy, for all its detractors, has generally been shown to be a successful (if expensive) treatment for many: a review of the history of psychotherapy shows that a consistent two-thirds of patients show improvement after six months of treatment. The critical factor does not appear to be the type of therapy employed but rather the strength of the treatment relationship—the 'therapeutic alliance'—between therapist and client (Barber 2008b). The disgraceful part of the Community Psychiatry Era has been the widespread discharging of patients from state-run psychiatric facilities into the community without proper supports. Psychiatrists overestimated the effectiveness of antipsychotic medications to allow patients to manage severe illnesses by themselves. Conversely, there was a profound under-estimation of the need for appropriate community support for these patients. Eventually there was simply no place for patients to go but to the parks and emergency rooms, leading to periodic epidemics of homelessness in the United States, in particular, since the 1980s. It is also no coincidence that in this same period the incarceration rate in US prisons and jails has skyrocketed, in many ways becoming a replacement to the old asylum for individuals with acute psychiatric problems (see Baillargeon *et al.* 2009: 103–9).

Most recently, Asylum Psychiatry and Community Psychiatry have both been swept away by a new Corporate/Biological Psychiatry. State hospitals now house about 5 per cent of the patients they once did; and Community Psychiatry in the form of psychotherapy has been eroded by 'managed care' and the embrace of psychiatric medications as the sole treatment of choice for many psychiatric disorders. There are two aspects to the new psychiatry: real (but over-hyped) progress in brain-imaging, neuroscience and genetics, and massive corporate profits for medications based on the premature belief that behaviour and disorders are ultimately a product of 'chemical imbalances'. As in previous eras, the medical model in psychiatry has literally been over-sold, leading to extraordinary profits for pharmaceutical companies, an expanding number of less meaningful psychiatric diagnoses and, arguably, an over-medicating and over-diagnosing of people who have sub-clinical symptoms or no formal symptoms at all. For instance, a 2010 systematic review concluded that although antidepressants appear to be more successful than placebos at treating patients with severe depression, the benefit of such drugs for those with milder, more common forms of depression 'may be minimal or nonexistent' (Fournier *et al.* 2010: 47–53).

It is easy to spin the story of these three movements as one of progress. Certainly development and change in biological psychology has been remarkably swift. Until 1950, the predominant theories about how the brain functioned were electrical, not chemical (Healy 2002: 198). When the first psychiatric drugs were discovered, no one had a clue what a neurotransmitter was. It was only in 1965 that the first biological theory of a major psychiatric disorder was published (ibid.: 143), yet today most school children are fluent in the language of ADHD, bipolar disorder and depression. Yet, rapid change is not the same as continuous progress. It is hardly the case that, as a result of 100 years of psychiatry, Americans (the world's leading consumers of psychiatric help) are healthier, happier and more psychologically fit—far from it. Mental illness appears, instead, to be increasing. In fact, in 2002, more than 11 per cent of American women and 5 per cent of American men were taking antidepressants (Stagnitti 2005). Even more worryingly, these illnesses are rapidly spreading among children. As Marcia Angell (2009: 11) points out, 'We are now in the midst of an apparent epidemic of bipolar disease in children . . . with a forty-fold increase in the diagnosis between 1994 and 2003.' In short, despite all of our pill popping, Americans have hardly become happier or more psychologically healthy.

Known Side Effects of Psychiatric Research

A perception has emerged that biological psychiatry is something akin to physics and chemistry and the more concrete areas of medicine, reassuring in its rules and clarity. This has contributed to a new image of psychiatry as a 'real' branch of medicine and a bona fide science built on white-coated certitude. At last, we are told, psychiatry has entered Big Science. As Tom Wolfe put it, those echoes you heard in the middle of the night in the late 1980s and early 1990s were the sounds of Departments of Psychiatry and Psychology in universities taking down their placards, and putting up new ones, saying Departments of *Neuro*psychology and *Neuro*psychiatry.[3]

A primary contributor to the bolstered scientific profile of psychiatry is the relatively recent emergence of randomized clinical trials (RCTs), which have become the *ne plus ultra* of psychiatry and indeed all medicine. However, RCTs in psychiatry have not always been of the highest quality. When the first 2,000 RCTs for the treatment of schizophrenia were reviewed, it was discovered that most trials were significantly flawed by inadequate sample size, too short durations and poor reporting of data. Only 1 per cent of the trials was given top marks on one 1–5 scale of quality (Thornley and Adams 1998). Moreover, about one-third of biomedical scientists have admitted to questionable research practices, such as changing experimental methods and reporting based on the preferences of their funders (Cook 2005). Still, RCTs remain the gold standard in psychiatric research to the point that it is difficult to be funded to do other types of research.

There is a subtle, inherent logical limitation in RCTs. RCTs are not set up to confirm how a medication or treatment is effective, but rather to confirm the null hypothesis—that is, that the intervention is better than nothing at all. In the standard RCT, one compares a treatment arm with a control arm, in which no treatment is provided. When a particular agent in an RCT is successful, all that has been demonstrated is that the treatment was in some way better than no treatment. In other words, unless it is independently evident that the treatment addresses the illness—in the way, for example, that penicillin treats pneumonia—then one does not actually learn very much from the trial (Healy 2002: chapter 7).

Indeed, to this day, no one knows exactly how most widely prescribed psychiatric medications work. The basic tenet of biological psychiatry, that depression is a result of a deficit in serotonin, for instance, has proven seductive to psychiatric practitioners and patients alike. Yet, while serotonin has *something* to do with depression, the relationship is neither a simple nor well-understood one. No deficiencies in the serotonin system have consistently been reported among depressed people; in fact, no simple one-to-one relationship between any psychiatric disorder and a single neurotransmitter has ever been proven. While SSRI antidepressants do act on serotonin regulation in the brain, the changes that the drug ultimately exerts on the brain

[3] Tom Wolfe, Lecture, Southampton, New York. 1993.

are unclear. The etiology of depression remains a scientific mystery, with new ways of understanding the disease—or *diseases*, as what we currently call 'depression' is likely dozens of discrete maladies—emerging regularly. A leading researcher, Jeffrey Meyer of the University of Toronto, captured the misplaced logic of the serotonin hypothesis: 'There is a common misunderstanding that serotonin is low during clinical depression. It mostly comes from the fact that many antidepressants raise serotonin. That's a bit like saying pneumonia is an illness of low antibiotics because we treat pneumonia with antibiotics.'[4] Correlation with serotonin is not causation by serotonin (Shorter 1977: 267).

The simplicity of the medical model in psychiatry, however, is immensely appealing. It is the premise upon which psychiatric medications have become among the most profitable areas of medicine. As a group, psychiatric medications are among the most prescribed class of medication in the developed world, with antidepressants the most prescribed medication in the United States.

Spurred by this profitability, the drug industry has infiltrated psychiatry. The industry has invaded the psychiatric academy, and the academy has for the most part only been too happy to let them in. 'Psychiatrists earn more money from drug companies than doctors in any other specialty', according to *The New York Times* (Harris 2007). More than half of psychiatrists involved in developing the 1994 edition of the *Diagnostic and Statistical Manual of Mental Disorders* ('DSM') had financial ties to drug companies (Carey 2006). Indeed, a sobering percentage of 'scientific' articles in even leading journals are now 'ghostwritten' — meaning that the authors are paid by the drug companies to write the piece. Some academics simply put their names on the articles already produced by the company, while others work from a draft given to them. Ghostwriting can be highly lucrative: an article published in one of the top journals (eg *The New England Journal of Medicine*; *The Lancet*; *The British Medical Journal*) can net the 'author' up to $20,000 (Johnson 2003).

As a result of the role of marketing and the embrace of the simplified medical model, more people have become diagnosed with mental illnesses and been medicated for them. For instance, Martin Seligman (2002) has observed a more than tenfold increase in the rates of self-reported depression in the last two generations. David Healy calls it a 'wholesale creation of depression so extraordinary and unwarranted' so as 'to raise grave questions about whether the pharmaceutical and other health care companies are more wedded to making profits from health than contributing to it' (Kendall 2004). Each edition of the DSM, psychiatry's bible, has proclaimed an increasing number of diagnoses that cover a widening terrain of normal, if painful, human behaviour. DSM-I, published in 1952, covered sixty-two diagnoses. DSM-IV, published in the 1990s, had over 300. (Not coincidentally, of the 170 contributors to the most recent edition of the DSM, 95 per cent had financial ties to drug

[4] Press Release: Link Between Serotonin and Suicide Found with New Brain Imaging Methods. Centre for Addiction and Mental Health, University of Toronto. 1 January 2003.

companies (Cosgrove *et al.* 2006).) It is only fairly recently that such day-to-day, emotional problems such as shyness were considered to be in the purview of psychiatry at all. With some exceptions, the original charge of psychiatry was to treat the severely mentally ill. But in a clear case of a business expanding its market base, much of psychiatry has abandoned its initial mission to serve the severely mentally ill and gravitated toward the more lucrative 'psychoneuroses', as the historian of psychiatry Edward Shorter has put it. Shorter (1977) contends that this shift is defensive and self-serving, a response to increasing competition from non-medical mental health professionals such as social workers and psychologists who began treating the 'worried well', 'garden variety' neurotics in the 1970s. As The *British Medical Journal* stated: 'a lot of money can be made from healthy people who believe they are sick' (Moynihan *et al.* 2002: 886).

The ultimate indicator of the new-found faith in biological psychiatry may be the mysteriously growing placebo effect. When psychiatrist Timothy Walsh analysed seventy-five trials of antidepressants conducted between 1981 and 2000, he discovered that the response rate to placebo, which is, of course, nothing more than sugar pills, increased 7 per cent per decade (Saxbe 2004). Simply because people thought they were taking pills, they thought they were going to get better.

Alternatives to the Medical Model in Psychiatry

The irony is that, masked by the attention to psychiatric medications and the medicalization of everyday problems, true progress has been made since the birth of Prozac by the 'low-tech' psychosocial realm in the remediation of mental illness and behavioural change. But as result of psychiatry's entry into the realm of Big Science, some of these developments, based on much earlier paradigms in psychology and psychiatry—mushy-headed things like old-fashioned psychoanalysis/psychotherapy—have been ignored.

A growing research base supports the effectiveness of these approaches—which include Prochaska's and DiClemente's (1992) Stages of Change model and Miller and Rollnick's (2002) Motivational Interviewing, for example—for a wide range of afflictions. These techniques have turned old-school medical dogma upside down. The traditional notions that the doctor is in charge; that the patient does what they are told; that change occurs along a straightforward linear path; that people have to be motivated at the beginning of treatment to engage successfully in it; that recovery from mental illness is independent of the social context, and is defined only by the successful remediation of symptoms: all these things have been turned on their heads in recent years. Researchers instead have found that the client's *relationship* to the care-giver, and to others is critical to the recovery process. Larry Davidson (2007), a Yale researcher in recovery from severe mental illness, writes:

> In the medical model, you take a person with a mental illness, you provide treatment in the hopes of reducing symptoms, and then they are supposed to approximate some notion of

normality. Our research shows the opposite. You take a person with a mental illness, you then reduce the discrimination and stigma against them, increase their social roles and participation, which provides them a reason to get better in the fist place, and then you provide treatment and support. The issue is not so much making them normal but helping them to get their lives back.[5]

When one listens to patients—instead of listening to Prozac—one often finds that another person is at the centre of their own recovery stories. That person who is central to the healing process may be a psychiatrist or a social worker, but more often than not it is a family member or a significant other.

These psychosocial models differ further from the medical model in that they are based on engaging strengths rather than redressing deficits. The strength-based approach is a departure from the standard medical model, which is based on the 'chief complaint', and 'symptoms' as the sole framework or guide for treatment. Medicine is simply not used to thinking about assets and resources—it is a problem-solving discipline and, therefore, it has mainly been involved with everything that is wrong with a person, rather than what is right about the person. George Vaillaint (2003) reviewed all scholarly psychological and psychiatric articles published between 1987 and 2002 and found 57,800 articles on anxiety and 70,856 on depression. But only 5,701 mentioned 'life satisfaction', and 851 mentioned 'joy'.

Progressive treatment plans place the patient's resources and abilities on a par with, or even above, their problems. The critical pathway to health is not dictated by the robustness of the disease but the resources the person can muster to deal with the affliction. Erik Erikson (1950: 93) put it a slightly different way: 'We cannot even really know what causes neurotic suffering until we have an idea of what causes real health. This we have only begun to investigate.' The new models also stress that clients are in charge of their own treatment. As Miller has written: 'MI encourages clients to develop their own solutions to the problems that they themselves have defined.' The client is held responsible for choosing and carrying out actions to change, while counsellors focus their efforts on helping the clients stay motivated. There is no 'right way' to change, and if a given plan for change does not work, clients are only limited by their own creativity as to the number of other plans that might be tried.[6]

Why have these approaches to psychiatric practice not been as influential as the traditional medical model? First, there's no money in it. The pioneer of cognitive behavioral therapy, Aaron Beck has said:

The drug companies spend several billion dollars a year on their consumer ads and promotions to professionals. This has created an aura of success [for drug-based solutions]. It is difficult to compete with such a juggernaut, but gradually it is becoming apparent that human problems are best solved by human solutions [Langreth 2007].

[5] Larry Davidson (2007), personal correspondence.

[6] See <www.motivationalinterview.org/clinical/principles.html>.

The other reason psychosocial approaches are not appreciated in the way they should be is that they require hard work. Developing supportive relationships, unlike prescribing drugs, takes time, focus, and real effort. Mostly, though, listening to patients cuts against the establishment grain. We live in an age of experts, in which we cede control of our bodies and our being to others. Different parts of our bodies go to different experts. It is almost sacrilegious, medically speaking, to think that one could be the expert on one's self—while also valuing and seeking the expertise of professionals.

Lessons for Criminology

For a contribution to a book entitled, *What is Criminology?*, we have spent an inordinate amount of space discussing psychiatry. We hope, however, that the cautionary tale we are implying has been obvious. It is a very real possibility that all of the mistakes of psychiatric research (the endless net-widening and expansion of territory, the influx and influence of corporate money, the denigration of basic research) could be repeated by criminology if we naïvely chase after the greener pastures of the medical model.

After all, one of the founding fathers of positivist criminology, Enrico Ferri (2004: 29) once wrote: 'This is the fundamental conviction at which the positive school arrives: That which has happened in medicine will happen in criminology.' This 'fundamental conviction' appears to remain at the heart of positivist criminology 100 years later. Although criminology remains highly diverse with numerous centres of influence, ranging from cultural criminology to resurgent feminist criminologies, it is beyond dispute that a medical model criminology (sometimes called 'experimental criminology') is very much on the rise. Far from a 'straw man', this vision is now associated with some of the most prestigious university departments, lucrative new prizes, and leading journals in the field. Adherents to this viewpoint refer to their research as the 'gold standard' of evidence and largely ignore other forms of criminological research in their assessments of 'what works' (for a critique, see Hough 2010).

It is this methodological privileging that most deeply offends critics in criminology. Kevin Stenson (2010: 163–4), for instance, forcefully argues that 'the broad church of criminology risks capture by a narrow sect' and that the field is at risk of becoming 'the tame police science of the new, centralized security state':

> The advocates of experimental criminology (and, more broadly, 'crime science')... borrowing the legitimacy of medical science... favour big datasets, big funding (leaving less available for non-Campbellites), self-referential systematic literature reviews, causal statistical analysis and a methodological hierarchy with random control trials at the apex, as if conscious human conduct is as determinable and predictable as branded prescription drugs in

experimental trials. In this vision, data gathering with real people carries low status. Data are mathematized and then analyzed by the priestly/rabbinical caste of senior investigators at a sanitized, safe distance from awkward humans [ibid.].

Yet, even the most strident critics of the medical model typically see nothing wrong with the use of RCT program evaluations or the systematic reviews borrowed from medical research. These methodologies produce useful information and the world would likely be a better place if more of this information existed and was taken seriously by policy-makers and politicians. The problem most have with the 'Randomista' movement in criminology is the idea of privileging this sort of research over all others, denigrating or detracting from the core business of our field—in particular, theory development and social observation.[7]

RCTs can only address a tiny fraction of the questions that are of crucial importance to criminologists, and this subset of questions that RCTs can usefully address is most definitely non-random.[8] RCTs are highly useful, for instance, in determining whether some very tightly packaged and structured 'programme' (conveniently, precisely the sort of programme that can be copyrighted and marketed) is effective or not in reducing crime in various settings. However, RCT methodology is of little value in determining whether extreme economic inequalities increase the incidence of violent victimization across cultures. Most criminologists would agree that the latter question is far more central to the scientific understanding of crime than the former. Yet, a privileging of methodology turns this on its head and channels precious resources to evaluating the government's latest 'programme'.

Moreover, like with the clinical trials of pharmaceuticals, RCTs and systematic reviews do not tell us how or why an intervention works. David Roodman (2009) puts this concern concisely:

> Already, grand men of economics such as Nobelist James Heckman and Angus Deaton are asking tough questions. Such as: are RCT researchers doing science if they treat people and households as black boxes—things to be experimented on and observed—without modeling or studying what goes on inside the black boxes? If you learn that pushing this button turns on that light, what have you really learned about electricity?

RCTs and systematic reviews are a crucial tool in the toolbox of criminologists and other scientific practitioners. However, as Chris McManus (2009) has argued, 'they

[7] Nick Tilley is particularly persuasive on this point, arguing that such advocates '[repudiate] theory and [encourage] the uncritical use of a particular methodological hammer as the preferred tool with which to crack evaluation problems' (Tilley 2009: 138).

[8] The *British Medical Journal* recently parodied the 'randomista' brigade by pointing out that the effectiveness of the parachute has never been tested in a peer-reviewed RCT. Ruling out the use of observational methodology as too unsystematic to prove the value of parachutes, the authors conclude, with tongues firmly in cheek: 'We think that everyone might benefit if the most radical protagonists of evidence based medicine organised and participated in a double blind, randomised, placebo controlled, crossover trial of the parachute' (Smith and Pell 2003: 1459).

must be seen for what they truly are: measures of desperate last resort when no better way exists to answer important questions...'

> Each RCT provides only one bit of information: 'Yes' or 'No' to a single question. Just as one could climb a mountain blindfolded by asking at each step which way to go, so RCT-based medicine is progress, but it's so very, very slow. Imagine Nasa using RCTs to land its Exploration Rover on Mars, without knowing Newton's Laws of Motion [ibid.].

A social science of crime requires more than the medical model, it also requires the development and testing of mid-level theories through social observation. This means talking to people, getting to know them, and immersing ourselves in their lives (in particular, through ethnography and first-person accounts from the 'subjects' of our research themselves). Although this is 'basic' science, ironically, it may also be the most practical methodology for applied questions of criminal justice interventions. As Dan Lewis argues in his essay 'From Programs to Lives', researchers may learn more about effective policy and practice from studying human lives (outside of interventions) than by narrowly evaluating the results of discrete programmes (Lewis: 1990). Lewis points out that almost all of the research evidence suggests that 'programmes' have a remarkably minor impact on aggregate measures of life outcomes, and yet policy researchers devote 99 per cent of our time evaluating these things anyhow. Lewis instead suggests that policy researchers turn our lens from programmes to human lives in their full biographical and historical context in order to better understand why and how programmes have such (minimal) impacts.

The eminent Harvard criminologist Robert Sampson recently made much the same case for the importance of understanding social context in his argument that 'experiments are not the gold standard' of social research (Sampson: 2009). Indeed, as one of the founders of 'life course' criminology, Sampson has been instrumental in promoting precisely the sort of basic science research that can be crucial for the development of criminal justice interventions (yet has nothing to do with policy evaluation (see Sampson and Laub 1993)). For instance, life course criminology, which seeks to understand how and why individuals move into and out of criminal behaviours over time, has generated considerable recent interest in something called a 'desistance paradigm' in probation work (see McNeill 2006). Like Miller's work in psychology, the desistance approach is deemed to be 'strengths-based' rather than 'deficit-focused' (Maruna and LeBel 2003), and it follows Lewis's maxim to reverse the traditional focus on 'programmes' to a focus on lives in context (social supports, friends, careers). McNeill (2006: 46) explains the desistance paradigm as follows: 'put simply, the implication is that offender management services need to think of themselves less as providers of correctional treatment (that belongs to the expert) and more as supporters of desistance processes (that belong to the desister)'.

It is this last point—the question of privileging or not privileging experts and agencies—that might best explain the enduring appeal of the medical model among those of us who work as criminal justice experts in agencies and academic departments. Although one might reasonably argue that criminology has less to worry about than psychiatry does in terms of the influx of huge corporate incentives toward certain types of research,[9] the problem with *profits* in criminology may not be as important as that of *prophets*. That is, there is something intoxicatingly powerful about holding the key to 'what works' and 'what doesn't' when the rest of the world is both so confused and also so distressed about the crime problem. In fact, in recent years the popular media has anointed a few criminological academics with just this sort of crime-fighting super-power—even drawing on the imagery of the 'new sheriff' (almost always white and upper middle class) riding into the backwards big city (almost always majority poor and non-white) and turning its crime problems around with the sheer power of Big Science. Although not as grubby as being paid outright by a pharmaceutical company to lend one's name to a ghost-written puff piece, the lure of this sort of power is still very real and potentially dangerous for criminology as a science.

What is the alternative to the sort of criminological hubris? The classic answer in criminology's history has been the crippling pessimism of 'nothing works': Since we probably do not have magic bullets for reducing crime, we should shift the focus instead to doing 'justice' (or, more accurately, 'retribution') better. We do not share this pessimism—although we have some sympathy for versions of the 'non-treatment paradigm' of the 1970s (Bottoms and McWilliams 1979). We *do* think that crime can be reduced, even substantially, through concerted effort, and such work can be helped substantially by the rigorous and systematic research of criminologists.

Our argument is simply that this will not happen by trying to mimic the psychiatric community and transform criminology into a branch of medicine. The 'broad church' of criminology has long welcomed a plethora of methodological approaches from discourse analysis to hierarchical linear modelling. Criminologists come to the field with training in anthropology, geography, philosophy, psychology, sociology, political science, history, and even medicine. This is perfectly appropriate. Crime is a multifaceted issue with political, normative, philosophical, biological and social dimensions. At the heart of our field, moreover, has always been the effort to develop our understanding of why communities, individuals and nations differ in terms of their propensity toward offending. As with any science, this theory development is and should be our primary contribution to the world and can be invaluable in designing interventions to reduce victimization. Still, like all social sciences, ours is necessarily a humble science. We have far more questions than we have answers, and although our understanding of crime may improve vastly over time, there are many things we will never be able to predict—let alone 'control'—nor would we want to. In other words, then, our recommendation for criminology is that rather than trying to

[9] At least, unlike psychiatric solutions, criminological cures can rarely be bottled (literally), packaged and marketed to the rest of the world.

make our own research more like that of our medical model colleagues, psychiatrists might do better to make their research more like ours in criminology—theoretically rich, methodologically diverse, grounded in the lived experiences of real people, but most importantly endlessly curious about the social world, seeking understanding first and cures and solutions second. In both fields, we feel, we should not be discouraged but rather comforted by the limits of what we can know, measure, and predict. No matter how much progress social sciences like ours make—and progress we can—there will always remain something ineffably mysterious and unknowable about us as human beings. And, that is precisely as it should be. It does not make what we do any less valuable. In fact, by promising less by way of miracle cures and ready-bottled solutions, and instead focusing on seeking to understand human lives in all of their rich context, we may have an even greater an impact on society.

References

Angell, M. (2009), 'Drug Companies and Doctors: A Story of Corruption', *New York Review of Books,* 15 January: 8–12.

Baillargeon, J., Binswanger, I. A., Penn, J. V., Williams, B. A., and Murray, O. J. (2009), 'Psychiatric Disorders and Repeat Incarcerations: The Revolving Prison Door', *American Journal of Psychiatry,* 166: 103–9.

Baird, C. (2009), *A Question of Evidence: A Critique of Risk Assessment Models Used in the Justice System,* Washington: National Council on Crime and Delinquency.

Barber, C. (2008a), *Comfortably Numb: How Psychiatry is Medicating a Nation* New York: Pantheon.

_____. (2008b), 'Review of 'American Therapy: The Rise of Psychotherapy in the United States,' by Jonathan Engel', *The Wilson Quarterly,* 32: 97

Bottoms, A. E. and McWilliams, W. (1979), 'A Non-Treatment Paradigm for Probation Practice', *British Journal of Social Work,* 9, 2: 159–202.

Burgess, A. (1962), *A Clockwork Orange,* New York: Norton.

Fournier, J. C., DeRubeis, R. J., Hollon, S. D., Dimidjian, S., Amsterdam, J. D., Shelton, R. C., and Fawcett, J. (2010), 'Antidepressant Drug Effects and Depression Severity A Patient-Level Meta-Analysis', *Journal of the American Medical Association,* 303, 1: 47–53.

Carey, B. (2006), 'Study Finds a Link of Drug Makers to Psychiatrists', *The New York Times,* 20 April.

Coid, J., Yang, M., Ullrich, S., Zhang, T., Sizmur, S., Roberts, C., Farrington, D. P., and Rogers, R. D. (2009), 'Gender Differences in Structured Risk Assessment: Comparing the Accuracy of Five Instruments' *Journal of Consulting and Clinical Psychology,* 77, 2: 337–48.

Cook, G. (2005), 'Surveyed Scientists Admit Misconduct: One-Third Cite Research Tactics', *The Boston Globe,* 9 June.

Cosgrove, L., Krimsky, S., Vijayaraghavan, M., and Schneider, L. (2006), 'Financial Ties between DSM-IV Panel Members and the Pharmaceutical Industry', *Psychotherapy and Psychosomatics,* 75: 154–60.

Erikson, E. H. (1950), 'Growth and Crises of the 'Healthy Personality'', in M. J. R Senn (ed.), *Symposium on the Healthy Personality: Supplement II of the Fourth Conference on Infancy and Childhood*, New York, Josiah Macy, Jr. Foundation.

Ferri, E. (2004 [1908]), in E. Untermann (trans.), *The Positive School of Criminology*, Chicago: Charles H. Kerr.

Harris, G. (2007) 'Psychiatrists Top List in Drug Maker Gifts', *The New York Times*, 26 June.

Healy, D. (2002), *The Creation of Psychopharmacology*, Cambridge, MA: Harvard University Press.

Hough, M (2010), 'Gold Standard or Fool's Gold? The Pursuit of Certainty in Experimental Criminology', *Criminology & Criminal Justice*, 10: 11–22.

Johnson, E. (2003), 'Inside the Business of Medical Ghostwriting', *CBC Marketplace*, broadcast 25 March (<www.cbc.ca/consumers/market/files/health/ghostwriting>).

Kendall, J. (2004), 'Talking Back to Prozac', *Boston Globe*, 1 February.

Langreth, R. (2007), 'Patient, Fix Thyself', *Forbes*, 9 April: 80–6.

Lewis, C. S. (1953), 'The Humanitarian Theory of Punishment', *Res Judicatae*, 6: 224–31.

Lewis, D. A. (1990), 'From Programs to Lives: A Comment', *American Journal of Community Psychology*, 18: 923–6.

Maruna, S. and LeBel, T. P. (2003), 'Welcome Home?: Examining the Reentry Court Concept from a Strengths-Based Perspective', *Western Criminology Review*, 4, 2: 91–107.

McManus, C. (2009), 'Bad Science', *Times Higher Education*, 22 January.

McNeill, F. (2006), 'A Desistance Paradigm for Offender Management', *Criminology and Criminal Justice*, 6: 39–62.

Miller, W. R. and Rollnick, S. (2002), *Motivational interviewing: Preparing people for change*, New York: Guilford Press.

Monahan, J., Steadman, H. J., Silver, E., Appelbaum, P. S., Clark, R. P., Mulvey, E. P., Roth, L. H., Grisso, T., and Banks, S. (2001), *Rethinking Risk Assessment: The MacArthur Study of Mental Disorder and Violence*, New York, Oxford University Press.

Moynihan, R., Heath, I., Henry, D. (2002), 'Selling Sickness: The Pharmaceutical Industry and Disease Mongering', *British Medical Journal*, 324: 886–91.

Petersen, M. (2008), *Our Daily Meds: How the Pharmaceutical Companies Transformed Themselves into Slick Marketing Machines and Hooked the Nation on Prescription Drugs*, Sarah Chrichton/Farrar, Straus and Giroux.

Prochaska, J. O. and DiClemente, C. C. (1992), 'Stages of Change in the Modification of Problem Behavior, in M. Hersen, R. Eisler, and P. M. Miller (eds), *Progress in Behavior Modification*, Sycamore: Sycamore.

Roodman, D. (2009), *The Rapid Rise of the Randomistas and the Trouble with the RCTs*, Center for Global Development (<http://blogs.cgdev.org/open_book/2009/03/the-rapid-rise-of-the-randomis.php>).

Rose, N. (1996), *Inventing Our Selves: Psychology, Power and Personhood*, Cambridge: Cambridge University Press.

Sampson, R. J. (2009), *Experiments are Not the Gold Standard: Causal Knowledge and Observational Science*, Paper Presented at the American Society of Criminology Meeting, Philadelphia, 6 November.

Sampson, R. and Laub, J. (1993), *Crime in the Making*, Cambridge, MA: Harvard University Press.

Saxbe, D. (2004), 'Placebo power: A Mystery Grows', *Psychology Today*, 1 September.

Seligman, M. (2002), 'Martin Seligman Forum on Depression', interview by J. McGrossin, *Life Matters*, Radio National (Australia), 16 August (<www.abc.net.au/rn/talks/lm/stories/s648530.htm>).

Shorter, E. (1977), *A History of Psychiatry from the Era of the Asylum to the Age of Prozac*, New York: John Wiley & Sons.

Smith, G. C. S. and Pell, J. P. (2003), 'Parachute use to Prevent Death and Major Trauma related to Gravitational Challenge: Systematic Review of Randomised Controlled Trials', *British Medical Journal*, 327: 1459–61.

Stagnitti, M. N. (2005), 'Trends in Antidepressant Use by the US Civilian non-Institutionalized Population, 1997 and 2002', *Statistical Brief #76*, May 2005, Rockville: Agency for Healthcare Research and Quality.

Stenson, K. (2010), 'Review of "Existentialist Criminology" edited by R. Lippens and D. Crewe', *British Journal of Criminology*, 50: 161–4.

Thornley, B., Adams, C. (1998), 'Content and Quality of 2000 Controlled Trials in Schizophrenia over 50 years', *British Medical Journal*, 317: 1181–4.

Tilley, N. (2009), 'Sherman vs Sherman: Realism vs Rhetoric', *Criminology and Criminal Justice*, 9: 135–44.

Vaillant, G. E. (2003). 'Mental Health', *American Journal of Psychiatry*, 160: 1373–84.

Whitaker, R. (2003), *Mad in America: Bad Science, Bad Medicine and the Enduring Mistreatment of the Mentally Ill*, New York: Perseus Publishing.

22

CRIMINAL JUSTICE, NOT CRIMINOLOGY?

ANDREW ASHWORTH

WHEN I am asked whether I am a criminologist, I always say no. That is not intended as some deep statement about disciplinary or methodological boundaries, but rather as a cursory attempt to differentiate my background and approach from those of people who clearly regard themselves as criminologists. I would not want to pretend to be a criminologist when I am not one. But flowing from the serious questions posed by the editors of this volume is this: how do I know I am not a criminologist?

My instinctive answer would be that I engage in the study of criminal justice rather than criminology. The focus of criminal justice may be seen as the institutions of the administration of criminal justice, and its study includes significant bodies of law (criminal procedure and sentencing, for example) and the practices of prosecutors, judges, parole boards, and others performing decision-making roles within what is often referred to as the criminal justice system. Two preliminary points can be made about this conception of criminal justice. The first is that, even if criminal justice as a topic can be differentiated from criminology, that does not mean that it must lie outside the disciplinary confines of criminology. It would be possible to regard criminology as the overarching discipline, with a number of discrete areas under its umbrella (criminal justice, victimology, and corporate crime, for example). But the relationship probably does not work the other way round: study of psychological theories of offending or of crime and the life course would not normally be regarded as 'criminal justice,' presumably because criminal justice concerns institutions and actors who assume certain roles within those institutions whereas theories of criminality focus on individuals, albeit within their social settings. The second point is that there are obvious overlaps between criminal justice and criminology, such that, even if they were regarded as separate disciplines, they would deal with some of the same topics. Sentencing is an obvious example—a core topic within criminal justice, yet overlapping with criminological research and theory in matters such as rehabilitative techniques, deterrent strategies and desistance studies. Indeed, as will be argued below, the dearth of basic empirical research on key issues of prosecution practice and sentencing practice is handicapping the proper development of public policy.

Accepting that there is a distinction between criminal justice and criminology, that would still not deal adequately with a third disciplinary field—that of criminal law. The study of the rules of conduct that make up the criminal law of a given country, and of the general doctrines that form part of that system of criminal law, is a major preoccupation of criminal lawyers.[1] But even within the criminal law there are different approaches. Those who are often (disparagingly) referred to as 'black letter lawyers' are concerned with detailed analysis of the criminal law, examining the boundaries of the law of criminal homicide, or exactly what conduct is penalized by the new offence of corporate manslaughter, or when ignorance of the law or intoxication will provide a person with a defence. But there are few 'black letter lawyers' who never ask about the purpose and justification for a particular offence—after all, that might be relevant to interpreting the ambit of the offence. Beyond the 'black letter' category lie other groups of criminal lawyers, notably those who adopt a philosophical approach to it and examine the rationales and the concepts involved, and others who adopt what may be termed a historico-social approach by tracing the forces that led to the emergence of a particular law or examining the impact of a particular law on social behaviour. But the focus of all these groups is on the law, and it is the law on which the different techniques are brought to bear.

Now, if one were to study the operation of the laws against drugs, for example, one might examine how the laws came into their present form, how the police approach their enforcement, how this impacts on patterns of drug use, what sentencing policies the courts adopt when dealing with convicted offenders, whether policing priorities and sentencing policies have a socially discriminatory effect (eg by punishing young black working class men involved with crack cocaine more than middle class users of powder cocaine), and so forth. Such a research programme would be a mixture of criminal justice, criminological and even socio-legal perspectives and techniques. It would start with an analysis of the criminal law, but would then examine the impact of the law and the use of the law by those working within the criminal justice system.

[1] For fuller discussions, see Zedner (this volume) and Lacey (2007).

The Role of the Criminal Law

There are forms of criminal law scholarship that shade into criminology, but a powerful case can be made for saying that some elements of criminal law scholarship are essential to criminology. Take the criminalization debate.[2] Philosophers of criminal law, and criminal lawyers with an interest in normative theory, are much occupied with examining the justifications for making any particular form of conduct (call it *X*) into a criminal offence. Are there any criteria that ought to be satisfied before the legislature takes the step of criminalizing *X*, a step that entails official censure and the prospect of a sentence that will take away significant rights? Are there any restrictive principles, which might tell against criminalization even if it is decided that conduct *X* fulfils the criteria? These are normative questions, not new but certainly current (Husak 2007; Duff 2007). The disciplines here are philosophy and law, and the philosophical justifications reach well down into moral and political philosophy and, ultimately, into basic philosophical orientations such as liberalism or Marxism. The philosophy of the criminal law has established itself as a sub-discipline,[3] with a focus on the viability of concepts used in criminal law (such as causation (eg Hart and Honore 1985) or intention (eg Duff 1991)) and on the rationales for certain rules (eg for admitting certain circumstances as an excuse or as a justification for given conduct (eg Horder 2004; Gardner 2008). Most English-language writers are in the liberal tradition, but not all (eg Norrie 2001; Ramsay 2009).

When one moves from the theoretical to the actual, one finds, not surprisingly, that there is no coherent strategy for criminalization in many countries. In the United Kingdom the decision to create a crime is often a political reaction to a few much-publicized cases—creating a criminal offence is taken to be unambiguous proof that the government is committed to 'doing something about' a certain form of (mis)conduct. 'Emergence studies' of particular criminal laws can be largely historical or more socio-legal, but they are not so much concerned with assessing the strength of the justifications for creating the new crime as with charting the forces and influences that led to the law finding its way on to the statute book in that particular form.

Why are these issues relevant to criminology? Some of the insights of labelling theory remain important. Even if it is an exaggeration to suggest that no form of conduct is inherently criminal (Rock 1974; cf Felson's chapter in this volume), it is certainly true that many forms of conduct are only criminalized in particular countries at a particular time. This leads, in crude terms, to the proposition that it is a possible weakness of criminological theories that purport to explain criminality (on psychological, social or other causal grounds) that there is no constant concept of crime. What is criminal is, to a considerable extent, historically and geographically

[2] Also discussed by Lucia Zedner in her chapter.

[3] eg from Hart (1968) to Feinberg (1984, 1985, 1986, 1988) and Shute, Horder and Gardner (1993) and Duff (1998); see also last note.

contingent. In England and Wales, some sexual conduct is criminal now but was not ten years ago, and vice versa; and some sexual conduct that is criminal in England and Wales is not criminal in Scotland. As one surveys European jurisdictions, one finds other examples in economic crime, in defamation of public officials (criminal in several countries but not in the United Kingdom), and so on. So any references to the 'causes of crime' must be premised on a suitably circumspect concept of crime. Thus criminologists, of some hues at least, need to be aware of certain slices of criminal law scholarship.

Even criminal lawyers cannot be confident of the boundaries of their own discipline, however. More and more offences in England and Wales today are created by government ministers exercising powers delegated to them by Parliament, which means that the details of the crime are not debated in the legislature and many people are unaware of them until they start being enforced. This is unsatisfactory: it is said to be necessary in order to allow this country to keep up with European directives and new forms of criminality, but it bypasses public debate and may give insufficient warning to citizens. There is also a different kind of readjustment of the boundaries taking place. In some spheres, the English government prefers to adopt a civil law approach instead of the criminal law, and thus we have seen the rapid development of 'civil preventive orders' (see, eg Burney 2005; Squires and Stephen 2005; Macdonald 2006; Ramsay 2009; Ashworth and Zedner 2008; cf Steiker 1998 on similar developments in the United States). In essence, these take the form of a two-step prohibition, and the anti-social behaviour order (ASBO) is the prime example (Simester and von Hirsch 2007): an order may be made where the court finds that the defendant has acted in an anti-social manner, ie 'in a manner that caused or was likely to cause harassment, alarm or distress,' and that an order is necessary to protect persons from further such behaviour. The court may then make an order 'which prohibits the defendant from doing anything described in the order' for the next two years. Breach of this civil order is a criminal offence, with a maximum punishment of five years' imprisonment. What is noticeable here is the delegation to the civil court of the decision on what prohibitions to insert into the order (in effect, a personal criminal code for the individual concerned), reinforced by a genuine criminal offence with a high maximum penalty in the event of any breach of the civil order. The government chose this approach because it believed that the criminal law and its procedures were failing to deal adequately with certain neighbourhood nuisances: the criminal law caters only for specific incidents, not capturing the whole course of conduct, and it requires those who have witnessed the events to give evidence, which they were frequently unwilling to do. Already there are more than a dozen of these civil preventive orders, a topic for enquiry in its own right (See Ashworth and Zedner 2010). Moreover, they have great significance for criminology, in terms not merely of over-criminalization (well documented and much discussed (eg Husak 2007)) but also of under-criminalization, as demonstrated tellingly in Lucia Zedner's chapter in this volume. Criminologists cannot take the boundaries of the criminal law for granted, therefore. Those boundaries are contestable, shifting and permeable. They are moving, not just one way (extending the criminal law) but also another and no less sinister way (civil preventive orders, backed by a powerful criminal offence).

The Criminal Justice 'System'

The emergence of civil preventive orders was as much about the alleged shortcomings of criminal procedure as about the alleged problems of the traditional criminal law, and that projects us into the realm of criminal justice. It is not being asserted here that criminal justice in England and Wales or anywhere else constitutes a 'system'; the term 'criminal justice system' is being used for convenience, and nothing more. As suggested earlier, it encompasses institutions such as the police, prosecutors, the probation service, the prison service, the judiciary and magistracy, parole boards and so forth. It should also encompass the procedures and powers of these institutional actors, particularly the law relating to criminal evidence, criminal procedure and sentencing, as well as the roles and working practices of the various criminal justice agents.

Major changes are afoot here. In recent years there has been a rapid increase in out-of-court disposals, such that the police, the Crown Prosecution Service, Her Majesty's Revenue and Customs and some other regulatory agencies have an increasing repertoire of powers to impose financial penalties for offences. Regulatory agencies have had powers of this kind for many years (see the study by Hawkins 2003), but in relation to the police the movement began in the 1990s with fixed penalty notices for certain motor vehicle and road traffic offences. It then spread to penalty notices for disorder, empowering the police (and, for some offences, community support officers) to impose a PND for various offences such as public drunkenness and causing harassment, alarm or distress, and was then extended to minor cases of theft from shops and criminal damage. Although the ticketed person can decline the penalty and opt to be prosecuted in court, that takes a strong will. It may also be an uninformed decision: many citizens will not know that, although a PND does not require an admission of guilt (unlike cautions) or rank as a conviction, PNDs are recorded on the Police National Computer and may become relevant when applying for a job or trying to enter the United States, for example. The role and powers of the Crown Prosecution Service have also been expanded through the arrival of conditional cautions, another 'alternative to prosecution' that may or may not have a benevolent function, depending on the actual manner of its use. Largely as a result of this transfer of powers, some sittings of magistrates' courts are being cancelled.

These developments raise a whole host of normative and empirical questions. The normative questions concern the proper domain of out-of-court penalties: although there is no reason to suppose that the line was historically drawn in the 'right' place, should law enforcement agents such as the police (and regulatory agencies) be given powers that really amount to sentencing? Since these are significant financial penalties (up to £80, or around $120), they raise questions of equality of impact on the economic resources of poorer people. Should that not be a matter for a court in all cases? Similar normative questions arise with prosecutors: the 'conditional caution' introduced in England and Wales is the first real power of disposal given to the Crown Prosecution Service, whereas public prosecutors in other European countries have long had powers to impose financial and other measures. These developments are often welcomed as a form of diversion from the courts, for people whose offence or whose culpability does not warrant a court hearing. But where is the limit to this, and has it been reached or exceeded by some of the available powers? Then we move on to the empirical issues: it is vital to an understanding of powers of this kind that there is research into the working practices of various agents. Very little is known about how the police use PNDs and other out-of-court penalties, what effect the possibility of a PND has on police–citizen contacts, how citizens typically react to being handed a PND, and so forth. Very little is known about how the Crown Prosecution Service exercises its power to give conditional cautions. Indeed, there has been no general survey of the practices of prosecutors for many years,[4] and yet independent evidence on the actual use of legal powers by those entrusted with them is crucial.

A similar dearth of empirical evidence is to be found in another important area of criminal justice, the sentencing practices of the courts. Although there were several large-scale studies of the magistrates' courts some years ago (see Ashworth 2003 for a summary and appraisal), there has never been a thorough piece of empirical research into how judges in the Crown Court approach their tasks and follow or adapt the law and the guidelines. Two major studies failed to proceed beyond the pilot stage, one by Oxford researchers in 1981 (Ashworth, *et al.* 1984) and one by Cambridge researchers in 2008 (Dhami and Souza 2008). When Lord Lane, the then Lord Chief Justice, was explaining his reasons for refusing further access to the Oxford researchers in 1981, he mentioned that 'sentencing is an art and not a science' and that if people wanted to know how sentencing is carried out, they should read books on the law of sentencing. It is now both elementary and axiomatic that whether a particular part of the criminal justice system operates in the way it is supposed to is a matter for empirical enquiry, and cannot simply be assumed. Nor is this merely a question of having reliable statistics on sentencing outcomes, important as that is. It is more a question of gaining an understanding of typical judicial approaches to sentencing, of what motivates or influences the approach they take.

The study of criminal justice should not simply be about the functioning of the various parts of the system, from policing to parole, from prosecutions to sentencing. Nor should it be simply a matter of exposing and commenting upon the gap between the law in the books and the law in action, informative though that is. It

[4] Research by Baldwin (1997) is probably the last major project on prosecutors, and before that, McConville, Sanders and Leng (1991).

should also include a more philosophical assessment, examining the justifications for particular rules and practices. This normative aspect was mentioned in connection with out-of-court penalties above, and another prime example of it is sentencing, where it involves the practical application of what are often termed 'theories of punishment.' There is a long history of normative theories, including the utilitarian approach developed by Bentham which emphasizes the avoidance of punishment, with the use of a deterrent strategy in default, and also the liberal approach of the neo-Kantians, which is traceable in various contemporary writings such as those of von Hirsch (1993; Von Hirsch and Ashworth 2005; see also Lippke 2007) and of Duff (2001). Theoretical debates about sentencing also reach into middle-range issues of great practical significance, such as the extent to which previous convictions should have a bearing on sentencing (see Roberts 2008), whether there should be a sentence discount for pleading guilty, which factors should or should not aggravate or mitigate sentence, and the proper approach to sentencing women (see Corston 2007). Can the answers to those various questions be deduced from some general theory of sentencing,[5] or do normative arguments from other sources (for example, principles of social equality, or human rights) properly flow into debates on those questions?

Sentencing principles and practice are crucial to a proper understanding of the size of the prison population in a given jurisdiction—even though they only represent an intermediate stage, between the creation of public policy on the one hand and the operation of imprisonment and release mechanisms on the other hand. One feature of sentencing in many US jurisdictions and latterly in England and Wales has been the introduction of sentencing guidelines. This development may be normatively attractive in the sense that it has gradually brought the rule of law into sentencing decisions, structuring the discretion that has for too long been their primary characteristic; but guidelines are merely vessels or channels, and just as a notably repressive state could still comply meticulously with rule-of-law values, so a sentencing guideline system could sustain sentence levels that are high, medium, or low. Furthermore, although some of the state guideline systems in the United States have good data on compliance, there is no systematic information in England and Wales on the extent to which guidelines constrain or influence judges and magistrates in their day-to-day sentencing. In the absence of empirical data, to make a statement about the 'effects' of sentencing guidelines may therefore be no more than to commit the classic error of assuming that sentencing practice reflects the formal rules and guidelines. A proper understanding and critique of criminal justice must therefore be premised on reliable empirical research as well as on relevant normative theorizing.

One of the perennial questions in criminology and criminal justice is whether those who have research interests in these fields ought to engage in public policy debates or even in practical decision-making within those fields. In these days when

[5] Or even from a general theory of criminal justice: see Braithwaite and Pettit (1990).

expert opinion is often regarded as elitist or detached from grim reality—particularly if it is not supported by detailed empirical research—this is a difficult path to tread. It is fair to say that in England and Wales the effect of 'expert' opinion in matters of criminal justice has declined. If the Criminal Justice Act 1991 was the high point of such influence, then much of the legislation in the first decade of the new century has been at the other end of the spectrum. Over some 30–40 years there has been strong academic criticism of the sentence discount for pleading guilty (eg, Baldwin and McConville 1977; McConville 2000; Ashworth 2010), on the basis that it introduces perverse incentives into defendants' decision-making and may lead some innocent people to plead guilty, but the critique has exerted no discernible effect on public policy. The Runciman Royal Commission offered a defence of the discount system (Royal Commission on Criminal Justice 1993: chapter 7), and this (although poorly reasoned and ultimately unconvincing) appears to have been just what governments and the courts wanted to hear, since the incentives to plead guilty have been increased in recent years.[6] The proposal for sentencing guidelines created by a broadly based Sentencing Council in this country had an academic origin (Ashworth 1983), but this is evidence that certain ideas may have their political day, rather than evidence of any ongoing relationship between policy-makers and the academy. The Sentencing Advisory Panel, created in 1999, operated for ten years without any political interference and with academic voices being heard at the table. It was a body with a diverse membership, including present and former criminal justice professionals as well as lay members (with backgrounds in business, education, medicine etc.), and academic arguments have certainly been listened to with respect, if not always adopted. A seat at the table is some recognition of the value of criminal justice scholarship, and the legislation creating the new Sentencing Council provides for at least one academic member to be appointed to that body.[7]

Criminal Justice or Criminology?

Much of the discussion in the last few paragraphs has been about criminal justice, and about different strains (empirical, normative) of criminal justice scholarship. Some would say that, when reference is made to empirical research as a necessary element in any rounded study of criminal justice, that imports a criminological element. This may suggest that a particular methodology (empirical research, presumably whether it is qualitative or quantitative) is the preserve of criminology, whereas criminal justice is more about the law and the theory of the particular institutions

[6] eg through the (repeated) statutory recognition of the sentence discount for pleading guilty, and the consequent guidelines issued by the Sentencing Guidelines Council (2008); see also the *Goodyear* system of sentence indications, discussed by Ashworth (2010: chapter 5).

[7] Coroners and Justice Act 2009, Sch. 15.

that go to make up the system. But if there is a distinction between criminal justice and criminology, it may not necessarily be about the methodologies typically employed. We may just have fallen into the habit of describing empirical research into criminal justice institutions as criminological research, when there might be a good argument for calling it criminal justice research. A similar view could be taken of another much-discussed body of scholarship not mentioned so far—the work of O'Malley (1992) and of Garland (2001) and others,[8] and more recently of Cavadino and Dignan (2006) and of Lacey (2008), who trace trends in criminal policy, expose tendencies and conflicts, and characterize particular positions on crime and state responses to it. That is commonly described as criminological theory, but in large measure it is criminal justice theory, since its primary concern is with governmental and institutional response to crime.

The argument here, then, is that a great deal of what is commonly regarded as criminology is in fact the study of criminal justice. This assumes that 'criminal justice' is chiefly concerned with the institutions of the criminal justice system, and the roles and practices of those who work within them. Some would say that it should also include the legal rules and guidelines that those working within the criminal justice system are supposed to apply, whereas others would insist that those fall squarely within the separate discipline of law, notably criminal law and criminal procedure. This taxonomy would leave 'criminology' as having two possible senses—the narrow sense of a study of the causes of offending, focusing on individuals in their social setting; and the broader all-encompassing notion of criminology that is taken to cover all studies of crime, criminals and official responses to them. None of these distinctions should be taken to suggest that those who self-identify as criminologists should be doing anything different from now, save for the argument that definitions of crime have such a fundamental relationship to criminology (howsoever defined) that more attention should be given to studying aspects of criminal law. The particular aspect that is relevant is criminalization, or the boundaries of the criminal law, and it is arguable that criminal lawyers should do more to make this topic accessible and to draw attention to significant trends and changes. Criminologists should be aware of the malleability of the basic concept of a crime and of the shifting boundaries of the criminal law—together with the arrival of civil preventive orders, sitting on or over the boundary of the criminal law, as elaborated in Lucia Zedner's chapter. Civil preventive orders (notably the anti-social behaviour order) allow prohibitions to be imposed on a person according to civil procedure, reinforced by an offence with a maximum sentence of five years' imprisonment in the event of breach; and since about half of those who breach orders receive custody, this recent phenomenon cannot be dismissed as a minor deviation from the norm. Thus the inter-relations between criminology, criminal justice and criminal law have complexities that run all the way through; but the absence of basic research into the practices of police,

[8] A fuller roll-call is surely not necessary here.

prosecutors, sentencers and others—whether it be called criminological or criminal justice research—is a major handicap to proper development of policy and theory.

References

Ashworth, A. (1983), 'Reducing the Prison Population in the 1980s: the Need for Sentencing Reform', in NACRO, *A Sentencing System for the Eighties and Beyond*, London: NACRO.

_____ (2003), 'Sentencing and Sensitivity', in L. Zedner and A. Ashworth (eds), *The Criminological Foundations of Public Policy*, Oxford: Oxford University Press.

_____ (2010), *Sentencing and Criminal Justice*, 5th edn, Cambridge: Cambridge University Press.

_____, Genders, E., Peay, J., and Player, E. (1984), *Sentencing in the Crown Court: Report of an Exploratory Study*, Oxford: University of Oxford Centre for Criminological Research.

_____ and Zedner, L. (2008), 'Defending the Criminal Law', *Criminal Law and Philosophy*, 2: 21–51.

_____ and Zedner, L. (2010), 'Preventive Orders: a Problem of Under-Criminalization?' in R. A. Duff, L. Farmer, S. Marshall, and V. Tadros (eds), *Criminalization*, Oxford: Oxford University Press.

Baldwin, J. (1997), 'Understanding Judge Ordered and Directed Acquittals in the Crown Court,' *Criminal Law Review*, 536–8.

_____ and McConville, M. (1977), *Negotiated Justice*, Oxford: Martin Robertson.

Braithwaite, J. and Pettit, P. (1990), *Not Just Deserts*, Oxford: Oxford University Press.

Burney, E. (2005), *Making People Behave*, Cullompton: Willan.

Cavadino, M. and Dignan, J. (2006), *Penal Systems: A Comparative Approach*, London: Sage.

Corston, J. (2007), *Review of Women with Particular Vulnerabilities in the Criminal Justice System*, London: Home Office.

Dhami, M. and Souza, K. (2009), *Study of Sentencing and its Outcomes: Pilot Report*, London: Ministry of Justice Research Series 2/09.

Duff, R. A. (1991), *Intention, Agency and Criminal Liability*, Oxford: Blackwell.

_____ (ed.) (1998), *Philosophy and the Criminal Law*, Cambridge: Cambridge University Press.

_____ (2001), *Punishment, Communication and Community*, New York: Oxford University Press.

_____ (2007), *Answering for Crime*, Oxford: Hart Publishing.

Feinberg, J. (1984), *The Moral Limits of the Criminal Law: vol. 1, Harm to Others*, New York: Oxford University Press

_____ (1985), *The Moral Limits of the Criminal Law: vol. 2, Offense to Others*, New York: Oxford University Press

_____ (1986), *The Moral Limits of the Criminal Law: vol. 3, Harm to Self*, New York: Oxford University Press

_____ (1988), *The Moral Limits of the Criminal Law: vol. 4, Harmless Wrongdoing*, New York: Oxford University Press.

Gardner, J. (2008), *Offences and Defences*, Oxford: Oxford University Press.
Garland, D. (2001), *The Culture of Control*, Oxford: Oxford University Press.
Hart, H. L. A. (1968), *Punishment and Responsibility*, Oxford: Oxford University Press.
_____ and Honore, T. (1985), *Causation in the Law*, 2nd edn, Oxford: Oxford University Press.
Hawkins, K. (2003), *Law as Last Resort*, Oxford: Oxford University Press.
Horder, J. (2004), *Excusing Crime*, Oxford: Oxford University Press.
Husak, D. (2007), *Overcriminalization*, New York: Oxford University Press.
Lacey, N. (2007), 'Legal Constructions of Crime', in M. Maguire, R. Morgan, and R. Reiner (eds), *The Oxford Handbook of Criminology*, 4th edn, Oxford: Oxford University Press.
_____ (2008), *The Prisoners' Dilemma*, Cambridge: Cambridge University Press.
Lippke, R. (2007), *Rethinking Imprisonment*, Oxford: Oxford University Press.
Macdonald, S. (2006), 'A Suicidal Woman, Roaming Pigs and a Noisy Trampolinist: Refining the ASBO's Definition of Anti-Social Behaviour', *Modern Law Review*, 69: 183–213.
McConville, M. (2000), 'Plea-Bargaining: Ethics and Politics', in S. Doran and J. Jackson (eds), *The Judicial Role in Criminal Proceedings*, Oxford: Hart Publishing.
_____, Sanders, A., and Leng, R. (1991), *The Case for the Prosecution*, London: Routledge.
Norrie, A. (2001), *Crime, Reason and History*, London: Butterworths.
O'Malley, P. (1992), 'Risk, Power and Crime Prevention', *Economy and Society*, 21: 252–75.
Ramsay, P. (2009), 'The Theory of Vulnerable Autonomy and the Legitimacy of Civil Preventive Orders', in B. McSherry, A. Norrie, and S. Bronitt (eds), *Regulating Deviance*, Oxford: Hart Publishing.
Roberts, J. (2008), *Punishing Persistent Offenders*, Oxford: Oxford University Press.
Rock, P. (1974), 'The Sociology of Deviancy and Conceptions of Moral Order,' *British Journal of Criminology*, 14: 139–49.
Royal Commission on Criminal Justice (1993), *Report*, London: HM Stationery Office.
Sentencing Guidelines Council (2007), *Reduction in Sentence for a Guilty Plea: Definitive Guideline (Revised)* (<www.sentencing-guidelines.gov.uk>).
Shute, S., Horder, J., and Gardner, J. (eds) (1993), *Action and Value in the Criminal Law*, Oxford: Oxford University Press.
Simester, A. P. and von Hirsch, A. (2007), 'Regulating Offensive Conduct through Two-Step Prohibitions', in A. von Hirsch and A. P. Simester (eds), *Incivilities: Regulating Offensive Behaviour*, Oxford: Hart Publishing.
Squires, P. and Stephen, D. (2005), *Rougher Justice: Anti-Social Behaviour and Young People*, Cullompton: Willan.
Steiker, C. (1998), 'The Limits of the Preventive State', *Journal of Criminal Law and Criminology*, 88: 771.
Von Hirsch, A. (1993), *Censure and Sanctions*, Oxford: Oxford University Press.
_____ and Ashworth, A. (2005), *Proportionate Sentencing*, Oxford: Oxford University Press.

23

CRIMINOLOGY, ACCOUNTABILITY, AND INTERNATIONAL JUSTICE

WILLIAM A. SCHABAS*

INTERNATIONAL criminal justice has barely engaged with the discipline of criminology, and vice versa. For example, international criminal justice does not find any place in *The Oxford Handbook of Criminology* (Maguire *et al.* 2007) or *The Handbook of Crime and Punishment* (Tonry 1998). Probably this is because the phenomenon of international crimes is viewed within the field as more a matter of politics than sociology. On the legal side, there is an attempt by some of the lawyers to exclude the social sciences, by reducing prosecution to absolute principles and dismissing the relevance of factors such as peace building, reconciliation and social reinsertion of offenders. Sometimes this is done in the name of legal rigour and sometimes its proponents invoke the rights of victims as justification. International criminal law could benefit from greater openness to the social sciences. Criminologists might

* OC, MRIA, Professor of Human Rights Law, National University of Ireland, Galway, and Director, Irish Centre for Human Rights.

break some paths here by developing more sophisticated approaches to the specifics of crime when perpetrated in time of conflict, or by brutal regimes.

One of the most important international legal developments of the past sixty years or so has been the adoption and progressive enlargement of international human rights norms. Beginning with the Universal Declaration of Human Rights, in December 1948, a complex web of treaties, declarations and other standard-setting documents, accompanied by a multitude of monitoring and enforcement bodies, has emerged. Today, the United Nations Human Rights Council sits more or less permanently in Geneva. Its work is backed up by the Office of the High Commissioner for Human Rights, with about 1,000 employees based in Geneva and the many field presences throughout the world. Hundreds of unpaid experts provide a support network of special rapporteurs, working groups and treaty bodies.

Historically, human rights law's interface with crime and criminal justice took place virtually exclusively within a context of arrest and pre-trial detention, fair trial standards and requirements of acceptable prison conditions. The focus was invariably on the suspect, the accused and the convicted detainee, who were viewed as victims of human rights violations perpetrated by the criminal justice system. Seminal instruments were developed within bodies like the United Nations Congress on the Prevention of Crime and the Treatment of Offenders, such as the Standard Minimum Rules for the Treatment of Prisoners[1] and the Safeguards guaranteeing protection of the rights of those facing the death penalty.[2] One of the primary human rights treaties, the International Covenant on Civil and Political Rights, adopted in 1966, declared that 'The penitentiary system shall comprise treatment of prisoners the essential aim of which shall be their reformation and social rehabilitation.'[3] Non-governmental organizations emerged with names like 'Amnesty' as if to underscore their tension with criminal justice.

During the 1980s, this one-sided focus on criminal justice as a source of human rights violations began to change. Human rights institutions became concerned with the role that prosecution might play in the enforcement of human rights, an idea that was probably present in human rights discourse from the beginning but that had hitherto remained undeveloped. Normative debates soon began to focus on such matters as the 'duty to prosecute', accountability, and combating impunity. This shift in orientation was further nourished by a growth in attention to the rights of victims, reflected in the 1985 Declaration of Basic Principles of Justice for Victims of Crime and Abuse of Power.[4] International human rights courts and commissions adopted rulings finding that states were in violation of their obligations because they had failed to investigate and prosecute alleged crimes.[5] Where national justice sys-

[1] ECOSOC Res. 663 C (XXIV); ECOSOC Res. 2076 (LXII). [2] GA Res. 1984/50.

[3] International Covenant on Civil and Political Rights, (1976) 999 UNTS 171, Art. 10(3).

[4] UN Doc. A/RES/40/34.

[5] *Velasquez Rodriguez v Honduras*, 29 July 1988, Series C, No. 4 (Inter-American Court of Human Rights).

tems were themselves unwilling or unable to prosecute crimes, especially those associated with conflict and political turmoil, international law stepped in to propose the establishment of international criminal tribunals, like the International Criminal Tribunal for the former Yugoslavia and the International Criminal Court.

In many ways, international human rights law has now turned full circle, from a vision of criminal justice rooted in opposition to prosecutors and prison officials to one that sometimes calls for rigorous prosecution and harsh, retributive sentences. This is not to say that it has become indifferent to issues of fairness and detention in criminal proceedings. But there is now a tension, and arguably some confusion in the perspective adopted. One form in which this manifests itself is debates about principles of sentencing, especially when international crimes such as genocide, crimes against humanity and war crimes are involved. Often, judges at the international tribunals insist that deterrence and retribution are the primary goals of sentencing, dismissing any significant consideration of rehabilitation and social reinsertion. There is also some resistance to such traditional, conservative approaches. A recent ruling of the European Court of Human Rights pursued the emphasis on the duty to prosecute, holding that Bulgarian prosecutors had been remiss in failing to proceed with an investigation in a 'date rape' case because there was no material evidence that the victim had offered physical resistance. Although she agreed with the majority that there had been a violation, Judge Françoise Tulkens, a distinguished Belgian criminal law professor, cautioned that 'criminal proceedings should remain, both in theory and in practice, a last resort or subsidiary remedy and that their use, even in the context of positive obligations, calls for a certain degree of "restraint" '.[6] But hers is a rather isolated voice, struggling for balance in a climate that is increasingly keen on the use of criminal justice to ensure respect for and to enforce human rights.

The Bulgarian date rape case shows that from the standpoint of human rights law, the obligation to investigate and prosecute applies to all serious crimes against the person. It is certainly present for intentional homicide and rape. The authorities have yet to clarify where the low end of this obligation might lie. Might it not also apply to theft or vandalism? The justification for what is sometimes called a 'procedural obligation' is rooted in the rights of victims: justice must be done because the victims are entitled to it. On what basis, then, could a bright line be drawn between 'serious' human rights violations for which victims have a right to see the perpetrators brought to justice and those deemed 'less serious' for which they do not? If anything, placing this priority on criminal justice within the framework of the human rights of the victim invites recognition that the right to prosecution, like most if not all human rights, is subject to limitations. Article 29(2) of the Universal Declaration of Human Rights states that human rights are subject 'to such limitations as are determined by law solely for the purpose of securing due recognition and respect for

[6] *MC v Bulgaria*, No. 39272/98, Judgment, 4 December 2003, Concurring Opinion of Judge Tulkens, para. 2.

the rights and freedoms of others and of meeting the just requirements of morality, public order and the general welfare in a democratic society'. But it is only reasonable that a human right to have violations addressed by a criminal justice system is dependent upon the resources of that system. It is too much to ask a state to provide uncompromising justice, where the potentially high costs may come at the expense of other priorities, such as health care and education.

Few if any of these issues, when they are considered within a human rights framework, are informed by criminological research. Occasionally, there is some perfunctory reference to the goals of punishment and the limitations of justice. Most of the comments in the human rights and international criminal case law on the theoretical foundations and the purposes of criminal justice, however, are marked by amateurishness. The perspective that human rights lawyers take to the phenomenon of crime is driven more by intuition than anything else. This is most acute in discussions about what is often called 'transitional justice' (or sometimes, 'post-conflict justice').

The term 'transitional justice' appears to have been coined in the early 1990s by legal scholars as part of efforts to analyse the issues of prosecution and vetting that arose in states of eastern and central Europe following the collapse of socialism, the truth commission processes in such countries as Chile and South Africa, and international prosecutions by bodies like the International Criminal Tribunal for the former Yugoslavia and the International Criminal Tribunal for Rwanda (Kritz 1995; Teitel 2000). For both criminal lawyers and criminologists, these have been relatively uncharted waters. What are sometimes called 'atrocity crimes'—genocide, crimes against humanity, war crimes—sit at the heart of the attempts to bring criminal justice to bear upon the behaviour of past regimes, or the conduct of combatants during civil wars.

The terrible consequences of these crimes may make 'ordinary' crimes committed in peacetime by social deviants look insignificant, even trivial. Their extraordinary gravity is often expressed by phrases like 'crimes that shock the conscience of humanity'.[7] At Nuremberg, where it all began, prosecutor Robert Jackson spoke of acts that were 'shocking and revolting to the common instincts of civilized peoples'.[8] He said the Nazi crimes were 'so calculated, so malignant, and so devastating, that civilization cannot tolerate their being ignored, because it cannot survive their being repeated.'[9] They were, of course, repeated, in Cambodia and Rwanda and many other places.

But the suggestion that such 'atrocity crimes' are distinguished by their particularly shocking nature does not seem to provide an entirely satisfactory explanation. Why is an atrocious murder of a single individual unworthy of international attention? How do we explain the first trial at the International Criminal Court, where

[7] Rome Statute of the International Criminal Court, (2002) 2187 UNTS 90, preambular para. 2.

[8] *France et al. v Göring et al.* (1948) 2 IMT 242.

[9] Ibid., p. 99.

charges are based upon the enlistment and recruitment of child soldiers, and where there is nothing in the accusations that reposes upon physical violence against the teenage combatants, many of whom joined voluntarily? There is no single explanation to account for the internationalization of crimes. Although sheer horror seems a relevant factor, perhaps the involvement of the state and the discriminatory dimension of the punishable act are also important.

So-called 'transitional justice' often seems to involve the application of criminal justice paradigms drawn from the context of 'ordinary' crimes to situations of mass criminality perpetrated in a political context. In a technical sense, of course, the subject-matter is the commission of acts that have the same common denominator as ordinary criminality: homicide, violence against the person, sexual abuse, etc. But there is little if any effort by practitioners to develop a sophisticated understanding of the criminological aspects of human behaviour when atrocity crimes are concerned. In fact, much of the discourse is characterized by simplistic formulations or clichés, such as 'we need to bring people to justice so that these crimes will not be repeated' and 'if we do not provide the victims with satisfaction, there will be a renewed cycle of violence a generation later'. A popular slogan in the field is 'no peace without justice'. In a sense, it links justice to the quest for peace in a context of conflict; but it usually metamorphoses into a more absolute proposition, by which peace without justice is profoundly flawed. It is also frequently stated that 'victims need to know the truth' so that they can obtain 'closure'. Very often, transitional justice is carried out in the name of 'reconciliation'. Hence, the establishment of truth and reconciliation commissions is posited as an almost indispensible component, a panacea in the process. But is any of this really borne out by scientific evidence of the sort that we expect from criminologists when assertions are made about ordinary criminality?

The first controversial proposition that bears closer examination is the claim that without justice there can be no reconciliation. International justice is a relatively recent phenomenon, and one that is still only very sporadic. It is difficult to prepare an adequate set of case studies in which justice was delivered and where reconciliation followed. But, of course, that really is not the problem. What about all of the cases in which there was no justice? That pretty much sums up this history of the world prior to Nuremberg. Did people never reconcile prior to Nuremberg, and before we had discovered international trials and truth commissions? In modern times, we have no shortage of examples where civil wars accompanied essentially by impunity for the atrocities that were committed were followed by significant periods of social harmony and stability. Spain is a good example here. After three years of brutal conflict in the 1930s, followed by more than three decades of dictatorship, it was transformed quickly into a modern, prosperous and well-adjusted society. There are rumblings of investigation, and occasional complaints from 'victims' that justice should be done. The ubiquitous Judge Garzon is trying to excavate graves that date back to the civil war. But it is very difficult to know whether the renewed interest in accountability is a consequence of impunity, or simply efforts by those who subscribe to 'no reconciliation without justice' to prove that the apparent anomaly of Spain is no exception to the rule. In reality, reconciliation following conflict is a complex process that seems dependent upon many variables.

This does not mean that post-conflict justice is undesirable, of course. But at the very least the argument that justice is necessary if reconciliation is to be achieved is unproven. In these discussions, there are occasional references to 'restorative justice', a concept that is familiar enough to criminologists (see, eg, Todorov 2009). Restorative justice is said to have salutary effects for both victim and perpetrator. This is probably also the case in situations of mass atrocity. Indeed, encouraging a relationship between the victims and their former tormentors is one of the functions of truth and reconciliation commissions. The author witnessed this first hand as a member of the Sierra Leone Truth and Reconciliation Commission, which held hearings during 2003. On many occasions, perpetrators of serious human rights violations (and international crimes) confessed to their deeds in well-attended public hearings, often expressing remorse and seeking the forgiveness of their victims. Often, these encounters were very inspiring, particularly when victims indicated their satisfaction. But there were two big limitations. The first was that the actual numbers of individuals involved were relatively small, really only a handful of individuals, if nothing else a consequence of the meagre resources of the Commission and the short period of time that it had in which to conduct its mandate. There was always the hope that such public exchanges between perpetrator and victim would set an example that would be replicated within communities. But there is no evidence that this actually took place. The second is the enormous difficulties in actually identifying the perpetrators in such cases of mass atrocities. In Sierra Leone, most victims had no idea of the identity of those responsible for atrocities except in the most general sense. The perpetrators came from another part of the country, and spoke another language, we were frequently told by witnesses. All told, restorative justice as it is understood in the context of ordinary crimes will probably be of limited relevance and application to situations of mass atrocity in civil wars.

Many advocates of uncompromising criminal prosecution do not insist that much on the utilitarian benefits of justice for future peace and reconciliation. Instead, they dwell upon the argument that victims have a right to justice, a right that exists regardless of whether or not society as a whole may benefit. Sometimes, this is couched in legal claims that are often intimidating for non-jurists. Using terms like *jus cogens*, 'peremptory norms' and 'non-derogability', proponents of this view claim that justice must be done because it is a requirement of international law. The principle is said to override all other considerations: *Fiat justitia, et pereat mundus*. This legalistic claim can be readily dismissed. There is, at present, no universal legal norm that prevents governments from declining to prosecute, whether by simple inactivity or by formal amnesty. Even the United Nations acknowledged this implicitly when it challenged the amnesty accorded in Sierra Leone, but then provided enough resources to try a dozen people, in effect ensuring impunity for tens of thousands of others. Had the organization, and the countries that funded the Special Court for Sierra Leone, truly believed in justice at any price, they could not logically have confined themselves to prosecutions that were, at best, symbolic.

Probably the best example of international tolerance of impunity concerns apartheid-era South Africa. Apartheid is a crime against humanity and, in principle, there should be just as much eagerness internationally to deal with crimes of the former South African regime as there is with respect to Pol Pot in Cambodia or any of the other issues that feature on international radar screens. Why, then, are white South Africans associated with the pre-1994 government not routinely arrested when they travel to Europe, and elsewhere? Why is Mandela himself not threatened with international prosecution for failure to punish such crimes? There is a simple answer, of course. The world accepts—and respects—the peaceful transition in South Africa, although it was carried out without any prosecution for the crime against humanity of apartheid.

The argument that justice must be done because individual victims so require is often accompanied by a total indifference to the consequences that this may have upon a peace process. Some go so far as to claim that peace negotiations should not be pursued if amnesty is an issue. Put another way, although few like it to be formulated so, it is posited that armed conflict should continue until peace can be achieved without compromising justice. For those who cherish peace, and see it as a goal that may sometimes be even superior to that of 'justice', this is a hard argument to swallow. This 'peace v justice' debate has figured in important discussions at the young International Criminal Court. In the first situation examined by the Court, the civil war in northern Uganda, the issuance of arrest warrants against five rebel leaders appears to have prompted the suspects to sue for peace. For nearly two decades, the government had been unable to secure a military victory. Once the threat of prosecution by the International Criminal Court was added to the calculus, the rebels were willing to negotiate. But because one of the reasons they were prepared to end the conflict was the pending charges at the Court, their removal was one of the important issues in the peace talks. The government was more than willing to compromise on this point. The International Criminal Court, backed by European states and international non-governmental organisations, was more intransigent. This did not stop the Court and its defenders from trying to take credit for the rebels' willingness to negotiate an end to the conflict. It was evidence of the Court's deterrent effect, they said. But when there was no flexibility about suspending or withdrawing the charges, the talks broke down and the conflict resumed. The threat of prosecution may well have been a deterrent, and to have contributed to a temporary end to the conflict. The problem is that unless the Court is willing to temper justice in the interests of peace, this sort of thing can only happen once. In the future, rebels who know of how things turned out in Uganda will not be induced to seek peace in response to international criminal charges, because they will have learned that such matters are not negotiable, at least as far as the Court is concerned.

International criminal justice has other examples along similar lines. In June 2003, the Prosecutor of the Special Court for Sierra Leone tried to arrest Liberian President Charles Taylor while he was out of his country attending a peace conference in Ghana. A trap was sprung, using a secret indictment. But Ghana refused to arrest Taylor, who returned to Liberia. The peace talks were temporarily aborted. The Prosecutor said it was just as well, because nobody could successfully make peace with Taylor anyway, charging that he was dishonest and in bad faith. Nevertheless, two months later, peace talks were successful and the lengthy and brutal conflict in Liberia came to an end. The price to be paid was impunity for Taylor. He was given asylum in nearby Nigeria. Years later, Nigeria caved in to international pressure and handed Taylor over to the Special Court. Here is an example of a conflict being successfully concluded, at the expense of justice, but where justice eventually triumphed. The problem will be repeating the gambit. In the future, African leaders to whom asylum or immunity is offered in exchange for leaving power will look to Taylor's case and see a double-cross. In effect, a useful and effective mechanism to bring an end to conflict has been discarded from the toolbox of the negotiator in the name of uncompromising criminal prosecution.

Although they are often presented as alternatives, some elements of transitional justice are shared by criminal prosecutions and truth commissions. Both institutions are involved in the search for truth, each in its own way. Like justice, truth is held out as both an entitlement of victims and a necessity of reconciliation. Indeed, this is one of the premises behind so-called truth commissions. There have been many initiatives within United Nations human rights bodies in recent years aimed at recognizing a 'right to truth', although nothing of the sort is expressed as such in the Universal Declaration of Human Rights and the other human rights instruments.

The South African Truth and Reconciliation Commission determined that there were different sorts of truth. At the lowest level, there is a form of forensic truth: who did what to whom? At the highest, there is a more political truth whose purpose is to establish common understandings about historical events and periods. This sometimes takes the form of legislative resolutions and similar measures where, for example, parliaments are asked to adopt statements declaring Turkey responsible for the crime of genocide against the Armenians in 1915. The international criminal tribunals themselves have contributed to this process of determining historical truth, either because of the near-universal acceptance of their findings as authoritative—Nuremberg is the example here—or by formal declaration. After repetitive production by the Prosecutor of evidence that genocide was perpetrated in Rwanda, the Appeals Chamber of the International Criminal Tribunal took 'judicial notice' of this fact. Henceforth, it was unnecessary to prove something that had become common knowledge.[10]

[10] *Prosecutor v Karamera et al.* (Case No. ICTR-98-44-AR73(C)), Decision on Prosecutor's Interlocutory Appeal of Decision on Judicial Notice, 16 June 2006.

Litigants do not always appreciate the historical truth mission of international justice. Defence lawyers complain that their clients are victims of a system that has assumed a function other than the determination of guilt or innocence in individual cases. Some prosecutors, too, object to this additional burden. In a recent strategy paper, the Prosecutor of the International Criminal Court explained that his 'mandate does not include production of comprehensive historical records for a given conflict', although he acknowledged that in selecting specific violations for prosecution, there was an effort 'to provide a sample that is reflective of the gravest incidents and the main types of victimization'.[11]

This is where there are benefits to a truth and reconciliation commission that, in effect, assumes the responsibility for the broader historical narrative. It is not bound by rules of evidence, nor is it circumscribed by the jurisdictional obstacles that may prevent a criminal court from properly addressing all relevant matters.

The selection of situations and cases is an important dimension of international criminal prosecution that sets it apart from national prosecution. Certainly, national prosecutors make policy decisions that mean that certain crimes will be the focus of attention, a matter with huge resource implications. They may also decide that, for the good of society, criminal law provisions be left to atrophy. An example of this process is the decision of the Director of Public Prosecutions to delimit prosecutions in cases of assisted suicide, something that was in fact directed by judicial decision.[12] At the international level, there is no prospect that all serious cases of genocide, crimes against humanity and war crimes will be prosecuted, unlike at the national level where we assume that all serious crimes against the person will be dealt with. Tribunals sometimes explicitly limit their scope by focusing on 'those who bear the greatest responsibility' or some similar, nebulous formulation. Moreover, and this is an even more difficult matter to provide a proper legal scheme, they address one 'situation' and not another.

For example, in 2006 the Prosecutor of the International Criminal Court said he would not proceed against British troops and officials for crimes committed in occupied Iraq, despite his conclusion that there were serious grounds to believe the international war crimes of wilful killing and torture had been committed. He said that there were not enough cases—only ten or twenty—and that therefore the situation of British troops in Iraq was not 'serious' enough. Instead, the Prosecutor explained, he would devote his energy to central Africa, where there had been more killings (Office of the Prosecutor 2006). But even in central Africa, choices had to be made. Thus, in northern Uganda, he determined to address his efforts to crimes committed by the rebel Lord's Resistance Army leaders rather than atrocities perpetrated by Ugandan government forces, against whom there was no shortage of evidence of misconduct.

[11] 'Prosecutorial Strategy 2009-2012', 1 February 2010, para. 20.

[12] *R (on the application of Purdy) (Appellant) v Director of Public Prosecutions (Respondent)*, [2009] UKHL 45.

This problem of selection of situations, as well as of individual cases, gives international criminal justice an inherently political dimension. Prosecutors have tried to dodge this suggestion by claiming they operate on the basis of judicial criteria, but their explanations fail to convince. Of course, the dilemma of political choices goes back to the beginning of international criminal prosecution. At Nuremberg, this was not the responsibility of the prosecutors. They had already been directed to bring to trial only 'the major war criminals of the European Axis'. Within this narrow ambit, they were free to choose the individual defendants. But they could not, of course, opt to prosecute British leaders for the firebombing of Dresden in February 1945. Critics of the Nuremberg trial, like David Irving, dismiss this as 'victors' justice'. Not only does this make the trial unfair, say its detractors, this selectivity distorts the historical record and deprives the trial of its ability to contribute to reconciliation.

When the new generation of international criminal tribunals was created, beginning in the early 1990s, it was said that the flaw of victor's justice had been removed. But that has turned out to be a misperception. It is true that the Yugoslavia, Rwanda, and Sierra Leone courts were not explicitly directed to prosecute specific parties to the conflict. But the overall situations were certainly selected for them by the United Nations Security Council, a profoundly and unashamedly political body. As a result, while some atrocity crimes have been addressed, others—in Gaza, or Burma, or Chechnya, for example—escape any judicial scrutiny because of the real or threatened intervention of one or another of the permanent members of the Security Council. At the International Criminal Tribunal for Rwanda, the Prosecutor has come under intense pressure to prosecute what are called 'flipside' cases, directed against the Rwandese Patriotic Front that now holds power in Rwanda for alleged crimes against humanity committed during and in the aftermath of the 1994 conflict. Recently, an influential non-governmental organization, Human Rights Watch, charged that unless the International Tribunal prosecuted the other side, its work would be incomplete and it would fail in its mandate to promote reconciliation.

But is this really the case? The wisdom of criminologists and criminal lawyers whose experience comes from national prosecutions is probably rather limited in this area, because they do not normally think in terms of opposing sides in a conflict. Perhaps the closest we get to this in national systems are charges of brutality directed against law enforcement officials. There may be some public sympathy for those who may violate the law in order to prevent crime, but at the professional level such a perspective would meet with little acceptance. In international justice, the problem lies with the didactic and symbolic functions of the project.

Returning to Nuremberg, those who claim that justice was one-sided and therefore defective ought to explain what even-handed justice would look like. There were twenty-four leading Nazis charged at Nuremberg, with a range of war crimes and crimes against humanity, as well as crimes against peace. Would the solution to the victors' justice dilemma have been to hold a second trial, with twenty-four British defendants, and yet another, with twenty-fourAmerican defendants? Assuming a conviction for fire-bombing Dresden, should the sentence be comparable to that of men who organized the physical extermination of an entire religious group? But even if this could have been accomplished, what exactly is the problem that would be corrected? The charge that 'victors' justice' prevented reconciliation is hard to sustain in light of the attitudes of modern Germans to their terrible past. Would Germany's understanding of Nazism have been enhanced by a second trial, this time of British leaders, that sought some moral equivalence? I doubt it. All things considered, the one-sided prosecutions at Nuremberg, governed in their choice of defendants by political rather than judicial considerations, delivered a just result. They also contributed to an accurate portrait of the historical truth. Like many assumptions in the transitional justice field, the view that prosecuting 'both sides' is necessary or useful remains as speculative an hypothesis for Rwanda as it is for the Second World War.

The idea that international criminal prosecution for atrocities can be organized in such a way as to eliminate political targeting of specific defendants, groups and situations is like searching for the end of the rainbow. In the final analysis, the selection of situations and of cases is a political exercise. Rather than suggest it can be reduced to the purely forensic, it is probably better to acknowledge that politics is not only present in such determinations, it is unavoidable. Criminologists and criminal lawyers who are uncomfortable with this political dimension would be advised to stick to domestic justice systems.

The rare appearances of criminologists at the international criminal tribunals have tended to be at the sentencing phase, where there have been efforts to transpose the wisdom gained in the punishment of 'ordinary' criminals.[13] But clearly, some of our understandings about criminal behaviour in a peacetime domestic context are inapplicable to the types of situations that interest international prosecutions. For example, recidivism is hardly an issue. Once the political substrate that feeds the criminal activity disappears, the perpetrators return to normal life, where they are harmless and no real threat to society. At the lower levels of these criminal hierarchies, it is probably true that some of the perpetrators are also 'ordinary criminals'. They may migrate from marginal criminal gangs to racist combatant units in conflict situations. But international criminal prosecution is not really concerned with thugs on the battlefield. The focus of international prosecution is the political and military leadership.

When discussing the objectives of sentencing, the international criminal tribunals have generally confined themselves to rather banal pronouncements about retribution and deterrence. Because of the unimportance of recidivism, general deterrence is the only serious concern. Even here, judges have cautioned that deterrence 'must not be accorded undue prominence in the overall assessment of the

[13] See, eg, *Prosecutor v Nikolic* (IT-94-2-S). Sentencing Judgment, 18 December 2003, para. 39.

sentences to be imposed on persons convicted by the International Tribunal'.[14] According to the Appeals Chamber of the International Criminal Tribunal for the former Yugoslavia, relying upon a ruling of the Supreme Court of Canada, retribution should be viewed as

> an objective, reasoned and measured determination of an appropriate punishment which properly reflects the... *culpability* of the offender, having regard to the international risk-taking of the offender, the consequential harm caused by the offender, and the normative character of the offender's conduct. Furthermore, unlike vengeance, retribution incorporates a principle of restraint; retribution requires the imposition of a just and appropriate punishment, *and nothing more*.[15]

There is little support in the case law for rehabilitation as an objective of sentencing.[16] Judges have been advised not to give this principle undue weight in the context of international prosecutions.[17]

References

Kritz, N. J. (ed.) (1995), *Transitional Justice: How Emerging Democracies Reckon with Former Regimes*, Washington: United States Institute of Peace Press.

Maguire, M., Morgan, R., and Reiner, R. (eds) (2007), *The Oxford Handbook of Criminology*, 4th edn, Oxford: Oxford University Press.

Office of the Prosecutor (2006), *Letter concerning communication on the situation in Iraq*, The Hague, 9 February.

Teitel, R. G. (2000), *Transitional Justice*, New York: Oxford University Press.

Todorov, T. (2009), 'Memory as Remedy for Evil', *Journal of International Criminal Justice*, 7: 447–62.

Tonry, R. (ed.) (1998), *The Handbook of Crime and Punishment*, Oxford: Oxford University Press.

[14] *Prosecutor v Kordić et al.* (IT-95-14/2-A), Judgment, 17 December 2004, para. 1078; *Prosecutor v Delalić et al.* (IT-96-21-A), Judgment, 20 February 2001, para. 801.

[15] Ibid., para. 1075, citing *R v M. (CA)*, [1996] 1 SCR 500, para. 80 (emphasis in the original).

[16] See *Prosecutor v Delalić et al.* (Case No. IT-96-21-T), Judgment, 16 November 1998, para. 1233; *Prosecutor v Serushago* (Case No. ICTR-98-39), Sentence, 5 February 1999, para. 39; *Prosecutor v Furundžija* (Case No. IT-95-17/1-T), Judgment, 10 December 1998, para. 291; *Prosecutor v Erdemović* (Case No. IT-96-22-T*bis*), Sentencing Judgment, 3 March 1998.

[17] *Prosecutor v Stakić* (Case No. IT-97-24-A), Judgment, 22 March 2006, para. 402; *Prosecutor v Nahimana et al.* (Case No. ICTR-99-52-A), Judgment, 28 November 2007, para. 1057.

2

THE LIMITS OF GEOGRAPHY: DOES CRIMINOLOGY TRAVEL?

24

TRANSNATIONAL CRIMINOLOGY AND THE GLOBALIZATION OF HARM PRODUCTION

BEN BOWLING*

Introduction

Since its birth, the discipline of criminology has attempted to establish general models of crime, punishment and justice. These models—symbolic, ideological or theoretical ways in which the control system makes sense of what it is doing or intends to do—inspire specific security and criminal justice practices. At the heart of this chapter is the question of whether these practices reduce or *produce* harm. Of course, the manifest goals of 'the criminal justice system', 'crime prevention programmes', and 'security strategies' are beneficent. They explicitly set out to prevent

* I am grateful to James Sheptycki for reminding me of iatrogenesis, to Carolyn Hoyle for pointing me towards Medical Nemesis and to Stan Cohen, John Braithwaite, Elaine Player, and Mary Bosworth for their comments on earlier versions of this chapter.

violent and property crimes; to reduce criminal harm, physical injury and financial loss; to decrease wrongdoing and make people safer. The irony, as Stan Cohen pointed out thirty years ago, is that—paradoxically—criminal justice practices 'often actually make things worse even if (especially if?) their intentions are benevolent' (1988a: 190).

This observation raises deeply troubling questions about the role of criminology, especially as the discipline seeks to understand crime and justice in the transnational realm and to contribute to safe and peaceful communities around the globe. It destabilizes the concepts of 'crime' and 'criminal justice': what words do we use to describe the harms inflicted on people through routine police and penal practices? It questions theories of crime causation and theories of justice: how do we explain how practices that we name 'crime control' and 'justice' can actually result in violence and injustice? It also raises normative questions: what is the relationship between academic criminology and the harms inflicted by criminal justice systems? What is the criminologist's role in describing and interpreting these harms? What role should we play in responding to them? How far, if at all, are we complicit (as participants or merely as observers) in harm-producing 'criminal justice' practices? Do we provide an alibi for harm production? Are we 'guilty by association'?

In attempting to answer these questions, this chapter first considers the emergence of 'transnational criminology'—a rapidly developing field that sets out specifically to understand crime and justice beyond national boundaries and, in some instances, to contribute to supranational criminal justice policies. The chapter then turns to the idea of 'criminal iatrogenesis': the harmful results of well-intentioned crime control practices. In doing this, the chapter looks in detail at the criminalization of psychotropic drugs as one example among many of how harm-producing crime control models have been exported transnationally even while failing domestically. The final substantive section examines a series of mass murders in Guyana, which provide a vivid illustration of criminal iatrogenesis rooted in the systemic effects of drug prohibition as well as the problems of attempting to understand crime from a transnational and comparative perspective. The chapter concludes with some reflections on the practice of harm production for an emerging global criminology.

Transnational, Comparative, and Global Criminology

Starting with its earliest pioneers, criminology has sought to develop general theories of crime causation and control that can be applied far beyond the cultural context and empirical data from which they were first conceived. Criminological theory developed in North America, Britain, and Europe often explicitly (and more often implicitly) claims to be universal. However, western criminology has been criticized because its theoretical presumptions are often misleading when applied to other contexts, miss the point, or are unhelpful in other ways (Cain 2000). Moreover, many important criminological problems in the developing world are not covered at all in conventional Anglo-American criminology texts (ibid.). Noting its failure to resonate with empirical observations in other contexts, many authors have challenged the generalizability of western criminological theory (Agozino 1993; Sheptycki 2005; Aas this volume; Nelken 2009). Maureen Cain argues that criminology's twin failings are *Orientalism* 'which romanticises the other' and *Occidentalism* 'which denies the possibility of difference, or seeks to explain it away' (Cain 2000). Along similar lines, David Nelken (2009) points to the risks of *ethnocentricity*—'assuming that what *we* do, our way of thinking about and responding to crime, is universally shared or, at least, that it would be right for everyone else'—and *relativism*, 'the view that we will never really be able to grasp what others are doing and that we can have no basis for evaluating whether what they do is right'.

Transnational, comparative and global approaches are various ways in which contemporary criminology has sought to cure its ethnocentric myopia. Each approach shares some common features, but while comparative criminology seeks to compare one place with another, transnational criminology aims to study the linkages between places, and global criminology aspires to bring together transnational and comparative research from all regions of the world to build a globally inclusive and cosmopolitan discipline. *Comparative criminology* provides a remedy for theoretical short-sightedness by providing primary and secondary data on crime and criminal justice with which to compare and contrast experiences in different places around the world. Critical analysis of similarities and differences helps to produce richer theories with stronger external validity and wider applicability (Mannheim 1965; Sheptycki and Wardak 2005; Larsen and Smandych 2008; Nelken 2009). *Transnational criminology* goes beyond comparative analysis to explore problems that do not belong exclusively in one place or another and can therefore only be understood by analysing *linkages between places*. The key to this is the observation that things happening in one locality are increasingly shaped by events occurring many miles away and vice versa (Held and McGrew 2002).

Transnational networks have become more extensive, intensive and faster-flowing as the world economy has integrated and as transport and telecommunications technologies have created a sense of global interconnectedness (ibid.). It is a fair assumption that growing world trade has been accompanied by an increasing global flow of illicit goods and services and of the people buying and selling them (Bowling 2009). Global interconnectedness through travel, trade and telecommunication creates new opportunities for illegality and criminal conspiracy, but it also opens up new possibilities for cooperation and collaboration among criminal justice agents and criminologists.

It is almost impossible to verify the claim, however plausible, that transnational organized crime is a growing threat. But it is beyond doubt that systems of policing and criminal justice are transnationalizing (Bowling 2009). The natural assumption is that the former is causing the latter: increasingly global criminal activity leads organically to a growth in transnational policing (Sheptycki 1995). However, police and governments are actively *driving* the globalization of crime control. Although the manifest justifications for this development are the problems of transnational organized crime and terrorism, there are other less conspicuous drivers. Globalization theorists contend that interconnectedness is causing a reconfiguration of the state as governments attempt to manage the contradictions emerging as national boundaries no longer constrain human activity within its borders (Sheptycki 1995). Faced with problems like global economic restructuring, climate change, population growth, and migration that cannot be controlled by nation states, structures and processes of governance are evolving. National governments are being forced to adapt to the emergence of supranational governance structures in ways that are unrelated to changing patterns of crime. The World Trade Organization, World Bank and International Monetary Fund are shaping the future of global economic governance and supranational structures (such as the European Union and United Nations) are playing a significant role in shaping the political context (Sheptycki 2000; Loader 2002; Goldsmith and Sheptycki 2007). While the 'third pillar' of justice and home affairs is the Johnny-come-lately of supranational governance, bodies such as the UN Office of Drugs and Crime, Interpol and the International Criminal Court are shaping ideas and developing new practices of criminal justice and law enforcement 'above' the nation state, all of which are of interest to transnational criminologists (Bowling 2009; Bowling and Sheptycki 2011).

Transnational and comparative criminology differ in their substantive preoccupations, theories, and methods of study. In researching illegal drugs, for example, *comparative criminology* might seek to describe and explain differences in the prevalence of cocaine use in various countries (eg, Barbaret *et al.* 2004). Such research, using comparative survey methods, case studies or ethnography, sheds light on patterns of drug consumption in countries with very different enforcement regimes. These comparisons are valuable, producing richer descriptions and explanations and therefore offer better prospects of producing general theories. *Transnational criminology*, by contrast, might seek to explain the ways that illegal drug production, distribution and consumption are *linked* across time and place. It would seek to understand, for example, the complex processes that enable cocaine produced in the Andes to travel across South America and the mid-Atlantic to reach the streets of European towns and cities. It would be concerned with the creation of transnational legal regimes and enforcement strategies and how decisions taken in one place impact on far distant localities. Transnational criminology requires detailed knowledge of various geographical locations and transnational processes as well as theoretical and methodological flexibility. It may also require an epistemological and affective leap to 'join the dots' connecting lived experiences in different parts of the world.

A distinction can also be made between *transnational criminology* and the related ideas of *international* and *global* criminology (Larson and Smandych 2007). In the field of international relations and political sociology, 'inter-national' is used to describe interactions among nation states, while 'transnational' denotes phenomena passing directly through national boundaries largely unaffected by them (Mann 1997). The distinction between the transnational and the global is one of scope, the latter speaking to the idea of proceses that involve, or at least aspire to involve, the whole world *considered in a planetary context.*[1] A fully global criminology—which should be *both* transnational *and* comparative, and should involve scholars from all regions of the world—is some way from being fully established (Larson and Smandych 2007).

Criminal Iatrogenesis

Stan Cohen's (1988a) article, 'Western Crime Control Models in the Third World: Benign or Malignant?' criticizes the tendency for criminologists from rich countries to export crime control theories to their poorer neighbours without the benefit of a comparative or a transnational perspective. Cohen argues that criminal justice practices often produce unintended negative consequences and is particularly critical of the application of damaging Western crime control models to developing countries. He points to the 'paradoxical counter productivity' of institutions; interventions designed for the best of motives, he argues, 'may have disastrous results' (1988a: 189). Cohen drew on Ivan Illich's declaration that the medical establishment is a major threat to health and well-being:

> the so-called health-professions have an indirect sickening power—a structurally health-denying effect. [This syndrome], I designate as medical Nemesis. By transforming pain, illness, and death from a personal challenge into a technical problem, medical practice expropriates the potential of people to deal with their human condition in an autonomous way and becomes the source of a new kind of un-health. [Illich 1974: 918]

Applying Illich's work to criminology, can we say that the crime control professions—in either domestic or international settings—have become a major threat to safety and to justice? Do they create new kinds of unsafety, insecurity and injustice? Cohen notes the irony and paradoxes in the development of criminology. From their eighteenth and nineteenth century origins, centralized and purpose-built crime control institutions have repeatedly failed to achieve their manifest goals (eg, Foucault 1977). Institutions for criminal law enforcement and punishment cannot show convincingly that they do, in fact, control crime, deliver justice or contribute to safe and peaceful communities. But the problem is not merely that 'criminal justice' fails to work; in some instances it demonstrably make things worse: police sometimes kill innocent people, courts cause 'secondary victimization' and prisons are

[1] *Oxford English Dictionary.*

known as 'universities of crime'. Central to Illich's critique of medical intervention, and applied by Cohen to the criminological context, is the idea of *iatrogenesis*—'something induced unintentionally by a physician through his diagnosis, manner, or treatment; of or pertaining to the induction of (mental or bodily) disorders, symptoms, etc., in this way.'[2] Cohen sets out a threefold typology of this phenomenon.

- *Clinical iatrogenesis*—in which hospitals, doctors and modes of treatment are 'themselves the sickening agents' by prescribing drugs with harmful side-effects, carrying out unnecessary surgery and otherwise inflicting pain on patients (Cohen 1988a: 191). In the criminological context, criminal justice agents can inflict pain, injury and sometimes even death on suspects including the innocent; they can damage families, blight careers, contribute to labelling and stigmatization, create and entrench deviance within individuals and entire communities.
- *Social iatrogenesis*—refers to the 'expropriation of health through overmedicalization and the encouragement of people to become passive dependents' (Cohen 1988a: 191). In this case, ill-health is caused by the socio-economic transformations made necessary by the institutional shape of health care. The criminological parallels are the growth and strengthening of crime control nets with finer mesh and faster churn. Dependence on criminal justice and the disappearance of informal dispute resolution are the products of diagnostic imperialism, preventative stigma and marketing of crime control panaceas in prisons and probation and centrally controlled planning of crime-prevention projects. Like Christie's (1977) assertion that the state has 'stolen' conflicts from those directly affected by crime, a highly expensive and often counter-productive crime control industry has been created
- *Cultural iatrogenesis*—refers to the 'deeper destructive effects of medical imperialism on healthy, autonomous cultural responses to suffering' (Cohen 1988a: 192). In criminology, new professions and technical solutions undermine traditional consensual forms of dispute settlement and paralyze the ability to help, cope and tolerate. This has the effect of 'creating deviance by creating the need for control agents. Old ways of learning to live with diversity, trouble and conflict eventually disappear' (Cohen 1988a: 192). The discipline of academic criminology is implicated here since the whole process of creating a professional knowledge-base about crime and control contributes to drawing away indigenous processes of conflict-resolution and problem-solving.

Cohen notes that crime control models and the criminological theories that inform them are exported by criminologists, crime control officials, international agencies, and various other 'experts', even though they are often 'the very ones that are now being discredited in the West' (Cohen 1988a: 172). Reflecting on this, Cohen considers three possible explanatory models. First, *benign transfer* (p. 177), the officially-stated motivation for exporting crime control, proposes that policy is transplanted

[2] *Oxford English Dictionary.*

for good reasons and results in good ends. Second, *malignant colonialism* (p. 184), building on Franz Fanon's (1967) critique of Imperialism, *The Wretched of the Earth*, proposes that both the means and ends of policy transfer are malign. From this perspective, colonial powers always seek to exploit the resources of the colonized and therefore any extension of international relations into crime and security policy will inevitably disadvantage the recipients. Accepting that there are circumstances where the export of crime control is intentionally exploitative, Cohen settles for the *paradoxical damage* model that proposes that arrangements designed for the best of motives can, and often do, have disastrous results (1988a: 185).

The phenomenon of criminal iatrogenesis has profound implications for the attempt to answer the question: what is criminology for? If crime control practices produce harm, especially as they are transferred from one context to another, then is it sufficient for criminology simply to document this? What role should criminologists play either in the domestic or transnational realm, in seeking to improve or implement policy change based on their knowledge of likely unintended consequences? It also speaks to the question of the impact of criminology. To what extent should it be seen as an intellectual pursuit that exists at a distance from crime control practice? The global attempt to prohibit the production, supply and consumption of psychoactive drugs, and the law enforcement edifice that this has created, is a key issue that brings these concerns into sharp focus.

Drug Enforcement and Iatrogenesis

Drug law enforcement is a good example of an iatrogenic practice inspired by a transnational crime control paradigm. Jock Young's (1971) book *The Drug Takers*, researched in the 1960s and published on the eve of the 1971 Misuse of Drugs Act in Britain, is prophetic. Applying the insights of labelling theory (Becker 1963), Young predicted that drug criminalization would have perverse consequences. Defining drug use as a crime, invoking the criminal law and encouraging police intervention, he argued, would have the effect of creating the very problems that law enforcement was supposed solve through a process of 'deviancy amplification' (Wilkins 1964; Cohen 1972). In late 1960s Britain, drug use was confined to relatively small numbers of bohemian cannabis smokers. Young predicted that, rather than reducing drug consumption, prohibition would entrench and possibly foster the popularity, availability and use of other drugs by linking cannabis markets with those for barbiturates and opiates and would have other undesirable effects.

Psychotropic and narcotic drugs, consumed for pleasure or out of habit, are commodities similar to legally obtainable mood-altering substances (such as alcohol or prescription drugs) and other kinds of commodities like food and medicine. The goal of prohibition—to wipe out drug use altogether—is justified by policy-makers on the grounds that drugs are evil, damage users' health and affect the wider community (Andreas and Nadelmann 2007; Mena and Hobbs 2010). Prohibitionists assume that users and traffickers will be deterred or incapacitated; but if prohibition fails to achieve these goals and both supply and demand persist, a number of socially harmful consequences follow. Most importantly, making drugs illegal means that the only possible mode of supply for those who choose to use them is through criminal sources; therefore, *prohibition creates a clandestine market* (Young 1971; Bowling 2010; Mena and Hobbs 2010).

Predictably, attempts to control importation, domestic distribution and personal possession since the 1970s have led to extensive policing, punitive sentencing, massive numbers of users and suppliers churning through the criminal justice system, and warehousing a large population of convicted prisoners. As enforcement policies have been pursued, the number of recreational and habitual drug users has increased. The more enforcement resources have been deployed, the greater the problems of morbidity, mortality, dependency and the systemic violence associated with drug markets have become.[3] Although it was evident by the 1980s that drug prohibition was not achieving its goals and was counter-productive, the policy has been pursued even more vigorously at home and abroad in subsequent decades. The high water mark of prohibition was in 1998, when the United Nations set a ten-year goal to achieve a 'drug free world'.[4]

While the prohibition of drugs has had an enormously damaging impact on Britain and the United States—powerful sponsors of this policy—the impact on drug producing and transhipment countries in the developing world has been even more acute (Mena and Hobbs 2010). The fines and other penalties for those caught supplying drugs means that only the most organized people can survive the risks involved (Young 1971). International strategic connections are made by entrepreneurs connecting producers, traffickers and domestic suppliers. Profit and job opportunities in the drug trade attract previously disinterested members of society from all social classes (Griffith 1997; Molano 2004). Smuggling fosters relationships between organized crime groups, legitimate business people, law enforcement agents and government officials leading to widespread corruption. The capital generated becomes very large and linked with other forms of organized crimes such as arms and people trafficking (Griffith 1997; Bowling 2010; Mena and Hobbs 2010).

Cocaine trafficking and the armed violence that accompanies it is currently ballooning in Mexico, Venezuela, Guyana, Brazil, and the coast of west Africa as a result of enforcement action (Buxton 2006; Mena and Hobbs 2010). Clandestine markets, created by prohibition, bring illegal drugs to new locations that then quickly become entrenched within local markets and 'spill over' into local usage. Tactical law

[3] Andrew Wilson's (2007, 2008) research on drug markets in the north of England provides a graphic example of the unintended negative consequences of criminalization.

[4] In 1998, the UN General Assembly Special Session on drugs committed to 'eliminating or significantly reducing the illicit cultivation of the coca bush, the cannabis plant and the opium poppy by the year 2008' and to 'achieving significant and measurable results in the field of demand reduction.' It hardly needs pointing out that a 'drug free world' was not achieved by 2008.

enforcement successes have specific predictable (unintended and unwanted) consequences. For example, the drug seizures remove profits that are recouped by more business activity and debt sparks violent conflict. Low-level operatives arrested by the police are replaced by hitherto law-abiding individuals (Molano 2004). Post-arrest intelligence-gathering and cultivation of informers creates distrust within organizations and can lead to violent conflicts. Arrest of mid-level and upper-level operatives destabilizes markets and triggers internecine conflict. Drug enforcement itself becomes militarized and armed police and soldiers sometimes perpetrate extra-judicial executions and other human rights abuses (Mena and Hobbs 2010). Intervention does not reduce overall supply but tends to displace trafficking to new routes with resulting 'spill over' of armed violence and corruption to new countries (Bowling 2010).

Ironically, police action can increase the organization and cohesion of drug markets. For example, the destruction of the Cali and Medellin cartels in the 1980s and 1990s had the effect of creating much more complex networks involving smaller and looser associations built around particular drug-importation projects (Molano 2004; Decker and Townsend Chapman 2008; Zaitch 2007). As in any business there are conflicts between the producers, shippers and distributors who have an interest in maximizing profit. Complex transnational supply chains require control mechanisms, but the clandestine nature of the market prohibits access to formal systems of regulation and control and therefore informal systems based on unrestrained violence spring up (Mena and Hobbs 2010). The scale of profits and the complexity of the drug business have led to increasingly powerful systems of policing involving battlefield weapons and routine use of side arms and a ruthlessness in their use. Arming street level operatives within the drugs trade has the effect of arming societies more generally (Agozino *et al.* 2009). Armed enforcers begin to identify themselves as soldiers who are prepared to kill for money and are also prepared to meet their own deaths (Gunst 1995; Molano 2004). The pattern of armed violence protecting the clandestine drug trade can be found across producer, transhipment, and consumer countries (Figuera 2004, 2006; Buxton 2006; Mena and Hobbs 2010; Bowling 2010; Pitts 2008).

Research linking local experiences transnationally indicates that the pursuit of a global drug prohibition regime has been accompanied by the emergence of a multi-billion dollar clandestine market, growing armed criminality and widespread human rights abuses (Mena and Hobbs 2010). The most generous assessment is that illegal drugs have become available and the use of lethal violence in the supply chain has exploded *in spite of* the best efforts of law enforcement. A more challenging conclusion is that global drug prohibition has not only failed to achieve its original purposes of stifling availability and reducing demand, but has spread drug trafficking to new places and created—as iatrogenic side-effects—new problems including corruption, money laundering, armed violence, and high levels of homicide. Another unfortunate side-effect is that the overwhelming emphasis on reducing drugs supply to North America and Europe has skewed policies in developing countries away from pressing issues such as firearm trafficking, natural and man-made disasters, food and water shortages, disease prevention, pollution, climate change, and sustainable economic development. The resources spent maintaining security forces tasked largely with the pursuit of drugs traffickers could have been used in these other spheres.

Drug prohibition is just one example among many of how harm-producing western crime control models have been exported even while failing domestically. There is a more general point that crime control always has iatrogenic qualities. We certainly should not be surprised that 'doing criminal justice' causes harm: punishment is *intended to inflict harm* upon alleged offenders. Sometimes this harm is very *explicit*—such as when police strike demonstrators with batons or execute suspected terrorists—but the pains of punishment are usually more subtle, such as the loss of liberty, money or reputation. The assumption is either that this legally inflicted *harm will result in good for others* or is justified simply because the offenders 'deserve it'. While the initial infliction of harm is certain, its hoped-for good consequence is not. Punishment damages the life chances of those upon whom it is inflicted without making a demonstrable contribution to safety or other goods for crime victims. Indeed, it often makes things considerably worse. The example of the criminalization of drugs brings the point home. Prohibition—mobilizing extensive policing, criminal justice, punitive and military resources—is founded on the idea that drug use will be reduced by inflicting pain on producers, suppliers and users. The deterrence paradigm at its heart has not only failed to achieve its manifest goals, but has had huge negative consequences including the spawning of armed violence, gangster states and a global rise in deaths from gunshot wounds. Although there is now conclusive evidence of this in numerous domestic settings, what is needed now is much greater attention to research that systematically compares experiences in different places and which unearths the global links between individual cases. In the final substantive section, we examine an example of severely iatrogenic impact of the global drug prohibition regime to illustrate some of the problems facing those attempting to do transnational and comparative criminology.

Mass Murder in Guyana

The Antillean islands and the South American countries on the Caribbean coast have been severely affected by the trans-continental clandestine cocaine trade (Griffith 1997; Klein *et al.* 2004). For some decades, the drug has transited from Colombia and Bolivia, through Venezuela, Guyana, Surinam, and French Guyana before moving through the Netherlands Antilles, Trinidad and the eastern Caribbean, and onwards by air or sea to Europe (Bowling 2010). The flow of cocaine has created an economically powerful underworld in the affected countries linking organized crime groups, business people, and corrupt politicians with armed enforcers responsible for guaranteeing the safe passage of one of the world's most valuable products (Griffith 1997; Molano 2004; Figuera 2004, 2006). This provides a sinister backdrop to the armed violence that has reached extreme levels in countries across the region (Agozino *et al.* 2009).

In 2008, there were three mass murders in the Co-operative Republic of Guyana, claiming the lives of thirty-one people. At 2am on 26 January, 2008 the east coast Demerara village of Lusignan was attacked by a group of about twenty armed men. Led by Rondell 'Fineman' Rawlins, and armed with shotguns and automatic rifles, the men walked through the village, knocking down doors and slaughtering men, women and children in their beds. After the fifteen- or twenty-minute onslaught, eleven people, including five children, were dead. On 17 February, the Essequibo town of Bartica—gateway to the South American interior—came under attack in a 'military-style' operation. Under cover of darkness, an armed group of between fifteen and twenty people dressed in military clothing and body armour arrived by boat, armed with AK47s. The gang shot a group of workers at the stelling[5] before attacking the police station, breaking into its armoury, stealing weapons, killing three police officers and robbing several businesses before leaving again by boat. The whole assault lasted around one hour and left twelve people dead. The third incident occurred between 15 and 17 June, when eight mine workers in Lindo Creek were beaten with hammers or shot to death and their remains burned. Extensive reportage of these three events, accompanied by horrific photographs and videos, can be found in internet editions of the *Stabroek News* and *Kaiteur News*. To address directly the question posed by the editors of this book: *what is criminology, if not the attempt to understand events like these?*

By any standard, mass murder is an example of serious crime. It is clearly a serious social *harm*. The atrocities described above caused untold pain to those who were killed, extreme suffering to those who were attacked and survived and lasting emotional harm to witnesses and to wider society. These events represent a particular kind of serious harm. They were deliberate, malicious and involved the infliction of violence with a degree of planning akin to guerrilla warfare. It is culpable violence of the most extreme kind and therefore qualifies as a serious crime using the penological formula of seriousness as the product of harm and culpability. Culpable homicidal violence offends against the norms and values of a democratic society and requires the kind of denunciation that invoking the criminal law is intended to signify. It invokes calls for retribution and decisive action from the state. The example of mass murder in Guyana raises a range of difficult criminological questions: Why does a person kill (Grossman 1996)? What are the killers' individual motives (if motives exist)? What are the proximal and distal causes of killing? How common is

[5] A wooden pier or landing-stage: *Oxford English Dictionary*.

mass murder in different parts of the world? What can be done to prevent atrocities of this kind from happening again? How should the harm inflicted on the survivors and their families be repaired? How can they be compensated for the loss of their loved ones? What is the appropriate response to the perpetrators? Punishment? Execution? Forgiveness? Disarmament and reintegration? Truth and reconciliation? Some of these questions are empirical (relating to the facts of the matter as far as they can best be ascertained) while others are normative (relating the norms and values that guide decision-making). The pursuit of answers to these questions through research, reflection, writing, teaching and public engagement is what I think of as the subject of criminology: *the study of crime, its causes and control*. This is not a plea for a narrow definition of the discipline; on the contrary, criminology can, should and does consider the broader context—through an engagement with the 'parent disciplines' of sociology, law, political economy, psychology, philosophy, psychoanalysis, geography, international relations, and so on. It must also engage with the question of 'praxis'—*what to do*, in a practical sense—with acquired knowledge and understanding.

Some serious problems face the English criminologist in attempting to explain the murders of Lusignan, Bartica, and Lindo Creek. As Maureen Cain says of teaching criminology in the Caribbean, the difficulties 'derive both from lack of materials, and a lack of a theory to make sense of these materials' (Cain 2000: 240). These events may be, in any case, too recent to be the subject of theoretical or empirical criminological research. Few British criminologists even heard the news from Guyana, a land of three-quarters of a million people in the only English-speaking country in South America. Although the Lusignan massacre was reported by the BBC, the *Economist* and several other sources outside the Caribbean region, it was not widely reported in the English newspapers. But there are good reasons for thinking that mass murder in Guyana is unlikely, in any case, to become the subject of a criminological study. The *British Journal of Criminology*, for example, has only ever published one article on 'multiple murder', which includes 'mass murder' and 'serial murder' (Greswell and Hollin 1994). The 1978 Jonestown massacre, probably the most infamous murder–suicide in recent history in which more than 900 people died, has been mentioned in the *British Journal of Criminology* only twice in passing (Barker 1983; Wallis 1981). Gresswell and Hollin point out that multiple murder is a relatively neglected topic; of over 900 articles published on homicide between 1967 and 1993 only twenty-six related to it. Criminology's neglect of this topic seems ironic given the fascination of the media and the general public with mass murder and serial killers. It illustrates the need, as Lucia Zedner argues in this volume, to bring crime (back) into the study of criminology. What could explain this omission? Is the level of violence too extreme? Are the subjects of serial killing and mass murder too interesting to the general public or the 'true crime' genre to be taken as the subject of serious scholarship? Does the political and military quality of heavily armed violence place it outside criminology (Cohen 1996)? To what extent can our existing theories of crime causation—often rooted in methodological individualism—be applied to the problems of armed violence and mass murder? If such extreme violence is, or should be, an appropriate subject for criminology, how do we go about explaining the atrocities that happened in Guyana in 2008?

English criminologists seeking to explain these events—without an empirical or conceptual map of the demographic, social, economic, and political terrain of Guyana—are likely to find themselves 'up the creek without a paddle'. First, you would need some knowledge of the territory's colonial history and its ethnic polarization triggered initially by CIA involvement during the 1950s and '60s leading ultimately to 'racial warfare' (Rabe 2005: 186). This would help to explain (if not entirely) why the armed gangsters who attacked Lusignan were Afro-Guyanese while the villagers were East Indian Guyanese. You would also need to know about the economic hardship, poverty and instability that have afflicted the country since independence in 1966 (Rabe 2005). You would need to know about Guyana's strategic position in the transatlantic cocaine trade described earlier, its vast rainforest interior, open borders with Surinam, Venezuela, and Brazil, complex coastlines and waterways, and the advantages that these provide the armed gangs involved in smuggling. And even after taking account of many other distal factors, you would need to know some of the proximal causes such as Rawlins' central role in a well-armed criminal gang formed after a jailbreak in 2002. The gang became entrenched on the east coast Berbice in the intervening years and was blamed for numerous armed robberies, paramilitary assaults on public places (including the capital, Georgetown), and the murder of the Agriculture minister and his family. You would need to be aware that a 'phantom' death squad of armed enforcers had been set up in collaboration with government ministers, local businessmen and security forces to respond to the jailbreak and the further allegation that it was responsible for more than 200 extra-judicial executions. Then there are the specific triggers, such as Rondell Rawlins' accusation that his pregnant girlfriend had been kidnapped by the police and his subsequent phone call to a national newspaper threatening the government that if she was not returned he would do something 'real bad'. One interpretation of Rawlins' action is that it was an act of retribution against the state. The fact is, of course, that it was innocent families who bore the brunt of the violence.

The example of armed violence and mass murder in Guyana points to some of the problems of attempting to do transnational criminology equipped only with the substantive knowledge and theoretical frameworks provided by British criminology. It demands a reevaluation of our theoretical constructs and the knowledge that we have available to us. It raises the question of whether Anglo-American crime control models are valuable in explaining crime problems in third world countries. Crucially, it draws our attention to the impact of drug prohibition, the resulting global clandestine trade and its role in creating heavily armed paramilitary gangs in transhipment countries such as Guyana, Mexico, Brazil, west Africa, and elsewhere (Buxton 2006; Bowling 2010; Mena and Hobbs 2010). This brings us back to the central question of whether crime control models contribute to the reduction or production of harm.

Conclusion

Why do certain crime control models become orthodox and remain unchallenged despite their obvious failures, and what is the role of criminology in this process? The unintended and ironic, but also predictable consequences of punitive intervention are well established. And yet, criminology often seems content blithely to describe the harm of criminalization as though this was a minor caveat to an otherwise well-functioning criminal process, especially when the harm is felt far away from where policies are initiated. Stan Cohen has pointed out that there are many forms of denial when people 'are presented with information that is too disturbing, threatening or anomalous to be fully absorbed or openly acknowledged' and is therefore 'repressed, disavowed, pushed aside or reinterpreted' (Cohen 2001: 1). The observation that the applications of criminology and the end-products of 'criminal justice' are often suffering, insecurity and injustice falls into that category. Stan Cohen's (1988b) 'The Last Seminar' describes a nightmare in which a scholar comes face-to-face with his research subjects. They turn up in the classroom and hallways of the university, bringing with them all the emotion, human suffering and visceral complexity that make up the human condition. In order to live with the awful products of the system that we observe, write about, advise on and sometimes contribute to, criminologists use 'techniques of neutralization' to deny the victim and deny the harm (Sykes and Matza 1957). But 'injustice anywhere is a threat to justice everywhere' (King 1963) and silence is an 'act of complicity' (Hooks 1995). Perhaps we need a *criminology of harm production* emphasizing the role of the discipline in documenting the harms produced by global crime control practices and the role of *criminologists* in speaking truth to power (Loader and Sparks, this volume).

In pursuit of a rational, humane and progressive criminology we would not start from where we are now. In the drugs field a powerful global prohibtion regime and a prison industry (with its appendages in the academy) has grown out of all proportion and has inflicted severe damage on those imprisoned, but also on their families and entire communities. But how do we undo the damage that has been caused in pursuit of the unattainable goal of a 'drug free world'? Are there criminologists brave enough to recommend that prison populations in the United States or United Kingdom be reduced by two-thirds to bring them back to 1980s levels? Significant progress in this direction could be achieved simply by releasing all the prisoners convicted of non-violent drugs offences, starting with the thousands of hapless drug couriers imprisoned in foreign jails. On the other hand, pause for a moment to think about the impact that this might have on communities—especially in Africa and the West Indies—of the return of more than 2,500 convicted prisoners from UK jails. The picture is even starker in the United States, where there are 100,000 prisoners scheduled to be deported at the end of their sentence. As far as the receiving countries are concerned, offenders convicted and imprisoned in the metropolis are hardly going to be welcomed if they are deported *en masse*. The broader question of drug legalization is also complex. It was a bad idea to criminalize the possession and supply of drugs in the first place. But having done so, decriminalization will not automatically solve the problems of organized crime and armed violence that have become entrenched in communities around the world (Transform 2009). One lesson from history is that ninety years after the passage of the Volstead Act (1920) prohibiting the use and sale of alcohol in the United States and more than seventy-five years after it was repealed (1933), organized crime groups still hold the power that they garnered during prohibition.

Many questions remain about the development of a transnational criminology concerned with reducing criminal harms. For starters, how far can theories of crime, criminal justice and punishment actually travel? To what extent, if at all, is western criminology applicable to Latin America, Africa or Asia? If criminology is to become more globally relevant, it is going to have to become multilingual and learn to listen to, and speak with, scholars from other parts of the world and to engage with other criminologies. It is important to recognize the specific biases within the discipline and its origins in particular epistemologies and traditions. As criminal law, courts, and law enforcement mechanisms are globalizing and transnational criminal justice norms are consolidating, we should be concerned by the dominance of Anglo-American explanations, systems and solutions. Criminologists should be working to understand the application of their theories and methods to other places. We should pay more attention to the role of resistance to processes of criminalization and to oppressive criminal justice practice. We should think more carefully about the implications for criminological practice of the failure of Anglo-American solutions in the fields of drugs prohibition and their iatrogenic effects of escalating drugs availability and promoting armed violence. We should reflect on a future beyond Anglo-American criminal justice norms, prohibition regimes and law enforcement tactics. In this light, what contribution should criminologists make to public policy discussions in global fora? To the extent that criminology does engage at the transnational level, how do we avoid the twin pitfalls of Orientalism and Occidentalism? I think that the future role for criminologists in the transnational realm is to contribute to undoing the damage wrought by criminal justice practices inspired by faulty crime control models. We could perhaps consider criminology as the practice of 'damage limitation'.

If we are to take this path, we could take some inspiration from what Illich calls 'counterfoil research'—the disciplined analysis of the levels at which the reverberations of an iatrogenic medical system damage humanity (1974: 921). For Illich, the 'tantalizing hubris' of a medical profession offering unlimited health is itself a major threat to wellbeing. This he called 'medical Nemesis'—the 'backlash of institutionally structured hubris' (1976: 230). This brings Rondell 'Fineman' Rawlins to mind, the embodiment of 'criminal Nemesis', his gang of men armed with military hardware brought into being by the practice of prohibition, supported by a model of deterrence and the 'institutionally structured hubris' of the goal of a 'drug free world.' A long way from its intended purpose, the global War on Drugs is at the root of this horrific, vengeful and nihilistic assault on an entirely innocent village and many other similar atrocities around the world. Ultimately, 'Fineman' met his own Nemesis on 28 August 2008 when he was shot dead by the Guyanese armed forces. This strikes me as an example of 'enemy penology' (Krassman 2007) based on a narrative about crime that sees its subject not as criminals but enemies who, rather than being brought to justice, must be 'combated [and] excluded, if not extinguished' (Krasmann 2007: 302). The extra-judicial execution of Rondell Rawlins was widely welcomed in the Guyanese press, and may have given some relief to those who felt vulnerable to a repeat of earlier atrocities; but it contributes nothing to ameliorating the conditions that made him so dangerous. As transnational criminology develops, and links with international relations and the parallel fields of war studies and security studies, and as the lines continue to blur between crime and war, an 'enemy criminology' is emerging as the flipside of 'enemy penology'. From this perspective, extreme forms of violence defy explanation and are pushed out of history into the realm of natural and inevitable events, or even—as the Guyanese President put it—the work of 'animals'.

Illich argued that the 'disciplined study of the distinctive character of Nemesis ought to be the key theme for research amongst those who are concerned with health care, healing and consoling' (1974: 919). A similar ambition might be apt for criminology. As a community of scholars, we have certain shared values including the pursuit of peace, safety, liberty and fair distribution of justice. A criminology seeking alternatives to increasingly armed police, severe penalties and growing prison populations will find some inspiration in the call for a 'non-violent revolution in our attitudes towards evil and pain' (Illich 1974: 921). The 'alternative to a war against these ills', Illich argues, 'is the search for a peace of the strong' (1974: 921). I agree. Peace, not war, is what communities ravaged by armed violence are seeking. We need a non-violent revolution in our attitudes to violence, dishonesty and harm. We need to think again about peace-making criminology (Pepinksy and Quinney 1991), and how to develop collective capacity, of young people especially, to build resilient, safe and peaceful communities. Criminology should be a discipline that contributes to developing systems of justice that resolve conflict and promote peace rather than producing harms and adding to the sum of human suffering.

References

Aas, K. F. (2007), *Globalization and Crime*, London: Sage.

Agozino, B. (1993), *Counter-Colonial Criminology: A critique of imperialist reason*, London: Pluto Press.

_____, Bowling, B., St. Bernard, G., and Ward, E. (2009), 'Guns, Crime and Social Order in the West Indies', *Criminology and Criminal Justice*, 3: 287–305.

Andreas, P. and Nadelmann, E. (2007), *Policing the Globe: Criminalization and Crime Control in International Relations*, Oxford: Oxford University Press.

Barberet, R., Bowling, B., Junger-Tas, J., Rechea-Alberola, C., van Kesteren, J., and Zurawan, A. (2004), *Self-Reported Delinquency in England and Wales, the Netherlands and Spain*, Helsinki: HEUNI.

Barker, E (1983), 'Review of Social Research Ethics: An Examination of the Merits of Covert Participant Observation', M. Bulmer (ed.), *British Journal of Criminology*; 23: 197–8.

Becker, H (1963), *Outsiders: Studies in the Sociology of Deviance*, New York: The Free Press.

Bowling, B. (2009), 'Transnational Policing: The Globalisation Thesis, a Typology and a Research Agenda'. *Policing: a Journal of Policy & Practice* 3: 149–60.

_____ (2010), *Policing the Caribbean: Transnational Security Cooperation in Practice*, Oxford: Oxford University Press.

_____ and Sheptycki, J. (2011) *Global Policing*, London: Sage.

Buxton, J. (2006), *The Political Economy of Narcotics: Production, Consumption and Global Markets*, London: Zed Books.

Cain, M. (2000), 'Orientalism, Occidentalism and the sociology of Crime', *British Journal of Criminology*, 40, 239–60.

Christie, N. (1977), 'Conflicts as Property' *British Journal of Criminology*, 17: 1–15.

Cohen, S. (1972), *Folk Devils and Moral Panics: Creation of Mods and Rockers*, London: MacGibbon and Kee.

_____ (1988a), 'Western Crime Models in the Third World: Benign or Malignant', in *Against Criminology*, New Brunswick New Jersey: Transaction, original paper presented University of Ibadan, Nigeria 1980.

_____ (1988b), 'The Last Seminar', in *Against Criminology*, New Brunswick: Transaction.

_____ (1996), 'Crime and politics: spot the difference', *British Journal of Sociology*, 47, 1: 1–21.

_____ (2001), *States of Denial*, Oxford: Polity

Decker, S. and Townsend Chapman, M. (2008), *Drug Smugglers on Drug Smuggling: Lessons from the Inside*, Philadelphia: Temple University Press.

Fanon, F. (1967), *The Wretched of the Earth*, Harmondsworth: Penguin.

Figuera, D. (2004), *Cocaine and Heroin Trafficking in the Caribbean: The Case of Trinidad and Tobago, Jamaica and Guyana*, New York: iUniverse.

_____ (2006), *Cocaine and Heroin Trafficking in the Caribbean (Vol. 2) The Case of Haiti, the Dominican Republic and Venezuela*, New York: iUniverse.

Foucault, M. (1977), *Discipline and Punish: The Birth of the Prison*, Harmondsworth: Penguin.

Goldsmith, A. and Sheptycki, J. (eds) (2007), *Crafting Transnational Policing: State-building and Police Reform Across Borders*, Oxford: Hart

Gresswell, D. M. and Hollin, C. R. (1994), 'Multiple Murder: A Review', *British Journal of Criminology*, 34: 1 - 14.

Griffith, I. (1997), *Drugs and Security in the Caribbean: Sovereignty Under Siege*, University Park: Pennsylvania State University Press.

Grossman, D. (1996), *On Killing: the psychological cost of learning to kill in war and society*, Boston: Back Bay Publishers.

Gunst, L. (1995), *Born Fi Dead: A journey through the Jamaican posse Underworld*, Edinburgh: Paperback Press.

Hooks, B (1995), *Killing Rage: Ending Racism*, New York: Henry Holt and Company.

Hardie-Bick, J, Sheptycki, J., and Wardak, A. (2005), 'Transnational and Comparative Criminology in a Global Perspective' in J. Sheptycki and A. Wardak (eds) (2005), *Transnational and Comparative Criminology*, London: Glasshouse.

Held, D. and McGrew, A. (eds) (2002), *The Global Transformations Reader: An Introduction to the Globalization Debate*, Cambridge: Polity Press.

Illich, I (1974), 'Medical Nemesis', *The Lancet*, 303, 7863: 918–21.

_____ (1976), *Limits to medicine: medical nemesis—the expropriation of health*, London: Marion Boyars.

King, Martin Luther (1963), 'Letter from Birmingham Jail', 16 April.

Klein A., Day, M. and Harriott, A. (eds) (2004), *Caribbean Drugs: from Criminalisation to Harm Reduction*, London: Zed Books/Kingston JA: Ian Randle Publishers.

Krasmann, S. (2007), 'The Enemy on the Border: Critique of a Programme in Favour of a Preventive State', *Punishment and Society* 9, 3: 301–18.

Larsen, N. and Smandych, R. (eds) (2008), *Global Criminology and Criminal Justice: Current Issues and Perspectives*, Peterborough, Ontario: Broadview Press.

Loader, I. (2002), 'Governing European Policing: Some Problems and Prospects', *Policing and Society*, 12, 4: 291–305.

Mann, M. (1997), 'Has Globalization Ended the Rise and Rise of the Nation-state?', *Review of International Political Economy*, 4, 2: 472–96.

Mannheim, H. (1965), *Comparative Criminology: Volume One*, London: Routledge & Kegan Paul.

Mena, F. And Hobbs, D. (2010), 'Narcophobia: drugs prohibition and the generation of human rights abuses', *Trends in Organised Crime*, 13: 60–74.

Molano, A. (2004), *Loyal Soldiers in the Cocaine Kingdom: Tales of Drugs, Mules and Gunmen*, New York: Columbia University Press.

Nelken D. (2009), 'Comparative Criminal Justice: Beyond Ethnocentrism and Relativism', *European Journal of Criminology*, 6, 4: 291–311.

Pepinsky, H. and Quinney, R. (eds) (1991), *Criminology as Peacemaking*, Bloomington: Indiana University Press.

Pitts, J. (2008), *Reluctant Gangsters: The Changing Face of Youth Crime*, Collumpton: Willan.

Rabe, S. G. (2005), *US Intervention in British Guiana: A Cold War Story*, Kingston, Jamaica: Ian Randle Publishers/University of North Carolina Press.

Sheptycki, J. (1995), 'Transnational Policing and the Makings of a Postmodern State', *British Journal of Criminology*, 35, 4: 613–35.

_____ (ed.) (2000), *Issues in Transnational Policing*, London: Routledge.

_____ (2005), 'Relativism, Transnationalisation and Comparative Criminology', in J. Sheptycki and A. Wardak (eds), *Transnational and Comparative Criminology*, London: Glasshouse.

_____ and Wardak, A. (eds) (2005), *Transnational and Comparative Criminology*, London: Glasshouse.

Sykes, G. M. and Matza, D. (1957), 'Techniques of Neutralization: A Theory of Delinquency', *American Sociological Review*, 22, 6: 664–70.

Transform (2009), *After the War on Drugs: Blueprint for Regulation*, London: Transform Drug Policy Foundation.

Wallis, R. (1981), 'Review of "The New Vigilantes" by A. D. Shupe and D. G. Bromley', *British Journal of Criminology*, 21: 401–2.

Wilkins, L. (1964), *Social Deviance*, London: Tavistock.

Wilson, A. (2007), *Northern Soul: Music, Drugs and Subcultural Identity*, Cullompton: Willan.

_____ (2008), 'Mixing the Medicine: The Unintended Consequence of Amphetamine Control on the Northern Soul Scene', *Internet Journal of Criminology.*

Young, J. (1971), *The Drugtakers: the Social Meaning of Drug Use*, London: McGibbon & Kee.

Zaitch, D. (2007), *Trafficking Cocaine: Colombian Drug Entrepreneurs in the Netherlands*, Amsterdam: Springer Verlag.

Zedner, L (2010), 'Putting Crime Back on the Criminological Agenda', this volume.

25

THE MISSING LINK: CRIMINOLOGICAL PERSPECTIVES ON TRANSITIONAL JUSTICE AND INTERNATIONAL CRIMES

STEPHAN PARMENTIER

Introduction

In its report to the UN Human Rights Council of September 2009 the Goldstone fact-finding commission on the use of force during the Gaza conflict in 2008–9 concluded that various gross human rights violations were committed by all parties, some amounting to international crimes.[1] Both the report and the conflict were just a recent manifestation of a long series of violent events and investigations that have taken place during the last decades in various parts of the world. It may help to recall some of them, like the killing fields in Cambodia, the genocides in Guatemala and Rwanda, the 'ethnic cleansings' in the former Yugoslavia, the ethnic-religious conflicts in East Timor, the apartheid regime in South Africa, and the successive civil wars in the Democratic Republic of Congo. The line of events goes back as far as the Second World War and subsequent wars in Korea, Vietnam, and the like. Each conflict has produced tens of thousands of victims with a total number of many millions.

Without exception all of these conflicts have led to massive human rights violations produced by a variety of perpetrators and entailing many victims. Because some of the violations can be categorized as international crimes, and because the violence involved is often extreme, one would expect that criminology, the academic discipline dealing with crimes and criminal behaviour, would have paid significant attention to these topics. However, this has simply not been the case. Compared with the steady and voluminous stream of research and publication on ordinary crimes in all their forms and sizes, very few studies have been concerned with international crimes and if they have most of them are the fruit of the last decade only.

In this chapter I will take this paradox as a point of departure to reflect on how criminology can and should expand its scientific attention into areas of mass-scale violent conflict. After a brief account of the subject at hand I will give a summary overview of existing criminological research on international crimes, before sketching some challenges for the future of criminology. It is my view that criminology must meet the challenge of these kinds of crimes if it is to remain a vital and relevant discipline.

Transitional justice and international crimes: mapping the field

Debates about gross violations of human rights and international crimes committed in the past usually start during periods of political transition when societies move away from an autocratic regime towards more democratic forms of government. At that time, new elites are openly confronted with the fundamental question of how to address the heavy burden of their dark past. This question was posed in most parts of Latin America in the 1980s, in all of central and eastern Europe in the 1990s, and

[1] Human Rights Council (2009), 'Human Rights in the Palestine and Other Occupied Arab Territories', Report of the UN Fact Finding Mission on the Gaza Conflict, 15 September 2009, A/HRC/12/48.

in several countries in Africa and Asia in the last two decades. Clearly, it also relates to the many wars fought in the first half of the twentieth century.

Since the mid 1990s these issues of 'dealing with the past' (Huyse 1996) have become a major object of scientific research under the heading of 'transitional justice'. Understood in some literature as 'the study of the choices made and the quality of justice rendered when states are replacing authoritarian regimes by democratic state institutions' (Siegel 1998: 431), transitional justice has become particularly influential as an explanatory tool to grasp the many challenges societies are facing during and after political transitions (Kritz 1995). More recently it has been conceived of as 'the full range of processes and mechanisms associated with a society's attempts to come to terms with a legacy of large-scale past abuses, in order to ensure accountability, serve justice and achieve reconciliation' (United Nations 2004: 4). This view is obviously wider than the first, as transitional justice is no longer restricted to situations of political transition but now extends to all situations of large-scale abuses. Hence, the latter definition is stretching transitional justice to cover two new sets of situations, first of all abuses in ongoing violent conflicts in various parts of the world such as Colombia (Ambos 2010) and Darfur, and, second, abuses in 'mature' or established democracies like the residential schools in Canada (Cunneen 2008) and Australia and sexual abuse in the Catholic church. In comparison, the frequently used notion of 'post-conflict justice' (Bassiouni 2002) refers to societies emerging from violent conflict and is therefore much more restrictive. In the remainder of this chapter I use the term 'transitional justice' in its broad sense to catch best the kinds of situations and the sorts of problems associated with serious human rights violations and international crimes.

Transitional justice has become the focus of study of several disciplines, starting with law (international law, criminal law) and political science (including international relations), and expanding more recently into sociology, psychology, and anthropology. In the rapidly booming literature on transitional justice two major strands can be discerned. The large majority of publications are concerned with analyzing and evaluating various legal strategies and mechanisms for dealing with international crimes of the past. Such works examine criminal prosecutions of offenders before national or international tribunals or courts, civil procedures to claim damages for victims, lustration and vetting policies to oust collaborators of the former regime from their post, truth commissions to sketch a general picture of the violations and the crimes, and policies of granting amnesty to perpetrators (see, *inter alia*, Kritz 1995; Bassiouni 2002). A smaller group of studies refers to the nature and the origins of the violent conflicts and also pays attention to the political and economic reconstruction of the societies at hand (see, for example, Mani 2002; Bloomfield et al 2003).

Large-scale past abuses can and have been referred to and thus defined in different ways. International policy documents often speak of 'gross and systematic' or 'serious' human rights violations without really defining them. In the eyes of

Medina (1988) such events imply four cumulative elements; a large quantity of violations, a longer period of time, very serious violations against vulnerable victims, and the element of planning. So, too, the notion of 'political crimes', used in contrast to common or traditional crimes, has gained ground over the last twenty years. Such political crimes refer to forms of extreme violence, that often goes back to deeply rooted conflicts in a given society, and to mass victimization, which is the result of large numbers of direct and indirect victims (Parmentier and Weitekamp 2007). In order to determine whether or not crimes are political, scholars usually check two cumulative components: the subjective one (intent or motivation of the offender) and the objective one (context of the act and outcome or consequences as observed by the outside world) (Van den Wyngaert 1980: 108–9). Finally, the Rome Statute of 1998 created a new category of 'international crimes', encompassing four major types of crimes: genocide, crimes against humanity, war crimes and the crime of aggression (the latter only recently being defined during the ICC review conference of June 2010).

These distinctions are far from semantic; they produce concrete legal consequences. To label certain acts as violations of human rights implies that they have transgressed national or international human rights law, which in turn entails the responsibility of the states where the acts were committed. In contrast, using the notion of 'crimes' establishes the principle of individual criminal responsibility of the offenders and opens the doors for criminal prosecutions by public prosecutors and trials by criminal courts.

Criminology 'in a state of denial'?

Despite many differences, the legacies of large-scale past abuses mentioned above share some common features, including the deep level of violence used, the large numbers of victims and the large numbers of offenders. It is therefore surprising that so little criminological research has been conducted on these topics, irrespective of either the exact terminology used or the precise political and social context in which they have arisen. I first provide a short overview of criminological studies that have addressed some aspects relating to serious human rights violations and international crimes. Then I argue that criminology, the discipline *par excellence* that describes and explains crimes and the behaviour of offenders and victims, should pay much more attention to international crimes and human rights violations.

Let us first have a quick look at some introductory handbooks on criminology. It is clear that they pay only limited attention to human rights, political crimes, and international crimes (Parmentier and Weitekamp, 2007). Thus, neither the classic text *Criminology* (Sutherland and Cressey 1978), nor the more recent *Oxford Handbook of Criminology* (Maguire, Morgan, and Reiner 2007), contain any profound analysis of such crimes (although Hoyle and Zedner's chapter on 'Victims# in the *Oxford Handbook* devotes a few hundred words to the subject). Over the years only a handful of exceptions has emerged, mostly in the older days and mostly limited to political crimes, such as *Crime and Justice* (Radzinowicz and Wolfgang 1977), *Criminology: Crime and Criminality* (Haskell and Yablonsky 1978), and the criminology handbook by Brown, Esbensen, and Geis (1991). A recent exception is Hagan's new handbook *Crime Types and Criminals* (2009) that contains a substantial chapter on political crimes and terrorism.

More important, however, is to see whether criminology has been host to concepts and theories that can be linked to this broad field of transitional justice and international crimes, either in a direct or an indirect way. In the following paragraphs I briefly discuss three theoretical frameworks. The first relates to the category of political crimes, which have first and foremost been studied by political scientists and have gradually but very slowly attracted attention from criminology. Original traces can be found as early as the 1970s, when political scientist Schafer (1977: 374–376) highlighted the special intent of political violence, calling it a 'convictional crime' committed 'for ideological purposes'. These ideas were picked up by criminologists such as Turk who on the basis of his theory of the unequal distribution of authority has differentiated between political crimes that 'defy' authority and those that 'defend' authority (1982). Echoes are found in typologies that distinguish between crimes committed by people against the state and crimes committed by the state against people (Brown, Esbensen, and Geis 1991) or between 'crime by government' and 'crime against government' (Hagan 1997). Ross (2003; 2005), another political scientist and one of the most prolific authors on political crimes, created a typology of four main categories based on the distinction between violent/non-violent crimes and oppositional/non-oppositional crimes. Subsections of the research on political crimes have paid attention to two specific forms, terrorism on the one hand (Laqueur 1978; Schmid and Crelinsten 1993; Rapoport 2006), and on the other hand the Nazi Holocaust and other genocides (Charny 1996; Jones 2004; Totten 2005).

The second relevant stream in criminology relates to state crimes, some forms of which come close to political crimes and even to international human rights violations. Chambliss' pioneering work (1975) on the political economy of crime and the nexus between organized crime, politics, and law enforcement serves as a prime illustration. Examples include the state's complicity in piracy, smuggling, assassinations, and criminal conspiracies, and violating laws that limit its activities. Similarly, the early work by Barak (1991) on state crimes in America, Kautzlarich's research on the state-corporate relationship (1992) and Kramer's publications (2002) are all illustrative of a critical strand viz-a-viz the practices of the American government and its related state agencies in getting involved in criminal activities. In the view of Friedrichs (1998), state crime is the inevitable result of power concentration and has led to high levels of war, violence and crimes of all types (also Rothe and Friedrichs 2006; Rothe and Mullins forthcoming).

The turn of the century has brought a third stream of criminological research with a clear focus on international crimes. Cohen's ground-breaking work *States of Denial* (2001) pays attention to violent crimes by asking crucial questions like 'how ordinary, even good people, will not react appropriately to knowledge of the terrible' (also Cohen 2003: 549). Building on the social psychology literature going back to Milgram's famous electro-shock experiments, and drawing on the neutralization theory of Sykes and Matza, he has argued that the same techniques of denial can easily be applied to understand why serious human rights violations or violent political crimes occur in the first place and why they can keep going on. Following in Cohen's footsteps various criminologists have started to contribute to this criminology of international crimes, or 'supranational criminology' in the words of Smeulers and Haveman (2008). Day and Vandiver (2000) have reinterpreted older socio-psychological theories of crime causation through the angle of genocide and mass killings in Bosnia and Rwanda. Roberts and McMillan (2003) have explored the theoretical and policy dimensions of international crimes and have looked into various cultures of crime causation to explain the commission of such crimes. Their plea for a 'criminology of international criminal justice' wishes to go beyond the legalistic paradigm of international criminal justice and to extend to other forms of crime causation and of accountability in a multidisciplinary way.

From another angle, Jamieson's work on the 'criminology of war' (2003) and recent research on the war on terror (Hudson & Walters 2009) have addressed the interlocking realities of war, terrorism and state terror. Some research has focused on one category of international crimes, namely genocide, also called the crime of crimes. Noteworthy is Alvarez' work on the complex dynamics between official authorities and ordinary citizens when it comes to explaining crimes as genocide (2001), Neubacher's plea (2006) for a theory of 'macro crimes' that combines the individual and the political level, and Smeulers' and Haveman's research on 'crimes of obedience' (2008). Woolford (2006) has argued for a 'critical criminology of genocide' that uses reflexive, critical and responsible approaches, partly echoing Hagan's plea (2003) for a 'public sociology of crime'. Slowly but surely these new perspectives are gaining ground in the larger criminological community; witness the 2009 Stockholm Prize for Criminology awarded to Hagan and Zaffaroni for 'their groundbreaking theories and models explaining the causes and motivations of genocides' in Darfur and other parts of the world (<www.criminologyprize.com>). Other research fitting this strand are my own and my colleagues' publications on transitional justice and on the applicability of restorative justice principles in situations of mass victimization (Parmentier 2003; Parmentier and Weitekamp 2007; Parmentier *et al.* 2009; Weitekamp, Parmentier *et al.* 2006). Also the work of Braithwaite (2002) on developing a 'restorative diplomacy of peace' and on studying the barriers to reconciliation and peace building (Braithwaite *et al.* 2010) can be seen in this context.

The above summary makes clear that the fields of transitional justice and international crimes have remained quite marginal in the criminological research tradition.

This stands in stark contrast to the enormous amount of attention devoted on a daily basis to conventional or classical forms of crime and delinquency, in research and publications, in teaching and training, in practice and policy work, in the press and the general media. Moreover, resembling the child who is about to celebrate its thirteenth birthday, the criminology of international crimes is only just entering its teens. For this reason a crucial question is bound to arise: why is it that the scientific discipline of criminology has paid so little attention to international crimes and violations of human rights in general? Referencing Cohen, Smeulers and Haveman, we might wonder whether and why criminology has been 'in denial' by not focusing on these important issues?

While it remains difficult to provide anything more than partial explanations for this striking lack of criminological attention, several hypotheses can be proposed. One lies in the methodological difficulties of researching international crimes, which are often violent and occur at distant places. Under such circumstances it may be particularly difficult and dangerous to gain access to the perpetrators and the victims and to investigate their motives, modus operandi and context. And it is even more difficult to obtain the general picture of the crimes committed and the exact figures involved. The sensitive nature of international crimes and serious human rights violations complicates matters too, as they are often directly linked to the political and economic activities of state organs and non-state actors with considerable power and influence and who operate mostly in covert conditions and grey zones. Coming closer to powerful structures and powerful people is most likely to make them uneasy. Furthermore, researchers may have a hard time finding funding for sensitive topics that deal with state power, even more if they are looked upon with a critical eye. Last but not least, there is the issue of framing. For a long time political violence and war-like situations, changing political regimes, and prosecutions of former enemies have been considered to belong to the realm of political and legal sciences and the administration of criminal justice, but outside of criminology. With the advent of transitional justice as a specific field of study, the establishment of international criminal tribunals since the end of the Cold War and the legal definition of international crimes under the Rome Statute, criminologists are gradually becoming aware of their criminological relevance.

Whatever the precise explanation, some have argued that by ignoring international crimes, and genocide in particular, criminology has missed opportunities to contribute to this field and 'to improve the specification of its own ideas' (Day and Vandiver 2000: 43). The reasons are simple: international crimes tend to be particularly violent and serious, they involve a substantial number of offenders from all levels, they generate many victims from vulnerable groups, and they strongly affect groups and societies at large. Therefore, each single aspect provides a strong argument to bring international crimes within the purview of criminological attention. The time seems to have come, in other words, for a fuller contribution from criminology to the field of international crimes and transitional justice. Thus criminology can also rejuvenate itself by exploring the applicability of existing theories to new situations of international crimes and new theories to old situations of common crime. How might this be done?

Opportunities for the Criminological Imagination

International crimes and transitional justice raise both challenges and opportunities for criminological research in the next decades. First of all, they constitute a goldmine of possible research topics for any criminologist old and young. Smeulers and Haveman (2008) put it in simple yet eloquent terms: 'Societies and political systems that commit international crimes need to be studied, just like organizations involved in committing the crimes, situations in which such crimes are committed and the dynamics leading to the perpetration of these crimes.'

In general terms, Smeulers (2006) has argued that the discipline of criminology can make a contribution to international crimes in six main research areas: (1) defining and conceptualizing international crimes; (2) measuring and mapping international crimes; (3) estimating social costs of international crimes; (4) investigating the causes of international crimes; (5) defining and analyzing ways of dealing with international crimes; and (6) developing preventive strategies in order to prevent international crimes. These six areas refer to three major dimensions of crime (Parmentier and Weitekamp, 2007): conceptualizing and describing criminal behaviour; explaining crimes and their consequences for individuals, groups and society as a whole; and designing criminal policies to prevent and repress crimes and rehabilitate the victims and offenders involved. Another way to think of the contribution of criminology to the study of international crimes and transitional justice is to distinguish between three other dimensions: (1) understanding the nature of crimes and of criminal behaviour; (2) understanding the nature of victimization and the needs of victims; and (3) understanding various strategies for dealing with the legacies of large-scale abuse.

It goes without saying that criminology is well-suited to contribute to the understanding of international crimes, their nature and the motives of their offenders. It can do so by mapping the crimes of the past and by reinterpreting the many existing sociological, psychological and biological theories about the causes of crime. Also various types of offenders can be distinguished, including the differences between direct and indirect perpetrators, masterminds and executioners, collaborators and bystanders. All of these constitute important aspects during situations of violent conflict, from the Second World War to the extermination camps in Cambodia, or other long-term abuse like the racial discrimination of indigenous peoples across the globe. Moreover, criminology has an important role to play at the conceptual level, in developing new theoretical frameworks to better understand the similarities and differences between political crimes (and the subjective and objective elements), state crimes (with the state as actors of commission and omission) and international crimes (a legal category encompassing genocide, crimes against humanity, war crimes and the crime of aggression), and to compare these to serious human rights violations. All of these issues have to be studied in the context of the doctrines of national sovereignty, state security and post-colonial economic development, and against the background of globalization, terrorism and the war on terror.

Criminology and victimology also have a great deal to contribute to a better understanding of victimization and categories of victims of international crimes. The classical distinctions between direct and indirect and between individual and collective victims are highly relevant during and after armed conflicts and other periods of abuse. But also the mechanisms and triggers of 'role reversal' between offenders and victims, a crucial element in the understanding of violence both between groups in the Balkans and between individuals in domestic cases, require further study. Furthermore, how to assess the various forms of harm done to victims, and which needs and rights they have at various moments in the recovery process, are additional topics that come within the ambit of criminology.

Third, there is a significant need to bring criminological knowledge to the analysis and the evaluation of the many strategies for dealing with international crimes and other legacies of large-scale abuse. Research on policies of repression and prevention, deterrence and rehabilitation, reparation and recovery, retributive and restorative justice, reconciliation and peace-building all have a long tradition in criminology and criminal justice studies, and to tap into the insights into 'what works', what does not work and 'what is promising' cannot be overrated. Moreover, criminology can also generate information about how the general public or specific groups view human rights abuses during and after violent conflict and policies of transitional justice designed to deal with them, in regions like Latin America and the Pacific Rim but also in central Europe and western-style democracies in general. In fact, the very question when the exceptional character of 'transitional' justice may whither into regular or permanent justice is also well worth investigating in further detail.

It is thus clear that the fields of international crimes and transitional justice provide many opportunities for criminology to apply and test existing knowledge as well as to develop new concepts and theories. A specific challenge is that the current-day training of criminologists through teaching and research is not commensurate with the complexities of these endeavours and will therefore need a serious upgrade. Students and researchers need to know more about interpreting figures of mass victimization, about determining levels of accountability of offenders, about assessing harm to individuals and societies, about measuring degrees of reconciliation, and about so many other issues drawn from other disciplines. And they need to acquire practical skills and reflect on ethical issues related to these fields. It is therefore of utmost importance to rethink the existing criminological curricula and to start training the new generation of criminologists as of today.

Conclusions

Although criminology portrays itself as the main academic discipline to describe and to explain all forms of crime, it is very striking that the overwhelming majority of its work is concentrated on crimes called common or traditional because they are incorporated in common or traditional criminal law. Crimes with a political component, because of the intent of the offender or of the object or the context in which they take place, have very rarely been addressed. Also crimes committed by states and state agencies to defend or to regain state authority have hardly been the object of criminological research. This is even more surprising as some crimes amount to international crimes and to serious human rights violations, and therefore tend to involve many perpetrators and victims and to have far-reaching consequences for individuals, groups and societies all over the world.

At the same time, it is clear that criminological attention to international crimes has gradually gained ground in the last decade and that the potential for criminology as an academic discipline is vast and wide, almost unlimited. Therefore, criminology should and can pay increasing attention to international crimes and transitional justice. By focusing on criminal behaviour and on victimization, as well as on strategies to deal with legacies of large-scale abuse and with the future, the 'criminological imagination' is likely to make a major contribution. This can be done by exploring existing theories in new situations and by bringing back new knowledge to old situations. There is little doubt that criminology, with its unique interdisciplinary approach to all these aspects, is particularly fit to explore this largely uncharted 'terra incognita'. But new discoveries also require new instruments and the training of criminologists is therefore in need of rapid and serious upgrades.

References

Alvarez, A. (2001), *Governments, Citizens and Genocide: A Comparative and Interdisciplinary Analysis*. Bloomington: Indiana University Press.

Ambos, K. (2010), The Colombian Peace Process and the Principle of Complementarity of the International Criminal Court. An inductive, situation-based approach, Heidelberg: Springer.

Barak, G. (1991), Crimes by the Capitalist State: An Introduction to State Criminality. Albany: SUNY Press.

Bassiouni, C. (ed.) (2002), Post-Conflict Justice. Ardsley: Transnational Publishers.

Bloomfield, D., Barnes, T., and Huyse, L. (eds) (2003), Reconciliation After Violent Conflict. A Handbook. Stockholm: International Idea.

Braithwaite, J. (2002), Restorative Justice and Responsive Regulation. Oxford: Oxford University Press.

Braithwaite, J., Braithwaite, V., Cookson, M., and Dunn, L. (2010), Anomie and Violence. Non-truth and Reconciliation in Indonesian Peacebuilding. Canberra : ANU E Press.

Brown, S., Esbensen, F.-A., and Geis, G. (1991), Criminology. Explaining Crime and Its Context. Cincinnati: Anderson Publishing Co.

Chambliss, W. (1975), 'Toward a political economy of crime', Theory and Society, 2(1): 149–70.

Charny, I. (ed.) (1999), Encyclopedia of Genocide, 2 vols. Santa Barbara CA: ABC-CLIO.

Cohen, S. (2001), States of Denial: Knowing about Atrocities and Suffering. Cambridge: Polity Press.

____ (2003), 'Human rights and crimes of the state: The culture of denial', in E. McLaughlin, J. Muncie, and G. Hughes (eds), Criminological Perspectives. Essential Readings, 3rd edn, Sage: London: 542–60.

Cunneen, C. (2008), State crime, the colonial question and indigenous peoples in A. Smeulers and R. Haveman (eds), Supranational Criminology: Towards a Criminology of International Crimes, Antwerp: Intersentia: 159–79.

Day, L. E. and Vandiver, M. (2000), 'Criminology and genocide studies: Notes on what might have been and what still could be', Crime, Law & Social Change 34: 43–59.

Friedrichs, D. (ed.) (1998), State Crime, 2 vols, Aldershot: Ashgate/Dartmouth.

Hagan, F. (1997), Political Crime: Ideology and Criminality. Boston: Allyn and Bacon.

____ (2009), Crime Types and Criminals. Thousand Oaks: Sage Publications.

Hagan, J. (2003), Justice in the Balkans. *Prosecuting War Crimes in the Hague Tribunal.* Chicago: University of Chicago Press.

Hoyle, C. and Zedner, L. (2007), 'Victims, Victimisation and Criminal justice', in M. Maguire, R. Morgan, and R. Reiner (eds), The Oxford Handbook of Criminology. Oxford: Oxford University Press.

Hudson, B. and Walters, R. (2009), 'Introduction to the Special Issue on Criminology and the War on Terror', 49 British Journal of Criminology: 603–717.

Huyse, L. (1996), 'Justice after Transition: On The Choices Successor Elites Make in Dealing with the Past', in A. Jongman (ed.), Contemporary Genocides, Leiden: PIOOM: 187–214.

Jamieson, R. (ed.) (2003), 'Special Issue: War, crime and human rights' of Theoretical Criminology 7: 259–405.

Jones, A. (ed.) (2004), Genocide, War Crimes and the West. London: Zed Books.

Kauzlarich, D., Kramer, R., and Smith, B. (1992), 'Toward the study of governmental crime: nuclear weapons, foreign intervention and international law'. Humanity and Society 16: 543–63.

Kramer, R., Michalowski, R., and Kauzlarich, D. (2002), 'The origins and development of the concept and theory of state-corporate crime', Crime and Delinquency 48: 263–82.

Kritz, N. (ed.) (1995), Transitional Justice: How Emerging Democracies Reckon With Former Regimes, 3 vols, Washington: US Institute of Peace.

Laqueur, W. (1978), Terrorism, London: Weidenfeld and Nicolson.

Maguire, M., Morgan, R., and Reiner, R. (eds) (2007), The Oxford Handbook of Criminology, 4th edn, Oxford: Oxford University Press.

Mani, R. (2002), Beyond Retribution. Seeking Justice in the Shadows of War, Cambridge: Polity Press.

Medina Quiroga, C. (1988), The Battle of Human Rights. Gross, Systematic Violations and the Inter-American System, The Hague: Martinus Nijhoff.

Neubacher, F. (2006), 'How Can it Happen that Horrendous State Crimes are Perpetrated? An Overview of Criminological Theories', Journal of International Criminal Justice 4, Symposium Nuremberg Revisited 60 Years on: 787–99.

Parmentier, S. (2003), 'Global Justice in the Aftermath of Mass Violence. The Role of the International Criminal Court in Dealing with Political Crimes', International Annals of Criminology 41: 203–24.

Parmentier, S. and Weitekamp, E. (2007), 'Political Crimes and Serious Violations of Human Rights: Towards a Criminology of International Crimes', in Parmentier, S. and Weitekamp, E. (eds), Crime and Human Rights, Series in Sociology of Crime, Law and Deviance, vol. 9, Amsterdam/Oxford: Elsevier/JAI Press: 109–44.

____, Valinas, M., and Weitekamp, E. (2009), 'How to Repair the Harm After Violent Conflict in Bosnia? Results of a Population-Based Survey', 27/1 Netherlands Quarterly of Human Rights: 27–44.

Radzinowicz, L. and Wolfgang, M. (eds) (1977), Crime and Justice, 2nd edn, 3 vols. New York: Basic Books.

Rapoport, D. (ed.) (2006), Terrorism. Critical Concepts in Political Science, 4 vols, London: Routledge.

Roberts, P. and McMillan, N. (2003), 'For Criminology in International Criminal Justice', Journal of International Criminal Justice 1: 315–38.

Ross, J. I. (2003), The Dynamics of Political Crime, New York: Sage.

____ (2005), 'Political Crimes against the State', in R. Wright and J. M. Miller (eds), Encyclopedia of Criminology, 3 vols, Routledge: New York/London: 1225–30.

Rothe, D. and Friedrichs, D. (2006), 'The state of criminology of state crime, Social Justice 33: 147–61.

Rothe, D. and Mullins, C. (eds) (forthcoming), Crimes of State: Current Perspectives, Piscataway: Rutgers University Press.

Schafer, S. (1977), 'The Political Criminal', in L. Radzinowicz and M. Wolfgang (eds), Crime and Justice, 2nd edn, 3 vols, vol. 1, New York: Basic Books: 368–80.

Schmid, A. and Crelinsten, R. (eds) (1993), Western Responses to Terrorism, London: Frank Cass.

Siegel, R. (1998), 'Transitional Justice. A Decade of Debate and Experience', Human Rights Quarterly 20: 431–54.

Smeulers, A. (2006), 'Towards a Criminology of International Crimes', Newsletter Criminology and International Crimes 1/1, 2–3 (<www.supranationalcriminology.org>).

____ and Haveman, R. (eds) (2008), Supranational Criminology: Towards a Criminology of International Crimes, Intersentia Publishers, Antwerp.

Sutherland, E. and Cressey, D. (1978), Criminology, 10th edn, Philadelphia: J. B. Lippincott.

Totten, S. (ed.) (2005), Genocide at the Millennium, vol. 5 of the Series Genocide. A Critical Bibliographic Review. New Brunswick/London: Transaction Publishers.

Turk, A. (1982), Political Criminality. The Defiance and Defense of Authority, Beverly Hills/London: Sage.

United Nations, Security Council (2004), 'The rule of law and transitional justice in conflict and post-conflict societies', Report of the Secretary-General to the Security Council, 23 August 2004, S/2004/616.

Van den Wyngaert, C. (1980), The Political Offence Exception to Extradition, Antwerp: Kluwer.

Weitekamp, E., Parmentier, S., Vanspauwen, K., Valiñas, M., and Gerits, R. (2006), 'How to Deal with Mass Victimization and Gross Human Rights Violations. A Restorative Justice Approach', in U. Ewald and K. Turkovic (eds), Large-Scale Victimization as a Potential Source of Terrorist Activities. Importance of Regaining Security in Post-Conflict Societies, Amsterdam: IOS Press: 217–41.

Woolford, A. (2006), .Making Genocide Unthinkable: three guidelines for a critical criminology of genocide', Critical Criminology, 14: 87–106.

Websites

<www.amnesty.org> (Amnesty International, London).

<www.csvr.org.za> (Centre for the Study of Violence and Reconciliation, Johannesburg).

<www.derechos.org> (Derechos Human Rights).

<www.hrw.org> (Human Rights Watch, Washington).

<www.icc-cpi.int> (International Criminal Court, The Hague).

<www.iccnow.org> (Coalition for the International Criminal Court, Brussels).

<www.ictj.org> (International Centre for Transitional Justice, New York).

<www.idea.int> (International Institute for Democracy and Electoral Assistance, Stockholm).

<www.supranationalcriminology.org> (academic network on the criminology of international crimes - University of Maastricht/Amsterdam).

<www.law.kuleuven.be/linc> (Leuven Institute of Criminology, KU Leuven).

<www.truthcommission.org> (Search for Common Ground, Washington—Project on Negotiation, Harvard University).

<www.usip.org/library/truth.html (United States Institute of Peace, Washington).

26

WHY COMPARE CRIMINAL JUSTICE?

DAVID NELKEN

COMPARATIVE studies of criminal justice seek to describe, explain, interpret and evaluate differences in the way offensive conduct is defined and sanctioned (Nelken 2010). We may, for example, be interested in differences in what is and is not forbidden, in the justifications of punishment or regulation, in measures used to deal with deviant conduct, in who is involved in the process (eg, lay people or private business), or in how crime and criminal justice are reported by the media. It is easy enough to find striking examples of contrasts in criminal justice. The United States is still sending people to their death in the electric chair but, in 2008, a fairground owner in Italy was convicted of a crime against public decency for exhibiting a pretend one! But what is less clear is how these could contribute to make up a coherent subject-matter. What is the comparative analysis of criminal justice (good) for? I shall first describe some of the theoretical and policy goals of this subject and then go on to discuss how far this sort of work can overcome the risks of ethnocentrism and relativism. My own take on this subject is one that highlights the opportunities and challenges it offers for engaging with the 'other' (Roberts 2002)

The Goals of Comparative Criminal Justice

Studying what others do about offending conduct may just be a matter of curiosity—variously motivated, even sometimes morbid. Whatever misgivings they may have about how their own system works, most people are even more suspicious of what goes on when their fellow citizens end up being tried abroad. But we may also have a more open-minded interest in apparently strange ideas and practices—including our own practices seen in the light of what others do and think. Comparative criminal justice—like criminology and criminal justice in general—is also an area of enquiry pursued because of its potential for policy application. Many of those seeking to understand how things are done elsewhere want to improve their own criminal justice systems. Hence we get articles with titles like 'English Criminal Justice: Is it Better than Ours?' (Hughes1984), or 'Comparative Criminal Justice as a Guide to American Law Reform' (Frase 1990).

Those who undertake studies of this kind seek to borrow some institution, practice, technique, idea or slogan so as to better realize their own values or—sometimes—to change them. They may aim to learn from those places with high incarceration rates what *not* to do, or else try to become more like places with low prison rates such as Scandinavia or Japan. Alternatively, they may want to help others change their systems, for example exporting new police systems to South Africa, or restoring the jury system in Russia. Or they may be concerned to cooperate and collaborate in the face of 'common threats'. In order to achieve such aims they may also have to explain and understand how others go about making comparisons as part of their roles.

But the practical importance of this subject brings us up against one of the most troubling questions regarding the goals of our comparisons. How far are we intending to learn more about our own system and its problems and how far are we trying to understand another place, system or practice 'for itself'? Some scholars (eg, Balvig 1987) argue explicitly that their aim is less to learn about somewhere else than it is to come to understand their own country or culture better in the (reflecting? distorting?) mirror of 'the other'. Or this may just be the outcome, as T.S .Elliot (1943) put it:

> the end of our exploring, Will be to arrive where we started, And know the place for the first time.

In the most well-known of debates between comparative proceduralists, the question was what could be learned from continental European practice in France, Germany, and Italy for the purposes of better controlling American police discretion. If the criterion was what would work in the United States, then Goldstein and Marcus were right that judicial (and prosecutor) surveillance did seem insufficient to avoid potential abuse (Goldstein and Marcus 1977). But, in so far as the issue was rather understanding what other places were actually trying to do (and sometimes succeeding in doing), *in the context of their own structures and expectations*, then

Langbein and Weinreb seem to have the better of the argument—and this despite their approach being less based on empirical research into the 'law in action' than those they were criticizing (Langbein and Weinreb 1978).

It could be argued that it is in fact impossible to make sense of another place except against some background of previous expectations. Any cross-cultural comparison emerges from a given cultural context and has to be able to make sense to the audience(s) for whom it is intended. What is found interesting or puzzling will often depend on local salience. But even questions couched in terms that *are* salient in both (or more) cultures being compared may lead to different answers depending on which culture one starts from. Someone from Mexico might find Italian criminal justice relatively efficient, someone from Denmark is unlikely to do so. What could it mean to understand a society only in (or on) 'its own terms'? Even the society being reported on may also—reflexively –*understand itself* in relation to points of similarity and difference in relation to (certain) other places.

Comparative research often uses other places as a foil. Both Cavadino and Dignan (2006), and Lacey (2008), for example, offers explanations of differences in prison rates in Europe so as to prove that growing punitiveness is not the only game in town, and not the only path that can be taken. The idea is to show politicians in England and Wales that they can—if they wish—get themselves out of the hole they themselves have helped dig, where each party finds itself obliged to outbid the other on being 'tough on crime'. What is picked out for this purpose is what can be helpful for us (eg, the significance of state investment in industrial training, the difference between multi-party and two-party polities), but not what is specific or not easily transferable (eg, the importance of religion or family structures in Italy). But should we then say that what is important in studying another place is less whether the author has actually got it 'right' and more what the author makes of it? Is it irrelevant if, according to Johnson (2001), Braithwaite may not have properly grasped the Japanese criminal justice practices he used as a model for his highly influential idea of 'reintegrative shaming' (Braithwaite 1989).

Taken too far, however, this line of argument becomes self-defeating. The reasons we do comparisons cannot provide the only criterion of a successful comparison. If we have failed to understand another system properly we can hardly make use of 'it' to throw light on our own arrangements. And it would be a drastic step indeed to say that there is no way of judging this (even if it is not obvious *who* should be the judge). Such agnosticism would also raise the question of why we even try to make sense of other places. Even if we admit that there is no view from nowhere, this does not prove that any starting point is just as good as any other, still less that all interpretations are of equal value.

Another problem that needs to be faced is whether a subject such as comparative criminal justice can exist or even needs to. It has been forcefully pointed out that all social science is concerned with explaining variation and difference (Feeley 1997). Comparison was central to the work of both Durkheim and Weber, albeit with rather different strategies. Many would say that comparison is the essence of all social enquiry or even of logical enquiry in general. So, in principle, no line can or needs to be drawn between criminal justice and comparative criminal justice—or, for that matter, between criminology and comparative criminology. Likewise, the traditional focus of what is called comparative criminal justice on different national jurisdictions is mainly a matter of political/legal convention and methodological convenience. There are considerable political, social and cultural differences *within* modern nation-states (even more so in less industrialised societies) that are just as worthy of exploration. Most obviously, we can and do compare variations amongst states (and regions) within the United States (Newburn 2006), in Australia (Brown 2005) or elsewhere, regarding their prison rates or uses of the death penalty. More than this, other 'units' such as towns, organizations, and professional groups can all provide occasions for comparison. On the other hand, it is increasingly being claimed that comparative criminal justice has been superseded not so much because of the existence of internal differentiation but because of the advent of globalization (Larsen and Smandych 2008). For example, transnational crime activities and responses to them help transform and transcend differences between units defined as nation states. The local, the national and the international interpenetrate.

But there may often still be good reasons to privilege the nation-state or the societal level. States are the locus both for collecting criminal statistics and administrating justice (and the two functions are related), and they also often, though not always, coincide with barriers of language and culture. The continued role of nation-states and the existence of significant and persisting cross-national differences means that we should not lose sight of this level. Franklin Zimring explains that he recently became a 'convert' to comparative criminology because only inter-country-level comparisons provided the possibility to know whether a country (the United States) was really 'exceptional' in its crime rates or not. Discovering that the crime rate in nearby Canada was not much lower than in the United States (with the exception of homicide and life-threatening robbery) made him more able to grasp the magnitude of the rise in US prison rates (Zimring 2006). As this example also shows, it could be argued that comparative enquiry is all the more important if it is inseparable from ordinary criminology. It is not so much a question of taking comparative criminal justice out of its ghetto. Criminology's major debates now are mainly about issues in comparative criminal justice.

Reference to cross-national and cross-cultural research may often be the best way to show criminology's claims to be more than local truths. But comparative criminal justice offers a number of other potential benefits (and challenges) that go beyond simply adding to the pool of potential variables that can be used in building criminological explanations. Trying to understand one place in the light of another allows us to move closer to a holistic picture of how crime and its control are connected (what do they know of England who only England know?) In England and Wales—as in the Netherlands—the answer to failures in the system is normally thought to be even more concern about efficiency and speed. Hence the recent reforms of the English youth justice system inspired by the reports of the Audit Commission. In Italy a rethinking or defence of 'values'—but rarely more managerialism—is invoked as the way forward when problems arise. Comparative study can help us escape from such self-sealing cultural logics (Field and Nelken 2007).

Another (under-emphasized) benefit of the comparative approach is that it permits or even requires the sort of dialogue about who is entitled to define crime and criminal justice that is too often truncated in domestic criminology because of the hierarchy of credibility between those who write about crime and the usually low status offenders and deviants they write about. By contrast, when comparative criminologists seek to describe or explain what goes on in other places they frequently find that there are locally-based criminologists (or others with high credibility) able and willing to take issue with them, whether they come to criticize or to praise.

In trying to contribute to the various goals of comparative criminal justice, scholars can and do use a variety of strategies, each of which is also subject to pitfalls. Classifications can be controversial, descriptions deceptive, explanations erroneous, interpretations interminable, translations twisted, and evaluations ethnocentric. The difficulties multiply in so far as a satisfactory account of difference usually requires the ability to draw on more than one of these strategies. Collecting data on legal rules, procedures and distinctive institutions, as is done by the comparative criminal justice textbooks (see, eg, Reichel 2008), is certainly a valuable first step and one that is both demanding and time-consuming, not least because of linguistic and conceptual difficulties. It can be instructive to learn about the social role of policemen in Japan, as well as the lesser known system of voluntary probation officers, or discover that the way chosen to stop traffic policeman in Mexico City taking bribes from motorists was to appoint less threatening women rather than men to do this job.

Careful description can help us get beyond often out-of-date classificatory stereotypes such as those that emphasize differences between the inquisitorial and adversarial systems of criminal justice. There are now few examples of pure forms of such systems—and wider political and cultural factors condition outcomes as much as legal rules and procedures. In many respects the Netherlands has more in common with the United Kingdom than with Italy even though the United Kingdom does not belong to the continental system. The characteristics of a given procedure depend on which level of court we are examining and the relative importance of trial and pre-trial procedures—consider the importance of plea-bargaining in the United States. The adversarial system has grown in prestige, has made at least one important conquest in Europe, and influences the work of the European Court of Human Rights. By contrast, American style problem-solving courts are currently a chief export (Nolan 2009), and for a period judges actually took over the running of the prison system in the United States.

If we were to set out only to provide descriptions our task would never finish. Even the effort to describe aspects of criminal procedure in Europe runs to over a thousand pages (Delmas-Marty and Spencer 2002). So we have to be selective; but in fact we need to do more than this. It is essential to have an understanding of the way the 'law in action' relates to the 'law in books', a general protocol for all social studies of law that was in fact first put forward in the context of studying police (mis) use of criminal procedure (Pound 1910; Nelken 1984, 2009a). Schlesinger famously argued that for those who are factually guilty the adversarial system offers more procedural chances for acquittal, whereas the inquisitorial has more protections for the factually innocent (Schlesinger 1976). But, in practice, everything depends on which offences and offenders we are talking about, and when and where they are being tried. Likewise, if we are worried by the state using psychological pressure against defendants (Vogler 2005), a closer look at what goes on in police cars will quickly show us that this is not a problem restricted to the inquisitorial system. At an even broader level, the key to what is assumed to be greater 'leniency' or tolerance towards offenders in countries with relatively low incarceration rates may lie more in everyday non-enforcement and collusion than (as is usually suggested) in the dominance of welfare ideology (Nelken 2009b).

As already noted, the distance between what continental systems of criminal justice claimed to be doing and what research into the law in action showed they were actually doing was the nub of the classical debate about what was called 'the myth of judicial supervision' in continental criminal procedure. The leading recent empirical in-depth study of French criminal justice, by Jacqueline Hodgson, goes over some of this ground and, *inter alia*, continues to place great stress on how there is little actual supervision of police by prosecutors (Hodgson 2005). To ensure politically appropriate outcomes of trials in communist East Germany, 'telephone justice' relayed by political controllers to judges and prosecutors was rarely required—the methods used to appoint and socialize recruits to these offices was sufficient (Markovits 1995). More recently, by contrast, corruption investigations in post-communist Poland were themselves used 'corruptly' against political adversaries under direct government impetus (Polak and Nelken 2010).

For many criminologists, the main interest of comparative criminal justice lies in the formulating and testing of explanatory hypotheses—for example, regarding which countries use prison more or still choose to retain the death penalty. Those looking for explanations of differences in criminal justice practices that translate quickly into policy arguments may be disappointed, however. Asking which penal disposal is better at reducing crime turns out to be more complicated than ever when asked across a range of countries *many of whose criminal justice systems seem to give low priority to this goal*. The same applies to the complexities that surround the question of how to predict what the effect will be of importing or exporting legal institutions.

Those with a normative agenda may be interested in evaluating a system of criminal justice as a whole, or—more plausibly—be seeking to assess what goes on in any of its 'stages', or what is achieved by any of its constituent organizations or networks. But it can be difficult to get bearings for our normative sympathies when applying them in different contexts. Is the problem in Italy (or elsewhere) that too many people are being sent to prison, or too few—or does it just depend on which offenders we are speaking about? And, criminal justice practices are also sites for contesting values. Significantly, there are also differences between criminal justice systems in what kind of evaluation is seen as appropriate for different actors in the system, for example whether judges can be evaluated, by whom, for what conduct, and for what purpose.

Description, explanation and evaluation are not always easily separable in practice. Even where debates seem to be about explanations, a normative agenda concerning either corrective justice (justice for and to the individual case), or distributive justice (justice in the allocation of goods), is not too far from the surface. Those that 'govern through crime' (Simon 2007) can be shown to be less concerned with crime in its own right than with larger issues of moral order. 'Ruling through leniency' (Melossi 1994) may be objectionable in other ways. Likewise many academic studies that purport to be descriptive or explanatory are really (also) attempts to prescribe a different way of organizing society—for example one that places more emphasis on solidarity or social welfare.

Beyond Ethnocentrism and Relativism?

To make progress in learning about and evaluating other systems of criminal justice we need to navigate between two opposite (or at least contrasting) dangers. On the one hand there is the risk of being ethnocentric—of 'confusing the familiar with the necessary'. Here we fall into the trap of assuming that the links between social factors, crime, and criminal justice that we find persuasive are also ones that apply generally, and that what *we* do, our way of thinking about and responding to crime, is universally shared, or, at least, that it would be right for everyone else. Alternatively there is the temptation of relativism (which again can be either cognitive or normative). Here the claim is that we will never ever really grasp what others are doing, or that there can be no trans-cultural basis for evaluating whether what they—or we—do is right (see eg Beirne 1983; Leavitt 1990; Cain 2000; Sheptycki and Wardak 2005).

In opposition to cognitive relativism, for some leading post-war authors the point of comparative work was precisely so as to 'uncover etiologic universals operative as causal agents irrespective of cultural differences between different countries' (Szabo 1975: 366–7). Criminology could only become a 'true science' by showing the effects of criminal justice responses in different countries so as to determine uniformities and differences in causal influences and predictive factors. At the more fundamental level, leading authors still seek to show that similar forms of criminal conduct are as a matter of fact universally disapproved, to similar degrees, and insist that a response by a well-organized state is the best way of helping those who are victims of such harm (Newman 1999). Likewise, claims are made by psychologists that, cross-culturally, people have similar preferences for fair trial processes and shared intuitions about how institutions such as the police must behave if they are to be considered legitimate (Lind and Tyler 1988).

The protocols of this kind of positivist 'scientific' approach to explanation guide cross-national literatures on matters such as the effects on crime of different penalties. Other comparative enquiries attempt to establish cross-national similarities in agency practices, for example in the ranking police give to the relative seriousness of various types of police misconduct (Klockars, Ivkovitch, and Haberfeld 2003). The currently renewed interest in establishing and spreading 'evidence-based', transcultural knowledge of 'what works' in responding to crime (Sherman *et al.* 1997) is another important example of the search for universalistic knowledge in this field. On the one hand, this represents a valuable attempt to reverse the unwarranted, and partially unintended, pessimism induced by the earlier slogan that 'nothing works' in terms of dealing with offenders. But this type of 'globalizing criminology' can be criticized for taking its local verities about what represents an effective criminal justice system to be universal ones (Nelken 2003). Strengthening dysfunctional families is seen as a major route to reducing crime. Yet Mafia groups, like those of corrupt politicians and all groups of collaborative criminals, seem if anything to suffer from having too strong family or family-like ties. The daughter of Toto Riina (the last head boss but one of the Sicilian Mafia) was the respected class representative in her school. This approach also often gives insufficient attention to what different cultures mean by 'working' (especially in reference to the procedures of criminal justice)—as well as for whom crime prevention and criminal justice is supposed to work.

By contrast, there are authors who contest this search for universals and suggest the point of comparative research is rather to undermine the pretensions of positivistic criminology. For them, careful examination of foreign criminal justice practices suggests that it is above all the certainties buried in universalizing approaches to explanation, such as the claim that all systems find ways of relieving case-load pressures (for example through plea-bargaining or its ' functional equivalents'), or that criminal law must always serve the interests of the powerful, that turn out to be cultural rather than scientific truisms. Differences between what different societies define and treat as crime can be striking—and not only in the obvious areas of political and sexual deviance. The same applies to solutions to deviance. Are UK writers right in thinking that military style policing always alienates police from the community and so cuts down the supply of information? In Italy the fact that the militarized carabinieri do not originate from the place where they are asked to police, and live in barracks apart from society, is seen as a guarantee of their independence from potentially corrupting local ties. This is especially important in the south where organized crime groups hold so much sway.

Those who argue that given practices are both explained and even justified by the way they relate to local circumstances are not necessarily relativists. An emphasis on the importance of the particular rather than the universal may actually presume the possibility of commensurability (Dembour 2006). The same arrangements may not be appropriate under different conditions and changing circumstances may also alter the relevance of values even within the same culture over time. Consider the claim by Roach that the rise of victims' groups challenges the continued utility of Packer's categories, focused as they were only on the roles of the state and the accused (Roach 1998). On the other hand, some minimal standards may indeed be applicable universally. And an appeal to better values (including those learnt from elsewhere) can be taken to justify actually trying to change existing conditions.

Deciding whether or not a writer is being ethnocentric or relativistic is not always straightforward. The standards textbooks writers advocate bear remarkable similarity to those accepted 'at home', even as they claim a wider validity. The presumed American readers are told firmly of the price, in terms of criminal procedure or political freedom, that other countries such as Saudi Arabia or Japan pay for their low crime or low prison rates. Yes, Saudi Arabia has less crime, but 'we' would not want to have as little 'freedom' as they do. It is true that Japan has low levels of punishment but some of the things the Japanese do in their criminal process to make this possible we would not find acceptable—and, more generally 'their 'conformist way of living is not for us (Dammer, Fairchild, and Albanese 2005: 9).

A surprising example of what could be seen as an ethnocentric approach is provided by the great criminologist Edwin Lemert, one of the inventors of the social reaction and labeling approach—and also a specialist in juvenile justice. In a paper about the Italian system Lemert noted the enormous disproportion between the number of juveniles arrested and processed in the United States and in Italy (Lemert 1986). But, rather than see this as an indictment of the American approach, he argued that the Italian system was what he called a 'spurious' example of juvenile justice because it could not be seriously considered as trying to implement a welfare system for juveniles on the American model. As it has turned out, it was the United States that moved away from the welfare model that the Italian system has been steadily consolidating (Krisberg 2006).

Every society has its internal critics and every culture is composed of a variety of not entirely consistent values, so even criticisms and attempts to learn from elsewhere are usually formulated in ways that take for granted local values (Pizzi 1999). This means that to avoid the problem of ethnocentrism it is not enough just to be critical of one's own legal system. A better way of trying to avoid ethnocentrism is to ask ourselves whether we have fallen into the so-called 'evil causes evil fallacy' (Cohen 1970). Just as with the search for the causes of crime, we should not assume that aspects of criminal justice that we disapprove of are *inevitably* the consequence of causes that we would also want to criticize (and vice versa for those practices that we admire)—even if this often will be the case. This is important even when we seek to understand developments in cultures we know well. But we need to be even more on the look out for counter-intuitive connections when engaging in cross-cultural research.

Ethnocentric chains on our imagination can prevent us from finding or wanting to find a place in our theories for certain kinds of variables. Criminologists who try to explain which states in the United States have the highest prison rates tend to single out factors that most criminologists would consider negative in their own right, such as lower welfare levels, less effort to ensure economic equality, and less public participation in political life, or the power of only certain groups to participate where it matters. But it can also be linked to the rise in concern for victims, or the introduction of determinate sentencing through sentencing guidelines (intended to reduce arbitrariness in decision-making and create more national standardization). Prison building restarted in the Netherlands in part to keep faith with the principle of one person to a cell. Comparative research may even suggest that increasing egalitarianism leads to an increase rather than a reduction in levels of state punishment (Whitman 2003).

Different societies have different routes to dealing with difference—either by excluding it or enforced assimilation (Young 1999). More individualist and more collective societies each have their characteristic pathologies. Learning from what others do is not straightforward. On closer acquaintance we may well find that we like the outcome achieved by other systems of criminal justice, but not the means they use to get there—or vice versa. In Italy it is the politicians' sense of their vulnerability to criminal prosecution that helps explains why they complicate criminal procedure and hence reduce the chance of (some) people ending up in prison. An approach that assumes that other places with lower prison rates operate more 'inclusive' systems of criminal justice can be the kind of short cut that can easily be misleading (such societies in continental Europe are now sending ever-increasing numbers of immigrants to prison).

Some practices that work locally will not travel well. It is hard to imagine other places copying the Japanese in seeking to reform a rapist by telling him to write a *haiku* (Johnson 2000). But the need to give attention to the local and the particular does not mean that we cannot talk about 'best practice', as evaluated according to widely shared standards. And, even if considerable caution needs to be used in interpreting cross-national ratings, some places may be doing better or worse in terms of such standards. If one in ten children in Denmark who grow up in local government care go on to further education, whereas in the United Kingdom only one in a hundred do so, then we would do well to try to learn why. More controversially, we can perhaps even evaluate systems of evaluation; thus those who evaluate the evaluation of courts tell us that Finland has most effective system (Mohr and Contini 2008: 37).

Comparative research should be seen not only as a means of identifying best practices to be adopted wholesale but also as an opportunity to reflect on our own practices and values in the light of what others do. Other places' practices can be a potential resource for this without hypothesizing that either problems or solutions are necessarily universal. We can learn from what happens elsewhere so as to engage in 'internal critique' according to our own standards. Those in common law systems could learn that paying more attention to 'due process' considerations could even help achieve the goal of 'crime control' (by increasing legitimacy, public confidence and cooperation). Conversely, strengthening the role of defence lawyers in the French system could help increase the chances of truth emerging from the process—a key value in that system. As important, *the best practice for 'us' to learn from may not always be best practice as such*, but rather that which stretches our imagination about what is possible. Moving a little nearer to what we would otherwise never normally think of doing may be just what we need to re-evaluate our own priorities.

References

Balvig, F. (1988), 'The Snow-White Image: The Hidden Reality of Crime in Switzerland', *Scandinavian Studies in Criminology*, 9, Oslo: Norwegian University Press.

Beirne, P. (1983/1997), 'Cultural Relativism and Comparative Criminology', reprinted in P. Beirne and D. Nelken (eds), *Issues in Comparative Criminology*, Aldershot: Dartmouth.

Braithwaite, J. (1989), *Crime, Shame and Re-Integration*, Cambridge: Cambridge University Press.

Brown, D. (2005), 'Continuity, Rupture or just more of the Volatile and Contradictory', in Pratt, J. *et al.* (eds), *The new Punitiveness*, Cullhampton: Willan.

Cain, M. (2000), 'Orientalism, Occidentalism and the Sociology of Crime', *British Journal of Criminology*, 40: 239–60.

Cavadino, M. and Dignan, J. (2006), *Penal Systems: A Comparative Approach*, London: Sage.

Cohen, A. (1970), 'Multiple Factor Approaches', in M. E. Wolfgang, L. Savitz, and N. Johnston (eds), *The Sociology of Crime and Delinquency*, New York: Wiley.

Dammer, H. R., Fairchild, E., and Albanese, J. S. (2006), *Comparative Criminal Justice*, Belmont: Thomson.

Delmas-Marty, M. and Spencer, J. R. (2002), *European Criminal Procedures*, Cambridge: Cambridge University Press.

Dembour, M.-B. (2006), *Who Believes in Human Rights? Reflections on the European Convention*, Cambridge: Cambridge University Press.

Eliot, T. S. (1943), *Little Gidding: section V.*

Feeley, M. (1979), *The Process is the Punishment*, New York: Russell Sage foundation.

Field, S. and, Nelken, D. (2007), 'Early Intervention and the Cultures of Youth Justice: A Comparison of Italy and Wales', in V. Gessner and D. Nelken (eds), *European Ways of Law*, Oxford: Hart.

Frase, R. S. (1990), 'Criminal Justice as a Guide to American Law Reform: How the French do it, How can we Find Out, and Why should we Care?', *California Law Review*, 78: 539–683.

Goldstein, A. S. and Marcus, M. (1977), 'The Myth of Judicial Supervision in Three "Inquisitorial" Systems: France, Italy, and Germany', *Yale Law Journal*, 87: 240–83.

Hodgson, J. (2005), *French Criminal Justice*, Oxford, Hart Publishing.

Hughes, G. (1984), 'English Criminal Justice. Is it better than Ours?', *Arizona Law Review*, 26: 507–614.

Johnson, D. (2000), 'Prosecutor Culture in Japan and USA', in D. Nelken (ed.), *Contrasting Criminal Justice*, Aldershot: Dartmouth.

_____ (2001), *The Japanese Way of Justice*, Oxford: Oxford University Press.

Klockars, C. B., Ivkovich, S. K., and Haberfeld, M. R. (eds) (2004), *The Contours of Police Integrity*, London: Sage.

Krisberg, B. (2006), 'Rediscovering the Juvenile Justice ideal in the United States,' in J. Muncie and B. Goldson (eds) (2006), *Comparative Youth Justice: Critical Issues*, London: Sage.

Lacey, N. (2008), *The Prisoners' Dilemma: Political Economy and Punishment in Contemporary Democracies*, Cambridge: Cambridge University Press.

Langbein, J. H. and Weinreb, L. (1978), 'Continental Criminal Procedure: Myth and Reality', *Yale Law Journal*, 87: 1549–69.

Larsen, N. and Smandych, R. (eds) (2008), *Global Criminology and Criminal Justice: Current Issues and Perspectives*, Buffalo: Broadview Press.

Leavitt, G. C. (1990/1997), 'Relativism and Cross-Cultural Criminology: A Critical Analysis', reprinted in P. Beirne and D. Nelken (eds), *Issues in Comparative Criminology*, Aldershot: Dartmouth.

Lemert, E. (1986), 'Juvenile Justice: Italian style', *Law and Society Review*, 20: 309–44.

Lind, E. A. and Tyler, T. (1988), *The Social Psychology of Procedural Justice*, New York: Plenum Press.

Markovits, I. (1995), *Imperfect Justice: An East-West German Diary*, Oxford: Oxford University Press.

Melossi, D. (1994), 'The 'Economy' of Illegalities: Normal Crimes, Elites and Social Control in Comparative Analysis', in D. Nelken (ed.), *The Futures of Criminology*, London: Sage.

Mohr, R. and Contini, F. (2008), 'Judicial Evaluation in Context: Principles, Practices and Promise in Nine European countries', *European Journal of Legal Studies*, 1, 2: 1–40.

Nelken, D. (1984), 'Law in Action or Living Law? Back to the Beginning in Sociology of Law', *Legal Studies*, 4: 152–74.

_____ (2003), 'Criminology: Crime's Changing Boundaries', in P. Cane and M. Tushnet (eds), *The Oxford Handbook of Legal Studies*, Oxford: Oxford University Press.

_____ (2009a), *Beyond the Law in Context*, Aldershot: Ashgate.

_____ (2009b), 'Comparing Criminal Justice: Beyond Ethnocentrism and Relativism', in *European Journal of Criminology*, 6, 4: 291–311.

_____ (2010), *Comparative Criminal Justice: Making Sense of Difference*, London: Sage.

Newburn, T. (2006), 'Contrasts in Intolerance: The Culture of Control in the United States and Britain', in T. Newburn and P. Rock (eds), *The Politics of Crime Control*, Oxford: Oxford University Press.

Newman, G. (1999), *Global Report on Crime and Justice*, Oxford: Oxford University Press.

Nolan, J. L. (2009), *Legal Accents, Legal Borrowing: The International Problem-Solving Court Movement*, Princeton: Princeton University Press.

Pizzi, W. T. (1999), *Trials without Truth: Why our System of Criminal Trials has Become an Expensive Failure*, New York: New York University Press.

Polak, P. and Nelken, D. (2010), 'Polish Prosecutors, Corruption and Legal Culture', in A. Febbrajo and W. Sadurski (eds), *Central Eastern Europe after Transition: Towards a new Legal Semantics*, Aldershot: Ashgate.

Pound, R. (1910), 'Law in Books and Law in Action', *American Law Review*, 44: 12–36.

Reichel, P. L. (2008), *Comparative Criminal Justice Systems*, 5th edn, Upper Saddle River: Prentice Hall.

Roach, K. (1998), 'Four Models of the Criminal Process', *Journal of Criminal Law and Criminology*, 9: 671–716.

Roberts, P. (2002), 'On Method: The Ascent of Comparative Criminal Justice', *Oxford Journal of Legal Studies*, 22, 3: 529–61.

Schlesinger, R. B. (1976), 'Comparative Criminal Procedure: A Plea for Utilizing Foreign Experience' *Buffalo Law Review*, 26: 361–85.

Sheptycki, J. and Wardak, A. (2005), *Transnational and Comparative Criminology*, London: Glasshouse Press.

Sherman L. (ed.) (1997), *Preventing Crime, What works, What doesn't, What is Promising*, National Institute of Justice Washington, DC.

Simon, J. (2007), *Governing through Crime*, Oxford: Oxford University Press.

Szabo, D. (1975), 'Comparative Criminology', *Journal of Criminal Law and Criminology*, 66: 366–79.

Vogler, R. (2005), *A World View of Criminal Justice*, Aldershot: Ashgate.

Whitman, J. Q. (2003), *Harsh Justice: Criminal Punishment and the Widening Divide between America and Europe*, Oxford: Oxford University Press.

Young, J. (1999), *The Exclusive Society*, London: Sage.

Zimring, F. E. (2006), 'The Necessity and Value of Transnational Comparative Study: Some Preaching from a Recent Convert', *Criminology and Public Policy*, 5, 4: 615–22.

27

VISIONS OF GLOBAL CONTROL: COSMOPOLITAN ASPIRATIONS IN A WORLD OF FRICTION

KATJA FRANKO AAS*

Criminology's recent history has been marked by a progressive move towards the 'exterior'. Both the scope of criminological knowledge, as well as crime control interventions, are expanding beyond the previously relatively contained world of the nation-state. In addition to the now well-established interests in issues of comparative justice, migration, transnational policing, and transnational crime, criminologists are also becoming increasingly fluent in topics such as human rights, environmental

* I am very grateful to Richard Jones, Adam Crawford, Lill Scherdin, Thomas Ugelvik and the editors of this volume for their helpful and insightful comments.

issues, terrorism, genocide and crimes against humanity, peace-building, and transitional justice (see, *inter alia*, Sheptycki and Wardak 2005; Morrison 2006; Green and Ward 2004; Findlay 2008; Parmentier, this volume).

My aim here is not to provide a comprehensive overview of the diverse criminologies of transnational connections or what might be even termed 'global criminology'. Instead I wish to reflect on the growing cross-border scope of criminological scholarship from a perspective of sociology of knowledge. What kind of knowledge is being produced by the turn into the exterior? What are the social contexts in which it is produced and, more importantly, in which is it being applied? Who is providing its paradigms and how is it constituted by power/knowledge relations? Moreover, what is criminology's relationship to law and its increasingly global reach?

If we were to look for historic parallels, Stan Cohen's (1985) account in *Visions of Social Control* can give us some useful pointers. The book examines a period of extensive, yet finely tuned and veiled, expansion of social control and the supporting expertise from the previously enclosed world of institutions into the community.[1] Then, the prefix *de*—(institutionalization, carceration, etc.) indicated the crumbling boundaries of control practices and their visions, just as today the prefix *trans* -, indicates the move beyond the state's boundaries. If we are to borrow Cohen's metaphor, the 'net is widening'; at times it may even seem as if it is spanning the globe. Yet, the net is a very uneven one, patchy and full of holes. It is precisely these holes and patches—more and less finely meshed—as well as 'zones of neglect', that I wish to address in this chapter.

By exploring criminology's global imagery, my intention is not only to ask 'what is criminology', but also 'where' and 'who' is criminology? By whom and for whom is it produced? Who are its audiences and where in the divided world are they situated? Moreover, is criminology, by lifting its gaze and extending its vision beyond the national, also in danger of re-entering the complex and paradoxical terrain defined by 'terms such as 'reform', 'progress', 'doing good', 'benevolence' and 'humanitarianism'' (Cohen 1985: 21), only this time on the transnational level?

Assembling the Global: Criminology that Travels

Global is not a self-evident perspective. It needs to be imagined in order to exist (Tsing 2005; Valverde, forthcoming) and throughout much of criminology's history the global has not figured as an important frame of reference compared to the nation-state and the national (Aas 2007). The question can thus be asked: what is global, who makes it, and how is it made? What particular qualities does it have when

[1] The use of the term 'social control' rather than 'punishment' is particularly apt in the context of global control, since punishment on the global level is in practice almost non-existent (see Morrison 2006).

applied in criminological scholarship and in penal policy? Moreover, how does a discipline assume a global reach and what are the consequences if it does so?

The existence of the global is daily represented and reiterated in innumerable images in the media—think of the CNN, BBC and Sky news introductions—in academic PowerPoint presentations and on book covers (this author guilty as charged, Aas 2007). This imagination frames the globe—or better the world—as a natural unity, a whole, which is somehow pre-established. Often the global is envisioned as a distinct scale or frame of reference and thus is incompatible with other scales. The idea is that the global is somehow distinguished from the national and the local and, consequently, exists in an antagonistic relationship with them (Aas 2010). They are distinct, binary opposite, master categories competing in a zero-sum game (Sassen 2007). The effect of this theoretical framework is that one seems necessarily to be losing at the expense of the other. The global functions as a homogenizing force that is eating away at the national and the local. This model is often not only overstating the powers and progress of globalization, but also carries much responsibility for feeding the sceptical voices about its salience and ultimately its very existence.

However, another scholarly tradition has argued for an alternative, more nuanced understanding of the global. This view does not see the global or the transnational as an autonomous, separate and privileged scale nor is one guided by the axiom of its homogeneity and unity (Tsing 2005; Sassen 2007). The global is not envisioned as antithetic to local/national nor is it necessarily inhabiting the space *above* the national and local (Sassen 2007; Aas 2010). The national and global are not monolithic but hybrid entities, shot through with diversity and movement. As anthropologist Anna Tsing points out 'global connections are made in fragments' not delivered whole (2005: 271). This requires grounding one's analysis of global connection not in abstract models of the global but rather in concrete engagements (ibid.: 267) which can enable us to distinguish the hybrid assemblages of the global, local and national (Sassen 2006). Tourism, for example, may produce localities which in one sense belong to a particular nation-state, but are in other respects divorced from their national contexts and can be described as '*translocalities*' (Appadurai 2003: 339). And although the acknowledgement that phenomena can be simultaneously global and local (ie glocal) has by now become part of conventional wisdom, the view of the national and the global as mixed is far less recognized.

I do not wish to suggest that this brief outline in any way covers the visions of the global that organizes the field and its representations. These epistemological assumptions are often left inexplicit in much of criminological writing about globalization. Instead the simple (and simplistic), ideal-typical, division between (a) the global as an autonomous unity, and (b) as hybrid assemblages, can serve as a useful starting point for our discussion. In what follows I shall explore how understanding the global in particular ways privileges certain types of criminological knowledge and is making certain forms of penal and security governance possible.

The vision of the global as a distinct, autonomous unity draws on the purported universality of the global. It is a vision that is perhaps more often encountered on the level of policy than in academic discourse. Although global connections involve a variety of transformations (Aas 2007), one of the main advantages and attractions of employing a global scale is that it supports the assumption that knowledge can be transferred from one specific context to another. As Tsing (2005) points out, universalism inspires expansion. 'Convincing universals must be able to travel with at least some facility in the world, and this requires negotiations across incompatible difference' (ibid.: 89). Specificity is erased and knowledge can 'travel'. It can be, particularly with the help of media and ICTs, communicated at a distance, transferred from one locality to another and reproduced *ad infinitum*. Often this specific kind of knowledge does not purport to describe the globe but rather to picture it in a model:

> In the process, they develop a globe that is unified, neural and understandable through the collection and manipulation of information. ... The global scale is privileged above all others... Local conditions can be predicted from the global mode; that is the point of its globality [Tsing 2005: 102].

The issue clearly relates to a perennial criminological debate about the transferability of criminological concepts and policies and the applicability of Anglo-American perspectives as universal theories of penal change (Bourdieu and Wacquant 1999; Newburn and Sparks 2004; Nelken 2009). It also relates to attempts at developing criminological knowledge as an international, timeless and spaceless system, where definitions of crime 'transcend natural variations' and find 'a common denominator among them' (Felson, this volume). The question acquires particular salience in the current international focus on concepts such as global terrorism and global crime, transnational policing, and penal policy transfers to the so-called societies in transition. Moreover, it raises an issue about the role of criminological expertise in the growing market of 'transnational security consultancy' (O'Reilly forthcoming) and 'transnational professionals of (in) security' (Bigo 2005).

Criminologists are, together with other criminal justice professionals, becoming increasingly eager exporters of knowledge. The fact that disciplinary boundaries are crumbling, that crime and its control are moving into the international domain, and that the emerging global (dis)order seem to be increasingly 'governed through crime' (Findlay 2008) is giving criminology a series of what might be called competitive advantages. However, this may be also a time for pause and reflection about the social and political context of these exports and the effects they may have on those on the receiving end. Paraphrasing Tsing (2005), a question can be asked: how does the universality of scholarly concepts operate in a world of 'friction'; a world marked by inequality on multiple levels? Her ethnographic analysis of environmentalism suggests that the belief in the universality of knowledge has been by no means politically neutral and that we should keep in mind 'the particularity of globalist projects' (ibid.: 76). They are not all-encompassing in their actual scope, but function in effect through particular political and institutional arrangements. Similarly, Sousa Santos (1999: 216) suggests that '[w]hat we call globalization is always the successful globalization of a given localism. In other words, there is no global condition for which we cannot find a local root, a specific cultural embeddedness.'

Criminology is not a universal science and several authors have explored its particular histories and the dangerous traps of the belief in the power of 'travelling reason', aiming to achieve progress and good government (see for example Morrison 1997). However, what I wish to explore further in this chapter is the inherent duality of these projects, their democratic potential and hegemonic undertones. As Tsing (2005: 9) points out: 'Universalism is implicated in *both* imperial schemes to control the world and libratory mobilizations for justice and empowerment. Universalism inspires expansion—for both the powerful and the powerless'.

The following section thus examines this duality in light of the prevailing global inequalities. It suggests that the lion's share of criminological insights about globality is produced by the west and is marked by its geographic origin. This western 'knowledge that travels' has a certain affinity with, and is supportive of, emerging forms of liberal global governance. Moreover, it carries a complex mix of liberating potentials as well as neocolonial undertones.

Exporting Justice: Penal Cosmopolitanism and its Discontents

The globalizing criminological scholarship can be situated in the increasingly cosmopolitan habitus of academics and policy-makers. 'Criminology that travels' refers also to criminologists who travel. A cosmopolitan criminology, in this sense, denotes more a field that has become 'familiar with and at ease in many different countries and cultures', rather than 'consisting of people from many different countries and cultures'[2]. Criminology has been historically, after all, first and foremost a discipline of the west (Agozino 2003). Cosmopolitanism, on the other hand, denotes a world view that aims to transcend national boundaries and achieve some form of 'planetary conviviality' (Mignolo 2000). Elsewhere I have argued for the need to move beyond the 'methodological nationalist' outlook if criminology is to address, empirically and theoretically, the multi-faceted nature of contemporary transnational connections (Aas 2007; see also Wimmer and Schiller 2002). These methodological and epistemological choices also have important implications in terms of social justice. However, a distinction should be made between having a methodologically cosmopolitan (or pluralist) outlook as distinct from global normative

[2] *Oxford English Dictionary.*

and political projects. A global analytical frame can produce a variety of normative and political choices, which in various degrees aspire towards ethical universalism, global governance and, ultimately, shared world citizenship.

On the other hand, Calhoun (2001: 3) argues that cosmopolitanism is not only a moral and political philosophy but is also too often 'the class consciousness of frequent travellers'. The figure of Mannheim's 'free floating intellectual' may be mobile and free-floating, but it is also one deeply rooted in terms of social class and nationality. Calhoun suggests that much cosmopolitanism 'misrecognizes its own social foundations, assuming these to be universal when in fact they are representative of particular social locations' (ibid.). Moreover, he suggests that the belief in the force of universal moral obligations, in individualism and in the language of rights, and suspicion of local culture, tradition and communities, carries potentially undemocratic tendencies. My question is therefore (how) are various emerging forms of penal cosmopolitanism infused with relations of power and global inequality? Just as, historically, Kant's cosmopolitanism 'presupposes that it could only be thought out from one particular geopolitical location', that of the heart of Europe and the imperial order of the time (Mignolo 2000: 735), so too the (penal) cosmopolitanisms of today need to be situated in the contemporary geo-politics of knowledge.

If we are to take a brief look at the various *actually existing* forms of what might be termed (imprecisely perhaps) penal cosmopolitanism, we would find they comprise a variety of criminal justice 'exports'. Aspiring to universality beyond the mere core of human rights, this type of intervention captures a broader set of conditions, such as police practice, prison conditions, criminal law legislation, as well as the agendas of the wars on drugs, terror and trafficking. Crime control and criminal justice reform are becoming increasingly popular modes of so-called political capacity building. Personnel exchanges, training and assistance programmes, liaison networks, joint operations, peace-keeping and capacity-building programmes are, according to Goldsmith and Sheptycki (2007), becoming essential elements of contemporary state crafting.

Several observers have pointed out the Janus-faced nature of global police and justice missions (Goldsmith and Sheptycki, 2007; Findlay 2008). They are, in a way, combining elements of cosmopolitanism and imperialism; the Kantian urge to create universal justice and the striving of a Hobbesian Leviathan to conquer its opponents and to provide security on the international level (Aas, forthcoming). There is therefore tension between a 'cosmopolitan or world-society view of policing' and a more critical politico-strategic one which sees these practices as 'new or relabelled forms of imperialism and colonialism' (Goldsmith and Sheptycki 2007). By exporting their 'sense of justice' and 'cloning' their own legal systems, western nations are engaging in a form of globalism (ie globalization turned into political action, Beck 2000) which is combining security self-interest and a desire to 'do justice'. As Andreas and Nedelmann (2006) point out, historically, through international prohibition efforts (against slavery, piracy, drugs) Western powers export their own definitions of crime for both political and economic reasons as well as to promote their own morals to other parts of the world. It would appear that these chains of criminal justice exports follow the more customary pattern of trade-routes between the global north and the global south, where the former is exporting highly valued know-how and the latter providing 'the raw materials'.

Criminal justice exports can be compared to what Tsing (2005: 238) describes as 'packages of political subjectivity' which structure for instance, global environmental and gender politics:

> Packages are created in a process of unmooring in which powerful carriers reformulate the stories they spread transnationally. ... These packages carry the inequalities of global geopolitics even as they promote the rhetoric of equality. Those who adopt and adapt them do not escape the colonial heritage, even as they explore its possibilities.

The exports can be seen as a welcome and overdue extension of criminal justice 'beyond the nation'. They involve for example a variety of human rights, anti-death penalty and anti-torture activities by international bodies, European Union and the Council of Europe (see for example van Zyl Smit and Snacken 2009). Yet, the geo-political imbalances of power between the 'exporters' and 'importers' of penal policies may also present a challenge for criminology which should, conscious of its past, be wary of becoming an auxiliary legitimating system for a new set of legal institutions, professionals and practices of global governance.

The imbalances of power between the 'exporters' and 'importers' of penal policies are, to a large degree, also mirrored in the imbalances of criminological knowledge production. For example, while policing practices are increasingly inter- and transnational, policing literature continues to be predominantly Anglophone, reflecting a lack of knowledge about other policing systems (Hinton and Newburn 2009). Similar observations can be made about several criminological topics, not least, about the universal application of retributive justice administered by the ICC. As Mark Drumbl powerfully points out:

> This universality eliminates the discretion necessary to make informed assessments of the salient characteristics of the post-genocidal society in question... Context, nuance and local particularities should be individualized, carefully planed and thoughtful. When the retribution and punishment of the trial model become universalised as the exclusive way to 'deal with' mass political violence, the creativity of conjunctive local solutions becomes marginalized [Drumbl 2000: 298].

Criminology in a World of Friction

How is (global) criminology then to address this geo-politics of knowledge and the imbalances of power permeating its knowledge production and use? If we return to our previous discussion, we can see that the vision of the global as a distinct and unitary sphere is far less suited to capture the nuances of on-the-ground, local and national varieties—or a cynic might say, far better suited to oversee them. The two models of the global might loosely be described as globalization 'from above' and globalization 'from below'. The latter brings to the fore the various strategies of resistance or what Tsing (2005) terms *friction*—'the sticky materiality' (p. 1) and 'awkward engagements' (ibid.: xi)—which need to be taken into account when examining the global and the universal. The globe we are dealing with is not the shiny, colourful ball depicted in CNN logos; it is divided and its divisions are replicated and evident in innumerable localities.

In order to avoid, in best case, charges of naivety and, in worst, imperialism, global criminology clearly needs to develop a better empirical and theoretical grasp of global power relations. There are several intellectual fields to borrow from—most notably, international relations (see Loader and Percy, forthcoming). However, criminology may also take up an old debt of omission and explore more systematically connections between globalization and colonialism. Colonial legacies have been, until recently, relatively neglected due to criminology's predominantly internal focus (Morrison 2007). Yet, the attention to colonial perspectives is essential if we are to address the imbalances of power and the dynamics of othering and social exclusion in the present world order (for recent contributions see Agozino 2003; Cunneen and Stubbs 2004; Bosworth and Flavin 2007).

The steadily growing body of work on post- and neocolonialism has a lot to offer to criminological scholarship on emancipatory grounds as well as in terms of creating elements of a critique of existing ethnocentric epistemological assumptions. Its potential, however, lies not only in illuminating injustices of the past and resituating silenced voices, but also in its vocabulary for analysing the present global order and its possible future developments. Exemplified by de Sousa Santos' (2006) attempts to develop 'an epistemology of the South' and in the recent South American writing on the concept of 'coloniality' (Quijano 1989; Mignolo 2000), this tradition aims to de-link knowledge production from western aspirations to universality and to bring to the foreground alternative epistemologies and principles. As Cunneen (this volume; italics orig.) points out: 'It is an idea that the postcolonial exists as an *aftermath* of colonialism and it manifests itself in a range of areas from the cultures of the former imperial powers to the psyches of those that were colonised.'

The concept of coloniality refers to the continuity of colonial forms of domination and 'the making and rearticulation of the colonial and imperial differences' (Mignolo 2000: 732). It outlines 'a power grid or a matrix that links modernity, colonialism, capitalism, and racism' (Krishnaswamy 2008: 5). And it is of particular interest at this point that the notion of coloniality encompasses both what Mignolo (2000) terms global designs (global coloniality) as well as neocolonial nationalist strategies (internal coloniality). As Agozino (2003: 11) observes, referring to the fraught police ethnic relations, 'a counter-colonial criminology is relevant not only to former colonial locations but also to the former colonial countries', and this is precisely where the majority of criminological contributions on colonialism has been located (Cunneen and Stubbs 2004; Bosworth and Flavin 2007). Their potential lies in offering essential perspectives for understanding the colonial legacies and the emerging, neocolonial relations in the midst of the prosperous west. The colonial south is, due to globalization, no longer a geographical location. Postcolonial perspectives thus offer conceptual tools for addressing one of the essential aspects of globalization: the shifting boundaries between national interiors and the exteriors. Not only is criminology moving into the exterior, but through complex processes of inversion, globalization brings the exterior back home (Aas, forthcoming). Several observers have recently noted the blurring boundaries between external and internal notions of security; between warfare and crime, and between the military and policing tasks. However, there are few innovative perspectives that move beyond the mere observation of the trend.

The colonial critique attempts to destabilize the established center-periphery relations. It offers not only a critique of ethnocentric knowledge production—which has been one of the major preoccupations of postcolonial studies—but, more interestingly, also points to the importance of establishing the periphery as a topic of vital analytical interest. The colonial periphery is, according to Homi Bhabha (1996: 87) 'that limit where the West must face a peculiarly displaced and decentered image of itself 'in double duty bound', at once a civilizing mission and a violent subjugating force'. It is a space which surrounds the centre yet its role is occluded by the universalistic imaginary. Structured around the notion of the colonial difference, it can be interpreted as 'irreducible difference of the exteriority of the modern/colonial world' (Mignolo 2000: 733). Representing 'the very limits of translatability of Western codes' (Krishnaswamy 2008:6) the postcolonial concept of the subaltern (as well as the recent theorizing on the abject)[3] should be close to classical criminological preoccupations with outsiders and outcasts of modernity and may be able to provide alternative framings of excluded subjectivities in the new global order, particularly the growing numbers of the 'transnationalised others' (Brotherton and Barrios 2009).

Nevertheless, rather than simply providing novel conceptions of otherness and exclusion, the incorporation of the colonial dimension can serve as a reminder of the importance of locality and resistance and the essential unpredictability of global encounters. Precisely because world centres do not, and cannot, provide a template for global change, the studies of the periphery offer invaluable insight into global-local dynamics and into the *productivity of friction* (Tsing 2005). 'As a metaphorical image, friction reminds us that heterogeneous and unequal encounters can lead to new arrangements of culture and power' (ibid.: 5). In a slightly different framework,

[3] For an innovative conceptual deployment of the concept of the abject in studies of transnational crime see Bially Mattern (2007), as well as Pratt Ewing (2008) for an account of Muslim masculinity as the 'abjected other' in German society.

Teresa Caldeira's studies of Sao Paolo make one such attempt at 'de-centring urban theory' and actively introducing the periphery into the analytical framework. Here, periphery stands not only as 'the symbol of precariousness, deterioration, violence, and inequality' (Caldeira 2006: 115); a space which cannot be rescued by NGOs and well-intentioned middle class help. As a Brazilian rap song observes: 'NGOs exist to tame things. There is a problem in the periphery, well, send an NGO to tame it, to give a little course in the periphery' (Caldeira 2006: 137). However, despite its irregularities and illegalities, the periphery is also a space that defies simplistic perceptions of chaos and social exclusion; it is marked by potential, innovation and creativity, organization of new social movements and new conceptions of citizenship (Caldeira 2008). It is the force behind the growth of what later on may appear as a natural unity of a global city.

By exploring global divisions, borders and boundaries (real and symbolic), scholars enter the terrain where the global and the universal is still in the making and where globalization creates its frontier lands. This is a territory covered with what Sassen (2008: 67) terms 'third spaces', which 'are not exclusively national or global but are assemblages of elements of each'. Frontiers are marked by the shifting terrain between legality and illegality. They are the 'meeting point between savagery and civilization'; 'zones of not yet—not yet mapped, not yet regulated' (Tsing 2005: 28). These types of spaces make possible 'kinds of engagements for which there are no clear rules' (Sassen: ibid.) and which open for collaborations among legitimate and illegitimate partners (Tsing 2005: 27). Western police and intelligence agencies can thus cooperate with disreputable partners and dictatorial regimes in the global wars on drugs and terror, Western humanitarian intervention can become a fertilizer for organized crime in the Balkans (Andreas 2008) and European border police forces can regularly divert thousands of migrants to Libya and other countries with poor human rights records (Aas 2010). Here, we can witness the paradoxical and contradictory nature of global connections, where often the objective of their globality—think of global surveillance and policing networks—is precisely to keep the world divided rather than connected and unified.

Conclusion

A lesson drawn from the counter-colonial critique should be that not only the 'what' of criminology matters, but also the 'where' and the 'who'. Criminology has until recently, as Agozino (2003: 61) suggests, been relatively underdeveloped in the global south 'by being aligned with imperialism instead of being made relevant to the daily struggles of the masses for social justice'. What does criminology have to say about—or more importantly to—those whom Paul Collier (2007) has termed 'the bottom billion'? Their social exclusion has gone hand in hand with the explosive production of criminological books and textbooks in the west, yet they are seldom directly addressed by them. This is not simply a question of 'applied' v 'free' research—critical or positivist. The question lies at another level: who and where are criminology's audiences? Are they national or international and, if the latter, which nations are included under the international label?

Instead of addressing the imagined universality of the global, criminological scholarship of global connections needs to make an attempt at decentring its epistemological and social parameters of knowledge production. In place of unity of the global, we need systematically to explore its divisions and frictions. The criminology of global universals is built around abstract notions such as global crime, human rights and global criminal justice. It is a terrain where criminology may be in danger of losing some of its distinctiveness by reifying concepts such as crime and justice, of which it has historically developed a fair amount of scepticism. Yet how these concepts are shaped around the world and inserted into national and local trajectories of meaning and political processes is far from inevitable or predictable from the abstract recipes for change.

This chapter has argued for a decentred view of the global, which rather than aspiring to provide universal models of social change, aims to address the varied effects of globalization in the global north and south equally. The concept of friction offers a useful starting point by recognizing the importance of interaction and the transformative power of global encounters. Friction not only slows down transnational flows and networks, but also recreates them so to speak 'from below'. In terms of knowledge and penal policy transfers, Cain (2000: 250) describes the process as interactive globalization where recipient groups 'may, if they choose, if they are strong enough, interact with that idea, re-stitute it within their own discourses and practices, modify it, make it their own, and so create an alternative model'. Global transformations are therefore neither to be understood as unresisted, unstoppable rolling out of western policies, nor as the always-resisted and infinitely different truths of the local.

If we return to Cohen's *Visions*, written almost twenty-five years ago, the book seems to have lost some of its interest to criminological audiences. Nevertheless, we may be wise to reflect on its lessons. The book points to the gap between, on the one hand, humanitarian visions, intentions, ideas and knowledge claims, and on the other hand, their implementation in penal policy, institutional programmes and daily practice. This is seemingly a familiar story in the history of social control—of good intentions going bad. Cohen's, and before him Foucault's, account of penal change exhibits a fair dose of scepticism towards benevolent interventions in the name of humanity. Tellingly, though, Cohen's later work (2001) did not follow the lessons he reported from criminology's history; that 'benevolence itself must be distrusted', and that a guide to future policy might be to 'do less altogether' rather than 'do more good' (1985: 21). Quite the opposite, he has been a passionate critic of moral relativism and inaction in face of atrocities and human suffering. His, and a growing number of other criminological contributions, have argued for expanding our visions beyond the confines of the western 'civilised space' (Morrison 2006).

However, if criminological cosmopolitan aspirations are to provide a template for 'planetary conviviality', they need to transcend the present Eurocentric modes of production and tendencies to 'give courses in the periphery'. Not only because the 'deep presumptions of western theories may be harmful for non-western consumers of them' (Cain 2000: 239), but more importantly, because of the potentially undemocratic and exclusionary nature of this model. As Calhoun (2001: 18) points out, theories of democracy should 'seek to empower people not in the abstract but in the actual conditions of their lives. To empower people where there are means to do so within communities and traditions, not in spite of them'. Similarly Mignolo proposes 'critical cosmopolitanism' which can provide a critical perspective on what he terms global designs as well as Eurocentric humanitarianism.

> Instead of cosmopolitanism managed from above (that is, global designs), I am proposing cosmopolitanism, critical and dialogic, emerging from the various spatial and historical locations of the colonial difference … [Mignolo 2000: 741].

Both authors suggest that focus should be on cosmopolitan pluralism rather than universalism. Critical and what has been termed 'subaltern cosmopolitan' perspectives (Santos and Rodriguez—Garavito 2005) retain the ethical commitment to cross-border tolerance, justice, and solidarity. Rather than 'discarding cosmopolitanism as just one more variety of global hegemony' (ibid.: 14), these perspectives seek to reinvent it by insisting on its 'unconditional inclusiveness' of marginalized voices and the centrality of southern epistemologies, a commitment I strongly share and agree with (see Baillet and Aas, forthcoming). This chapter is therefore not a critique of 'global visions' *per se*, but rather a critique of their selective and exclusionary underpinnings. Cosmopolitan claims to universality are based on a number of exclusions, most importantly those relating to nationality and citizenship (see *inter alia* Douzinas 2007). Addressing the global geo-political imbalances of power is one of criminology's greatest challenges and also where its claim to importance among the social sciences may lie in the future.

References

Aas, K. F. (2007), *Globalization and Crime*, London: Sage.

_____ (2010), 'Victimhood of the National?: Denationalizing Sovereignty in Crime Control', in A. Crawford (ed.), *International and Comparative Criminal Justice and Urban Governance: Convergence and Divergence in Global, National and Local Settings*, Cambridge: Cambridge University Press.

_____ (forthcoming) '"Security—at—a Distance": Globalization and the Shifting Boundaries of Criminology', forthcoming in Ian Loader and Sarah Percy (eds), *Redistributing Security*, Cambridge: Cambridge University Press.

Agozino, B. (2003), *Counter-Colonial Crimiology: A Critique of Imperialist Reason*, London: Pluto Press.

Andreas, P. (2008), *Blue Helmets and Black Markets: the Business of Survival in the Siege of Sarajevo*, Ithaca: Cornell University Press.

_____ and Nedelmann, N. (2006), *Policing the Globe: Criminalization and Crime Control in International Relations*, Oxford & New York: Oxford University Press.

Appadurai, A. (2003), 'Sovereignty without Territoriality: Notes for a Postnational Geography' in S. M. Low and D. Lawtrence-Zuñiga (eds), *The Anthropology of Space and Place: Locating Culture*, Oxford: Blackwell Publishing.

Bhabha, H. K. (1996), 'The Other Question: Difference, Discrimination and the Discourse of Colonialism' in H. A. Barker *et al.* (eds), *Black British Cultural Studies: A Reader*, Chicago: The University of Chicago Press.

Bially Mattern, J. (2007), 'Stealing Sovereignty: On Abject Transnational Criminals in World Political Order', *International Studies Association*, Chicago.

Bigo, D. (2005), 'Frontier Controls in the European Union: Who is in Control?' in D. Bigo and E. Guild (eds), *Controlling Frontiers: Free Movement into and within Europe*, Aldershot: Ashgate.

Bosworth, M. and Flavin, J. (2007), *Race, Gender and Punishment: From Colonialism to the War on Terror*, Chapel Hill: Rutgers University Press.

Bourdieu, P. and Wacquant, L. (1999), 'On the Cunning of Imperialist Reason', *Theory, Culture and Society*, 16, 1: 41–58.

Brotherton, D. B. and Barrios, L. (2009), 'Displacement and Stigma: The Social-Psychological Crisis of the Deportee', *Crime Media Culture*, 5, 1: 29–55.

Cain, M. (2000), 'Orientalism, Occidentalism and the sociology of crime', *The British Journal of Criminology*, 40: 239–60.

Caldeira, T. (2006), '"I Came to Sabotage Your Reasoning!": Violence and Resignifications of Justice in Brazil' in J. Comaroff and J. L. Comaroff (eds), *Law and Disorder in the Postcolony*, Chicago and London: The University of Chicago Press.

_____ (2008), 'Worlds set apart' in *Urban Age* (December 2008), at: <http://www.urban-age.net/10_cities/08_saoPaulo/_essays/SA_Caldeira.html>.

Calhoun, C. (2001), 'The Necessity and Limits of Cosmopolitanism: Local democracy in a Global Context', Paper presented to the UNESCO/ISSC conference, 'Identity and Difference in the Global Era', Candido Mendes University, Rio de Janeiro, 20–23 May 2001 (<www.ssrc.org/calhoun/publications/articles/>).

Cohen, S. (1985), *Visions of Social Control: Crime, punishment and Classification*, Cambridge: Polity Press.

_____ (2001), *States of Denial: Knowing about Atrocities and Suffering*, Cambridge: Polity Press.

Collier, P. (2007), *The Bottom Billion: Why the Poorest Countries are Failing and What can be Done about it*, Oxford: Oxford University Press.

Cunneen, C. and Stubbs, J. (2004), 'Cultural Criminology and Engagement with Race, Gender and Post-colonial Identities' in J. Ferrell *et al.* (eds), *Cultural Criminology Unleashed*, London, Sydney, Portland: GlassHouse Press.

Douzinas, K. (2007), *Human Rights and Empire: The Political Philosophy of Cosmopolitanism*, Abingdon: Routledge-Cavendish.

Drumbl, M. (2000), 'Sclerosis: Redistributive Justice and the Rwandan Genocide', *Punishment & Society*, 2, 3: 287–307.

Findlay, M. (2008), *Governing through Globalised Crime: Futures for International Criminal Justice*, Cullompton: Willan Publishing.

Goldsmith, A. and Sheptycki, J. (eds) (2007), *Crafting Transnational Policing: Police Capacity -Building and Global Police Reform*, Oxford and Portland, Oregon: Hart.

Green, P. and Ward T. (2004), *State Crime: Governments, Violence and Corruption*, London: Pluto Press.

Hinton, M. and Newburn, T. (2009), *Policing Developing Democracies*. London: Routledge.

Mignolo, W. D. (2000), 'The Many Faces of Cosmo-polis: Border Thinking and Critical Cosmopolitanism', *Public Culture*, 12, 3: 721–48.

Morrison, W. (1997), *Theoretical Criminology: From Modernity to Post-modernism*, London and Sydney: Cavendish Publishing Ltd.

_____ (2006), *Criminology, Civilisation and the New World Order: Rethinking Criminology in a Global Context*, London: Glasshouse Press.

Newburn, T. and Sparks R. (eds) (2004), *Criminal Justice and Political Cultures: National and International Dimensions of Crime Control*, Cullompton: Willan Publishing.

O'Reilly, C. (forthcoming), *Policing Global Risks: The Transnational Security Consultancy Industry*, Oxford: Hart Publishing.

Pratt, E. K. (2008), *Stolen Honor: Stigmatising Muslim Men in Berlin*, Stanford: Stanford University Press.

Sassen, S. (2007), *A Sociology of Globalization*, New York & London: WW Norton and Company.

_____ (2008), 'Neither Global nor National: Novel Assemblages of Territory, Authority and Rights', *Ethics and Global Politics*, 1: 61–79.

Santos, B. de S. (1999), 'Towards a Multicultural Conception of Human Rights', in M. Featherstone and S. Lash (eds), *Spaces of Culture: City—Nation—World*, London: Sage.

_____ and Rodriguez-Garavito, C. A. (eds) (2005), *Law and Globalization from Below*, Cambridge: Cambridge University Press.

Sheptycki, J. and Wardak, A. (2005), *Transnational and Comparative Criminology*, London: Glasshouse Press.

Tsing, A. L. (2005), *Friction: An Ethnography of Global Connection*, Princeton: Princeton University Press.

Van Zyl Smit, D. and Snacken S. (2009), *Principles of European Prison Law and Policy: Penology and Human Rights*, Oxford: Oxford University Press.

Wimmer, A. and Schiller, N.G. (2002), 'Methodological Nationalism and Beyond: Nation-State Building, Migration and the Social Sciences', *Global Networks*, 2, 4: 301–34.

3

THE LIMITS OF THE ACADEMY: WHAT IS THE IMPACT OF CRIMINOLOGY?

28

CRIMINOLOGY AS INVENTION

LAWRENCE W. SHERMAN

CRIMINOLOGY was invented as a new way of reducing human suffering. If an invention is a 'new design for doing something', the 'something' criminology was designed for was less crime and injustice (Sherman 2003). Criminology has been most successful in producing those results when it has focused on inventing and testing new laws, institutions and social practices for dealing with crime (Sherman 2006).

This chapter is written for the millions of people who devote their lives to the goals of reducing crime and injustice. Some of them are criminologists. Most are not—but could be. The purpose of the chapter is to persuade both current and potential criminologists to use criminology for invention, as well as for building the basic science of crime.

Criminology was invented (independently) by Henry Fielding (1751) and Cesare Beccaria (1764) in the European 'Enlightenment' of the eighteenth century. The Enlightenment was an intellectual movement encouraging people to think for themselves, rather than accepting the opinions of church and state authorities (Gay 1996). It was also an effort to apply intellectual *reasoning* to the analysis of complex problems long seen as matters of faith or emotion (Sherman 2003). This outlook led to an 'age of invention', ranging from the industrial revolution to the abolition of the slave trade (Uglow 2002).

As part of the broad cultural transformation surrounding its creation, criminology quickly set about to invent more humane methods for dealing with crime. Its early inventions led to less reliance on torture and the death penalty, and more reliance on crime prevention—especially by means of police patrols (Hurd 2007). Since then criminology has had an uneven record, both at producing inventions and in the success of the inventions produced.

Accomplishing the purpose of this chapter requires that we first consider the idea of invention, especially of social institutions rather than just mechanical technologies. The essay then reviews a few notable historical examples of criminology as invention. Those examples lead to a modern statement of the scientific process of invention in criminology. With these foundations, the chapter then examines a few prime examples of recent 'invention criminology' across the criminal justice system and beyond it. The chapter concludes by acknowledging the great debt criminological inventors have to the many criminologists who help make invention possible.

This chapter is especially relevant to a rapidly growing field called *experimental* criminology, which I have defined as 'scientific knowledge about crime and justice discovered from random assignment of different conditions in large field tests' (Sherman 2010). That definition is correct, but insufficiently detailed to demonstrate the role of invention in creating 'crucial experiments'. Some might read my definition as confirmation of a vulgar assessment of experimental criminology as an enterprise devoted to atheoretical evaluations of poorly conceptualized government programmes. The evidence shows otherwise.

In recent years, experimental criminology has repeatedly demonstrated its capacity to 'develop and test' (Sherman, 2006). By that I mean that criminology as invention begins with an understanding of a problem in a specific context, and of theories about the causes of a problem, which then frame a review of previous research on those theories and that problem. That review then leads to *invention* of a 'new design' (as the Cambridge online dictionary defines invention) for dealing with the problem. Inevitably, most new designs will fail to improve on old designs. But some of them will. A few will have a revolutionary impact in benefit to humanity.

It is the lure of such major breakthroughs that attracts inventors to their task. The successes of the past should inspire us all to try, and to keep trying, to do better tomorrow at what we are doing today.

What is Invention?

'Don't think. Try.'
—John Hunter to Edward Jenner [Carter, 1993: 564]

'Don't just try. Test.'
—Motto, Cambridge University Police Executive Programme

Invention is a *process* (a verb) that leads to a *result* (a noun) that is known by the same name: invention produces inventions. The results are not just new gadgets, or mechanical devices. They encompass any and all *new designs* for doing things—accomplishing goals, solving problems, reducing costs, and endless other results.

The invention of public education in the nineteenth century was no less an invention than the invention of the telegraph at about the same time. Nor was the eighteenth century medical invention that fundamentally altered the nature of life itself, by making humans immune to diseases, increasing life expectancy, and geometrically increasing the size of human populations: the invention of vaccination. The enormous success of that invention—initially with smallpox, and then with other (but far from all) diseases—makes it a prime example for several principles of invention.

The principles of invention that vaccination illustrates are (a) problem-focus, (b) multiple versions, (c) grounded theory, (d) systematic testing, and (e) theoretical revision. These principles are needed to counteract the 'eureka' model of invention, in which a moment of epiphany turns on a metaphorical lightbulb in the inventor's head. Such moments may, in fact, occur. Yet they rarely comprise the whole story of how the invention was invented. A single breakthrough may well create a tipping point of effectiveness. But it is only in the context of many previous efforts that most such breakthroughs occur, even in the invention of theories. Few people remember, for example, that Charles Darwin's grandfather wrote a book on evolution; the grandson hardly discovered the origin of species all by himself (Jones 2009).

The 'eureka' model of invention is the conventional story of a doctor named Edward Jenner, who is credited with inventing vaccination in rural Gloucestershire, England in the late eighteenth century (Williams 2010). In systematically thinking about his many patients who were dying of smallpox, Dr Jenner's flash of insight came from a common observation that milkmaids who had suffered *cow*pox were never stricken by *small*pox. Cowpox was a minor disease that was rarely fatal. Smallpox was far more fatal, killing large portions of the population. Jenner theorized that something about the minor disease protected people from getting the major disease. His invention was intentionally inducing cowpox in humans by vaccination, a term he invented (Carter 1993).

Jenner's invention of vaccination was a giant step for humankind. But it was only a small incremental step in a long process of inventing vaccination. The full context of the many steps leading to this invention demonstrates the principles of invention this chapter addresses.

Problem-Focus

The most obvious principle of invention is the focus on a problem to be solved. It is not so obvious just how different a way of learning that is from other ways of learning. Vast areas of knowledge can be created by observation without intervention: history, geology, astronomy, linguistics, sociology, and many other fields can study the world without trying to change it. For other kinds of knowledge, however, intervention in the world is an essential element of discovery. That is why Dr William Harvey's (1578–1657) dictum—'Don't think, try!'—is so widely cited in medicine, largely through the surgeon John Hunter's teaching of Dr Edward Jenner (Williams

2010). This reflects the strong reliance of medicine on experimental knowledge, the disciplines whose own motto might be 'no causation without manipulation'. Therein lies even the unlikely connection between medical research and the inventor Karl Marx, who argued that the purpose of studying the world is to solve its problems.

Multiple Versions

The problems Edward Jenner solved were not just the consequences of smallpox itself: a massive death toll and disfigurement for survivors. He also focused on a problem with previous designs for preventing the disease. Inoculation with a small dose of smallpox itself had been recognized as an *effective* preventative earlier in the eighteenth century, partly because of contact with Africans who had long practised it (McCullough 2001: 142). The problem for Jenner was not just effectiveness, but *side effects* of inoculation that made it so very unsafe. Much the same is true for many criminological inventors. Quakers once promoted prison as a humane alternative to hanging, but now must invent alternatives to the excess of mass incarceration.

Jenner's solution to the problems of preventing smallpox fits the general pattern of building on prior work. People had been inoculated for many centuries in China, India, and Africa. But Jenner was the true inventor of the first 'safe' vaccine, in the way this chapter defines the process of invention. Not only did he *try* the invention, he both *theorized* about it and *tested* its outcomes in a more rigorous way.

Grounded Theory

Most inventors appear to theorize about their inventions in a process that Glaser and Strauss (1967) describe as 'grounded theory'. This approach is a combination of both inductive and deductive reasoning. Inductive reasoning generalizes from specific observations to hypothesize general patterns. Deductive reasoning uses general patterns to predict specific observations. Grounded theory is a process of going back and forth between the two methods of reasoning.

Jenner had a grounded theory of why smallpox could be prevented by contracting cowpox. It was wrong, but it did not matter. What seems important about theory for inventors is that they use it to organize their data. What seems less important is that the theory itself be right in the first place. By helping inventors to organize their data, a theory insures a systematic approach to developing a new design.

It is striking just how often inventors have been right in practice but wrong in theory. In many areas of invention, people have discovered how to *predict* results far in advance of their ability to *explain* results with a general theory that fits all the facts. Moreover, a theory helps to organize a strategy for *testing* the design in ways that are more compelling than simply *using* the design and saying it 'works'. People who snap their fingers to keep away tigers in England may justly claim to say their invention 'works', especially if they have never been attacked by tigers. But that is hardly a test that any theory would allow.

Systematic Testing

Jenner's main contribution was not just to *try* inoculation with cowpox. It was to *test* the hypothesis that the inoculation would prevent smallpox. The analogy to 'tiger prevention' would be to teach people to snap their fingers at tigers, and then introduce tigers into the room. What Jenner did was equally dangerous, but far more successful.

Jenner's conclusive experiment was to infect eight-year-old James Phipps (the son of Jenner's gardener) with *smallpox* pus, after the boy had already been inoculated with cowpox pus. While unlikely to survive a modern ethics committee review, this experiment provided a far more conclusive test than mere correlations. It is one thing to be vaccinated and never get smallpox. The result could be explained by either successful vaccination, or a lucky absence of any exposure to smallpox germs. By injecting smallpox pus into an immunized human, Jenner eliminated the main competing hypothesis. Whatever remains after other possible explanations have been eliminated is highly likely to be the truth.[1]

Even when the crucial experiment was completed, scepticism prevailed in medicine. The good result of that scepticism was to add the adjective 'systematic' to the testing Jenner did. He repeated his attempt to infect Phipps, again with no effect. He then repeated the experiments on twenty-two others. The uniform success of immunization in resisting inoculations of smallpox finally convinced the scientific world, and attracted Royal research grants to support his work on vaccination for two more decades. More important, his work became a tipping point for vaccination around the world, and the complete eradication of smallpox in humans by 1979 (Williams 2010).

Theoretical Revision

The pattern of invention can be described as a circular process of data→theory→invention→data→theory. The pattern is clear enough to predict that testing inventions will almost necessarily lead to revisions in the theory on which an invention is based. In one sense, the effect of success in practice is often failure in theory. But the failure is only 'technical.' The success of the theory was to help structure a test that had substantively important results.

In the prevention of infectious disease, Pasteur and others showed where Jenner's theory had been wrong. They elaborated on it with such key concepts as 'herd immunity', by which a large majority of a population must be vaccinated to obtain maximum benefit. They applied the theory of evolution to account for the mutations of diseases to overcome immunities, and to find effective vaccines for other kinds of

[1] As Arthur Conan Doyle said in his references medical school professor-mentor Dr Joseph Bell often observed through the voice of 'Sherlock Holmes', thus anticipating future philosophies of science.

infectious diseases, such as influenza (Barry 2004). Today, the quest to invent new vaccines may be more intense than ever.

Can the same intensity be reported for inventions in criminology?

Example: Braithwaite and Restorative Justice

A prime modern example of invention criminology is very similar to the invention of vaccines. Braithwaite's (1989) theory of reintegrative shaming was prompted by his *focus on the problem* of penal responses to crime, and the failures of modern criminal justice. His theory of 'hating the sin but loving the sinner' attracted him to *previous versions* of that design, including ancient customs of indigenous populations in New Zealand, Asia, the Middle East, and North America (Braithwaite 2002). He then supported a police sergeant in a small Australian city who had been inspired by the New Zealand model of 'family group conferences'. Promoting Sergeant Terry O'Connell's work as an application of reintegrative shaming theory, Braithwaite found funding and staff for systematic testing of the invention. The tests found that face-to-face restorative justice conferences could be very successful, but more so for some groups than others (Sherman and Strang 2007). The detailed data on how offenders reacted to these conferences also required Braithwaite to revise the theory (Ahmed *et al.* 2001).

The restorative justice example also illustrates other principles of invention discussed below. It is a modern, scientifically advanced version of the invention process, more similar to the invention of pharmaceuticals in the twentieth century than to the invention of vaccines in the eighteenth. Yet it builds on a long tradition of criminology as invention, on which we should look back before we look forward.

Historical Examples of Inventions in Criminology

As a proportion of criminological work, criminology may be at the least inventive time in its history. Most English-speaking criminologists appear to be focused on basic science, testing and refining theories of crime causation and desistance across and within individuals. The head of the largest criminology project in history, the Project on Human Development in Chicago Neighborhoods (PHDCN), has repeatedly said he does not use his research to invent policy (Sampson, personal communication, 1996). But there was once a time when inventing new policy was all that criminology did.

Eighteenth Century: A Paid Police

In what was arguably the first treatise on criminology published in English, London playwright and magistrate Henry Fielding published, in 1751, *An enquiry into the causes of the late increase of robbers, &c., with some proposals for remedying this growing evil. In which the present reigning vices are impartially exposed; and the laws that relate to the provision for the poor, and to the punishment of felons are largely and freely examined.* This remarkable book was based on extensive field work in London, including interviews of defendants charged in his court. Its analysis was far more sociological than retributive. The result is a series of 'grounded theory' proposals for regulating the sale of gin (the heroin of its day), managing opportunities for crime, and revamping the failing police system of London.

The early result of publishing this book was a government request to put his proposals to the test. Reacting to a wave of robbery-murders in London, the king's ministers asked Fielding to organize a response. That response became the first well-paid police force in British history. The people Fielding hired put them on the trail of the robbery gangs, who were promptly arrested, convicted and hanged. The spate of murders stopped, and the government kept the police force going (Fielding 1755). They became known as the 'Bow Street Runners'.

In the process, Fielding invented crime statistics, including a fully transparent account of the time and place details of all crimes reported to his office. He also invented rapid response policing, whereby police would be dispatched on horseback whenever a serious crime was reported to the court. His brother John replaced Henry Fielding upon Henry's death in 1754, and institutionalized most of Henry's inventions.

Fielding, like Jenner, had a wealth of data from clinical practice. He used those data to develop a theory, and used the theory to develop a design. He then tried the design—at the behest of criminology's perennial partner, the government. What he did not do that Jenner did was to test the design against a counterfactual. Crime might have gone down even without the creation of his police. It was left to later centuries to test his idea, and to refine the theory by which police prevent crime (Sherman 2011 (forthcoming)).

Nineteenth Century: Customized Sentencing

By the late nineteenth century, the development of universities helped to create an academic specialty in teaching criminal law. Professor Franz von Liszt, a cousin of composer-pianist Franz Liszt, was one of the most influential members of the new professoriat. He was especially important as the first to squarely challenge the dominance of punishment policy by the anti-utilitarian philosophy of Immanuel Kant. Rather than accepting Kant's view that punishment should be determined without regard to its consequences, von Liszt's Marburger Programme of 1882 argued that punishment should fit the criminal, not the crime.[2] His programme, presented at the University of Marburg, was a major invention. Its design greatly reduced use

[2] The programme is available in the original German text at <http://koriath.jura.uni-saarland.de/textsammlung/pmwiki.php?n=FranzVonLisztDerZweckgedankeImStrafrecht.Start>.

of prison, both then and now (by the standards of current US and UK policy, if not Europe or India).

Liszt relied on the early criminology of differences in offending patterns. Rather than treating each crime in isolation, he focused on the offenders committing the crimes. Based on the differences across offenders in the frequency and seriousness of their detected crimes, he proposed using different kinds of criminal punishment for different kinds of offenders. His plans arguably laid the foundation for a century of emphasis on the rehabilitation of criminals as a major purpose of criminal justice. For him, this meant suspended sentences or probation for many first offenders, longer sentences for habitual offenders, and very long sentences for very serious offenders. It is, to a greater or lesser extent, largely what many judges and sentencing guidelines try to do today.

Yet Liszt, like Fielding, was a pre-modern inventor in criminology. He offered no specific theory of rehabilitation, nor of selective incapacitation. He offered no plan to test his proposals, to see if they worked. It was again up to later centuries to both try *and* test an offender-specific approach in the age of rehabilitation.

Twentieth Century: An Alternative to Prison

The age of rehabilitation peaked in the United States in 1975, when the age of mass imprisonment began. In its waning years, there were a series of experiments suggesting that imprisonment could be used less often than it was in that age of low prisoner populations. One of the most important was the Provo (Utah) Experiment (Empey and Erickson 1972) of the early 1960s, led by a University of Southern California criminologist named Lamar Empey. The experiment was designed to apply a range of sociological theories about crime and its treatment to invent a more effective alternative to incarceration. Using random assignment of juvenile delinquents who would normally be incarcerated in a training school, the experimental group was allowed to remain in the community. Their programme included meetings each evening with other delinquents for discussions, described as 'Guided Group Interaction' (GGI). Based in part on Sutherland's theory of differential association, the GGI was designed to decrease the positive evaluations of crime and increase the negative messages young people would receive about crime.

This theory was tested in a way that was highly advanced, but imperfectly implemented. A breakdown of random assignment was the major problem, when too few offenders were randomly assigned to the incarcerated control group. The response was to incorporate offenders from other communities beyond Provo, which made the control group less comparable to the experimental group living in Provo. Despite these problems, the findings were at least suggestive. They showed higher repeat offending rates among those randomly assigned to incarceration than those who remained in the community. Whether that difference was due to the rehabilitation programme or the freedom from incarceration remains unclear. But the experiment itself was a bold vision of how a criminological invention can be tested.

Inventions vs Innovations

These three historical examples demonstrate a clear progression in the role of science in invention. In the eighteenth century, Henry Fielding invented the police with little formal theory or reliable data for testing. In the nineteenth century, Franz von Liszt invented customized sentences with extensive bureaucratic records kept by Bismarck's Germany. Yet he still lacked the capacity to test his programme, or to demonstrate how favourably (or not) it compared to existing penal practices.

Not until the mid-twentieth century did Lamar Empey become the first criminological inventor who used both formal theory and rigorous experimental testing. His test was limited to juveniles, the test was compromised, and the historical tide turned against rehabilitation. Yet the example of using random assignment to compare prison to a new form of probation was a radical step forward for the modern science of criminological invention.

Modern Science and Inventions in Criminology

This section attempts to identify the key elements of using modern science for criminology as invention. Using modern examples, it touches briefly on the use of both data and theory at every step of the process. Its premise is that inventing does not stop once a design has been tested, just like political campaigns do not stop with an election. The process must be constantly repeated, always looking ahead for something better than what we have already.

Identifying Problems

Einstein observed that the most important part of science is framing the right question. That observation is no less true in the applied science of invention than it is in theoretical physics. The questions for inventors require broad imagination, of the kind that leads to 'what if?' questions. Such questions are the grist of an inventor's mill, leading to the grinding assessment of feasibility. 'What if everyone graduated from university?' is the kind of question that will fail a feasibility test. So too, in the current political climate, would a question like 'What if we abolished prisons?'

What *will* pass such a test may depend on how skilful an inventor may be in raising funds and gaining access to public policy decisions. Lamar Empey had access to a judge in Utah, and to a major foundation (Ford) in New York. Both were essential for even designing the experiment, let alone carrying it out.

The chronological sequence in which these tasks are accomplished may not be as important as the interaction among them. Just as Thomas Edison had to manage the municipal governments regulating electrical supplies (in addition to inventing a feasibly marketable light bulb), criminological inventors must work on many fronts to make something new happen. All of that requires the vision needed to frame the problem in all its parts. That problem may be stated like this: 'What if we tried to do this—what pieces of the plan would we have to put together?'

Diagnosis

Diagnosing a problem requires a review of all the facts known about the problem. When data are available to review, they can reveal important clues to the design of a new invention. But the data need to be directly tied to the problem at hand, rather than vaguely and loosely related to that problem.

Murder: An Example. The forecasting of domestic homicide and attempted murder is a new task that British police took up in the early twenty-first century. The tool they chose to use was based not on who was committing those homicides and how they could be identified in advance. It was based, instead, on risk factors for domestic violence in general, most of which is non-injurious and certainly non-lethal. These risk factors led to clinical judgments to select the persons placed on a watch list requiring extra supervision by multi-agency partnerships, including probation, social services and others.

But were the watch lists reliable predictors of homicide? Possibly not. Subsequent reviews of forecasting accuracy in several police agencies showed that most homicides and attempted homicides were committed by people who were not on the watch list. Whether that means the watch list effectively protected the people on them is unclear. What is clear is that most homicidal attackers were 'false negatives': cases that had been predicted (by definition) not to merit placement on the watch list.

The chief constable of Thames Valley Police, Sara Thornton, personally examined the data on domestically homicidal offenders. She found that the majority of them had records of prior crime, but *not* of prior domestic violence. Similar findings had been reported in the United States and Australia. Her diagnosis suggested that a more accurate forecasting tool would need to be based on a far larger population than known domestic violence offenders. Such a data-driven tool has already been developed for murder among a population of 30,000 probationers in Philadelphia (Berk *et al.* 2009), and could be applied to the UK data as well. Such a procedure reflects the advanced tools of scientific diagnosis that are now available to criminologists.

Theory

The role of theory in an invention may be 'deductive' from a formal theory in criminology, or 'grounded' in the data. Inventions may borrow pieces from a variety of theories or diagnostic facts. They may also fit the framework of several theories simultaneously. In that respect, they are not designed to test theories or even compare them. Inventions are designed to 'work:' to achieve the greatest good for the greatest number. There is nothing so useful as a good theory, and perhaps the more the better. As the discussion of restorative justice demonstrates below, there are some inventions that even fit theories not yet born at the time the experiment begins. The role of theory in such inventions may be said to be accidental rather than intentional. But a constant awareness of how an invention connects to the current state of theory may help to improve the invention's results—as well as to help specify and refine the theory. That is just what happened with Randall Collins' (2004) theory of interaction ritual chains, which had used the restorative justice experiments in Australia as an example of the theory.

Design

Most criminal justice innovations are designed without theories or even logic models. Many of them have unclear objectives, unspecified actions that must be accomplished, and unspecified outcomes. Many federal programmes documented in Sherman *et al.* (1997) have those characteristics. By the standards of this chapter, they would not be considered inventions. They may not even be innovations. As one multiagency partnership group told me in the United Kingdom in 2009, a new programme called 'Integrated Offender Management' would manage offenders in exactly the same way that they had been managed before the new programme. The only difference would be that there would be 'more meetings' of the people supervising the offenders.

A criminological invention requires a blueprint. Like a patent, the description of the invention should literally be able to show who must do what to whom and how. It must also show how these tasks will be measured, at least in a testing phase, in order to tell whether the invention is actually in operation. But far too many new 'programmes' fail to meet this key definition of a criminological invention.

Testing

The key distinction between modern and historical invention is *testing*. The contrast between just 'trying' and really 'testing' is crucial, but not obvious to the general public—or elected officials.

A 'try' is operating the invention, like vaccinating a human with cowpox. A test examines the *effects* of the invention: trying to give smallpox to an immunized human to see if the invention fails. The 'try' is often called a 'proof of concept,' while the test is called an 'evaluation'.

Sadly, most of the major innovations in modern crime and justice have been tried without testing. Sentencing guidelines, for example, have been widely adopted, with the possible result that they have vastly increased incarceration, costs, and possibly crime. The inventors of this idea, however, were never required, or allowed, to fully test its consequences.

The *scientific* inventor's motto has been adopted in the Cambridge Police Executive Programme, which provides post-graduate degrees and training to senior police commanders. That motto is 'Don't just try. Test.' The programme's students have had ample experience of central governments trying without testing. But many, like chief constable Thornton, are becoming inventing criminologists as well.

The programme helps respond to frustrations over repeated 'pilots' of new crime and justice policies that failed to embed any test of whether they 'worked' in achieving better results. 'Community payback justice', for example, was a new requirement in 2009 for offenders sentenced to community service to wear bright orange jackets. The government's claim was that the visibility of the offenders—as in the chain gangs of old—would reassure law-abiding citizens that justice was being done, that retribution was accomplished. It was not clear whether the programme also was intended to deter crime or prevent recidivism. What was clear is that there was no transparent impact evaluation of the programme, no way to determine a cost-benefit of the investment in this new design.

This approach sharply contrasted with earlier UK practice, and with current US Department of Justice strategy: a much more explicit 'try and test' model of invention. Since the 1990s, the US Department of Justice's Office of Justice Programs has let millions of dollars of contracts with twin coordinated contractors. One organization is hired to deliver the 'try', while the other is to deliver the 'test'. The success of the model depends entirely on the quality of the test, especially in achieving an unbiased control or comparison group. Very often this model starts the try long before the test, which leaves the evaluation unable to measure before-and-after-differences, let alone a comparison. The evaluation methods literature (eg, Berk and Rossi, 1999) repeatedly warns against this problem, but criminologists are often powerless to prevent it.

What criminology needs to do about it is to promote the teaching of its science to government officials who make these decisions. A modern Enlightenment of evidence-based government would embrace the idea that senior officials require rigorous training in programme evaluation. Until then the experts will be at the mercy of generalists who fail to appreciate the distinction between trying and testing.

Results

Even when rigorous testing occurs, there are often endless debates about how to interpret results. The opponents of inventions may object to them for other reasons, yet focus on the test results as the most vulnerable target of attack. Any new programme that threatens the funding of existing programmes is clearly in that category. Testing alone is no guarantee that test results will be fairly interpreted. Criminologists who wish to see the results of their tests treated fairly should be prepared for a long and relentless battle over interpreting the results. The playing field of politics is not as level as the design of a fair test. The victors in such contests will not be the best scientists or inventors, but the best communicators.

How the results of tests are *interpreted* may depend more on advocates of an invention than on the inventors themselves. Criminologists are rarely inclined to become their own advocates, nor is there much record of their success at propagating inventions on the strength of research alone. But when people with an emotional stake in the invention can support good test results, the potential for adoption of an invention is enormous. That is the lesson of the Vera Institute's test of release on recognizance (Ares, Rankin, and Sturz 1967), which remains a model for the process of criminological invention.

The UK's restorative justice experiments in 2001–5, for example, were tried and tested at a cost of over £5 million. Heather Strang and I led the 'try' in the form of randomized controlled trials, while Joanna Shapland and her colleagues (2008) ran the 'test' as independent evaluators of the trials. Her team's results were complex and subject to quotation out of context. There was, for example, no significant difference in prevalence of repeat offending, but there was a statistically significant average reduction of 27 per cent in the frequency of reconviction over two years (a number that is never presented in the evaluation report, but is calculable from the data in Figure 2.6 and Table 2.3). There was no significant reduction in the Home Office scale of seriousness of repeat offending, but there was a large benefit to cost ratio of 8 to 1 savings in cost of crime in relation to the cost of the programme (again not stated, but calculated from data in Table 4.8), which Shapland *et al.* (2008: 65) describe as 'value for money.'

Ironically, some members of Parliament have recited these findings, chapter and verse, to senior civil servants. The latter have been less familiar with the details than the MPs, but have accepted what junior officials told them: that peer reviews of the Shapland (*et al.* 2008) study were 'mixed'. Since that can be said about most papers in science, accepted for publication or not, its meaning is entirely in the hands of the messenger. Whether the clear statements on value for money can become the conventional wisdom about what the studies found may depend upon the advocacy of such groups as the Restorative Justice Council and 'Why Me?', the organization of victims for restorative justice.

An alternative view is that criminologists should never stop pouring evidence of tests into the policy-making process. Howarth (2010) suggests that the timing of a policy decision is never predictable, and will hardly ever follow on the heels of new research findings. His thesis is that constant inflows of data may build up a wealth of evidence that can be marshalled when the time is right. His optimism, as a former shadow Justice minister of the Liberal Democratic Party, should provide a more realistic grounding for inventing criminologists. It may also defend them against sceptics who define testing as a 'failure' if the policy implications are not translated into policy almost immediately.

What Next?

The time to stop testing, then, may be never. Rather than waiting for the policy-making process to get around to serious consideration of the testing so far, inventing criminologists may be well advised to keep on testing. The need for evidence is, after all, enormous, given the uncertainty of predictions from one sample to the next, or to entire populations. The only reason to stop testing altogether may be when an invention should clearly be placed on the 'reject list' of how not to accomplish a goal.

Reject List

The key question is whether testing is intended for refining an invention, or judging it for a life-or-death sentence (Sherman and Strang 2004). The Maryland Report to the US Congress (Sherman *et al.* 1997) had a long list of 'What Doesn't Work'. The standard was relatively low: two or more quasi-experimental studies showing no positive effects, without a substantial body of other evidence to the contrary. Such a standard does run the risk of cutting off further testing of an invention that might still work. But it may also save a lot of time and money.

The 1997 report, for example, concluded that the Drug Abuse Resistance Education (DARE) programme does not work. Uniformed police teaching young school children to resist drugs made good television. But repeated tests had found almost no benefit in preventing drug abuse. The programme reacted to the report by saying that the effects took a long time to materialize, and that the dosage should be higher in any case. That claim attracted over $10 million in new research funding for a randomized controlled trial. Ten years later, the RCT reported that the new, improved version of DARE was no more effective than the original version.

Good testing is always useful, no matter what the result. It is very important to know what does not work. Edison, for example, said recording what does not work adds to our knowledge one more way *not* to make a light bulb. And Einstein defined insanity as repeating the same action in hopes of obtaining a different result. The more replication, the less reason there is to keep testing an invention that does not work. Yet when the results are mixed, the course of future action is less clear.

More Testing

In a scientific approach to invention, the reason to keep testing is to learn when an invention might work, or for whom, more predictably than can be discerned from one or only a few tests. While the ethics of testing become more problematic when clear benefits have been established (Federal Judicial Center 1981), the risk of subgroups having an adverse reaction remains high. Testing with large enough samples, for example, revealed that Australian Aboriginals reacted very badly to restorative justice (Sherman and Strang 2007). Further testing of arrest for minor domestic violence (Sherman 1992) also found adverse reactions among unemployed suspects. These complications provide inconvenient truths that both policy and theory must accommodate.

Redesign

Ideally, testing an invention leads to its being redesigned, again and again. Josiah Wedgwood invented modern Chinaware in the eighteenth century by keeping careful records of over 5,000 tests. James Dyson developed a new carpet sweeper in the twentieth century with over 5,000 tests of his design as well. Inventing criminologists have been constrained by the governmental expectation that every policy must be right the first time, and make no mistakes. If that is the standard, then there may need to be a political plan for allowing policy development to continue long before policy adoption.

Scale Up

Once a newly invented crime policy is 'ready'—however defined—the standard engineering recommendation is to take two steps rather than one. The first step is to 'scale up' the design. When inventions are operated on larger scale, the volume of production may reveal complications and variations that can lead to more refinements. This can also become part of a continuous quality improvement.

Roll-Out

The final step in scientific invention is the roll-out. The crucial data needed at this stage is whether the invention is being delivered as designed. Equally important is whether rare events arise—harmful or otherwise—that were not evident when the invention was in development.

It is just as important for inventors to track the mass usage of the invention as for them to test the prototype. For Jenner, it was tracking the number of people who contracted smallpox despite being vaccinated with cowpox. For Edison and his companies, it was tracking the rate of electrical fires and electrocutions after electricity was installed in millions of homes. For sentencing guidelines, it could have been tracking the effect they had on causing imprisonment rates to rise.

For many inventing criminologists, the questions of what effects a roll-out has would be a welcome challenge. What is more difficult is to get to that point at all. One thing that may help a good invention along is a good theory.

But Does it Work in Theory?

There is an old saw about inventions that work very well in practice, but which provoke the objection that they do not work 'in theory'. The truth in that joke is that people find it hard to accept facts that violate their own 'theory' of how things work. The experimental evidence that arrest can cause an *increase* in domestic violence—rather than deterring it—was rejected by people whose theory was that deterrence works. The problem, to them, was that the evidence must be wrong because it did not fit their theory. But it is little use telling people they must let the evidence take precedence over a theory. Emotionally and instinctively, most people (including academics) need an acceptable theory to make sense of, and accept, an unexpected piece of evidence.

The final task of the inventing criminologist may be to develop a theory that accounts for the anomaly. Squaring new evidence with old theory is a challenge that is not beyond most scientists. One example was my development of defiance theory (Sherman, 1993) to account for a series of anomalous findings in relation to the deterrence doctrine. By showing how the twice-replicated facts could be reconciled with an integration of existing criminological theories, defiance helped many criminologists (if not advocates) to accept the evidence as correct. Absent such a reconciliation, a major paradigm shift may be necessary to accept a new invention as one that 'works'.

Conclusion

Criminology is a field of invention, just as much as it is a field of research and theory-building. Its inventions can do great good, or great harm. The examples of criminology as invention go far beyond the limited space of this essay. Many are in progress at time of this writing. Most are associated with experimental criminology, even as they link to the major (or minor) theories in criminology. With more and more successful inventions to its credit, the field of criminology may attract even more inventive people to its ranks. Many of them may be mid-career professionals, such as the police chiefs who have enrolled at Cambridge to take a PhD after several decades of police service. Others may be inventors who would like to do something about crime. Some of them may even read this essay. I wish them all the best of luck.

References

Ahmed, E., Harris, N., Braithwaite, J., and Braithwaite, V. (2001), *Shame Management Through Integration*, Cambridge: Cambridge University Press.

Ares, C. E., Rankin, A., and Sturz, H. (1963), 'The Manhattan Bail Project: An interim report on the use of pre-trial parole', *New York University Law Review* 67:38.

Barry, J. (2004), *The Great Influenza*, New York: Viking.

Beccaria, C. (1764), *On crimes and punishments*, trans. J. Grigson, Milan, Italy: Oxford University Press, 1964.

Berk, R. and Rossi, P. (1999), *Thinking About Program Evaluation*, Thousand Oaks: Sage.

Berk, R., Sherman, L., Barnes, G., Kurtz, E., and Ahlman, L. (2009), 'Forecasting murder within a population of probationers and parolees: a high stakes application of statistical learning', *Journal of the Royal Statistical Society* (Series A). 172: 191–211.

Braithwaite, J. (1989), *Crime, Shame and Reintegration*. Cambridge: Cambridge University Press.

____ (2002), *Restorative Justice and Responsive Regulation*, New York: Oxford.

Carter, R. (1993), 'Surgical Sketches: John Hunter, 1728–1793', *World Journal of Surgery*, 17: 563–5.

Collins, R. (2004), *Interaction Ritual Chains*, Princeton: Princeton University Press.

Empey, L. T. and Erickson, M. (1972), *The Provo Experiment: Evaluating Community Control of Delinquency*, Lexington: DC Heath.

Federal Judicial Center (1981), *Experimentation in the Law*, Washington: Federal Judicial Center.

Fielding, H. (1751), *An enquiry into the causes of the late increase of robbers, &c., with some proposals for remedying this growing evil. In which the present reigning vices are impartially exposed; and the laws that relate to the provision for the poor, and to the punishment of felons are largely and freely examined*, London.

____ (1755), *Journal of a Voyage to Lisbon*, London.

Glaser, B. and Straus, A. (1967), *The Discovery of Grounded Theory: Strategies for Qualitative Research*, Chicago: Aldine.

Howarth, D. (2010), 'How Should Ministers and Parliament Be Educated on Evidence?' Paper presented to the Third International NPIA-Cambridge Conference on Evidence-Based Policing. 6 August, Institute of Criminology, Cambridge University.

Hurd, D. (2007), *Peel*, London: Weidenfeld and Nicolson.

Jones, S. (2009), *Darwin's Island: The Galapagos in the Garden of England*, London: Little, Brown.

Lombard, M., Pastoret, P.-P., and Moulin, A.-M. (2007), 'A Brief History of Vaccines and Vaccination' Rev. sci. tech. Off. int. Epiz., 26 (1): 29–48.

McCullough, D. (2001), *John Adams*, New York: Simon and Schuster.

Shapland, J., Atkinson, A., Atkinson, H., Dignan, J., Edwards, L., Hibbert, J., Howes, M., Johnstone, J., Robinson, G., and Sorsby, A. (2008), Does restorative justice affect reconviction? The fourth report from the evaluation of three schemes', London: Ministry of Justice.

Sherman, L. (1992), *Policing domestic violence: Experiments and dilemmas*, New York: Free Press.

____ (1993), 'Defiance, Deterrence and Irrelevance: A Theory of the Criminal Sanction', *Journal of Research in Crime and Delinquency*, 30: 445–73.

Sherman, L. W. (2003), 'Reason for Emotion: Reinventing Justice with Theories, Innovations and Research. 2002 ASC Presidential Address' *Criminology*, 41 (1): 1–38.

____ (2005), 'The Use and Usefulness of Criminology, 1751–2005: Enlightened Justice and Its Failures', ANNALS of the American Academy of Political and Social Science, 600: 115–135.

____ (2006), 'To Develop and Test: The Inventive Difference Between Evaluation and Experimentation', *Journal of Experimental Criminology*, 2(3): 393–406.

____ (2010), 'An Introduction to Experimental Criminology', in A. Piquero and D. Weisburd (eds), *Handbook of Quantitative Criminology*, New York: Springer: 399–436.

____ (2011), 'Police and Crime Control: Getting Research Into Practice', in M. Tonry (ed.), *Oxford Handbook of Criminal Justice*, New York: Oxford University Press.

____, Gottfredson, D., MacKenzie, D., Reuter, P., Eck, J., and Bushway, S. (1997), 'Preventing Crime: What Works, What Doesn't, What's Promising', A Report to the US Congress, Washington: US Department of Justice, 655 pp.

____ and Strang, H. (2004), 'Verdicts or Inventions? Interpreting Randomized Controlled Trials in Criminology', *American Behavioral Scientist* 47 (5): 575–607.

____ and ____ (2007), *Restorative Justice: The Evidence*, London: Smith Institute.

Uglow, J. (2002), *The Lunar Men*, London: Faber.

Williams, G. (2010), *Angel of Death: The Story of Smallpox*, London: Palgrave Macmillan.

29

CRIMINOLOGICAL CLIQUES: NARROWING DIALOGUES, INSTITUTIONAL PROTECTIONISM, AND THE NEXT GENERATION

KELLY HANNAH-MOFFAT*

THIS chapter presents three related challenges faced by the 'discipline' of criminology, with the goal of promoting dialogue about the field's future. I first argue that although criminology has achieved disciplinary status with discrete areas of

* I would like to thank the editors and my colleagues for reading earlier drafts of this paper and for continuing to challenge my position.

specialization, it is vitally important that criminological research and education draw on the range of other disciplinary knowledges that intersect with criminology. Second, I explore how the development of research branches in many criminal justice agencies, who are rightly concerned with the everyday pragmatics of policing or punishing can (and in some cases do) shape and restrict research possibilities. I examine how emerging forms of institutional protectionism restrict the production of critical criminological knowledge. These observations may be applicable to other countries, but this chapter focuses on the research landscape in Canada. Finally, I consider how commitments to intellectual diversity and the restrictions imposed on certain types of 'critical' scholarship can complicate future criminologists' research and education. These three themes are linked by my broader interest in criminological knowledge, its structure and progression as well as by a need to discuss how various institutional 'boundaries' shape our theorizing, research questions, types of analysis and scholarly standards.

Narrowing Dialogues: Splintering and Specialization

Criminology is a field of inquiry that draws deeply from the conceptual and methodological strategies of multiple disciplines (cf Edwards 1985). Although it can be difficult to define with precision, criminology is often characterized as a cross- or inter-disciplinary field of study that encompasses a wide range of theoretical, methodological, and policy perspectives. In this context, 'inter-disciplinary' refers to the ways that criminological inquiry crosses and builds on disciplines including geography, philosophy, psychology, history, and law, meaning that it is not simply or even primarily a subfield of sociology.[1] Richard Ericson and Kevin Carriere (1994: 89) noted that criminology 'is a depository of multiple academic discourses and a generator of blurring among disciplines'. While it could be characterized as fragmented, I argue that criminology's epistemological boundaries are necessarily fluid.

Criminological inquiries have been broadened and advanced by research and theory that cross substantive fields of investigation and academics have worked for decades to create an inter-disciplinary space for the study of criminology to flourish (see, *inter alia*, Weir and Curtis 2002; 2003; O'Malley and Hunt 2003; Crocker 2003). Early and unconventional forays in criminology encouraged scholars to think creatively when analysing criminal justice institutions. Some fifteen years ago, for instance, Clifford Shearing and Philip Stenning (1985) encouraged a wide-ranging understanding of policing that included private police, communities, regulation, and security. Elsewhere, other scholars argued for a broader understanding of penality as

[1] See Hagan (1988) and Downs and Rock (1982) for discussions of the relationship between sociology and criminology.

an alternative to the narrow framework of punishment or the technical institutional study of penology (Garland 1990; Braithwaite 2003). Recent dialogues about security and risk demonstrate how a diverse group of scholars can bring insights from several substantive fields (insurance, finance, public health, management, and environment) to the study of law, 'crime', and 'criminal justice' (eg, Zedner 2003; Shearing and Johnston 2006; Ericson 2007; Loader 2007). Others such as Mariana Valverde have challenged 'the criminological habit of reading [M. Foucault's] *Discipline and Punish* in isolation, and the related practice of using this book only to answer existing criminological questions', calling instead for more nuanced and comprehensive theoretical inquires (Valverde 2009: 201; also see Valverde 2010).

In order to take up this call for more nuanced and comprehensive theoretical inquiries, criminology needs to 'cope with an almost unlimited range of potentially relevant disciplines from which it does and could borrow concepts and methods' (Nelken 1994: 11; also see Ericson and Carriere 1994). Arguably, the field of criminological inquiry also transcends the criminal to include other forms and sites of regulation (eg, schools, health and voluntary sectors, financial markets, and private companies). Some of the most effective criminological inquiries have crossed the boundaries of legal and institutional disciplines to investigate how various systems of regulation evolve, overlap, and interact.[2]

Over the past several years, the field of criminology in Canada and elsewhere has become more narrowly 'disciplinary' as it strives for autonomy from related subfields. New departments of criminology are emerging and splintering off from law schools and sociology departments, while a seemingly ever-increasing number of criminology journals and specialized subfields are being established. Although criminology, socio-legal studies, and newly emergent social justice studies continue to coexist in some settings, they are more often than not considered distinct fields of study with separate research agendas, journals, and conferences. The increasing number of specialist journals and conferences may be narrowing audiences and reducing dialogues between subfields and in some cases between traditional disciplines. The American Society of Criminology now has six distinct divisions,[3] each with separate governance structures and some with their own journals. A Canadian Criminology Association has recently formed and although general criminological journals are still available, so are approximately thirty-one specialist criminology/penology journals and 104 law review journals. These numbers do not include the

[2] The work of legal geographers and theorists of space may add to our understanding of how aspects of punishment are spatially organized and how parole and policing practices are central to the production and regulation of criminogenic spaces (Turnbull and Hannah-Moffat 2008). Beckett and Herbert (2010) recently investigated how civil trespass orders are becoming a mechanism of 'banishment' enforced by police and how they intersect with traditional criminal sanctions.

[3] These divisions include: Division on Corrections and Sentencing; Division on Critical Criminology; Division of Experimental Criminology; Division of International Criminology; Division on People of Color and Crime; Division on Women and Crime.

multitude of sociology journals and unranked specialized substantive criminology journals. The increased production of specialist journals could lead to even narrower debates and fewer broadly based dialogues. The ideal of expertise and the shear quantity of scholarship in subfields makes this form of comprehensive engagement challenging. Although individuals are often members of multiple groups and read a range of journals, the proliferation of subfield expertise produces 'boundaries' that could ultimately restrict theorizing and research.

The current organization of criminological knowledge has produced parallel literatures on substantive topics involving related and/or relevant theoretical empirical research, with limited interaction. For example, a lively debate about therapeutic justice and problem-solving courts has emerged in the area of specialized courts, whereas distinct and separate literatures have emerged loosely organized by the type of court (eg, domestic violence, drugs, Aboriginal, mental health). Although informative, the study of specialized courts also requires an analysis of how these courts reconfigure relationships with the community and produce alternative views of race, addiction, and mental health. This kind of analysis can benefit from insights in literature about punishment, social policy, culture, immigration, public health, risk, the voluntary sector, feminism, and critical race and organizational theories, but unfortunately little cross-fertilization takes place. Some scholars working in this area have incorporated this kind of analysis (Walsh 2001; Birgen and Ward 2003; Carson 2003; Moore and Lyons 2008; Nolan 2009), but debates are becoming more narrow and specific to the types of court being studied (Fischer 2003; Gover *et al.* 2003; Galloway and Drapela 2006; Schneider 2006; Marlow *et al.* 2006; Gottfredson *et al.* 2007). Similarly, the area of punishment and risk includes distinct feminist, critical race, psychological policy, and governance literature, which rarely intersect, despite their examination of similar substantive topics (for exception see Blanchette and Brown 2006; Hannah-Moffat 2009). Some scholars[4] working in substantive areas of criminology such as sentencing have recognized the limits of narrow substantive debates, and efforts are being made to reconnect with a broader disciplinary base. For any subfield of scholarship to continue to flourish and remain relevant, cross-area and cross-disciplinary dialogues are required.

Perhaps ironically, other areas of criminology informed by feminist, critical, and Foucauldian scholarship are also becoming more insular, even when they do not share a common subject of study. Thus, constriction is apparent in traditionally marginalized areas of criminology. For instance, feminist engagements with criminology have produced many theoretical, methodological, institutional, and political changes and the success of feminist criminology has positioned debates about the criminalization of women, victimization, and women's penality within 'mainstream' criminology. Feminist criminology has become an established and active

[4] See for example, <www.albany.edu/scj/SentencingSymposium.htm> (accessed 12 February 2010), and forthcoming special issue of *Criminology and Public Policy* (2011).

subfield based on the type of analysis brought to bear on an issue irrespective of the substantive content. The American Society of Criminology (ASC) has a separate division for women and crime with its own journal entitled *Feminist Criminology*. In short, pioneering feminist contributions to criminology put gender on the criminological map, so to speak (Heidensohn 1968; Bertrand 1969; Smart 1976; Gelsthorpe and Morris 1988; Daly and Chesney Lind 1988; Rafter and Heidensohn 1994, Naffine 1997; also see contributions on masculinity and crime Messerschmidt 1993; Jefferson and Carlen 1996).

Critiques of feminist criminologies, especially those pertaining to white, middle class, and heterosexual privilege, established intellectual space for a wider range of feminisms that includes active engagement in the study of the diversity of women's (and to a lesser extent the diversity of men's) experiences. Many feminist criminologists embrace intersectional perspectives and have built allegiances with other critical scholars. For instance, the ASC division of Women and Crime routinely promotes intersectional (race/gender) engagement and scholarship. Yet, even though feminist criminology, more than any other area, has fostered conceptual frameworks that recognize multiple and intersecting inequalities and forms of regulation (see Burgess-Proctor 2006), substantive boundaries exist within feminist criminology (see Moore 2007). Feminist criminologists are having even fewer discussions with 'feminists' and other critical scholars who are positioned outside criminology and studying 'gender' or other diversities and the welfare state, social policy, immigration, and health. Similarly, other veins of 'critical criminology' have limited interaction with feminist scholars. Narrower focuses on the experiences of women within the criminal justice system are instructive but should continue to be connected to other institutional forms and theorizations about the regulations of gender, sexuality, race, and marginality (for example, see Haney 2004).

Notwithstanding the 'success' of critical scholarship, the field of criminology (including critical elements) is grappling with the meaningful integration of persistently marginalized areas within the discipline. Criminology texts continue to neglect and separate questions of gender, race, and sexual diversity and may include these issues in one or two token chapters (indeed they rarely consider issues around sexual diversity). Criminological policy discussions persist in framing gender categorically as sex and race as something separate from gender. Feminist criminology has also experienced a backlash; like many critical discourses, it has encountered the pains of institutional cooptation by governing authorities (Moore 2007). Although some researchers are engaged in a thriving theoretical dialogue on the politics of intersectionality (Daly 2008; Burgess-Proctor 2006; Yuval-Davis 2006), few studies have incorporated these insights into general criminological theory, substantive research, or policy.[5] Some individual researchers are inclusive and move easily between subfields and disciplines, but scholars are increasingly writing for, and

[5] The separation of these categories (theory, research, and policy) is somewhat artificial.

speaking to, audiences who are interested in a specific theoretical or substantive area or subfield. The same groups of people gather at conferences and exchange ideas; few venture into unfamiliar territory. Narrow discussions are constructive but should not be isolated from broader discussions. These developments have indisputable effects on researchers working in these areas, especially young scholars. For the discipline to flourish, the next phase of criminology will require both sustained, active reflection and inclusion of broad interdisciplinary dialogues. The evolution of criminological theory and research will require crossing crudely defined epistemological boundaries, as well as reading literature and studying fields (ie, insurance, organizational risk management, urban governance, voluntary sector) that have seemed too many to be peripheral to the mainstream study of crime and criminal justice.

Criminological Knowledge and Institutional Protectionism

The previous section focused on the expansion and prospective splintering of criminological research into a series of subfields. I argued that in favour for more cross-disciplinary and cross-field dialogue, especially in the area of critical scholarship. A related divide in criminology pertains to the relationship between the criminal justice agencies and the discipline of criminology. Although empirical researchers, and to a lesser degree theorists, benefit from the co-operation of criminal justice institutions, these agencies' interest in the production of criminological knowledge is tenuous and influenced by politics and the structure of the agency (Walters 2003). Many Canadian criminal justice agencies have established research branches to develop, evaluate policies, practices and specific programmes. This chapter is not objecting to this form of criminological knowledge. Instead the following examines how these institutional research practices can produce a context wherein some forms of intellectual inquiry are seen as 'legitimate' and others as 'threatening' or redundant. Arguably, critical criminologies that examine discrimination, marginalization and question various institutional practices are most at risk of being negatively characterized. By viewing some types of criminological knowledge as 'risky', organizations can limit access and opportunities for research (see, for example, the discussion of 'knowledge destruction' Andrews and Bonta 1998; Zinger *et al.* 2001; Gendreau *et al.* 2000; Bonta 2007). These practices shape criminological knowledge and lead to various forms of institutional protectionism and intellectual polarizations and limit the potential for interdisciplinary dialogues.

In Canada, a growing degree of institutional protectionism has begun to shape research by restricting and 'policing' some academics' access to criminal justice agencies in Canada. Criminological research is often motivated by intellectual curiosity, but also by deeply rooted concerns about social justice. It is important to consider the extent to which criminological research can and should influence policy (see Petersilia 2008).[6] Other chapters address the issue of public criminology and administrative criminology (eg, see Hope in this volume and Hough in this volume). This section explores a slightly different, but still related, focus on finding and maintaining a space for critical self-reflexive institutional research. Here I explore how access to research sites can shape the type of questions researchers explore and the kinds of criminological knowledges produced. I argue that although the 'field' of criminology in Canada is intellectually diverse and by and large convivial to critical perspectives, criminal justice institutions (perhaps understandably) only reluctantly and purposefully engage with 'critical' scholars.

In Canada, research on punishment is complex and difficult to negotiate for critical scholars who challenge the assumptions underpinning hegemonic correctional approaches, or whose research may bring the system into disrepute. Many scholars are experiencing forms of 'managerialist interventions'[7] that are affecting research funding as well as shaping the type of research conducted and the forms of research access negotiated. Research driven by intellectual curiosity is becoming more difficult, as is research that cannot be compartmentalized into areas of study currently being conducted by 'in-house' researchers working within criminal justice organizations. For example, Corrections Canada[8] has a large and multifaceted research branch that organizes and regulates the study of correctional populations in Canada as well as access to data about correctional populations, policies, and programmes. In-house research departments, which often hire graduates of Canadian criminology or psychology programmes, increasingly dictate the type of research conducted either by censoring access to information or dominating the production and dissemination of information. Students and scholars interested in critical institutional research face many barriers, and the situation is worsening.

Over the past few years a growing number scholars have found it difficult to gain access to data and secure the cooperation of criminal justice agencies (police, court, correctional). Academic researchers are required to submit their proposals to institutional research committees who review and vet proposals. These proposals *do not* include requests for funding, but simply request access to individual staff, clients, or documents. Most research requests coming from university faculty and doctoral students have already cleared university ethics committees; still, many critical researchers are being denied access. Although the reasons for not granting institutional access to researchers include characterizing research as irrelevant or useless, they are usually diplomatically positioned and admittedly sometimes valid. They can include concerns about confidentiality, resources validity of research questions,

[6] I firmly support criminology's engagement with policy.

[7] Term borrowed from O'Malley and Hunt (2003).

[8] The Correctional Service of Canada (CSC) is responsible for administering the custodial sentences of offenders imprisoned two years or more. CSC is also responsible for supervising offenders under conditional release (parole) in the community (<www.csc-scc.gc.ca/text/index-eng.shtml>, accessed 16 February 2010).

and ability to accommodate requests to visit the institution. Often, the issue of research access is framed as a 'resource issue': resources are typically interpreted in terms of the staff time required to enable the research. For example, if a researcher requests interviews with prisoners and/or visits to institutions, the response may well be based on concerns about the amount of time required for staff to supervise these activities. Requests to interview correctional staff are perceived as inefficient encroachments on staff time, even when researchers offer to interview and contact individuals during off hours. In some cases, access to staff can be facilitated through unions or other means outside of work hours; however, if a researcher has been denied access by an agency, then staff who agree to interviews under such circumstances are placed in a precarious position because they are being asked to engage in a research process that is not officially sanctioned. In many cases, deeper probing reveals that 'resource limitations' is a code for concerns about the utility of the research and/or the 'risk' it represents to the institution. Researchers denied access have little recourse; institutions presently possess the power to shut down a considerable amount of critical scholarship.

In some cases, access is granted but strictly limited to the data or individuals deemed by the institution as relevant. Institutionally selected interview participants may provide researchers with useful data, but often the nature and scope of the available information is limited, and the structure of the access granted to the researchers can limit their ability to study a wider sample. Further, some agencies now require researchers to sign contracts that stipulate that the agency has the right to review any articles or materials produced for publication. This stipulation is included to purportedly ensure a 'high standard' and that the information being presented/published is correct.[9] There is no guarantee that the organization will be timely in its review of the material. These requirements and restrictions give institutions a considerable amount of power over the production of knowledge. They also severely limit the autonomy of researchers and the research methodology, impede and censor publication, and can compromise the quality of data collected.

This trend reflects the 'commodification of criminological knowledge' (Walters 2003) and increased protectionism among criminal justice organizations, which are becoming more and more concerned with the task of reputation management and the production of research that demonstrates efficient, evidence-based interventions. These trends are perhaps understandable because critiques of penal practices made by academics and penal advocates have made correctional agencies vulnerable to legal challenges and public scrutiny. For example, criticisms of risk/need assessment tools, practices, and policies in the early 1990s resulted in inquiries by the Canadian Human Rights Commission (CHRC 2003). These inquiries raised concerns about how security classification, risk/needs assessment practices, and contingent programmes may contravene human rights law by failing to account adequately for

[9] Correspondence with author and government research branch 2004.

gender, race/ethnicity, and mental health. In this instance, a criminological critique had an impact on correctional research and practice in security classification and risk/needs assessment. Canada has now produced a new gender-specific security classification assessment instrument. However, researchers find it extremely difficult to obtain access to the data used to produce that tool, its content, and application. Secondary analysis of the data used to produce the tool or of the data produced from the tools used on correctional populations is restricted. Not surprisingly, this tool was developed in-house, as were the original tools. Although many practitioners and policy-makers are critically minded, a growing institutional hegemony is characterizing research as relevant only if it is practical. Critical research is increasingly being characterized by criminal justice organizations as a 'reputational risk' (Power 2008) that must be governed accordingly. Institutional relationships with external researchers and research access protocols are designed to protect correctional reputations: institutions have a reputational stake in research. Research that examines sensitive issues such as deaths in custody, institutional racism, prisoners' rights, risk classification, and reform implementation often reveal administrative/organization problems that put the institution being studied at risk. This problem is not entirely new to institutions or researchers; currently the salient point for criminology is how these concerns shape the type of research that is possible and how institutions play a role in regulating and defining research agendas, and ultimately the field.

A considerable amount of work could and should be happening in the field of penality in Canada, but research access is becoming a significant deterrent. Many Canadian scholars reject contract research, particularly when these contracts restrict independent publication. These practices can and often do lead to the forfeiture of intellectual property, publishing, and morality rights. Good critical research requires intellectual freedom to formulate questions that are not necessarily in line with institutional agendas and the ability to observe, document, and interpret data independently without worrying that a responsible theoretical or empirical interpretation of the data will prevent future access to data. Critical scholars interested, for example, in the organizational restructuring of correctional practices, the development of gender- or race-specific policies, staff training, decision-making, risk/need assessment, health practices, prisoners' rights, staff and prisoner views, and critical assessments of the impact of policy changes are required to find alternative methods of inquiry. Researchers are becoming more reliant on document analysis and the assistance of community-based organizations and other legal strategies, while others have shifted their research focus as a result of access difficulties. For instance, instead of interviewing correctional staff or prisoners researchers have engaged in content analysis of policy documents and institutional narratives. Some topics such as the policing of racialized groups, experiences of segregation, and self-injury/suicide in prison are either not studied or only studied by government research branches. Other important areas of research are risky for graduate students and junior faculty who must publish and establish a viable programme of research.

Criminal justice agencies should continue to conduct research, interact with external researchers and assume responsibility for identifying relevant research questions. However this research activity should not limit other forms of research. Critical research can inspire normative policy blueprints and lead to new ways of imagining penality. The comments above are general and it is important to note that institutions are not entirely resistant to critique. Critical engagement with practitioners does not require researchers to frame results in predetermined policy boxes, but it does require an understanding of how institutions think about and respond to the problems under study. Critical researchers have a crucial role to play in conceptualizing alternative approaches. For example, in the area of risk and prison classification, critical researchers played a central role in creating an awareness of how race and gender affect the assessment and management of risks and needs. Although researchers have little control over how results may be used, and in this case how gender and race are operationalized and integrated into classification or used to produce new classification schemes that are also highly problematic, the engagement continues to be important. Critical researchers should not be comfortable in their positions. The continuing need for reflexive analysis of engagements with criminal justice agencies has generated new space for critical scholars and gender and race specialists. For example, a gender-responsive penality in Canada and the United States has emerged; yet it is under-theorized and under-researched and is largely disengaged from wider debates within feminist theory (Hannah-Moffat 2009). Although well-intentioned, such practices contribute to what Walters (2003) called a 'market-led criminology' that is notably devoid of a critical voice.

The Next Generation of Criminology Education and Research

International interest in criminology and its institutionalization in the form of departments and centres of criminology have (perhaps unintentionally) not only created a discipline but have contributed to the professionalization of the field. The result of the academy's success is the now critical mass of individuals trained in criminology, myself[10] included, and growing numbers of criminology departments. Criminology programmes are immensely popular at my university and elsewhere in North America. Criminology courses are in hot demand: according to the American Sociological Association (ASA), criminology and criminal justice programmes 'typically have more majors than sociology programs yet fewer faculty; indeed, it has been noted that in joint departments offering both a sociology

[10] I was among the first Canadian cohort to graduate with an interdisciplinary degree officially in criminology.

major and CCJ major, the CCJ program has about two-thirds of the majors but only one-third of the faculty' (ASA website). Criminology jobs also dominate the academic job market. Criminology attracts a multitude of students wanting to pursue research and careers in criminology and forensics. Students perceive criminology as better preparing them for employment outside of the academy, and, more broadly, as a field of inquiry that can help them understand the causes and cures for crime. More critically-minded individuals view the field as an opportunity to explore broader questions of social justice and reform. Some of these students will go on to advanced degrees in practical areas of law, social work, and psychology. Others will stay in the academy. Others still will leave the academy to become police officers, customs officers, shelter workers, correctional workers, private security professionals, and, perhaps, policy analysts. In the past, individuals would have entered directly into a police force or corrections field, but these fields are now professionalizing and requiring university degrees from incumbents. Long debates could be held about how and whether criminology is meant to 'train' or educate practitioners, or whether criminology is an autonomous discipline that should seek greater independence from disciplines such as sociology. However, more compelling debates may be related to the form and content of graduate education in criminology and whether the 'discipline of criminology' has (or should have) a 'core' set of theoretical or methodological literatures.

I argued above that criminology as a discipline must maintain broad conversations with other established disciplines; however the diversity of intellectual resources informing criminology complicates graduate education and the development of criminology curriculums. The saturation of research and interest in criminology has inspired the formation of many masters and doctoral programmes in criminology. In 2008, the ASA established a task force[11] to study the relationship between sociology and criminology departments and to develop a 'model curricula and sample course content for courses in criminology taught in sociology departments' (ASA website) in conjunction with the American Society of Criminology (ASC). Such developments exemplify the evolution of criminology and signal how universities in Canada and elsewhere are actively engaged in defining criminology and in producing criminologists at the undergraduate and graduate level.

If criminology continues to be widely defined and draw from multiple disciplines, then practical questions about the parameters of graduate education, for example with regard to comprehensive/area exams and course work require reflection. Graduate comprehensive exams reflect tensions in criminology and reveal a

[11] Task Force on Sociology and Criminology Programs—'The resulting report will provide guiding principles and recommendations, as well as illustrations ('promising practices') for how departments of various types offer strong criminology programmes within sociology departments. The report will also include information on the optimal relationships between separate sociology and criminology programmes', (<www.asanet.org/cs/root/leftnav/committees/council_approves_establishment_of_three_new_task_forces>, accessed 16 September 2009).

considerable amount about how the field and its 'core' are being constructed. Some criminology programmes tend to include exams organized around substantive topics (ie, policing/security, risk, penality, youth, addictions) and a wide range of literature from multiple disciplines. Criminology however is also positioned as a 'subfield' rather than a 'discipline' in other departments such as sociology where exams tend to be substantively broader but also focused on sociologically-grounded work. These differences reflect how various institutions and departments organize and frame the field of criminology. Comprehensive exams normally form the basis for dissertation research and allow students to identify their teachable areas. In these ways, comprehensives and graduate research play key roles in producing criminological knowledge and defining the future of this intellectual field. Clearly, the boundaries of this field are difficult to define; consequently considerable latitude should be allowed and preserved to enable creative spaces for new analysis and a range of intellectually rigorous inquiries and broadly based education. What remains unclear is how to maintain cross-disciplinary breadth while simultaneously evolving criminology as an academic discipline.

Institutional protectionism represents another challenge for the future of criminological research and education. This trend has contributed to parochialism within criminological research. It continues to have the potential to shape the forms of knowledge produced about specific criminal justice populations, policies, and practices and to prescribe lines of inquiry. Practices that limit research access to those who present questions that fit with institutional agendas or to questions that do not risk exposing undesirable policies, technologies, or behaviours need to be contested. These practices impact on students because the uncertainty of gaining access to mainstream institutions may deter them from studying certain issues.

Enterprising groups of graduate students and faculty studying Canadian penal practices have begun to use legal tools such as the *Access to Information Act* to acquire reports, documents, and even relevant policy information. But this practice is expensive and time-consuming, especially if they are unsure what documents they are looking for, which is often the case at the beginning of a research project. Moreover, using access to information protocols (ATIP) does not guarantee access to needed documents because government agencies censor and vet the information requested. Although screening is conducted to protect security and privacy, agencies are also aware of the fact that if they release information under ATI they cannot prevent researchers from using the information or censor its interpretation. Research strategies such as the use of ATIP and public documents that are being used by new scholars are informative, but methodologically limited. Because the process of securing access is lengthy and unpredictable, graduate students are advised to consider the question of access well before they commit to their programme of research. Critical scholars who are often more skilled at assessing the limits of existing policies and social structures than developing alternatives that can be implemented within existing institutional frameworks risk being further marginalized and discredited for their 'lack of empirical evidence'. Paradoxically, the evidence required to produce such critiques is difficult to access. In future, researchers interested in studying penality, police, and courts will need to be more creative in gaining access to individuals and information. Discussion groups and special issues of journals are already under way to help researchers learn how to penetrate institutional boundaries. This issue is becoming a central concern for critical scholars who are investigating politically-charged research questions and need access to criminalized groups, police, courts, and correctional fields.

Although critical scholarship does not neatly match what institutions and policy-makers require or think they need, it plays an important role in ensuring accountability and transparency and in producing alternative visions. Future generations of 'critical' scholars should continue to interact with more 'applied' scholars even when their perspectives diverge. Criminology programmes ought to integrate both forms of knowledge into curriculums in order to produce a richer context for intra-disciplinary and cross institutional dialogues in the academy.

Conclusions

As the field of criminology evolves it is worthwhile to reflect on how disciplinary developments such as specialization, cross-disciplinary debates, and various forms of institutional protectionism will affect knowledge and shape debates. Scholars are saturated with unprecedented amounts of information, articles relevant to their research areas, and material that is simply 'interesting.' It is necessary to keep current with new developments in our field, but it is equally important to be engaged with the fringes of our discipline and with material that takes us beyond the intellectual comfort of our clique. Finally, movements toward institutional protectionism, including restrictions on access to 'public' institutions for research purposes should be challenged and resisted when possible. Criminological knowledge should not pivot around the policy needs of governments or be required to conform to hegemonic rationalities. Researchers and institutions can ultimately benefit from wide-ranging interdisciplinary dialogues.

References

Andrews, D. and James B. (1998), *Psychology of Criminal conduct*, Cincinnati: Anderson Publishing.

Beckett, K. and Steve, H. (2010 at press), 'Penal Boundaries: Banishment and the Expansion of Punishment', *Law and Social Inquiry*, 35, 1.

Bertrand, M. A. (1969), 'Self Image and Delinquency: A Contribution to the Study of Female Criminality and Women's Image', *Acta Criminologica*, 2: 71–144.

Blanchette, K. and Brown, S. L. (2006), *The Assessment and Treatment of Women Offenders: An Integrative Perspective*, West Sussex: John Wiley and Sons.

Braithwaite, J. (2003), 'What's Wrong with the Sociology of Punishment', *Theoretical Criminology*, 7, 1: 5–28.

Birgden, A. and Ward, T. (2003), 'Jurisprudential Considerations: Pragmatic Psychology through a Therapeutic Jurisprudence Lens: Psycholegal Soft Spots in the Criminal Justice System', *Psychology, Public Policy and Law*, 9: 334–60.

Bonta, J. (2007), 'Offender Risk Assessment and Sentencing', *Canadian Journal of Criminology and Criminal Justice*, 49, 4: online.

Burgess-Proctor, A. (2006), 'Intersections of Race, Class, Gender, and Crime: Future Directions for Feminist Criminology', *Feminist Criminology*, 1, 1: 27–47.

Canadian Human Right Commission (2003), *Protecting their Rights: A Systemic Review of Human Rights in Correctional Services for Women*, Ottawa: Canadian Human Rights Commission.

Carson, D. (2003), 'Therapeutic Jurisprudence and Adversarial Injustice: Questioning Limits', *Western Criminology Review*, 4, 2: 124–33.

Chan, J., Ericson, R. V., and O'Malley, P. (1996), 'Special Issue on the Future of Criminology', *Current Issues in Criminal Justice*, 8, 1: 7–88.

Crocker, D. (2003), 'The Accidental Sociologist: Fragmented Identities in the 21st Century', *Canadian Journal of Sociology Online* (<http://www.cjsonline.ca/pdf/crocker.pdf>).

Curtis, B. and Weir, L. (October 2002), 'The Succession Question in English Canadian Sociology', *Society/Société*, 26: 3–13.

Daly, K. (2008), 'Seeking Justice in the 21st Century: Towards an "Intersectional Politics" of Justice', *Sociology of Crime, Law, and Deviance*, 11: 3–30.

______ and Lind, M. C. (1988), 'Feminism and Criminology', *Justice Quarterly*, 5, 4: 498–538.

Doob, A. N. and Greenspan, E. L. (1985), *Perspectives in Criminal Law: Essays in Honour of John Ll. J. Edwards*, Aurora, Ont.: Canada Law Book.

Downes, D. and Rock P. (1982), *Understanding Deviance*, Oxford: Oxford University Press.

Ericson, R. (2007), *Crime in an Insecure World*, Cambridge, Polity Press.

Fischer, B. (2003), 'Doing Good with a Vengeance: A Critical Assessment of the Practices, Effects and Implications of Drug Treatment Courts in North America', *Criminal Justice*, 3, 3: 227–48.

Galloway, A. and Drapela L. (2006), 'Are Effective Drug Courts an Urban Phenomenon? Considering Their Impact on Recidivism among a Nonmetropolitan Adult Sample in Washington State', *International Journal of Offender Therapy and Comparative Criminology*, 50, 3: 280–93.

Garland, D. (1990), 'Frameworks of Inquiry in the Sociology of Punishment', *British Journal of Sociology*, 41, 1: 1–15.

Gendreau, P., Goggin, C., and Smith, P. (2000), 'Obstacles to Effective Correctional Program Delivery', in Compendium 2000 on effective correctional programming, Ottawa: Correctional Service of Canada. (<www.csc-scc.gc.ca/text/rsrch/compendium/2000/chap_6-eng.shtml>).

Gladstone, J., Ericson, R. V., and Shearing, C.D. (1991), *Criminology: A Reader's Guide*, Toronto: Centre of Criminology, University of Toronto.

Gottfredson, D. C., Kearley, B. W., and Najaka, S. S. (2007), 'How Drug Treatment Courts Work: An Analysis of Mediators', *Journal of Research in Crime and Delinquency*, 44, 1: 3–35.

Gover, A. R., MacDonald, J. M., and Alpert, G. P. (2003), 'Combating Domestic Violence: Findings from an Evaluation of a Local Domestic Violence Court', *Criminology and Public Policy*, 3,1: 109–35.

Lee, E. (2000), *Community Courts: An Evolving Model*, US: Department of Justice, Centre for Court Innovation.

Hagan, J. (1988), *Structural Criminology*, Cambridge: Polity Press.

Haney, L. (2004), 'Introduction: Gender, Welfare, and States of Punishment', *Social Politics*, 11, 3: 333–62.

Hannah-Moffat, K. (2009), 'Gridlock or Mutability: Reconsidering 'Gender' and Risk Assessment', *Criminology and Public Policy*, 8, 1: 221–9.

Heidenshon, F. (1968), 'The Deviance of Women: A Critique and Enquiry', *British Journal of Sociology*, 19, 2:160–75.

Holdaway, S. and Rock, P. (1998), *Thinking about Criminology*, Toronto: University of Toronto Press.

Jefferson, T. and Carlen, P. (1996), 'Masculinities, Social Relations and Crime', *Special Issue of the British Journal of Criminology*, 36, 3

Loader, I. (2007), *Civilizing Security*, Cambridge: Cambridge University Press.

Marlow, D., Festinger, D., and Lee, P. (2006), 'Matching Judicial Supervision to Client's Risk Status in Drug Court', *Crime and Delinquency*, 52, 1: 52–76.

Messerschmidt, J. (1993), *Masculinities and Crime*, Manham: Rowman and Littlefield.

Moore, D. (2008), 'Attacked on all fronts? Feminist Criminology and the Problem of Backlash', *Sociology Compass*, (online journal).

Moore, D. (2007), 'Translating Justice and Therapy: The Drug Treatment Court Networks', *British Journal of Criminology*, 47,1: 42–60.

Moore, D. and Lyons, T. (2007), 'Sentenced to Treatment/Sentenced to Harm: Women, Risk and the Drug Treatment Courts', in K. Hannah-Moffat and P. O'Malley (eds), *Gendered Risks*, Abingdon: Cavendish Routledge.

Naffine, N. (1997), *Feminism and Criminology*, Dartmouth: Aldershot.

Nelken, D. (1994), *Futures of Criminology*, London: Sage.

Nolan, J. (2009), *Legal Accents, Legal Borrowing: The International Problem-Solving Court Movement*, Princeton: Princeton University Press.

Nolan, J. L. (2003), 'Redefining Criminal Courts: Problem-Solving and the Meaning of Justice', *American Criminal Law Review*, 40: 1541–65.

O'Malley, P. and Hunt, A. (2003), 'Does Sociology Need to be Disciplined?', *Society/Société*, 27: 7–13.

Petersillia, J. (2008), 'Influencing Public Policy: An Embedded Criminologist Reflects on California Prison Reform', *Journal of Experimental Criminology*, 4: 335–56.

Rafter, N. and Heidenshon, F. (1995), *International Feminist perspectives in Criminology*, Buckingham: Open University Press.

Shearing, C. and Johnston, L. (2003), *Governing Security: Explorations in Policing and Justice*, London, Routledge.

Schneider, Hon R. D., Bloom, Hy., and Heerema, M. (2006), *Mental Health Courts: Decriminalizing the Mentally Ill*, Toronto: Irwin Law Inc.

Smart, C. (1976), *Women, Crime and Criminology*, London: Routledge Kegan Paul.

Walsh, C. (2001), 'The Trend Towards Specialisation: West Yorkshire Innovations in Drugs and Domestic Violence Courts', *Howard Journal*, 40: 26–38.

Walters, R. (2003), 'New Modes of Governance and the Commodification of Criminological Knowledge', *Social and Legal Studies*, 12, 1: 5–24.

_____ (2003), *Deviant Knowledge: Criminology, Politics and Policy*, Abingdon: Willan.

Weir, L. and Curtis, B. (2003), 'Reply to O'Malley and Hunt', *Society/Société*, 27, 2: 91–5.

Valverde, M. (2009), 'Beyond Discipline and Punish: Foucault's Challenge to Criminology', *Carceral Notebooks*, 4: 201–24.

_____ (2010), 'Comment on Loic Wacquant's 'Theoretical Coda' to *Punishing the Poor*', *Theoretical Criminology*, 14, 1: 117–20.

Yuval-Davis, N. (2006), 'Intersectionality and Feminist Politics', *The European Journal of Women's Studies*, 13, 3:193–209.

Zedner, L. (2003), 'The Concept of Security: An Agenda for Comparative Analysis', *Legal Studies*, 23: 153–75.

Zinger, I., Wichmann, C., and Gendreau, P. (2001), 'Response Réplique Legal and Ethical Obligations in Social Research: The Limited Confidentiality Requirement', Canadian Journal of Criminology, 43, 2: 269–74.

30

OFFICIAL CRIMINOLOGY AND THE NEW CRIME SCIENCES

TIM HOPE*

THE notion that criminological ideas provide the discursive conditions for the governance of crime has featured prominently in criminological scholarship (Melossi 2008; Simon 2007; Hughes 2002; Garland 2001; Young 1999; Lea and Young 1993; Cohen 1985; Currie 1985; Morris and Hawkins 1970). In the matter of government, thinking about crime coalesces into *official criminologies* that function to justify and validate state policies and practices of crime control. In representative democracies, these official criminological discourses are 'public' and, in principle, take their place alongside others, including those of lay people, the media and politics generally; as well as the criminology produced by academics. As a form of knowledge, official criminologies are definable by the purpose to which they are put; that

* I am grateful to Adam Edwards and Gordon Hughes both for sharing ideas about science, politics, and expertise and for convening a panel at the Annual Conference of the European Society of Criminology, Ljubljana, 9–12 September 2009, where a version of this chapter was first presented; and to Derek Cornish, not only for commenting upon an earlier draft but also for kindly donating a copy of Clarke and Cornish (1983). I would also like to thank Mary Bosworth and Carolyn Hoyle for providing an opportunity to develop some of the ideas in this paper.

is, as '... [Politically] effective, truth-producing categories that provide the discursive conditions for real social practices' (Garland 2001: 25). They seem to serve the purpose of 'framing' issues for public action (Jasanoff 2005), and of helping to form the paradigms that shape policy-making (Rein 1976). As with democracy, while the totality of these discourses comprise the knowledge that the polity has of itself, the nature of political conduct, especially competition for the distribution of power, means that all such discursive knowledge has real social consequences. There are always likely to be winners and losers—amongst politicians, administrators, judges, and criminologists; police officers, citizens, victims, and offenders—as a consequence of the preference for one sort of public or official criminology over another.

Where political truth is contestable, the key questions to be asked of any system of truth-producing categories have always been: first, how do we know what is true; and, second, who or what do we trust to help us decide what is true? A principal strategy for addressing these questions in the philosophical and social scientific study of science has been that of deciding upon the criteria of *demarcation*; particularly, of distinguishing scientific from pseudo-scientific truth claims. Broadly, there have been two traditions of enquiry: the first takes an epistemological path, seeking to find criteria for assessing the validity of truth-producing categorical claims, thereby eradicating error from the advice that science offers to politics (Popper 1983, 1974, 1945); the second approach interrogates the institutions and practices of scientists, or of political efforts to use science to inform or resolve technical and social problems (Jasanoff 2005), in order to identify normative principles about the nature of scientific expertise—especially how scientists maintain the integrity of their work, the place of science in society, and its contribution to governance (Collins and Evans 2007).

Yet it is not easy to distinguish questions of an epistemological kind from normative and institutional considerations: questions about the organization of scientific effort to attain knowledge for ulterior purposes raise questions about the status of such knowledge (Collins and Evans 2002). This is because of the increasing importance of science and technology both in conceptualizing the social risks to which government is required to respond (Giddens 1990), and in the salience of science in the governance of a society that is predominantly orientated towards understanding, managing and preventing risk (Rose 1999). Yet this makes the issue of demarcation even more important politically and morally: as scientific and political activities merge together in governance, it becomes all the more necessary to analyse the bases on which their conjoint rationality is being constructed, and what interests are served or ignored (Collins and Evans 2007). And it remains just as much of a threat to liberty when reasoned (critical) scepticism is brushed aside or suppressed by power-holders, particularly in the supposedly superior interests of social progress and reform (Mathiesen 2004; Popper 1992, 1945).

Official Criminology

In *The Culture of Control*, David Garland demonstrates the role played by official criminology in the legitimation and justification of beliefs, values and ideologies (Garland 2001). Central to his argument is that official criminology serves the latent function of easing and resolving the fundamental policy-predicament of the state with regard to crime control: how to reconcile the expectations of citizens (fostered by politics) that the state can control and reduce crime, against the public's widespread reaction (and politicians' own fears) that it has failed to do so. Yet while Garland (2001) is clear (and largely correct) about the political functions these official criminologies serve, he is less certain about *how* precisely they have been produced. In particular, the state itself features largely as a passive receptacle for popular political sentiment; while state agents and politicians themselves appear uncharacteristically apolitical with respect to the development of official criminology, which somehow emerges nevertheless to meet their ideological needs.

Yet, in Britain at least, there has been a proactive and conscious effort by the state to promote official criminology. Symbiotically, this has given an opportunity for certain criminologists to promulgate their own ideas and expertise, gaining prominence as scientific advisors to government, and acquiring a political authority that vies against the scientific authority of their erstwhile academic peers. In constructing this new 'pseudo-scientific' infrastructure for official criminology, the criterion of demarcation has featured prominently, though on this occasion, it has been government agents and their collaborators that have been the ones doing the demarcating.

The Problem of Causation for Official Criminology

The key issue for official criminology has been *to identify the causes of crime, while not implicating the state as one of them*. Variously termed the 'socio-liberal approach to criminal policy' (Radzinowicz 1999), the 'medico-psychological model' (Clarke and Cornish 1983), or 'penal-welfarism' (Garland 2001), the approach assumed the existence of certain 'causes' in the psychological make-up of individuals that gave rise to an *a priori* 'disposition' towards crime, that subsequently manifested itself in the commission of criminal acts, and for which it should be the purpose of criminal justice to 'treat' so that the disposition would be removed or controlled, and the offender 'rehabilitated', thus becoming equipped to return to normal life absent of the will to offend. Criticism of its logic notwithstanding (Matza 1969; Wootton 1959), the approach had become the principal official criminology of Britain in the post-war period, serving to justify a socially-interventionist role for the criminal justice system within the overall ideal of a 'welfare state' (Garland 2001).

Yet, not only was this perceived by emergent sociologists of deviance to be deliberately ignoring the 'root causes' of crime residing in social conditions (the source of 'primary deviance'), which could be ameliorated by public policy (Hope 1995), but, of more significance, ignoring also the recursively causal effect (and hence responsibility) of the state itself upon the definition, labelling and amplification of social deviance (Wilkins, 1964) (the source of 'secondary deviance'). The countervailing critique was that the official approach, in requiring the systematic censure and 'criminalization' of deviance by the apparatus of governmental systems of criminal justice, justified a moral order that relied upon repressive forms of social control (Cohen 1988, 1985). The insurrection of the new criminologists (eg, Taylor *et al.* 1973) against the hegemony of penal-welfarism represented by the Cambridge Institute of Criminology (Radzinowicz 1999) led to their intellectual secession from official criminology (Wiles 1976); and to the institutional demarcation of an independent, academic criminology in Britain, often housed within the newly established sociology departments of the colleges and universities of an expanding higher education system (Cohen 1988).

The seriousness of their criticism was confirmed by the failure of a key mechanism of the medico-psychological model: the failure of statistical methods to predict the causes of reoffending from risk-factors derived from the medico-psychological model. Rather, the evidence suggested more immediate social factors to do with offenders' current circumstances, and their prior involvement with crime and the criminal justice system (Clarke and Cornish 1983). The evident failure of the criminal justice system to control crime through penal treatment, demonstrated by high rates of recidivism, appeared to be 'caused' both by the treatment actually received in penal contexts, and in its effect on the post-release experiences of offenders when returned to society (Clarke and Cornish 1983). In sum, nothing much of a penal nature seemed to 'work'; the explanations offered by the new criminologists finding confirmation in the methods of official criminology.

The response within the government scientific community in the United Kingdom was to set about testing a revised theoretical model of crime causation—an individual-behavioural 'choice model'—that would identify causes of crime that were more amenable to remedy by crime prevention measures aimed at modifying the opportunities and risks present in the immediate environments in which particular crimes typically occur; an approach known as *situational* crime prevention (see von Hirsch *et al.* 2000). The principal architects of this approach, Clarke and Cornish (1983), portray this as an *evolutionary* development of the scientific responsibilities of the Home Office Research Unit (see also Croft 1978)—the government's in-house research organization for crime and criminal justice, which had been established in 1957 (Cornish and Clarke 1987; Lodge 1974).

In its idealized form, the approach would entail the systematic development and testing of causal theory (Wilkins 1964). During the post-war period, the notion that government should be considered as if it were engaged in experimentation was the guiding metaphor for those who sought to apply principles of scientific enquiry to politics (Campbell 1969; Popper 1945). The ideal would be that both government and science would be engaged in the *same* process of enquiry—a logical, experimental path to find out *what works*, pursued mainly by ruling out *what did not*. In this respect, the approaches adopted seemed to aspire to Popper's (1945) conception of 'piecemeal social engineering'. Applying these principles more or less faithfully, government social science nevertheless reached a point at which it had found that, actually, nothing much did 'work' in the repertoire of penal and criminal justice interventions that had been tried by government up to that point (Clarke and Cornish 1983).

At this juncture (the early-1970s), an ideal experimental politics might have been expected to search for alternative ways of finding out what *did* work to reduce crime and promote safety, while abandoning approaches that seemed to have been falsified. From both critical and official perspectives, crime was becoming normalized as social deviance, an everyday part of life (Garland, 2001). Critical criminologists were calling for radical non-intervention, decarceration, and the abolition of penal institutions; and even within official criminology, the predominant trend was towards non-custodial sentencing. Indeed, the turn to crime prevention in civil society, in its variety of forms, appeared to indicate a readiness of official criminology to continue along the path of open, experimental governance (Tonry and Farrington 1995; Hope and Shaw 1988; Clarke and Hope 1982; Clarke and Mayhew 1980). Nevertheless, this would also have meant the state accepting three uncomfortable arguments:

- Penal institutions play a positive, causal role with regard to deviance.
- If the state plays no role in the genesis of crime, likewise it must be impotent in its control and prevention, relative to civil society.
- If crime is more likely to be controlled by civil rather than penal activity, then the state must have been in breach of the social contract, and negligent in its support of civil society: particularly by failing to protect the vulnerable poor from the growth of crime in their communities, while simultaneously failing to protect the better-off from the threat of predation.

Instead, we have seen the governance of crime taking a *revanchist* turn, refocusing on the deviant and threatening few (Melossi 2008), and a reassertion of the authority of the 'sovereign state', especially of its policing and penal institutions (Garland 2001). In its wake, we have seen the emergence of a new official criminology to help government avoid confronting these unpalatable propositions.

The Teleological Turn

The clarion call for the reconstruction of official criminology was made by James Q. Wilson in his seminal essay *Crime and the Criminologists*, (1974), a reaction to the apparent political *debacle* in the United States of attempts to reduce crime by attacking its 'root causes' in society with programmes to tackle poverty, deprivation and discrimination (Hope 2000). For Wilson, the root cause of the 'failure' of these interventions was what he saw as the misguided assumption that '... no problem is adequately addressed unless its causes are eliminated' (1985: 47), which he saw as committing government to '... futile acts that frustrate the citizen while they ignore the criminal' (ibid.: 47; see also Moynihan 1969). His reason was the infinite regress that he saw in causal theories of crime which led to the apparent paradox (he called it the 'causal fallacy') that '... ultimate causes cannot be the object of policy analysis because, being ultimate, they cannot be changed' (ibid.: 46). In preference, Wilson proposed that official criminology should be guided by a *policy analysis* that asks

> ...not what is the 'cause' of a problem, but what is the condition one wants to bring into being...and what policy tools does a government...possess that might, when applied, produce at reasonable cost a desired alteration in the present condition or progress toward the desired condition [ibid.: 49].

In Wilson's definition, policy analysis is thus the assessment of the cost-effectiveness of the available means of approximating to desired outcomes. Policy analysis seeks to fit emergent problems to pre-existing solutions—that is, those that government already possesses, primarily in the shape of policing and criminal justice (Wilson 1985: chapter 13). Yet this essentially conservative motive is teleological. The risk is that policy analysis may simply focus upon those aspects of crime and offending that are most congenial to already established or preferred policies, thus continuing to support what may be fallacious causal explanations and ineffective policies—for example that police patrol may be effective (Hope 2009a)—merely because it has blinded itself, *tout court*, to the range of alternative possibilities for crime control that new discoveries and innovative thinking about crime causation may generate.

The most serious problem with this view of policy analysis lies in its purpose—'progress toward the desired condition'—which is an *historicist* definition of the purpose of knowledge (Popper 1957). The flaws of historicism emerge in two main ways: first, as the problem of *prediction*—that is, the belief that we can uncover causal propositions that will shape or determine the future *before* it happens so that, if we take action now, we can forestall what would otherwise be its inevitable development; and second, the problem of inductive *selectivity*, that is, that we can safely select knowledge from the past that will satisfactorily explain the present. Both serve the purpose of justifying action in the present by recourse either to a selective view of the past or by a prophecy of the future. Their seductive appeal to 'common sense' makes them dangerous politically since their evidence can be cast as irrefutable justification for governmental action; while cloaking ideological or expedient choices with the justification of science gives their protagonists a spurious authority that brooks little opposition (Popper 1945).

The Problem of Prediction

The starting point for the 'new crime sciences' (Hope and Karstedt 2003) that have dedicated themselves to policy analysis is the apparent general tendency of crime, howsoever measured or conceptualized, to be concentrated disproportionately in a small proportion of the population, whether of offenders, places or victims. The apparent 'horizontal j-curved' shape of observed distributions of crime is seductive; the long right-hand tail suggesting the possibility that, if only we could identify, predict or locate the 'big targets' (Sherman 2007)—that is, those relatively few cases who appear to be contributing disproportionately to the frequency distribution—we would maximize the efficiency of our crime control apparatus. Such a case has been made specifically with respect to crime victimization (Farrell 2005; Laycock 2001), and more generally for all crime phenomena (Sherman 2007). In this view, previous crime control efforts have dissipated resources over too wide a population, and led to 'nothing works' results by failing to concentrate on the 'power few' (Sherman 2007).

A key problem lies in how we interpret this distribution, particularly whether we think we are selecting the 'power few' (deviants) from a single population or from many. On the one hand, if we think of the distribution as a composite of many different sub-populations, only a few of which might contain the 'deviants' and if, as looks likely, these are going to be relatively small both in absolute number and in proportion to the population, then it is going to take very large samples or (of more concern) very wide-ranging population surveillance techniques to pick them out from amongst the normal population. Clearly, rigorous scanning (police surveillance) of the many to find the few runs counter to principles that (we trust) underpin the administration of criminal justice in liberal democracies.

That is why the customary response has been to *let the 'power few' select themselves*; that is, to continually come to the attention of the authorities until their troublesomeness becomes sufficiently noticeable so as to justify special attention. This is not necessarily a problem for policy analysis, whose avowed purpose is to experiment with varying disposals upon the population of 'targets' that has already presented itself; that is, to justify the special attention that the state has already made available to deal with deviance (Sherman 2009, 2007). But this approach forecloses broader innovation since consideration of putative causes is foreclosed by pre-determined policy (Hope 2009a). Thus, the teleological bias towards criminal justice has served to foreclose the investigation of policies that would reduce crime through economic and social policy—the policies supposedly favoured by sociologically-minded criminologists (Wilson 1985). It invites the criticism that the state has neglected to do anything until subjects have already 'become deviant'; and it does not absolve the state of its selectivity; that is, of actually creating 'high risk' populations through repeated attention, thereby reinforcing and amplifying their deviance (Matza 1969).

On the other hand, if such distributions are samples from a single population, then those who appear at the far right-hand end of the distribution must have started out at the left-hand side—that is, amongst the majority of the population who do not progress to the extremely deviant end of the spectrum. The key issue is that of being able to *predict* who it is amongst the non-crime population who will progress to membership of the crime population. Essentially, the strategy of longitudinal research has been to wait long enough to see who turns out to be deviant, and then to go right back to their pre-crime state to identify its precursors—the so-called 'risk factors' of offending (Farrington 2009). Using information on criminal career trajectories gleaned from this longitudinal research, a new population can then be scanned for the presence of risk factors, which policy should then act upon pre-emptively. The prize for government is to target deviants in as formative a pre-crime state as possible (Zedner 2007), such as in their early family experiences, preferably avoiding the causal role of later influences—such as schooling, housing and employment—where the state might have to share some of the responsibility.

Yet some limit on early prediction needs to be set in order to avoid Wilson's charge of infinite regress. Even with longitudinal data it is necessary to have an appropriate model of temporal development, since the same distribution can support explanations that *either* see early developmental risk factors maintaining a stable, continuous influence over the subsequent life-course, *or* a path-dependent sequential development, where each successive stage is influenced by its immediate predecessor, which gives much greater weight to experiences and opportunities in later life, and includes the negative impact of criminal justice. Here, the historicist perspective is of great help (Home Office 2007): on the one hand, if early intervention works to forestall crime, then history will be the judge, with the verdict coming long after the respective politicians have left office. So, present-day politicians can take comfort and credit for their effort to 'do good' in the here-and-now while appearing to be working altruistically for the future. On the other hand, if events do not turn out as predicted, governments can equally take comfort in the thought that the public of the future will blame their own government of the day for the present state of crime (as they always do) rather than their predecessors. Consequently, predictions about future adult offending made before the onset of criminal responsibility cannot be falsified in policy analysis since there is no need to prove that they will work in the future (such is the nature of prophecy), and nothing in the future to be achieved by blaming a long distant past.

Even when possible future outcomes are estimable (on the basis of completed longitudinal studies), the false positive rate of prediction, for any of the variables available within existing data sets, seems high. In previous eras, governments tended to calculate that, given the cost of early provision (which in lieu of predictive certainty would have to be applied universally), they would rather put resources into dealing with crime in the here-and-now, tackling the circumstances and situations of crime and offending that had already come to attention. The advent of risk society and the security state has tended to give greater weight to the *precautionary principle*—better to take as much precaution as possible now against a low but potentially harmful risk emerging later on (Zedner 2007). To the extent that such precaution becomes electorally valuable, the comfort that politicians can derive from an historicism that cannot be falsified in the present merely helps them in their task of reassuring the electorate, without entailing much of a hostage to fortune.

The Problem of Selection

The pursuit of 'what works' has been taken forward through the evaluation of policy 'experiments'. Evaluation is the opposite side of the coin to prediction, with the similar purpose of causal attribution. For some time, the Home Office has publicly described its social research function as follows:

> ...How we use research to make policies:
>
> For example, by accurately measuring burglary levels over time we can find out whether our burglary-reduction strategies are working or not:
>
> - If we found levels of burglary were dropping, we could develop the successful strategies further.
> - If we found levels stayed the same or increased then that would be evidence that our anti-burglary strategies weren't working, so we would then change and improve them'.[1]

This simple statement purports to describe the government practice of *evidence-based policy-making*, harking back, in a *faux-naïve* way, to the ideal of piecemeal social engineering of yesteryear.

However, like the problem of prediction, evaluation methodology can neither resolve nor avoid the problem of empirical causal attribution, which is:

> ...the impossibility of observing what would happen to a given person in both the state where he or she receives a treatment (or participates in a program) and the state where he or she does not. If a person could be observed in both states, the impact of the treatment could be calculated by comparing his or her outcomes in the two states, and the evaluation problem would be solved [Heckman and Smith 1995: 87].

In the operation of the experimental design, those persons assigned to non-treatment conditions represent the *counterfactual condition*—what would have happened if what happened had not happened? While the definition of the treatment group depends on actual policy implementation (reality), the definition of the 'control' group is conjectural—an effort to construct a hypothetical 'unreality' of what might have been, had the intervention not occurred. The reliability of random assignment relies upon statistical theory, hence the methodology's scientific pretensions and the reification of the method of the randomized controlled trial (RCT) (Sherman *et al.* 1998).[2] Yet if 'random assignment' is crucial to the capacity

[1] <www.homeoffice.gov.uk/science-research/RDS> (accessed 2 September 2009).

[2] Although, advocates of the RCT method tend to ignore or downplay advances made in recent years in the methodology for estimating causation from non-experimental data (see Winship and Morgan 1999).

to control the estimation of effects, then it is also critical to control randomization operationally in 'field experiments' of policy to ensure that a reliable experimental set-up is obtained.

Not all criminal justice policies are commensurate in their capacity to support reliable random assignments; but since the 'gold standard' of the RCT relies upon the control of subjects, and control over those who control them institutionally, the methodological criteria employed will bias judgements of what works in favour of some kinds of policy intervention over others. For instance, community crime prevention interventions differ from criminal justice interventions in terms of the styles of *governance* associated with the different institutional settings and programmes typically implemented within each sphere (Hope 2005). Community interventions tend to be premised upon mechanisms of collective, voluntary participation; in contrast, the 'treatment' programmes taking place in courts and corrections are characterized by individual, constrained participation. Typically, they are concerned with altering the rewards and/or sanctions bearing upon individuals so that they can 'fit in' to prevailing institutional arrangements, backed up by the state's authority of coercion. It is no wonder, then, that reviews based upon the RCT gold standard (Sherman, *et al.* 1998) tend to support criminal justice interventions and to negate efforts to reduce the causes of crime in community settings (Hope 2005), much as Wilson (1974) would have liked.

A crucial difference between a community crime prevention initiative and, say, a controlled laboratory experiment is that, in the former, the 'treatment' has far less integrity *a priori*.[3] The experience of project implementation shows that any 'treatment' intervention, especially in field settings, is *produced* over time in specific contexts, in complex practical and organizational ways, utilizing varying combinations of authority, capital and resources (Hope *et al.* 2004; Hope 1985). Pawson and Tilley (1997) argue that the task of evaluation is therefore to uncover the variety of particular *context-mechanism-outcome* (CMO) configurations inherent in an intervention and then seek additional similar cases (replication) where regularities of policy input can be discerned. Thus, replication studies of the Kirkholt Burglary Reduction Project (Tilley 1993; Farrell 2005) have been reported as part of a process to assess the effectiveness of a policy of repeat burglary prevention (Laycock 2001), another variant of the 'power few' intervention policy.

Nevertheless, this method contains no methodological guarantee against *bias* in its selection of case studies and in its investigation of causal mechanisms (Hope 2002). Failure to assure against bias stems from the liabilities of its methodology—that is, a reliance on case-study methods—and an inductive epistemology that does not guard against selectivity in the formation of CMO configurations (Hope 2009b).

[3] It may also be hardly possible to ensure treatment integrity anywhere, even in closed and controlled institutions, without draconian control or blind manipulation of criminal justice practitioners (Clarke and Cornish 1972).

In contrast, specification and testing of the central hypothesis of the Kirkholt Project, on a range of data, has found no further instances that replicate its supposed effect (Hope 2007; Hope *et al.* 2004; Hope 2002). So far, the hypothesized 'Kirkholt effect' has been more often and more reliably falsified than it has been verifiably replicated.

Is Official Criminology a Science?

The question posed to the contributors to this book was, *what is criminology?* This chapter has focused on recent versions of official criminology; so the question here becomes, *what is official criminology?* Since recent versions make claims to be regarded as science, we have first sought to address the question, *is official criminology a science?* We have sought to compare what might be called Phase 1 with Phase 2 official criminology. More or less explicitly (Wilkins 1964), Phase 1 tended to conform to Popper's criteria of demarcation and produced 'nothing works' results. Phase 2 has sought to produce 'what works' results but has violated Popper's criteria, especially falling foul of the fallacies of induction and historicism, the key 'enemies' of his definition of science and, by extension, his principles for public policy-making in an open democratic society (Popper 1945). So, at least in terms of Popper's (admittedly highly stringent) criteria of demarcation, we might suppose that official criminology struggles to claim scientific status on epistemic grounds, even if it ever could.

Clearly, this is unfortunate in the risk society, where the possession of scientific authority has come to greater prominence in the support and legitimation of public policy (Beck 1992). Arguably, this explains the outward style of recent official criminology, with its efforts to credentialize itself by using the appurtenances and terminology of the natural sciences. Recent examples include: *The Journal of Experimental Criminology*, *The Academy of Experimental Criminology*, the *Scientific Methods Scale*, and the demarcation of a new *Crime Science* (Smith and Tilley 2005). However, its empirical content remains exclusively the product of *social research methodology*. Nor do the new crime sciences resemble the more formal kind of (deductive) social science to which the discipline of economics has aspired. While much is made of comparisons with 'medical science' (Sherman 2009), it is as if the actual scientific bases of medicine can be safely ignored, so that all that matters is the social study of the effect of clinical practice. Lacking in any reflexivity of their own conditions of existence, the new crime scientists seem unwilling to take on the task of demarcating their own research practice epistemically, even while they use the popular trappings of 'science' to claim superiority over criminological research that is rooted in the disciplinary traditions of the social sciences (Hope 2006).

Is Official Criminology Political?

It has been argued that the purpose of official criminology is to deal with the problem of crime causation without implicating the state as one of its causes. Does this mean that official criminology is better thought of politically—is official criminology a form of *politics in another guise?* Nowadays, the use of research by government in Britain seems to be unashamedly political:

> ...serving political masters whose primary interest is confirmation that the policies they are pursuing are working so that the public at large...can be persuaded that they made the correct choice at the last General Election and will make the same choice at the next...the research programme is ultimately managed for political ends...that means that at best it aims at the fine-tuning of policy, not challenging it and certainly not discrediting either it or the agencies that deliver it and for which the government is responsible to Parliament. This is a fact of Home Office life. [Morgan and Hough 2008: 55].

While such a bald statement of purpose may be true enough nowadays (we are given no reason to suppose otherwise), it does not accord with that published by previous directors of Home Office research (Lodge 1974; Croft 2005, 1978: Cornish and Clarke 1987; Clarke and Cornish 1983). Although some might see these past accounts as self-serving or self-deluding, the above view also marks a radical sea-change in the administration of criminal justice policy in Britain, comprising what Ian Loader has called (based on the reminiscences of former government civil servants and researchers) the *fall of the platonic guardians* (Loader 2005). That is to say, wider changes in British public administration, including the administration of criminal justice, that have occurred since the 1970s, have seen both the collapse of a 'liberal-elite' ideology and style of government, and the rise of greater political partisanship and populism in the government of crime.

One of the central characteristics of the risk society is that it is becoming difficult to demarcate science from politics because much politics looks to science for advice in helping to solve social problems, and as such, science becomes implicated in politics. To understand this process there needs to be a way of conceptualising the use of science in politics. Sheila Jasanoff proposes the concept of *civic epistemology*, as the '...systematic practices by which a nation's citizens come to know things in common and to apply their knowledge to the conduct of politics' (Jasanoff 2005: 9). The *political* nature of such practices is confirmed in her comparative study of the politics of biotechnology through the intimate relationship between the way in which science is used and particular forms of democratic institutions and conduct of government. This varied not only according to differences in political cultures but also the balance struck between expert knowledge and political position:

> ...to a remarkable extent, British expertise remains tied to the person of the individual expert, who achieves standing not only through knowledge and competence but through

a demonstrated record of service to society. It is as if the expert's function is to discern the public's needs and to define the public good as much as it is to provide appropriate technical skills [Jasanoff 2005: 268].

As if echoing this sentiment, the (then) Director of Research, Development, and Statistics at the Home Office answers his question 'Can Criminologists engage in policy-making?' by opining, 'British criminology seems to have lost the knack of engaging in public debate' (Wiles 2002: 247). Academic criminology fails in its aims or its methods, either as an effective external critic that can guide policy in constructive directions or as the provider of useful knowledge that might address the government's requirements for evidence. To have any point criminology has to be a public activity; '... and, if it has to be so, then it better try and serve the public good' (ibid.: 251). This seems consistent with the civic epistemology of British government:

...much energy is devoted in Britain to producing experts whose right to speak on behalf of the public will be virtually unquestioned. Their authority is not a matter of skills and knowledge alone, but of those attributes coupled to significant demonstrations of social responsibility [Jasanoff 2005: 289].

In Britain, then, official criminology is now advanced by whether its proponents offer credible support for political ideas that fit in with the government's way of thinking. In turn, government will provide political machinery to persuade the public of the scientific authority of official criminology. The effect is reciprocal: political authority is given scientific legitimacy; and the scientific credentials of official criminology are endorsed by political authority.

Under this new dispensation, research and statistics are pressed into political service, and 'official criminologists' are now called upon to serve political purposes, often in helping government to deal with controversies and arguments that have a scientific aspect to them. One example of this is to present official data so as to come up with inferences and interpretations that are more congenial to, or supportive of, government policy. For example, a team of expert consultants and government researchers published a reanalysis of data (Kodz and Pease 2003), which had been collected by an independent research consortium, on contract to evaluate the Home Office Reducing Burglary Initiative, even before the consortium's analysis had been published (Hope *et al.* 2004). It seemed that the purpose of committing this rather heinous scientific offence was pre-emptive, giving a more promising prognosis for a recently-appointed minister to brag about (Hope 2004). Even after I had given evidence on the matter to a parliamentary select committee (Science and Technology Committee 2006), officials continued to spin their own version in private, and to brief against ours (Hope 2008), the gist of which was faithfully reported (without courtesy to ourselves) in a criminological textbook (Morgan and Hough 2008), and as expert evidence to the government's own review of science at the Home Office (Morgan and Hough 2007).

The Procurement of Truth

In the past, the Home Secretary exercised responsibility for the publication of research and statistics in official or command series by virtue of Parliamentary statute (Lodge 1974). Nowadays, although these statutory responsibilities still persist, the chief purpose to which government puts research and statistics is to assist it in directing the criminal justice system, forming part of the performance management regime that governs the various criminal justice agencies (Home Office 2000). While such a regime is justifiable in terms of the management of public expenditure, it has nevertheless provided an opportunity by stealth to convert official research and statistics into a kind of internal 'corporate intelligence' for the government of the day (Walters 2003) rather than as information created for wider public consumption and debate, not least to the general public via their Parliamentary representatives, academia or the mass media.

Home Office and Ministry of Justice ministers have now put in place machinery for procuring research and vetting the publication of results that superficially seems to be 'scientific' (Government Office for Science 2007) but on closer scrutiny turns out to be nothing of the sort (Hope 2008; Walters 2008).[4] Through such subterfuge government ministers are able to steer, distort or, in the worst case, suppress research findings (Hope 2008) in order to validate their policies (Science and Technology Committee 2006). They now have the power to deny independent access by other legitimate interests, including academic research, as well as parliamentarians, the media and other interest groups, who may wish, or have a public duty, to put government claims to test, and to develop alternative explanations and policies. This trend is having very harmful consequences: it is denying independent scrutiny of the criminal justice system that is especially harmful for democratic accountability. It is particularly harmful to the development of criminology as a social scientific discipline in Britain, access to whose subject-matter is now directly controlled by government ministers. The government of the day is not best qualified to predict what scientific knowledge might turn out to be useful in the longer run since concerns to censor challenging research, or to validate policy, override the methodological considerations that are properly applied by scientific disciplines.

Despite this, a former Home Office Chief Scientific Advisor (and former academic) found he could assert that academic criminology had become the private vice of its practitioners, especially since, alongside the growth of the discipline, 'a larger criminological community can *indulge itself* by writing for each other' (Wiles 2002: 248, emphasis added). This kind of populist denigration of academic research seeks to speak directly to the public and ministers, turning on its head the basic principle

[4] For details see http://webarchive.nationalarchives.gov.uk/+/http://www.berr.gov.uk//dius/science/science-reviews/Completed per cent20Reviews/page42390.html (accessed 25/09/09). Similar protocols have been put in place by the Ministry of Justice, and with respect to research on the police services in England and Wales (NPIA 2008).

upon which scientists have sought to guarantee the integrity of their research; that is through an independent, self-regulating academy of critical peers—*the republic of science* (Polanyi 1962). More than simply an effort at demarcation, the use of such language seems indicative of a direct challenge to the scientific authority of academic criminology; a stratagem to legitimize official criminology by delegitimizing academic criminology.

The contemporary politics of criminological research in Britain seems to be following the logic identified by Matthiesen (2004)—the *silent silencing* of independent voices concerning criminal justice policy and practice. Instead, government officials and their collaborators are actively promoting their own favoured official criminology not only to gain the ear of ministers but also to widen public support for the policies of their masters. But this leads to bad government—an Emperor's New Clothes syndrome. Through lack of challenge, government ministers have allowed themselves to become blind to anything other than the most congenial construction placed upon research and statistics, and risk becoming committed to policies with a weak or uncertain evidentiary basis, with an increasing danger of policy failure and unintended consequence. In this drive, the credibility of the government's research is being jeopardized through the release of reports that fail even to comply with its own regulatory standards.[5] And since government has thus been able to 'fix' the evidence that underpins its assertion of 'evidence-based policy', when the efficacy or legitimacy of its policies is challenged, it cannot resist the temptation to fix the evidence rather than fix the policy.

References

Beck, U. (1992), *Risk Society*, London: Sage Publications.

Campbell, D. T. (1969), 'Reforms as experiments', *American Psychologist*, 24: 409–29.

Clarke, R. V. G. and Cornish, D. B. (1972), *The Controlled Trial in Institutional Research—Paradigm or Pitfall for Penal Evaluators*, Home Office Research Study No. 15. London : HMSO, reprinted in R. V. G. Clarke and D. B. Cornish (eds) (1983), *Crime Control in Britain: A Review of Policy Research*, Albany: State University of New York Press.

_____ and _____. (eds) (1983), *Crime Control in Britain: a Review of Policy Research*, Albany: State University of New York Press.

_____ and Hope, T. (eds) (1984), *Coping with Burglary: Research Perspectives on Policy*, Boston: Kluwer-Nijhoff.

_____ and Mayhew, P. (eds) (1980), *Designing Out Crime*, London: HMSO.

Cohen, S. (1985), *Visions of Social Control: crime, punishment and classification*, Cambridge: Polity.

[5] Recently, the UK Statistics Authority (http://www.statisticsauthority.gov.uk/) has found the Home Office to have breached the Code of Practice for Official Statistics (UK Statistics Authority 2009); while a similar incident (Pease 2009), was met with scorn (Goldacre 2009).

_____ (1988), *Against Criminology*, New Brunswick and London: Transaction.

Collins, H. M. and Evans, R. (2002), 'The Third Wave of Science Studies: Studies of Expertise and Experience', *Social Studies of Science*, 32, 2: 235–96.

_____ and _____. (2007), *Rethinking Expertise*, Chicago and London: University of Chicago Press.

Cornish, D. B. and Clarke, R. V. (1987), 'Social Science in Government: The Case of the Home Office Research and Planning Unit', in M. Buler (ed.), *Social Science Research and Government*, Cambridge: Cambridge University Press.

Croft, J. (1978), *Research in Criminal Justice*, Home Office Research Study No. 44. London: HMSO.

_____ (2005), 'The Hunting of the Snark: Reflections on a Half Century of Crime', *The Political Quarterly*, 76, 1: 114–23.

Currie, E. (1985), *Confronting Crime: An American Challenge*, New York: Pantheon Books.

Farrell, G. (2005), 'Progress and Prospects in the Prevention of Repeat Victimisation', in N. Tilley (ed.), *Handbook of Crime Prevention and Community Safety*, Cullompton: Willan.

Farrington, D. P. (2007), 'Childhood Risk Factors and Risk-Focused Prevention', in M. Maguire, R. Morgan, and R. Reiner (eds), *The Oxford Handbook of Criminology*, 4th edn. Oxford: Oxford University Press.

Garland, D. (2001), *The Culture of Control: Crime and social Order in Contemporary Society*. Oxford: Oxford University Press.

Giddens, A. (1990), *The Consequences of Modernity*, Cambridge: Polity.

Goldacre, B. (2009), 'Bad Science', *The Guardian*, 18 July 2009. (<www.badscience.net/2009/07/is-this-a-joke/>, accessed 8 September 2009).

Government Office for Science (2007), *Science Review of the Home Office and Ministry of Justice*, London: Department for Innovation, Universities and Skills.

Heckman, J. and Smith, J. A. (1995), 'Assessing the case for social experiments', *The Journal of Economic Perspectives*, 9: 85–110.

Home Office (2000), *Review of Crime Statistics: A discussion Document*, London: Home Office.

_____ (2007), *Cutting Crime: A New Partnership, 2008–11*, London: Home Office.

Hope, T. (1985), *Implementing Crime Prevention Measures*, Home Office Research Study No. 86, London: HMSO.

_____ (1995), 'Community Crime Prevention', in M. Tonry and D. P. Farrington (eds), *Building a Safer Society: Strategic Approaches to Crime Prevention*. Chicago: University of Chicago Press.

_____. (ed.) (2000), *Perspectives on Crime Reduction*, The International Library of Criminology, Criminal Justice and Penology. Aldershot: Ashgate Publishing.

_____ (2002), 'The Road Taken: Evaluation, Replication and Crime Reduction', in G. Hughes, E. McLaughlin and J. Muncie (eds), *Crime Prevention and Community Safety*, London: Sage Publications.

_____ (2004). 'Pretend it Works: Evidence and Governance in the Evaluation of the Reducing Burglary Initiative', *Criminology and Criminal Justice*, 4, 3: 287–308.

_____ (2005), 'Pretend it Doesn't Work: The 'Anti-Social' Bias in the Maryland Scientific Methods Scale', *European Journal on Criminal Policy and Research*, 11: 275–96.

_____ (2006), 'Review of *Crime Science* (Smith and Tilley)', *Theoretical Criminology*, 10, 2: 245–50.

_____ (2007), 'The Distribution of Household Property Crime Victimization: Insights from the British Crime Survey', in M. Hough and M. Maxfield (eds), *Surveying Crime in the 21st Century*, Crime Prevention Studies vol. 22, Monsey: Criminal Justice Press and Collumpton, Devon: Willan.

_____ (2008), 'A Firing Squad to Shoot the Messenger: Home Office Peer Review of Research', in W. MacMahon (ed.), *Critical Thinking about the Uses of Research: Evidence Based Policy Series 1*, London: Centre for Crime and Justice Studies, King's College London.

_____ (2009a), 'The Illusion of Control: A response to Professor Sherman', *Criminology and Criminal Justice*, 9, 2: 125–34.

_____ (2009b), 'Evaluation of Safety and Crime Prevention Policies in England and Wales', in P. Robert (ed.), *Evaluating Safety and Crime Prevention Policies in Europe*, Brussels: Vubpress: Bussels University Press.

_____, Bryan, J., Crawley, E., Crawley, P., Russell, N., and Trickett, A. (2004), *Strategic Development Projects in the Yorkshire and the Humber, East Midlands and Eastern Regions*, Home Office Online Report 41/04. London: Home Office.

_____ and Karstedt, S. (2003), 'Towards a New Social Crime Prevention', in H. Kury and J. Obergfell-Fuchs (eds), *Crime Prevention: New Approaches*, Mainz, De.: Weisse Ring Verlag-GmbH.

_____ and Shaw, M. (1988), *Communities and Crime Reduction*, London: HMSO.

Hughes, G. (2002), *Crime Control and Community: The New Politics of Public Safety*, Cullompton: Willan.

Jasanoff, S. (2005), *Designs on Nature: Science and Democracy in Europe and the United States*, Princeton: Princeton University Press.

Kodz, J. and Pease, K. (2003), 'Reducing Burglary Initiative: Early Findings on Burglary Reduction', *Findings 204*, Research, Development and Statistics Directorate. London: Home Office.

Laycock, G. (2001), 'Hypothesis-Based Research: The Repeat Victimisation Story', *Criminology and Criminal Justice*, 1: 59–82.

Lea, J. and Young J. (1993), *What is to be Done about Law and Order? Crisis in the nineties*, London: Pluto Press.

Loader, I. (2005), 'Fall of the 'Platonic Guardians': Liberalism, Criminology and Political Responses to Crime in England and Wales', *British Journal of Criminology*, 46: 561–86.

Lodge, T. (1974), 'The Founding of the Home Office Research Unit', in R. Hood (ed.), *Crime, Criminology and Public Policy: Essays in Honour of Sir Leon Radzinowic*, London: Heinemann.

Mathiesen, T. (2004), *Silently Silenced: Essays on the Creation of Acquiescence in Modern Society*, Winchester: Waterside Press.

Matza, D. (1969), *Becoming Deviant*, Englewood Cliffs: Prentice-Hall.

Melossi, D. (2008), *Controlling Crime, Controlling Society: Thinking about Crime in Europe and America*, Cambridge: Polity Press.

Morgan, R. and Hough, M. (2007), *Evidence Submitted to the Home Office and Ministry of Justice Science Review: File 44676.doc*, Government Office for Science. London: Department for Innovation, Universities and Skills.

_____ and _____. (2008), 'The Politics of Criminological Research', in R. D. King and E. Wincup (eds), *Doing Research on Crime and Justice*, 2nd edn, Oxford: Oxford University Press.

Morris, N. and Hawkins, G. (1970), *The Honest Politician's Guide to Crime Control*, Chicago: Chicago University Press.

Moynihan, D. P. (1969), *Maximum Feasible Misunderstanding: Community Action in the War on Poverty*, New York: Free Press.

NPIA (2008), *Research Protocols: Specialist Operational Support,* National Police Improvement Agency.

Pawson, R. and Tilley, N. (1997), *Realistic Evaluation*, London: Sage Publications.

Pease, K. (2009), 'Annex C: DNA Retention after S and Marper: Ken Pease Jill Dando Institute April 2009', Home Office (2009) *Keeping the Right People on the DNA Database: science and public protection*, May 2009. London: Home Office.

Polanyi, M. (1962), 'The Republic of Science: Its Political and Economic Theory', *Minerva*, 1, 1; 54–73.

Popper, K. R. (1945), *The Open Society and its Enemies*, London Routledge and Kegan Paul.

_____ (1957), *The Poverty of Historicism*, London: Routledge and Kegan Paul.

_____ (1983 [1974]), 'The Problem of Demarcation', in D. Miller (ed.), *A Pocket Popper*, Oxford: Fontana.

_____ (1992), *Unended Quest: An Intellectual Autobiography*, London: Routledge.

Radzinowicz, Sir L. (1999), *Adventures in Criminology*. London and New York: Routledge.

Rein, M. (1976), *Social Science and Public Policy*, Harmondsworth, Middlesex: Penguin Books.

Rose, N. (1999), *Powers of Freedom: Reframing Political Thought*, Cambridge: Cambridge University Press.

Science and Technology Committee (2006), House of Commons Science and Technology Committee, *Scientific Advice, Risk and Evidence Based Policy Making*, Seventh Report of Session 2005–06, Volume I Report HC 900-I; Volume II Oral and Written Evidence HC 900-I. The House of Commons, 26 October 2006.

Sherman, L. W. (2007), "The Power Few: Experimental Criminology and the Reduction of Harm' The 2006 Joan McCord Prize Lecture', *Journal of Experimental Criminology*, 3: 299–321.

_____. (2009), 'Evidence and Liberty: The Promise of Experimental Criminology', *Criminology and Criminal Justice*, 9, 1: 5–28.

_____, Gottfredeson, D. C., MacKenzie, D. L., Eck, J., Reuter, P., and Bushway, S. (1998), *Preventing Crime: What Works, What Doesn't, What's Promising*, Research in Brief, July 1998. Washington, D.C.: National Institute of Justice, reprinted in T. Hope (ed.) (2000), *Perspectives on Crime Reduction*, Aldershot: Ashgate Publishing.

Simon, J. (2007), *Governing Through Crime; How the War on Crime Transformed American Democracy and Created a Culture of Fear*, Oxford: Oxford University Press.

Smith, M. and Tilley, N. (eds) (2005), *Crime Science: New Approaches to Preventing and Detecting Crime,* Cullompton: Willan.

Taylor, I., Walton, P., and Young, J. (1973), *The New Criminology*, London: Routledge.

Tilley, N. (1993), 'After Kirkholt—Theory, Method and Results of Replication Evaluations', Crime Prevention Unit Series Paper No. 47, London: Home Office.

Tonry, M. and Farrington D. P. (eds) (1995), *Building a Safer Society: Strategic Approaches to Crime Prevention*, Chicago: University of Chicago Press.

UK Statistics Authority (2009), *Statement on Knife Crime Statistics, 11 December 2008—Analysis Against the Code of Practice for Official Statistics*. Monitoring and Assessment Note 1/2009. (<www.statisticsauthority.gov.uk/>).

Von Hirsch, A., Garland, D., and Wakefield, A. (eds) (2000), *Situational Crime Prevention: Ethics and Social Context*, Oxford: Hart Publishing.

Walters, R. (2003), *Deviant Knowledge: Criminology, Politics and Policy,* Collumton: Willan.

_____ (2008), 'Government Manipulation of Criminological Knowledge and Policies of Deceit', in W. MacMahon (ed.), *Critical Thinking about the Uses of Research*, Evidence Based Policy Series 1. London: Centre for Crime and Justice Studies, King's College London.

Wiles, P. (ed.) (1976), *The Sociology of Crime and Delinquency in Britain: vol. 2. The New Criminologies*, London: Robertson.

_____ (2002), 'Criminology in the 21st Century: Public Good or Private Interest?', The Sir John Barry Memorial Lecture, *Australian and New Zealand Journal of Criminology*, 35: 238–252.

Wilkins, L. T. (1964), *Social Deviance: Social Policy, Action, and Research*, London: Tavistock.

Wilson, J. Q. (1974), 'Crime and the Criminologists'. *Commentary*, 58: 47–53, reprinted in J. Q. Wilson, (1983, 1985), *Thinking About Crime: revised edition*. New York: Basic Books (1983). New York: Vintage Books (1985).

Winship, C. and Morgan S. L. (1999), 'The estimation of causal effects from observational data'. *Annual Review of Sociology*, 25: 659–707.

Wootton, B. (1959), *Social Science and Social Pathology*, London: Allen and Unwin.

Young, J. (1999), *The Exclusive Society: Social Exclusion, Crime and Difference in Late Modernity*, London: Sage.

Zedner, L. (2007), 'Pre-Crime and Post-Criminology', *Theoretical Criminology*, 11, 2: 261–81.

31

CRIMINOLOGY: SCIENCE + POLICY ANALYSIS

ALFRED BLUMSTEIN

Introduction

My educational background is not in criminology, but in engineering, a profession that is typically concerned with drawing on scientific knowledge to solve a practical problem. I was introduced to criminology in 1965 when I was recruited to serve as the director of a science and technology task force for the President's Crime Commission. My protests that I knew nothing about crime or criminal justice were met with the assurance that the Commission had many experts in those areas who could answer any question I had. Since then I have become a card-carrying criminologist, having served as president of the American Society of Criminology and having been awarded the Stockholm Prize in Criminology in 2007. Thus, I prepared this piece as an immigrant to criminology, bringing a different perspective to the field.

Much of criminology involves research into the behaviour of individuals. Criminologists are particularly interested in those individuals who end up committing various kinds of crime. They also study the behaviour of the elements of the criminal justice system. Many criminologists are quite content to stop there, informing their colleagues about their findings or building on the work of others to advance the state of the science. I do not stop there; rather, I have sought to apply my criminological knowledge to improve policies, particularly those associated with the choices made within the criminal justice system. I will confess that this has been a demanding challenge because so many policies are made with little regard for scientific knowledge; rather, they are driven much more often by ideological preference. Perhaps, even worse, they are frequently shaped by cynical appeal to politically popular policies that are contradicted by scientific knowledge.

In this chapter I devote most of my attention to issues in which I have been involved. In some cases, I was motivated initially by scientific curiosity. In others I was driven by a desire to confront what I viewed as wrong-headed policy. In those cases, I sought to deploy scientific knowledge to help shape and improve public policies.

A Basic Model of Policy Analysis

The basic thrust of policy analysis can be summed up briefly and generically in the following general relationship:

$$Y = f(X, Z)$$

where:

Y = Objectives or outcomes of concern
X = Policy choices
Z = Factors that affect the impact of X on Y

Here, the outcomes (Y) are typically concerned with lowering crime, reducing cost, enhancing justice, and other aspects of societal concern that criminologists care about. The policy choices (X) relate to considerations like sentencing policy, intensity of police presence, investment in early socialization or in rehabilitative methods, capital punishment, and all the policy choices that float around criminology meetings and debates. The richest array of variables includes the many factors Z that affect the degree to which the policies influence the objectives. Thus, Z could include demographic factors, social environment, police training, correctional environment, judicial temperament, and all the factors that could end up on the right-hand side of regression equations. Because crime interacts with so many aspects of the social environment and can be influenced by so many individual, family, community, situational, and national phenomena, selecting an appropriate set of such variables becomes an extremely difficult analytic choice. The choice is particularly difficult because of the many possible candidates, the effort to collect the appropriate data, and the risk of overwhelming the available sample size with the number of possible variables. Indeed, many debates in criminology centre on an author's failure to include some particularly salient variables.

The functional relationship (f) in the model that links all these together is, of course, the hardest part of any such analysis. That is because the number of factors Z affecting the influence of X on Y covers so much territory and also because the typical assumption of linearity in these relationships is inherently arbitrary and often inadequate. Nevertheless, considerable progress can and has been made in identifying such models and estimating them with reasonable data. But the field has still been minimally penetrated, and much of even that limited penetration will, no doubt, subsequently be shown to have been incorrect. This could occur because there were important Z's left out of the model or because the formulation f—usually a simple regression equation—was found to be excessively simplistic.

In the following discussion I identify two areas in which I have been involved, one about the science and its implications for policy, the other about policy concerns and the science that has developed that can contribute to recommending improved policies. The relevant issues include the following:

- the science of criminal careers and its relationship to incapacitation effects and the contribution to sentencing policy;
- the policy concern of the dramatic growth of incarceration in the United States and the use of science to identify the factors contributing to that growth and to provide focus for controlling that growth.

Criminal Careers

Considerable research has been directed at studying the nature of individual criminal careers (see, for example, Blumstein *et al.* 1986; and Blumstein and Cohen 1987). A 'criminal career' is not necessarily how an individual offender earns his living, but rather is simply a longitudinal characterization of the offending patterns of individuals. This is typically done either with (a) self-reports from a set of sampled individuals who report periodically on what offences they committed since the last report or (b) from official records of the longitudinal sequence of arrests or convictions of the individuals of interest.

Self-reports provide the opportunity for much richer collection of information from the individuals of concern. They also inform us about individuals who have never come to official attention and are thus missing from official-record databases. Reports tell us about the offences committed that never come to official attention and so their density of reported events would be much higher (roughly the reciprocal of the mean arrest probability following a crime) than in the official records. They also provide much richer information about the respondents that can provide insights into the dynamic factors affecting their lives that could be contributing to their criminal activity. The sample sizes, however, are typically limited by the cost of the individual interviews and the limited capacity of any research organization to pursue the self-report methodology with a very large sample.

The other major source of data is derived from official records, typically containing information on arrests or other encounters with the criminal justice system. These records would include the date and the jurisdiction of the arrest, the offence charged by the police, and ideally the disposition of the arrest and any sentence imposed if the perpetrator was found guilty. The official records, especially in a populous jurisdiction, can generate an enormous sample in the hundreds of thousands of individuals, but the information provided is only limited to what was recorded for those events. Also, the event frequency observed with official records will be appreciably lower than the frequency displayed by self-reports since only a fraction of offences committed lead to an arrest.

The official record data are more limited in content but much richer in the available sample size. They typically contain information on arrests or other encounters with the criminal justice system. These records would include the date and the jurisdiction of the arrest, the offence charged by the police, and only occasionally the disposition of the arrest and any sentence imposed if the perpetrator was found guilty. The official records, especially in a populous jurisdiction, can generate an enormous sample in the order of hundreds of thousands of individuals, but the information provided is limited to what was recorded for those events. Also, the event frequency observed with official records will be appreciably lower than the frequency displayed by self-reports since only a fraction of offences committed lead to an arrest.

Because of the size of criminal history repositories, they provide access to potentially millions of offenders and the longitudinal characteristics of their offences that came to official attention. Thus, they can deal richly with the sample size problem, but in exchange have much more restricted information on the characteristics of the members in their sample and the events surrounding their crimes.

The parameters of a criminal career that have been explored most richly have been the following:

- offending frequency λ (the Greek letter lambda), the crimes committed per year while actively offending; λ can be measured directly in self-reports, but a counterpart frequency μ (the Greek letter mu), represents the arrest or conviction rate;
- probability of arrest or conviction following a crime (q), an important parameter linking the events in a self-report sequence with those in an official-record sequence, where the key offending-frequency parameter of interest, λ, can be estimated as μ/q, where μ is the arrest or conviction frequency;
- career length, or time from initiation of the criminal career until its termination; a related measure is the *residual* career length, or the time from a criminal justice intervention during the career until the career terminates;
- participation rate or fraction of the population or of any particular population subgroup engaging in crime—or with a non-zero offending frequency—at any time.

Given the inherent saliency of these parameters to any work in criminology (like the speed of light or gravitational acceleration to physics), one would think their values and their distributions would have been well measured in different settings for different subsets of the offending population. Yet while there was a flurry of such measurements and analysis in the 1970s and 1980s of both official records (see, eg, Chaiken and Chaiken 1982; Greenwood and Abrahamse 1982; Blumstein and Cohen 1989) and self-reports (see, eg, Farrington 1989, on the Cambridge Study in Delinquent Development; Loeber and Stouthamer-Loeber 1986, on the Pittsburgh Youth Study; and Elliott 1994, on the National Survey of Youth), we have seen very little since then. Not only would we like measurement of the parameters themselves, but it would be important to know something about their determinants and how the parameters vary, for example, between urban and rural areas, across race, and among prison populations, prison entrants, and offenders in the general population.

An important step forward would involve information on the probability of arrest following commission of a crime, designated by the symbol q. If the individual offending frequency is indicated by the symbol λ and the arrest frequency by μ, then the two are related by $\lambda = \mu/q$. One can generate a rich array of these three parameters for different crime types and for different subgroups in the population. Unfortunately, however, even though there are many self-report data sets providing information on λ and official-record data sets on μ, there is very little information linking the two through the use of q. Having that linking opportunity on similar populations would provide an opportunity to generate large samples from the official records and to record related information on identifiable subgroups from the self-report information.

Policy Analysis Using Information on Criminal Careers

The previous discussion focused heavily on obtaining scientific knowledge about criminal careers. It should be obvious that such knowledge could contribute significantly to enhancing crime control efforts. This would be especially helpful in developing incarceration policy intended to remove active offenders—and especially the most active offenders—and their offences from the community through an incapacitation effect. One would seek to remove those with the highest offending frequency in the most serious offences and especially so during the active portion of their criminal careers. This provides the opportunity to exploit scientific knowledge about criminal careers to develop intelligent and informed policies targeted at enhancing public safety, certainly one important role for criminology.

Focus on Offending Frequency (λ)

We recognize that an offender incarcerated for S years during his active period has the potential to avert λ^*S crimes.[1] This leads to the obvious possibility of trying

[1] Since many individuals engage in a mixture of crime types we might apply a weight, W_i, to the ith crime type with its associated offending frequency λ_i, and so the weighted value of the crimes averted by the sentence of S years would be $\Sigma_i\ \lambda_i{}^*S^*W_i$ In our discussion we deal only with a homogeneous value of λ.

to estimate an individual offender's λ and incarcerating those with the highest values. This was proposed as 'selective incapacitation' by Peter Greenwood (1982), estimating individual values of the λ using data on prior record and other recorded variables based on a survey of prison inmates. The proposal was met with a storm of protest because of the disparate treatment that would result, whereby individuals convicted of the same offence could receive sharply different treatment based on their estimated value of λ, with the high- λ people getting an extended prison sentence and the low- λ people receiving probation. Furthermore, as with any statistical prediction, there would be errors and the opposition highlighted the false-positive errors (ie, people who were truly low λ but predicted to be high λ) that would result in them being punished unjustly. That was an era characterized by great concern over issues of disparate treatment—with particular concern about disparity across the races—and that emphasis undoubtedly contributed to the demise of the 'selective incapacitation' proposal. In the current era, where 'risk assessment' has become much more popular as a means of reducing prison populations without increasing crime, selective incapacitation would undoubtedly receive a friendlier welcome. The current climate in the United States is looking for means of accommodating the widespread desire to reduce prison populations without increasing crime; this desire is motivated on the political right by a desire to reduce costs and to balance budgets and on the left by a revulsion at a high rate of incarceration.[2] This desire on the left is especially intense because of the disproportionate incarceration of African-Americans, who comprise about half the prison population, even though they comprise only 12 per cent of the general population, an incarceration rate ratio of greater than 6:1. In order to avoid reigniting calls for more incarceration, risk assessment is being called on to avoid a corresponding decrease in public safety.

Further research by Canela-Cacho *et al.* (1997) using self-reports by prisoners highlighted the stark difference between the λ estimates of those in prison and those active offenders in the larger community. This gave rise to the realization that the high—λ offenders 'roll the dice' more often, and so with some limited assumption of arrest, conviction, or incarceration risk per crime (all related to q) being reasonably homogeneous across individual offenders, there would be a natural tendency for the high- λ offenders to disproportionately show up in prison. This characterization of 'stochastic selectivity' demonstrated that the goals of selective incapacitation would be achieved just as a matter of natural course due to the greater risk of incarceration by those who commit crimes at a higher rate.

[2] The current rate of incarceration in prisons and jails in the United States is currently about 750 per 100,000 population (Walmsley 2003), or about 1 per cent of the adult population (Pew 2009), giving it the world's largest incarceration rate, recently having surpassed Russia, and compared to about 100 per 100,000 in much of western Europe, a rate that prevailed rather steadily for over 50 years in the United States until the 1970s (Blumstein and Cohen 1973).

Focus on Career Length

A second parameter of obvious interest for sentencing policy is that of career length, and so information about the distribution of career length should be taken into account. In particular, *residual* career length, or the time left in an individual's career at some intervention point when a sentencing decision is being made, should pose limits on the length of time an individual is assigned to prison. Once a particular individual's career is terminated, any further time spent in prison can be characterized as 'wastage' from the viewpoint of incapacitation. That prison space could well be occupied by a still-active offender, even if he had a lower value of λ, and that would do more to reduce crime than keeping the cell occupied by an individual whose value of λ has dropped to zero.

Of course, it is most difficult to know precisely when or whether any particular individual's career will terminate. But it is possible, based on self-reports and official records, to make estimates of that residual career length as a function of individual characteristics. Age is certainly one such important characteristic since we do know, from the classic age–crime curve[3], that offending (at least as measured by arrest) as a function of age rises rapidly to a peak in the late teen years and then declines fairly steadily. The decline could be attributable to some combination of slowing down and career termination, but there are reasonable indications that the major effect is attributable to the latter.

In at least one study, it was found that residual career length *increases* with age during the 20s. This finding is somewhat counterintuitive in the sense that if one anticipates that all offenders began their criminal careers at about age 20, then one would expect the residual career length to decline with age. Yet, not all careers are the same length. One would anticipate that many active offenders in their early 20s would have a short career, would terminate early, and that those still active into their late 20s would be more committed to offending and thereby display a longer career.

That study also found that the longest residual career occurs in the 30s and is fairly constant over that period. Into the 40s, 'wear out' would begin to take effect and start to bring down the residual criminal career length. This effect is not dissimilar to the life patterns of items of technology such as airplanes or of athletes. In the early parts of their careers, they may perform well but there will be a larger number of 'break-in' failures with early dropout. Those good enough to continue into their mid-career would have demonstrated good staying power. Finally, late in the career, wear-out becomes common, even to the best.

This understanding of the progression of a criminal career becomes important in developing sentencing policy and in making individual sentencing decisions. The

[3] The age–crime curve is measured simply as the ratio of the number of arrests of people of a particular age divided by the population of that age, or AC(a)= A(a)/N(a), where a = age, A(a) = number of arrests of people of age a, N(a) = number of people of age a in the general population, and AC(a) is the value of the age-crime curve at age a.

tendency in the United States in the 1980s and 1990s for legislatures to curry favour with voters by passing mandatory sentencing laws calling for lengthy draconian sentences (eg, the 'three strikes and you're out' rule mandating a life sentence following a third conviction, thereby invoking a baseball metaphor as an ostensible manifestation of 'justice'). These long sentences almost certainly incur a high degree of wastage as a result of keeping these offenders in prison well after their criminal careers would have terminated, but the political benefit of appearing 'tough on crime' seems to outweigh the crime control effectiveness or cost efficiency.

The Special Case of Market Crimes

In the above discussion, it was clear that a sentence of S years should be able to avert $S^* \lambda$ crimes through incapacitation, but that can only happen if the following are true:

- the career does not terminate during the S years;
- the time spent in prison does not change λ or the residual career length through either specific-deterrence or rehabilitation (the crime reduction is then greater than $S^* \lambda$) or through criminalization (the crime reduction is less than $S^* \lambda$);
- there is no replacement of the offender's criminal activity in the community;
- The last item here relates to various means by which replacement can occur. In the case of a personal crime like rape, for example, replacement is not likely to be an issue of concern and the rapist's crimes are taken off the street when he is incarcerated. In the case of burglary, in contrast, a burglar who sells his proceeds to a fence could be replaced by the fence recruiting someone else to steal the goods he markets. With drug crimes in particular, and also other vice crimes serving a market, replacement is an issue of major concern. As long as the demand for the marketed goods or services persists, and as long as there is a supply of replacements, there can be no significant incapacitation effect associated with incarcerating the sellers.[4]

In line with this observation, one would hope that those establishing policy regarding drug offenders would be fully aware of this interaction, and that they would seek other means such as treatment or decriminalization to deal with the admittedly serious problem of drug abuse and its consequences. While that awareness seems to be widespread in most countries, it has yet to surface as an important policy consideration as the United States tries to deal with its widespread drug problem. As drug abuse became an issue of concern in the late 1970s and 1980s and particularly as violence associated with competition or dispute resolution pervaded the market for

[4] This was the major theme of Blumstein's (1973) presidential address to the American Society of Criminology in November, 1972, shortly after Bill Clinton was elected as president and there were hopes that he might lead a reconsideration of the then intense US policy for incarceration of drug offenders. Those hopes were never realized.

crack cocaine, the legislative response was most often to enact mandatory minimum sentencing laws. These were initially enacted to challenge the judges who often sentenced drug sellers to probation, perhaps because the judges appreciated the problem of replacement. The initial laws imposed mandatory sentences of two years; those did not have much effect and so they were replaced by five-year and ten-year mandatory minimum sentences. There was still no clear evidence of an effect on drug transactions, although the effect on prison populations was quite clear: offenders serving prison time for drug offences currently comprise over 20 per cent of the population in state prisons and over 50 per cent of those in federal prisons, representing the single largest offence type in prison (Sabol *et al.* 2009). The incarceration of drug offenders is currently about ten times the rate that prevailed in 1980.

One important but unintended consequence of this massive incarceration of drug sellers was the nature of their replacements. The replacements were typically males who were appreciably much younger than those they replaced. Crack was typically marketed by African-American males in contrast to powder cocaine, which was marketed primarily by whites and Hispanics. One consequence of the arrival of those replacements was that these younger sellers were far less restrained than their older predecessors in their use of the guns they carried to protect themselves against street robbers. Also, in view of the tight networking among these young people, their neighbourhood peers, even though they had no involvement with drug markets, also began carrying guns. This armaments race gave rise to a major increase in homicides involving young black males killing other young black males (Blumstein 1995).

That rise in violence turned downward in the early 1990s after the demand for crack subsided as a result of the growing recognition of the harm that drugs visited on siblings, parents, and older peers (Blumstein and Wallman 2006). Fortunately, the United States had a robust economy at the time and so the young people who would have been recruited into the drug markets could readily find roles in the legitimate economy. That transition, along with major police efforts at searching out and confiscating guns that were on the street, contributed to a decline of over 40 per cent in violence between 1993 and 2000.

Policy Concern Stimulating Analysis

The previous discussion was focused on the ways in which scientific knowledge most specifically about criminal careers provides useful guidance to policy. The flow could as easily move in the other direction, where one sees inappropriate policies that warrant scientific analysis to point out how best to improve the policies. The analysis would be focused on identifying and understanding the factors contributing to the current undesirable policy. Its undesirability could be manifested by cost inefficiency (excessive costs being incurred to achieve a particular result) as well as harms in terms of social justice (eg, in terms of unreasonable impact on some minority group or an excess of punitiveness more generally in the population.)

For example, the United States for at least fifty years from the 1920s to the 1970s maintained an impressively stable and trendless incarceration rate of 110 per 100,000 of the population (Blumstein and Cohen, 1973). Beginning in the mid-1970s, that incarceration rate increased at an annual rate of 6 to 8 per cent to a level that is currently about 500 per 100,000, almost five times the previously stable rate. This rate is about five times that of most other industrialized nations with which the United States identifies.

This growth of incarceration concerned many criminologists and raises the question of what factors contributed to that growth. The likely candidates would include the following:

- more crime;
- more arrests per crime;
- more commitments to prison per arrest;
- longer time served in prison, including for parole violation.

If the growth was all attributable to more crime, that would be understandable and a reflection of a continuation of prior policy and would warrant efforts mostly directed at reducing the crime, perhaps with less attention to reducing the punitiveness. If it were all attributable to more arrests per crime, particularly victim crimes, that could reflect an improvement in police performance, perhaps by more effective management of police forces, maybe aided by forensic and information technologies. Again, that growth would be understandable and might have some long-term benefits in terms of enhanced deterrence and incapacitation, and might warrant further consideration of the trade-off between the social costs of incapacitation and the crime control consequences.

Blumstein and Beck (1999 and 2005) showed that there was a small contribution to the growth from increases in crime and that the contribution from better policing was negligible. Rather, virtually all of the growth was attributable to an increase in punitiveness, reflected in more commitments per arrest (more aggressive prosecution and more punishment by judges, stimulated largely by policies mandated by legislatures) and longer time served per commitment. Initially, in the period between 1980 and 1994, these two factors contributed about equally. Later, with the increase in commitments having gone about as far as it could go, the further growth was attributable twice as much to time served than to commitments. Also, a major contributor to the growth has been the tenfold increase in incarceration rate for drug offences.

It is clear that a regime change in the policy environment occurred, mostly beginning in the early 1980s. The earlier control by the functionaries within the criminal justice system that maintained a stable incarceration rate was transferred to control by the political environment. Statutory changes such as mandatory minimum sentences required the judges to make commitments where they might not have, or to impose sentences longer than they might otherwise have. These statutory changes transferred control over sentencing from the judges to prosecutors who decided what charges to assign to defendants, and the role of prosecutors as elected officials gives them powerful incentives to act 'tough' by calling for more punitive sentences.

Thus, if one wants to reduce incarceration, one has to focus on the punitiveness of the sentencing policies. One factor contributing to attention to those issues is the budget problem faced by most states as a consequence of the current recession. States are constitutionally mandated to maintain a balanced budget; the political environment strongly inhibits their raising taxes, and so they look for opportunities for cost reduction. The greatest growth in expenditures in most states in recent years has been a consequence of the rise in prison populations, and so about half of the states, with Texas, New York, and Michigan in the lead (Sabol *et al.* 2009), have found the political means to reduce their prison populations, and interestingly have not seen a consequent increase in crime.

Again, this illustrates the interaction between the science and the policy analysis where the policy concerns raise scientific questions that can then lead to a potential improvement in the policy choices. Of course, that improvement does not necessarily occur because the political choices are not always rational, at least from the perspective of a policy analyst. Politically motivating events can force the policies to move in the other direction.[5]

Interaction of Science and Policy Analysis

This chapter has tried to highlight some important interactions between scientific knowledge about offenders and their criminal careers and the implications of that knowledge for developing more intelligent policy that can and should be used in the operation of the criminal justice system. I have also highlighted how policy concerns can stimulate scientific research that can provide a focus on where policy improvement can best be targeted. These have provided an opportunity for identifying policies that have been put in place that failed to exploit that knowledge. There are many other examples that could be developed in a similar manner. They relate to knowledge about the declining risk with 'time free and clean' for individuals with a prior encounter with the criminal justice system, and the use of that knowledge to

[5] For example, a parolee shot and killed a police officer in Philadelphia in 2008. So heinous an event gave rise to a major political outcry against parole that it forced the governor of Pennsylvania to order a freeze on all prisoners released on parole until parole policies could be reevaluated. That reevaluation was a long drawn-out process during which parolees were released but in a much more limited way than previously. As a result, the state of Pennsylvania led the nation with a 30 per cent increase in its prison population in 2008, when the national increase was only 0.8 per cent and when state prison populations actually declined for the first time in decades.

establish 'redemption times' when that prior record no longer contains useful information and should be ignored (Blumstein and Nakamura, 2005). Other examples include the many approaches that have been pursued to identify and test a variety of rehabilitative or crime-prevention methodologies.

These are models of criminology that admittedly take criminologists out of the isolation of academia and force interaction with public officials who tend to have strong political objectives that exploit the public's ignorance of most of the complexities of criminal justice knowledge and too often respond simply to any policy that looks like it is 'tough on crime'. That political approach, whether naïve or cynical, too often conflicts with criminologists' desire to stimulate more rationality in the formulation of policies.

References

Blumstein, A. (1993), 'Making Rationality Relevant—The American Society of Criminology Presidential Address, 1992', *Criminology*, 31(1): 1–16.

_____ (1995), Youth Violence, Guns, and the Illicit-Drug Industry. *Journal of Criminal Law and Criminology*, 86 (4): 10–36.

_____ and Beck, A. J. (2005), 'Reentry as a Transient State between Liberty and Recommitment' in J. Travis and C. Visher (eds), *Prisoner Reentry and Crime in America*, Cambridge: Cambridge University Press: 50–79.

_____ and _____ (1999), 'Population Growth in U.S. Prisons, 1980–1996', in M. Tonry and J. Petersilia (eds), *Crime and Justice: An Annual Review of Research*, Chicago: University of Chicago Press: 17–61.

_____ and Cohen, J. (1987), 'Characterizing Criminal Careers', *Science*, 238 (4818): 985–91.

_____ and _____ (1973), 'A Theory of the Stability of Punishment', *Journal of Criminal Law, Criminology and Police Science*, 63 (2): 198–207.

_____ and Cohen, J. (1979), 'Estimation of Individual Crime Rates from Arrest Records', *Journal of Criminal Law and Criminology*, 70 (4): 561–85.

_____, Cohen, J., Roth, J., and Visher, C. A. (eds) (1986), *Criminal Careers and 'Career Criminals'*. Report of the National Academy of Sciences Panel on Research on Criminal Careers, Washington: National Academy Press.

_____ and Nakamura, K. (2009), 'Redemption in the Presence of Widespread Criminal Background Checks', *Criminology*, 47(2):327–59.

_____ and Wallman, J. (2006), *The Crime Drop in America*, Revised Edition, New York: Cambridge University Press.

Canela-Cacho, J. A., Cohen, J., and Blumstein, A. (1997), 'Relationship Between the Offending Frequency (λ) of Imprisoned and Free Offenders', *Criminology*, 35 (1): 133–75.

Chaiken, J. M., Chaiken, M.R., Peterson, J. E. (1982), *Varieties of Criminal Behavior*. Rand Report No. R-2814/1-NIJ. Rand Corporation.

Elliott, D. S. (1994), 'Serious Violent Offenders: Onset, Developmental Course, and Termination—The American Society Of Criminology 1993 Presidential Address', *Criminology*, 32(1):1–21.

Farrington, D. (1989), 'Early Predictors of Adolescent Aggression and Adult Violence', *Violence and Victims*. 4(2): 79–100.

Greenwood, P. W. and Abrahamse, A. (1982), *Selective Incapacitation*, Rand Report No. R-2815-NIJ. Rand Corporation.

Loeber, R., and Stouthamer-Loeber, M. (1986), 'Family Factors as Correlates and Predictors of Juvenile Conduct Problems and Delinquency', *Crime & Justice: An Annual Review of Research*, 7: 219–39.

Pew Center on the States (2009), *One in 100: Behind Bars in America*, 2008 Pew Public Safety Performance Project.

Sabol, W.J., West, H. C., and Cooper, M. (2009), *Prisoners in 2008*. Bureau of Justice Statistics Bulletin No. NCJ 228417. US Bureau of Justice Statistics.

Walmsley, R. (2003), *World Prison Population List*, 4th edn, London: Home Office.

32

CRIMINOLOGY, BUREAUCRACY, AND UNFINISHED BUSINESS

IAN O'DONNELL

WHEN exploring the interplay of criminology and policy the debate often revolves around the changing influence of the former on the direction of the latter. This debate generally occurs in countries where the discipline is firmly entrenched and the policy context is well understood. But what about when the criminal justice system operates in the absence of a sustained academic critique? How do things appear where criminology is in a fledgling state and where bureaucratic arrangements in respect of criminal justice have an unformed quality? What does the absence of criminology tell us about the possible impact of its presence?

An underlying theme of this book is that criminology is beginning to fragment just as it establishes its credentials as a vibrant academic discipline with all of the necessary apparatus of scholarship. However, it would be fair to say that in the Republic of Ireland the consolidation that might precede such fragmentation remains a long way off. Before an institute of criminology was set up in University College Dublin in 2000, Ireland was unusual among European countries in having no institutional framework for the study and teaching of criminology. Furthermore, when criminology finally emerged it was not because the state or university sector decided it was time to act, but because philanthropic funding for the venture was made available, anonymously.

The research infrastructure remains slight. A national crime council was established in 1999 but abolished in 2008. There is neither a society of criminology nor a specialist journal. There is no research unit in the Department of Justice, Equality and Law Reform and the amounts of funding made available by research councils and other bodies are extremely modest. So, what do policy and practice look like when there is no discipline to dialogue with, when the conversation is stuttering and one-sided? An examination of the Irish context suggests several salient characteristics.

To begin with, there is a litany of broken political promises, false starts, legislative stillbirths, unexpected outcomes, perplexing priority shifts, unevenly executed commitments, sporadic (but seldom sustained) eruptions of punitive sentiment, and a grindingly slow pace of reform even when its desirability is not disputed. To give but two illustrations, the Probation of Offenders Act 1907—a hangover from a time when Ireland was a British colony—remains in force and the 1947 Prison Rules were not replaced until 2007, despite calls for a new version as far back as the early 1960s and the publication of draft new rules in 1994. It is not just legislative change that moves slowly; high-level policy discussions have little impetus. A white paper on crime was promised by the minister for Justice, Equality and Law Reform in 1997 and remained a stated priority for several years. Yet it did not generate a programme of work and resulted in no publications. In 2009 a new minister repledged the commitment to producing a white paper on crime, without reference to his predecessor's promise, and setting a deadline of two years. Taken in isolation any of these phenomena might be viewed as aberrations but together, and over time, they evince a pattern that demands explanation.

Furthermore, the cumulative impact of initiatives that elsewhere seem to have led to predictably harmful outcomes has been surprisingly benign. It is not that politicians in Ireland have never been keen to express punitive sentiments or take what they perceive to be firm action, but the gap between rhetoric and effect is wide. For example, the Criminal Justice Act 1999 introduced minimum ten-year prison sentences for possession of drugs valued over €13,000, unless there were 'exceptional and specific circumstances' that would make such a sentence unjust. The courts found such circumstances for 125 of the first 130 persons convicted under this law. Anti-social behaviour orders were introduced in the Criminal Justice Act 2006 and heralded as a significant additional weapon in the fight against community disharmony. In the first two years of their existence, just six were issued nationwide; three for adults and three for children.

To what extent are there lessons here that might be of wider relevance? Does the experience of Ireland offer any clues about the circumstances under which punitive promises are not translated into painful practice? What can be learned from turning the criminological gaze to new territories? Trying to solve the riddle of why criminal justice policy-making does not always have the pernicious consequences that it promises brought me back to Weber (on bureaucratization), Mills (on the failure of the sociological imagination), Merton (on the unanticipated consequences of public policy), and to a reconsideration of Mathiesen's politics of the unfinished. Before engaging with the theoretical context, it is worth elaborating one particularly puzzling policy choice.

Odd Decisions, Badly Made

Many of the concerns about incoherence in the criminal justice policy arena are brought into clear focus when attention is turned to prison building. Despite the expense of imprisonment, which is much greater in Ireland than in other developed countries (the average cost per prison place in 2008 was €93,000), and against a background of steep falls in recorded indictable crime, the government revised upwards its estimate of the number of additional prison places required by a factor of ten in the space of three years: from 210 in 1994 to 2,000 in 1997. In a country where the prison population averaged around 2,100 throughout the first half of the 1990s, this was a phenomenal policy change. We do not know much about the composition of the prison population at this time as no detailed data were ever published for the years 1995 to 2000. But we do know that the per capita number of sentenced prisoners was virtually the same in 2004 as it had been in 1994 and that over the same period the number of committals to prison under sentence fell. In other words, it does not appear that the desire to increase capacity was stimulated by rising crime or that the courts responded to the prospect of more prison places by imposing more prison sentences.

The situation becomes even more curious when one considers that Irish Prison Service (IPS) forecasts of the growth in prisoner numbers have fallen far short of the reality (unlike in other Anglophone countries where the growth in the number of prisoners has tended to outstrip even the most pessimistic projections). In its *Strategy Statement 2001–2003* the IPS set a 'target' number of prisoner places for December 2003 of 4,042. When this month came around, according to the IPS annual report, there were 3,146 persons in custody, suggesting that the scale of the targeted expansion was considerably higher than required. Indeed, in 2002 a young offender institution was shut down, followed by two prisons for adult males in 2004. This was hardly the mark of a penal system unable to cope with the demands being put upon it. The fact that growth was below what had been predicted, and the number of institutions was contracting, might have been expected to subdue enthusiasm for penal expansionism, especially given the huge associated costs. But this did not happen.

In January 2005 the government pledged to build a cluster of institutions on a scale never before imagined on farmland that had been purchased at great expense at Thornton Hall in north county Dublin. The new prison complex was to accommodate 1,400 prisoners in single cells but the plans allowed for deliberate overcrowding (described by the IPS in its promotional material as 'multiple occupancy arrangements') that could raise this total to 2,200. This titanic development, which could have housed most of the country's prisoners, was intended to replace a Victorian prison in Dublin's city centre and adjacent facilities, which between them held around 850 men, women and children. The latter existed in varying states of decrepitude, but included a prison for women that was innovative in terms of its architecture and regime and opened to great acclaim in 1999, almost thirty years after a site had been purchased (albeit in a different location).

As if to underline the lack of clarity around penal planning the IPS went out to tender for projections of the prison population in March 2009, years after the commitment had been made to expand, the Thornton Hall site purchased, and the technical drawings finished down to details of individual cell and landing layouts and furnishings. Another act in this drama began in May 2009 when the government announced that, after spending €41 million purchasing and preparing the site, it would not be going ahead with the project as originally envisaged. The stated reason was that the consortium that had been formed to finance and build the new prison complex could no longer offer value for money at a time of deepening recession. To understand how and why such important decisions emerge, morph and are reversed it is necessary to consider the context in which policy choices are made, in particular the role of bureaucracy.

Rational-Legal Authority and Criminal Justice

Modern bureaucracies are supposed to function in a spirit of indifference to the moral worth of their task. They are goal-oriented, hierarchically organized, impersonal, and governed by formal rules. This, coupled with a division of labour that segments activities into discrete parts, ensures that bureaucracies are the most efficient means of carrying out morally distasteful acts ranging from the denial of benefits to supplicant citizens, to the administration of punishment and the organization of genocide. Bureaucratization is both an inevitable concomitant of increased complexity in political and economic arrangements as well as a midwife for further differentiation.

Weber's characterization of bureaucracy stresses the overriding importance of rational-legal authority. This involves a graduated structure, within which each office possesses a tightly circumscribed jurisdiction. Authority inheres in the office rather than the office-holder. Procedural fairness is guaranteed by written rules; the lines of accountability are clear; outcomes are calculable; and discretion is limited to minimize the possibility of bias. Record-keeping and accurate filing are prioritized. Efficiency and predictability are of paramount importance. There is little scope for judgement or favouritism. How people feel about their colleagues is of minor consequence; the operation runs smoothly because mutual role expectations are entrenched and stable. As Weber (1968: 975) put it: 'Bureaucracy develops the more perfectly, the more it is 'dehumanized', the more completely it succeeds in eliminating from official business love, hatred, and all purely personal, irrational, and emotional elements which escape calculation.'

The 'iron cage' that Weber describes is the apotheosis of bureaucratization and rationalization. It denotes a society where laws and rules are accorded privileged status, exceptions cannot be tolerated and we all become either cogs in the machine or sources of input. Fairness is defined in terms of predictably similar treatment. Impersonality, precision, reliability and efficiency are the bywords. Of course, Weber's portrayal of bureaucratic order is an ideal type; things are never this neat. Circumstances will invariably arise that pose challenges for even the most encyclopaedic rule book. Then interpretation, discretion and discernment must be allowed a role.

When the line of action is inchoate the bureaucratic intellectual may have considerable scope to define it, identify and rule out alternatives, and map the route from concretizing an idea to measuring its impact. Where there is a greater degree of specificity the room for manoeuvre is correspondingly reduced. In his study of the routine initiation of criminal justice policy in England and Wales and Canada, Rock (1995) drew attention to the different forces that sculpt policies as they emerge from the bureaucratic milieu, compete for attention, receive official sanction, are balanced against prior commitments, debated by committees, gradually introduced to wider arenas where support cannot be guaranteed, and finally become anonymous (in that the connection with a sponsor or champion is sundered) and dispersed outside of the originating environment. The final product is the culmination of a series of overlapping and interlocking dialectical processes. The role of the civil servant in this chain of events can range from cipher to author. While they operate within clearly delineated constraints in terms of political priorities, parliamentary scheduling and research support, a zealous bureaucrat can nonetheless leave a mark. The Thornton Hall project in Ireland did not emerge from such a process. The critical decisions about scale and location remained tied to the minister who made them; they were not tested and tweaked in an informed debate, and failed to develop a currency or legitimacy of their own.

An interesting question is raised about the implications for bureaucratic decision-making and, furthermore, for the subjective experience of the application of rules, if the iron cage is never properly fortified. If there are substantial imperfections in a country's bureaucratic arrangements what does this imply for the size and shape of its criminal justice system? When there are few developed structures is there more room for the personalities and proclivities of key individuals to play a determining role? When this is coupled with a clientelist political system what are the consequences for penal arrangements? Before attempting to answer these questions it is necessary to say a little more about how we might conceptualize the policy process.

The Policy Process

When thinking about the relationship between criminology and public policy it is useful to return to the distinction drawn by Mills (1959) between 'grand theory' (in its most polysyllabic, abstract and unintelligible forms, where ornate argumentation is more important than limpidity of thought) and 'abstracted empiricism' (in its most narrowly focused manifestations, where levels of statistical significance are fetishized). While contemporary criminology abounds with examples of each of these styles of work, it would be going too far to interpret their all too evident presence as a failure of the criminological imagination, especially given the coexistence of the kind of analysis that is both supple and subtle enough to encapsulate an understanding of what Mills (1959: 8) describes as the crucial relationship between 'personal troubles' and 'public issues of social structure'. The task of the social scientist is 'continually to translate personal troubles into public issues, and public issues into the terms of their human meaning for a variety of individuals' (ibid.: 187).

But the increasing specialization of the criminological endeavour and the growing emphasis on collaboration may exercise an unwelcome effect on the residuum of intellectual space where curiosity can be given free rein. The bureaucratization of scholarship, as Mills portrayed it, results in the emergence of teams of technicians focused on priorities that are not of their own making and in thrall to funding bodies. They are led by a new breed of entrepreneur who excels at grantsmanship but whose individual prowess in the arena of ideas cannot easily be ascertained. It is said that certain forms of criminological expertise are taken less seriously today by the powers that be and that other varieties are denigrated by the academy. Could it be that, generally speaking, politicians and policy-makers are unmoved by 'grand theory' in the same way that critical criminologists find 'abstracted empiricism' patently unsatisfactory? It is interesting to speculate that when the enterprise of criminology was younger, the volume of work smaller, and the aficionados less numerous but more puzzled, it was easier to keep the person and the political in simultaneous focus. Expansion, fragmentation and replication have militated against this kind of coherence.

Sometimes the debate about the proper role of criminology in public life is between those who feel they should try to make a difference in terms of influencing policy and practice and those who believe that this is at best a distraction or at worst a dangerous irrelevance. One common theme is that while criminologists and governments share many core concerns, the danger of the former becoming the servant of the latter must be guarded against. The objectivity of the social scientist could be seriously compromised should a relationship of dependency emerge. Despite the importance of this concern, the literature on how influence is distributed in criminal justice decision-making is not well developed, a point made by Solomon (1981) and strongly reiterated by Ismaili (2006). Solomon argues that the stuff of deliberation should be the evolution of the policy process, which he sees as embracing four phases: agenda-setting, decision-making, implementation and evaluation. The first phase involves sensitizing the policy community to the relevance of a new idea. The second revolves around the extent to which the idea should be adopted, if at all. The third is the translation of policy preferences into practical actions; this involves making subsidiary choices, drafting guidelines, clarifying parameters and dealing with opposing views. Finally, there is an opportunity for appraisal that may or may not incorporate an impartial assessment, and provides feedback on the efficacy of the policy.

This is a good way to think about the incremental development of policy and the sequencing of opportunities for politicians, professional actors and the attentive public to reinforce or derail the process. It suggests that the prospects for successful innovation are poor when decisions are made suddenly, in a context where the items on the agenda cannot be agreed, and where the policy is imposed from above, with little clarity about what it is supposed to achieve, in an environment where the capacity to evaluate it does not exist. This helps to explain why some initiatives, such as a stated determination to expand the prison system, which can be made without immediate regard to the preferences of key interest groups or the need to effect behavioural change on the part of the relevant actors, can remain influential until the point at which resource allocation becomes pressing. At this moment, if the promise is to be realized, the early phases of the process must be expedited, an unlikely scenario given the limited progress that has been made in terms of rendering the idea acceptable to the policy community, deemed to be a priority, and amenable to implementation.

Solomon suggested that it might be helpful to see social scientists as contributing to policy-making in two distinct ways. First of all, as problem-solvers (perhaps most prominently involved at the evaluation phase) whose deliberations and conclusions will struggle to survive among competing, and shifting, political priorities, professional interests and public concerns. Second, as providers of new perspectives on what might constitute priority areas in the policy arena (this gives them a role much earlier on, in the agenda-setting and decision-making phases). In countries where the criminal justice system has developed a capacity to carry out research and planning internally, there might be activity along each of these dimensions (problem specification and solving) in house. Where such intellectual capital does not exist—as in Ireland—these influences are more remote and policy formation has an *ad hoc* feel to it.

Furthermore, it cannot be assumed that researchers are unified in their view of how any set of criminal justice phenomena should be addressed. Good research will probably raise new questions and add uncertainty where decision-makers seek clarity. Often the findings of criminologists are hedged with caveats and liable to revision; there are competing interpretations; the idiom can be difficult for policy-makers to penetrate; there are few replicated experimental results (and even doubt about the relevance of such findings, where they appear clear). Nuance and contestation are integral to the academic process but anathema to politicians and policy-makers.

Making Choices in an Informational Vacuum

In a paper published in the first volume of the *American Sociological Review* Merton (1936) elucidated the conditions under which public policy was likely to misfire. The first is the existing state of knowledge. While we often act without complete information, the hazards are inversely related to the knowledge base. In other words the less we know the greater the possibility that unforeseen consequences will follow. (It must be said, of course, that these are not necessarily negative in their effects; poorly-informed decisions can have unambiguously beneficial consequences.) The second factor is error. Whether through force of habit, selective attention or a determination to proceed despite the evidence, decisions can lead in unexpected directions. The third factor is immediacy of interest. This refers to situations where 'paramount concern with the foreseen immediate consequences excludes the consideration of further or other consequences of the same act' (Merton 1936: 901). In other words the urgency of the immediate can trump the less pressing but possibly more significant demands of the future.

Merton argued that if we are ignorant, error-prone and preoccupied with immediate effects, the unanticipated consequences of social policy will be magnified. The poor quality of available information and the desire to make a swift impact render criminal justice policy-making peculiarly vulnerable in these respects. We need to add to the mix another factor identified by Merton, namely that 'public predictions of future social developments are frequently not sustained precisely because the prediction has become a new element in the concrete situation, thus tending to change the initial course of developments' (ibid.: 903–4).

Consider the prison-building programme described above in light of Merton's ideas. This was a policy decision designed to provide an immediate response to a political desire to do something tangible about crime. It was taken in the absence of an informed debate about the size and shape of the prison population, and in the face of a surprising stability in the level of sentenced prisoners. It was clung to despite unanswered questions about its intended scale. Here we see at play the factors of immediacy of interest, underdeveloped knowledge and error. Finally, the sheer fact of the prison-building programme may be responsible for introducing an upward shift in the use of imprisonment, even if there is no change in the pattern of offences coming before the courts. This is Merton's point about the decision itself influencing outcomes. It follows from all of this that the stated purposes of this policy, namely more humane conditions, lower recidivism, improved treatment of prisoners through differentiated regime design and enhanced sentence planning, are not necessarily those that will flow from it.

Another unanticipated development came to play a vital role at the end of 2008 when Ireland plunged into recession. Some months later the economy had reached such a low ebb that it was decided to postpone building at Thornton Hall; penal policy decisions could no longer be insulated from financial considerations. That economic factors called a halt to this development, rather than the many principled objections about its necessity, scale, location and mix of prisoners, is an emphatic statement of the pointlessness of the plan. Just as the bottom line, rather than a clear penal philosophy, drove reckless expansion, so too might it be the motor for contraction.

Parish Pump Politics

Bureaucracy is meant to minimize the possibility of favouritism, but it could be argued that the pursuit of the latter is one of the defining features of Irish political arrangements. Elected representatives see their role as intervening with public agencies on behalf of their constituents. For many politicians this micro-activity is the paramount concern, with their role as legislators coming a distant second. The desire to respond to client concerns, and the expectation that they can be called upon to do so, know few bounds.

Politicians in Ireland take a detailed interest in voters' lives because they are closer to them than their counterparts elsewhere. There are proportionately a large number of them: 166 members of parliament for a population of four million, compared with 650 in the United Kingdom for a population of 61 million. Also, Irish political representatives are returned from multi-seat constituencies where the single transferable vote system of proportional representation is used. This means that they are in competition with party colleagues as well as the opposition. Politicians who do not work their patch assiduously take their chances with the electorate. No matter is too trivial and the stock response whenever a constituent raises a query is to initiate a trail of correspondence. In January 2007, a junior minister wrote to the minister for Justice, Equality and Law Reform arguing for the early release of two constituents, a child rapist and a murderer. In the ensuing controversy it emerged that since first returned to the Dáil in 1992 he had sent *more than 200,000 letters* from his constituency office.

These factors foster a strong sense of localism and personalism, where serving and prospective parliamentarians dedicate themselves to case work on behalf of those who they hope to represent. By asking for their vote they incur the obligation of service. Politicians act as brokers for their constituents, mediating between them and the state. In all likelihood these interventions make little appreciable difference to the outcome. But the result is delivered more quickly (sometimes) and with a personal touch (always). The constituency clinic is not a place where debates about national (or, perish the thought, international) affairs are aired. It is where complaints about road surfaces, school buildings, public housing lists and welfare benefits are grist to the mill. Clientelism is rampant in Ireland, particularly in rural areas, because people feel they cannot navigate the bureaucratic maze; they need a more powerful figure to intervene on their behalf, whether to secure an entitlement or to win a favour. This is an attempt to weave back into official business the 'purely personal, irrational, and emotional elements' that Weber (1968: 975) saw as undermining bureaucratic administration. But it relates also to the countryman's traditional confidence in face-to-face encounters rather than exchanges of correspondence. (In any event the latter function—largely a secretarial one—will be discharged on their behalf by a local political hopeful.)

Clientelism inhibits meaningful debate on issues that transcend the proximate and this has serious implications for civil servants who spend much of their time dealing with trivial representations from politicians. Some civil servants are seconded to teams that deal exclusively with the concerns of their minister's constituents, thereby further reducing departmental capacity to deliver national objectives, formulate and follow through policies. A bureaucratic system that is vulnerable to quotidian interference becomes compromised in terms of delivering predictable and swift outcomes. If anything the system becomes clogged with queries and slows down even more, thus increasing citizens' desire for politicians to broker results, and confirming their antipathy towards direct engagement with the bureaucracy itself. The system contains within it the seeds of its own perpetuation. In such bureaucratic environments strategic thinking will be difficult to sustain; there will always be numerous matters requiring immediate attention. Returning to the four phases that Solomon (1981) suggests characterize the evolution of policy-making, it is the penultimate one—implementation—that is most seriously compromised by clientelist politics.

Inertia and Inconsistency as Intolerable Virtues

At one level what has been described thus far might be taken to suggest that an underdeveloped criminology represents a missed opportunity. This is an argument in favour of an expanded production of criminological knowledge in the sense that when it exists it may be ignored but at least there is a chance that it will be heard. My point, however, is the contrary one that there may be advantages to invisibility and incoherence, especially in a system like Ireland's that is heavily based on discretion and where the data deficits are large. In addition, the degree of resistance to innovation is marked. Judges have set themselves against giving reasons and imposing minimum sentences. Police have frustrated attempts at civilianization, the introduction of volunteer reservists and zero tolerance. Probation officers retain strong roots in social work practice and have not succumbed to correctionalism. Prison officers have been so militant for so long that meaningful sentence management and purposeful regimes remain a distant aspiration; the prospect of having to negotiate any proposed change to prison rosters with the Prison Officers' Association acts as a powerful disincentive to action.

Where the state's in-house capacity for research is almost non-existent, views from the academy are scarce, public concern is intermittent, and vested interests are strong, it is difficult to overcome the inertia that is present in the criminal justice policy domain. Even when politicians appear committed to a particular approach, the administrative machinery required to drive the agenda forward may not exist and, if it does, it is vulnerable to manipulation by the self-same politicians. Slowness of response is a protection against a 'punitive turn' (or a turn in any direction for that matter). Change does not come slow in the Irish criminal justice system because the deliberative process is careful, future-oriented and results driven. It comes slow because of the lack of an infrastructure to deliver on commitments and the staccato nature of criminal justice policy-making.

The absence of expertise means that the final stage in policy formation, that of providing feedback about whether desired outcomes were actually achieved and the impact of any unforeseen consequences, is not executed. Therefore the process remains incomplete, the lack of a robust evaluative mechanism meaning that lessons go unlearned and the raw materials required to produce a set of metrics for criminal justice do not emerge. This serves to dampen the managerialist impulse.

Keeping Things Unfinished

In his account of the pitfalls associated with the codification of the law Goff (1983: 174) warned against succumbing to what he memorably described as the 'temptation of elegance'. What he meant by this was that what appear to be elegant solutions to legal problems automatically acquire the sheen of credibility. But there are dangers here. The law has to reflect life in all its messy uncertainty and it is imperative to guard against embracing a formulation—however exquisitely stated—that does not allow for the possibility of future exceptions or qualifications.

Similar to Goff's notion of leaving space for fluidity and the possibility of revision is Mathiesen's (1974) idea of keeping the business 'unfinished'. Mathiesen's argument (as applied to penal abolition) is underpinned by a conviction that the most compelling alternative to an existing system is one which is in competition with it but is not fully-formed. The implications of the putative arrangements are unclear, the parameters are shadowy, and the debate is hindered by an absence of shared understandings; ambiguities abound. Even its proponents find it difficult to articulate the likely, or desirable, outcomes of the alternative arrangements. But, with clarity and finalization come redundancy. 'Freedom', in Mathiesen's (1974: 25) words, 'is the anxiety and pleasure involved in entering a field which is unsettled or empty'. The priority of the abolitionist is to return continually to the potentially transformative power of the unfinished. In so doing they must set their own terms of engagement, refusing to be drawn into a dialogue about the relative efficacy of different approaches.

What connects Mathiesen's writings to the shambolic nature of penal policy-making in Ireland is the potentially protective value of a domain that is opaque and uncertain and where unanticipated consequences are paradigmatic. There is something to be said for a poorly understood criminal justice system in the sense that when understanding has crystallized, structures become rigid and reform is more difficult. When flexibility is removed, mercy—by its nature individualized—follows; there is less space left for the person. Any attempt to clarify the issues, identify fault lines, provide definitions, furnish research tools and methodological critiques—all areas where criminology can make a contribution—may lead to the disappearance of some of the humanity (the flipside of unpalatable harshness) that characterizes the system.

It is more difficult to be idiosyncratic when there exists a recognized framework against which to view behaviour. This applies to everything from the sentences passed by individual judges to the bills published by legislators; exceptions seem more glaring in an ordered environment. There is room for manoeuvre in the liminal state between the ascendancy of rational-legal authority in a machine-like bureaucracy and an environment where political meddling is omnipresent and decision-makers retain a high degree of discretion. With clarity, the room for manoeuvre evaporates.

If there is a developed criminal justice bureaucracy, drawing sustenance from a vigorous discipline of criminology, things are more likely to happen dispassionately. New approaches will be designed so that their impact is evaluable. If they are demonstrably ineffective they may be revisited and revised. Predictability will be emphasized and strenuous efforts will be made to compress complex and shifting realities into tidy academic categories. Quite simply, the world will look different. This is why the argument against criminology carries force. A sustained debate about priorities and how to address them is more likely when the parameters of the key issues can be successfully drawn. When sufficient data exist to allow success and failure to be defined, parsed and quantified, metrics can be devised and used to determine resource allocation (and reallocation). If the debate never gets to this level—and the absence of a muscular criminology is one restraining force—the likelihood that a new, state-sponsored, architecture of control will evolve is reduced. If we cannot take the appropriate measurements with confidence, or press the resultant counts into service as indicators of moral or political imperatives, then the state's focus on criminal justice is more likely to waver.

Conclusion

The imprisonment rate in the Republic of Ireland is among the lowest in the developed world. It stood at 76 per 100,000 population in 2007 compared with 153 for England and Wales and 756 for the United States (Walmsley 2009). This is despite an avowed political commitment to penal expansionism and the existence of a judicial bias towards custody (in 2007, as is usual, more prison sentences were imposed than probation and community service orders combined). How can this paradoxical state of affairs be explained?

The argument advanced in this chapter is that the lack of capacity for criminal justice policy formulation, implementation and evaluation together with the lack of criminological expertise and the unformed nature of the discourse may, in concert, have beneficial consequences, acting as bulwarks against a punitive shift. Clientelist politics are another restraining force, chipping away at the capability of government to deliver change and blunting the effect of new initiatives. External factors are important too. This is why the most ambitious prison-building programme in the history of the state became a priority when the economy was booming but was shelved when Ireland tumbled into recession.

There is not necessarily a positive correlation between plentiful good quality data and rational approaches to crime and punishment. While indubitably frustrating, it may be better to know little about a small criminal justice system than lots about a bigger one, if knowledge is a driver of expansion. The same factors that have stunted the growth of criminology in Ireland may have insulated the country from some of the punitive excesses that have disfigured Anglo-American responses to crime over recent years. There is a major caveat here; stasis is not guaranteed. The sharp increases in imprisonment in countries as different as the Netherlands and the United States show that a trend can go into reverse and generate an unstoppable momentum in an unforeseen direction. If Ireland's economy had continued to grow it is likely that the Thornton Hall project, as originally envisaged, would have progressed further and it is too early to say if the emphasis on prison building as the primary response to crime will itself act as a stimulus to rising prisoner numbers.

Criminology, particularly if it aspires to policy-relevance, needs an advanced bureaucracy if it is to thrive and the existence of criminology breathes life into bureaucratic forms. The culmination of such a state of affairs is predictability, uniformity, rigidity and dehumanization. Ireland's criminal justice arrangements, however, are characterized by uncertainty and fluidity coupled with significant resistance to change, routine political interference in administration, and the lack of an infrastructure to sustain action even when the need for it is not disputed. The question is whether we should welcome, however reluctantly, the forces that buttress inertia, maintain a focus on the 'purely personal', and keep the business unfinished? The answer is that perhaps we should, that it may be in our collective interest to resist the temptation of elegance.

References

Goff, R. (1983), 'The Search for Principle', *Proceedings of the British Academy*, 69: 169–87.

Ismaili, K. (2006), 'Contextualizing the Criminal Justice Policy-Making Process', *Criminal Justice Policy Review*, 17: 255–69.

Mathiesen, T. (1974), *The Politics of Abolition*, London: Martin Robertson.

Merton, R. K. (1936), 'The Unanticipated Consequences of Purposive Social Action', *American Sociological Review*, 1: 894–904.

Mills, C. W. (1959), *The Sociological Imagination*, New York: Oxford University Press.

Rock, P. (1995), 'The Opening Stages of Criminal Justice Policy Making', *British Journal of Criminology*, 35: 1–16.

Solomon, P. H. (1981), 'The Policy Process in Canadian Criminal Justice: A perspective and Research Agenda', *Canadian Journal of Criminology*, 23: 5–25.

Walmsley, R. (2009), *World Prison Population List*, 8th edn, King's College London: International Centre for Prison Studies.

Weber, M. (1968), *Economy and Society: An Outline of Interpretive Sociology*, G. Roth and C. Wittich (eds), Vol. 3, New York: Bedminster Press.

33

CRIMINOLOGY AND GOVERNMENT: SOME REFLECTIONS ON RECENT DEVELOPMENTS IN ENGLAND[1]

TIM NEWBURN*

TOWARDS the front of the second of his series of volumes on penal policy, Lord Windlesham (Windlesham 1993) has a map entitled 'Tributaries to Legislation,

* I am particularly grateful to Paul Rock, David Downes, and Mike Hough for comments on an initial version of this paper.

[1] In relation to developments in criminal justice and penal policy, although it is often tempting to talk about 'Britain' it is almost always misleading. Scotland's distinctive legal system marks it off

1987–1991'. In it there are a series of streams and rivers eventually coming together and ending at the 'Sea of Statutes'. Towards the top of the map, where a series of smallish streams are descending from a mountain range called 'penal reform', there is a cloud overhead, entitled 'research', scattering rain over the hills below. Despite the growing 'penal pessimism' of the period there is no doubt that the intention was that the sketch should indicate that research was still considered an important component in enabling penal reform ideas to begin their long and unpredictable journey toward the statute book.

If such a map were being drawn now what location would criminological research occupy? Assuming it appeared at all, I think it would be significantly less prominent than was the case a decade and a half ago. More than this, however, there is arguably a broader sense of disenchantment in the 'relationship' between policy-makers and the academy: government appears less and less satisfied with what it sees in academic criminology and, in turn, many criminological scholars are critical of government attitudes toward research.[2] My concern in this chapter is to explore some of the developments that lie behind this growing mutual disenchantment. In the limited space all I can do is attempt to sketch out some of what I take to be the more important developments. In doing so, I have divided the chapter into five parts. In the first I will explore the changing social and cultural context in which criminological research is conducted and penal policy made. I then turn my attention to the changing governmental context, including the reform of the civil service and the rise of so-called 'evidence-based policy-making'. Criminological research, of course, has itself not been static and in the third section I offer a brief sketch of developments in criminological scholarship outside government. In the fourth section I look at the changing nature of criminological research within government and, in particular, at the location and nature of research within the Home Office. Finally, and building on these four initial themes, I will finish with some reflections on what the future might hold in relation to the changing nature of the relationship between government and criminological research.

from England and Wales and, these days, most general criminological discussions deal with Scotland separately from other jurisdictions (where it is dealt with at all). Indeed, despite its shared legal system the move toward greater devolution in Wales is increasing its distinctiveness from policy-making in England. In this chapter my observations, though they have some bearing on developments in Wales, focus on England and, more particularly, are primarily concerned with government in Westminster.

[2] I am not seeking to imply here that this is a relationship that could ever be entirely unproblematic. Clearly—and this is reflected in the experience of researchers and scientists from a variety of disciplines—the relationship between the priorities and requirements of the state on the one hand and academic independence on the other is by no means straightforward, and there are significant risks in any academic subject—though this is perhaps especially true of criminology—becoming overly identified with government.

The Socio-Political Context

The most obvious change in the socio-political context of criminal justice and penal policy in the last decade and a half is the politicization of crime control (Downes and Morgan 2007). Penal policy in England, as in so many liberal democracies, has also taken a strongly punitive turn, particularly in the period during which crime has been in general decline. Although stirrings of a more punitive penal environment were noticeable from the mid-1970s, it appears that the decisive shift occurred in the early 1990s, when both the two main political parties locked themselves into a second-order consensus (Reiner 2006; Newburn 2007) around the need to be seen to be 'tough on crime'. The result has been a general ratcheting-up of punishment—both community and custodial—with a two-thirds increase in the prison population in little over a decade. Broadly speaking, although there are clearly distinctive trajectories and important differences of scale (Cavadino and Dignan 2006; Lacey 2008), such developments in Britain appear to be in line with trends elsewhere in Europe and beyond (Garland 2001; Tonry 2007).

As numerous commentators have noted, the trends in recent times have tended to be both punitive and 'populist' with politicians increasingly 'tapping into and using for their own purposes, what they believe to be the public's generally punitive stance' (Bottoms 1995: 40). Though such populism can sometimes be viewed as a straightforward political or electoral strategy, arguably it has both deep and complex roots (Sparks 2001; Pratt, 2007). Lord Windlesham, himself previously minister of state in a Conservative administration, observed that the manner and tenor of penal policy-making changed after Kenneth Clarke left the Home Office in early 1993. Clarke's successor, Michael Howard, was, he said,

> generally dismissive of professional expertise, including at times advice from his own officials, sensing that the general public was looking for a greater emphasis on punishment than on the rehabilitation of offenders. All elected politicians need to keep an ear to the ground, but Howard's was more closely attuned than most. Before long a consistent pattern could be detected of conforming to perceived public opinion, taking particular notice of the coverage of crime and editorial comment in the broadsheet and tabloid press. As an inevitable result, decisions began to be taken piecemeal, often dictated by what was thought most likely to appeal to an insecure and resentful general public [1996: 41].

Moreover, and significantly, the punitive and populist stance was bipartisan (Downes and Morgan 2007).

The very fact of increasing political scepticism towards certain forms of expert opinion led to the creation of a more distant relationship between government and scholars. A growing alienation was reinforced by the shifts in the process of penal policy-making (in which short-termism and particular types of public responsiveness came to have greater prominence) and in the nature of penal policy (toward greater punitiveness), each of which sat ill with the predominantly liberal outlook of academic criminology.

If the two most significant characteristics of penal policy from 1993 onward were its populism and its increasing punitiveness, then a close third has been its systemic managerialism (Bottoms 1995). At the heart of this shift in all aspects of criminal justice have been increasing attempts by government to promote greater consistency in the delivery of public services and ever more vigorous attempts to enable local practice to be monitored, measured, and compared. Such managerialism has many features but, centrally, as Faulkner (2008: 233) notes, the overall aim has been

> to reduce the influence and discretion of supposedly self-interested service providers and career civil servants; to separate 'purchasing' from 'providing' or 'delivery'; to focus on outcomes rather than process; and to create a 'performance culture' based on rewards for success and penalties for failure.

Centrally driven, league-table-oriented targets have been established for most criminal justice agencies. In part, this development was a product of political belief in the power of the private sector and of markets to deliver organizational efficiency and value for money, and also reflected an increasing impatience on the part of No. 10 with the apparent slowness of departments and agencies to 'deliver' (Rock 2004). In the 1990s the Audit Commission was a key player in this regard, initially in relation to policing, and subsequently in the fields of youth justice, crime prevention/community safety and 'offender management'. The Audit Commission initially restricted its work so as to stay away from what senior police officers 'would regard as their operational territory' (Campbell-Smith 2008: 214). However, the Commission gradually broadened its focus to cover many aspects of the organization, management and operation of the police service. Having successfully entered the world of policing, the Audit Commission went on to examine community safety and crime prevention and also to have a remarkable influence in youth justice. Subsequently, some of its erstwhile senior staff went on to take senior roles in both policing and youth justice fields.[3]

One outcome of public sector reform has been to shift the focus of activity. In policing, for instance, the increasing emphasis on outcome measurement saw a gradual shift in which the core 'mission' of the police service was gradually redefined so that 'crime control' rather than 'order maintenance' came to predominate (Morgan and Newburn 1997). In youth justice, the reorientation was even more unequivocal. The explicitly managerialist Crime and Disorder Act 1998 gave the youth justice system, for the first time, an overarching objective; it required that it be the duty of all agencies in that system to have regard to that aim, and it established a new command and control system to oversee and monitor performance against this overarching, and a series of subsidiary, objectives. Growing centralization, a

[3] Kate Flannery joining HMIC as one of its civilian inspectors, and Mark Perfect and Judy Renshaw, both of whom had been heavily involved in the Audit Commission report *Misspent Youth*, becoming senior figures in the Youth Justice Board when it was established in 1998.

desire on the part of government to control both priorities and processes, together with the increasing preoccupation with 'risk management' and 'risk avoidance' have combined both to reorient penal practices and to shift expectations within and beyond the criminal justice and penal systems. In turn, governmental attitudes toward the types of knowledge perceived as necessary to the efficient functioning of such systems has meant a shift of emphasis, where 'particularly in the field of administrative criminology, socially oriented and explanatory criminology is being displaced by predictive, risk-oriented rational choice models' (O'Malley 2009; see also Zedner 2006).

Criminology and Criminological Research

Here I simply want to offer a few reflections on the historical backdrop to the position we find ourselves in now. How has the government–academy relationship in the crime field developed since the Second World War? This will be necessarily brief and, undoubtedly, somewhat superficial.[4]

Writing in the 1930s, Thorsten Sellin observed that the 'criminologist does not exist who is an expert in all the disciplines which converge in the study of crime' (Sellin 1970: 6). Early criminology had its origins in applied medico-legal science, psychiatry, a scientifically-oriented psychology and in Victorian social reform movements (Garland 1994). Although early positivist attempts to distinguish the identifying characteristics of the 'criminal type' were overtaken by other considerations in the early twentieth century, much criminology has been concerned with identifying the individual, social and environmental factors associated with offending. In parallel, criminology's 'governmental project' has focused on the empirical study of the administration of justice, the working of prisons, police etc. and the measurement of crime. It has, therefore, for much of its history, had concerns which are partly drawn from and consequently mesh with the state's need to maintain order and control.

It was after the Second World War that government began to invest in criminological research and, notably, under R.A. Butler's tenure as Home Secretary (1957–62), the Home Office expanded its own research capacity, began increasingly to invest in outside research—including stimulating the creation of the Institute of Criminology in Cambridge—and took research evidence to be central to progressive penal policy (Home Office, 1959). The white papers of 1959 and 1964 both explicitly acknowledged the importance of criminological research, the former noting that such work was 'not necessarily best conducted by official agencies. The outlook, training and environment of the academic worker give him advantages in some kinds of research over

[4] For a more extended treatment of aspects of this relationship see Zedner (2003).

the staff of a Government Department'[5], as well as distancing the Home Office from any less than ideal findings.

The broadly positivistic assumptions that underpinned this mid-century faith in the potential of criminological knowledge gradually came under increasing pressure as research regularly offered less impressive results than had been hoped for (Brody 1975; Folkard *et al.* 1974 and, subsequently, Clarke and Hough 1984) and as new, interpretive voices emerged urging a more critical engagement with the problem of 'crime' and its control. Although the establishment in the late 1950s of the British Society of Criminology (BSC) in part signalled an attempt to counter the dominance of psychiatric and other clinical perspectives in existing forums, much criminological activity continued to have a 'heavy bias in a clinical direction' (Cohen 1971). A more sociologically-oriented, radical criminology was emerging, however, and becoming increasingly vocal and influential. These more radical perspectives were, in part, a reaction against somewhat apolitical, empiricist approach of earlier scholars and they offered 'an escape route from the positivist methodology and functionalist orthodoxy of much British sociology' (Downes 1988b: 47).

Despite these competing pressures, it was arguably at roughly this point that the closest relationship developed between the government's research arm—the Home Office Research and Planning Unit as it then was[6]—and, at least elements of, the academic criminological community. As its then head noted (Croft 2005: 114), 'In the 1970s and early 1980s the conduct of research business in the Home Office... had the full support of both Labour (Merlyn Rees) and Conservative (Whitelaw) Home Secretaries.' Though by no means an unproblematic relationship, this was nevertheless a sustained period in which high quality research was produced 'in-house' (Burrows *et al.* 1985; Riley and Shaw 1985; Brown 1988), was commissioned from universities (Downes 1988; Genders and Player 1995; Shapland *et al.* 1985), and where shared concerns led to collaborative activity between researchers inside and outside government (Hope and Shaw, 1988). This generally positive relationship lasted through the 1980s and only experienced significant rupture when the politics of crime changed course, dramatically, in the early 1990s.

Meanwhile, there have been a variety of developments in the face of British criminology that bear brief note here. First, and most obviously perhaps, has been the remarkable growth in the teaching of the subject at both undergraduate and postgraduate levels within the universities with a consequent substantial increase in the numbers of criminologists working in higher education.[7] Criminology's greatest strength, arguably, has been found in its multi-disciplinary roots, its eclecticism and its porous 'disciplinary' boundaries. Contemporary British academic criminology

[5] *Penal Practice in a Changing Society,* London: HMSO, 1959, para. 18; see also *The War Against Crime in England and Wales 1959–1964* London: HMSO, 1964.

[6] For an account of its establishment see Lodge (1974)

[7] Though they have not been the subject of study as yet, there are some undoubted differences between these new cohorts and earlier generations (Rock 1988).

continues to exhibit these characteristics. A number of tensions are visible, however, some of which, broadly speaking, focus on the style and purpose of criminological endeavour. To a certain degree these tensions either derive from, or reflect residual elements of, the 'paradigm wars' in British social science since the 1970s (Oakley 1999)—disputes which unhelpfully and inaccurately pit differing methodological approaches *against* each other. Variations on this theme can be seen, from time to time, in the current arguments over the value of experimental methods in criminology and in the rise of 'crime science' as a distinctive orientation.[8]

My concern here is not to assess these competing arguments and positions, but merely to observe that all too frequently such debates have generally been conducted as if they were a battle that could be won; that is, as if there were one preferred way of 'doing criminology'. The conversations are, of course, not confined to the academy—nor should they be. However, in a context of government scepticism about what criminology can offer—and I return to this below—the tone and tenor of such debates can be profoundly unhelpful not least in encouraging government to think in simplistic terms about methodological preferences rather than to accept (at least what I take to be) the reality of the necessity of methodological pluralism or heterodoxy. In short, all too often recent debates within British criminology have confused the issue of methodological choice with the question of rigour. There is undoubtedly much still to be learned, and practised, in relation to rigorously conducted empirical research but, too often, such matters have been reduced to ill-thought through spats about one method versus another.

The Governmental Context

At the same time as these changes were occurring within British criminology, and the disputes were gathering fire, the governmental context itself was changing. I want briefly to focus on the general modernization of the civil service and the rise, and subsequent fall, of evidence-based policy-making.

In the aftermath of the Fulton Report in the 1960s (Fulton 1968) a series of reforms were set in train which, with increasing speed in the last decade and a half, have transformed many aspects of the civil service. During the 1980s a process of 'opening up' the civil service got underway. The appointment of Derek Rayner to head the Cabinet Office Efficiency Unit from 1979, and the Cassels and Fraser[9] Reports to sub-

[8] Although there are occasional bouts of exaggeration, much of the recent debate around experimental methods has been conducted in a robust but thoughtful manner (see, for example, Sherman 1999; Hope 2009; Tilley 2009; Hough 2010). Some of the debates around 'crime science' have not always been conducted with the same good grace.

[9] This was an unpublished report to the Prime Minister on progress in relation to 'Next Steps', 1991.

sequent Conservative administrations (Cassels 1983) affected both the management of, and recruitment to, the civil service (Tyson 1990), and the increasing application of new public management principles, together with the creation of a large number of 'next steps' agencies, changed the character of the civil service. Under successive Labour governments there has been increasing emphasis, as Tony Blair put it in a speech on civil service reform in 2004, on the challenge of shifting 'from policy advice to delivery'. This, rather radical, change has been captured as requiring

> that a modernised Civil Service should be accountable in terms of the outcomes it delivers in the world, rather than the outputs it produces. So, for example, the passing of a piece of legislation is not in itself a sign of success, but rather whether that legislation achieves the changes in the real world that it was designed to produce [Wiles 1999: 3].

The danger here for the external research contractor lies in the pressure that can be brought to bear to co-opt them in support of hoped-for policy outcomes. It also, it could be suggested, has potential knock-on consequences for teaching, practitioner training, and for university research assessment.

Indeed, criminal justice and penal policy-making has changed in a number of other important respects in the last decade or more. One reason has been the growing profile of the Treasury in this, as in other public policy fields. Continuing a process that began under Chancellors Lamont and Clarke, the Treasury under Gordon Brown sought and achieved much greater control over how spending related to broad governmental objectives and, more particularly, in using such power to drive the domestic policy-making agenda (Thain 2009), including home affairs. In addition to growing Treasury influence in Home Office activity, there was also a higher profile occupied by other parts of government, notably the Cabinet Office and No.10 policy units under New Labour.

A further important development has been the rise of 'special advisers' on the political scene (Blick 2004).[10] Once again, a process which began in the 1970s, gathered pace under the Conservative administrations of the 1980s and early 1990s, and rapidly increased under New Labour in the 1990s and beyond. Hugo Young in his notebooks recorded his recollection of a discussion in 1996 with David Blunkett about what might happen if he were appointed as Secretary of State for Education. Blunkett, he noted, 'doesn't want to arrive at the department to be told he can't do things, or that he must wait a year to get the Act passed. He also intends to come in armed with a lot of his own experts' (Trewin 2009: 468). What was true of Blunkett at Education, applied equally to the Home Office where political and policy advisers were increasingly visible after 1997 (Sausman and Locke 2004).

These shifts in the nature of public policy-making were, in part, made possible by the changes to the character of the civil service that occurred in the 1980s and the early

[10] Concern about this development was aired in the report of the Public Administration Committee of the House of Commons: *Special Advisers: Boon or Bane?* HC463, 13 December 2001.

1990s. In particular, the retirement of a cohort of well-established civil servants enabled the government to appoint and promote a new breed of senior mandarin. There are differences of opinion as to what impact these changes brought about—Hugo Young (1989), for example, taking the view that considerable politicization took place whereas, by contrast, Hennessy (1988) argues that the changes were more superficial. The importation of 'outsiders' has gathered pace in recent years leading, on occasion, to most unmandarin-like behaviour by the new, senior incumbents.[11] It was against this background of quite radical changes to the staffing, management and focus of the civil service that 'evidence-based policy-making' made its appearance.

Evidence-based policy-making emerged as part of New Labour's 'modernising government' agenda (Cabinet Office 1999a), once again building on reforms instituted initially under earlier Conservative administrations. Its core assumption was elaborated in a report from the Cabinet Office Strategic Policy Making Team (Cabinet Office 1999b: para. 7.10) arguing that 'policy making must be soundly based on evidence of what works'. In the criminological field the rise of the 'what works' agenda represented a shift away from the generalized penal pessimism that had characterized much of the 1970s and 1980s in particular. Reviews of research on both sides of the Atlantic provided limited, but nonetheless relatively optimistic promises of the possibility of identifying improved means of intervening in the lives of offenders and of focusing and refining policing methods (Sherman *et al.* 1997; Goldblatt and Lewis 1998). Following the Comprehensive Spending Review in 1998[12] the Treasury initially allocated £250 million to its 'Crime Reduction Programme', of which up to 10 per cent was to be spent on research (Bullock *et al.* 2002), in what one commentator described as 'the most comprehensive, systematic and far-sighted initiative ever undertaken by a British government to develop strategies for tackling crime' (Maguire 2004: 214).

The Home Office, Research, and Criminology

The background then to recent developments in the relationship between government and academic criminology is one of significant—if not lengthy or sustained—optimism. With its avowed commitment to 'evidence-based policy-making', the

[11] On one particularly notorious occasion Louise Casey, then government adviser on anti-social behaviour, garnered considerable press attention for what was described as an 'expletive-ridden' speech which included criticism of Downing St staff. See <www.timesonline.co.uk/tol/news/uk/article541166.ece>(accessed 26 February 2010).

[12] Spending reviews set firm and fixed three-year expenditure limits for government departments. The 1998 comprehensive spending review, which involved a review of departmental aims and objectives and an analysis of each spending programme, was the first time a spending review on that scale had been attempted in the United Kingdom (<www.hm-treasury.gov.uk/spend_csr98_index.htm>, accessed 27 January 2010)

Labour government's Crime Reduction Programme aimed to fund projects to both use and develop the evidence base about those methods that are most effective in reducing crime. A review of extant research (Goldblatt and Lewis 1998) identified areas deemed worth pursuing, and the subsequent programme included a number of areas (reducing burglary, targeted policing, treatment of offenders, drug arrest referral, domestic violence, and CCTV). In the event, a somewhat ill-thought-out and poorly executed research programme was then instituted which had a number of consequences. One of the first was a substantial increase in the capacity of the Home Office's research and statistics directorate. There was a huge growth in the numbers of researchers employed in the Home Office. Though often highly trained in research methodology relatively few had any experience of *criminology* or *criminological* research. At the same time there was also a noticeable increase in the aims and expectations attached to research. Not perhaps since the early 1960s when the Home Office was first establishing its research arm was a naïve faith in the power and promise of social research so evident. The very swift recruitment of a great number of relatively inexperienced research staff did little to check such over-optimism. Methodological expectations also changed. Predictably, and on one level understandably, the investment of such large sums of public money, led government increasingly to seek to set the methodological parameters for research. To this end the Home Office published a series of booklets and 'toolkits' covering a variety of methodological issues in which prescriptions for how research was to be conducted were detailed, not least in relation to the analysis of cost-effectiveness (Dhiri and Brand 1999).

The next bit of the story, and one that need not be rehearsed at any length,[13] concerns the fate of the Crime Reduction Programme. In short, it failed to live up to expectations. Looking back on the experience, Hough (2004: 240) captured its essence when he observed that the criminological researchers commissioned to undertake the evaluations 'consumed a large amount of public money to mount research that yielded lower benefits than expected either by ourselves or our funders'. From a government perspective the 'results' were clearly disappointing (where there were results at all). Certainly, the projects, individually and collectively, that made up the CRP did not provide the 'evidence-base' that government had imagined using as the basis for future policy development.

Analysing the reasons for the failure of the CRP is not the concern here. Rather, the issue is the consequences of this (perceived) failure for the relationship between academic criminology and government. In short, the outcome has been disillusionment. This it could be argued is visible on at least three levels. First, and predictably, it led to disillusionment within Home Office of university-based research, as illustrated both by the expressed views of senior officials (Wiles 1999, 2002) and, in part, by the

[13] Much of this history is discussed in detail in the special issue of *Criminology and Criminal Justice* (vol. 4, no. 3) published in 2004.

increasing willingness to turn to consultants and other outside contractors rather than university-based researchers. Second, it led ministers quickly to temper their faith in research. Third, the experience of the CRP and other aspects of the relationship with government research customers led to disillusionment among academics and other outsiders about various aspects of the Home Office's treatment of research and researchers (for a range of views see Hope 2004; Hough 2004; Walters 2008).

Simultaneously with, and quite possibly independently of, these developments, the organization of the internal Home Office research capability was also changing. Historically, the Home Office had a stand-alone central research unit. Originally separate, by 1990 research and statistics had been merged to establish a new, larger department. As already noted, it grew markedly from around 1998 with the creation of the Research and Statistics Directorate. More recently, and significantly, a separate research group effectively disappeared as research teams were 'embedded' within specific policy directorates. This changed the nature of Home Office research—albeit bringing it closer into line with other government departments—although the impact of this reorganization is difficult to assess—particularly for outsiders. The potential advantage of embedding teams is that bringing researchers closer to policy the aim is that research—both internal and external—will be more likely to meet the department's needs and be responsive to its timetables. The danger, critics argue, is that research becomes narrowly attuned to short-term political and policy priorities, is concerned with a narrow range of questions, and loses sight of medium and long-term goals. Whatever the reality, the organizational shift has almost certainly contributed to what is perceived to be a growing rift between Home Office and academic researchers. The outcome of these various developments has been at best a significantly changed relationship between government and academic criminology and, quite clearly, one that many perceive to have been badly damaged.

The Future

What, then, might the future hold? As I have suggested above, in recent times the criminological research agenda has shifted. Put crudely, the research interests of government departments have narrowed somewhat—at least in one sense. That is to say, technical and often relatively short-term policy-related interests have come to predominate. As a consequence, research with broader aims has become squeezed. Now, there is a natural governmental defence of this shift and, in essence, it boils down to the question of what rationale there might be for government investment in research that has no obvious or immediate policy relevance? This is the other side of the Janus face of 'evidence-based policy'. Such an apparently laudable aim can be presented, and rightly so, as supportive of scholarly activity. However, it can also be used to argue that it is only research that will potentially provide evidence for informing policy that is important, and to prescribe, in exceedingly narrow ways if desired, what sorts of evidence count.

The issue really concerns how the phrase 'policy relevance' is defined. It is perfectly possible for governments, whilst sticking to the Rothschild formula (Rothschild 1971), under which applied research is undertaken on a customer–contractor basis, still to accept that medium and longer-term policy interests can be aided by sponsoring research that asks broad questions that have no apparent application to immediate policy matters. The contemporary Home Office (and Ministry of Justice), even if it were to accept such an argument in principle, often fails to act in such a manner in practice. Furthermore, governmental concern with technical, often short-term, 'what works' style research has also led officials to attempt to influence other funding bodies, such as the ESRC, in an attempt to influence their research agendas.[14] None of this is to argue that applied research, closely tied to matters of contemporary policy concern is of less value than other research, merely to observe that there is a danger in skewing research agendas so far toward applied models that other forms of scholarship are marginalized.

So how might academic criminologists reasonably respond? Such a question speaks directly to the question 'what is criminology?' and also to what criminology wishes to be. One, radical proposal has been for some form of boycott of government. Whilst perhaps understandable, such isolationism carries considerable risks, not the least of which is confirming a perception that criminological scholarship is largely irrelevant. A variety of challenges face us and in briefly highlighting a few I will borrow Michael Burawoy's (2005) categorization of differing styles of sociological scholarship—the *critical, professional, policy* and *public*[15]—as a means of organizing some very brief reflections on criminology. Much of what I have had to say thus far has been stimulated by what appears to be a deteriorating relationship between parts of government and at least elements of the academy.[16] Whilst some of the most trenchant analyses of the current situation have come from 'critical' criminology, the challenge lies in maintaining its critical stance whilst involving itself in the process of improving criminology's engagement with governmental interests, with politics and policy-making, rather than standing outside.

A challenge for 'professional' criminology lies in overcoming elements of the paradigm conflicts alluded to earlier. The current stand-offs between, for example, those promoting 'experimental criminology' over alternative methods (or vice

[14] A similar concern arguably underpins HEFCE's emphasis on measuring 'impact' in the forthcoming Research Excellence Framework exercise.

[15] This fourfold categorization has been the subject of considerable critical discussion. See, for example, the debates in *British Journal of Sociology*, vol. 56, no. 3, and in Clawson *et al.* 2006.

[16] The outspoken comments by the then chair of the Advisory Council on the Misuse of Drugs, and his subsequent sacking by the Home Secretary, Alan Johnson, in late 2009, were one indicator of some of the tensions that existed. See, <www.guardian.co.uk/politics/2009/oct/30/drugs-adviser-david-nutt-sacked> (accessed 5 March 2010).

versa), and that between 'crime science' and 'criminology' are often-times unnecessarily oppositional. There has clearly been a view within government in recent times that academic criminology is of less relevance and utility than should be the case. Such a view poses challenges for both 'policy' and 'public' criminology. For the former the challenges include, but are not confined to, attempting to establish a healthy and realistic view of the policy/research relationship, delivering high quality empirical research whilst still seeking to 'speak truth to power' (Wildavsky 1987) and resisting attempts to impose narrowly technocratic views of research methods. Finally, for 'public' criminology the challenge lies in finding new and more effective forms of engagement with the politics of crime and its control (Loader and Sparks 2010) in speaking, constructively and powerfully, with the various constituencies that it seeks to influence, whilst remaining always mindful of the need to avoid the hubris involved in overestimating its own importance (Rock 2010).

References

Blick, A. (2004), *People Who Live in the Dark: The History of the Special Adviser in British Politics*, London: Politico's.

Blunkett, D. (2000), *Influence or Irrelevance Can Social Science Improve Government?*, Secretary of State's ESRC Lecture, 2 February, London: DfEE.

Bottoms, A. E. (1995), 'The Philosophy and Politics of Punishment and Sentencing', in C. Clarkson and R. Morgan (eds), *The Politics of Sentencing Reform*, Oxford: Oxford University Press.

Brody, S. (1976), *The Effectiveness of Sentencing*, London: HMSO.

Brown, D. (1988), *Detention at the Police Station under the Police and Criminal Evidence Act 1984*, London: Home Office.

Bullock, K., Farrell, G., and Tilley, N. (2002), *Funding and Implementing Crime Reduction Initiatives*, Home Office Online Report 10/02, London: Home Office.

Burawoy, M. (2005), '2004 American Sociological Association Presidential Address: For Public Sociology', *British Journal of Sociology*, 56, 2: 259–94.

Burrows, J., Heal, K., and Tarling, R. (1985), *Policing Today*, London: HMSO.

Cabinet Office (1999a), *Modernising Government*, London: Cabinet Office.

_____ (1999b), *Professional Policy Making for the Twenty-First Century*, London: Cabinet Office.

Campbell-Smith, D. (2008), *Follow the Money: The Audit Commission, Public Money and the Management of Public Services, 1983–2008*, London: Allen Lane.

Cassels, J. (1983), *Review of Personnel Work in the Civil Service: Report to Prime Minister*, London: HMSO.

Cavadino, M. and Dignan, J. (2006), *Penal Systems: A Comparative Approach*, London: Sage.

Clarke, R. and Hough, M. (1984), *Crime and Police Effectiveness*, London: HMSO.

Clawson, D., Zussman, R., Misra, J., Gerstel, N., Stokes, R., Anderton, D. L., and Burawoy, M. (eds) (2006), *Public Sociology*, Berkeley: University of California Press.

Croft, J. (2005), 'The Hunting of the Snark: Reflections on a Half Century of Crime', *Political Quarterly*, 76, 1: 214–23.

Dhiri, S. and Brand, S. (1999), *Analysis of Costs and Benefits: Guidance for Evaluators*, London: Home Office.

Downes, D. (1998a), *Contrasts in Tolerance: Post-war Penal Policy in the Netherlands and England and Wales*, Oxford: Clarendon Press

_____ (1988b), 'The Sociology of Crime and Social Control in Britain 1960–1987, *British Journal of Criminology*, 28, 2: 45–57.

_____ and Morgan, R. (2007), 'No Turning Back: The Politics of Law and Order into the Millennium', in M. Maguire., R. Morgan, and R. Reiner (eds), *The Oxford Handbook of Criminology*, Oxford: Oxford University Press.

Faulkner, D. (2001), *Crime, State and Citizen: A Field Full of Folk*, Winchester: Waterside Press.

_____ (2008), 'Government and public services in Britain: What happens next?', *Political Quarterly*, 79, 2: 232–40.

Folkard, M. S., Fowles, A. J., McWilliams, B., Smith, D. D., Smith, D. E., and Walmsley, G. (1974), *IMPACT*, Vol. 1, London: HMSO.

Fulton, Lord. (1968), *The Civil Service: Report of the Committee*, London: HMSO.

Garland, D. (1994), 'Of Crimes and Criminals: The Development of Criminology in Britain', in M. Maguire., R. Morgan, and R. Reiner (eds), *The Oxford Handbook of Criminology*, Oxford: Oxford University Press.

Genders, E. and Player, E. (1995), *Grendon: A Study of a Therapeutic Prison*, Oxford: Clarendon Press.

Goldblatt, P. and Lewis, C. (1998), *Reducing Offending: An Assessment of Research Evidence on Ways of Dealing with Offending Behaviour*, Home Office Research Study No. 187. London: Home Office.

Hennessy, P. (1988), 'Mrs Thatcher's Poodle? The Civil Service since 1979', *Contemporary Record*, 2, 2: 2–4.

Home Office (1959), *Penal Practice in a Changing Society*, London: HMSO.

_____. (1964), *The War Against Crime in England and Wales 1959–1964*, London: HMSO.

Hope, T. (2009), 'The Illusion of Control: A Response to Professor Sherman', *Criminal Justice*, 9, 2: 125–34.

_____ and Shaw, M. (eds) (1988), *Communities and Crime Reduction*, London: HMSO.

Hough, M. (2004), 'Modernization, scientific rationalism and the Crime Reduction Programme', *Criminal Justice*, 4, 3: 239–53.

_____ (2010), 'Gold Standard or Fool's Gold? The Pursuit of Certainty in Experimental Criminology', *Criminology and Criminal Justice*, 10, 1: 11–22.

Lacey, N. (2008), *The Prisoners' Dilemma: Political Economy and Punishment in Contemporary Democracies*, Cambridge: Cambridge University Press.

Loader, I. and Sparks, R. (2010), *Public Criminology*, London: Routledge.

Lodge, T. (1974), The founding of the Home Office Research Unit', in R. Hood (ed.), '*Crime, Criminology and Public Policy*', London: Heinemann.

Lowe, R. (2005), 'Grit in the Oyster or Sand in the Machine? The Evolving Role of Special Advisers in British Government', *Twentieth Century British History*, 16, 4: 497–505.

Maguire, M. (2004), 'The Crime Reduction Programme in England and Wales: Reflections on the Vision and the Reality', *Criminology and Criminal Justice*, 4, 3: 213–37.

Morgan, R. and Newburn, T. (1997), *The Future of Policing*, Oxford: Oxford University Press.

Newburn, T. (2007), 'Tough on Crime: Penal Policy in England and Wales', in M. Tonry (ed.), *Crime and Justice: A Review of Research*, Chicago: University of Chicago Press.

Oakley, A. (1999), 'Paradigm Wars: Some Thoughts on a Personal and Public Trajectory', *International Journal on Social Research Methodology*, 2, 3: 247–54.

O'Malley, P. (2009), 'Risk, Crime and Prudentialism Revisited', *Legal Studies Research Paper No. 09/122*, Sydney: University of Sydney Law School.

Pratt, J. (2007), *Penal Populism*, London: Routledge.

Reiner, R. (2006), 'Beyond Risk: A Lament for Social Democratic Criminology', in T. Newburn and P. Rock (eds), *The Politics of Law and Order: Essays in Honour of David Downes*, Oxford: Clarendon.

Riley, D. and Shaw, M. (1985), *Parental Supervision and Juvenile Delinquency*, London: Home Office.

Rock, P. (1988), 'The Present State of British Criminology', *British Journal of Criminology*, 28, 2: 188–99.

_____. (2004), *Constructing Victims' Rights: The Home Office, New Labour and Victims*, Oxford: Clarendon Press.

_____. (2010), 'Comment on C. Uggen and M. Inderbitzin; "Public Criminologies", *Criminology and Public Policy*, 9, 4: 751–767.

Rothschild, V. (1971), *The Organisation and Management of Government Research and Development*, London: HMSO.

Sausman, C. and Locke, R. (2004), 'The British Civil Service: Examining the Question of Politicization', in B. G. Peters and J. Pierre (eds), *The Politicization of the Civil Service in Comparative Perspective: The search for control*, London: Routledge.

Sellin, T. (1970), 'A Sociological Approach', in M. E. Wolfgang, L. Savitz, and N. Johnston (eds), *The Sociology of Crime and Delinquency*, New York: Wiley.

Shapland, J., Willmore, J., and Duff, P. (1985), *Victims in the Criminal Justice System*, Aldershot: Gower.

Sherman, L. (2009), 'Evidence and Liberty: The Promise of Experimental Criminology', *Criminology and Criminal Justice*, 9, 1: 5–28.

_____, Gottfredson, D., MacKenzie, D. L., Eck, J., Reuter, P., and Bushway, S. (1997), *What Works, What Doesn't, What's Promising*, Report to the US Congress. Washington: US Deptartment of Justice.

Sparks, R. (2001), '"Bringin' it all Back Home": Populism, Media Coverage and the Dynamics of Locality and Globality in the Politics of Crime Control', in K. Stenson and R. Sullivan (eds), *Crime, Risk and Justice: The Politics of Crime Control in Liberal Democracies*, Cullompton: Willan.

Thain, C. (2009), 'The Core Executive in the UK: The Roles of the Prime Minister and HM Treasury', unpublished research paper, available at: <www.treasuryproject.org/ecpr.pdf> (accessed 27 February 2010).

Tilley, N. (2009), 'Sherman vs Sherman: Rhetoric vs Reality', *Criminal Justice*, 9, 2: 135–44.

Tonry, M. (2007), 'Determinants of Penal Policies', in M. Tonry (ed), *Crime, Punishment and Politics in Comparative Perspective*, Chicago: University of Chicago Press.

Trewin, I. (ed.) (2009), *The Hugo Young Papers: A Journalist's Notes from the Heart of Politics*, London: Penguin.

Tyson, S. (1990), 'Turning Civil Servants into Managers', *Public Money and Management*, 10, 1, 27–30.

Walters, R. (2008), 'Government Manipulation of Criminological Knowledge and Policies of Deceit', in W. McMahon (ed.), *Critical Thinking about the Uses of Research*, London: Centre for Crime and Justice Studies.

Wildavsky, A. (1987), *Speaking Truth to Power*, New Brunswick, NJ: Transaction Publishers.

Wiles, P. (1999), Speech given at the Centre for Crime and Justice Studies and the ISTD, Kings College London, 17 November 1999 (available at: <www.homeoffice.gov.uk/rds/pdfs/pwilesspeech.pdf>, accessed 27 January 2010).

_____. (2002), 'Criminology in the 21st Century: Public Good or Private Interest? The Sir John Barry Memorial Lecture', *Australian and New Zealand Journal of Criminology*, 35, 238–52.

Windlesham, Lord. (1993), *Responses to Crime*, vol. 2, Oxford: Oxford University Press.

_____. (1996), *Responses to Crime*, vol. 3, Oxford: Oxford University Press.

Young, H. (1989), *One of Us*, Basingstoke: Macmillan.

Zedner, L. (2003), 'Useful Knowledge? Debating the Role of Criminology in Post-War Britain', in L. Zedner and A. Ashworth (eds), *The Criminological Foundations of Penal Policy*, Oxford: Clarendon Press.

Zedner, L. (2006), 'Opportunity Makes the Thief-Taker: The Influence of Economic Analysis on Crime Control', in T. Newburn and P. Rock (eds), *The Politics of Crime Control: Essays in Honour of David Downes*, Oxford: Clarendon Press.

34

BEING A CRIMINOLOGIST: INVESTIGATION AS A LIFESTYLE AND LIVING

ALISON LIEBLING

I was thinking about your research and contemplated the impact of your work on the stakeholders... Do you reflect on your ability to influence the 'status quo'? How much—objectively—does your work achieve?... Please let me know your rationale, your 'war effort', or the rationalisation process you undergo before doing such work? What matters to you?

[Extract from a letter handed to the author following a group discussion by one prisoner-participant in a recent study of long-term imprisonment in conditions of maximum security, 2009]

THE aim of this chapter is to reflect on some aspects of 'being a criminologist' who specializes in prisons research. I consider the purpose of research, as I see it, and some of the outcomes of research projects I have led or conducted. I end with a few reflections on the research experience. My main argument is that research—understood as 'authentic description'—has a moral and explanatory value. Nothing gives us firmer credentials for forging change than having a firm empirical grasp of actual practices and experiences. We should, however, be wary of 'correctional agendas'.

The Purpose of Research

A small team and I were conducting a repeat of an ethnographic study of staff–prisoner relationships in a maximum security prison.[1] Throughout the first study, conducted in 1998–9, there had been a regular Dialogue Group meeting in the prison, consisting of one morning and one afternoon group discussion with prisoners from all areas within the establishment (Liebling and Price 1999; 2001). It had been facilitated by an external organization (Prison Dialogue). We had joined in, and benefited greatly from its existence, both in terms of deep understanding of life in the prison and in forging enduring relationships with a small number of prisoners. This time, there were no such groups operating in the prison, for reasons relating to the changing penal climate (and a stringent 'public acceptability test' for all external contracts). So we started one: Cambridge Dialogue. During these regular afternoon sessions, we got to know a group of prisoners well, sharing ideas, readings, and thoughts about the prison, life before and after it, and the process and purpose of criminological research. We were seriously challenged ('what does this achieve, apart from the personal benefits to you?'), as well as defended ('more people like you should do this kind of work'). We felt a bit like Stan Cohen and Laurie Taylor, in their 1972 study, *Psychological Survival*, as outside sociologists forming a close allegiance with a group of articulate, critical men serving 'heavy', serious prison sentences over an extended period of time. There were some differences, however. We had formal access to the prison for specific research purposes (unlike Cohen and Taylor), we had a clear research agenda ('what were the nature and quality of staff–prisoner, and prisoner–prisoner relationships in the establishment?'), we had limited time available (about eighteen months, for the project as a whole), and we were also talking sympathetically to staff. These often-passionate conversations about the meaning and purpose of prison research, and the complex identities and allegiances of the researchers and the participants, made me want to return to the questions posed by the editors when they invited a contribution to this volume.

The questions I address in this chapter are: What is criminology for? What is its impact? How should it be done? Our prisoner group members asked precisely these questions: 'Does this type of research achieve any fundamental change?' 'Do you believe that striving for perfection is what matters, even though you never achieve it?' Or more immediately, in a fraught environment, 'Is it safe for me to talk to you, with that tape recorder on?' Our regular attendees were attracted to our discussion group, by curiosity, but also by hope that expressing their views to us, as part of a research project, might change their world in some 'progressive' way. The question of trust really mattered, for if the prisoners did not trust us, they would not share their experiences fully. If we wanted to describe the prison, and understand it, we

[1] The research is being conducted with Helen Arnold and Christina Straub, and will be the subject of a separate publication.

required honesty and openness. This cannot be a one-way process, and to ask for these things generates obligations.

My answer to the basic question posed by the prisoner–participant above about the impact of research is that direct impact is often limited, that in some ways this is appropriate (for reasons I shall elaborate below) but that *clarifying and developing conceptual understanding* is, in itself, perhaps the most important part of any change or reform process. As Blumer argued in *Symbolic Interaction*, the role of the concept in social science is to 'sensitise perception' (1969: 152)—to change the perceptual world, so that, for example, consciousness of fairness and unfairness, the meaning of the term 'justice', accurate descriptions of differential uses and abuses of power, clearer understanding of the prison's moral and emotional universe, and accounts of the intended and unintended effects of changing punishment provisions, are brought into existence. Once in existence, they can be taken into account. Applying theory in ways that 'make sense' of long-term changes in punishment practices, or of patterns in painstakingly analysed empirical data, is a way of 'speaking truth to power'.

Our prisoner 'stakeholders', as they described themselves, wanted direct action; changes that would benefit them in visible ways.[2] They thought if we understood the unimaginable problems and injustices of 'doing an IPP sentence', or 'being post-tariff', we would be able to get the sentence abolished, or help them to move on. That if we could see how unreasonable it was to be 'still on Cat A' after seven years of programmes and self-control, and on the basis of poor quality and inaccurate information, we would be able to assist in a downgrade (a recategorization to B, or a 'progressive move'). We said this was unlikely.

Sometimes, under the right conditions, research leads to policy change. More usually, it leads to policy adaptation—small changes that make it more palatable for the existing policy to operate in a slightly better way (see Bottoms 1999 for an example). But there are many intermediate positions between my somewhat 'purist' starting position (research is for knowledge, which informs decisions) and the aspiration of most members of our prisoner dialogue group (research will change our lives). One outcome of the research described above, for example, might be for us to recommend that the Chief Inspector of Prisons take 'the quality of file information', 'security categorization', or 'prisoners serving IPP sentences' as the focus of a forthcoming thematic review.

Research-for-knowledge can be directed at campaigning organizations, for example. It can be placed in the hands of those who are by occupation more activist. When I began my criminological career in the late 1980s, it was clear that academics and campaigning organizations were often 'on the same side', sharing information and working in coordinated ways to exert pressure 'upwards'. This networking

[2] For a related discussion of what motivated prisoners to participate in research in a US project, see Bosworth *et al.* 2005.

arrangement has changed, so that campaigning organizations are less uniform or powerful, and some researchers are courted directly by policy and operational figures who are themselves under unprecedented pressure to improve their performance.[3] But this does not necessarily mean that the researcher has to be 'tame' or the research 'administrative'. Meeting the (sometimes superficial or politically motivated) needs of the research sponsor is often highly compatible with exploring the topic deeply and challenging some taken-for-granted practices. Often our theoretically-driven research designs generate data that are more welcome by those in policy positions (it can serve as a warning, for example) than data generated by their proposed, more limited research questions.

According to a recent source, even Michel Foucault proposed, as part of his work with the GIP, that:

> A survey be prepared 'to gain concrete knowledge about prisoners' real situation (and not simply what the administration tells us about it')... The questionnaire was directed at revealing key aspects of imprisonment, such as living conditions, medical care, hygiene, food, physical abuse, punishments, visitation policies and a host of prisoners' concerns... The survey was not intended to be an idle exercise of social science; rather, it was firmly embedded in action against the prison regime and 'resistance to the intolerable' [Welch 2010: 55, drawing on Macey 1993].

Investigation, in this view, was a 'weapon against the prison administration'. Indeed, findings from the questionnaire, conducted via visitors in twenty prisons, became the basis for the GIP's first pamphlet (ibid.: 55). Welch cites Macey as follows:

> These investigations are not designed to improve or soften an oppressive power, or to make it tolerable. They are designed to attack it at those points where it is exercised under a different name—that of justice, technology, knowledge or objectivity. Each investigation must therefore be a political act [Macey 1993: 268].

This account resonates with my experience. Careful investigation exposes self-deceit in the powerful (as well as among others), and can constitute a way of challenging 'official discourse' with complex realities and the many disappointments of 'criminal justice in action'. By observing, listening, checking, and by careful design, well-organized research teams can gather evidence and example of action and experience. We can test the formal or stated aims of policy against the individual case, as well as the aggregate experience. Away from the formal discourses of risk, punishment, resettlement, progress, relationship, and treatment, we find a complex human being trying to make sense of his or her predicament, or struggling to cope with it, or actively resisting it, and other complex human beings, in (a professional) role, trying to get through their day, or trying to make a difference. Sometimes, they make things worse. Or organizational structures and cultures work against them.

[3] For a critical discussion of what happens to prison researchers who are not courted by policy figures see Hannah-Moffat, this volume.

These 'on-the-ground' realities are always difficult to piece together and describe. Often it is only in the writing of a project—the comparing of sources, extended team discussions, the checking of transcripts, or reanalysis of the data, that the patterns start to 'make sense'. Prisoners in this prison, for example, may feel unrecognized as people. Yet in this other one, they feel helped and supported. Why? When did the tone change, and how? Why are two prisons, in the same policy universe, operating in such different ways? Or why does this wing stand out as a place where you can show emotion, expect help, talk with staff, and retain hope? All of these questions must be answered in the research: that is our primary goal. Once we have satisfactory answers—a good enough description, and some explanation—the search for a future direction can begin:

> [Social science research] must manifest both its relevance and concern for the human predicament.' [Gouldner 1973: 13]

The motivation for research can include the urge to improve: as Durkheim said, 'Why strive for knowledge of reality, if this knowledge cannot serve us in life?' (Durkheim 1964: 71). But this should not be its *primary* goal. Its primary goal is accurate description, and plausible explanation. The research can then contribute, in a responsible way, to the dialogue about reform. It is often persuasive, and sometimes 'speaks for itself'. Whether policy-makers respond to its key messages often depends on other contextual matters (the stage of the election cycle, media and political interest, cost, and so on) as well as on the plausibility of the findings. Sometimes cumulative knowledge is needed—one project becomes the first in a slow process of losing faith in a policy that was attractive and fashionable, but that became unsustainable in the face of a growing evidence base, or unintended consequences.

Sociologists are divided amongst themselves about the extent to which research should have 'policy reform' as its chief target. Burowoy argues that there are four types or divisions of labour in sociology: professional, policy, critical, and public. Professional sociology is theoretical and empirical, and adheres to scientific norms. Policy sociology is instrumental ('in the service of a goal'), looks mainly at the effectiveness of policies, and is 'servile'. Critical sociology has 'moral vision' and is foundational, providing intellectual challenge but often for internal uses. It can provide a critique of existing value assumptions. Public sociology is aimed at enriching public debate about moral and political issues, by infusing public dialogue with theory and empirical research in a reciprocal manner. Each of these four 'ideal type' approaches involves entering into relations of domination and subordination, but in distinct ways. His case 'against' professional sociology, or empirical social science, is that it can end up being self-referential and self-interested. I agree with him, but I also have some concerns about his case for sociology's direct engagement in public work. Professional social science should *inform* policy and value discussions, but this often happens organically. It should, amongst other things, promote discussions of what 'the good society' might look like. But it is not always easy to work out what the implications of research might be. It is crucial, in my view, to distinguish between high quality and poor quality research, to place high standards above political influence, and to show how complex the 'real world' is, however disappointing policy-makers (and 'utopian idealists') find this. Professional social science should produce 'responsible speech' (Bauman 1990: 12) and 'communicative knowledge' (Burowoy 2004). Responsible speech is an 'attribute of science'. It is 'vigilantly self-controlled', 'corroborated by evidence', self-critical, and not grounded solely in emotionally intense beliefs (Bauman 1990: 12). This kind of work requires time, high standards (and, ideally, security of employment).

Having said all of the above, it is not always in the researcher's gift to determine the nature of the relationship between research and practice. I consider below some of the possibilities.

The Impact of Criminological Research

There are at least four ways in which research *can* support reform in my experience: the direct reflection on practice it allows—challenging assumptions, and placing micro-action in the context of macro-level characteristics of criminal justice institutions; in the direct presentation of evidence to senior managers, policy-makers and campaigning organizations, who may find they can use the research in strategic ways; in the development of new ways of looking at and thinking about the social world; and, we reflected in a recent long interview-based study on values and practices among senior managers (being conducted with my colleague Ben Crewe), allowing reflective space in a frantic operational climate to ask and answer questions about practitioners' assumptions and frameworks, which makes 'going on uncritically' less possible than before. One private sector director, for example, left our three-hour career-biographical interview wondering whether she was, after all, reconciled to the use of private prisons. A second senior manager wondered why he did not feel able to speak out when in disagreement with his colleagues. *Being researched* involves being asked questions that may be more difficult to answer than many busy practitioners and policy-makers assume. The very process of a long, reflective interview can change practice.

Examples of the former include the analysis of the impact of a newly-introduced policy of incentives and earned privileges for prisoners. The policy was intended to improve prisoner behaviour, by rewarding and punishing it, but the evaluation found that a lack of fairness in its administration could lead to further disaffection (see further Liebling 2008). The results from an evaluation of a new suicide prevention initiative in ten 'high-risk' prisons showed that, in one prison, levels of distress among women prisoners were significantly reduced by providing better care on entry into custody, and a more supportive (as well as physically improved) environment. These positive findings had a major impact on the enthusiasm of other establishments for the new 'safer custody' strategy. Feedback on the research was provided at regular intervals throughout the study (and subsequently) and provided moral as well as empirical support for practitioners working in other establishments who were actively seeking funding, or who were simply trying to improve practice in their own establishments. There emerged a team of 'safer custody roadshow' speakers and practitioners, committed to suicide prevention, who accumulated evidence, best practice and momentum. This collective enterprise contributed significantly to a 'will to improve' that seemed to have real effects on operational staff confidence and on the prisoner experience. In another example, describing the best aspects of prison officer work as 'peacekeeping', or the judicious under-use of power, helped to focus attention on the training needs of staff, and the complexity of their work (see Liebling and Price 2001).

Of course research can sometimes have *unintended effects* on practice: learning to measure the 'moral climate' of prisons for reasons of curiosity appealed to people in higher places in ways I could never have anticipated (Liebling, assisted by Arnold 2004). A research exercise funded by a short-lived (but highly welcome) Home Office Innovative Research Challenge Award led to the development of a detailed but structured questionnaire aimed at identifying and, if possible, measuring the 'moral performance' or quality of prison life, as experienced by prisoners. This exploratory, 'ground-up' process captured the imagination of senior managers trying to fill a gap in their performance management agenda. The dimensions devised reflected values, and therefore aspects of prison life, 'that mattered' to prisoners, like respect, humanity, staff–prisoner relationships, and safety, and the results apparently had high face validity—or 'looked like' the prison felt, according to prisoners and staff. Almost overnight, the questionnaire was formally adopted by the Prison Service's Standards Audit Unit, a team was appointed, and surveys were conducted in an extraordinarily high number of prisons each year thereafter (around 40–50 annually). I was asked to steer and advise on the process, as well as help to reflect on the results, with colleagues from the Prisons Research Centre providing statistical and practical support where needed.

The 'MQPL' as it is now known, is now a well-established 'measuring tool'—more or less the opposite of what had been intended (an exploratory mechanism for deepening our understanding of prison life)—but, nonetheless, it acts as a useful barometer of the inner life of prisons, as experienced by prisoners. There are countless and ongoing 'teething problems' with this translation into senior management practice of a tentative research outcome (we like to revise and improve, they like to compare; we like to interpret and reflect, they like to measure; we are painfully aware of its limitations, they like to rely on it; and so on). But there are also many points of agreement and signs of positive change. If a prison gets a 'low score' on 'respect' or 'fairness', then the senior management team set about trying to improve matters.

There is a risk that the main appeal of this kind of information—survey-based, systematic and routinely administered—is simply that it is (a) potentially legitimating, and (b) amenable to quantification. On balance, I am satisfied that if the Prison Service is measuring 'respect', 'fairness' and 'relationships' then this research has made an impact on focusing the minds of senior managers on these concepts in a positive and important way. It has provided valuable support to those who were already intent on trying to provide decent and humane regimes and on taking feedback from prisoners seriously. But these things are never straightforward. I meet 'heads of MQPL' and 'heads of decency' on senior management teams in establishments and sometimes feel humbled, nervous and apologetic. I feel impatient when individuals look at the survey results too technically, and do not absorb their meaning (for example, that in this prison, prisoners are unhappy and frustrated, and staff are indifferent towards them). But at other times I feel proud that a curiosity-driven research project led to an action, and clarified a way of seeing, that matters. It is interesting and significant that Grendon (therapeutic community) is the highest scoring prison, that private sector prisons have the highest variation in scores, from poor to good, and that prisons of the same type are experienced so differently by prisoners. There is much to be learned, and some glaring departures from official claims made for the prison, compared to the experience as reflected in prisoners' survey responses.

The main purpose of research is rigorous description, and *explanation*, in which the notion of explanation includes some account of the subjective meaning of action, and a grasp of the complex of meanings in which action occurs. This is close to Weber's concept of '*verstehen*' (interpretative understanding) and should be distinguished from *prediction*, another aim altogether (see Liebling 1992). This model of social research (a form of analytic induction) requires some qualitative depth, but does not preclude quantitative methods, provided these methods are well grounded, and appropriately interpreted. Any complexity should be permitted to lie with the research participants, rather than with the analysis methods adopted (Walker 1977). As Fromm argued: 'It is as inhabitants of this human world that we... must finally recognise that there is a certain kind of scientific 'objectivity' that can lead us to know everything, but to understand nothing' (Fromm 1962: viii).

Hempel argued that research may be motivated by the desire to understand, by 'man's insatiable intellectual curiosity, his deep concern to *know* the world he lives in, and to *explain*, and thus to *understand* (Hempel 1966: 95). My argument is that where this is done well, it stands a better chance of changing the world. Matza describes a kind of naturalistic appreciation aimed at 'comprehending the moral and social life' of participants rather than 'trying to correct' (1969: 5). It requires time, intuition and insight, observation, engagement and empathy.

The commitment of this kind of research is to 'the phenomena and their nature; it is loyal to 'the world with whatever measure of variety or universality happens to inhere in it' (p. 5). Inquiry, under this framework, produces knowledge about 'what they are' not what they are not, or ought to be. The integrity of the participant takes precedence over the integrity of 'any philosophical viewpoint' (p. 6); 'It does not and cannot commit itself to any single preferred method for engaging and scrutinizing phenomena' (p. 5). Its opposite is reductionism—a mechanistic and distorting search for single categories and explanations—a form of deliberate misconception about the nature of the individual as 'an object'. How then, does this style of research work in practice?

Being a Human Being: Research in Practice

Do you think about us when you are not here? [Long-term prisoner, maximum security prison; member of Cambridge Dialogue Group]

How the punishment hurts, how it feels, the suffering and the sorrow, these are the elements most often completely lacking in the texts [Christie 1981: 15].

Turning to the question of method: how should criminological research be conducted? Slowly, carefully, and in extended, intimate (that is open and honest) but boundaried contact with the researched; rigorously, with 'from-a-distance analysis' built in throughout, and in conceptual dialogue with others. Wherever possible, it should be done 'appreciatively' (Matza 1969; Liebling *et al.* 1999), taking all accounts seriously, and seeking what gives our participants life and energy, as well as what frustrates and disappoints them. Matza speaks of an 'intimate familiarity with the field'. Researchers have their own style, position, and capacity for both closeness and distance, but there are some rules of engagement we should all follow. No one should be exposed, or placed at risk, if at all possible. Individuals should be respected, and given the freedom to decline participation, or change their mind. All individual accounts should be anonymized. The research questions should form the core of any interaction between the researchers and the participant, but straying off topic is human and considerate, if other pressing issues dominate. All research data should be handled with care. Our most important ethical consideration is to careful and authentic representation. Like an artist who seeks to extend human sympathy through the depiction of ordinary things (see Liebling 1999) the researcher claims a kind of skilled representation of the life experience of others. This is our craft.

We pay a price for attempting this kind of research—the time this kind of approach takes, that we are not granted, exposure to distressing confessional accounts, immersion in the complex experience of others, confusion by contradictions in the presentation and self-description of our participants, and a feeling of helplessness when the circumstances individual participants find themselves in seem dire. We do not build in to research contracts (or have available, at an organizational level) professional supervision, as social workers or psychologists might, through which we might inwardly digest and process complex narratives. If we go in deep, as we should, it is sometimes hard to emerge, unchanged, unmoved, intact.

Sometimes the impact of the particular policy or organization we are evaluating can have negative effects on us, for example if it conflicts (or they conflict) with our own basic values in some way. Team members can have distinctive responses to 'what is going on' in the field (is a challenging and controversial intervention simply unethical, for example, or are 'extreme measures' sometimes justified?) and this can generate conflict if the dynamics for each individual are not discussed and understood. In one highly challenging project, evaluating a training initiative by the organization Youth at Risk, the four members of the research team struggled to identify their personal (positive and negative) value priorities in order to make sense of their powerful but distinctive feelings about the training and its effects. Each of us had attractions, or aversions, to aspects of the training, which was confrontational. So one team member might privilege respect over kindness, another might choose humility over the urge to rescue. Individual aversions might range from control to abandonment, or from masculine authority over-used to profiteering. These deeply hidden rawnesses in ourselves can shape our interpretations and risk becoming treated as data. This aspect of the research experience is hidden or ignored in many projects, but if addressed, perhaps with outside facilitation, constitutes part of the hard work involved in making sense of complex realities.

The answer to the prisoner's question above about whether I kept them in mind outside of the prison was 'Yes... especially on the drive home [pause]... But at other times too. You haunt us sometimes.' Our participant was satisfied with this answer. He was checking—our credentials, and level of engagement. What did our encounters mean? How authentic was our interest? Did these conversations have meaning beyond the collection of data? 'Are we human, to you?' These questions came up all the time. After a pause: 'I think more people like you should do this kind of research.' This welcome affirmation came despite our many conversations about the limits of research in helping individual prisoners. Another participant added, 'I don't know what we are gonna do when you guys finish here.' Were we getting this right? What about the risks of 'being there' and then 'not being there', as an outside, interested presence, perhaps even alleviating the loneliness and meaninglessness of the prison experience, briefly? The risk here—common to many research studies and also to time-limited interventions—is that whilst conducting the study we come to represent a missing open or affirming form of interaction that is felt as a lack when it ends (see, eg, Digard and Liebling 2010). Expectations have to be continually lowered.

In all research, but especially in its qualitative phases, the researcher *is* the research instrument. Meaningful research in prison is by its nature intimate. That is sometimes one of its attractions. But it is also a risk and a strain. It tests us, methodologically and emotionally, and it can create emotions and expectations in participants. But this is a difficulty to be managed, not a reason to take refuge in anonymous surveys. It is an extraordinarily difficult part of the research process to get right. How can an appreciation of the inner world of another occur unless we engage deeply in each encounter? But we should bear in mind that we are not just our 'selves' in the research encounter. We represent hope, and interest from the outside world, when that world feels a long way away. We have obligations to be *careful*, arising from the vulnerability and powerlessness of our participants, as well as obligations to be *cautious* about the environment we enter, and the many complex motivations individuals might have for presenting those aspects of their experience they are willing to share with us.

In the study referred to in this chapter, we brought our students in at one stage, taking advantage of the relationships we had built up in the prison over time. I wanted to show our regular dialogue group participants, many of whom were studying for Open University degrees, that they were closer to the world of 'studentdom' than they realized, that the young and educated thought about and were curious about and compassionate towards them, and that as Open University students themselves, they were part of a significant network of people studying. I wanted to show my students that prisoners serving long sentences in conditions of maximum security were complex, thoughtful people, with moral depth, and powerful stories to tell.

Conclusion

Social science research aims to provide authentic description, understanding and explanation of social phenomena. This is useful and it has a moral as well as policy value. Nothing gives us better credentials for forging change than having a firm empirical grasp of actual practices, or 'the habits and practices of punishment' (Garland, pers. comm. 2003). As criminologists, we have a privileged and a constrained role. We sometimes have access to people in high places, and we can get our voices heard. We owe it to our profession to use our skills and networks responsibly, and for the greater good. Many of us believe in working for greater social justice, whether by trying to identify what that might look like, or where and how practices fall short, or by more direct means. Different projects lead us in different directions on this trajectory, and sometimes it is when we are able to take a more reflective stance, in an advisory or informal networking role, that we can shape policy or practice in ways the evidence supports. Social research is demanding and challenging, and it is not necessarily well supported by current organizational structures. It works best when sustained and accumulative attention can be paid to the field, and where this kind of model has institutional support. It needs a certain openness to unanticipated questions, and unexpected directions. It requires appreciative as well as critical energy. It is an art and a craft, and a way of life.

References

Bauman, Z. (1990), *Thinking Sociologically*, Oxford: Blackwell.

Blumer, H. (1969), *Symbolic Interactionism: Perspective and Method*, Englewood Cliffs: Prentice-Hall.

Bosworth, M, Campbell, D., Demby, B., Ferranti, S. M., and Santos, M. (2005), 'Doing Prison Research: Views from Inside', *Qualitative Inquiry*, 11(2): 1- 16.

Bottoms, A. E. (1999), 'Interpersonal Violence and Social Order in Prisons', in M. Tonry and J. Petersilia (eds), *'Prisons', Crime and Justice: A Review of Research*, xxvi, Chicago: University of Chicago Press: 205–82.

Burawoy, M. (2004), 'Public Sociologies: Contradictions, Dilemmas, and Possibilities', *Social Forces*, 82, 4: 1603–18.

Christie, N. (1981), *Limits to Pain*, Oxford: Martin Robertson.

Cohen, S. and Taylor, L. (1972), *Psychological Survival: The Experience of Long-Term Imprisonment*, Harmondsworth: Penguin.

Digard, L. and Liebling, A. (2010), 'Harmony behind bars: Evaluating the therapeutic potential of a prison based music programme', in L. Cheliotis (ed.), *The Arts of Imprisonment: Control, Resistance and Empowerment*, Aldershot: Ashgate Publishing.

Durkheim, E. (1964), *The Rules of Sociological Method*, New York: The Free Press.

Fromm, E. (1962), *Beyond the Chains of Illusion: My Encounter with Marx and Freud*, Abacus edn (1986): London.

Garland, D. (2003), *Comments at Scottish Criminology Conference, Edinburgh* (personal communication, 2003).

Gouldner, A. W. (1973), *For Sociology*, London: Allen Lane.

Hempel, C. K. (1966), *Philosophy of Natural Science*, Englewood Cliffs: Prentice-Hall.

Liebling, A. (1992), *Suicides in Prison*, London: Routledge.

_____ (1999), 'Doing Prison Research: Breaking the Silence?', *Theoretical Criminology*, 3, 2: 147–73.

_____, Elliott, C. and Price, D. (1999), 'Appreciative Inquiry and Relationships in Prison', *Punishment and Society: The International Journal of Penology*, 1, 1: 71–98.

_____; assisted by Arnold, H, (2004), *Prisons and their Moral Performance: A Study of Values, Quality and Prison Life*, Oxford: Clarendon Press.

_____ (2008), 'Incentives and Earned Privileges Revisited: Fairness, Discretion, and the Quality of Prison Life', in *Journal of Scandinavian Studies in Criminology and Crime Prevention*, 9: 25–41.

_____ and Price, D. (2001), *The Prison Officer*, Leyhill: Prison Service (and Waterside Press).

_____ and _____ (1999), *An Exploration of Staff-Prisoner Relationships at HMP Whitemoor*, Prison Service Research Report, No. 6: HMPS, London.

Macey, D. (1993), cited in M. Welch. (2010), 'Pastoral Power as Penal Resistance: Foucault and the Groupe d'Information sur les Prisons', *Punishment and Society*, 12, 1: 47–63.

Matza, D. (1969), *Becoming Deviant*, Englewood Cliffs: Prentice-Hall.

Walker, N. (1977), *Behaviour and Misbehaviour: Explanations and non-explanations*, Oxford: Basil Blackwell.

Welch, M. (2010), 'Pastoral Power as Penal Resistance: Foucault and the Groupe d'Information sur les Prisons', *Punishment and Society*, 12, 1: 47–63.

MAPPING THE BORDERS OF CRIMINOLOGY: CONCLUDING THOUGHTS

CAROLYN HOYLE AND MARY BOSWORTH

WHILE we are tempted to end with the slogan we used for the student-helpers' t-shirts at the Oxford conference—'What is Criminology... I dunno!'—we shall instead take the opportunity to offer some final observations about the state of and challenges to the discipline. In so doing, we do not aspire to close the conversation that we have begun in these pages, but to invite further debate and interaction and, maybe, one day, a second edition!

In putting together this collection, we asked each of the contributors to respond to a range of prompts—What is criminology for? What is the impact of criminology? How should criminology be done? What are the key issues and debates in criminology today? What challenges does the discipline of criminology currently face? How has criminology as a discipline changed over the last few decades?

It is of no surprise that the questions did not inspire uniform answers. Each of our contributors has responded to them slightly differently, generating an image of the discipline that is multiple and contested, rather than singular and settled. So what conclusions, if any, can we draw?

Our plan originally was to group essays into sections based on the prompts. This way of arranging chapters, we thought, would replicate some of the theoretical and methodological divisions within the field. We envisaged putting key criminological figures head to head to fight over methodological or theoretical territories. It was not to be. Instead, we found much more willingness among our contributors to engage with alternative viewpoints and strategies than we had expected. It is not that criminologists are in universal agreement, but rather that they perhaps look elsewhere more often than we might think.

Instead of finding fixed allegiances or camps within a fractious whole, then, we identified a series of borders along which many of us range, but over which we also cross. Borders, in criminology as elsewhere, are policed, yet they are also frequently transgressed; criminologists can and do move across them to plunder, admire, or learn from other regions. While some boundaries may be more difficult or dangerous to cross than others it is rare to find an entirely secluded locale or community.

In traversing ideological, political, geographical and disciplinary borders, those of us who call ourselves 'criminologists' take with us our own training, tools, and concepts, as well as 'our' seminal texts. We share these with 'foreigners' outside our comfort zones and dip into or pillage their resources to help us to further make sense of our own worlds as well as those beyond our borders. From such exchanges, over time, borders may break down, shift, or spring up, enriching those who take the journey and those who are visited. Hence, we came, rather late in the day, to structure the book within a framework of borders.

Internal Borders

Essays in the first section are primarily concerned with internal borders *within* criminology; contributors' positions on appropriate theoretical frameworks, methodological approaches and on the relationship between activism and academia. Authors raise a number of familiar concerns: the position of critical criminology/cultural criminology/public criminology within the wider field; ethnography v statistics; social justice viz-a-viz the academy. In so doing, they grapple with theoretical, methodological and normative questions over what it is criminologists should study, what intellectual resources we should draw on, how we should approach our research, and what our intentions should be.

Ian Loader and Richard Sparks open this section by revisiting old questions about the place and purpose of criminology in politics and public life. They remind us of the disquiet many of us feel about the apparent inverse relationship between criminological academic activity and potency in the spheres of policy and practice beyond the academy. Drawing on Locke's 'under-labourer', Loader and Sparks' 'democratic under-labourer'—with the help of other dramatis personae—aims to persuade us that our role, as criminologists, is 'to foster and sustain a better politics of crime and its regulation', essentially to engage in public life. In an epilogue evocatively entitled 'the value of criminological pluralism', they set the mood for much of this edited collection: whilst 'there are genuine points of epistemological and political disagreement', criminologists, by and large, appreciate the value of other stances. There is, they argue, public value in criminology's plurality of theoretical perspectives, focal concerns and methodologies—as long as serious debate and exchange is encouraged. The contributions that follow take up the challenge of this first chapter, producing just such an engaging and rigorous debate.

In considering what it is we are, or should be, doing when we 'do criminology', Michael Gottfredson alerts us to the importance of determining our terms of reference; we need to be clear about what crime is before we can know on which disciplines to draw in explaining its causes or in devising remedial policies. Gottfredson is adamant that we should not be restricted by criminal law in our definitions of crime. Rather, he advocates a 'crime-free criminology' to reduce 'the focus on delinquency and crime as special or especially motivated behaviour'. Such a criminology, in his view, would look beyond its own borders and incorporate 'the methods and findings of a broad range of disciplines'.

Eugene McLaughlin demonstrates how the 'theoretical and political parameters' of critical criminology, at least in the United Kingdom, hardened into an uncompromising orthodoxy, scathing of the deferential stance towards the state of conventional criminology. While many critical scholars have considered abandoning the 'compromised discipline of criminology to the managerial criminologists and crime scientists', McLaughlin calls on critical colleagues to 'engage with and when necessary draw upon a range of viewpoints in order to generate a rigorous critique of its core assumptions and positions'. While maintaining its distinctiveness, critical criminology must critique and interrogate what too often has been considered self-evident. Drawing on the work of Stan Cohen, McLaughlin sides with Loader and Sparks insisting that criminologists—critical and otherwise—should be politically engaged and not allow 'intellectual scepticism' to be 'an alibi for political inaction'.

Taking up McLaughlin's critique of orthodoxy, Jeff Ferrell urges criminologists to drift across the borders imposed by our disciplinary forefathers and violate 'criminology's social scientific self-image and its standards of "scientific" inquiry'. In a detailed rereading of Sykes and Matza he applauds cultural criminology's determination to engage in 'an open-ended process of wandering intellectual exploration'. David Brown similarly encourages criminologists to wander the 'highways and byways', to be open to 'inspiration and refreshment... in seemingly unlikely places', and to move beyond our secure boundaries. Yet, Brown sounds a note of warning too; calling for bridge building rather than burning, he reminds us of the benefits and security of the foundational disciplines from which criminology springs.

Pat Carlen closes this section with further critique, this time directed at those who become evangelical about their own 'alternative' positions within the broader field.

Carlen sees much to admire and benefit from scholars working under the alternative labels of 'public', 'critical' or 'cultural criminology', but expresses concerns about certain 'writings' that 'make apostolic and imperialistic pronouncements about what are the fit and proper questions, sources of funding, methods, and epistemological and ontological assumptions' not just for their own approach but for all of our work. Her chapter invites us to consider whether some among us have transgressed old borders only to establish new ones. In so doing, have criminologists simply created new orthodoxies that malign the old, often without creating something new?

Building on Nils Christie's (2010) observation that 'so much in criminology is dull, tedious and intensely empty as to new insights', Kathy Daly opens the second set of chapters advocating a 'rock 'n' roll criminology'. Introducing the section on how criminology should be done, she urges criminologists to step out of our 'well-grooved tracks', release ourselves from our 'psychic jails', and engage with those whose work is unfamiliar. Expressing concerns about the field's overreliance on 'distant data research', she encourages criminologists to try different ways of thinking about and doing criminology, and in particular to come closer to the phenomenon we are studying. Clifford Shearing and Monique Marks do just this in their qualitative work in South Africa. For them, positivist methods cannot capture the divergent meanings of the range of actors involved in crime and criminal justice in this fragmented, deeply scarred and still unequal postcolonialist society. In their view, ethnographic and case study research not only enables better understanding of fluid social realities, but may enable criminologists to change their worlds for the better.

For Nicole Rafter too much contemporary criminology is of the 'gold-digging' type: we keep looking for 'truth', discarding, or ignoring the efforts of those before us. She would rather we conceive of criminology as a river, 'an ongoing effort flowing through time, hitting rocks, absorbing currents from other fields, picking up new methods or concepts as it travels, eddying back to reconsider earlier findings, sometimes allowing work... to wash up on the river's banks'. A fluid approach to research naturally erodes the borders of hardened conceptual and methodological allegiances, as well temporal restrictions, revealing its sedimentary intellectual development.

Consideration of how to 'do' criminology not only concerns methodological choices, but how authors choose to disseminate data and how we manage the impact that our research might have. Do we write only for each other? Do we publish solely within the safe confines of our peer-reviewed academic journals, and even then in a particular sub-field of criminology? Or, do we, as Linda Mills invites us, consider the relevance of our work for a broader audience and draw on varied technological resources for wider dissemination? If so, how might we capture our audience with a 'good story'? Whilst her normative position is clear, Mills nonetheless warns of some dangers in getting up close and personal with our subjects. Proximity to the data is not a problem for Marcus Felson, who looks at his subject through a wide lens. Despite his belief that criminology succeeds best when it considers crime as a local matter, Felson, taking from the life sciences, pursues a universal and comprehensive classification of crimes that is not 'burdened by jurisdictional differences in how crimes are classified', nor 'limited by local variations in law' or criminal justice responses. In this sense, he transcends many of the borders that most of us stay within.

We had thought that this methodological section would divide our authors, and certainly divisions persist. Yet, rather than presenting such distinctions as absolute, most contributors recognize the possible benefits and contributions of alternative approaches. Indeed, the rising popularity of mixed methods approaches suggests that empirical borders might be the easiest to break down. Yet, we remain cautious, since our sample of criminologists is unlikely to be 'representative'. In particular, as we observed in the introduction, we fell short in recruiting equal numbers of highly statistically oriented scholars; though not for want of trying. Those most wedded to the quantitative approach have shied away from contributing to this collection. So too, the absence of younger scholars may skew this section. Forced to compete in a world of declining funding and university jobs, emerging scholars are less likely to be able to reject methodological demands of funders, most of whom prefer quantitative methodologies and 'scientific' evidence over ethnographic or small-scale qualitative inquiry.

Ray Paternoster and Shaun Bushway address head-on the mistrust between criminologists, noting that many of us were trained to think in binary and oppositional terms and to be derisive or dismissive of those using the 'other' method. Despite their own association with quantitative methods (Paternoster was for some years editor of *Quantitative Criminology*) they argue that this type of 'one-sided thinking' 'is dunderheaded, and frankly a waste of time'; 'qualitative and quantitative data are equally useful' they assert, for testing theory and influencing policy. On the other side of the Atlantic, Mike Hough has also done more than his fair share of quantitative research yet he too criticizes those who insist on advocating one research strategy above all others. Concentrating on experimental research methods in particular, he disputes that it offers a 'gold standard' of reliability in evaluating criminal justice policy. The randomized controlled trial, he asserts, has value in answering questions of middling complexity but not very simple or very complex ones.

As Hough warns us, methodological debates are not only of interest to those of us who prefer one approach to another; they may determine the shape and impact of public criminology: 'If only that evidence which has been accumulated through experimental research is treated as reliable,' he points out, 'then criminal policy will only make choices from a sub-set of relatively crude and simple policy options.' In a message that reappears throughout the essays in this collection, Hough rejects government-funded research that 'implicitly accepts the conceptual frameworks within which political and governmental debate about crime and its control are conducted'. We cannot challenge the status quo if we are stuck within the borders of the state agenda.

The final set of essays in this first half of the book take Hough's criticisms further, arguing that criminologists have a duty to challenge those state practices that are imbricated in and amplify social inequality and injustice. To do this, requires both an engagement with social movements and a rethinking of some basic methodological and intellectual tenets. Beth Richie begins this section urging criminologists 'to craft a social justice agenda for the divergent intellectual positions in the field'. For Thomas Mathiesen and Kristian Hjemdal, meaningful and just social change cannot succeed while criminologists accept the boundaries of state hegemony. Scholars must not only reject the state agenda, but also challenge their own theoretical boundaries to think differently about victims as well as about offenders.

Natalie Sokoloff and Amanda Burgess-Proctor believe that the criminological pursuit of social justice is best accomplished through an 'intersectional' approach. Method is not enough. A commitment to race and gender equality as well as to the thorough investigation of how these qualities intersect must be placed at the heart of research. Rather than maintaining a veneer of neutrality, criminologists should use their research as a weapon in a war against injustice. Yet, as Chris Cunneen points out in the final paper in this section, race and gender as analytical categories themselves require further refinement. Rather than 'intersectionality' Cunneen advocates a postcolonial criminology. This approach, he argues, invites an exploration of 'fundamental questions such as the relationship between race and criminalization, the development of identities of resistance, and various processes of transformative justice [and] broader questions of social and political power, ... matters of legitimacy, political authority and consent'. In so doing, it disrupts the western, Eurocentric focus of our field drawing on and championing accounts and understandings from nations and peoples who are currently marginalized.

It seems, from the contributions to the first half of this collection, that allegiances remain in criminology to certain ways of seeing the social world and our role within it, to methodological approaches to investigating and explaining social life, and to political standpoints concerned with uses of our academic work. Yet, such views are not (always) fixed. Instead, there is considerable tolerance for moving beyond the boundaries of our training, mother disciplines, and preferred intellectual sources. There is an appetite for plundering from neighbouring fields and for enriching them in exchange; many wish to challenge themselves as well as those they work with or for.

While essays in the first half primarily advocate a broad view, some voices of caution can also be heard. In the second half, these words of warning proliferate. While some seem to aspire to a criminology sans frontières, others call for a check on our emerging instinct to travel. The organizing principle as we turn to the relationship between criminology and the wider world becomes one of limits. What are the limits to our engagement with other disciplines and fields of inquiry? How, if at all, has globalization changed criminology? Does any of our work have an impact? Are policy-makers (or anyone else, for that matter) listening?

External Borders

The second half of the book begins with a discussion of the position and nature of criminology in the academy. Reflecting their disciplinary homes (if not always their own academic training) authors are particularly interested in the relationship between criminology and law. In the spirit of openness, criminology has ventured into new domains: considered acts that are deviant but not criminal; that breach laws and regulations but not criminal laws; that cause social harms but cannot be policed. Lucia Zedner has often applauded the 'rendez-vous' nature of our discipline but in her opening chapter to the second half of this book she considers what might be lost if we stray too far from our roots. In particular, she laments the lost art of criminological consideration of what crime is and what it should be. We have left the field open, she argues, to those who use other organizing concepts such as 'conflict', 'dispute', or 'harm'; perspectives she exposes as inadequate to the task. Her role however is not to put us back in a particular box. Rather, she invites us to take our criminological expertise to the criminalization debates occurring in criminal law.

If Zedner is cautious about criminology expanding too far beyond its core concerns, Aaron Doyle, Janet Chan and Kevin Haggerty, argue for a criminology that is nearly unbounded. Drawing on the wide and diverse scholarship of Richard Ericson, they believe we can and should travel 'beyond the conventional foci of criminology' to 'fully understand crime, deviance, and their regulation', and to have 'wider reach and import'.

In his chapter, David Garland warns both against narrowing criminology too far and against straying from its disciplinary sources. Taking aim at the seemingly inexorable rise of criminology into a 'free-standing, autonomous subject', particularly in US universities, Garland laments the field's growing intellectual insularity and fragmentation. Instead of dismissing our heritage, he urges criminologists to cultivate a multidisciplinary, policy-orientated subject that draws on and, in turn, enriches a range of academic disciplines and that resists the temptation to break up into many different topic specialisms, with little relevance to each other.

Taking up the question of criminology's relationship to other disciplines, Shadd Maruna and Charles Barber report on the emerging intersection between criminology and psychiatry. They conclude that criminology should be wary of adopting wholesale the psychiatric approach to research; it is psychiatry, in their view, which has much to learn. Conversely, Andrew Ashworth, who returns to the relationship between criminology and criminal justice and between criminology and criminal law, advocates a closer engagement with criminal law. William Schabas positions himself, like Ashworth, on the outside, looking in. From the perspective of international criminal justice, he sees considerable mutual gain from engagement with criminology and regrets the dearth of traffic across these borders to date. He makes clear that few if any of the issues around responding to crimes against humanity, when 'considered within a human rights perspective, are informed by criminological research'. Is this because there are limits to what we as criminologists can and should take on? While we can borrow from other disciplines and consider how our tools can be applied to wider infractions of the law or deviance beyond criminal law, perhaps our approaches do not travel well across geographical borders?

Geography and globalization provide the backdrop for the next section that begins with Ben Bowling's account of transnational criminology. Bowling describes a field looking beyond its geographical borders, one that seeks to understand crime and justice in the transnational realm and 'to contribute to safe and peaceful communities around the globe'. Yet, as he demonstrates, a criminology that travels must be ready to challenges to its core concepts, vocabulary, prognoses of the problems, and diagnoses of the cures. It can be dangerous or simply ineffective to transplant policies and frameworks of analysis to other jurisdictions.

Stephan Parmentier takes up the question of whether the discipline is 'up to the job' of moving beyond its core concerns in his chapter on crimes against humanity. Though there is a vibrant field of criminological literature on transitional justice, it is small and easily outnumbered by work produced by scholars in other fields. Methodologically and geographically, criminologists seem reluctant to engage.

In his essay on comparative criminology, David Nelken highlights the practical opportunities and challenges of looking elsewhere. Just as crimes against humanity expand criminological understanding of crime, comparative research broadens our understanding of criminal justice. Yet, he asks, what should we do with the knowledge acquired through comparison? Can we use good practice from other jurisdictions to look afresh at our own policies, practices and values? As he points out, 'some practices that work locally will not travel well'. Katja Franko Aas stays with this issue of whether ideas and practices can travel, tackling it from a theoretical perspective. Are criminological concepts, policies and theories rooted in the Anglo-American traditional transferable? While Aas does not reject global visions of crime and justice, she stresses that we must focus our intellectual and activist attentions on the varied effects of globalization in the north and south equally.

Many years ago that 'founding father' of British criminology, Sir Leon Radzinowicz said:

> I would like to see criminologists taking a public stand on controversial and important issues of the moment more often than they do at present, particularly when views are expressed which rest upon an erroneous or distorted impression of what criminology has to say about them. [1994: 101]

His former student, Roger Hood, did much to facilitate productive dialogue between the academy and the state during his time as director of the Oxford Centre for Criminology but as contributions in the final section of the book demonstrate, the political climate has changed considerably in the United Kingdom, Canada, and beyond.

Some remain optimistic. Larry Sherman, for instance, begins by encouraging criminologists to be innovators; developing, testing and refining new and better responses to crime, in order to improve society. Kelly Hannah-Moffat is rather more pessimistic. She points out that the ability of many scholars to have an impact is under threat as those with a 'critical' perspective are increasingly denied access to state institutions. Tim Hope's chapter shows that these concerns are being felt in the United Kingdom. Those criminologists who, in Hannah-Moffat's terms, are seen by the state and its agents to be 'legitimate', he argues, are provided with considerable opportunities to 'promulgate their own ideas and expertise, gaining prominence as scientific advisors to government, and acquiring a political authority that vies against the scientific authority of their erstwhile academic peers'. This official criminology has the job of providing data that does not point a critical finger at the state. In turn, the government has the power to decide what methods we use (these days the preference seems to be for randomized controlled trials), which criminal justice institutions we have access to, and then to sift through and hold back from publication some of what we do if they have held the purse strings for our research.

Al Blumstein has sought throughout his career to have influence beyond the academy. He shares Sherman's view that the task of criminologists is to do research to advance scientific knowledge with a view to developing 'intelligent policy that can and should be used in the operation of criminal justice systems'. Yet, he concedes, this task is made all the more challenging by governments' proclivity for building policy on ideological preference rather than scientific knowledge.

For Ian O'Donnell the pertinent question is what happens in a jurisdiction where criminology has been underdeveloped and had little or no influence on criminal policy? His surprising conclusion, for those of us opposed to the Anglo-American ratcheting-up of punitive sentencing, is that 'the lack of capacity for criminal justice policy formulation, implementation and evaluation together with the lack of criminological expertise and the unformed nature of the discourse may... have beneficial consequences, acting as bulwarks against a punitive shift'. Of course this is not the only factor, and O'Donnell is careful to point out that stasis is not guaranteed.

Tim Newburn further explores the declining influence of much criminological research on policy-makers and the increasing disenchantment between the two. This, he explains, has come about, at least in part, because of the government's appetite for relatively short-term policy-related research and its power to define—narrowly, as it happens—what sorts of evidence count and what constitutes 'policy relevance'. Newburn is not dismissive of the kinds of research that the government of the United Kingdom currently favours, but is concerned that skewing research agendas towards more applied criminology results in other forms of scholarship being marginalized. He invites us therefore to resist government attempts to keep our research beyond the borders of influence and to engage with policy and practical concerns of government without selling out our particular epistemological or methodological preferences.

We were not surprised that some of our contributors were keen to use this collection as an opportunity to reflect on the difficulties, especially today, of crossing the border between the academy and the state. We were perhaps a little surprised though that only one explicitly sought to contemplate the relationship between researcher and individual research subjects. Alison Liebling ends this collection by reminding us that when we do empirical research that directly engages with people outside of the academy, especially people in disadvantaged positions or people with little power, such as those in prison, we have a responsibility both to provide 'authentic description, understanding and explanation' of the phenomenon under investigation and to 'use our skills and networks responsibly, and for the greater good'. In aspiring to shape policy, she advices us, we should take note not only of what the evidence supports, but also—as Richie, Sokoloff and Burgess-Proctor and others in this collection have argued—we should use our research for greater social justice. We should, to keep with the theme of this collection, work to challenge, to explore beyond, and sometimes to cross, the borders that divide people.

Final Thoughts: Making Sense of Borders, Understanding Criminology

What has this exercise been for? Has it been to survey the discipline; to map the contours of criminology and show where the borders are and what they mean to us? To show that borders are not fixed in time and space but can shift, in part under our influence? Or are we trying to dissolve the borders or at least pension off the border police so that traffic can flow across borders unhindered by philosophical, empirical, geographical, normative or other objections?

Moreover, how do we conceive these borders? Do we respect the limits they impose or do we consider borders are for pushing? Do we gather and pillage from outside of our discipline in order to enrich our own field or do we take our own resources out into other domains to break down cultural, political, and academic borders and to enrich other disciplines? Is criminology's insecure disciplinary status a weakness that we, as criminologists, should try to do something about, or is it in fact its strength?

Is criminology simply a discipline, as Paul Rock claimed more than two decades ago, that has 'evolved quickly and erratically, appearing sometimes to advance in opposing directions' so that 'it has been more than a little difficult to make sense of its progress'? (Rock 1988: 58). Perhaps Sir Leon Radzinowicz had it right when he suggested that there is 'less need' in this field 'for further expansion and more need for a robust consolidation' (Radzinowicz 1994: 100).

Indeed, this question of the stability and coherence of inquiry clearly concerns a number of our colleagues. Scholars in Canada, for example, recently referred to criminology as an 'umbrella discipline' (Huey and Paré 2010: 237); implicitly characterizing it as a field that shelters loosely connected individuals and approaches from an unidentified external force rather than as one with a coherent sense of purpose, method or framework.

For some, matters are even worse. Famously, Nils Christie provocatively proposed many years ago now that 'Maybe we should not have criminology. Maybe we should rather abolish institutes, not open them. Maybe the social consequences of criminology are more dubious than we like to think' (Christie, 1977: 1). This view, which he broadly reiterated in 2010, (Christie 2010) highlights the inverse relationship between the progress of criminology and the regressive nature of criminal justice. Is this just a coincidence, or is there a causal relationship at work here?

We could go on with this kind of self-critique; criminology is, for many, not just tied to the state, but also plays a role in perpetuating racial disparities (Agozino 2003); it stands accused of reifying notions of victim and offender which are simplistic and, themselves, harmful (Hillyard *et al.* 2004). It is overly technical (Pasquino 1991), often dull (Foucault 1991) and too easily deployed by the forces of managerialism and neo-liberalism to tinker with institutions of state control without imagining alternatives (Cohen 1988). With its focus on crime as an action by an individual, criminology all too often overlooks the crimes of the powerful (Green and Ward 2004; Sutherland 1985; Box 1983), while finally, scholars have failed in the most fundamental tasks of the field, to reach an agreement on the cause(s) of crime (Wikstrom and Sampson 2006).

Such a litany of limitations and disappointments may seem a strange way to end an edited collection on the state and nature of the field, particularly since we are not minded to be pessimistic. We agree—and think the chapters in this book show—that there is a lack of coherence across the field. We also recognise—as do a number of the contributors to this book—concerns about the relationship between criminological 'expertise' and state control. Clearly it is true that individual criminologists are poles apart in their methodology, ideology and theoretical viewpoint. So, too, we would like to see more attention paid to certain topics and probably less attention to others.

Yet, none of these criticisms render the field of inquiry any less dynamic to us. Instead, quite the opposite; this collection of essays, with its wide range of ideas, styles and beliefs, demonstrates the enduring promise and potential of criminology. It is, in fact, their variety that is key.

As David Garland has pointed out, from its inception criminology has been 'highly differentiated in its theoretical, methodological, and empirical concerns'

(2002: 15). This is, in part, a consequence of its disparate heritage, with roots in sociology, law, history, economics and other social scientific disciplines. As far as we know, none of the contributors to this collection have a first degree in criminology. In practical terms, this means that they have come to the discipline with divergent conceptual, methodological and political allegiances. Al Blumstein with his training in engineering has a totally different set of interests from Lucia Zedner with her background in history.

It may be that as increasing numbers of undergraduate degrees in criminology and criminal justice spring up, some of the diversity will be lost. We think this would be a shame. Questions about the nature, purpose and method of our work—whether posed in the classroom or in academic publications—should not seek to map out and seal the borders of the discipline, but rather to invite discussion across and within the boundaries that we may habitually construct.

We are not suggesting blind optimism—there are real barriers between some scholars that may not be breached. Questions of method and the relationship of the academy to the state are particularly contentious. So too, as we mentioned in the introduction, matters of race and gender remain distressingly outside the sphere of interest of too many among us. Ultimately, however, we believe that we should not insist on common ground—imagine how boring that would be—but encourage interaction and debate. This indeed was the aim of this book and we think it has succeeded in providing a rich and diverse set of essays that raise some interesting questions and provide some astute answers, and illustrate that criminology cannot and should not be constrained by conceptual, methodological, and political borders. Nor should it be bound by geography, epistemology, or its own academic walls. Nonetheless, these chapters have drawn on theoretical and empirical research that shows that above all criminology should not lose sense of its focus and purpose; to explore crime and criminal justice and to keep an eye on broader matters of social justice.

References

Agozino, B. (2003), *Counter-Criminology: A Critique of Imperialist Reason*, London: Pluto.

Box, S. (1983), *Power, Crime and Mystification*, London: Routledge.

Christie, N. (1977), 'Conflicts as Property', *British Journal of Criminology*. 17(1): 1–15.

_____ (2010), 'Scandinavian Exceptionalism: Five Dangers Ahead', 5th Roger Hood Annual Public Lecture, Gulbenkian Lecture Theatre, University of Oxford.

Cohen, S. (1988), *Against Criminology*, New Brunswick: Transaction Publishers.

Foucault, M. (1991), 'Questions of Method', in G. Burchell, C. Gordon, and P. Miller (eds), *The Foucault Effect: Studies in Governmentality*, Chicago: University of Chicago Press.

Garland, D. (2002), 'Of Crimes and Criminals: The development of criminology in Britain', in M. Maguire, R. Morgan, and R. Reiner (eds), *The Oxford Handbook of Criminology*, 3rd edn, Oxford: Oxford University Press.

Green, P. and Ward, T. (2004), 'State Crime: Governments, Violence and Corruption', London: Pluto Press.

Hillyard, P., Pantazis, C., Tombs, S., and Gordon, D. (2004), *Beyond Criminology: Taking Harm Seriously*, London: Pluto Press.

Huey, L. and Paré, P-P. (2010), 'Bridging Divides in Canadian Criminology: Some Thoughts on a Possible Future', *Canadian Journal of Criminology and Criminal Justice*, 52(3): 237–41.

Pasquino, P. (1991), 'Criminology: The Birth of a Special Knowledge', in G. Burchell, C. Gordon, and P. Miller (eds), *The Foucault Effect: Studies in Governmentality*, Chicago: Chicago University Press.

Radzinowicz, Sir Leon (1994), 'Reflections on the State of Criminology: Speech made at the Dinner to Mark the British Criminology Conference held in Cardiff 28–31 July 1993', *British Journal of Criminology*, 34(2), 99.

_____ (1988), *The Cambridge Institute of Criminology: Its Background and Scope*, London: HMSO.

Rock, P. (1988), 'The present State of Criminology in Britain', *British Journal of Criminology*. 28(2): 58–76.

Sutherland, E. (1985), *White Collar Crime: The Uncut Version*, New Haven: Yale University Press.

Wikstrom, O. and Sampson, R. (eds) (2006), *The Explanation of Crime: Context, Mechanisms and Development*, Cambridge: Cambridge University Press.

Index